Palestine and Sinai as photographed during space flight of Apollo 7. In both views the Mediterranean Sea is readily recognized, as well as the rugged and complex character of the earth's crust that forms the bridge between Africa and Asia: the Gulfs of Suez and Aqabah to the north of the Red Sea; the Jordan rift southward from Mount Hermon; river beds and mountains — the geographical locale of biblical history. *Photos courtesy:* National Aeronautics and Space Administration.

Front cover (north portal of the hundred-column Throne Hall at Persepolis): Rev. Robert North, S.J.; (facsimile of Manual of Discipline Dead Sea Scroll and jar): John Dominik. *Rear cover* (ziggurat at Ur; Ishtar Gate at Babylon): Matson Photo Service, Alhambra, California; (facsimile of decalog in Old Hebrew script): John Dominik; (stables of Solomon at Megiddo; Valley of Josaphat burial site at Jerusalem): Maison de la Bonne Presse, 27 boulevard des Italiens, Paris, France.

Layout and title page by Brother Placid, O.S.B.

The Men and the Message of the Old Testament

THE MEN AND

OF THE

THE LITURGICAL PRESS,

THE MESSAGE

OLD TESTAMENT

Third Edition — Illustrated

by Peter F. Ellis, C.SS.R.

Fordham University, Bronx, New York

COLLEGEVILLE, MINNESOTA

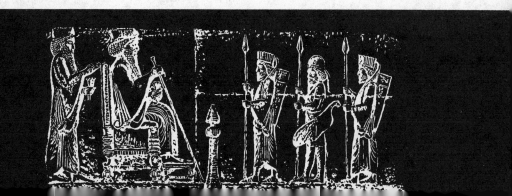

Other titles by Father Ellis

MATTHEW: HIS MIND AND HIS MESSAGE
— *A Study in Composition Criticism*

FIRST AND SECOND BOOK OF KINGS
— *Introduction and Commentary*

THE YAHWIST
— *The Bible's First Theologian*

LIST OF ABBREVIATIONS

ANEP	The Ancient Near East in Pictures
ANET	Ancient Near Eastern Texts
CBQ	The Catholic Biblical Quarterly
CCHS	A New Catholic Commentary on Holy Scripture (1969 edition)
HOTOT	History of the Old Testament — Claus Schedl
JBC	The Jerome Biblical Commentary
LXX	The Septuagint translation of the Old Testament
LFAP	Light from the Ancient Past — J. Finegan
OTRG	Old Testament Reading Guide
SDB	Supplement Dictionnaire de La Bible
WHAB	Westminster Historical Atlas to the Bible

Imprimi potest: Very Reverend James T. Connolly, *Provincial. Nihil obstat:* William G. Heidt, O.S.B., S.T.D., *Censor deputatus. Imprimatur:* † George H. Speltz, D.D., Bishop of St. Cloud. July 31, 1975.

To
Minnie and Nan Nan

PREFACE

To find a sure-fire *Open Sesame* to the treasures hoarded in the Bible has been the dream of every professor of Scripture and the naive expectation of every student. No one has ever found the magic password. The professor, however, can learn to live with his dream by trying to formulate an *Open Sesame* of his own. This book is one such attempt.

The Men and the Message of the Old Testament, as initially conceived, was for beginners only — students on college level studying the Bible for the first time. Hence our first approach: the introduction to and familiarity with each of the sacred books. But while preparing the text for tyros, a wider audience came into focus. Thus, our second approach was added: the literary analysis of the books with a rapid glance at pertinent biblical theology. This was added for those whose biblical studies would be ancillary to the study of sacred theology. Finally, our third approach — the study of 75 psalms — has been added both for the benefit of clerics and religious who daily recite the divine praises, and for that growing battalion of lay Catholics whose piety has drawn them instinctively to this inspired wellspring of liturgical prayer.

The three approaches have been integrated; they have not been united. It is the author's conviction that familiarity with the books, the backbone of the first approach, is an indispensable prerequisite to any other study of the Bible. The dictum, "Always read the sources — everything flows from them naturally," is basic to intelligent study. It is elementary to a study of the Scriptures. As we have arranged the text, the student must make a threefold trip through the Bible. However, once the first trip has been made, the second trip by way of literary analysis and the third by way of the psalms become pleasant journeys through familiar territory.

Since the study of Sacred Scripture has yet to find its "place in the sun" in most college and seminary curricula, the threefold approach has a practical advantage. Where only one or two semesters are given to the Old Testament, the first approach — an introduction to the books — will provide an adequate course. Where more than a year is allotted to the Old Testament, opportunity will be afforded for literary analysis as well. For those sufficiently interested, the study of the psalms can be independently pursued.

Two firm convictions underlie the making of this book. First, that studying about the Bible without actually reading the Bible itself is a bleak and fruitless chore. Second, that the student will benefit from the Word of God only in so far as he knows it and loves it. With this in mind we have passed over much that is found in the conventional textbook and have sought to fix the student's attention on the text itself of the Old Testament. Thus the student will find little about textual criticism, philology, the history of exegesis, and the like. Such studies are for the advanced student of the Scriptures. Textbooks too often concentrate on the knotty and abstruse portions of Scripture, monopolizing all the student's time and effort, side-tracking him from enjoying the glorious ninety percent of the Bible that for two thousand years has been the solace and delight of learned and unlettered alike. The beginner should not be forced to hack and chop for the difficult ten percent of the Scriptures when, like the iron ore of the great Mesabi range, the major portion of the Bible's riches lie at the surface.

Still, for the readily available wealth of the Bible, method is necessary both to be sure of lasting results and to complete the study of the Bible in the allotted time. To the student using this text without benefit of professors, the following method is recommended. 1. A brief study of the introduction to each book. 2. An immediate reading and re-reading of the book itself. 3. A study of those points of Biblical theology stressed in the book. 4. A study of psalms which recapitulate the book.

1. The brief introduction to each book is a necessary preliminary. Modern books provide the reader with three things that the biblical books omit. Every modern book has a title and subtitle. Its jacket bears a photograph of the author with a thumbnail sketch of his life and work. It has a preface and a table of contents.

Biblical authors have not been so considerate. Titles are rare. Prefaces, with the exception of 2 Maccabees and Luke's Gospel, are virtually unknown. A table of contents, division into chapters, and a biographical sketch of the author are not to be found.

Introduction does for the modern reader what the biblical author would do if he were writing today: providing a suitable title to describe the theme of the book; writing a few words about the author where anything certain is known; composing a preface to explain the purpose of the book, and dividing the book into sections and chapters to show the author's plan and give some idea of the progress of his thought.

The importance of introduction should not be underrated. It supplies the first two requirements for the appreciation of any book, namely, an idea of the author's specific aim in writing and something about the method he used to achieve this aim. The third step — the reliving of the author's creative activity by means of an intelligent reading of his work — is left to the reader himself.

2. Reading and re-reading to attain familiarity with the Bible depends very much on the student's determination to do it over and over again. Daily Bible reading is not only desirable; it is a practical necessity. It is the only sure way to develop a love for the Word of God and it is the only practical way to finish so long a book in the brief time allotted to Old Testament studies. The Old Testament contains about 900,000 words divided into approximately 900 chapters. The student who reads three chapters per day should easily finish the whole of the Old Testament in a year. Doubling this pace or continuing the same pace over two years will ensure two complete readings and secure for the student a serviceable familiarity with the Old Testament.

On the *why* and *how* of Bible reading, it should suffice to point out that the Bible is not only a classic but something infinitely more. In a world of human literature, it is the only book God thought important enough to seal with the charism of inspiration. Since the student knows the divine Author has a purpose for everything He inspires, he must learn to have patience when parts of the Bible seem digressive or irrelevant. He must not skip tedious parts because he does not at the moment see how they fit in. In the divine Author's mind each part has its place in the total build-up. God sees it from the beginning. The reader sees it only after reading the whole book. Nor should the reader lose heart if he does not grasp the Bible's whole meaning. To fully grasp any classic at one reading, one would have to be equal in genius to the author. For intellectual giants like Saints Augustine, Jerome, John Chrysostom, and Thomas Aquinas, life itself was not long enough to grasp completely the message the Holy Spirit transmitted to man by the Sacred Scriptures.

3. An adequate course in biblical theology is out of the question. Biblical theology — the knowledge of the Word of God in as much as it establishes revealed principles of theology — will, it is hoped, in the years to come, receive the attention it deserves. For the present it will be possible only to cover a few high points. These will be dealt with in conjunction with those books that treat of them in an emphatic rather than a passing way. Covenant theology, for example, will be taken with Genesis and Exodus, divine love with Deuteronomy and Hosea, messianism with the prophets, the books of Samuel, Kings, and Chronicles.

4. The study of psalms related to a book or group of books serves as an easy way to review and at the same time provides an ideal way to appreciate the very essence of the psalms. The psalms have been called the Bible in song. It is not literally true, of course, but in many ways the psalms are a digest of the Bible. There are historical psalms that touch

upon the highlights of Israel's history, doctrinal psalms that sing of her faith, prophetic psalms that ring with her hopes, prayerful psalms that sound the depths of her love for God. Where a psalm sums up the history or the principal doctrine taught in a book, it can be more easily understood if the student studies it immediately after finishing the book in question.

Something must be said about the section entitled "Significant Passages." They are intended to direct the student's attention to the major personages, places, and events in the Bible. History is made by great men in the right places at critical times, by sequences of interlocking and extraordinary events. Whole periods can be summed up in the career of one exceptional man. One cataclysmic event can earmark a decade or categorize a century. These personages and these events are the landmarks of history. They are not always perfectly placed, nor do they always give unmistakeable directions, but they stake out the field, show its divisions, its contours, its high and low spots. The significant passages selected are stakes driven into the field of historical memory. This done, the field can be more easily and more accurately explored.

The student should note that the selection of significant passages has not always been made on the basis of what is most important in the book, but on the basis of what is important for an appreciation of the book itself and for its relation to other parts of Sacred Scripture. He should note especially that no attempt is made to give extensive exegesis of these passages. They are meant to be simple streetlights spaced along the biblical highway, giving adequate illumination to their immediate vicinity, diminishing light to the space intervening, and at the same time serving as a group to outline the whole highway.

In addition to the significant passages, the student will notice the recurrence of detailed and overlapping chronological tables. They are not meant to encumber the memory but to emphasize the place of the Kingdom of God in history and the unilinear direction of history as a result. The Kingdom of God is a tree, planted in the time of Abraham, putting forth its first shoots in the time of Moses, a vigorous sapling in the time of David, pruned to the roots in the intervening centuries to the coming of Christ, rising in the centuries following the Incarnation to spread its branches and cover with its shade the whole world. It is of no small importance that the student become vividly aware that all other institutions pass; the Kingdom alone perdures. As the chronologies show, empires rise and fall, the Kingdom of God alone continues — ever contemporaneous, ever the witness to the passing of temporal kingdoms, itself eternal. It is only when the student becomes aware of the duration and continuity of the Kingdom of God that he will be able to reflect upon its significance and elaborate a theology of history. The chronologies have been introduced to foster such reflection.

Something must be said about three minor points. First, concerning opinions expressed, the accepted critical positions are followed for the most part, without extensive explanation and without reference to the excellent scholars who have labored so indefatigably to establish them. Biblical scholars will recognize with ease the paternity of these positions. Where new positions are advanced, some explanation has been attempted, though not such as would be required for scholarly presentation.

Second, concerning the text, the New American Bible has been followed with a few noted exceptions.

Thirdly, concerning bibliography and footnotes, a policy of minimal references has been followed in order to detract as little as possible from attention to the Bible itself. As far as possible references have been restricted to books and periodicals readily available to the college student. For those whose time permits additional research, a more extensive bibliography has been added at the end of the book.

There remains the pleasant task of expressing my gratitude to the numerous friends and confreres whose generous assistance, valuable suggestions, and continual encouragement played no small part in the production of whatever is of value in this work. I am indebted first of all to my students whose needs elicited the book and whose reactions helped to shape it. I am indebted to my superior, Rev. Francis Sweeney, for lightening my daily chores and thus making available the time necessary for the preparation of the book. I am equally indebted to many other confreres but especially the Rev. Louis Hartman, the Rev. William Barry, the Rev. John Craghan, the Rev. Francis X. Murphy, the Rev. Edward Crowley, the Rev. Eugene McAlee, and my one time confrere and associate, the Rev. Callaghan Burke, O.C.S.O. I am particularly indebted to Sr. Ritamary Bradley, C.H.M., to whose gentle persuasion and unflagging encouragement I owe the initial burst of energy that launched the first draft of the book, and to Mrs. Joseph Woods, to whose patience, devotion, and tireless energy in typing the final copy I owe the completed manuscript.

Peter F. Ellis, C.SS.R.

Fordham University
Feast of the Assumption
August 15, 1975

INTRODUCTION

The traveller who sets out on a long journey must have a destination in mind and some idea of the principal stopovers along the way. What he encounters in his travels will make an impression on him only in the degree that he experiences it. And what he will think of the journey as a whole will be determined not only by his powers of observation along the way but by his capacity for reflection on the trip as a whole when he has finally reached his destination. The highlights of the journey will stand out; the little details will fade into the shadows of memory.

It is much the same for the reader who sets out for the first time to read the Bible, the record of God's journey with men through the centuries, leading them in His own way and by degrees to the rock upon which is built His kingdom on earth — the Catholic Church. The reader will have to remember that this kingdom is the basic theme of the whole Bible, the final destination on the road laid out by God for mankind. The beginning of the road will be in Genesis, the end in the Gospels. Along the way will be the various books of the Old Testament.

These books have usually been grouped into the historical, prophetical, and sapiential books. The division is traditional and sound, but for the reader who wishes to proceed methodically through the Bible, it will be better to follow a more exact division, determined by the time each book was written or by the period of Israel's history with which it deals.

Beginning with the Pentateuch, therefore, the student will read the history of the foundation of God's kingdom on earth: the origins of the people in Genesis, the institution of the theocratic kingdom in Exodus, the liturgical organization of the kingdom's worship in Leviticus, the communal organization of the theocratic nation around the Ark and the Tabernacle in Numbers, the spirit of love that is to animate the citizens of the kingdom in Deuteronomy.

In the book of Joshua, the student will read the story of the new nation's conquest of the Promised Land of Palestine. In Judges, he will see the Israelites battling the surrounding nations in order to retain possession of the newly conquered homeland. In the books of Samuel, he will meet Saul, the rejected first king of the Israelites, and David, the man after God's own heart, whose reign solidifies the Israelite hold on Palestine, and whose person becomes for future ages the embodiment of the ideal king to come.

In 1 Kings, the student will read of the glorious reign of Solomon and the subsequent division of his kingdom into two parts: the northern kingdom called Israel and the southern kingdom called Judah. Most of 1 Kings (ch. 12–22) and of 2 Kings (ch. 1–17) will deal with the northern kingdom: its kings, its prophets, and its final destruction, in 722 B.C., before the onslaughts of the Assyrian army. Here the reader should pause to read the sermons of Amos and Hosea, the last prophets of the northern kingdom.

Continuing 2 Kings 18–25, the reader can finish the history of the divided kingdom by reading the history of the last kings and the fall of the kingdom of Judah to the Babylonians in 587 B.C. But it will be better at this point to take up the two books of Chronicles, which deal almost exclusively with David and the kingdom of Judah, and read the history of the southern kingdom from beginning to end.

When in the course of the Chronicler's history of the kingdom of Judah the student comes to the reign of King Ahaz (735-715), he will do well to stop and read the collected sermons of the great Judean prophet Isaiah and his contemporary Micah.

Continuing the history of the southern kingdom into the seventh century, the student will come to the time of Jeremiah (c. 650-582), the great prophet of the last days of Judah. Along with the sermons of Jeremiah, he will read the briefer collections of sermons extant from the preaching of Zephaniah, Nahum, Habakkuk, and Obadiah.

For the period that follows – the time of the Babylonian captivity (587-539) – the student will find no historical sources such as the Pentateuch, Samuel, and Kings. He will have, however, the collected writings of Ezekiel and Deutero-Isaiah, the two great prophets of the exile who comforted the Jews in captivity and prepared them for the return to Judah, when in God's good time the exile should end.

What happened when the exile did end in 539 B.C. and the Jews returned home to Palestine, the student will discover in the books of Ezra and Nehemiah, supplemented by the collections of sermons extant from the preaching of Haggai, Zechariah, Malachi, and Joel. Since the Pentateuch was put into its present form at this time, it will be of no small value to re-read it here, noting the different traditions fused together in the course of the centuries to form the Pentateuch as we have it in our present Bible.

With the end of the book of Nehemiah, there is an historical blackout from approximately 400 to 175 B.C. During this period and perhaps even a little earlier, such books as Job, Jonah, Proverbs, Tobit, Esther, Judith, the Canticle of Canticles, Ecclesiastes, Sirach, and parts of Daniel were either composed or put into their final form (e.g., Proverbs). It will be advisable to accompany the reading of these books with a study of the literary forms in use in Israel at this time.

Finally the student will read the two books of Maccabees, Daniel, Judith, and Wisdom, all written sometime in the last two centuries before Christ. With these books the Old Testament comes to an end and the reader is ready to take up the last and the climactic part of the Bible, the New Testament.

If the reader is observant in reading these books of the Old Testament, he will notice the gradual formation and development down through the centuries of what he knows now as the Catholic Church — the Kingdom of God on earth. He will see it promised in the announcement of the victory of mankind over Satan (Gen. 3:15); extended to all mankind through the descendants of Abraham: "In you shall all the nations of the earth be blessed" (Gen. 12:3); and begun in embryonic form in the Israelite nation at Sinai: "You shall be to me a kingdom of priests, a holy nation" (Exod. 19:6). He will see it developed doctrinally throughout the rest of the Old Testament by means of experiments with human kings — insufficient and destined to be replaced by the one Divine and Human King — and by the preaching of the inspired prophets, the men whose mission it was to preserve the true faith from perversion and adulteration until the coming of the King of kings in the fullness of time, when the Kingdom of God in all its glory and perfection would be inaugurated. In the Old Testament, the student will see the seeds planted and the roots taking hold. In the New Testament, he will see the blossoming.

CONTENTS

PART ONE

THE PENTATEUCHAL HISTORY

Chapter

PART TWO

THE DEUTERONOMIST'S HISTORY

PART THREE

THE CHRONICLER'S HISTORY AND
THE PROPHETS OF JUDAH

PART FOUR

THE DIDACTIC LITERATURE AND THE HISTORY OF THE MACCABEES

Now will I praise those godly men,
    our ancestors, each in his own time.
Rulers of the earth by their authority,
    men of renown for their might,
Or counselors in their wisdom,
    or seers of all things in prophecy;
Resolute governors of peoples,
    or judges with discretion;
Authors skilled in composition,
    or poets with collected proverbs;
Composers of melodious psalms,
    or discoursers on lyric themes;
Stalwart men, solidly established
    and at peace in their own estates —
All these are buried in peace
    but their name lives on and on.
At gatherings their wisdom is retold,
    and the assembly sings their praises.

— Sirach 44:1-6, 14-15

PART ONE

The

Pentateuchal History

1

The Pentateuch

1. The Pentateuch as a Whole

The history of the composition of the Pentateuch — the identification of the Yahwistic, Elohistic, Deuteronomic, and Priestly sources, the fusion of these sources in the course of the centuries, and the final revision and unification of all the sources into one connected narrative by a priestly theologian in the sixth or fifth century before Christ — is matter for higher literary criticism (cf. pp. 52ff). It will suffice for the present to note that it is these parallel sources and their successive compilations and revisions that account for the duplicated narratives and the differences in style, vocabulary, and syntax that we find in the Pentateuch. What is important is that the reader should realize that the present Pentateuch represents the last edition of the original, substantially Mosaic tradition.

As it stands now, the Pentateuch is an elaborate account of the founding of God's kingdom on earth by means of the solemn covenant made with Israel at Sinai sometime in the thirteenth century before Christ. The present division of the Pentateuch into five parts represents a later partition of the one immense and composite work into smaller intelligible subunits or sections.

The Pentateuch, however, was conceived as a single book and the reader will understand and appreciate its message only if he sees and interprets each of its five parts in relation to the whole. Thus Genesis explains the origin of the people who became the first citizens of God's theocratic kingdom of Israel. Exodus recounts the actual birth of the kingdom at Sinai. Leviticus impresses upon the reader the "holy" nature of the kingdom. Numbers describes its communal organization and emphasizes the need for a hierarchy of authority. Deuteronomy inculcates the spirit of love by which the citizens of the kingdom are to be animated in relation to God and to each other.

The following outline sees the Pentateuch in this way. It considers the whole as divided into five parts (with Gen. 1–11 as its prologue), telling the story of the birth of the kingdom of God on earth, and combining the history and the laws of the Chosen People from the beginning down to the year 1250 B.C.

The Pentateuchal history as a whole

Prologue / Gen. 1–11

> The combined theological prologues of the Priestly author (Gen. 1) and the Yahwist author (Gen. 2–11).

Part One / Genesis

Theme	The origin of the people of the kingdom..
Purpose	In relation to the Pentateuch as a whole, Genesis has as its purpose to show God's providential preparation of the Israelite people.
Division	1–11 Prologue describing the theological situation of mankind in relation to God. 12–25 The saga of Abraham. 25–36 The saga of Isaac and Jacob. 37–50 The saga of Joseph and the other sons of Jacob in Egypt.

Part Two / Exodus

Theme	The inauguration of the theocratic kingdom of Israel at Sinai.

Purpose	In relation to the Pentateuch as a whole, Exodus has as its purpose to describe the events that led to the birth of the Israelite nation.
Division	1–12 Events preparatory to the exodus from Egypt.
	12–18 The exodus from Egypt and the journey to Sinai.
	19–24 The birth of the Israelite nation at Sinai by means of the covenant.
	25–40 The Ark and the Tabernacle: God's dwelling-place in the midst of the newly constituted nation.

Part Three / Leviticus

Theme	The organization of Israel's cult around the Ark and the Tabernacle.
Purpose	In relation to the Pentateuch as a whole, Leviticus has as its purpose to define the holy nature of the new kingdom.
Division	1– 7 Laws governing sacrifices.
	8–10 Laws governing ordination to the priesthood.
	11–16 Laws governing legal purity.
	17–26 Laws governing legal holiness.
	27 Laws governing the redemption of votive offerings.

Part Four / Numbers

Theme	The social organization of the Israelite community and the march from Sinai to the plains of Moab.
Purpose	In relation to the Pentateuch as a whole, Numbers has as its purpose to show the necessity of a hierarchy of authority for the communal organization of the new nation.
Division	1–10 Communal organization of the people and the departure from Sinai.
	10–22 The authority of Moses, the priests, and the elders and the march from Sinai to the plains of Moab.
	23–36 On the plains of Moab before the invasion of Canaan.

Part Five / Deuteronomy

Theme	An eloquent review of Israel's covenantal relationship with God.
Purpose	In relation to the Pentateuch as a whole, Deuteronomy has as its purpose to show the Israelites that their spirit as a nation must be a spirit of love, honor, and obedience to God.
Division	1– 4 Historical review and exhortation to love God.
	4–11 Sermon on God and the covenant stressing bond of love.
	12–26 Explanation of the Sinai pact and the law.
	27–34 Last words of Moses before his death on Mt. Nebo.

2. Genesis

Genesis begins with the first man in paradise and ends with the twelve sons of Jacob in Egypt in the early seventeenth century before Christ. The ending is significant. It shows what the author had been leading up to: an explanation of where these twelve sons, the immediate forefathers of the Israelite people, originated. Thus the main theme of the book of Genesis is the origins of the Israelite people.

With this main theme in mind, the author purposes to show how from the very beginning of time God providentially prepared this special people to be the first citizens of His kingdom and the repository and vehicle of His revelation. That this is the general purpose of the author can be shown from the format he follows. Beginning with a universal history in ch. 1–11, he rapidly narrows it down to the one chosen people. One by one all the other peoples mentioned in Genesis are eliminated from the record, leaving only the direct line from Adam through Seth, Noah, Shem, Abraham, Isaac down to Jacob and his twelve sons. Thus, after 4:24, nothing more is said about Cain and his descendants. The history then carries on with the Sethites (5:6-32) down to Noah. Of Noah's three sons, Japheth is first eliminated (10:2-5), then Ham (10:6-20), and the history continues with the line of Shem alone (11:21-31) down to Abraham (11:26). Of Abraham's two sons, Ishmael and Isaac, Ishmael is eliminated (25:18). Of Isaac's two sons, Esau and Jacob, Esau is eliminated (36:40), and the history of origins comes to an end with Jacob (Israel) and his twelve sons, from whom come the twelve tribes of Israel, who are selected by God on Mt. Sinai to be His Chosen People (Exod. 19–24).

Concurrently with his major theme, the origins of the Chosen People, the author pursues several minor themes. In ch. 1–11, he purposes to show how mankind after the fall and the promise of ultimate triumph (ch. 1–3) gradually deteriorated when left to itself without any special divine help (ch. 4–11). In ch. 11–25, he shows how God began to fulfill His promise of ultimate triumph for mankind over the forces of Satan (Gen. 3:15) by setting aside one particular family through whom His saving power would be extended to the whole of mankind (Gen. 12:3). With Abraham, therefore, a new and eternal covenant is made (Gen. 15–17). This covenant, however, is made only with those whom God freely and independently chooses, not by inheritance or primogeniture (ch. 25–36). Finally in ch. 37–50, the author shows how God's providence can turn even the sins of men and the apparent accidents of fate to the fulfillment of His designs for Israel.

Three dominant motifs, therefore, can be seen in the book: promises of salvation (3:15, 12:3); the free choice of those through whom the promises would be fulfilled (25–36 and *passim*); and lastly, the way in which these promises will be brought to realization – by way of covenants between God and man (Gen. 3; 15; 17).

If the reader will keep in mind the fact that we have a learned author intent on teaching simple people not only their own racial origin but also the profound religious truths which were to be passed on to the world, he will have gone a long way toward understanding the enduring message of Genesis. The nature of the audience will explain, for example, why in the first part of the book, the description of the theological situation of mankind in relationship to God, the author uses concrete picturesque language to teach such basic truths as the creation of all things by the one, omnipotent God (ch. 1); God's plan of salvation thwarted by the intrusion of evil into the world by the free will of man (ch. 2–3); the reign of sin that would prevail in the world if man were left to himself (ch. 4–11). The simplicity of the audience also explains the author's emphasis on a family history in the second part of the book (ch. 11–50).

With this in mind, and paying special attention to the emphasis placed on promises, covenants, free election of those through whom God will realize His salvific designs and on the providence of God watching over this uniquely chosen people, the reader will be ready to appreciate the basic message of the book of Genesis.

The book divides easily into four convenient parts: I. the theological prologue (1–11); II. Abraham (11–25); III. Isaac and Jacob (25–36); IV. Joseph and his brothers (37–50). Without attempting extensive exegesis, we shall give a short explanation of the significant passages in each part, and, where opportune, refer the reader to other sections of the book for explanation of passages requiring longer treatment.

Part One / Gen. 1–11 / The Theological Prologue

1:3 "God said: 'Let there be light!'" While the author indicates that all things are created by the mere word of God, he nevertheless describes all of creation in a concrete, picturesque way, visualizing God working as a craftsman who divides His work into eight parts spread over the available six days of a laborer's week, leaving the seventh day for rest (cf. pp. 85ff).

2:7 "Then the Lord God created man out of the dust of the ground" (cf. pp. 98ff).

2:8 "The Lord God planted a garden in Eden. . . ." For lack of knowledge of the material state of early man, the great love of God is expressed metaphorically in the well-being that goes with living in a garden of delights. Throughout the Bible, such material prosperity will be described as a manifestation of God's love for man (cf. pp. 98ff).

Scholars are now using the phrase "early man" as equivalent to "Adam," "our first parents," "the first men," etc., simply because we are as ignorant of the date of the appearance of the first human beings upon earth as was the biblical author. The vast amount of anthropological information amassed during the nineteenth and twentieth centuries in no way contributes to a solution of this problem since the natural sciences are based upon observable, factual phenomena, e.g., skeletal remains, archaeological data, geological strata, etc. But the biblical writer is speaking of "moral man," namely, a human being capable of grave moral decisions on matters of good and evil, right and wrong in consciousness of God. Further, a correct and adequate definition of man — whether "early" or modern — must not omit another requirement, i.e., personal immortality (even though this point is absent from revelation existing at the time of the Priestly and Yahwistic writers). Since anthropology as a science can supply no answer to the question as to the chronological date when man began to exist as "man" with moral responsibility in relationship to God and with the personal ontological endowment of immortality and since divine revelation has not answered our curiosity in this regard, the matter of the age of the human race remains wholly open for theological speculation. Intelligent persons will continue to evaluate more wisely the bland, baseless assumption that all the paleolithic bones on the staircase of anthropological evolution must necessarily be human.

3:1 "Now the serpent was more cunning than any beast of the field. . . ." Evil is symbolized as a serpent because of the place held by serpents in the idolatrous worship of the Canaanites at the time the author put his teaching into written form.

Since there is little or no evidence available to support an exegesis identifying the serpent symbolically with the devil or Satan (because the revelation of evil spirits occurred at a later date), current procedure uses the word *evil* to convey the contrast-judgment in the mind of the biblical author. In the light of the revelation given in passages such as Wis. 2:24; John 8:44, however, Judaic-Christian faith down through the centuries spontaneously thinks of Satan or the devil when considering this passage.

3:15 "I will put enmity . . . between your seed and her seed; he (the seed of the woman) shall crush your head." Mankind (the seed of the woman) will eventually triumph (through Christ as we know from later revelation) over evil. How and when this triumph will come about is the slowly unfolding message of the rest of the Bible (cf. pp. 351ff).

4:8 "Cain turned against his brother Abel and slew him." In this symbolic story and in the symbolic stories of the next seven chapters (flood, tower of Babel), the author shows how rebellion against God multiplies (cf. 6:5, 11; 8:21; 11:3ff). If God does not intervene, man will by his crimes bring about his own destruction.

5:5 "The whole lifetime of Adam was 930 years; then he died." In ch. 5 and 11, we have two sets of genealogies, each consisting of ten generations; those in ch. 5, the generations before the flood, those in ch. 11, the generations after the flood. From Babylonian literature we know that the usage of attributing great ages to men, distributed according to series of ten generations each, was a literary device used to express the passage of a long period of time. Not knowing the length of time between early man and Abraham, the author uses the conventional literary device of his time to span this period. The diminishing length of years given to successive individuals may perhaps be intended to show that as sin increased, the gift of long life decreased.

6:5 The consequences of early man's revolt against God reaches its climax in the sins of his descendants, bringing as punishment the flood. God, however, spares Noah and makes a covenant with him (9:8ff). The original promise comes down, therefore, through the family of Noah and Shem (Japheth and Ham and their descendants are quietly eliminated from the story in 10:1ff).

11:1 The story of the tower of Babel is a symbolic story describing the **revolt of society against God.** Originally a folk legend from Babylon, the story is used by the author to show that men still wanted, like Adam, to decide their own destinies independently of God, a continuation, therefore, of the primal revolt.

11:10 The genealogy of Shem, from whom eventually comes Terah, the father of Abraham. With this genealogy, the theological prologue ends. The new section, Gen. 11–25, will introduce Abraham, the first of the important forefathers of Israel, the man with whom God makes the new and eternally valid Abrahamitic covenant which is fulfilled and perfectly implemented by Christ nineteen hundred years after the call of Abraham from Mesopotamia to Palestine.

Part Two / Gen. 11–25 / The Saga of Abraham

11:31 ". . . from Ur of the Chaldeans. . . ." Ethnically and geographically a Mesopotamian Semite, Abraham's homeland is in ancient Chaldea in southern Mesopotamia, near the Persian gulf, in the vicinity of the modern oil centers of Basra, Kuwait, and Abadan. His cultural background is that of the Old-Babylonian empire which produced Hammurabi, the great law-giver, and shared with Egypt the highest level of culture and civilization in the ancient world of the nineteenth century B.C., the approximate period of Abraham (cf. J. Bright, *A History of Israel*, 2nd ed. 67-102).

12:1-3 With the mystic call of Abraham from Mesopotamia to Palestine, God begins the formation of the ethnic group in which He will found His kingdom on earth. The promise, "In you will all the nations of the earth be blessed" (v. 3), is the first step in the fulfillment of the more general promise made in Gen. 3:15. The same promise will be repeated to Abraham's son Isaac (26:4) and to his grandson Jacob (28:14). It will begin to be fulfilled under Moses (Exod. 19—24), and be perfectly fulfilled by Christ, the descendant of Abraham through Isaac, Jacob, Judah, and David (cf. Luke 1:55, 72-73; Matthew 1:1-14).

12:6-10 Abraham's travels: his first trip from Ur to Haran to Shechem in Palestine is made as a result of his divine call (12:1). His subsequent travels from Shechem to Bethel (12:8), Bethel to the Negeb (12:9), the Negeb to Egypt (12:10), Egypt to the Negeb (13:1), the Negeb to Bethel (13:3) and Bethel to Mamre-Hebron (13:18) are explained by his mode of life. As a rich caravan-trader, with a large entourage of men (Gen. 12:14-16; 14:14; 23:6; 24:34), he is obliged to move according to trade opportunities.

13:14-16 God promises to give to Abraham's descendants the land of Canaan (Palestine). This promise is fulfilled around 1225 B.C., when Israelite armies under Joshua conquer and rule the major part of central Palestine.

14:18ff The war of the kings against the plain cities at the southern end of the Dead Sea, the capture of Lot and his family, and Abraham's successful rescue are probably all narrated because of their relation to the meeting of Abraham with Melchizedek. The author includes the meeting because it shows the great patriarch in contact with Jerusalem, the future capital of David's kingdom (cf. Ps. 110:4; Heb. 7).

15:6 Abraham's faith is not so much intellectual adherence to a body of doctrines as confidence and trust in God to fulfill an apparently impossible promise. St. Paul will use this text to prove that man is justified by faith alone independent of the works of the law (Rom. 4:3; Gal. 3:6); St. James, to prove that faith without works is dead (2:23).

15:9-20 The strange and ancient covenant rites mentioned here are alluded to later in Jer. 34:18ff. The parties of the covenant, by passing between the slaughtered carcasses, called down upon themselves a similar fate if they did not observe the covenant promises. (Concerning the Abrahamitic covenant described here in ch. 15 and also in ch. 17, cf. pp. 22ff).

16:1-6 Sarah's invitation to her husband to have children by her maid-servant — a practice expressly mentioned and regulated by the Code of Hammurabi (ANET nn. 146; 170) — is evidence of the patriarch's Babylonian background.

17:1-10 The command, "Walk in my presence and be perfect" (17:1), is the Hebrew way of saying, "Live virtuously," and shows that morality was primary in the true religion from the first. The changing of Abraham's name from Abram to Abraham (17:5) was to indicate a change in his destiny. According to the Semitic mentality, the name not only designated the thing, it in some way determined its nature (a.v., *nomen est omen*; cf. the change of Jacob's name to Israel, and Simon bar Jonah's to Peter — the rock).

17:10 Circumcision was already an ancient rite and practice when God chose it as the outward sign of those who entered into His covenant. It was practiced among the Egyptians and others of the ancient world, not, however, by the Philistines. Its origins are obscure but probably have something to do with prenuptial rites or with initiation into the adult element of the tribe.

19:23-29 The destruction of Sodom and Gomorrah is recorded to impress upon the Israelites of the author's time God's detestation of unnatural vice, the cancer that ran through Canaan's history down the centuries. Evidence indicates the two cities were probably located at the southern end of the Dead Sea, in ancient times dry land, now covered by water (cf. WHAB 26; 65). They were probably destroyed by one of the frequent earthquakes that plague the Jordan valley.

22:1ff Since Isaac was the son through whom the promise of numerous posterity was to be realized, the test of Abraham was a test not only of his obedience but of his faith (Gen. 15:1-6). The incident is related for its sublime example of obedience (cf. 1 Sam. 15:22ff; Ps. 51:18ff) and to inculcate the lesson for the author's contemporaries that the firstborn truly does belong to God; but, contrary to the abominable practice of infanticide among the Canaanites (sometimes practiced by the Israelites as well — cf. 2 Kings 16:3; 21:6; 23:10; Jer. 7:30; 19:5), God demands as a substitute the sacrifice of an animal (cf. Exod. 13:13).

24:3 The incident is related to impress upon the Israelites of the author's time the necessity of marrying their own rather than the depraved women of the Canaanites.

Part Three / Gen. 25—36 / The Saga of Isaac and Jacob

26:3ff The promise made to Abraham (12:1 *passim*) is made with Isaac as well. In showing the choice made of the second-born rather than the first-born, the author brings out his teaching on the freedom of the divine election.

27:24 Unquestionably a lie, Jacob's shrewdness (perhaps so viewed in that age of undeveloped moral conscience) is not praised by the author and need not be defended by the exegete. The *non* could well be stricken from St. Augustine's famous explanation, "*non est mendacium, est mysterium.*" It is a lie, but it is a mystery too, in that God makes use even of the sins of men to further His designs.

28:13-14 The promise is renewed with Jacob as it was with Abraham and Isaac, and will be renewed down the course of sacred history until its fulfillment in Christ.

29:31ff These verses up to 30:20 list the births of the twelve sons of Jacob by his wives and concubines: Leah and Zilpah, Rachel and Bilhah. Of these, it will not be the firstborn, but the fourth-born, Judah, through whom the promises will be fulfilled, when from the tribe of Judah and the family of the Judean David there is born in the fullness of time Christ.

Part Four / Gen. 37—50 / The Saga of Joseph and his brothers

N.B. 1) The student should make a brief review of Egyptian geography and history while reading Gen. 37-50. It is important because the Israelites will spend 400 years in Egypt and become Egyptianized in many ways, though never in religion. Moses, the father of the new nation, will be Egyptian in culture and training. Down through the centuries Egypt will enter into the history of the Israelites.

2) The author's purpose in including the Joseph story in Genesis

is not only to show how the Chosen People came to be in Egypt, but to point out the providential hand of God guiding the family of Jacob to Egypt where it could increase from a family to a people and thus be prepared to become a nation at Sinai (cf. Gen. 45:5-8; 50:20-21; Exod. 1:1-9).

37:3-11 The origin of Joseph's brothers' hatred is envy. Though it results in evil for Joseph, God turns this evil to good not only for Joseph but for the completion of His designs on Israel (cf. 45:5-8; 50:20-21).

38:1ff This chapter, an interruption in the story of Joseph, is interpolated to keep in the foreground the family of Judah from whom David will eventually come. Thus, throughout the story of Joseph, Judah stands out among his brothers: in 37:26ff, he defends his brother; in 43:8ff, he speaks for his brothers; 44:16ff the same; in 49:8-10, the promise of ruling power is given, not to Joseph, but to Judah. It is from Judah by Tamar that Perez is born (38:27-29). Perez is the ancestor of David (Ruth 4:18ff; Num. 26:21; 1 Chr. 2:3ff) from whom eventually is born Christ (Matthew 1:3; Luke 3:33).

41:37 The rise of Joseph, a Hebrew slave, to viceroy of Egypt is more easily understandable if it is recalled that between 1720-1550, Egypt was under the control of the Hyksos, foreigners and Semites like Joseph.

45:1-4 The author shows how God, the Maker of history, moves events good and evil toward the fulfillment of His providential designs (cf. Gen. 50:20).

46:1-4 In Egypt, as God promises, Israel does indeed become a people. In the exodus, they succeed in escaping Egypt and becoming a nation. The seventy members of Jacob's household (46:27) increase prolifically during the 400 years in Egypt until, as we shall see in Exod. 1:8, their numbers pose a threat to Egypt's security.

48:5-13 Jacob adopts Ephraim and Manasseh as his sons and they are reckoned among the twelve tribes in place of Joseph and Levi. As a map of Palestine in the time of the Judges will show, Ephraim and Manasseh were the largest tribes and thus allotted the most territory. While politically overshadowed by Judah in the time of David, Ephraim and Manasseh remained the largest of the tribes numerically until the fall of Samaria and the northern kingdom in 722 B.C.

49:8-12 In vv. 3-7, the ruling power is denied to the three older sons because of their crimes. In vv. 8-9, the symbol of a ruler, the lion (cf. the Sphinx and Assyrian Karibu), is applied to Judah, as yet only a young lion, but eventually to be a true ruler. The power promised to Judah will remain "until he comes to whom it belongs," not in the sense that it will then cease (a possible implication of 'until'), but in the sense that it will be inherent in Judah until "he comes to whom it belongs" preeminently, i.e., the Messiah. This is in accordance with all Jewish and Christian tradition. The Hebrew *shelo* is best translated according to Ezechiel 21:32 as "to whom it belongs," although some would translate it as an Accadian word *shelu* or *shilu* meaning 'ruler'; thus, it would read "until the ruler comes." While the prophecy refers directly to David, it certainly refers typically to Christ. This is confirmed by vv. 11-12 a typical prophetical description of the messianic era as a time of bountiful material prosperity (cf. pp. 357ff).

3. Exodus

While the Pentateuch as a whole is concerned with the over-all story of the foundation of the kingdom of God on earth, the book of Exodus is concerned with the central fact of that story: the foundation of the nation as a theocratic kingdom, and the events which led immediately to this extraordinary happening. Around this fact the other parts of the Pentateuch are grouped as spokes around a wheel.

Genesis, as we have seen, leads up to Exodus by explaining the origin of the people who in Exodus become the first citizens of the kingdom of God on earth. It explains how Abraham was called from Mesopotamia to be the forefather of this people and how the promises made to Abraham that his descendants would be a great people were repeated to his son, Isaac, and to his grandson, Jacob. The last part of Genesis narrates how the sons of Jacob (Israel) happened to go down to live in Egypt, and how God, by means of Joseph, providentially prepared a place for them (Gen. 37–50). The immediate link between Genesis and Exodus is given in Joseph's last words to his brothers: "I am about to die, but God will certainly come to you and lead you up from this land to the land which he promised on oath to Abraham, Isaac, and Jacob" (Gen. 50:24; cf. Gen. 46:3).

While the book derives its name from the escape or going out (*exodos*) of the Israelites from Egypt, the reader should not forget that this going out is only one of the providential events, along with the oppression, Mosaic leadership, and plagues, which lead up to the central event of the book—the foundation of God's kingdom on earth among the Israelites narrated in ch. 19—24. Keeping this in mind the reader will see that the plan of the book is simple:

PART I
1—12
The events preparing the way for the exodus: the oppression (ch. 1), the vocation of Moses (ch. 2—6), the plagues inflicted on Egypt inducing Pharaoh to release the Israelites from slavery (ch. 7—11).

PART II
12—18
The critical event: the actual escape (exodus) of the Israelites from Egypt and their migration to Sinai.

PART III
19—24
The basic and central event of the book and of the whole of the Old Testament: the election of this people by God at Sinai to be His own divinely instituted kingdom on earth; and the covenant according to which this people is bound to God and God to them.

PART IV
25—40
A description of the Ark and the Tabernacle, in which God takes up His dwelling among His people.

The reader of the Exodus story should note that much that goes into the birth of any nation went into the birth of Israel; with this exception, that in the birth of no other nation was the hand of God so manifest. The foundation of a nation requires among other things a group consciousness among the people, some great unifying experience, a system of government, and a homeland. Israel had all of these.

a) *Group consciousness*: the Israelites were related by blood to the same common ancestors (the patriarchs), and were brought up on the same historical and religious traditions (the saga of the patriarchs). At least remotely, the Israelites were conditioned to form a unified group. All that was necessary was a sufficiently strong unifying experience and an opportunity.

b) *Unifying experience*: the oppression (forced labor, execution of male children), the revolt against Pharaoh led by Moses and climaxed by the plagues, the exodus, and the miraculous passage through the Red Sea—all these were unifying experiences that left an indelible imprint on the Israelite soul.

c) *System of government*: basically theocratic, Israel was ruled by God through vicars, who saw to the observance of the basic law, the ten commandments, and the subsidiary laws in Exod. 21—23 (the Code of the Covenant).

d) *Homeland*: Palestine, the strip of land between Egypt and Syria, was to be the divinely appointed homeland for this unique people. The story of how they finally reached it is begun in Numbers and finished in Joshua.

Significant passages in Exodus

Part One / Exod. 1—12 / Events preparatory to the Exodus

1:8-22 The oppression: around 1550 the Egyptians expelled the Hyksos who had oppressed them since 1760. Egyptian hatred of the Semitic Hyksos probably included the Semitic Israelites as well. This, added to the danger presented by a possible alliance between the Israelites and any invading army from the north, led to the oppression and the decimation of Israelite manpower by infanticide.

2:1-15 The providential preparation of Moses to lead the new nation: adopted by Pharaoh's daughter (9-10), Moses is intellectually prepared for his mission at Pharaoh's court, the center of culture of the ancient world in the thirteenth century B.C. Living at court, with entree to Pharaoh, Moses learns the legal codes of his time as well as the religious practices of the Egyptians, some of which will be manifest in his drawing up of Israel's juridical and religious institutions. His flight to Midian by way of Sinai (v. 15) and his stay in Midian prepare him to lead and protect his people in the future migration to Palestine.

3—4 The call of Moses, like the call of Abraham (Gen. 12), marks the beginning of a new stage in the working out of the divine economy of salvation.

7—11 The plagues: for the most part natural phenomena connected with the inundation of the Nile, the plagues are miraculous by reason of the manner in which they occur. They begin and end at Moses' command; they are extraordinarily intense; they afflict only the Egyptians.

12:11-13 Passover: celebrated to commemorate the exodus from Egypt, the feast gets its name from the fact that God spared, i.e., passed over the Israelites when He inflicted a pestilence on the firstborn of Egypt. In the mind of the Israelites, the paschal lamb takes the place of their firstborn (12:24-27). The sprinkling of blood on doorposts (12:7) to invoke divine protection is an old practice going back to Babylonian times. The feast commemorates Israel's deliverance from slavery and her constitution as a nation.

Part Two / Exod. 12—18 / Exodus from Egypt, march to Sinai

12:40 "Four hundred and thirty years": presuming Joseph rose to power in Egypt around 1700, when the Hyksos were ruling the country, 430 years would point to about 1270 B.C. as the approximate time of the exodus. This date is confirmed as an approximation by the fact that the Egyptian capital was located in the Delta, as it is in Exodus, only during the Hyksos period and the thirteenth century B.C. Also the store-cities upon which the Israelites worked, Raamses and Pithom, are known to have been constructed or reconstructed during this same century (1:11). Moreover, when the Israelites enter Transjordan, they enter into contact with the kingdoms of Moab, Ammon, and Sihon, shown by archeologists to have been founded around the beginning of the thirteenth century. Finally, mention of Israel in an inscription of Pharaoh Mernepthah around the year 1227 refers to them as a conquered people, assuring us they had certainly left Egypt before this time. It is on this basis that most scholars date the oppression to the time of Pharaoh Sethi (1319-1301) and the exodus to the reign of Pharaoh Rameses II (1301-1234).

13:1 The reason for the consecration to God of every first-born was to remind the people of the exodus and the tenth plague. By claiming the first-born, God reminded the Hebrews of what had happened to the Egyptians, who had lost their first-born by tempting God (cf. 13:14-16).

14:21 The separation of the waters of the sea was something most likely of itself natural, brought about by the east wind (v. 21) and the receding tide. The miraculous element is manifest in the timing, favorable for the Israelites, disastrous for the Egyptians.

15:1ff The Canticle of Moses, the *Te Deum* of the liberated Israelites, probably dates in essentials to the actual victory celebration of the people, but was freely elaborated and lengthened at a later date when it became part of the liturgy (cf. p. 126).

16:4 The manna is a natural substance produced by a species of cochineal (wood-louse) that feeds on the leaves of the tamarisk tree which grows in the Sinai peninsula. The miracle consists in the quantity of the otherwise scarce manna, which at this time is providentially sufficient for such a large group.

16:13 The quail are a type of edible bird which migrates from Africa in the spring across the Sinai peninsula. While the arrival is natural, the prediction of the arrival by Moses is extraordinary.

17:1-7 The memory of the miracle is a bitter one since it recalls how the people doubted God's providence and put Him to the test: *Massah* (the test) and *Meribah* (the quarreling) come to be symbols of Israel's lack of trust.

Part Three / Exod. 19—24 / The birth of the nation at Sinai

19:3ff Immediately preparatory to the institution of the Sinai covenant are three events: (a) the promise of God that He will enter into a covenant with Israel which will be conditional (19:3-8); (b) a retreat commanded as preparation for the covenant; (c) the great Sinai theophany, in which God appears or manifests Himself as master of nature, and to whose presence wind, clouds, thunder, lightning, smoke and earthquake all give eloquent testimony.

20:1-17 The ten commandments: the basic law of the new kingdom (cf. Deut. 5:6-21) along with the Code of the Covenant (ch. 21—23), a more minute code of laws, are given to the Israelites as a charter. Many of these laws are similar in form to the laws contained in the Code of Hammurabi, indicating that Moses incorporated much of the common law of his time.

24:3-8 Ratification of the covenant: the covenant is sealed with a sacrifice and the pouring out of blood upon an altar. At the Last Supper when our Lord sealed the new covenant with the symbolic sacrifice of Himself, He spoke of the "blood which shall be poured out for the remission of many" (Matthew 26:28).

Before continuing with the significant passages in part four of Exodus, the reader is invited to initiate a study of biblical theology with the following brief treatment of covenant theology and the Ark and the Tabernacle.

Covenant theology

When the reader arrives at the institution of the Sinai covenant between God and the Israelite horde recently escaped from Egyptian slavery, he is face to face not only with a landmark in the history of Israel but with a landmark in the history of religion. At Sinai a revealed religion with laws, rites, and a hierarchy becomes historical fact. It is communicated to Moses, transmitted by him to the Israelites, and eventually committed to writing under the inspiration of the Holy Spirit. Religion, therefore, is no longer a matter of individual choice. God has made known His will and man must ordain his life to God according to the manner revealed by God.

The reader may ask how God communicates His will to man. The answer is twofold. God communicates His will directly to certain chosen men such as Abraham and Moses. This initial revelation remains always the personal mystical experience of the men to whom it was originally given. For the rest of mankind, God's revelation is indirect, made through selected, inspired men. Apart from immediate revelation to each individual, this is the only way God can make His revelation public.

The reader may further ask how these men inspired by God make known God's will to the rest of men. Here there is question of making public the revelation received in a personal mystical encounter with God. To begin with, the revealed will of God must be made known to man in a way proportionate to man's way of being. To accomplish this, to make itself accessible to men, divine truth must of necessity become incarnate in some way. It must be adapted to man's way of thinking and living if he is to grasp it. It must go from the natural which is known by man to the supernatural which is unknown. If God is to teach, He must in a sense get down to the level of His pupils. He must take men as they are, use what they know, make use of their human institutions and customs and transform them by His living truth. A study of covenant theology will show that this is precisely what God has done. It will show, moreover, that the Church, the Mystical Body of Christ in the world, is not something that burst upon men unheralded and unrehearsed.

Covenants

As a matter of historical fact, God's way of dealing with men through men (Abraham, Moses, David, and Christ the Man-God) was by means of covenants, also called pacts or treaties or testaments. God took man's way of dealing with man and adapted it to the supernatural. The covenants between Abraham and Abimelech (Gen. 21:22-32), between Jacob and Laban (Gen. 31:43-54), between David and Jonathan (1 Sam. 18:3-4), between Ahab and Ben-hadad (1 Kings 20:34) were no less covenants with regard to outward form and formalities than the divine covenants made by God with Adam, Abraham, and Moses. When God entered into covenants with Abraham and Moses, He was not introducing something entirely new. He was raising up to an eminently higher plane something already old and purely human. When He commanded Abraham to cut in two certain birds and animals and caused a flaming torch to pass between the pieces, He was not instituting a new ceremony but adapting the ancient ceremony that had long before given rise to the popular expression "to cut a covenant" (cf. Gen. 15:9-20; Jer. 34:18). The same, as we shall see, was true of many other ceremonies and rites connected with the making of covenants. God adapted. He did not invent.

Covenants between men or between nations in ancient times were simply pacts or treaties whereby rights were recognized or obligations established in a public and ceremonial manner (cf. Gen. 21:22-32; 31:43-54; 1 Kings 20:34). The covenants used by the men, to whom God had directly revealed His will, as a means to communicate God's will to the public were modeled upon these purely human covenants. One may define a divine covenant, therefore, as a concession on the part of God whereby He binds man to Himself by laws and promises. It must be noted, however, that Israel and God by means of these covenants do not in any real sense meet on equal terms. God is "bound" by His promises only because He makes them. He is bound to Himself because He cannot be false to His promises. It is only in this sense that we can speak of a bilateral covenant between God and man. Man on the other hand is strictly bound to observe his part of the covenant. When he does, God fulfills freely the promises He has made.

A study of the covenants made by God with men shows that the principal purpose of divine covenants is to ordinate man to God effectively, and ultimately to establish the kingdom of God on earth. It also shows that divine covenants are usually bilateral, i.e., with obligations on both sides. Sometimes a penalty is laid down for breaking the covenant, e.g., death in the covenant with Adam. Sometimes an outward sign is given, e.g., circumcision in the Old Testament, baptism in the New Testament. Finally and most important, covenants are always initiated by God and always for man's good, so much so that man would be foolish to refuse a covenant, even though he has no say whatever concerning its terms.

Once man breaks a covenant with God, all he can do is hope that God in His goodness and love will forgive and initiate a new one.

In the Bible the kingdom of God is prepared for, elaborated, and perfected by four great covenants: the Adamitic (a tacit covenant), the Abrahamitic, the Sinaitic, and the Christian covenants, of which the most important are the last two, more commonly known as the Old and the New Testaments.

The Adamitic covenant

Gen. 2 represents God making a covenant with Adam, promising him immortality, integrity, and the use of the garden of paradise with all it implied, provided Adam on his part observed the single law laid down to test his obedience. Upon this law God laid the penalty of death as a sanction. The covenant with Adam may be summarised as follows: (a) it is bilateral, i.e., with obligations on both sides — on the part of God promises of paradise and immortality; on the part of man the obligation to obey God's precept; (b) it is a conditional, not an absolute covenant; (c) it carries with it a sanction — the penalty of death; (d) it is characterized by familiarity between God and Adam (cf. A. Schökel, "Sapiential and Covenant Themes in Gen. 2–3," *Theology Digest* 13; 1965).

Of special importance is the fact that the shattering of this covenant by Adam ends the initial economy of salvation. The promise of redemption in Gen. 3:15 initiates a new economy of salvation — coloring the whole future of the human race. Further, this initial relation between God and man, which is disrupted by Adam, is restored by future covenants: partially by the second covenant made with the family of Abraham, more fully by the third (Sinaitic) covenant made with the Israelite nation, completely by the fourth and last covenant — the New Testament, in which not merely one man, or one family, or even one nation, but all mankind, one with Christ, is called to form *the* kingdom of God on earth. (cf. Rom. 5:15-21; 1 Cor. 15:22-28).

The Abrahamitic covenant

The second great covenant ordaining man to God and restoring partially the initial relations between God and man disrupted by Adam's disobedience is made with Abraham and his posterity sometime in the nineteenth or eighteenth century B.C., and is later renewed with Isaac (Gen. 26:1ff) and Jacob (Gen. 28:12ff; 39:9ff). It may be summarized as follows: (a) it is bilateral: on the part of God, promises of a great posterity (Gen. 12:2; 15:5), possession of Palestine (Gen. 12:7; 15:7, 18), extraordinary blessings on the patriarchs and through them on all mankind (Gen. 12:3; 15:5-6); on the part of Abraham, Isaac, and Jacob: the obligation of serving God (Gen. 17:7), moral integrity (Gen. 17:1; 18:19; 26:5), and faith in God's promises (Gen. 15:6; cf. Rom. 4:1-25). (b) It is absolute, not conditional. (c) Circumcision[1] is given as the external sign of those who enter the covenant (Gen. 17:10). (d) There is, as in the Adamitic covenant, familiarity between man and God (Gen. 18:17ff).

It should be noted that the Abrahamitic covenant, unlike the Adamitic covenant, is absolute, unconditional, and eternal — perfected and fulfilled in the New Testament (cf. Luke 1:55-73 where the coming of Christ is recognized in the Magnificat and the Benedictus as the fulfillment of the promises made to Abraham). It should further be noted that this pact, made first with a single family, is extended to a nation at Sinai (Exod. 19—24) and finally to all mankind through Christ and the New Testament.

The Sinaitic covenant

In Egypt the descendants of the patriarchs increase to such an extent that for political reasons they are enslaved by the Pharaohs. When in God's providential design they have been oppressed and enslaved to the point where they typify as a people the sinfully enslaved condition of all mankind, God raises up Moses and commands him to bring His people out of bondage and lead them to Sinai.

On Sinai God fulfills His promise to Abraham (Gen. 12:3), extending His covenant to the Israelite people, amplifying laws and obligations, taking the Israelites to Himself as His covenanted nation (Exod. 19—24), and promising them His blessing, protection, prosperity, and peace. His greatest promise is one of intimate familiarity: "I will make my dwelling among you. I will not reject you. But I will walk among you as surely as I am God; I will be to you God, and you will be to me my people" (cf. Lev. 23:3-13).

The Sinaitic covenant may be summarized as follows: (a) it is bilateral; on the part of God, the promises made to Abraham are extended to the whole Israelite nation; on the part of the nation, what was required of Abraham is now required of Israel, plus obedience to the Mosaic law (Exod. 20—23). (b) It is conditional. *De facto* it is broken by the Israelites and repudiated by God (cf. Exod. 19:5; Jer. 30:31; Matthew

[1] Cf. R. de Vaux, *Ancient Israel* (New York: McGraw-Hill, 1962) 46-48

26:28; Mark 14:24). (c) Circumcision is continued as the external sign of those who enter the covenant. (d) There is extraordinary familiarity. God Himself dwells in the midst of the nation in the Tabernacle above the Ark of the Covenant.

Other notable circumstances of the Sinaitic covenant are the providential preparation and vocation of Moses as mediator and prophet (Exod. 2–6), the miraculous liberation of the Israelites from Egyptian slavery (Exod. 14), the inauguration of the covenant with a great and memorable theophany (Exod. 19:16ff), ratification of the covenant by the people as a group (Exod. 24:1-8), and lastly a special book of laws known as "The Book of the Covenant" (Exod. 21–23:19; 24:7).

Historical background of the Sinaitic covenant

We have given a brief description of the Sinaitic covenant. There remains the question of its origin. Did it derive directly from God by revelation? Was it the invention of Moses working under the influence of inspiration? Or was it an adaptation by Moses of a covenant form already common in the world of his time? If it was an adaptation, from what covenant form did it derive?

It has already been shown in a general way that the covenants made by God with men in the Old Testament were not new creations but simply adaptations of existing covenant forms in common use in the ancient world. It is now possible, as a result of recent investigations, to show that the Sinaitic covenant, which was made between God and a whole people or nation, may have been based upon a specific form of covenant made between a king and his vassals (cf. G. E. Mendenhall's "Covenant Forms in Israelite Times" BA (1954) 50-75) This form of covenant, which is known as a suzerainty pact, is best illustrated by the Hittite suzerainty pacts from the fifteenth to the thirteenth centuries B.C.

Before describing the Hittite suzerainty pacts, it is well to note that no claim is made for any direct dependence of the Sinaitic covenant on any specific Hittite pact. What is suggested is that there existed in the time of Moses a well known form of international covenant made between kings and vassal peoples for which we have clear documentary evidence from the kingdom of the Hittites.

In form and content the Hittite suzerainty pacts generally consist of the following six elements:

1. A preamble giving the name of the covenanting king along with a list of his titles and attributes.

2. An historical prologue in which are recounted the benevolent deeds

performed by the king in favor of his vassals, because of which the vassals are obligated in perpetual gratitude to obey the commands of the king. Two significant characteristics of this section are the careful descriptions of the actual benefits conferred by the king, and the basic statement of commitment demanded of the vassal by the covenanting suzerain.

3. A list of stipulations detailing the obligations imposed upon the vassals. These include specific prohibitions (cf. the decalogue) as well as demands that the vassals show unlimited trust in the king, appear before him or present tribute once a year, and submit to him for judgment any controversies between his vassals.

4. A provision for deposit of the pact in the temple and for periodic public readings of the pact.

5. A list of gods. Just as ordinary contracts were witnessed by individuals in the community, so international contracts were witnessed by the gods. Significant in this section is the inclusion of the deified mountains, rivers, sea, heaven, and earth as witnesses (cf. Deut. 32:1; Is. 1:2).

6. Formulas of blessings and curses which will follow upon the observance or non-observance of the covenant. Significant in this section is the fact that the only sanctions for the covenant are religious sanctions. The curses and blessings are considered the actions of the gods and are similar to those mentioned in Deut. 28. In addition to the above six elements there was also some form of oath sworn by the vassals and some kind of solemn ceremony for the ratification of the covenant.

Of all the many covenants described in the Bible, only two follow the form detailed above for the Hittite suzerainty pacts: the Sinaitic covenant and the covenant described in Jos. 24. The fact that these suzerainty treaties are instanced frequently in the time of Moses and before and are rarely mentioned later, plus the remarkable resemblance between the Sinaitic covenant and the suzerainty treaties make it possible but not certain that Moses adapted this treaty form to express the relations that were to exist between God and His Chosen People. The following parallels will indicate the similarity between the Sinaitic covenant and the suzerainty treaties:

1. *The preamble identifying the author of the covenant*: "I, Yahweh, am your God. . . ." (Exod. 20:2a).

2. *The historical prologue describing the king's benevolence in favor of his vassals*: "who brought you out of Egypt, that place of slavery" (Exod. 20:2b). It is this previous divine act of benevolence that establishes the obligation of gratitude and the obligation of accepting the stipulations of the king. As in the Hittite pacts the prologue uses the "I— Thou" form of address and calls for a basic statement of commitment —

the first commandment, "You shall not have other gods besides me" (Exod. 20:3).

3. *The list of stipulations:* the ten commandments (Exod. 20:3-17) detail in the first part the obligations of the vassals to their God-King and in the second part the obligations of the vassals to each other. It should be noted as well that the vassal-Israelites are called upon to appear before God annually with tribute (Exod. 23:17) and to submit controversial cases to adjudication at God's shrine (Deut. 17:8-13).

4. *Deposit of the pact in the temple and periodic public reading:* according to Deut. 10:5 the tablets of the commandments are deposited in the Ark of the Covenant. And according to Deut. 31:9-13 the priests are required to read the law aloud to the people at the feast of Booths.

5. *A list of witness-gods:* for obvious reasons this list is missing from the Sinaitic covenant. It is, nevertheless, significant that in Deut. 32:1 and in Is. 1:2 the heavens are called upon to witness Israel's infidelity to the covenant.

6. *Formulas of blessings and curses:* in Deut. 28 long lists of blessings and curses are given which will follow as sanction upon the observance or non-observance of the covenant.

While the people do not take formal oaths to observe the Sinaitic covenant, it is significant that they publicly declare their willingness to observe it (Exod. 24:3) and that the covenant is solemnly ratified with the ceremonies of sprinkling blood on the altar (Exod. 24:4-8) and probably also by a sacred banquet (Exod. 24:11b).

In the brief description of the renewal of the covenant at Shechem in Jos. 24, there is a preamble identifying the author of the covenant (v. 2a), a long historical prologue in which the "I — Thou" form of address is used (vv. 2b-13), no list of stipulations but the one basic stipulation concerning the putting away of other gods, which was the foundation of all other obligations (v. 14), a quasi-oath formula recapitulating the one stipulation and giving a summary of the historical prologue (vv. 16-18). In a sequel (vv. 21-28), mention is made of witnesses (vv. 22 and 27), a quasi-oath formula (vv. 21 and 24), and stipulations (vv. 23 and 26), along with an implicit reference to the deposit of the written text of the covenant in the sanctuary (v. 26). There is no reference made to blessings or curses.

The covenant renewal in Jos. 24 (cf. also Deut. 4—8; 9—11; 26:16—28:69; 29—30 plus 31:9-13 and 31:24-29) is significant for the light it casts on Israel's historical traditions. The longer historical prologue in Joshua (24:2b-13), summing up the divine deeds of benevolence toward the Israelites from the time of the patriarchs down to the time of Joshua,

B.C.	Personalities	Events	In the Neighborhood	Literature
1900 → 1300	ABRAHAM	Abraham called from Mesopotamia to Canaan	3rd Dynasty of Ur (2090–1960)	*Gilgamesh* *Enuma Elish* *Code of Hammurabi* Song of Lamech (Gen. 4:23-24)
	Isaac		Hammurabi (1728–1686) unified lower Mesopotamia	
	Jacob	Jacob and sons settle in Egypt		Blessings of Noah (Gen. 9:24-27)
	Joseph		Hyksos rule Egypt from 1760 to 1550 Amenophis IV (1377–1360)	Oral traditions about the Patriarchs *Tel el Amarna letters*
1300 → 1200	MOSES	Oppression of Israel in Egypt Plagues and exodus from Egypt Sinai Covenant — Israel becomes a nation	Seti I (1315–1290)	Canticle of Moses (Exod. 15:1-11) Refrain on Amalek (Exod. 17:16)
			Ramses II (1290–1234)	Code of the Covenant (Exod. 20:22–23:19)
	Aaron		Suzerainty pact between Ramses II and Hattusil III of Hatti (c. 1280)	Refrain on the Ark (Num. 10:35-36)
	Caleb Balaam JOSHUA	Israel in the wilderness Israel in Moab Conquest of Canaan (c. 1225)	The Trojan wars	Oral traditions about the exodus and the conquest

B.C.	Personalities	Events	In the Neighborhood	Literature
	JUDGES	Israel's period of transformation, and adaptation to Canaanite customs	Philistines enter Palestine (c. 1190) Philistines capture the Ark and destroy Shiloh	*Homeric traditions* Canticle of Deborah Blessings of Jacob (Gn. 49) Blessings of Moses (Deut. 33)
	SAMUEL Saul	The monarchy Saul fails as first king	Philistines defeat Saul at Gilboa	David's lament over Saul and Jonathan (2 Sam. 1:17–27) David's lament over Abner (2 Sam. 3:33)
1200	DAVID	David, king of Judah alone David, king of all Israel		Ark narrative (1 Sam. 4–7; 2 Sam. 5–6) Book of "Yashar" and book of the "Wars of Yahweh"
		David captures Jerusalem		Davidic psalms Oral traditions about Samuel, Saul, and David
1000	NATHAN	Nathan's oracle promises perpetuity to the Davidic dynasty		
	SOLOMON	Soloomn builds the Temple (960)		Court history of David (2 Sam. 9–20; 1 Kings 1–2) Proverbs of Solomon (Prov. 10–22; 25–29)
	Ahijah REHOBOAM—JEROBOAM I	Division of David's kingdom into Judah and Israel (c. 926)	Pharaoh Shishak's invasion of Palestine (c. 922)	YAHWIST's synthesis of patriarchal and exodus traditions
	Abijam—Nadab ASA—Baasha; Elah JEHOSHAPHAT—Zimri			Book of the "Acts of Solomon" (1 Kings 11–41)
1000	OMRI ELIJAH AHAB ELISHA Jehoram—Ahaziah Ahaziah—Jehoram ATHALIAH—JEHU Jehoash—Jehoahaz	Omri founds Samaria (c. 870) Elisha versus Ahab Elisha, through Jehu, destroys the Omrid dynasty in Israel	Asyrians repulsed at Karkar (854) Jehu subject to Shalmaneser III of Assyria (c. 842)	Chronicles of the Kings of Judah and the Kings of Israel The Elijah-Elisha cycles
800				

indicates that the covenant form itself may have furnished the nucleus around which Israel's historical traditions crystallized. Thus Israel's unique feeling for history, and indeed religious history primarily, is seen to be intimately bound up with the covenant form. The same may be said for Israel's legal and cultic traditions, since the stipulations followed upon the historical prologue, which laid the foundation for the obligation of gratitude at the basis of the stipulations, and the cultic traditions were bound up both with the basic stipulation — no alliances with strange gods — and with the solemn ceremonies for the ratification of the covenant.

The covenant and the kingdom

A study of the parallels between the Sinai covenant and the Hittite suzerainty pact suggests that Moses may have done on a national level what Abraham had done on a family level. Just as Abraham presented his relations with God under the well known form of a personal covenant, so Moses presented the newly revealed religion under the well known form of an international suzerainty covenant. The realization that Moses could use an already existing covenant form to define God's relations with His Chosen People is important for the understanding of an outstanding characteristic of revealed religion in both the Old and the New Testaments, namely, the adaptation and use of existing customs, laws, and institutions, even those having a strictly pagan background, for the organization and development of the kingdom of God on earth.

An extensive list could be drawn up of the adaptations made by Moses. A few examples, however, will have to suffice. In the field of law it is more than obvious, from a study of the common law of the ancient Near East, that Moses sanctioned many existing laws giving them a new bent by making them the stipulations of Yahweh, Israel's God-King.[1] In the field of cult it is reasonably certain that the Ark of the Covenant is adapted from Egyptian cult arks. Israel's feasts are for the most part either pre-Mosaic feasts or baptized Canaanite feasts, but they are all given a new orientation. When the Temple is built, it is built by Phoenician architects; and in its appurtenances it will be for the most part similar to those of Canaanite temples of the time.

Examples could be multiplied, but enough have been given to show that it was not without precedent that the early Church drew much of her liturgy from the synagogue, much of her law and organization pattern from the Roman empire, and many of her customs and practices

[1] Cf. Claus Schedl, *History of the Old Testament* (Staten Island: Alba House, 1973) vol. 2, 121–202.

from the daily life of the people among whom she took root. One need only point to the Church's baptizing of the 25th of December, the Roman feast of the Unconquered Sun, by making it the birthday of the Son of God, to realize that in the New Testament as well as in the Old, God's way is not to destroy but to adapt and reorientate.

How Israel became, however, is not nearly so important as what Israel became. As a result of the Sinai covenant, the Israelite people become God's immediate subjects and constitute a unique theocratic nation. In the theocratic kingdom of Israel, God Himself becomes both religious and civil ruler of His people. He makes Himself King, Lawmaker, and Judge of Israel. He gives her a political constitution not unlike that of other nations and exercises judgment either directly or through His appointed vicars (Moses at first, later the charismatic judges and the Davidic kings). He remains King of Israel until the moment when the scepter passes from the human vicar-kings to the hands of Him to whom it belongs preeminently — Christ the King, King not only of the Israelites but of all men and all nations (cf. 1 Cor. 15:22-28; Eph. 5:24-33; Heb. 12:18ff; Gal. 3–4).

In God's providential design the Church-nation instituted on Mt. Sinai was meant to grow and find true spiritual fulfillment. Eventually, therefore, the alliance between Church and nation will have to be dissolved. The dissolution will take place during the apostolic age. In the years between 50 and 75 A.D., due principally to the persistence of St. Paul in dissociating the true Israel of God from the outmoded forms and laws of the dispossessed Sinaitic covenant, the Old Testament Church-nation will break its nationalistic bonds and become universal in the Church founded by Jesus.

A careful reading of the outline on page 33 will show the relation between the different covenants and their progressive ordination toward the Church as we know it now.

Part Four / Exod. 25–40 / The Ark and the Tabernacle

It should be noted before reading this section that the historical narrative interrupted at 24:18 is continued at 32:1 down to 34:35. The narrative interrupted there is not taken up again until the book of Numbers (10:29). Everything between Exod. 24:18 and Num. 10:28, with the exception of Exod. 32–34 represents a re-ordering of the text and may be considered a huge parenthesis into which the priestly editor has inserted a vast block of material from the "P" document: Exod. 25–40, concerning the Ark and the Tabernacle; the whole book of Leviticus, concerning the duties and privileges of the levitical personnel; and Num. 1–10, concerning the arrangement of the tribes around the Ark and the Tabernacle and the census upon which was based the tax measures for the support of divine worship.

The episode of the golden calf-idol related in Exod. 32–34 can be considered, at least psychologically, as the event which showed an innate need for something external like the Ark and the Tabernacle as a focus for worship in an idol-less cult. It will be useful pedagogically, therefore, to treat Exod. 32–34 first and then give a brief description of the Ark and the Tabernacle and their place in the religious life of Israel.

32:1-6   The people demand an idol of God in place of the invisible God whom they have been commanded to worship without representation of any kind (Exod. 20:4). Their sin is one of disobedience, making a visible representation of God contrary to the first commandment of the decalogue.

32:21ff   Aaron's lame explanation and Moses' punishment of the disobedient, with the assistance of the Levites, provides a lasting lesson on the evils of idolatry.

33:1ff   Through the intercession of Moses (vv. 12-17) the people are forgiven and the covenant is renewed (34:10-28).

The Ark and the Tabernacle

Most of part four of Exodus (ch. 25–40), in which there is much repetition (ch. 25–31 give instructions for the construction of the Ark and the Tabernacle [1] and ch. 35–40 recount how these instructions were carried out to the letter), can be found summed up in ch. 40:16-33. The chapters should all be read, nevertheless, for the information they give us concerning Israelite religious rites so influential in the formation of our own liturgy and so important as a preparation for the book of Leviticus containing the laws that governed Israelite liturgy, centered for the most part around the Ark and the Tabernacle.

It is not unlikely that God inspired Moses to construct the Ark of the Covenant in order to supply the innate need of the Israelites for something external upon which they could focus their religious sentiments (cf. Exod. 32). Since God could not permit His people to worship Him under a sensible form because of the danger of idolatry to which a sensible representation might lead simple people in pagan, idolatrous surround-

[1] Cf. De Vaux, op. cit., 294–302.

I   **TACIT PACT WITH ADAM**
Kingdom of God
Grace of God
Test stage
    a) conditional
    b) bilateral
    c) penalty: death
    d) some familiarity

THE FALL   Mankind's future, however, is assured by the promise given in the protoevangel (Gen. 3:15).

II   **PACT WITH ABRAHAM**
Kingdom of God
Grace of Christ
Foundation stage
    a) absolute — fulfilled in Christ and the Church
    b) one family, potentially universal
    c) outward sign: circumcision
    d) limited familiarity: theophanies

III   **PACT WITH MOSES**
Kingdom of God
Grace of Christ
Elaboration stage
    a) conditional, broken
    b) one nation, potentially universal
    c) external sign: circumcision
    d) much greater familiarity:
       1. God present with them in the Ark and Tabernacle
       2. God Himself is Ruler
       3. Vicars: priests, prophets, kings

IV   **PACT WITH CHRIST**
Kingdom of Christ
Grace of Christ
Completion stage
    a) absolute and eternal
    b) all men
    c) external sign: baptism
    d) greatest possible familiarity:
       1. one Mystical Body
       2. indwelling of the Blessed Trinity
       3. ruler: Christ the King
       4. vicar: the Pope

At the **STAGE OF ULTIMATE PERFECTION,** Head and members reign triumphantly in heaven and the Kingdom of Christ is handed back to the Father (1 Cor. 15:22-28).

ings, He devised the Ark as the place above which His presence would in some mysterious way be localized, and in such a way that the Ark represented the footstool of His royal throne (cf. 1 Chr. 28:2; Ps. 99:5; Ps. 132:7).

The Ark was constructed in the shape of a small trunk or chest about four feet in length, two and a half feet in width and depth, covered with gold inside and out (cf. Exod. 25:10-22; 37:1-9), with a slab of gold (the propitiatory) on the top, where God's feet were conceived as resting (cf. Exod. 25:17-22).

As described, the Ark shows a definite resemblance to Egyptian arks (box-like structures upon which were carried idols of the Egyptian gods), with the difference that God was not represented by an idol riding the Ark as in Egypt, but was considered as localized there, enthroned in the empty space above the Ark, His feet conceived as resting upon it as a footstool, with the cherubim (figures of angelic beings) as His throne (cf. Exod. 25:18-20). From there God communicated with His vicars: Moses, the priests, and the prophets (cf. 1 Chr. 28:2; Ps. 14:7).

The Ark contained the tables of the law (cf. Exod. 40:20 and the fourth stipulation of the Hittite suzerainty pacts) and later a container of the manna, the rod of Aaron, and a copy of the Book of the Covenant (Exod. 21—23).

While the Ark remained in the Tabernacle for the most part, it was on occasion taken out, particularly on the occasion of battles (cf. Jos. 6:6 and 1 Sam. 4:4). Around 1050 B.C., the Ark was captured by the Philistines (cf. 1 Sam. 4). Upon its return it was taken to Kiriath-jearim (cf. 1 Sam 7). From there it was brought by David to the house of Obed-edom and later to Jerusalem (cf. 2 Sam. 6). When Solomon completed the Temple in Jerusalem about 960 B.C., the Ark was placed in the Holy of Holies where it remained until 587 when it disappeared at the time of the destruction of the Temple by the Babylonians. In 2 Mach. 2:4-8, a legend is cited according to which Jeremiah saved the Ark from destruction by hiding it. The epistle to the Hebrews (ch. 8—10) contains a fine commentary on the worship that centered upon God present above the Ark of the Covenant.

The Tabernacle may be defined as the portable temple of the Israelites, built to serve as God's dwelling place among His people until the building of the permanent Temple in the time of Solomon. Externally, the Tabernacle probably resembled the common nomadic tents of the Israelites. Inside, it was divided into two parts: the Holy Place and the Holy of Holies (cf. 26:33-34), with the Ark and the protecting cherubim in the Holy of Holies (cf. 25:18-20), and the golden, seven-branched candlestick (25:31-40), the table with the loaves of proposition (25:23-30), and the altar of incense in the Holy Place (30:1-4). Outside, in the court in front of the Tabernacle (27:1-8), was the large altar of holocausts (27:1-8) and the bronze basin in which water was stored for liturgical purposes (30:17-21).

Constructed at Sinai (Exod. 35–39), accompanied by and set up by the Levites (Num. 4:24-33; 20:21, 36), the Tabernacle was carried up through the desert to the plains of Moab and across the Jordan to Gilgal, where it remained during the period of the conquest (1250-1225). During the lifetime of Joshua it was brought to Shiloh (Jos. 18:1) where it is found in the time of Samuel (1 Sam. 1–4). Later it was set up at Gibeon where it remained until taken by Solomon to be preserved in the vaults of his Temple, which replaced the tabernacle after 960 B.C.

Importance of the book of Exodus

In view of what has already been said, it is obvious that the basic importance of Exodus lies in the fact that it gives us the blueprint of the Kingdom of God, the basic plan upon which the Church instituted by Christ is built. It is important also because of its use in the liturgy: in the Holy Week services, in the prayers at baptism, in the Mass and Office during the paschal season. This use is prompted by the abundance of types found in Exodus, outlining in a veiled manner the history of our redemption wrought by Christ.

The basic parallelism of the types may be summed up as follows: as Moses led the Israelites from captivity in Egypt, through the Red Sea to a new life as God's redeemed, and from the sea to the promised land, directed by a pillar of fire, fed by miraculous bread (manna) and miraculous meat (quail) and water from a rock. . . . so Christ, the new Moses, the paschal lamb, sacrificed on Mt. Calvary, leads His Chosen People through the Red Sea of His redeeming Blood, by baptism, to the new Christian life in which, leading the life of the resurrected Christ, the redeemed follow Christ, the light of the world, through this life as a desert, eating His flesh, drinking His blood, until they ascend with Him into the Promised Land, the kingdom of heaven. When engaged in liturgical prayer, the worshipper should go immediately from the types to the anti-types. St. Paul in 1 Cor. 10:1-13 is an excellent guide on how to read Exodus and Numbers.

Finally, Exodus is most important for an understanding of the rest of the Bible. Future inspired writers, prophets, historians, evangelists, look back upon these events, draw comparisons and make innumerable allusions. No one can read the prophets and the wisdom writers nor even much of the Gospels and St. Paul with real appreciation and understanding unless he has read and digested the great theological impact of the Exodus and the Sinai covenant.

In conclusion, we can say that the theme of Exodus is the story of the greatest event in the whole history of the Chosen People: its sublime elevation to the dignity of a theocratic nation, directed, ruled, and protected by the one true God. The book gives the foundation of this kingdom, its laws and regulations, some of its vicissitudes. It ends with the construction and dedication of the Ark and the Tabernacle, in which from this time on, God will dwell in the midst of His people. This last event is by no means something loosely related to the covenant, but rather its immediate consequence and its glorious consummation. With the dedication of the Tabernacle and God's coming to dwell there, the Kingdom of God on earth begins. In a similar manner, twelve hundred and fifty years later, God dedicates the tabernacle of Mary's body, and at the annunciation His only-begotten Son takes His place there to fulfill the promise made to Abraham, becoming no longer the "expected" but the arrived "blessing of all nations," in whose Mystical Body all men are called to salvation.

4. Leviticus

Leviticus is a collection of laws and rites that have to do with the organization and carrying out of divine worship. In the Pentateuch, Leviticus serves to emphasize the 'holy' nature of the newly founded kingdom. It follows immediately upon the Exodus account narrating the setting up of the Ark and the Tabernacle (Exod. 25–40) and explains what the coming of God to dwell in the midst of them entailed for the Israelites.

The nature of the new kingdom is explicitly declared by God on Mt. Sinai, when He says: "If you hearken to my voice and keep my covenant . . . you shall be to me a kingdom of priests, *a holy nation.*" The echo of these words runs through the whole book of Leviticus and becomes explicit several times in the words: "You shall make and keep yourselves holy, because I am holy" (11:44-45); "Be holy, for I, the Lord, your God, am holy" (19:2; 20:7; 20:26; 22:31-33).

While the whole last part of Exodus (ch. 25–40 concerning the Ark and the Tabernacle) is intimately connected with Leviticus, it is the last words of Exodus (40:34-38), describing the coming of God to take up His abode in the midst of His people, that provide the immediate link with the book of Leviticus. Such an event immediately raises several questions. First: how treat so important a Guest? This question is an-

2

Nos. 1–6. Prehistoric Palestine.   **1**. Palestine provides excellent archaeological evidence for the physical or skeletal evolution of man. From
the Paleolithic Age we have the "Galilee Skull" found in this cave in
1925.   **2**. More important are a series of skeletal discoveries in the Mugh-
ara caves on Mount Carmel near Haifa.   **3**. From these caves bones and
dozens of complete skeletons have been recovered, bridging the period
from Paleolithic man, through Neanderthal, Cro-Magnon, and more recent
types.   **4**. Neolithic man in Palestine was fond of dolmen structures
(note dolmen in background, framed by another; from about 6000 B.C.,
on hills above Damiya, East Jordan.   **5–6**. By 3500 before Christ, the Ghas-
sulians, a bit northeast of the Dead Sea, were designing stars and typical
Chalcolithic pottery. Abraham and the patriarchs were not to arrive there
for about another two thousand years. No. 1 *courtesy:* Matson Photo Service,
Alhambra, California. Nos. 2–6: Pontifical Biblical Institute, Piazza Pilotta,
Rome, Italy.

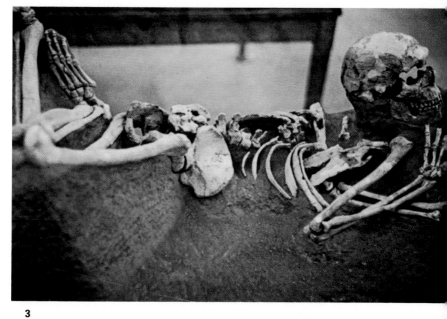

3

4

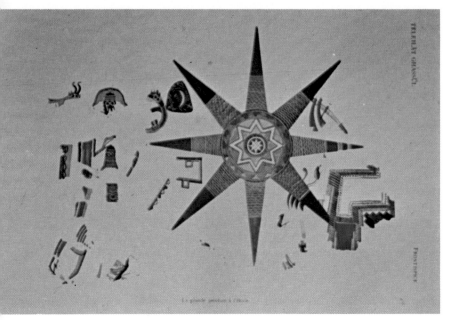

5

6

swered in Part I (1–7), describing the ritual of sacrifices which make up the major external element of Israel's worship; and in Part II (8–10), describing the ordination ritual by which worthy men are singled out and publicly invested with power as mediators (priests) between God and His people. Emphasis is laid on the "holiness" required of priests because of their nearness to God.

How the people should comport themselves outwardly now that they are so close to God present in their midst is the question answered in Part III (11–16), the code of laws regulating legal purity or cleanliness. The last part of the book (17–26), called the Code of legal Holiness, gives the answer to the question: what moral laws should govern the conduct of a people called to such familiarity with God? The basic law regulating the conduct of the Israelites toward each other is given in this section: "You shall love your neighbor as yourself" (Lev. 19:18).

Leviticus, therefore, tells the Israelites just how God wishes to be worshipped; not according to any way they might personally choose, but according to the ritual of sacrifice and feasts that God prescribed through Moses. In the New Testament God has done no less. The note or mark of "holiness" which characterizes the Old Testament kingdom of God will remain one of its characteristic notes or marks in the New Testament as well, when it presents itself to the world as one, *holy*, universal, and apostolic.

Significant passages in Leviticus

Part One / Lev. 1–7 / The Ritual of Sacrifices

1:3-9 *The holocaust*: a blood sacrifice entailing the total destruction of the victim in order to acknowledge God's supreme dominion over His creatures. The reader should note the elements of sacrifice detailed here and repeated in the descriptions of the other types of sacrifice described in this part of the book. They will be found in the perfect sacrifice of Calvary and in its repetition, the holy Sacrifice of the Mass.[1]

a) *The victim*: it must be perfect, without blemish, because only a perfect gift befits God (v. 3; cf. Lev. 22:17ff).

b) *The offering lay-man*: he lays his hands on the victim to indicate solemnly that the victim is offered in his name. Where the priest does it, he shows that the victim is offered either in his own name or in the name of the community for whom he acts.

c) *The immolation*: the destruction or killing of the victim is

[1] Cf. De Vaux, *op. cit.*, 415ff.

done to remove it from profane use and to prepare it to be handed over to God. It should be noted that the immolation, since it was not an essential but only a preparatory act of sacrifice, could be and was done by anybody, priest, levite, or lay-man.

d) *The oblation*: the essential act of sacrifice is the oblation or handing over of the victim to God (v. 5). It is done by pouring the blood of the victim on the altar, because the blood represents the life of the victim (cf. Lev. 17:11), and the altar represents God as the receiver of the victim.

e) *The priest-offerer*: under the Sinai Testament, as interpreted in the post-exilic Priestly Code, only a legitimately ordained priest had the power of offering sacrifice. In patriarchal times, the patriarchs and heads of clans had this power.

N.B. While the indispensible elements of sacrifice consist in the internal acts of worship, thanksgiving, and propitiation, it must never be forgotten that man because of his very nature, part spiritual and part material, must be allowed to express externally his interior, spiritual sentiments of worship. When Leviticus, therefore, speaks of the externals of sacrifice, it means those external actions which express what should be going on simultaneously and invisibly in the soul of the individual. Where these are lacking — sentiments of internal worship, thanksgiving, propitiation — there is no true sacrifice.

Books which speak as if only the externals of sacrifice were required in the Old Testament speak erroneously. Mere externals constitute formalism, effecting and expressing not sanctity and worship but legalism and sanctimoniousness. Leviticus says little about the internals of sacrifice precisely because it takes them for granted and because it is essentially a book of rubrics. In a similar way our Christian rubrical books take for granted the requisite internal dispositions and for the most part give nothing more than directions (rites and ceremonial) for the externals.

That the Old Testament considered the internal disposition of basic importance can be seen from the statement of Samuel to Saul, "Obedience is better than sacrifice" (1 Sam. 15:22); from a reading of the prophets (Is. 1:10-20 and the prophets passim); and from a study of such psalms as Pss. 40; 50; 51.

7:11-21 *The 'peace' offering* and the sacrificial banquet: while the way of offering a peace offering, whether it was a thanksgiving sacrifice (cf. Ps. 50:14, 23), or a sacrifice made in fulfillment of a vow (cf. Pss. 61:9; 57:13), or a free will offering of sacrifice (cf. Ps. 54:8) was basically the same as that for a holocaust, it differed in this that the victim was not wholly destroyed. Part was destroyed to indicate it was given over to God (7:14), part was given to the priest as his stipend (7:14), and the remainder was returned to the offering layman to be consumed at a sacrificial banquet in the Tabernacle or Temple courts (7:15, cf. 1 Sam. 1:4 and 1:18; 9:22-24). Only those, however, who were ritually clean (v. 20) could partake of this banquet at which God was the host and the offerer and his friends were the guests. Further rules for this banquet are given in Deut. 12:4-7, and examples of the usage can be found not only in the Old Testament (1 Sam. 1:3-5; 2:12-16; 9:22-24), but in the New Testament as well (1 Cor. 11:17-22).

N.B. It should be noted that the sacrifice of the Mass is the perfection of both the holocaust and the peace offerings of the Old Testament. While the victim — Christ — is given over entirely to the Father as in a holocaust, He is nevertheless returned to the faithful under the appearance of bread and wine to be consumed at the Communion banquet at the end of the Mass-sacrifice.

As examples of psalms recited on the occasion of these peace offerings followed by sacrificial banquets, the reader should study Pss. 66; 116 (cf. pp. 154ff).

Part Two / Lev. 8–10 / The ritual of ordination

10:1-3 The story of Nadab's and Abihu's punishment is told to stress the holiness expected of God's priests. For additional emphasis on the sanctity required of priests, cf. 10:8-11; 21:1-15; 22:1-9.

Part Three / Lev. 11–16 / Laws regarding legal purity

12:1-8 This chapter, concerned with the purification of women from the ritual uncleanness contracted as a result of childbirth, is a good example of the purely legal, and in no immediate sense moral, uncleanness with which this section of Leviticus is concerned. In the Old Testament, certain conditions or actions made one unfit to take part in divine worship. Such unfitness was called uncleanness (cf. Num. 9:6-14). The origin of this ritual uncleanness goes back to ancient customs, taboos, and prejudices common throughout much of the Near East (cf. Aeneid, Book II, line 718; Odyssey, Book XII, line 198) plus reasons of congruity (Lev. 15:31), and perhaps even hygienic reasons. Moses' purpose in incorporating these ancient taboos in his ritual was evidently to promote spiritual cleanliness from bodily cleanliness, to destroy pagan influences by giving a monotheistic bent to what formerly had a pagan bent and background, and finally to practice his people in obedience by directing as much as possible of their civil, social, moral, and religious life toward the worship of the one, true God. The success of this pedagogical tour de force can be gauged by the difficulty we have now in discovering the original backgrounds of these baptized customs, taboos, and prejudices.

Part Four / *Lev. 17–26* / *The Code of legal Holiness*

17:11-16 "The life of a living body is in its blood. . . ." Since God is the Lord of all life, every taking of life was considered a ritual act. It is from this chapter and this outlook that the "Kosher" laws derive.

18:1ff Laws condemning illicit and particularly incestuous sex relations. These laws were especially necessary for a people used to the immorality of the Egyptians and surrounded by the even more immoral Canaanites (cf. Num. 25).

19:17-19 Great law of love, basis of both testaments. While some tended to understand neighbor here only as fellow-countryman, the statement in Lev. 19:34 about the treatment of aliens was a clear indication of its at least potential universality. Of this, our Lord banished all doubt in His parable on the Good Samaritan (Luke 10:30ff).

20–22 Special laws for priesthood: 21:1-15 sanctity required; 21:17ff irregularities; 22:17ff unacceptable sacrificial animals.

23:1ff Feast days to be celebrated: (a) *Sabbath* (v. 3), complete day of rest to be given to God. (b) *Passover* (4-14), 14th day of Abib, later Nisan (March or April), first of the three great feasts and first day of the liturgical year (cf. Exod. 12:14ff; Lev. 2:41). (c) *Pentecost* (15-22), second great feast celebrated 50 days after the Passover, also called the "Feast of Weeks," i.e., seven weeks after the passover, when the first harvest was taken in and the best fruits offered to God (cf. Acts 2:1). (d) *The Day of Atonement* (26-32 and Lev. 16), also called Yom Kippur, follows the octave of the civil New Year (Rosh Hashanah) usually celebrated during September. Yom Kippur is for the Israelite a day of great penance and sincere sorrow for sin. (e) *The Feast of Tabernacles* (33-44), celebrated in September or October at the time of the late or grape harvest; the people live in tents or huts of branches to commemorate their arrival in the Promised Land (cf. John 7:2) — a time of great rejoicing and the third great feast of the Israelites.[1]

25:1ff *The Sabbatical and Jubilee Years*: every seventh year was celebrated as a sabbatical year, a year when the fields went untilled as a recognition of God's dominion over them, when even the fields were allowed to rest, and when whatever grew spontaneously was to be given to the poor. Every seventh sabbatical year (50 years) was celebrated as a Jubilee year. Houses, fields, etc., had to be returned to the original owner, and slaves were to receive their freedom.

In conclusion, we can sum up Leviticus in the words of our Lord: "You are not of this world, but I have chosen you out of the world" (John 15:19). The Christian as well as the Jew must be separated from the world. This separation is one which brings him close to God. The closer to God, the holier he must be. Even the primitive meaning of the word "holy," meaning to be separated from profane things and set aside for the service of the Lord, indicated this double movement away from the world and toward God.

The negative aspect of sanctity, separation from the world, is emphasized in the laws of cleanliness: laws about not touching corpses, because the corruption of the tomb has no place in the presence of the living God, source of all life; laws rendering unclean those who have anything to do with pagan cults and idolatry (cf. Lev. 18:21; 20:2-8), and in the sacrifices for sin.

The positive aspect, the nearer one is to God, the more holy must he be, is emphasized in the greater sanctity prescribed for priests (Lev. 21:10-15, 23; 22:9, 16) in the moral laws, particularly that of charity (Lev. 19:17-19), and in the insistence on a spirit of interior sentiments of sacrifice preached by the prophets and inculcated by the psalms.

[1] Cf. De Vaux, *op. cit.*, 468–517.

5. Numbers

By the time the reader finishes Genesis and Exodus, he knows the origins of the Israelites and how they came to be chosen by God to be His unique theocratic nation. When he finishes Leviticus, with its emphasis on the sanctity required of the new nation — its ritual of sacrifices, ritual of ordination of priests, ritual of legal cleanliness and laws of holiness — he understands well the meaning of God's command concerning the nature of this kingdom: "You shall be to me a kingdom of priests, a holy nation" (Exod. 19:6).

He has yet to discover, however, how the new nation was organized. What was the numerical strength of the different tribes? Who were their leaders? How did they contribute to the support of the priestly kingdom? How was the land to be divided among them and how was the hierarchy of authority to be transmitted? These are the questions answered in the book of Numbers — a book the reader will agree is well named when he makes his way through the different censuses, divisions of duties, and allotments of land recorded with precise enumeration in its pages. What Leviticus tells us about the organization of cult, Numbers tells us about the organization of the community. In each case the organization is centered about the Ark and the Tabernacle, the abode of God in the midst of His Chosen People.

The reader may be puzzled by the mixture of legislative and historical matter found in the book, but if he recollects that most biblical works were written primarily to teach (without detriment, however, to their basic historical value), he will look beyond the numbers tabulated, the laws listed, and the episodes narrated, to the teaching purpose of the author. The cut and dried numbers, the divisions of duties, taxes, and allotments of land, plus the emphasis given in the narrative section (ch. 10–22) to the establishment of a hierarchy of authoritative leaders, will convince the reader that the author was intent in his own way on teaching the Israelites the necessity of being a closely knit community, subject to the authority of its God-given leaders.

The book is perhaps best divided geographically, i.e., according to the places in which the principal events described took place. The reader will note that the events narrated in Part I (1–10) all take place at Sinai within one year after the Exodus from Egypt and the arrival at Sinai. The events narrated in Part II (10–22) take place between Sinai and the plains of Moab slightly north and east of the Dead Sea in the Transjordan. Part III (22–36) records the events that took place on the Plains of Moab while the Israelites were preparing to invade Palestine on the other (western) side of the River Jordan.

The reader will notice that in its legislative section (Num. 1–10; 26–36) Numbers continues the legal and liturgical codes begun in Exod. 20–40 and carried on in Leviticus. Exod. 20 to Num. 10 could well be considered a long digression aimed at describing the organization of cult and community in Israel. Num. 10 continues the narrative interrupted in Exod. 24.

Significant passages in Numbers

Part One / Num. 1–10 / Organization at Sinai

1:45-46 603,550 men, not counting women and children, would give a total number of approximately two or three million Israelites, a number impossible in the circumstances of the Exodus. The meaning or at least use of the term for 'thousands' has been rightly challenged. Division of the census numbers by 100 will give the more probable number.

2:1ff The community is camped around the Ark and the Tabernacle as parishioners around a parish church. Nearest are the priests and levites in the inner circle, surrounded in the outer circle by the twelve tribes, located according to order of precedence.

3:5-13 The Levites are made the assistants of the priests (who are taken from the Levitical family of Aaron alone) and take the place of the first-born (Exod. 13:2, 11-16; Num. 8:17-19) to serve before God. Note the emphasis on the hierarchy in 3:10 and 18:1-5. Cf. 3:21–4:33 on the duties of the Levites.

6:1ff The Nazarites are the first evidence of the monastic spirit in the kingdom of God, the first blossoming of the kingdom whose nature is to be 'holy.'

6:22-26 The priestly blessing calling down God's protection, favor, and peace (the abundance of all good things both spiritual and temporal).

9:1-5 The second celebration of the Passover, one year after the exodus from Egypt. Note 9:15 the link with Exod. 40:34-38, following the digression in Leviticus and Num. 1–9, and taking up once more the interrupted historical narrative.

Part Two / Num. 10–22 / The Journey to the Promised Land

The teaching purpose in this section can be discovered from an analysis of the incidents chosen for inclusion by the author. Almost all have to do with the failure of the people to obey and trust their leaders: God first of all, and then His vicar, Moses, and the priests. The teaching element in this section can be summed up in the words of Phil. 2:14: "Do all things without murmuring and without questioning."

10:11f The Israelites move from Mt. Sinai to the desert of Paran, fourteen months after their arrival at Sinai (cf. map, plate 3). 10:35 gives the *itinerarium* intoned by Moses at the beginning of each day's march (cf. Ps. 68:2).

11:16ff Appointment of the seventy elders. Note that the taking of, or sharing of, the spirit of Moses with the elders was a way of showing they were subordinate to him (cf. Exod. 18, Jethro's advice to Moses).

12:1ff To teach the necessity of obeying God's vicars, the author cites the punishment of Miriam for rebelling against Moses.

13:1ff Intending to invade Canaan from the South, Moses sends out twelve spies to reconnoiter the country. With the exception of Caleb (v. 30) and Joshua, they bring back a pessimistic report. As a result, the people rebel against Moses (ch. 14) and are condemned to spend forty years in the desert until a new generation more trusting and obedient is ready to invade successfully the Promised Land.

16:1ff Two more rebellions against Moses are cited: one of a political nature (Dathan and Abiram) against the ruling authority of Moses; the other of a religious nature (Korah and his followers) against the priestly authority of Moses and Aaron.

17:16-26 Following the episode of Korah's rebellion, the flowering of Aaron's staff is related as a confirmation of his sacerdotal power. This is followed in ch. 18:1-7 with a strong statement concerning the hierarchy of priests and levites. Laymen have no part in this hierarchy (vv. 5-7).

20:2-13 On the occasion of a drought at Kadesh in the Negeb, the people rebel against Moses. By the power of God, Moses brings water from a rock. But for some sin committed on this occasion (possibly for doubting God's power or mercy), both Moses and Aaron are condemned to die like the others without setting foot in the Promised Land (12-13; cf. Num. 20:24).

20:14-21 After a long period spent at Kadesh, during which a new generation grows up, the Israelites set out once more to conquer Palestine. Unwilling to attack again from the south, they decide to circle the Dead Sea and attack from the east (cf. map, plate 3). Refused permission to go up along the King's highway (a natural road running up the eastern side of the Dead Sea from the Gulf of Aqabah all the way to Damascus), they are forced to detour along the border of Edom and around the kingdom of Moab to the east (21:10f).

21:4-9 The people, complaining again, are punished by *saraph* serpents.

21:21ff Refused passage by Sihon, king of the Ammorites, the Israelite army takes to the field and defeats successively Sihon, and then Og, king of Bashan, taking possession of all of Transjordan from the borders of Moab to Bashan east of the Lake of Galilee. After these victories the Israelites camp in the plains of Moab just north and east of the Dead Sea and prepare for the crossing of the Jordan and the invasion of Palestine proper.

Part Three / Num. 22—36 / On the plains of Moab

22—24 Balak, king of Moab, calls Balaam, a famous Mesopotamian soothsayer, to curse the Israelites; but Balaam, divinely inspired, repeatedly blesses the invading Israelites, concluding in ch. 24:17 with a prophecy about a future Israelite ruler, who will lead his people to great victories (cf. p. 358).

25:1ff Israel takes part in the licentious idolatry of the Moabites at the shrine of Baal of Peor at the instigation of Balaam (Num. 31:16). Phinehas, the grandson of Aaron, gives example of great zeal by executing two of the sinners. This incident is a preview of the degraded paganism of the Canaanites against which the divinely revealed religion of Israel will war for the next six centuries. Centered around the worship of Baal (the male deity) and Astarte (his female consort), who were considered as giving fertility to the land, beasts, and even humans, the cult consisted in placating these gods with such abominations as infant sacrifice and sacred prostitution (cf. Deut. 23:18). Under Jezebel in the ninth century, Baalism is at its height. In the eighth century Hosea preaches incessantly against it (Hosea 1—2). In the late seventh century and in the last years before the downfall of Judah, Jeremiah (ch. 2—4; 19 *passim*) preaches in vain against the prevalence of this same degraded cult among his people.

27:15-23 Moses publicly designates Joshua to succeed him.

31:1ff Organization of an army by Moses in order to war against the Midianites responsible for the defection of the Israelites at Baal-Peor. The narrative, interrupted at ch. 25:18, is here resumed.

32:1ff The Reubenites and Gadites request and finally receive permission to settle in the conquered lands of Transjordan (cf. Jos. 1:12-18; 22:1-9).

It is only fair to say, in concluding, that the theme of Numbers, the organization of Israel as a community, is hardly of great interest to moderns. But above and beyond that theme, Numbers has a message that is timeless: the call of God to each one of us to serve Him unreservedly like Caleb (Num. 14:24), with boundless trust in His goodness and power. It is said that baptism makes us saints — until we are put to the test. It is true of us as it was true of the Israelites. What they were before their new birth as the kingdom of God on Sinai is told in Exod. 1—18; a servile, complaining horde. What they were like after Sinai is the discouraging record in Exod. 32 and Num. 10—25. As they were before, so they are after Sinai — weak in faith, lukewarm in love, carnal, crass, unceasingly complaining. Like so many Christians today, they were still children of this world, born to a new life, but in fact unchanged and living the old life of the flesh. Numbers, therefore, tells the failure of Israel to realize the demands put upon her by God and by her new and exalted status. It is the story of the new nation's failure to live up to its sublime destiny. It is in figure, as St. Paul will point out in 1 Cor. 10, the story of multitudes of Christians after baptism.

6. Deuteronomy

Lest anyone be deceived into interpreting the history of the Pentateuch coldly or its laws legalistically, the book of Deuteronomy[1] sets out to show that the nation was conceived and brought to birth through nothing more nor less than God's warm and boundless love and was meant to grow and develop only through a return of that love, manifested by

[1] Cf. Bright, *op. cit.* 141ff; 320ff; Raymond Brown, *The Book of Deuteronomy*, OTRG No. 10.

loyalty and obedience. Deuteronomy is to the Pentateuch, therefore, what our Lord's discourse in John 13–17 is to the Gospels – a testimony to the primacy of love in God's dealings with men. And its theme may be summed up in our Lord's words from the priestly discourse: "If you love me, keep my commandments!"

Deuteronomy's place in the Pentateuch is to define the spirit of the new nation. Genesis gives the origin of the people; Exodus, the birth of the nation; Leviticus, the holy nature of the nation; Numbers, the organization of the community; Deuteronomy, the spirit of the community – which is to be a spirit of love, a spirit expressed for all time in the great words of Deut. 6:5: "Therefore, you shall love Yahweh, your God, with all your heart and with all your soul and with all your strength. Take to heart these words which I enjoin on you today. Drill them into your children. Speak of them at home and abroad, whether you are busy or at rest. Bind them at your wrist as a sign and let them be as a pendant on your forehead. Write them on the doorposts of your houses and on your gates."

The purpose of the book is precisely "to drill these words" into the Israelite consciousness, to make the Israelites, man, woman, and child, understand how much God *loves* them and how much he wants them *to return that love*. This should be readily manifest to the reader, but it will be well to underline the emphasis given to love in Deuteronomy by reading rapidly through the following texts: 1:31; 4:32-40; 6:4-9; 7:7-13; 10:12-15, 11:1, 13, 22; 13:2-4; 30:6, 16, 20; 32:1-20.

Deuteronomy's links with Numbers are close. Numbers closes with the observation that the commandments and decisions contained in the book were given through Moses on the plains of Moab beside the Jericho stretch of the Jordan (Num. 36:13). Deuteronomy opens with Moses explaining these laws to the Israelites encamped in the plains of Moab awaiting the signal to advance on the Promised Land (Deut. 1:1-5).

Psychologically, the connection is even closer. In Deuteronomy, Moses is represented as giving his last will and testament. He realizes he will soon have to leave his people. He had worried about them for most of his adult life. He had brought them out of bondage, lived with them in the wastelands of the Sinai peninsula, led them to the borders of the Promised Land. He knows their weaknesses. He knows that in the land they are about to enter they will meet with new temptations. The simple life of the desert will be over. The land they are about to enter will be rich and depraved. The cities they are about to conquer will bring them a wealth and luxury they have never known. In Deuteronomy, therefore, Moses, before his death, is pictured as preaching to his people out of the abundance of his heart to persuade them never to betray God, never to lose faith in Him, to love Him, observe His covenant, and be His people with the same love and devotion that a son shows for his father. They have a glorious destiny in store for them, but it will be attained only through a return of love to their loving Father.

Because Deuteronomy contains a recapitulation of Israel's history, plus a partial repetition, completion, and explanation of the laws given on Sinai, the book has been named by the Greek translators "the second law" (*deuteros nomos*). But the book is far from a mere repetition. It is rather a preacher's commentary on Israel's laws and history seen in the light of Israel's basic law and guiding spirit—the law of love (cf. pp. 135; 216f).

The book is divided into four parts, each ostensibly a long sermon. In Part I (1–4), the preacher tells of God's loving care for Israel from Sinai to Moab (mostly historical). In Part II (5–11), the preacher expounds the covenant as the great proof of God's love for Israel. In Part III (12–26), he explains Israel's theocratic laws. And in Part IV (27–34), he makes his last impassioned exhortation to Israel to love and obey God, giving them as a liturgical reminder his famous canticle (ch. 32). The book closes with Moses blessing the tribes and with an account of his death (ch. 33–34).

While reading Deuteronomy the student should note the preaching style, the frequent use of the personal pronoun "you," the frequent appeal to the emotions, the constant use of the motives of love and fear. He should use Deuteronomy not only for its doctrine on the place of love in God's dealings with His chosen ones, but in a practical way as a review of all the Pentateuch, checking for familiarity, first mentally, and then with the help or confirmation of the footnotes and textual concordances.

Significant passages in Deuteronomy

Part One / Deut. 1–4 / God's care for Israel from Sinai to Moab

1:1ff Verses 1-5 connect Deuteronomy with Numbers, setting date and place for Moses' sermons. Vv. 29-36 immediately emphasize a basic theme: the necesity of trusting God unreservedly (cf. Numbers *passim* and the Sermon on the Mount, Matthew 5–7).

4:9-10 For this command to teach children God's goodness to His chosen people, cf. Exod. 12:26; Deut. 6:7, 20.

4:15ff The resume of doctrine about creation (15-19) is taught in a more figurative way in Gen. 1. The conclusion of the first sermon on God's love for Israel is contained in the last words of the chapter (32-40).

Part Two / Deut. 5—11 / The Covenant — proof of God's love

6:4-9 The great command of love, keynote of Deut. and of the whole Bible.

8:2-5 God's care and discipline is like that of a father (cf. Deut. 32:1-20).

9:4-6 The gratuity of God's love for Israel.

10:12-20 What God expects of Israel in return for His love.

Part Three / Deut. 12—26 / Moses' explanation of the law

15:7-11 Charity to the poor.

17:18-20 The future king is to be subject to the law of God just as are others.

18:9-22 The institution of prophetism.

19:11-13 The avenger of blood (cf. Num. 35:12).

24:1-4 Marriage and divorce.

25:5-10 Levirate marriage (cf. ANET 182; Ruth 4; Matthew 22:24).

Part Four / Deut. 27—34 / Moses' last words and death

29:9-14 Covenant binding on future Israelites as well as the immediate audience.

30:11-14 God's law is clear and manifest and Israel's fate, blessing or curse, depends on her own free choice to accept or reject God's teaching (cf. 30:15-20; Deut. 11:26-30; 27—28).

31:23f Joshua commissioned to lead the Israelites to the Promised Land (cf. Num. 27).

32:1ff The Canticle of Moses — the "Our Father" of the Old Testament.

34:1ff The death of Moses and a eulogy.

7. Summary and Review of the Pentateuch

By means of the first step in his study of the Pentateuch — a familiarity with the text as a whole — the student has seen that the Pentateuch is a fairly well knit literary unit, substantially the work of Moses (cf. p. 54f), but edited into its final form as late perhaps as the fifth century.

One final step must be taken before the student can claim a mastery of the Pentateuch as a book — the over-all look, seeing it as the final editor saw it: its purpose, basic plan, and the execution of that plan.

Clearly the author's purpose was to leave a record of the Sinai pact and of the people with whom it was made, telling who they were, where they came from, and to what they were destined by God.

His basic plan was to give first an account of the events leading up to the Sinai pact, then a description of the pact itself, and finally an exposition of the consequences flowing from it.

The execution of the plan is manifest in the format of the Pentateuch as a whole. The author begins with the events leading up to the Sinai pact: the origin and early history of the chosen people from Abraham to the Exodus from Egypt. The principal events are as follows:

Gen. 1–11 (Prologue). Basic truths about God and man (1–2); and of the initial economy of salvation (the pact with Adam), and the promise of ultimate triumph of mankind over evil (3:15); the progressive deterioration of mankind after the initial fall (4–11), showing the need for active intervention on the part of God if man is truly to conquer the forces of evil.

Gen. 12–36 Preparation of a chosen family set apart from the pagan world and eventually to bring salvation to that pagan world — the family of the Mesopotamian patriarch Abraham, from whom descend Isaac and Jacob and the twelve tribes of Israel. Institution of an absolute pact with the patriarchs and their descendants (15–17).

Gen. 37–50 Providential location and expansion of Jacob's descendants, the twelve tribes of Israel, in Egypt so that at the critical moment they are ready to be welded into a theocratic nation.

Exod. 1–12 Immediate events leading to the making of a nation out of this people: oppression by the Egyptians, preparation of Moses as leader, miraculous intervention of God through Moses and the plagues.

Exod. 12–18 The critical event — the exodus from Egyptian slavery to freedom.

Following upon the preparatory events leading up to the Sinai pact is the pact itself (Exod. 19–24) climaxing all preceding events by the birth of Israel as a nation and its institution as God's kingdom on earth. A conditional pact based on the Abrahamitic pact, the Sinai pact is eventually broken by the Israelites and rejected by God. God, however, through the prophets Jeremiah and Ezekiel, promises a new pact, the pact we know as the New Testament, instituted by our Lord in fulfillment of the absolute pact made with Abraham.

After describing the Sinai pact in Exod. 19–24, the author gives an exposition of the consequences flowing from the Sinai pact. They may be stated as follows:

Exod. 19–24	Israel becomes a theocratic nation.
Exod. 25–40	God dwells among the Israelites in the Ark and Tabernacle.
Lev. 1–27	God demands that His people be holy as He is holy. Israel's religious life is organized around God present in the Ark and the Tabernacle.
Num. 1–36	God sends the Israelites from Sinai to Palestine to take possession of the Promised Land. Even Israel's communal life is to be organized around God present in the Ark and the Tabernacle.
Deut. 1–34	Recapitulation of the Pentateuch in sermon form emphasizing love as the basis of all God's dealings with men.

To understand the Pentateuch and, indeed, the whole of the Bible, the reader must look at it with the eye of God's eternity. He must see it as one book, from Genesis at the beginning to the Apocalypse at the end, by one divine author, who sees all things simultaneously present before Him — the promise in Gen. 3:15, the fulfillment on Calvary; the theocratic kingdom established on Sinai, the Church of Christ inaugurated on Pentecost; the Promised Land set aside for the citizens of the kingdom, the beatific vision reserved for the elect in heaven.

The Pentateuch, therefore, in conclusion, represents the first five chapters of the great book of the Bible. It lays the scene, introduces the main characters, sketches the basic plot. The New Testament represents the last chapters of the same book, the same history of salvation. Without the New Testament, the Bible is a story without an ending, a mystery without a solution. Without the Old Testament, the New Testament hangs in the air. Only with a thorough knowledge of the Old Testament is the New Testament fully understood. Only with an appreciation of the New Testament as the climax of God's love is the Old Testament, the story of love's initial overtures building up to this climax, appreciable and precious.

2

Literary Analysis

of the

Pentateuch

1. Literary Analysis and the Pentateuch

Literary analysis or criticism of biblical books consists in the investigation of a book in order to determine exactly what the author had in mind when he wrote and what value is to be placed on his statements.[1]

In the temptation story of Genesis, the author states that when Adam and Eve "heard the sound of the Lord God walking in the garden in the cool of the day," they hid themselves among the trees of the garden (Gen. 3:8). The reader quite naturally asks: did God actually take human form and walk in the garden as a man walks? If God did not take human form and walk as a man, then what value is to be placed upon this statement of the inspired author? How in other words is the reader to determine the precise meaning of these words according to the mind of the inspired author?

To determine exactly the author's judgment when he penned these words and so to avoid putting a meaning upon his words that was far

[1] Cf. Schedl, HOTOT, vol. 2, 229ff; JBC 1–6; E. LaVerdiere, OTRG No. 1 and additional bibliography on p. 575.

from his mind and intention is obviously of prime importance if the reader is to correctly understand the inspired text. It is for this reason that literary criticism is indispensable for the understanding of the Bible. Without it we should be in danger of thinking that God assumed flesh and blood in paradise, that He took six days to create the world, that He physically breathed into man's face in order to make him a living creature, that He did many other things which to even the simplest mind appear incongruous.

Before we can determine an author's meaning, however, we must first be sure of his exact words. Since these can be changed and garbled in the course of time due to the mistakes of copyists, it is first necessary to establish the exact words of the author. This criticism which attempts to restore the exact words of the original author by recovering the text as it left his hands is called textual or lower criticism.

Higher criticism as distinguished from lower or textual criticism is aimed not so much at the restoration of the words as the establishment of the meaning of the words. It deals, therefore, with the far more difficult questions of date, authorship, literary form, historical and psychological background. When it has been satisfactorily completed, the correct interpretation of the author's mind and words becomes a relatively simple task. One knows, then, when to understand him non-figuratively, when to understand him figuratively. One knows where he speaks as a poet, where as a teacher, where as an historian. One knows in a word what was in his mind and what was not in his mind.

Literary analysis or higher criticism of the Pentateuch is admittedly difficult for the beginner. Its advantages, however, compensate for its difficulties. Even the beginner is puzzled to find at the beginning of Genesis two different accounts of the creation of the world (Gen. 1:1–2:3 and Gen. 2:4-25). He is further puzzled to find two genealogies of Cain — Cainan (Gen. 4:17f and 5:12-17), two narratives of the flood with conflicting details concerning its duration and the numbers of the animals taken into the ark (Gen. 6–8), two accounts of Abraham risking Sarah's honor by trying to pass her off as his sister (Gen. 12 and 20), not to mention Isaac's similar episode (Gen. 26:6-11). Moses' father-in-law is sometimes called Reuel (Exod. 2:18 and Num. 10:29), sometimes Jethro (Exod. 3:1 and 18:1). There are two accounts of the vocation of Moses (Exod. 3 and 6), several different accounts of the plagues (Exod. 7–12), and the story of Israel's rebellion at the waters of Meribah is told once in Exodus (17:7) and once more in Numbers (20:13). Did all these events actually take place twice? Or do we have two different accounts of the same events? Answers to these questions and solutions to these puzzles are supplied by higher criticism. As a result of long and intense study, higher critics of the Pentateuch have established in the Pentateuch the fusion of several different documentary sources or traditions, each recounting the same basic story but with differences in detail, emphasis, and style. When an editor fused these different sources into the one literary work we now know as the Pentateuch, he took from each source whatever suited his purpose, even when it meant telling the same story twice or putting together details from two different sources in order to obtain a fuller account of one event.

An analogy will perhaps illustrate the steps that went into the making of the Pentateuch as we have it now, and at the same time show the value of literary analysis. Around the year 173 A.D., a monk named Tatian made a harmony of the four Gospels. His objective was to group into one narrative all that was known about Christ from the four Gospels and thus not only avoid repetition of the same event but choose the best description of each event from whichever Gospel contained it and thus present his readers with a unified and harmonious account of the life of Christ. He called his work the *Diatessaron* ('one "through four"').

In the case of the Pentateuch an ancient author took four different accounts of the founding of the kingdom of God on earth and fused them into one. His work was a true Diatessaron, though it was never given the name. The difference between Tatian's Diatessaron and the Pentateuchal Diatessaron is a matter of history. Tatian's Diatessaron became popular in Syria alone. Its popularity, however, never outweighed the popularity of the original four Gospels. As a consequence, the Gospels remained, the Diatessaron disappeared. The Pentateuch on the other hand became more popular than its four original sources. The Pentateuch remained, the four sources disappeared. The work of restoring these lost sources is substantially the task of those who undertake a literary analysis of the Pentateuch.

The analogy may be carried further. On the hypothesis of lost Gospels supplanted by a Diatessaron, it is not difficult to see how a literary analysis of the Diatessaron would reveal the hands and the minds of four different authors. The stark and simple style of John the Evangelist, like the style of the Priestly author in the Pentateuch, would be readily distinguishable. Luke's special vocabulary, colorful style, and delicate psychological descriptions would stand out in contrast to John in a way similar to the contrast between the Yahwist and Priestly authors of the Pentateuch. Matthew and Mark would cause difficulties, but even these two authors could be distinguished by a careful literary analysis.

We may complete our analogy by citing a modern day Diatessaron. In the little book entitled *Christ in the Gospel, the Life of Christ by the Four Evangelists* edited by F. Frey, the infancy narrative harmonized from the four Gospels runs as follows: John 1:1-18; Luke 1:1-80; Matthew 1:1-25; Luke 2:1-38; Matthew 2:1-23; Luke 2:40-52. Since Fr. Frey indicates his sources by citation in the margin and the four Gospels are available for comparison, there is no danger that anyone will ever lose sight of the sources and falsely consider Fr. Frey's Diatessaron an original composition coming from the mind and the pen of one individual.

Just the opposite is true of the Pentateuch. The original sources were lost. The editor left no marginal notes. And in the course of the centuries all remembrance of an editor faded away and the Pentateuch came to be considered a unified original composition. There remained in the work itself, however, internal evidence of the style, the language, and the theological preoccupations of the original authors of the lost sources. It is upon these that literary analysis bases its conclusions. We shall begin, therefore, with the question of the Mosaic authenticity of the Pentateuch, take up the most widely accepted solution to the problem of the literary formation of the Pentateuch, and then study each of the four original sources.

2. The Mosaic Authenticity of the Pentateuch

By authenticity is meant the actual authorship of a book by the man to whom that authorship is attributed. Sometimes by mistake a book is attributed to the wrong author, or the author uses a pseudonym and his name is lost (e.g., the books of Wisdom and Qoheleth). As a result the author named is not the authentic but the reputed author.

That Moses is the author of the Pentateuch in some true sense cannot be reasonably doubted. Such has been the constant tradition of the Jewish and Christian Churches, testified to in the Old Testament (Exod. 17:14; 24:4, 34:27; Num. 32:2; Deut. 31:9, 24) and in the New Testament (Luke 24:44; Mark 12:26; Matthew 8:4; 19:8; John 5:45-47).

In what exact sense Moses is author of the Pentateuch is another matter. Until the seventeenth century almost everyone believed Moses had written everything in the Pentateuch. In the eighteenth and nineteenth centuries, with the application of the principles of higher literary criticism, it was realized that Moses could not have written the entire Pentateuch as it stands today. It became obvious that many of the laws were posterior to him. The style, syntax, and vocabulary, moreover, differed radically in different sections of the Pentateuch (e.g., the vast difference between Leviticus and Deuteronomy). In addition, when matter characterized by the same style, vocabulary, and mode of composition was isolated, it was found to be characterized by different theological concepts betraying the existence of different minds at work in different parts of the Pentateuch (e.g., the difference between the creation account in Gen. 1 and the creation account in Gen. 2).

As a result of the discoveries of the higher critics, many began to deny the Mosaic authorship entirely, claiming that the Pentateuch as a whole was a compilation made in the fifth century B.C. from original works dating no farther back than the eighth century. Conscientious scholars, however, refused to admit this extreme about-face. In time, then, and by dint of patient study it came to be realized that while much in the Pentateuch was indeed written down long after the time of Moses, it was, nevertheless, truly Mosaic because it had derived from him by way of an oral tradition that had developed for centuries before being finally written down.

This reaction to the extreme view of the higher critics of the nineteenth century represents the present state of the controversy — a more refined and critically established version of the traditional opinion, namely, that Moses is truly the author of the Pentateuch, not in its entirety, not word for word, or even book for book, but according to its substance.

Some understand this "according to substance" quantitatively, in the sense that Moses actually wrote the major part of the Pentateuch as we have it today. Others with better right understand it qualitatively, in the sense that the Pentateuch is "the net result of a long literary process begun and inspired by Moses and continued and developed in his spirit."

3. The Literary Formation of the Pentateuch

Up to the present no completely acceptable documentary theory of the formation of the Pentateuch has been produced. The following theory, however, is supported by good authors and may be followed with reasonable security. First of all, the nucleus of the Pentateuch — its basic historical narrative and legal code — was composed sometime in the thirteenth century. Parts may have been committed to writing, but since the people had little access to manuscripts, the bards and the minstrels must have kept the story alive orally.

In the recitations of the bards and the minstrels the initial narrative section developed in the course of time into a national saga. In the keeping of the priests, the original legal code likewise developed with the continual addition of new laws made necessary by changed circumstances and social conditions.

Sometime in the tenth century, probably during the reign of Solomon, the narrative part of the national saga was put into writing for the first time. Because the author favored "Yahweh" as the divine name, his account has been called the Yahwistic or "J" document (from Jahweh — the spelling of the German authors who originated the term).

When the kingdom of Solomon was divided in 926, with the secession of the northern tribes from the rule of Rehoboam, the Davidic successor of Solomon, the national saga came down in the northern kingdom separately and was put into writing sometime in the eighth century. This version of the saga has been called the "E" document because of the author's preference for "Elohim" as the divine name.

After 722, the year the northern kingdom was overrun and destroyed by the Assyrians, the "E" document was brought south to Judah and fused with the "J" document. In the meantime, the priests of the northern kingdom who had come to Jerusalem codified their legal traditions in what is now known as the book of Deuteronomy, commonly referred to as the "D" document or "Original Deuteronomy."

The "P", or priestly document, was the last of the traditions to be put into written form. It contains the legal traditions of the Jerusalem priesthood and is generally held to have been composed from very ancient sources, attaining its present status sometime in the sixth century. At this time or perhaps as late the fifth century, the Priestly theologian fused into one the "P" tradition and the already fused "JE" documents. To this combination of "JEP" was appended the "D" document making a diatesseron of four documents "JEDP." Our present Pentateuch, therefore, is made up of four traditions: the two sagas of the national history — "J" and "E", and the two priestly codes, the northern "D" code and the southern "P" code. It is on this basis that our existing Pentateuch is held to represent the last edition, with many necessary additions and changes, of the original, substantially Mosaic traditions.

Color outline of the sources of the Pentateuch

The following outline in color of the JEDP sources of the Pentateuch indicates visually the arrangement by the final Priestly theologian of the sources utilized by him in composing his pentateuchal diatessaron. It should be consulted in studying each of the sources.[1]

At times it is practically impossible to distinguish between the J and

[1] I am indebted to my confrere, the Rev. Eugene McAlee, for this outline which he has kindly permitted me to include here.

E traditions. For this reason, no attempt has been made to try to settle the disputes among the scholars. Therefore, when the two colors, blue and yellow, are combined, it signifies that the text is composed of the two traditions. This is true of the entire book of Numbers. It was judged too complicated to indicate which of these traditions predominates in a given passage.

Gen. 1:1—7:11 KEY ■ J; □ E; ■ D; ■ P; □ redactor; ▨ special source

| 1 | 1 | 2 | 3 | 4 | 5 | 6 | 7 | 8 | 9 | 10 | 11 | 12 | 13 | 14 | 15 | 16 |

| 17 | 18 | 19 | 20 | 21 | 22 | 23 | 24 | 25 | 26 | 27 | 28 | 29 | 30 | 31 |

| 2 | 1 | 2 | 3 | 4a | 4b | 5 | 6 | 7 | 8 | 9 | 10 | 11 | 12 | 13 | 14 | 15 |

| 16 | 17 | 18 | 19 | 20 | 21 | 22 | 23 | 24 | 25 | 3 | 1 | 2 | 3 | 4 | 5 |

| 6 | 7 | 8 | 9 | 10 | 11 | 12 | 13 | 14 | 15 | 16 | 17 | 18 | 19 | 20 | 21 |

| 22 | 23 | 24 | 4 | 1 | 2 | 3 | 4 | 5 | 6 | 7 | 8 | 9 | 10 | 11 | 12 | 13 |

| 14 | 15 | 16 | 17 | 18 | 19 | 20 | 21 | 22 | 23 | 24 | 25 | 26 | 5 | 1 |

| 2 | 3 | 4 | 5 | 6 | 7 | 8 | 9 | 10 | 11 | 12 | 13 | 14 | 15 | 16 | 17 | 18 |

| 19 | 20 | 21 | 22 | 23 | 24 | 25 | 26 | 27 | 28 | 29 | 30 | 31 | 32 |

| 6 | 1 | 2 | 3 | 4 | 5 | 6 | 7 | 8 | 9 | 10 | 11 | 12 | 13 | 14 | 15 | 16 | 17 |

| 18 | 19 | 20 | 21 | 22 | 7 | 1 | 2 | 3 | 4 | 5 | 6 | 7 | 8 | 9 | 10 | 11 |

Gen. 7:12—15:21 KEY ■ J; □ E; ■ D; ■ P; □ redactor; ■ special source

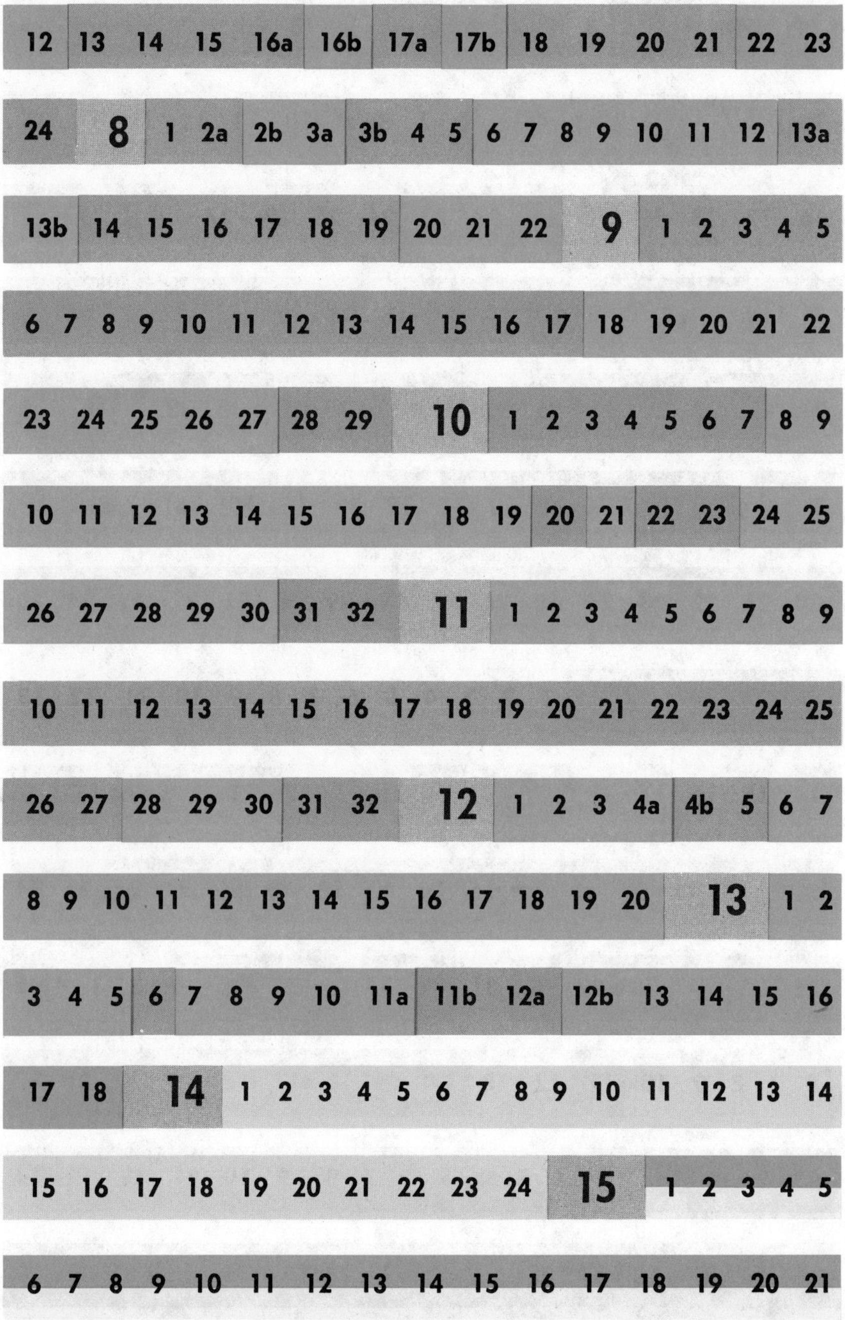

Gen. 16:1a—24:10 KEY ☐ J; ☐ E; ☐ D; ☐ P; ☐ redactor; ☐ special source

| 16 | 1a | 1b | 2 | 3 | 4 | 5 | 6 | 7 | 8 | 9 | 10 | 11 | 12 | 13 | 14 | 15 |

| 16 | 17 | 1 | 2 | 3 | 4 | 5 | 6 | 7 | 8 | 9 | 10 | 11 | 12 | 13 | 14 | 15 |

| 16 | 17 | 18 | 19 | 20 | 21 | 22 | 23 | 24 | 25 | 26 | 27 | 18 | 1 | 2 |

| 3 | 4 | 5 | 6 | 7 | 8 | 9 | 10 | 11 | 12 | 13 | 14 | 15 | 16 | 17 | 18 | 19 | 20 |

| 21 | 22 | 23 | 24 | 25 | 26 | 27 | 28 | 29 | 30 | 31 | 32 | 33 | 19 | 1 |

| 2 | 3 | 4 | 5 | 6 | 7 | 8 | 9 | 10 | 11 | 12 | 13 | 14 | 15 | 16 | 17 | 18 | 19 |

| 20 | 21 | 22 | 23 | 24 | 25 | 26 | 27 | 28 | 29 | 30 | 31 | 32 | 33 | 34 | 35 |

| 36 | 37 | 38 | 20 | 1 | 2 | 3 | 4 | 5 | 6 | 7 | 8 | 9 | 10 | 11 | 12 | 13 |

| 14 | 15 | 16 | 17 | 18 | 21 | 1a | 1b | 2a | 2b | 3 | 4 | 5 | 6a | 6b | 7 |

| 8 | 9 | 10 | 11 | 12 | 13 | 14 | 15 | 16 | 17 | 18 | 19 | 20 | 21 | 22 | 23 | 24 |

| 25 | 26 | 27 | 28 | 29 | 30 | 31 | 32 | 33 | 34 / 34 | 22 | 1 | 2 | 3 | 4 | 5 |

| 6 | 7 | 8 | 9 | 10 | 11 | 12 | 13 | 14 | 15 | 16 | 17 | 18 | 19 | 20 | 21 | 22 |

| 23 | 24 | 23 | 1 | 2 | 3 | 4 | 5 | 6 | 7 | 8 | 9 | 10 | 11 | 12 | 13 | 14 |

| 15 | 16 | 17 | 18 | 19 | 20 | 24 | 1 | 2 | 3 | 4 | 5 | 6 | 7 | 8 | 9 | 10 |

Gen. 24:11—29:25 KEY ■ J; □ E; ■ D; ■ P; □ redactor; ■ special source

| 11 | 12 | 13 | 14 | 15 | 16 | 17 | 18 | 19 | 20 | 21 | 22 | 23 | 24 | 25 | 26 |

| 27 | 28 | 29 | 30 | 31 | 32 | 33 | 34 | 35 | 36 | 37 | 38 | 39 | 40 | 41 | 42 |

| 43 | 44 | 45 | 46 | 47 | 48 | 49 | 50 | 51 | 52 | 53 | 54 | 55 | 56 | 57 | 58 |

| 59 | 60 | 61 | 62 | 63 | 64 | 65 | 66 | 67 | **25** | 1 | 2 | 3 | 4 | 5 | 6 |

| 7 | 8 | 9 | 10 | 11a | 11b | 12 | 13 | 14 | 15 | 16 | 17 | 18 | 19 | 20 | 21 |

| 22 | 23 | 24 | 25 | 26a | 26b | 27 | 28 | 29 | 30 | 31 | 32 | 33 | 34 |

| **26** | 1 | 2 | 3 | 4 | 5 | 6 | 7 | 8 | 9 | 10 | 11 | 12 | 13 | 14 | 15 | 16 |

| 17 | 18 | 19 | 20 | 21 | 22 | 23 | 24 | 25 | 26 | 27 | 28 | 29 | 30 | 31 | 32 |

| 33 | 34 | 35 | **27** | 1 | 2 | 3 | 4 | 5 | 6 | 7 | 8 | 9 | 10 | 11 | 12 | 13 |

| 14 | 15 | 16 | 17 | 18 | 19 | 20 | 21 | 22 | 23 | 24 | 25 | 26 | 27 | 28 | 29 |

| 30 | 31 | 32 | 33 | 34 | 35 | 36 | 37 | 38 | 39 | 40 | 41 | 42 | 43 | 44 | 45 |

| 46 | **28** | 1 | 2 | 3 | 4 | 5 | 6 | 7 | 8 | 9 | 10 | 11 | 12 | 13 | 14 | 15 |

| 16 | 17 | 18 | 19 | 20 | 21 | 22 | **29** | 1 | 2 | 3 | 4 | 5 | 6 | 7 | 8 | 9 |

| 10 | 11 | 12 | 13 | 14 | 15 | 16 | 17 | 18 | 19 | 20 | 21 | 22 | 23 | 24 | 25 |

26 27 28 29 30 31 32 33 34 35 **30** 1 2 3a 3b

4 5 6 7 8 9 10 11 12 13 14 15 16 17 18 19 20

21 22 23 24 25 26 27 28 29 30 31 32 33 34 35 36

37 38 39 40 41 42 43 **31** 1 2 3 4 5 6 7 8 9

10 11 12 13 14 15 16 17 18a 18b 19 20 21 22 23

24 25 26 27 28 29 30 31 32 33 34 35 36 37 38 39

40 41 42 43 44 45 46 47 48 49 50 51 52 53 54 55

32 1 2 3 / 2 3 4 5 6 7 8 9 10 11 12 13a 13b 14a 14b

15 16 17 18 19 20 21 22 / 22 23 24 25 26 27 28 29 30

31 32 **33** 1 2 3 4 5 6 7 8 9 10 11 12 13 14

15 16 17 18 19 20 **34** 1 2a 2b 3 4 5 6 7 8 / 1 2 3 4 5 6 7 8

9 10 11 12 13 14 15 16 17 18 19 20 21 22 23 24 / 9 10 11 12 13 14 15 16 17 18 19 20 21 22 23 24

25 26 27 28 29 30 31 **35** 1 2 3 4 5 6 7 8 9 / 25 26 27 28 29 30 31

| 10 | 11 | 12 | 13 | 14 | 15 | 16 | 17 | 18 | 19 | 20 | 21 | 22a | 22b | 23 |

| 24 | 25 | 26 | 27 | 28 | 29 | 36 | 1 | 2 | 3 | 4 | 5 | 6 | 7 | 8 | 9 | 10 |

| 11 | 12 | 13 | 14 | 15 | 16 | 17 | 18 | 19 | 20 | 21 | 22 | 23 | 24 | 25 | 26 |

| 27 | 28 | 29 | 30 | 31 | 32 | 33 | 34 | 35 | 36 | 37 | 38 | 39 | 40 | 41 | 42 |

| 43 | 37 | 1 | 2a | 2b | 3 | 4 | 5 | 6 | 7 | 8 | 9 | 10 | 11 | 12 | 13 | 14a |
| | | 1 | 2a | | | | | | | | | | | | | |

| 14b | 15 | 16 | 17 | 18a | 18b | 19 | 20 | 21 | 22 | 23a | 23b | 24 | 25 |

| 26 | 27 | 28a | 28b | 28c | 29 | 30 | 31a | 31b | 32a | 32b | 33 | 34 | 35 |

| 36 | 38 | 1 | 2 | 3 | 4 | 5 | 6 | 7 | 8 | 9 | 10 | 11 | 12 | 13 | 14 | 15 |

| 16 | 17 | 18 | 19 | 20 | 21 | 22 | 23 | 24 | 25 | 26 | 27 | 28 | 29 | 30 |

| 39 | 1 | 2 | 3 | 4 | 5 | 6 | 7 | 8 | 9 | 10 | 11 | 12 | 13 | 14 | 15 | 16 | 17 |

| 18 | 19 | 20 | 21 | 22 | 23 | 40 | 1 | 2 | 3 | 4 | 5 | 6 | 7 | 8 | 9 | 10 |

| 11 | 12 | 13 | 14 | 15 | 16 | 17 | 18 | 19 | 20 | 21 | 22 | 23 | 41 | 1 |

| 2 | 3 | 4 | 5 | 6 | 7 | 8 | 9 | 10 | 11 | 12 | 13 | 14 | 15 | 16 | 17 | 18 | 19 |

| 20 | 21 | 22 | 23 | 24 | 25 | 26 | 27 | 28 | 29 | 30 | 31 | 32 | 33 | 34 | 35 |

Gen. 41:36—47:15 KEY ■ J; □ E; ■ D; ■ P; □ redactor; ■ special source

36 37 38 39 40 41 42 43 44 45 46 47 48 49 50 51
46

52 53 54 55 56 57 **42** 1 2 3 4 5 6 7 8 9 10

11 12 13 14 15 16 17 18 19 20 21 22 23 24 25 26

27 28 29 30 31 32 33 34 35 36 37 38 **43** 1 2
27 28

3 4 5 6 7 8 9 10 11 12 13 14 15 16 17 18 19 20

21 22 23a 23b 24 25 26 27 28 29 30 31 32 33 34

44 1 2 3 4 5 6 7 8 9 10 11 12 13 14 15 16 17

18 19 20 21 22 23 24 25 26 27 28 29 30 31 32 33

34 **45** 1 2 3 4 5 6 7 8 9 10 11 12 13 14 15

16 17 18 19 20 21 22 23 24 25 26 27 28 **46** 1

2 3 4 5a 5b 6 7 8 9 10 11 12 13 14 15 16 17 18

19 20 21 22 23 24 25 26 27 28 29 30 31 32 33 34
28 29 30 31 32 33 34

47 1 2 3 4 5 6a 6b 7 8 9 10 11 12 13 14 15
5 6a 12

Gen. 47:16—50:26 KEY ▪ J; ▫ E; ▪ D; ▪ P; ▫ redactor; ▪ special source

| 16 | 17 | 18 | 19 | 20 | 21 | 22 | 23 | 24 | 25 | 26 | 27a | 27b | 28 | 29 |

| 30 | 31 | **48** | 1 | 2 | 3 | 4 | 5 | 6 | 7 | 8 | 9 | 10 | 11 | 12 | 13 | 14 |

| 15 | 16 | 17 | 18 | 19 | 20 | 21 | 22 | **49** | 1a | 1b | 2 | 3 | 4 | 5 |
| | | | | | | | | | | 1b | 2 | 3 | 4 | 5 |

| 6 | 7 | 8 | 9 | 10 | 11 | 12 | 13 | 14 | 15 | 16 | 17 | 18 | 19 | 20 | 21 | 22 |
| 6 | 7 | 8 | 9 | 10 | 11 | 12 | 13 | 14 | 15 | 16 | 17 | 18 | 19 | 20 | 21 | 22 |

| 23 | 24 | 25 | 26 | 27 | 28a | 28b | 29 | 30 | 31 | 32 | 33 | **50** | 1 |
| 23 | 24 | 25 | 26 | 27 | 28a | | | | | | | | |

| 2 | 3 | 4 | 5 | 6 | 6 | 7 | 8 | 9 | 10 | 11 | 12 | 13 | 14 | 15 | 16 | 17 | 18 |

| 19 | 20 | 21 | 22 | 23 | 24 | 25 | 26 |

Exod. 1:1—3:15 KEY ▪ J; ▫ E; ▪ D; ▪ P; ▫ redactor; ▪ special source

| **1** | 1 | 2 | 3 | 4 | 5 | 6 | 7 | 8 | 9 | 10 | 11 | 12 | 13 | 14 | 15 | 16 |

| 17 | 18 | 19 | 20 | 21 | 22 | **2** | 1 | 2 | 3 | 4 | 5 | 6 | 7 | 8 | 9 | 10 |

| 11 | 12 | 13 | 14 | 15 | 16 | 17 | 18 | 19 | 20 | 21 | 22 | 23a | 23b | 24 |

| 25 | **3** | 1 | 2 | 3 | 4 | 5 | 6 | 7 | 8 | 9 | 10 | 11 | 12 | 13 | 14 | 15 |

Exod. 3:16—10:29 KEY ▮ J; ▯ E; ▮ D; ▮ P; ▯ redactor; ▮ special source

16 17 18 19 20 21 22 **4** 1 2 3 4 5 6 7 8 9

10 11 12 13 14 15 16 17 18 19 20a 20b 21 22 23

24 25 26 27 28 29 30 31 **5** 1 2 3 4 / 1 2 3 4 5 6 7 8

9 10 11 12 13 14 15 16 17 18 19 20 21 22 23

6 1 2 3 4 5 6 7 8 9 10 11 12 13 14 15 16 17

18 19 20 21 22 23 24 25 26 27 28 29 30 **7** 1 2

3 4 5 6 7 8 9 10 11 12 13 14 15 16 17 18 19

20a 20b 21a 21b 22 23 24 / 24 25 26 27 28 29 **8** 1

2 3 4 5 6 7 8 9 10 11a 11b 12 13 14 15 16 17

18 19 20 21 22 23 24 25 26 27 28 **9** 1 2 3 4

5 6 7 8 9 10 11 12 13 14 15 16 17 18 19 20 21

22 23a 23b 24 25 26 27 28 29 30 31 32 33 34 35

10 1 2 3 4 5 6 7 8 9 10 11 12 13a 13b 14 15

16 17 18 19 20 21 22 23 24 25 26 27 28 29

Exod. 11:1—18:22   KEY ■ J; □ E; ■ D; ■ P; □ redactor; ■ special source

THE LITERARY FORMATION OF THE PENTATEUCH   67

23 24 25 26 27 **19** 1 2a 2b 3 4 5 6 7 8 9

10 11 12 13 14 15 16 17 18 19 **20** 21 22

23 24 25 **20** 1 2 3 4 5 6 7 8 9 10 11

12 13 14 15 16 17 18 19 20 2 22 23 24 25 26

21 1 37 **22** 1 30

23 1 32 **24** 1 2 3 4 5 6 7 8

9 10 11 12 13 14 15a 15b 16 17 18a 18b

25 1 40 **26** 1 37

27 1 21 **28** 1 43

29 1 46 **30** 1 38

31 1 2 3 4 5 6 7 8 9 10 11 12 13 14 15 16 17

18a 18b **32** 1 2 3 4 5 6 7 8 9 10 11 12 13 14

15 16 17 18 19 20 21 22 23 24 25 26 27 28 29 30

31 32 33 34 35 **33** 1 2 3 4 5 6 7 8 9 10 11

Exod. 33:12—40:38 KEY ■ J; □ E; ■ D; ■ P; □ redactor; ■ special source

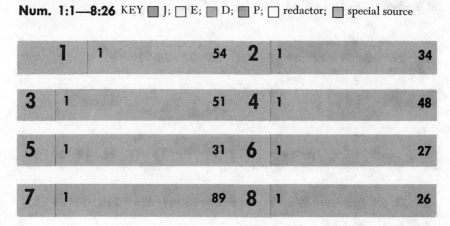

| 12 | 13 | 14 | 15 | 16 | 17 | 18 | 19 | 20 | 21 | 22 | 23 | **34** | 1 | 2 |

| 3 | 4 | 5 | 6 | 7 | 8 | 9 | 10 | 11 | 12 | 13 | 14 | 15 | 16 | 17 | 18 | 19 |

| 20 | 21 | 22 | 23 | 24 | 25 | 26 | 27 | 28 | 29 | 30 | 31 | 32 | 33 | 34 | 35 |

| **35** | 1 | | | | | | 35 | **36** | 1 | | | | | 38 |

| **37** | 1 | | | | | | 29 | **38** | 1 | | | | | 31 |

| **39** | 1 | | | | | | 43 | **40** | 1 | | | | | 38 |

The book of Leviticus is not included in this chart; it belongs entirely to the Priestly tradition.

Num. 1:1—8:26 KEY ■ J; □ E; ■ D; ■ P; □ redactor; ■ special source

1	1				54	**2**	1			34
3	1				51	**4**	1			48
5	1				31	**6**	1			27
7	1				89	**8**	1			26

KEY ▨ J; ☐ E; ▨ D; ▨ P; ☐ redactor; ▨ special source

| 9 | 1 | | | | | | | | | | 23 | 10 | 1 | 2 | 3 | 4 | 5 | 6 | 7 | 8 |

| 9 | 10 | 11 | 12 | 13 | 14 | 15 | 16 | 17 | 18 | 19 | 20 | 21 | 22 | 23 | 24 |

| 25 | 26 | 27 | 28 | 29 | 30 | 31 | 32 | 33 | 34 | 35 | 36 | | 11 | 1 | 2 |

| 3 | 4 | 5 | 6 | 7 | 8 | 9 | 10 | 11 | 12 | 13 | 14 | 15 | 16 | 17 | 18 | 19 | 20 |

| 21 | 22 | 23 | 24 | 25 | 26 | 27 | 28 | 29 | 30 | 31 | 32 | 33 | 34 | 35 |

| 12 | 1 | 2 | 3 | 4 | 5 | 6 | 7 | 8 | 9 | 10 | 11 | 12 | 13 | 14 | 15 | 16 |

| 13 | 1 | 2 | 3 | 4 | 5 | 6 | 7 | 8 | 9 | 10 | 11 | 12 | 13 | 14 | 15 | 16 | 17a |

| 17b | 18 | 19 | 20 | 21 | 22 | 23 | 24 | 25 | 26a | 26b | 27 | 28 | 29 | 30 |

| 31 | 32a | 32b | 33 | 14 | 1 | 2 | 3 | 4 | 5 | 6 | 7 | 8 | 9 | 10 | 11 |

| 12 | 13 | 14 | 15 | 16 | 17 | 18 | 19 | 20 | 21 | 22 | 23 | 24 | 25 | 26 | 27 |

| 28 | 29 | 30 | 31 | 32 | 33 | 34 | 35 | 36 | 37 | 38 | 39 | 40 | 41 | 42 | 43 |

| 44 | 45 | 15 | 1 | | | 41 | 16 | 1a | 1b | 2a | 2b | 3 |

| 4 | 5 | 6 | 7 | 8 | 9 | 10 | 11 | 12 | 13 | 14 | 15 | 16 | 17 | 18 | 19 | 20 | 21 |

| 22 | 23 | 24 | 25 | 26 | 27a | 27b | 28 | 29 | 30 | 31 | 32a | 32b | 33 | 34 | 35 |

Num. 17:1—32:15 KEY ▨ J; ☐ E; ▨ D; ▨ P; ☐ redactor; ▨ special source

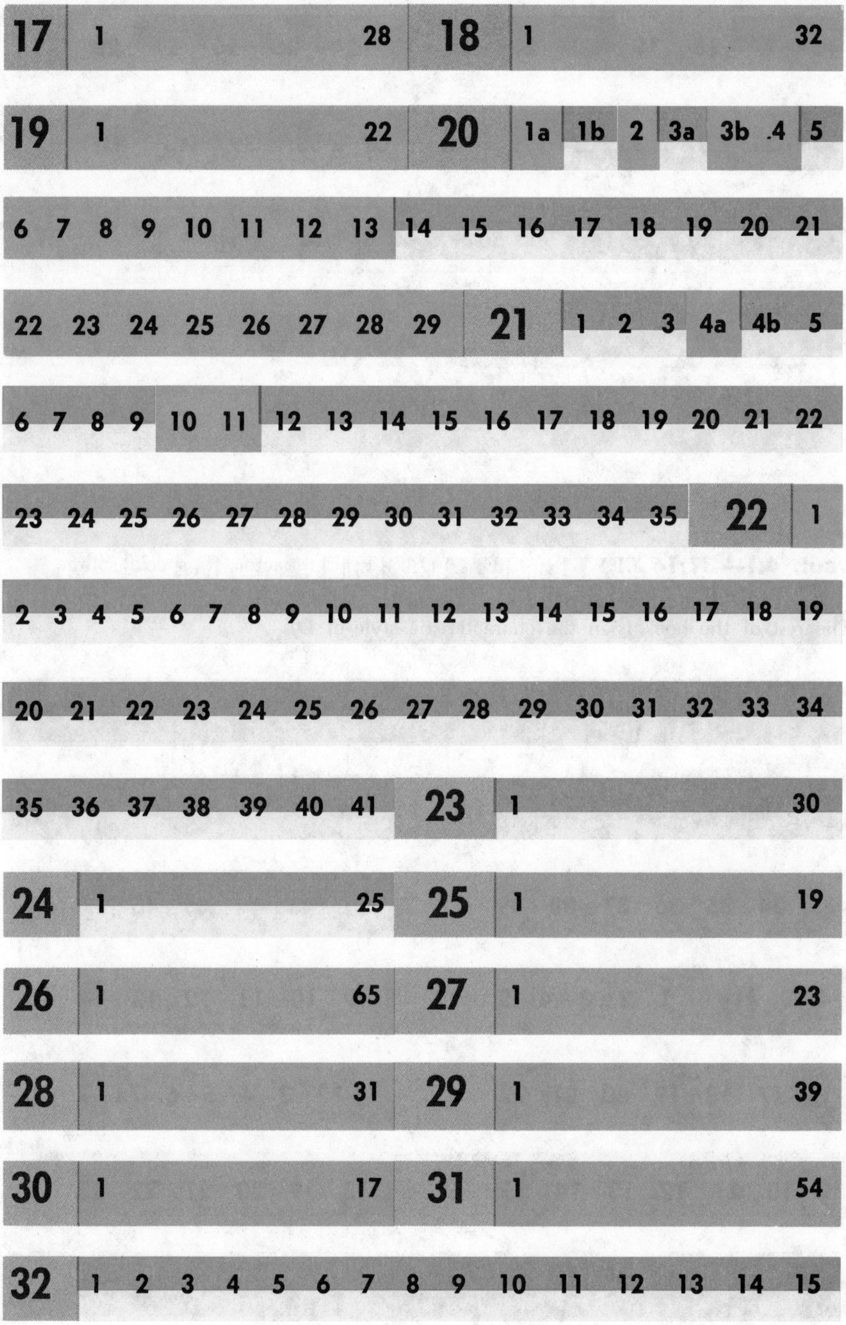

Num. 32:16—36:13 KEY ▢ J; ▢ E; ■ D; ▢ P; ▢ redactor; ▢ special source

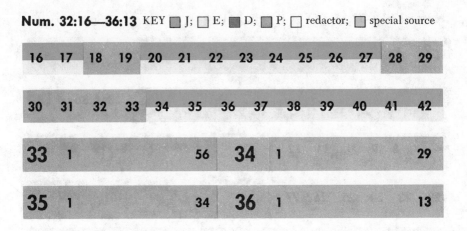

Deut. 4:1—31:14 KEY ▢ J; ▢ E; ■ D; ▢ P; ▢ redactor; ▢ special source

The rest of the book is in the characteristic style of D.

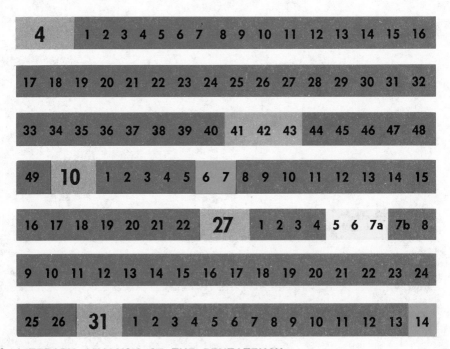

Deut. 31:15—34:12 KEY ☐ J; ☐ E; ■ D; ☐ P; ☐ redactor; ☐ special source

4. The Priestly Tradition[1]

As indicated above, the different traditions which ultimately were fused to form the Pentateuch came down for many years by word of mouth before being put into writing. The last of these traditions to be put into written form was the tradition that came down through generations of priests connected with the Temple of Jerusalem. It is called the priestly tradition because of its emphasis on those things which were of peculiar interest to priests: the Temple, the Ark and the Tabernacle, the ritual, the covenant, the genealogies that established a bond between Abraham, the father of the faithful, and the Jews who had returned from exile in 539 B.C. Its proudest boast was contained in the words of the great Sinai promise: "If you hearken to my voice and keep my covenant, you shall be my special possession, dearer to me than all other people, though all the earth is mine. You shall be to me a kingdom of priests, a holy nation" (Exod. 19:5-6).

A priest who was also a theological genius put this tradition into written form and gave the Pentateuch its final form sometime in the sixth-fifth century B.C. Respecting for the most part the earlier fused historical sagas of the Yahwist and Elohist, he begins with a grand prologue, the creation account of Gen. 1, continues with the Yahwist-Elohist accounts for most of the remainder of Genesis, and interpolates genealogies as he goes along (5:1-32; 6:9-10; 10:1-7; 11:10-32; 25:7-20; 36; 46:8-27) to show that from the very beginning of time God had singled out Israel from among all the nations of the earth to be His special covenanted nation.

Continuing with the Yahwist-Elohist sagas through Exod. 1–24, the Priestly theologian interrupts the national saga at Exod. 24 to introduce the bulk of the priestly traditions (see p. 68ff). These chapters running from Exod. 25 to Num. 10 deal, as we might expect, with those things which were of paramount interest to Israel, the kingdom of priests, namely, the Ark and the Tabernacle (Exod. 25–31; 35–40), the sacrificial cult (Lev. 1–7), the ritual of ordination for priests (Lev. 8–10), the codes of legal cleanliness and legal holiness (Lev. 11–26), genealogies, the organization of the priests and levites, and the division of the land among the tribes (Num. 1–10; 15; 17–19; 25–31; 33–36). In order to show the Mosaic origin of the priestly institutions and their intimate association with the very constitution of the priestly nation, the author designedly inserts these priestly traditions at that very point in the national saga where the Sinai covenant, constituting Israel a priestly nation, is instituted by God and ratified by Israel (Exod. 24).

If the reader will isolate and read separately the chapters containing

[1] Cf. Select bibliography on p. 575.

the priestly tradition indicated above, he will find them characterized not only by a similarity of content but by a similarity of language and style as well.

The priestly tradition can be distinguished from the other traditions by the following characteristics: a pronounced emphasis on the law and the liturgy, a preoccupation with chronological indications and genealogical tables, a transcendent idea of God, and a style that is somber, redundant, and abstract.

The Priestly Theologian

The Pentateuch is the product of five centuries of inspired theologizing. The Priestly theologian is the student of the Yahwist, the Elohist, the author of Original Deuteronomy, and the traditional teaching of the Jerusalem Temple priesthood. In addition he lived in a century which for some unaccountable reason saw a flowering of genius unlike any century before or after; a century which in Greece saw the birth of Socrates, in Persia the birth of Zoroaster, in China the birth of Lao-tse and Confucius, and in Israel the blossoming of such great minds as Ezekiel, Deutero-Isaiah, and the author of the Book of Job. He was no primitive theologian. His Pentateuch was destined to influence millions before and after Christ and to become the catalyst for the creation of what has come to be known as the Judaeo-Christian civilization of the western world.

His Audience

The Priestly theologian wrote either during or shortly after the exile (587–539), and there is no question about the audience for whom he wrote. They are Jews in Babylonia, severely shocked by the successive catastrophes that fell upon the nation in 587 — the destruction of Jerusalem and the Temple, the deportation of the people into captivity in Babylon, and the extinction of the independent rule of the Davidic kings in Judah.

The Priestly theologian's audience as a consequence is a people that no longer enjoys the status of an independent nation; a people for whom there is little or no hope in a revived and independent monarchy; a people for whom salvation history would appear to have come to an abrupt and grinding stop. It was a people, moreover, who lived in the heart of a pagan society, and in a city, Babylon, which was not only the greatest city of the middle-eastern world, but the center of a magnificent cult of the pagan gods.

Under such circumstances the paramount need of his audience was not merely survival but survival with continuity and purpose. It was an audience, therefore, that needed to be shown its links with the past, its present unique nature dependent upon the past, and its destiny for the future. Assured of these, Israel as a people could survive and survive meaningfully and purposefully.

His Sources

To supply for these needs the Priestly theologian took the traditions of his people — the Yahwist's and Elohist's sagas, the priestly traditions and the book of Deuteronomy, and fused them into a continuous narrative with a center of gravity that no longer could be associated with the idea that Israel had to be a politico-religious kingdom but upon the far more exalted conviction that Israel's nature was to be a holy people and her mission to be a worshipping community.

The Worshipping Community

If we examine the theological techniques by which the Priestly theologian inculcated his conviction that Israel was to be a worshipping community rather than a politico-religious kingdom, we shall find that he uses both simple and abstruse techniques.

His simplest technique is the technique of silence. He says nothing about the political kingdom that was. He says almost nothing about the kings and nothing at all about the long history of the Davidic kingdom that stretched from the year 1000 down to the year 587. If to be ignored is worse than to be maligned, the Priestly author has disposed of Israel's false political ambitions in a devastating manner.

His second simple technique is the technique of attracting attention by sheer command of space. In the outline of the Pentateuch that follows, two characteristics of the Priestly theologian's salvation history stand out: first, the *amount* of material in the Pentateuch that deals with the origin, the nature, the worship, and the organization of Israel as a worshipping community; and second, the *position* of the priestly author's material.

The Pentateuch as a Whole

In the Pentateuch as we have it from the Priestly theologian's hand, approximately eighty-seven out of one hundred and eighty chapters are given over to his teaching about Israel as a worshipping community. The Yahwist's and Elohist's sagas which total approximately sixty-five chap-

CATEGORY	Saga material	Priestly tradition	Deuteronomic material
NATURE	Historical	Liturgical-legal	Paranaetic
AUTHOR	Yahwist and Elohist (c. 950–850 B.C.)	Priestly author (c. 550–500 B.C.)	"D" theologian (c. 700 B.C.)
QUANTITY	Total of 65 chapters	Total of 87 chapters	Total of 34 chapters
	Gen. 1–11 Theological prologue Gen. 11-50 Birth of the people Exod. 1–18 Deliverance from Egypt Exod. 19–24 Birth of the nation — the "Worshipping Community"		
		Exod. 25–40 Ark and Tabernacle: God in the midst of the Worshipping Community Lev. 1–7 Cult of the Worshipping Community Lev. 8–10 Priesthood of the Worshipping Community Lev. 17–26 Internal holiness of the Worshipping Community Num. 1–10 Organization of the Worshipping Community	
	Num. 10–25 The March of the Worshipping Community to the Promised Land		
		Num. 26–36 Priestly division of land among tribes of the Worshipping Community	
			Deut. 1–34 Covenant theology emphasizing the spirit of love of the Worshipping Community [1]

[1] It is the salvation history particularly in the saga material that gives to the worshipping community its *élan vital*; the Priestly traditions that give to it its *raison d'être*; and the Deuteronomic sermons that define its *esprit*.

ters are used by the Priestly theologian as an introduction to his detailed description of the worshipping community. If as Jesus observed, "It is out of the abundance of the heart that the mouth speaks," then the eighty-seven chapters dealing with the worshipping community show that the Priestly theologian's heart was filled with the conviction that Israel was to be a worshipping community rather than a politico-religious nation or state.

The second characteristic of the Priestly theologian's material is its *position*. The major portion of the material dealing with the worshipping community is situated in the very center of the Pentateuch at that point where God comes down on Mount Sinai to make Israel His chosen nation. Immediately following Exod. 24, the chapter that describes the making of the Sinai covenant, the Priestly theologian introduces the major portion of his material from the priestly traditions. The rest of Exodus (Exod. 25–40) deals with the Ark, the covenant, and the Tabernacle. Leviticus follows with its laws for sacrifice in ch. 1–7; its laws for priestly ordination in ch. 8–10; its laws of ritual cleanliness in ch. 11–16; and its laws of legal holiness in ch. 17–26. In Num. 1–10 the Priestly author places his material dealing with the organization of the tribes around the Ark and the Tabernacle and the laws dealing with the upkeep of the house of God. As A. Bentzen says in his introduction to the Pentateuch:

> . . . the climax of revelation is reached (for the priestly theologian) in the covenant at Sinai, where the cultus is revealed. . . That the priestly author also has ethical laws is quite clear. . . But that the Priestly author values the cultus higher cannot be denied. It follows from the place which the cultic laws occupy in the final revelation.[1]

A third and more abstruse technique used by the Priestly theologian is his utilization of the priestly tradition's salvation history narrative. It is a narrative which is made to parallel the Yahwist's and Elohist's sagas but in such a way that the great events of Israel's salvation history are described to *foreshadow* the creation of Israel as a worshipping community. Thus in Gen. 1, the sun, the moon, and the stars are placed in the sky to regulate time for liturgical feasts and seasons, and the creation of the world itself is described as a work of six days followed by a day of Sabbath rest. As G. von Rad says:

> The fact that this history of cultic institutions begins with the creation of the world shows the tremendous theological claim made by the Priestly author. P is utterly serious in wanting to show that the cult which entered history in the people of Israel is the goal of the origin

[1] *Introduction to the Old Testament*, vol. II, p. 35 and footnote.

and the evolution of the world. Creation itself was designed to lead to this Israel.[2]

In the Priestly author's description of the flood story (Gen. 6–9), everything leads up to the laws for sacrifices and the covenant with Noah (Gen. 9:1-16), which is a reprise of Gen. 1. In Gen. 17 the Priestly author's Abraham story centers on two liturgico-moral elements in the covenant with Abraham — the institution of circumcision which distinguished Jews from the non-circumcising Babylonians during the exile and the obligation to be holy expressed in God's words to Abraham: "Bear yourself blameless in my presence."

In the Priestly author's narrative of the Exodus, three elements which deal with the nature of the worshipping community, stand out. First, the long description of the Passover feast (Exod. 12), the principal feast of the worshipping community; second, the explanation given for offering the first-born to God for service in the priesthood (Exod. 13:1-16); and third, the programmatic text of the whole priestly narrative, "Say this to the house of Jacob, declare this to the sons of Israel: You yourselves have seen what I did with the Egyptians, how I carried you on eagle's wings and brought you to myself. From this you know that now, if you obey my voice and hold fast to my covenant, you of all the nations shall be my very own for all the earth is mine. I will count you *a kingdom of priests, a consecrated nation*" (Exod. 19:3-6).

The words are programmatic and at the same time summarize the Priestly theologian's theology in the proclamation that Israel as a nation is to be a nation of priests; that is, a nation that is to be as close to God as the priests are in the sanctuary, a nation that is to have as its principle function the principal function of priests — namely, divine worship. It is another way of saying that Israel's nature is to be holy, and that her function is to be a worshipping community. Martin Noth comments as follows on Exod. 19:5-6,

> Israel is to be the special possession of Yahweh (v. 5), to whom the whole earth and so all nations belong; she is therefore a 'holy' people, i.e., set apart from the rest of the nations (v. 6). The singular expression 'kingdom of priests' (v. 6) obviously also refers to this. There is no particular emphasis on the word 'kingdom' in this expression; it may be understood to mean 'state' in just the same way as the nations on the earth are usually organized into states. Israel is to have the role of the priestly member in the number of earthly states. Israel is to have the special privilege of priests, to be allowed to 'draw near' God, and is to do 'service' for all the world (cf. also Is. 61:5f); this is the

[2] *Theology of the Old Testament*, vol. I, 223-334.

purpose for which Israel has been chosen, as has been demonstrated by the earlier acts of God towards the people.[1]

If we have understood the Priestly theologian correctly, he has taught 2500 years before Vatican II what the Council Fathers declared in the Constitution on the Liturgy: "The liturgy is the summit toward which the activity of the Church is directed."

Confirmation for such exalted theological thinking so early in the history of the kingdom of God can be found in the preaching of Ezekiel, in the needs of the exile community for whom the Priestly author wrote, and in the theological teaching of the Chronicler's history.

A similar theology of the worshipping community in Ez. 40–48 proves that the question of the nature of the kingdom of God was a burning question during the exile and that the Priestly theologian was not alone either in his theologizing or his theology.

The fact that the Pentateuch was written during or shortly after the exile, when Israel's political fortunes were at the nadir, indicates that such instruction was both relevant and necessary for those exiles who might have wondered about the specific nature of the kingdom of Israel in the eyes of God now that independence, power and influence had been reduced to memories.

The fact that the priestly author describes the nation as "a kingdom of priests" and repeats through the mouth of God the constant injunction, "You shall be holy because I the Lord your God am holy," further corroborates this interpretation.

The fact that the Chronicler, in his history of Judah written at least one hundred years after the exile, teaches that Israel is to be a worshipping community and even represents David as a king whose principal interests were liturgical rather than political, shows that the Chronicler had gone to school in the theology of the Priestly theologian's Pentateuch.

Lastly, it is no accident that in the years following the exile there was a great era of psalm writing in Israel. The psalter became the hymnbook of the restored community, and its very existence testifies to the seriousness with which Israel after the exile took its function as a worshipping community.

If we look once more at the above outline of the Pentateuch, we shall understand why Judaism, Jesus, the Apostles, the Church Fathers and the Church down the centuries have considered the Pentateuch so central to God's revelation contained in the Bible. By incorporating the work of the Yahwist and the Elohist, the Priestly theologian preserved the great history of election contained in the work of those early theologians. Thus,

[1] *Exodus*, p. 157.

'election' provided the *elan vital* for the kingdom on earth. By elaborating the nature and function of the Kingdom of God as a worshipping community — as it were through the mouth of God Himself from the covenant mountain, Sinai — the Priestly theologian settled once and for all the place of holiness and worship in the Church. He thus provided the *raison d'etre* of the kingdom. He made all creation God's cathedral and all men the 'meant to be' worshippers in the cathedral. By concluding the Pentateuch with the Deuteronomic theologian's teaching about love and response to love by obedience to the word of God, the Priestly author inculcated in unforgettable terms the *esprit* of love that was to be for all time the dynamic principle of the kingdom's activity in the world.

When Jesus said, "Do not think that I have come to destroy the Law or the Prophets, I have not come to destroy but to fulfill," it was of the Priestly author's Pentateuch and of such great seminal theological concepts as these that He spoke.

The Priestly Theologian's Anthropology

For the Priestly theologian, as we have seen, the world is meant to be a cathedral and all mankind is meant to constitute the choir whose privilege it is to praise God in His heaven. From the Priestly author's teaching about Israel as a worshipping community, it is clear that the priestly bent in theology is more transcendent than immanent, more theocentric than anthroprocentric. Unlike the Yahwist who has God walk in the garden with Adam, close the door of the ark behind Noah, and visit Abraham like a friendly neighboring sheik, the Priestly author sets an altar rail between man and God and tends to see all mankind streaming in procession toward God rather than God leaving His heaven to come down and dwell familiarly with man.

In the Yahwist's saga, God deals with man as a sinner, but in a manner that is friendly, forgiving, and tender. In the Priestly author's theology, there is little about man the sinner. It is almost taken for granted that all men will want to enter the Cathedral of the universe and praise God as they should. As a consequence, in the Priestly author's view, only the forces of evil are thoroughly alien to the Cathedral and only the man who joins the forces of evil in their opposition to God is ejected from the Cathedral. It is as a consequence a truism of Old Testament theology to speak of the immanent God of the Yahwist and the transcendent God of the Priestly author. And it is perhaps this truism that has tended to obscure the magnificent theology of man taught by the Priestly author. Since his theology of man touches on both cosmology and anthropology and links the two, we will begin with the Priestly theologian's idea of the world and creation. This will lead to his concept of man and man's place in the world.

Briefly, the Priestly author's theology is a theology of goodness — the goodness of God to begin with, the goodness of all creation as a first corollary, and the goodness of man, God's "image and likeness," as a second corollary. In the Priestly author's theology of goodness three points seem to be both proclaimed and combined: 1. All that God has created is good. 2. Out of His goodness and love God has made man "in the image and likeness of God," which means man is God's vicar and representative on earth to rule the earth and created things. 3. Man, the vicar of God on earth, has the right, the power, and the obligation to rule the earth and created things as God would rule them if He himself ruled on earth rather than through His designated vicar, man.

Goodness of All Things

The Priestly theologian teaches the goodness of all creation in a thoroughly Semitic way in the first chapter of Genesis. He represents God creating all things by dividing God's work of creation into eight works; one on the first day, one on the second, two on the third; one on the fourth; one on the fifth, and two on the sixth. On the last or seventh day God rests. What is notable about this description is its pedagogical intent. The priestly author goes out of his way to say after each work of creation that God looked at it and "saw that it was good." God says this seven times (Gen. 1:3, 11, 12, 19, 22, 25, 31), the number which for the Jews represented perfection. Thus, it is no accident that, although there are eight works of creation, the author has God see that what He has created is good and say so *seven* rather than eight times. The seven represents in itself the perfection of all created things — their unalloyed goodness as they come from the hand of God. It is no accident either, that the seventh time the author says this he adds the qualifier "very good": "God saw all he had made, and indeed it was very good." To an Israelite these words left no doubt about the goodness of all things in the universe.

If we have understood the Priestly theologian, then it is right to say that nothing in the whole cathedral of the universe, whether in the skies above, on the earth below, in the seas, or in the heart of the earth, is bad. All created things are inherently good and one can never say of anything, in itself, that it is anything but good. According to the Priestly theologian there is no evil principle in nature. For those who accept this teaching, the Priestly author has given the death blow to every form of dualism, whether it be Gnosticism, Manichaeism, or Jansenism. Dualists can fatten on many things in the rest of the Old Testament and even in the New Testament. They cannot possibly swallow Gen. 1 without choking.

The Goodness of Man

The Priestly theologian's teaching on the position of man in the created universe is enunciated briefly, almost dogmatically, in four different passages. In Gen. 1:26 he has God say: "Let us make mankind in our image and likeness; and let them have dominion over the fish of the sea, the birds of the air, the cattle, over all the wild animals and every creature that crawls on the earth." In Gen. 5:1 he repeats this teaching in the words: "When God created man, he made him in the likeness of God." In Gen. 9:5, speaking about murder, the Priestly theologian puts the following words into God's mouth: "Whoever sheds the blood of man, by man shall his blood he shed; for in the image of God man was made." Lastly in Lev. 19:18 the priestly author has God command: "You shall love your neighbor as yourself."

It is clear from Gen: 9:5 that murderers are to be executed because they have killed him who was created in the image of God. If we are to understand this prohibition, as well as the command to love our neighbor as ourself, we shall have to discover what the Priestly author means by saying man has been made in the "image and likeness of God."

In our western, Greek based culture, it has been the custom for centuries to interpret "in our image" as the spiritual nature of man and especially as a reference to the faculties of will and intellect. In recent years it has come to be realized that Israel's theologians did not think after the manner of the Greeks. They did not think of man as a body and a soul but a total person. They would not as a consequence have seen this image and likeness as referring to such spiritual faculties as will and intellect. The solution, therefore, of man's likeness to God must be seen against the cultural background of the sixth century Priestly author, not against the philosophical background of Greek culture.

In Hebrew there is no question about the meaning of image and likeness. The word used for image is *tselem* and is the same word used for the image or idol of a god, or the image or statue of a king. The word for likeness is *demut* and means precisely 'likeness' or resemblance. A semantic investigation of the terms leads to the conclusion expressed by Paul Humbert: "The semantic verdict is perfectly definite: man, according to P, has the same outward appearance as the deity of whom he is the tangible effigy, and the noun *tselem* — image — refers to no spiritual likeness in this case any more than in the others." [1]

What the Priestly author meant by saying man was created in the image and likeness of God, is now clear. In the middle eastern world of the sixth century B.C., images not only represented the pagan gods but also represented the king. In the great kingdoms of the middle east it was not uncommon for a king to set up images or statues of himself in the different provinces of his empire. An Assyrian king, for example, states this fact in the words: "I will set up my statue in their midst." The significance of the "image' then is that it represents the king. It is his *alter ego* in places in which he himself either is not or cannot be present.

If man then is created in God's image, it means that he is the *alter ego* of God on earth. He is God's vicar or viceroy. This conclusion is confirmed by the common practice of middle-eastern authors of expressing themselves in parallel, i.e., saying the same thing twice in different words. Thus, when the Priestly author has God say to man, "Let us make mankind in our image and likeness" — and then follows that statement with the statement, "Let them have dominion over the fish of the sea, the birds of the air, the cattle, over all the wild animals and every creature that crawls on the earth," the second statement is saying the same as the first: as image and likeness of God, man is made God's vizier or representative on earth, which is to say that man is king of creation by reason of his appointment by God to be His representative vicar in having dominion over created things.

That this interpretation was not unknown to the Jews before Christ can be shown from a midrashic story told about the Rabbi Hillel in the year 20 B.C.

> When Hillel took leave of his disciples he usually accompanied them far along the road, and as they asked him: "Rabbi, where are you going?" he answered: "I am going to fulfill a commandment." "Which one?" they asked. "I am going to take a bath at the bathing place," he replied. When his disciples asked: "But is that a commandment?" he replied: "Certainly, for if the man appointed for the statues of kings set up in the theatres and circuses washes and rubs them down and for that work is not only provided for but honoured amongst the great men of the realm, how much more must this duty be incumbent upon me who am created after the image and likeness of God." [2]

The interpretation is further corroborated by the Priestly theologian's argument that murderers are to be executed for taking the life of man, because man is the image and likeness of God. Just as the man who in-

[1] *Etudes sur le recit du paradis et de la chute dans la Genese*, 1940, p. 157.
[2] Strack-Billerbeck, t. I, p. 654.

7

9

10

Nos. 7–10. Bronze Age Mesopotamia. **7**. Sumerian statuette from Lagash, southern Babylonia, from about 2500 B.C. A non-Semitic people, the Sumerians had attained a high degree of civilization during the Early Bronze Age; much of the literature, art, law, and agriculture of the later Semites was borrowed from Sumer, just as Rome was heir to Greece. **8**. Statue of Ebih II, governor of Mari; Middle Bronze. **9**. Alabaster head of Ur-Nin-Girsu, Neo-Sumerian, *ca*. 2100 B.C. **10**. Ziggurat at Nippur, 108 kilometers northwest of Warka, built by Ur-Nammu (2100 B.C.). The level marshlands and plains between the Tigris and Euphrates in Lower Mesopotamia were dotted with dozens of temple towers, or ziggurats, many of them centuries old when Abraham was directed: "Leave your country and your father's house for the land which I will show you" (Gen. 12:1). *Photos courtesy:* Pontifical Biblical Institute, Rome, Italy.

sults the statue of the king insults the king, so he who attacks man attacks God whose image man is.

It is not clear in the Priestly author's theology why man should "love his neighbor as himself." It would appear, since man is indeed the *alter ego* or representative of God on earth, that in loving himself and in loving others as himself he is loving God.

If this interpretation is correct, then the Priestly author has laid down the basic premise for a theology of transcendent humanism. Man as God's vicar is by God's decree and will the lord and master of creation. All created things are at man's service. Man is little less than God. As the author of the eighth psalm puts it: "What is man that you should be mindful of him, or the son of man that you should care for him? You have made him little less than a god. You have crowned him with glory and honor. You have given him rule over the works of your hands putting all things under his feet. . . ." Or as Sirach expresses the same truth. "God gave into the power of men what is on the earth. He clothed them with power like his own; in his image he created them. He put the fear of man on all creatures" (Sir. 17:2-4).

Transcendent humanism as opposed to immanent, natural humanism, can be based on the Priestly theologian's teaching because the Priestly author makes it clear that all man's power, all man's dignity comes from God and must be referred to God. Man must rule creation as God would rule it were He ruling it in person. This means that man must know creation, its constitution, its nature, its laws. Without this knowledge he cannot rule it as God would rule it, nor perfect it as God would perfect it. It means also that man must see in all other men that dignity which belongs to a vicar of God. He must reverence, respect, and protect the rights of all men because each and every man is a vicar of God. He must love every man because every man is God's *alter ego* on earth.

In the New Testament, Jesus Himself is the perfect exemplar of man "the image and likeness of God." He is the second Adam. He is the perfect vicar. He is king of Kings and Lord of creation. He is all goodness, all concerned for the world, all self-sacrificing for other vicars of God, and He is totally obedient to the will of the Father of all, thus reversing the *hubris* of Adam which amounted to repudiating the lesser dignity of vicar to grasp for a power that would make him equal to God Himself.

The creation account of Gen. 1:1—2:3

To understand rightly the Priestly author's creation account,[1] the reader

[1] Cf. *Beginnings* by C. Hauret; *A Path Through Genesis* by B. Vawter; W. Heidt, *Genesis 1–11*, OTRG No. 9.

must keep in mind three basic principles. 1. The inspired author's purpose is to teach religion not science (he is interested in the "what" and "why" of things, not the "how"). 2. The inspired author, like other authors, writes according to the literary norms and style of his time. 3. Sacred Scripture and science cannot contradict each other, because God is author of both.

If one asks what religious truths the Priestly author teaches in his creation account, the answer is simple. He teaches that there is only one God, that the one God created all things good, that He created man in His own image and likeness and made him master of created things.

If one asks what scientific truths the Priestly author teaches in his creation account, the answer is equally simple. He has nothing to say about the "how" of creation. He has nothing to say for two good reasons. First, he knows no scientific explanation of creation and God gives Him no revelation on the "how" of creation. Secondly, his purpose is to teach religious truths, not scientific truths. A scientific explanation of creation would be a digression and could serve no good purpose for him.

If one asks what literary form and style the author uses to serve his religious purpose, the answer is forthcoming from an analysis of the text. His literary form is popular description in typical Hebrew poetic style. Thus he describes the principal eight works of creation in a balanced and artificial arrangement based upon the ordinary six day work-week of his time followed by the Sabbath as God's stipulated day of rest. The eight works of creation are spread over the six working days not only to facilitate memorization of the account and to emphasize the Sabbath, but to substitute a theologically correct 'popular' account of creation for the theologically false and depraved 'popular' Babylonian creation myths current at the time of the author (6th-5th century B.C. in Babylon). The poetic schematic arrangement of Gen. 1:1—2:3 can be seen in the following outline.

Day	WORK	WORK OF DIVISION
1	Light (3)	Separation of light from darkness (4-5)
2	Firmament (6)	Separation of upper from lower waters (7)
3	Earth—plants (9-12)	Separation of sea from land (9-12)

Day	WORK	WORK OF ADORNMENT
4	Luminaries (14-15)	Firmament with sun, moon, stars (16-18)
5	Fish and birds (20-22)	Waters with fish, air with birds (21-23)
6	Animals—men (24-27)	Earth with animals, man (24-31)

The cosmology or picture of the universe behind the schematic arrangement in Gen. 1 is new only to moderns. At the time of the author it was shared by the Egyptians, Babylonians, and the Phoenicians, and it continued to be the common, popular cosmology of the Near East down to the time of Christ and beyond. Entirely unscientific, it was based upon what appeared to the eye. For example, it was held that the earth was an island in the midst of a vast encircling sea.

Since the earth was steady except when shaken by earthquakes, it was popularly believed that the earth, like a firm building, must have foundations and that when it shook it must be because someone was shaking these foundations (cf. Ps. 24:2; Job 38:4-11).

Since rain and snow came down from the sky, it was popularly believed that this was so because there was another ocean above the sky. This ocean was supported by the firmament which appeared to the eye to be a solid, metallic vault supporting the upper (heavenly) waters and separating them from the lower (earthly) waters. When it rained, it was because trapdoors in the solid firmament had been opened and the upper waters allowed to pour through and down (cf. Job 37:18; 38:22; Prov. 8:27; Gen. 7:11; Ps. 78:23).

Since the sun, the moon, and the stars appeared to move like an army along the solid surface of the firmament, they were considered to be in the firmament and were popularly referred to as the armies or "hosts of the heaven." The light from these luminaries was seen before and after their rising and was considered distinct from them (cf. Gen. 1:3; Job 38: 12, 19, 24).

The heavens themselves appeared to be arranged like a three storied building with the first story consisting of the atmospheric heaven where the birds fly, the second story the sidereal heaven where the sun, moon and stars move along the firmament, and the third story the empyrean heaven — in excelsis — high above the upper waters where God dwells directing the universe and sending His angels to dispense the rain, the snow, the hail, and the lightning (cf. Job 37:2-5; 38:22, 35, 37).

That these were the popular concepts of the time is evident from a reading of Egyptian and Babylonian literature. That they were common to the Biblical authors is more than evident from their frequent occurence in the Bible (cf. Job 38; Prov. 8:23ff; Pss. 19; 104). They are clearly evident in the Priestly author's creation account. Thus, light exists before and independently of the sun (Gen. 1:3). The firmament divides the upper waters from the lower waters (Gen. 1:6). The lights (sun, moon, stars) are "in" the firmament (Gen. 1:14).

Since the Priestly author is using the popular language of his day (the only language he and his unscientific contemporaries could understand), and since his purpose is to teach religious doctrine and not science, it is pointless to object on a scientific basis that light is created on the first day and the sun on the fourth, or that the plants and trees created on the third day live without the light of the sun created only on the following day. The author has no intention of teaching these things as scientific truths. He merely uses them to express his teaching in the same way that moderns use such popular expressions as "the sun rises," "the stars come out," the "vault of the heavens," and the like.

It is likewise pointless to argue that the author intended to teach that the earth was created over a period of six days. His six days are literary days, a poetic artificial arrangement, as arbitrary as a listing from "a" to "f" or from "one" to "six." Since there is nothing taught about the actual time of creation, there can be no question of opposition between the six literary days of the Genesis account and the long eons of time postulated by scientists for the formation of the universe. The author knows nothing about the "how" of creation and tells us nothing. Only science čan explain this "how," since God did not make it an object of revelation.

Philosophically stated, the problem is solved as follows: *error lies in judgment. The author makes no judgment on the essential nature of visible phenomena* (as is the object of science). *Therefore he can make no error.* It is on this philosophical foundation that the above apology rests.

It has been stated that a probable purpose of the Priestly author in using the six day schema was to supply a theologically correct popular account of creation for the theologically false popular Babylonian creation epic ("Enuma Elish"; cf. ANET 60ff) of the time. To correct this false creation story and still communicate in a medium intelligible to his contemporaries, the Priestly author had to be singularly adroit. He corrects, therefore, by describing pagan deities such as the sun, moon, and stars as mere luminaries, created by the one true God to provide light for man and to help man reckon the time and distinguish the seasons — thereby implicitly denying to them the divinity attributed to them by the polytheists.

Other polytheistic ideas are subtly refuted in an equally clever manner. Where the ancient polytheists conceived of gods and the world as coming from a common, primordial material, the Priestly author uncompromisingly declares: "In the beginning God created heaven and earth." The one God, therefore, is anterior to and independent of all matter.

According to the ancient polytheists, primordial matter was watery and made up of two gods, Abzu and Tiamat. The Priestly author ignores Abzu entirely and eliminates Tiamat by merely alluding to her in his name for the sea (*Tehom*, Hebrew for "Tiamat"). He thus leaves to Tiamat about as much substance as moderns give to "Father Neptune."

For the Priestly author as well as for the polytheists of his time, the creation of man was important. The gods, according to the polytheists, went into consultation; then the god, Enlil, created man from the blood of some dead deity. The Priestly author has God deliberating with Himself (or perhaps with His angels) before creating man (Gen. 1:26), thereby retaining the correct popular notion about the importance of man among the works of God, but eliminating the crass, polytheistic notions that accompanied it.

Because of the resemblance between the creation account of the Priestly author and some creation accounts from Babylonia, the fatherland of the patriarch Abraham, particularly the Enuma Elish creation story and the Gilgamesh epic (ANET 60ff and 72ff), there arises a question of dependence. Does the biblical account depend on these or any other oriental epic? The consensus of scholars on this question is expressed by Fr. Lagrange. "We can conclude," he says, "that the Mosaic cosmogony in its doctrine is unique because its doctrine comes from God; in its exposition, however, it has similarities with other Semitic cosmogonies, because that exposition can be said to be the fruit of the Semitic mind and imagination."

As a result of modern studies the fundamentalist interpretation of the Priestly author's creation account has been completely abandoned. The arguments against the fundamentalist interpretation may be summed up briefly. (a) The author unequivocally states that God creates instantaneously by His word alone. (b) The schematic order of the six days and eight works (four on the first three days, and four more on the second three days) indicates poetic rather than historical intent. (c) The evidence from comparison with Egyptian and Babylonian literature shows that the author's popular cosmological concepts are common to all the ancient Near East and indicates that he has no intention of revealing or teaching anything new along this line. (d) The entirely different creation account in Gen. 2, which the Priestly theologian does not exclude, shows that he does not present his six day arrangement as a scientific explanation of creation. (e) Scientific findings give conclusive proof that the formation of the universe took billions of years and not six days. Since Sacred Scripture and established scientific conclusions cannot contradict each other, it follows that the author of Gen. 1 is using words and phrases in a figurative or non-literal manner.

The age of the earth

Until two centuries ago the age of the earth was reckoned on the basis of biblical chronology at approximately four thousand years. In the nineteenth century geologists and palaeontologists produced alarming hints and then certainties to show that the earth had been in existence at least several million years. In the present century astronomers and astrophysicists have pushed these millions to billions. On November 22, 1951 Pius XII, speaking to the Pontifical Academy of Science, accepted tentatively an approximate birthday for the universe between five and ten billion years ago. The Holy Father gave the following reasons as the scientific basis for this conclusion.

The first reason is based on the recession of the spiral nebulae or galaxies. These nebulae are known to move at a speed up to 25,000 miles per second. Determining the point from which they started and visualizing a backward flight of the galaxies like a motion picture in reverse, one can imagine the galaxies returning to the spot from which they started out at the time the cosmic processes had their beginning. Knowing the speed at which they travel, plus their distance from the same common point of divergence, astronomers have computed the zero hour of departure from the same common point at between five and ten billion years ago.

The second reason is based upon the breakdown rate of radioactive Uranium 238. Knowing the breakdown rate of Uranium 238 into an isotope of lead, scientists placed under a geiger counter a specimen of uranium ore from one of the oldest rock formations on earth and determined its age at approximately five billion years. The same method applied to meteoritic uranium from outer space produced a similar figure.

The third reason was based upon the stability of the systems of double stars and starry masses as exemplified in the whirling motion of the Milky Way. To understand this proof we must imagine the Milky Way galaxy as an enormous wheel. The wheel spins around a flaming hub, its gravitational center, consisting of clusters of stars. The spinning movement tends to pull these stars apart, so that with each revolution they should be pulled farther apart. Examination of the Milky Way reveals how many times it has revolved. Knowing the time for each revolution the astronomers compute that the Milky Way began to whirl between five and ten billion years ago.

The Holy Father concludes this part of his address with the words:

> Although these figures may seem astounding, nevertheless, even to the simplest of the faithful, they bring no new or different concept from the one they learned in the opening words of Genesis: 'In the beginning . . . ', that is to say, at the beginning of things in time. The figures we have quoted clothe these words in a concrete and almost mathematical expression, while from them there springs forth a new source of consolation for those who share the esteem of the Apostle for that divinely inspired Scripture, which is always useful 'for teaching, for reproving, for correcting, for instructing.'

The Priestly author's framework for the Pentateuch

The theological and liturgical framework imposed by the Priestly author on Israel's history appears at its clearest in the prologue to that history provided in the creation account of Gen. 1, in the "descendants of" formula for genealogies that marks off the divisions of Genesis (2:4; 5:1; 6:9; 10:1; 11:10, 27; 25:12, 19; 36:1, 9; 37:2), and in the division of Israel's theological history into four covenants: the tacit creation covenant of Gen. 1, the covenant with Noah in Gen. 9 (a sort of repetition of the covenant with Adam), the covenant with Abraham in Gen. 17, and the great covenant of Sinai in Exod. 19–24.

In the creation account of Gen. 1 the Priestly theologian not only provides the history of Israel with a magnificent exordium but strikes a liturgical note from the very beginning by likening God's creative work to the true Israelite's typical week. God's works are spread over six days, but on the seventh day, the Sabbath, He rests. Thus the author begins Israel's history with an account of creation that not only refutes the crass polytheistic creation accounts with which the Israelites were acquainted from their exile in Babylon, but inculcates upon his readers the privilege and obligation of fashioning their weekly activities upon the activity of the creator, who "worked" six days but rested on the Sabbath.

In the "descendants of" formula the Priestly theologian not only divides off the different periods of Israel's early history, but by eliminating all except the line of ancestor of the Israelites shows how from the very beginning the nation Israel had been part of God's plan for the salvation of the world. His interest in genealogies continues in Exodus (6:14-27 where there is a notable interest in the priestly clan of Aaron) and reaches its peak in Numbers (1:1-46; 2:14-39; 26:1-51).

Besides the division by means of the genealogies, the Priestly author uses another and broader division of Israel's history by means of covenants. Just as the genealogies show God's special interest in Israel, so also do the successive covenants made: (a) with all mankind before the flood (the tacit covenant of Gen. 1); (b) with all mankind after the flood (Gen. 9:1-17); (c) with Abraham and his descendants (Gen. 17); (d) with the nation Israel (Exod. 19–24).

In each of the covenants the author emphasizes God's goodness to man and establishes some kind of sign of the covenant. Thus in the tacit covenant with the first man God shows His goodness by creating man "in the image and likeness of God" and giving him dominion over all living creatures. The sign of this covenant is either the "lights in the firmament" which serve as "signs" (Gen. 1:14) or the Sabbath observance (cf. Ez. 20:12). Striking still another liturgical note, in preparation for Israel's sacrificial system, the Priestly author points out that God gives to the first man "every seed-bearing plant on the earth and every tree which has seed-bearing fruit" as food. Nothing is said about flesh as food.

In the covenant with Noah after the flood, God shows His goodness to man by giving to him as food "every creature that moves and lives," but "flesh with its life, that is, its blood" he is not to eat (Gen. 9:3-5). Thus the liturgical note is struck again and louder. Blood, even that of animals, was considered the seat and sign of life and, therefore, something sacred (cf. Lev. 17:3ff). As a sign of the covenant Noah is given the rainbow (Gen. 9:12-13). Thus in the first two covenants, which may be termed cosmic covenants because they are for all men, the signs given are such that all mankind can see them — the lights in the heavens and the rainbow.

The third covenant with Abraham again emphasizes God's goodness, this time by the promise of a great progeny (the Israelite nation) and by the promise of the land of Canaan (Gen. 17:1-8). The sign of the covenant is circumcision, a sign emphasized by the Priestly author because of its liturgical significance (Gen. 17:9-14).

In the last covenant at Sinai, God's great gift to His kingdom of priests is twofold: the law and the land. The sign again is circumcision. It is at this point that the Priestly theologian inserts the liturgical law of the worshipping community, beginning at Exod. 25 and continuing down to Num. 10, with additions throughout the remaining chapters of Numbers.

5. The Yahwist Tradition and Genesis 2—3[1]

It requires little study to see that the Priestly author liberally exercised his privilege as final editor of allocating to himself not only the climactic position in the Pentateuch for the subjects dear to his heart but also the lion's share of the space. Thus it is immediately after the institution of the Sinai covenant, the high point of Israel's history, that the Priestly author places the major part of his own material (Exod. 25 through Leviticus up to Num. 10, with further additions in Num. 13; 15; 17—19; 25—31; 33—36). Of the total 187 chapters in the Pentateuch, the "D" (Deuteronomy) tradition is allocated 34 chapters, the Yahwist and Elohist combined receive 65 chapters, the Priestly tradition 87 chapters (see p. 58ff)!

One is inclined to say "to the editor belong the spoils," but in the case of the Pentateuch, poetic justice has won out. Of all the parts of the Pentateuch read on the run by the average person, none is read faster than the Priestly parts. The "J", "E", and "D" parts on the contrary have been the favorites down the centuries. And if there were a vote for the

[1] Cf. select bibliography on p. 575.

favorite among these three parts, the winner without a contest would be the "J" or Yahwist tradition.

The student perhaps does not yet know how to distinguish the Yahwist from the other traditions, but if he will recollect for himself his favorite stories from the Pentateuch (Adam and Eve, Cain and Abel, the flood, the tower of Babel, the call of Abraham, the destruction of Sodom and Gomorrah, etc.), he will unknowingly be putting his finger on some of the salient episodes of the Yahwist's tradition. The parts of the Yahwist saga retained in the Pentateuch by the Priestly theologian are the parts almost everybody remembers. If the Yahwist does not entirely steal the Priestly theologian's thunder, it is only because the Priestly theologian had the last word and was able to subordinate the Yahwist's saga to his own purposes, taking what served his purpose, omitting what did not.

If the student is to understand and appreciate the great contributions of the Yahwist both to history and theology, it is of first importance that he know the historical background, the purpose, and the sources of both his history and his theology. It will be no small help as well as for the student to realize that the Priestly author is dependent for much of his theology on the Yahwist, and that while he did not retain the whole of the Yahwist's saga, he retained an amount sufficient for a reasonable conjecture concerning the remainder.

Historical background of the Yahwist

The majority of exegetes date the Yahwist to the reign of Solomon between the years 965-926. The principal reason for this dating is the Yahwist's obvious interest in things pertaining to the tribe of Judah, an interest that is easily understood in the tenth century when the Davidic dynasty reached the apex of its power and glory. Thus the Yahwist speaks at length about the patriarchal sojourn in and around Hebron, one of the oldest Israelite sanctuaries in Judah (cf. Gen. 13:14-18; 18—19); gives the hero's part to Judah in the Joseph story (Gen. 37:26; 43:1-12; 44:14-34; 46:28); and goes out of his way in Gen. 38 to record the early genealogy of the family of David, even though it involves telling a scandalous story about the patriarch Judah. In Gen. 49:8-12 and in Num. 24:7 and 24:17, he uses the storytelling device of foreshadowing to inject into earlier poems from the period of the Judges references to the royal power that would be centered in Judah (see p. 357f).

Similarities between the author of the court history of David (2 Sam. 9—1 Kings 2) and the Yahwist indicate either the same school of writers or perhaps even a common author. Thus each exhibits a remarkable gift for story-telling and the same genius for bringing out psychological insights. Each uses the expression "good and evil." Each has the same interest in women (Sarah, Rebecca, Rachel, Tamar, Mikal, Bathsheba) and the same interest in showing that the first-born is not always the one chosen by God. The significance of this last point may have something to do with an apologia for Solomon, who succeeded to the throne of Judah after David, despite the better natural claim of his older brother Adonijah. While the relation between the court history of David (2 Sam. 9–20; 1 Kings 1–2) and the Yahwist's saga cannot be established absolutely, there is no question but that they come from the same literary circles, that the court history did not begin *ex abrupto* with 2 Sam. 9 or even with 2 Sam. 7, and that the Yahwist's saga would find a perfect climax in 2 Sam. 7 and the following chapters of the court history. If the relation could be established, it would throw infinitely more light on the whole of the Yahwist's saga.

The nearest indication of an exact date for the work of the Yahwist is found in the foreshadowing prophecy concerning Edom in Gen. 27:40. Edom was conquered by David (cf. 2 Sam. 8:12-14), but regained its independence sometime in the reign of Solomon (cf. 1 Kings 11:14-25). The saga was written therefore sometime in the reign of Solomon (c. 962-922).

The purpose of the Yahwist author

Since the Priestly editor did not retain the whole of the Yahwist's saga in his massive synthesis of Israel's traditions, it is not easy to determine from the remains a perfect formulation of the Yahwist's purpose. It is possible, however, with the help of the Yahwist's foreshadowings, the general outline of his work, and a knowledge of his historical background to come to a reasonably accurate estimate of his purpose.

In the texts in which the Yahwist makes use of foreshadowing (a storyteller's literary device whereby knowledge of the future, which is of course past to the author, is given or hinted at, in order to arouse interest, sustain suspense, and prepare his audience to look for an interconnection of the parts of his story with the whole), there is a gradual narrowing of the foreshadowing focus from the seed of the woman (Gen. 3:15) to the seed of Abraham (Gen. 12:3) to the tribe of Judah and the dynasty of David (Gen. 49:8-12; Num. 24:7, 9, 17). In Gen. 9:25-27, the Yahwist adds a complementary foreshadowing to the curse of the serpent in Gen. 3:14 by cursing Canaan.

When the general outline of the Yahwist's saga is studied, it can be seen that the line of development indicated in the foreshadowing texts is followed. Thus from the seed of the woman, only the genealogical line that leads from Adam to Seth to Noah to Shem to Abraham receives special attention in Gen. 2–11; all the other peoples descended from the first couple are gradually eliminated. The foreshadowing in Gen. 12:2-3 is complemented by the special election of Isaac to the exclusion of Ishmael and the special election of Jacob to the exclusion of Esau. In Gen. 49:8-12 the foreshadowing of the rise of Judah and the Davidic dynasty is complemented by the additional foreshadowings of Num. 24:7,9,17. The further implementation of this foreshadowing is lost to us but there seems good reason to believe that from beginning to end, the intention of the Yahwist was to establish the place of the theocratic kingdom and the Davidic dynasty in God's plan for the salvation of the world. It would appear, moreover, from the Yahwist's repeated disparagement of the Canaanites that he intended as well to warn his readers that there must be an undying enmity between them and the Canaanite religion (cf. Gen. 3:14; 9:25-27; 18:1ff; 19:30-38; 24:3; 27:46; 28:1, 6-9; 38).

Another thread of evidence leading to the unraveling of the Yahwist's intentions is his emphasis on the promises made to Abraham. These promises were a cherished part of Israel's remembered history, testified to in each of the four great traditions, but in none more insistently than in the Yahwist's (cf., in the Yahwist tradition Gen. 12:1-3, 6-7; 18:17-19; 26:3-5; 28:13-15; in the Elohist tradition Gen. 15:5-7, 13-20 [possibly "J"]; in the Deuteronomist tradition 6:10; 26:5-9; in the Priestly tradition Gen. 17:1-14). In the time of David and Solomon, never before and never after, Israel existed as the great nation promised to Abraham. Her borders extended from the river of Egypt on the south to the Euphrates on the north, and from the sea on the west to the desert on the east (cf. Gen. 15:18-20). In the first chapter of Judges, a list is given of the conquered and the unconquered sections of Canaan after the invasion under Joshua. If this list belongs to the Yahwist's tradition as many authors believe, then it is significant that the author goes out of his way to show that the promises made to Abraham were not completely fulfilled by the conquest under Joshua. The implication, clear to the author's audience in the time of Solomon, is that the fulfillment of this promise has been brought about through David.

It is impossible to know for certain what it was that occasioned the writing of the Yahwist's saga, but it is reasonable to believe that it resulted from the profound transformation of Israel's life brought about by the change from a loose confederation of independent tribes in the time of the Judges to a well-knit and powerful kingdom in the time of David and Solomon. With the concentration of power in the hands of the kings and the concentration of cult in the new royal city of Jerusalem, there arose great danger that Israel would imitate the other kingdoms of the period, forget her theocratic history, and abandon the unique spiritual destiny determined for her by God. To offset that danger the Yahwist reminded his readers that they were a people apart, different from the other nations, chosen, protected, made into a theocratic kingdom by the hand of God, and destined by God for the unique mission of bringing all mankind into subjection to Him as universal king. The divine plan, therefore, was the one thing Israel must not forget.

For this reason it was important to show that the monarchy in Israel was not an accident but a part of that divine plan. The same Lord who had called Abraham out of Mesopotamia and Moses out of Egypt had called David from the flock to rule His people Israel. The dynasty of David, as the Yahwist knew from Nathan's oracle to David concerning the perpetuity of his dynasty (2 Sam. 7), had a very real part to play in God's plan — but it must remember that it was only a part of that plan. How the Yahwist put this message across in his saga has been indicated already in a sketchy manner in the brief explanation given of the foreshadowing texts (Gen. 3:15; 12:2-3; Gen. 49:8-12; Num. 24:7, 9, 17) and their place in the outline of Israel's history developed by the Yahwist. It is time now to consider the sources of the Yahwist's history and theology.

The historical and theological sources of the Yahwist

The Yahwist is a creative writer but he is not an innovator. Israel's traditions are already well established and even partially written down when he prepares to write his interpretation of those traditions in the light of his own times and in the light of Nathan's oracle guaranteeing perpetuity to the dynasty of David. His *credo* is the *credo* of all Israelites. It is summarized in the ancient cultic *credos* articulated in the time of the conquest and in the period of the Judges (Jos. 24:2-15; Deut. 6:20-25; 26:5-9; 1 Sam. 12:7-11) and consists fundamentally in the patriarchal promises, the Sinai covenant together with God's kingship, the partial fulfillment of the patriarchal promises by the conquest of Canaan, and finally the perpetuity of the Davidic dynasty, the latest addition to Israel's deposit of faith.

With these historico-theological data as his foundation stones and with a multitude of well-worn, traditional stories from the time of the patriarchs, the exodus, and the conquest, the Yahwist constructed his saga. He could not change these data even if he had wanted to, for he was as much bound by the unwavering memory of tradition as the simplest among his readers. But he could interpret them. He could show their interrelation and their inner dynamism. He could so arrange them that their full significance would be more clearly evident. He could indeed theologize on the data of Israel's traditional revelation and come by the power of deduction under the guidance of inspiration to new revealed truths and to a deeper and more profound knowledge of the divine plan for Israel and the world. All this he did not only in his account of the patriarchal history and the exodus experience but in his masterful historico-theological re-creation of mankind's pre-history in Gen. 2—11. Because of the many insoluble difficulties in these chapters it will not be practicable to enter into an explanation of everything in Gen. 2—11. It will not, however, be without benefit to list briefly the dominant characteristics of the Yahwist author, and then exemplify a few of these characteristics by means of Gen. 2—3.

Distinguishing characteristics of the Yahwist

The Priestly tradition, as we have already indicated, is characterized by its own special vocabulary, its somber, redundant, and abstract style, its special interest in law, liturgy, chronology, and genealogies, its transcendent concept of God and theocratic concept of Israel, and its historically based use of names for God — using "Elohim" and "El Shaddai" in Genesis, and "Yahweh" only from the time when it was first revealed to Moses according to Exod. 3:15.

In contrast, the Yahwist projects the name Yahweh into the past and has men using it almost from the beginning (cf. Gen. 4:26), has a very distinctive vocabulary, and a style that is flowing, colorful, pungent, and economical. His dialogue is terse, earthy, and consistent with the character of his speakers. He has a genius for psychological insight and an unerring eye for the dramatic element in any story.

In contradistinction to "P" and "E" which bring out the transcendence of God, the Yahwist brings God very close to man, has Him form man from the dust like a potter, walk in the garden, seal the door of Noah's ark, visit and dine with Abraham, and go down to see if the sin of Sodom and Gomorrah is as heinous "as he has heard." In addition to his national interest in Judah and his undisguised delight in all of Israel's ancient traditions, the Yahwist loves to give the popular etymologies of the names of people and places, sometimes punning on the meaning of the Hebrew names (cf. Gen. 3:20; 11:9; 25:26; 25:30; 32:27; Exod. 32:27; Num. 20:13).

Finally and most distinctive is the Yahwist's penchant for the theological undertones that sound throughout the history of Israel from the creation of man in the beginning to the choice of Israel at Sinai and the election of the Davidic dynasty in his own time. Law and liturgy in the

Yahwist's saga give way before theological interests. His symbolic stories in Gen. 2—11 are almost naive, but beneath the popular imagery lie theological truths basic to the whole of Christian revelation, and beneath apparent naiveté, answers to some of the most profound of human problems.

In Gen. 2—3 the reader will find an excellent cross-section of the Yahwist's principal characteristics: his style, his genius for psychological insight, his unerring eye for the dramatic, his interest in probing causes, his penchant for the theological.

The special creation of man

In Gen. 2:7 the author is obviously speaking anthropomorphically, picturing God in a popular manner as working, like a potter, with clay and breathing as man would into the face of his modeled product. Such anthropomorphisms are part of the Yahwist's popular style and need not be taken verbally. This interpretation is confirmed by the similar popular way of describing the creation of man in an old Babylonian text in which "Mami," the mother-goddess, says: "Let him be formed out of clay, be animated with blood . . ." (ANET 99). A similar description is given in the Babylonian epic, Enuma Elish, where man is said to have been created out of the blood of the conquered god, Kingu: "Out of his blood they fashioned mankind . . ." (ANET 68).

With regard to the formation of the woman described in Gen. 2:20-24, the author's popular mode of expression is obvious from his anthropomorphic description of God leading the animals before Adam for Adam to impose names upon them, and from his equally anthropomorphic description of God taking a rib from Adam and "making" it into a woman. The whole context witnesses to an imaginative description designed to teach the equal dignity of woman with man because basically they are the same; as the man says: "She now is bone of my bone, and flesh of my flesh."

The original happiness of our first parents

There are a number of elements in the description of "the original happiness of our first parents in a state of justice, integrity and immortality" which have been understood in too fundamentalist a manner, taking the dictionary definition of the words rather than the meaning intended by the author. We may question, for example, whether "the tree of life" was an actual tree or a symbol for immortality; "the tree of knowledge," an actual tree or a symbol for omniscience; the "serpent," a real serpent or a symbolic serpent; the "cherubim," a real angel with a flaming sword or merely a symbolic way of describing the interdict laid on our first parents. A study of ancient, extra-biblical literature indicates that these expressions all belong to the kind of simple metaphorical language used by ancient storytellers. To discover the doctrinal teaching of the Yahwist, therefore, we must distinguish between the symbols he uses and the truths he intends to teach by means of such symbols.

The tree of life (Gen. 2:9)

There is evidence from Babylonian literature to show that the expression, "tree of life," was a popular metaphorical expression for unending life or immortality. In a religious hymn, for example, Marduk the Babylonian god is celebrated as the "Lord of the plant of life." In an Assyrian letter we read: "We were dead dogs, but my lord the king gave us life, presenting to our nostrils the plant of life." King Assarhaddon declares: "My kingdom shall be as salutary for the flesh of men as the plant of life." And in the Gilgamesh epic, Gilgamesh, looking for immortality, is directed to a certain plant which he finds but then loses to a serpent who steals it while he is bathing (ANET 96). These examples from ancient literature indicate that the idea of life and immortality was popularly symbolized by a plant — not at all a far cry from the "tree of life."

The tree of knowledge of good and evil (Gen. 2:9-17)

There is no mention of the tree of knowledge of good and evil in Mesopotamian literature, but there is mention of a "tree of truth" in the name "Nin-gish-zi-da," a name which means "Lord of the tree of truth" (ANET 40; 41; 51; 337; 341). The Yahwist's use of this symbolic tree of good and evil as a symbol of omniscience can be deduced from other passages in the Bible where "good and evil" is shown to be the Hebrew way of expressing the knowledge of all things (cf. Gen. 31:24; 2 Sam. 13:22; 14:17, 20). It is paralleled by the Hebrew expression "to go out and come in," an expression used to express in a popular way 'all that one does' (cf. 2 Sam. 3:25).

Evil symbolized as a serpent (Gen. 3:1-14)

It is probable that the Yahwist symbolizes evil as a serpent to show his opposition to the fertility rites of Israel's Canaanite neighbors, among whom the serpent was a popular symbol for life and fecundity (cf. ANEP nn. 511, 571).[1] In this respect it is significant that it is a serpent who steals the plant of immortality from Gilgamesh in the Gilgamesh epic (ANET 96).

[1] Cf. L. Hartman, "Sin in Paradise," *CBQ* 20 (1958) 39.

Evidence from inscriptions indicates that the ancients used the cherubim and the flaming sword pretty much as moderns use the symbolic skull and crossbones, to warn intruders against dangerous or unwanted entry. In Babylon and Assyria statues have been found of mythological creatures called *Karibu*, which have the head of a man, the feet of an ox, the wings of an eagle, and the body of a lion, and which were used as tutelary divinities to guard the entrances of palaces and temples (ANEP nn. 644-651). On ancient boundary stones both the Karibu and the flaming sword — a zigzag bolt of lightning — are found (ANEP nn. 519-521). Their significance can be deduced from an Assyrian text dating from about the year 1000 B.C., in which Tiglath-Pilesar I says of a conquered city: "I have made a thunderbolt of bronze and I have written upon it, 'The booty taken with the help of my god Asshur.' I have also written upon it the prohibition to occupy the city and to reconstruct it. In that place I have built a house, and placed above it the thunderbolt of bronze." The Yahwist speaks of a sword and Tiglath of a thunderbolt, but it is significant that both are used to warn away those who would re-enter a forbidden place.

The above examples from Gen. 2–3 illustrate the colorful, concrete, and popular style of narration that is characteristic of the Yahwist. Exegetes are not agreed on a label for the literary form he uses in these and the following chapters (Gen. 4–11) to communicate to his readers the doctrinal facts that underlie his popular mode of narration. Since the form is, as far as can be seen, a kind of symbolical story constructed to communicate in a vivid way certain doctrinal truths that Yahwist has learned either through direct revelation or through inspired deduction from the deposit of revelation at his disposal, one may with some security label his narratives symbolic stories.

6. The Elohist Tradition[1]

The Yahwist's saga, as we have seen, was put into writing in the tenth century and preserves for us the southern or Judean version of the Mosaic tradition. The Elohist saga, which is parallel to the Yahwist saga since each is a variant version of the original Mosaic tradition, was put into written form sometime between 850 and 750. It represents the Mosaic tradition preserved in the northern kingdom, that larger part of the Israelite kingdom which rebelled against Rehoboam, the successor of King Solomon, in

[1] Cf. select bibliography on p. 575.

926, and became a separate kingdom independent of the Davidic kings in the south.

The differences between the two sagas, which are for the most part accidental differences, can be traced to the time, the place, and the occasion that gave rise to the formation of each tradition. One may illustrate the situation by American history on the hypothesis that the South had won the Civil War and that following the year 1865 there had come into being a confederate nation independent of the northern union. Pre-civil war history on this hypothesis would be the common heritage and tradition of both nations. One may question, however, whether the historians of the north and the south would have presented their common pre-civil war history in identically the same manner. Presumably they would have recounted substantially the same history but with variations of emphasis reflecting the respective interests and prejudices of each "American" nation. In Israel this is precisely what did happen. And it is the principal reason both for the existence of the Elohist's saga and for its differences from the Yahwist's saga.

The critical belief that the Elohist's saga originated in the northern kingdom is based upon the prominence given by the author to such northern figures as Joseph, his mother Rachel, and his sons Ephraim and Manasseh, and to such places as Bethel and Shechem, both shrine or sanctuary cities of the northern kingdom.

Characteristics of the Elohist's saga

The Elohist's saga has been called the "E" document because its author prefers the word "Elohim" for God in the pre-Mosaic part of his history rather than Yahweh as in the Yahwist's saga. The "E" may also stand for Ephraim, the most influential of the northern tribes and the very heart of the dissident northern kingdom, from which the Elohist's saga originated.

In vocabulary E differs from J not only by his use of Elohim for God, but by his use of Horeb for the mountain of the covenant (Sinai in J), Amorites for the people of Canaan (Canaanites in J), Jethro for Moses' father-in-law (Hobab or Reuel in J), 'amah for serving-girl (shiphah in J).

E's style is popular and pungent like J's, but more restrained. E avoids the anthropomorphisms of J, keeps God more apart from men, has Him speak to men in a less direct way through dreams or through the intervention of angels (cf. Gen. 15:1; 20:3, 6; 28:12; 21:17; 22:11, 15).

Unlike J, E reflects strongly the influence of prophetism in Israel, perhaps as a result of the preaching of Elijah and Elisha. Thus Abraham is called a prophet (Gen. 20:7), Miriam a prophetess (Exod. 15:20), and

Moses, the prophet *par excellence*, is not only given the most prominent place in E's saga but is extolled with the highest praise as the one to whom God spoke "mouth to mouth," in contradistinction to others to whom God spoke through angels or by the medium of dreams.

Whether the Elohist wrote his saga in the early years of the northern kingdom or in the time of Jeroboam II (787-747), the most successful and influential of the northern kings, we do not know. In either event it is probable that the saga was written to justify the nationalism of the northern kingdom. Unfortunately for the Elohist his saga was fused with the Yahwist's saga after the fall of the northern kingdom to the Assyrians in 722. Since the fusion of the two sagas was made by a Judean editor whose sympathies were naturally on the side of the Yahwist, only parts of the Elohist's saga were preserved. The fragmentary remains are sufficient to identify the Elohist's saga as an independent tradition but they are not sufficiently complete to establish adequately the precise purpose of the original author. The reader can sample for himself E's style by a reading of Gen. 22:1-14; 40–42; 48. His account of Abraham's response when told to sacrifice his son Isaac (Gen. 22) is one of the masterpieces of literature.

7. The Deuteronomic Tradition[1]

The JEP traditions do not appear in Deuteronomy. As a result critics are agreed that Deuteronomy was not fused with the other traditions but appended to them as a conclusion by the final editor of the Pentateuch. It was not fused with the JEP traditions because it was not a continuous narrative in any sense of the word. It purported rather to be a series of sermons given by Moses before his death exhorting the Israelites to know, love, and serve God. Since the subject matter upon which the exhortations were based — Israel's history and her covenant laws — was similar to that of the JEP traditions, the final editor appended Deuteronomy to his fusion of JEP on the basis of homogeneity of subject matter. This was not the only reason, however, for appending Deuteronomy to the already existing tetrateuch of Genesis, Exodus, Leviticus, and Numbers. Deuteronomy made explicit in an uncompromising manner what was only implicit in the JEP fusion — the love of God behind Israel's history and law. It drew the conclusion for which the JEP fusion provided the premises. It not only declared divine love to be the only adequate answer to the enigma of God's dealings with Israel, but it defined in unforgettable terms what was to be the "spirit" of the new nation — a spirit of generous love responsive to the boundless love that had brought it into existence.[2]

[1] Cf. select bibliography on p. 575.　　　　[2] Cf. De Vaux, *op. cit.*, 337 ff.

The original book of Deuteronomy is at the same time the mystery book par excellence of the Bible and the key to much of the Old Testament. It is the first book of the Bible we know for certain to have existed in manuscript as opposed to oral form as early as 621 B.C. It was found 'as a book' in the Temple in the course of Josiah's reform by Hilkiah, the High Priest, and immediately caused a sensation (see 2 Kings 22:8ff). In the biblical world it has not ceased to this day to excite scholars. It has been recognized that in all probability "Original Deuteronomy" was the first book of the Old Testament to be considered canonical in the full sense of the term. As such it may well be the 'acorn' from which the Bible as a whole sprang.

Whatever its earliest form, the book of the law found in the Temple by Hilkiah in 621 went through several redactions to reach the state in which we find it now. If the critics are correct, the original book of Deuteronomy consisted of Deut. 4:44 – 26:19; 28:1-69. By the time the Deuteronomist took it up, around 550 B.C., and incorporated it as the introduction to his great history of Israel (Deut.; Jos; Judg.; 1 and 2 Sam.; 1 and 2 Kings), it had come to look very much as we have it now. However, sometime later the Priestly author-editor of the Pentateuch detached it from the Deuteronomist's history and used it for the conclusion of his Pentateuch.

In the light of its history, it is not difficult to see that the original book of Deuteronomy is in many ways the key not only to the Deuteronomist's history and the Pentateuch but to the very formation of the Bible itself. Since it is the covenant book par excellence as well, it is also in many ways the key to Israel's covenant theology. Finally, its influence on the book of Jeremiah has been discussed for decades, and when the critical dust has settled it may well provide a key to Jeremiah and much of the exile theology that developed as a result of the preaching of Jeremiah and the reading of Deuteronomy by the exilic community in Babylon.

Since the history of the book is vital both for the deuteronomic theology it contains and for the Deuteronomist's history and the Pentateuch for which it was in all probability the immediate catalyst, it will be well to study first the sources of Original Deuteronomy and then the book itself. The later episodes in the history of Deuteronomy will be treated with the Deuteronomist's history and the Pentateuch.

Before entering into a study of Deuteronomy, it will perhaps assist the reader to contrast the "D" theologian with that earlier theologian, the Yahwist, who did so much to set the stage, draw up the general outline, and write the first draft of Israel's inspired theology. It will be noted immediately that the Yahwist worked with old traditions and composed a great theological saga. The "D" theologian worked, not so much with old historical traditions, but with old covenant-renewal sermons, compiling them into a unified book of sermons aimed at a seventh century audience.

It will be noted as well that the Yahwist is cosmopolitan, the "D" theologian is parochial. The Yahwist has a far-ranging mind that goes back and out into the far reaches of the past at the same time that it thrusts into the future. The "D" theologian is more pastoral and priestly, going into his material theologically in order to elicit from his audience an immediate response to God. He is preacher first and theologian second.

Finally, the reader will notice a decided contrast between the Yahwist and the "D" theologian in relation to both the dynasty and the covenant. The Yahwist allows the covenant to take its normal place in Israel's history, but goes out of his way to emphasize and throw the spotlight on the Davidic dynasty. The deuteronomic author on the contrary has nothing to say about the Davidic dynasty and a great deal to say about the covenant. The contrast is not unlike that between eastern and western Christendom; both staunchly Christian, but only the West staunchly papal. The difference ultimately traces to the place of origin and reflects the southern origin of the Yahwist's saga and the northern origin of Deuteronomy. The ideals of the amphictyony lived on in both north and south, but while they barely survived in the south under the Davidic dynasty, in the north, perhaps because of the north's painful experience with the monarchy, they flourished.

The Origin and Audience of Original Deuteronomy

It is agreed by almost all that the "Book of Law" found in the Temple in 621 B.C. (cf. 2 Kings 22:8ff) was a copy of Original Deuteronomy.[1] It has been argued, with no consensus as yet appearing, that it issued either from levitical circles in the northern kingdom,[2] whose covenant renewal sermons were edited and promulgated in the kingdom of Judah sometime after the fall of Samaria in 721; or from circles close to the Judean monarchy, whose fusion of the Sinai and Davidic traditions was completed sometime after the reform of King Josiah in 621–609;[3] or

[1] G. Fohrer, *Introduction to the Old Testament*, 165-178; W. Moran, "Deuteronomy" in *A New Catholic Commentary on Holy Scripture*.

[2] Cf. G. von Rad, *Studies in Deuteronomy*, 60ff.

[3] Cf O. Bächli, *Israel und die Völker: eine Studie um Deuteronomium* (Zurich, 1962).

from prophetic circles in the north, whose members came south after the fall of Samaria in 721 and in the century following formulated their northern traditions as the true expression of Yahwism in the hopes that it would be accepted and bring about the reform of Yahwism in the kingdom of Judah.[1]

Because of the emphasis on the centralization of cult in Jerusalem (Deut. 12), a move first made in the reign of King Hezekiah of Judah (715–687), most authors place the origin of the book either in the reign of Hezekiah (cf. 2 Kings 18 and 2 Chr. 29–31) or in the reign of his successor, King Manasseh (687–642).

If written under Hezekiah, the book was aimed at furthering the religious reform of 705 (2 Chr. 30–31) which was extended to the north and took as its particular aim the destruction of all idolatrous cult objects and worship (cf. Deut. 7:1-5; 20:1-20; 13:13-19). Hezekiah's push to take over the northern kingdom would account for the emphasis on the land and the covenant in Deuteronomy. The covenant guaranteed the land in response for fidelity. Since the land had been lost as a consequence of Israel's infidelity, the quickest way to ensure the return of the land was to carry out a new holy war spearheaded by destruction of idolatry and a reform of covenant morality and love.[2] This would account not only for the emphasis on centralization of cult, regaining of the land, and renewal of the covenant, but for the emphasis on the holy war (Deut. 20:1-9; 21:1-14; 23:10-15; 24:5; 25:17-19).[3]

If the book originated in the reign of King Manasseh (2 Kings 21; 2 Chr. 33), a time of general apostasy, the same reasoning would be valid.[4] In either case the aim would be to return Judah to her covenant fidelity and to remove from the land the abuses of old that had led to the fall of the Northern Kingdom and were, at the time the book was written, threatening to call down a similar destruction on the Southern sister Kingdom of Judah. E. W. Nicholson summarizes his solution to the immediate origin of Deuteronomy as follows:

> After 721 B.C. the Deuteronomic circle fled south to Judah in the belief that the possible future religious and political revival of the nation lay there. Such a belief was soon confirmed when Hezekiah inaugurated and attempted to carry out such a revival. When this attempt ultimately failed and reaction set in under Manasseh they

[1] Cf. E. W. Nicholson, *Deuteronomy and Tradition*, 94-106. See also, M. Weinfeld, "Deuteronomy — The Present State of Inquiry," *JBL* 86 (1967), 249-262. Weinfeld attributes the book to sapiential circles.

[2] Cf. F. Moriarity, "The Chronicler's Account of Hezekiah's reform," *CBQ* 27 (1965), 399-406.

[3] On the Holy War, cf. R. de Vaux, *Ancient Israel*, 258ff.

[4] Cf. H. H. Rowley, *Studies in Old Testament Prophecy*, 164.

drew up their own plans for reformation in the form of Deuteronomy. In order to have it accepted and put into operation by the Judaean authorities, they made certain concessions to the Jerusalem traditions notably in demanding the centralization of the cult. When Josiah came to the throne and the Assyrian power began to decline, the aims of Hezekiah were revived. In the course of this revival in Josiah's reign the book was discovered in the Temple where it had been deposited by its authors. It was accepted by the authorities in Jerusalem and became the basis for further reformation enactments which supplemented those already enforced by them.[1]

The Sources of Original Deuteronomy

Wherever Original Deuteronomy reached its final form — and the evidence is good that it reached its final form in Judah in the period preceding the reign of King Josiah — the source material of the book comes from the sanctuaries of the Northern Kingdom. These sanctuaries were, to name the principal ones, Shechem and Shiloh, Gilgal, Bethel, and Dan.

At these sanctuaries, perhaps since the time of the conquest (cf. Jos. 24), Israelites gathered periodically to renew the covenant. Yahweh's mighty works were rehearsed. His law was recited. And the gathered worshippers responded as in the time of Joshua: "It is Yahweh our God we choose to serve; it is his voice that we will obey" (Jos. 24:20-24).

The studies of Mendenhall, Baltzer, Korosec, and McCarthy have satisfied almost all that the form of this covenant renewal followed the format of a Hittite suzerainty pact: 1. preamble; 2. historical prologue; 3. stipulations; 4. command to preserve and re-read periodically the stipulations of the covenanting king with his vassals; 5. witnesses; 6. curses for the recalcitrant and blessings for the obedient; 7. perhaps some form of covenant sacrifice.

McKenzie has argued convincingly, as have de Vaux and others, that the minor Judges (cf. Judg. 10:1-5; 12:8-15) were the men who preserved the laws of the amphictyony and recited them periodically before the Israelites assembled in worship or for the renewal of the covenant.[2] G. von Rad has made an equally good case for the Levites as the reciters of the law in the centuries that followed.[3]

In Deuteronomy we are faced with a series of sermons put in the mouth of Moses after the manner of a farewell address, reminiscent of the literary form adapted for the farewell speeches recorded in Jos. 23; 1 Sam. 12

[1] *Deuteronomy and Tradition,* 102.
[2] J. L. McKenzie, *The World of the Judges,* 118-119.
[3] G. Von Rad, *Deuteronomy,* 24-25.

and 1 Chr. 22 and 29. Since the book as a whole and even the individual sermons cannot be authentically Mosaic on the testimony of internal evidence, it would seem compelling to accept the form of the book as a farewell address, put on the lips of Moses, containing a series of covenant renewal sermons that had come down from the reciters of the law and the levites of the northern sanctuaries.

On the basis of this reconstruction, one would have to look for the sources of Deuteronomy proximately in the covenant renewal sermons delivered at the covenant renewal festivals by the reciters of the law and the levites, and ultimately, in the traditions and spirit of the early amphictyony.[1]

There still remains the problem of dissecting Deuteronomy to recover the original covenant renewal sermons from which the book was eventually compiled. The attempt will not always be successful since the compiler was under no obligation to take everything at his disposal. Nevertheless, the basic outline of the covenant renewal sermon is known, and where one finds the outline relatively intact one may presume to have found one of the units from which Deuteronomy was built up.

The outline, as is now widely agreed, followed the main points of the Hittite suzerainty pact. It began with a preamble in which God introduced Himself as Lord of Israel. It followed with an historical prologue of God's saving deeds in favor of Israel. In view of these saving deeds the declaration of basic principle was made that Israel should have no other gods but Yahweh and that she should love Him with all her heart, with all her soul, and all her strength. A list of laws then followed upon this declaration of basic principle. The sermon concluded with a promise of blessings on the obedient and a threat of curses upon the disobedient.

The following would seem to be individual sermons or parts of covenant renewal sermons amalgamated in Deuteronomy: (a) 1:1—4:40, a sermon from the hand of the 6th century Deuteronomist; (b) 4:44—11:32, a sermon belonging to Original Deuteronomy; (c) 12:1—26:19, a heterogenous collection of cultic and legal material amassed during centuries of updating the amphictyonic covenant law; (d) 27:1ff, an appeal to renew the covenant, interjected in all probability by the Deuteronomist; (e) 28:1ff, a collection of blessings and curses, with some expansion of the text after v. 19, representing the conclusion of Original Deuteronomy; (f) 29—30, a renewal sermon, probably added to the text of Original Deuteronomy before the Deuteronomist's redaction; (g) 31—34, the second half of the framework put around Original Deuteronomy by the Deuteronomist.[2]

[1] See J. L. McKenzie, *The World of the Judges*, ch. VI-IX.
[2] See E. W. Nicholson, *Deuteronomy and Tradition*, 18-36, but especially p. 36.

Chapter 4:44–6:3 serves as the introduction to Original Deuteronomy in two ways. It introduces almost immediately the basic covenant law of Israel — the ten commandments (5:1-22) — and it explains, by means of a fictional *mise en scène*, the precise function to be carried out by Moses throughout the rest of the book — the function of mediator and expositer of the covenant relationship between Israel and Yahweh (5:23-31). "The purpose of the entire section, 4:45–6:3," according to von Rad,, "is to represent Moses' whole speech in Deuteronomy as a communication to Israel, not really of the Decalogue, but of that conversation on the mountain with Yahweh." [1] "That conversation," of course, is the conversation mentioned in 5:31, "But you will stand here by me and I shall tell you all the commandments, the laws and the customs that you must teach them, which they must observe in the land I am giving them for their possession."

The basic stipulation establishing the relationship between Yahweh and His people is stated in 5:6 and followed immediately by the Decalogue of which it is the first and greatest commandment: "I am Yahweh your God who brought you out of the land of Egypt, out of the house of slavery. You shall have no gods except me." Nevertheless, having prefaced Original Deuteronomy with the Decalogue (5:1-22) and the explanation of Moses' precise function as mediator and expositer of what God had said to him on the mountain (5:21-31), the author now has Moses deliver a series of exhortations (ch. 6–11) which set the tone for the exposition of the ". . . commandments, the laws and the customs" (5:31) which follow in the long covenant code of ch. 12–26.

The exhortations amalgamated in ch. 6–11 prepare the audience for the Detueronomic Code of law in ch. 12–26 and may be presumed to have been collected on the basis of what was meaningful to the seventh century audience for which the book was written. The Deuteronomic theologian, therefore, will have much to say about opposition to the Canaanites and all that is opposed to Yahwism. But in addition to the negative side of the reform, the author will emphasize the positive — and it is in his positive message that the essence of the Deuteronomic theology is found.

The basic message can be reduced to three propositions, each of which will be repeated throughout the book but especially in ch. 6–11: 1. Israel has been chosen by God by an election that was entirely unmerited and entirely dependent on God's gracious love; 2. Israel should respond to this love by loving God in return; 3. Israel's response of love should be.

---

[1] G. von Rad, *Deuteronomy*, 61.

manifested outwardly by fidelity to the stipulations of the Sinai Covenant.

The Greatest Commandment

Since the second of these three propositions is the most important, the author begins with a sermon on the great commandment. It should be noted that the great commandment is a positive expression of the first commandment of the decalogue: "You shall have no gods except me" (5:7). In giving the first commandment a positive expression: "Listen, Israel: Yahweh our God is the one Yahweh. You shall love Yahweh your God with all your heart, with all your soul, with all your strength" (6:4), the Deuteronomic theologian reduces all the commandments and all of Israel's law to the first commandment. His positioning of this commandment at the beginning of the sermon should be considered in this light. Although he does not explicitly say it, his emphasis on the command "Let these words of mine remain in your heart and in your soul; fasten them on your hand as a sign and on your forehead as a circlet. Teach them to your children and say them over to them, whether at rest in your house or walking abroad, at your lying down or at your rising. Write them on the doorposts of your house and on your gates, so that you and your children may live long in the land that Yahweh swore to your fathers he would give them for as long as there is a sky above the earth" should be understood to be his way of saying what Jesus later said: "This is the greatest and the first commandment. The second resembles it: You must love your neighbor as yourself. *On these two commandments hang the whole Law, and the prophets also*" (Matthew 22:38-40). Lest his audience forget, even after so insistent a call to love God as that given in the brief sermon in ch. 6:4-13, the command to love God is repeated in one form or another at regular intervals (cf. 5:10; 7:9; 10:12; 11:1, 13, 22; 13:2-4; 30:6, 16, 20; 32:1-20).[1]

Election

It is the Deuteronomic theologian's conviction that the only worthy response to love is a return of love. It is for this reason he is so insistent on the first and greatest commandment. But he is not less insistent on his conviction that Yahweh truly loves His chosen people, and his great proof for God's love of Israel is based upon God's election of Israel.

[1] The repetition in 11:18-21 of the opening lines in 6:4-9 looks very much like an inclusion-conclusion; if so, it makes it even more probable that ch. 6-11 is to be considered a unit.

The Deuteronomic theologian's teaching on election is implicit in his credal formulas in ch. 6:20-25 and 26:5-10 and in all his references to Israel's salvation history.[1] Not content with the implicit message of Israel's salvation history, he goes out of his way to state explicitly in a number of places that God's election of Israel was purely the effect of His love (cf. 7:7-8, 13; 10:15; also 9:5; 23:1-20).

Going beyond the Yahwist, who also taught the election of Israel as a sign of God's love, the author of Deuteronomy goes into the question of why God has chosen Israel. In doing so, he is perhaps the first theologian to grapple with the mystery of grace. He explicitly teaches that Israel's election is a matter of pure benevolence and entirely gratuitous (cf. 7:6-9; 8:17; 9:4-6ff). It is, in brief, the direct result of God's love for Israel (cf. 10:15).

Obedience — The Proof of Love

It is important to note that the emphasis on an election flowing from the gratuitous love of God is part of the preacher's argumentation in preparation for his application to his audience of what election based on love demands of them in the concrete. He will argue that since God has elected Israel out of love, Israel must respond with love and prove this love by keeping the commandments out of love. As Edmond Jacob says:

> Election confers on him who is its object a particular dignity, but, so that this may never harden into a haughty conceit, election carries service as its necessary corollary; to be the 'am of Yahweh involves being his 'ebed: the two terms are sometimes put in parallel: "Yahweh will see his people righted, he will take pity on his servants' (Deut. 32:36). But . . . to be a servant necessarily implies a mission to fulfil; the servant should love Yahweh, should cleave to him, fear him, requirements which in Deuteronomy return at least as frequently as the assertion of election, and this mission will always be exercised in a specific task.[2]

Thus the third proposition inculcated by the Deuteronomic theologian is that Israel's response of love must be manifested outwardly by fidelity to the stipulations of the Sinai covenant. It is his way of saying what Jesus says in His own farewell discourse, so similar in teaching to Deuteronomy: "If you love me you will keep my commandments" (John 14:15).

[1] See H. H. Rowley, *The Biblical Doctrine of Election*; also "Election" in the *Interpreter's Dictionary of the Bible*.

[2] E. Jacob, *Theology of the Old Testament*, 204ff; See H. H. Rowley, *The Biblical Doctrine of Election*, 45ff.

For the Deuteronomic theologian Israel's love for God will be proved in the concrete by her observance of the Sinai covenant and the laws that flow from it, which will be explained in ch. 12–26. There is, however, something peculiar about the author's presentation of this teaching. As G. von Rad says: ". . . there seems to be something new in the unequivocal manner based on fundamental principle in which stress is laid on love for God as the only feeling worthy of God."[1]

The "Something New" in Deuteronomy

It has already been stated that Deuteronomy as a whole and even many of its individual sermons follow the format of the Hittite-Suzerainty pact: preamble; historical prologue establishing the debt of gratitude that the vassals owe to their covenant king; the payment of this debt of gratitude by obeying the stipulations laid down by the suzerain; witnesses; blessings and curses. What is new, therefore, cannot be the simple element of obedience to the stipulations of the suzerain king of Israel, nor even that these stipulations are obeyed out of gratitude. The suzerainty pact format had been used long before Original Deuteronomy was composed. Joshua probably used it as early as the time of the conquest (cf. Jos. 24).

What is new is the author's emphasis on loving God "with all your heart, with all your soul, with all your strength." In five places the author harps on the necessity of a truly interior love – a love from the heart, a love that is genuine. In addition to the emphasis on interiority in the expression of the great commandment in 6:4-5, the author says in 6:6, "Let these words I urge on you today be written on your heart." In 10:12 he says again: ". . . to love him, to serve Yahweh your God with all your heart and all your soul. . . ." In 11:13 he speaks of ". . . loving Yahweh your God and serving him with all your heart and all your soul. . . ." And in 13:4 he says: "Yahweh your God is testing you to know if you love Yahweh your God with all your heart and all your soul."

If to this emphasis on interiority of love there is added the author's recurrent appeal to the utter gratuity of God's elective love for Israel (cf. 7:6-9; 8:17; 9:4-6ff; 10:15), it would appear that the author has of set purpose applied himself to the preacher's task of establishing Israel's covenant relationship with Yahweh on a basis of heartfelt love. No such emphasis on love will be encountered in the Bible again until the farewell discourse of Jesus at the last supper (cf. John 13–17).

But how are we to explain this emphasis on love? G. von Rad has traced

[1] G. von Rad, *Deuteronomy*, 63.

it to the preaching of Hosea.[1] W. Moran makes an excellent case for the suzerainty pact as the background for the deuteronomic emphasis on love.[2] Moran shows that the love of God in Deuteronomy is a commanded love just as the love of the suzerain is a commanded love. He shows, moreover, that the observance of the covenant law out of gratitude to God is similar to the observance of the stipulations out of gratitude and loyalty to the suzerain. His conclusion, however, that the Deuteronomic author's dependence for his doctrinal elaboration is more directly upon the suzerainty pacts than upon the preaching of Hosea does not necessarily follow. The suzerainty pacts certainly do provide a background for a relationship of 'love' between suzerain and vassal and vassal and suzerain, and in this Moran is certainly correct. But Deut. 6:4–11:32 in its emphasis on love as the basis of relations between Yahweh and his servants goes beyond anything in the suzerainty pacts.[3]

What has to be explained, as Moran has argued, is the background, but even more the degree of emphasis put upon the love between Yahweh and His people. It is this "something new in the unequivocal manner based on fundamental principle in which stress is laid on love for God as the only feeling worthy of God," as von Rad says, that requires explanation.

Chronologically Hosea's emphasis on love would appear to precede the emphasis on love in Deut. 6–11, and the credit, therefore, for the conception of this fundamental theological insight must go to the prophet. In either case the insight is expressed by means of an analogy – in Hosea by the analogy of a marriage and in Deuteronomy by the analogy of the suzerainty pact.

In Hosea's analogy, God's love for Israel is like Hosea's love for his unfaithful wife Gomer. In the covenant analogy, God's love for Israel is like the love of a covenanting king for his vassals. In Hosea's analogy, the reciprocity of this love is only implied. In the Deuteronomic analogy, the love of Israel for her covenant King is spelled out in no uncertain terms. Israel's existence depends upon her commitment to God in love which is to be manifested by the loving acceptance and carrying out of His law.

There is no certain explanation for this sudden emphasis upon love in

[1] G. von Rad, *Deuteronomy*, 63f.

[2] W. Moran, "The Ancient Near Eastern Background of the Love of God in Deuteronomy" *CBQ* 25, 1963, 77-87.

[3] In the extant suzerainty treaties there is nothing quite like Original Deuteronomy's emphasis on interior love. At the most there is the occasional call to be "faithful with all thy heart," or to act "with a true heart," or "with your whole heart" (see D. McCarthy, *Treaty and Covenant*, 199-206 but especially 182; 195; 196; 199; 200). There are also regular, but not emphasized appeals to love between the parties of the pact (*op. cit.*, 80ff).

the relations between God and His people. If Hosea's preaching is dated to the third quarter of the eighth century and the writing of Original Deuteronomy to the first half of the seventh century, the emphasis upon love would occur at the time when Israel's religious leaders were beginning to see the breakdown of the covenant. For some reason, which has not been thus far adequately explained, the prophets as a general rule did not appeal directly to the covenant. It has been said, and it may well be the correct explanation, that the prophets avoided too close an adherence to the covenant terminology and format because the people had come to glory in the covenant and to claim from it rights they had never been given.

Love — The Heart of the Covenant Relationship

Whatever the misunderstanding of the people about the covenant, it would appear that both Hosea and the Deuteronomic author wanted to get back to first principles. Hosea returned to first principles by avoiding the covenant analogy and using the marriage analogy. The Deuteronomic author continued to use the covenant analogy but attempted to correct Israel's misunderstanding of the central aspect of that analogy.

The one point where the suzerainty covenant analogy was in danger of limping was in the possibility that the people would begin to equate the kind of love due to Yahweh with the political 'love' due to a human suzerain. In the suzerainty pacts the love of the king for his vassals and the love of the vassals for the covenanting king contained no great or genuine feeling. It was a matter of expediency, a matter of *quid pro quo* rather than a genuine love of the heart. It was a political 'love' just as the suzerainty pact was a political gambit.[1]

In using the analogy, therefore, the Deuteronomic author was obliged to make sure that God's love for Israel was never equated with the political 'love' of a human sovereign, nor Israel's love for God with the political 'love' of constrained human vassals. To change what had to be changed in the analogy, the author of Deut. 6—11 reiterated again and again both the intensity and the gratuity of God's love for Israel. He also insisted that there be no doubt about the nature of the love God commanded in return. Love could not be a matter of expediency. It had to be genuine, interior, from the heart. It had to be proved by deeds done not out of fear or expediency but out of love. It was to inculcate this difference between Israel's covenant relationship with God and the ordinary suzerainty love of convenience that the Deuteronomic theologian repeatedly and

[1] Cf. W. Eichrodt, *Theology of the Old Testament*, vol. I, 372-374.

explicitly insisted: "You shall love Yahweh your God with all your heart, with all your soul, with all your strength . . ." (6:5-9; 10:12; 11:13; 13: 4).[1]

Thus, where the prophets avoided the covenant analogy because it appeared to them the analogy might lead the people to look upon the law of God the way they looked upon the stipulations of an earthly ruler — worthy only of lip service and formalism — the Deuteronomic theologian preferred to continue to use the analogy but with an emphasis on genuine interior love as a corrective for the limp to which the analogy was prone by reason of its origin. In either event, Israel's theologians, both the Deuteronomic theologian and the prophets — especially Hosea — were out to accomplish the same religious purpose: namely, to bring Israel to a genuine love for God and to a genuine manifestation of their love through obedience.

Ultimately, the Deuteronomic theologian bases his appeal to Israel on the same principle as Jesus in His farewell discourse in John 13—17: "If you love me you will keep my commandments." This is the message the Deuteronomic theologian inculcates by his appeal to salvation history, by his emphasis on election ("You have not chosen me, but I have chosen you"), by his emphasis on God's love, and by his emphasis on the covenant relationship as God's commitment to Israel which demands from Israel a commitment on her part.

The proof of commitment on the part of Israel is the keeping of God's law out of love. Where the law is not kept — either not at all or not out of love — the response and the commitment are dubious. Jesus' words are as applicable in Old Testament times as they are now: "If you love me, you will keep my commandments."

In view of such a magnificent theology of love as the heart of the covenant relationship, it is hardly to be wondered that Israel produced not only great saints like Jeremiah and Ezekiel but a whole generation that persevered throughout the Babylonian captivity and returned to Palestine to form the worshipping community of postexilic Judaism. Love builds and soars on eagles' wings. It is perhaps not facetious to rejoice that in our day we are seeing a renewed emphasis on the law of love first enunciated by Deuteronomy and later confirmed everlastingly by Jesus Himself.

Distinguishing characteristics of the Deuteronomic author

The outstanding characterstic of the Deuteronomic theologian is his eloquent preaching style. He heaps phrase upon phrase, each beautifully bal-

[1] M. J. O'Connell, "The Concept of Commandment in the Old Testament" in *Theological Studies*, 21 (1960) 351-403, especially 394 ff.

anced and skillfully arranged to storm the hearts of his hearers and persuade them to commit themselves generously and wholeheartedly to the love and service of God.

Certain turns of phrase appear regularly and distinguish the author's vocabulary from all other biblical writers, e.g., "that you may have long life on the land which Yahweh, your God, is giving you . . . these are the commandments, the statutes and decrees which Yahweh, your God, has enjoined upon you. . . when Yahweh, your God, brings you into the land which you are to enter and occupy . . . remember that you were once slaves in the land of Egypt . . . with all your heart and all your soul . . . you are to be a people peculiarly his own, as he promised you."

Another characteristic, deriving perhaps from the literary format of the suzerainty pacts, is the "I — Thou" form of address. Finally, like the E author the Deuteronomist calls the mountain of the covenant Horeb instead of Sinai, refers to the people of the Promised Land as Amorites rather than Canaanites, and makes Moses the most prominent personage in his book. This last characteristic brings us to the question of the literary form of the book of Deuteronomy.

The literary form of Deuteronomy

It requires no great discernment to see that Deuteronomy is some kind of didactic literature in sermon form. History, when it is mentioned, is mentioned only as an argument or as a springboard for the preacher's call to love and obedience. It is not mentioned for itself and there is no pretense of giving a continuous historical account as in the J and E traditions. Nevertheless, the author appears to be preserving for us a series of sermons actually delivered by Moses just before his death.

But appearances are deceiving. A closer examination of the book shows much that could hardly have been of great interest to Moses in the thirteenth century. There are references to exile and return from exile. There is a description of a covenant ceremony at Shechem that certainly took place after the death of Moses. There are laws that presume sociological backgrounds that were not in existence until long after the time of Moses. And the book gives a little treatise on monarchy in Israel that is premature for the time of Moses. How are we to explain these anomalies? How are we to explain, in particular, the fact that the author of Deuteronomy claims Moses said certain things when actually Moses did not say them at all?

These questions raise serious difficulties only if we refuse to the inspired writers the liberty of using the customary literary devices and artistic forms of their time. One of these literary devices in common use in ancient times was the attribution to individuals of speeches they never actually made, but which they would be presumed to have made if they had decided to express their thoughts and feelings in a speech. The attribution of such speeches to those who never actually made them is a common practice not only of Hebrew writers but of Greek and Roman writers as well. It is a literary device found in the works of Plato, Xenophon, and Thucydides among the Greeks, and among the Latin writers in the works of Cicero, Livy, and Tacitus. In the Bible it is utilized in many books on a small scale, but extensively only in Deuteronomy and Chronicles. The clearest proof of the use of this literary device in any book is the similarity in style of speeches attributed to different individuals, and in books giving the speeches of only one individual the similarity of the narrative style of the book with the style of the speeches.

If, as is quite probable, there existed the tradition of a final exhortation delivered by Moses in the plains of the Jordan, such a tradition would have provided an excellent basis for the literary procedure used by the author of Deuteronomy. Be that as it may, the custom at the northern shrine cities of renewing the covenant mediated by Moses at Sinai and bringing up to date in his name the developing Mosaic legislation provided more than sufficient justification for the literary form employed. The author could not have chosen a more effective way to emphasize the Mosaic origin of his doctrine and legislation.

The expression "literary form" has been used before in the designation of such particular compositional types as "saga," "family history," and "parable." Since the study of literary forms in general and ancient symbolic literary forms in particular is of vital importance for a truly adequate understanding and appreciation of the Bible, we shall conclude our literary analysis of the Pentateuchal history with a brief study of this subject.

8. The Literary Forms of the Bible

The Bible is a library in miniature containing different types of poetry (hymns, prayers, lamentations, love songs), a wide assortment of didactic literature (proverbs, riddles, fables, sermons, allegories, parables), a number of different kinds of historical narratives (popular traditions, biography, religious history, ideal history, moralizing history, even staid collections of annals and genealogies), as well as prophecies, apocalypses, letters, and pseudonymous writings.

Each of these different types of literature (literary forms) has its own history of development and its own proper rules of interpretation. The recognition of these various types and the correct application of their proper norms of interpretation is as important for the study of biblical literature as it is for the study of modern writing.

11

Nos. 11–14.   **11**. The façade of Al-Haram Al-Ibrahami (the Mosque of Abraham) in Hebron, which encloses the tombs of Abraham and his wife Sarah. The mosque is of great architectural interest and a center of religious devotion because Abraham, "The Friend of God," is venerated as the first Moslem.   **12**. A reproduction of a wall painting in the tomb of an Egyptian noble at Beni-hasan, midway between Memphis and Thebes, showing the family of a chieftain named Absna entering Egypt about the time of Abraham. The number in the family of this Asiatic band, who presumably are Amorites, is given as thirty-seven (cf. Gen. 46:27). Note the dress recalling Joseph's "coat of many colors" (Gen. 37:3).   **13**. Monastery of St. Catherine in the valley below the mountains traditionally associated with locale where Moses received the Ten Commandments from God.   **14**. "When the Lord came down to the top of Mount Sinai, he summoned Moses to the top of the mountain, and Moses went up to him. Mount Sinai was all wrapped in smoke, for the Lord came down upon it in fire. The smoke rose from it as though from a furnace, and the whole mountain trembled violently. Then the Lord delivered all these commandments" (Exod. 19:20, 18; 20:1).

13

14

Since the principles upon which the study of literary forms is based are the same at all times and for all literature, and since what differs from one literature to another are not the principles but the various types or forms developed, it will be advantageous to approach the study of biblical literary forms in the following manner: 1. the basic principles in relation to modern literary forms; 2. the application of the same principles to ancient literary forms; 3. an explanation of the Church's attitude toward the study of literary forms; 4. a brief explanation of some of the more difficult literary forms found in the Scriptures; 5. a brief discussion of the objections and difficulties raised against the study of biblical literary forms.

Literary forms in general

Literary forms, whether ancient or modern, are the commonly accepted patterns or ways of writing used by writers of a given age and culture to express their ideas and at the same time indicate to their audience the purpose for which they are writing. The message or measure of truth of what an author writes, it is generally agreed, is determined by his purpose, and his purpose or intention is known principally from his literary form. It is for this reason that an author does not tumble at random into a literary form but chooses the one that best suits his purpose. Some literary forms, depending on the purpose the author has in writing, are obviously and for good reasons more suitable than others. If the author, for instance, intends to write a technical historical treatise, he will hardly use a poetic literary form. A lover will certainly not use textbook language. For teaching purposes ideas are stated in a clear, direct, persuasive manner employing a literary form in which easy intelligibility is the prime characteristic.[1]

Among the modern literary forms subconsciously recognized and understood by anyone with a fair amount of education are the novel, the poem, the essay, the satire, various types of plays as the tragedy, the comedy, and the musical, and various kinds of historical writing such as the popular, the edifying, the entertaining, and the so-called strict research history.

Those who are students of the literary arts know that these forms of communication, like other more sophisticated forms, have a history. They do not appear as finished and perfect literary methods. They originate in an imperfect state, develop over a period of time, eventually reach a peak, and then after a shorter or longer period of time either become classical, fall into a decadence and disuse, or undergo adaptation to some new and different literary purpose.[2]

The more perfectly developed a literary form becomes and the more

[1] A. Shökel, *The Inspired Word*.   [2] Cf. B. Lonergan, *Insight* 572ff.

widely it is used, the better it serves as an instrument for communication. In such cases there is an immediate and easy rapport between author and audience. The audience subconsciously follows the road taken and absorbs the author's message without difficulty and with the highest degree of accuracy (e.g., stock market or athletic reports).

By his recognition of the literary form, the reader understands immediately the purpose the author has in writing and guides himself accordingly in the interpretation of what has been written. He judges poetry by the accepted norms for poetry and editorials by the accepted norms for editorials. When he reads Carlyle's *History of the French Revolution* and Dickens' *The Tale of Two Cities,* he knows from the literary form that one is to be judged according to the norms for professional history, the other according to the norms for the historical novel. When he picks up von Pastor's *Lives of the Popes*, he knows automatically from its literary form the tenor of its contents. When he scans an historical romance such as Tolstoy's *War and Peace*, he knows immediately from the literary form that the author intends to give him part history and part fiction.

What is of utmost importance is that the reader, recognizing the literary form, judges the content accordingly. He must not accuse the author of an historical romance, for example, of lying when he fictionalizes, nor of deliberately distorting the facts of history when he subordinates them to the entertainment value of his work. He does not judge poetry by the rules for professional history, nor satire by the rules for poetry. From the literary form he knows the purpose the author had in writing and evaluates the composition accordingly.

Ancient literary forms

What is true of modern literary forms is equally true of ancient literary forms. The sense message or measure of truth in any ancient book must be determined by the purpose of its author, and that purpose lies imbedded in and is extracted from its literary form. To each ancient literary form there belongs its own measure of truth which the author affirms according to the norms of that particular literary style. As a consequence the sense or message of an ancient composition cannot be ascertained apart from an understanding of the literary form employed.

What the reader of the Bible must understand is that the human authors of the Bible, while writing under divine inspiration, nevertheless used the established literary forms of their day and age. From the intimate relationship we have seen between the literary form and the purpose of the author, according to which the message and measure of truth of what he has written is known, they could hardly have done otherwise without risk of puzzling and confusing their readers. If David, for instance, had composed his psalms in modern verse forms, the Israelites might have recognized them as poetry, but certainly not as Hebrew poetry. If Jesus, instead of using parables, a common teaching form of His time, had preached in polysyllogisms — major, minor, conclusion following each other in fine array — the people might have understood Him, but they would not have been moved. The writer who wants to be understood and accepted is not free. No matter who he is, he is bound by the literary forms or conventions of his day.

The significance of this literary fact of life can perhaps best be illustrated by suggesting how certain books of the Bible might have been written if they were composed today instead of two or three thousand years ago. David's psalms, for example, would be written according to modern poetic forms, as odes or sonnets or in free verse, with rhyme, alliteration, and measured verse for euphony and structural beauty. Job would probably be in the form of a drama, Jonas in the form of a satire. Tobit, Esther, and Judith would be composed either as religious historical novels, or as the lives of the saints were written before the Bollandists' school made its influence felt. Genesis 1—11 would not unlikely resemble a midget Denzinger, its imagery, symbolism, anthropomorphism expunged by a dogmatic redactor.

This, of course, is not to say that these biblical works conform *exactly* to any of our modern literary forms, but only to emphasize the fact that an author must conform to the literary forms and conventions of his time; and to point out also the obvious but often forgotten rule that an author's work is to be judged according to his purpose in writing it, and that that purpose is inherently related to the literary form he chooses.

Our Lord's parables, for example, are to be judged according to the literary norms for a parable; the application of these norms is essential in determining what He had in mind when He used a given parable. The parable was a form of realistic fiction in vogue among the Jews of the first century to teach moral and dogmatic truths. It was not used to teach history. The reader must judge the parable accordingly. He must ask himself what is the moral or dogmatic truth taught in the parable. He must not investigate "scientifically" whether there was such a person as a specific Good Samaritan or a particular Prodigal Son and then repudiate the whole composition because there was not. Those two personages are fictitious characters invented by Jesus, in the one case to teach that love of a neighbor means helping anyone who needs help regardless of who he is, and in the other to teach the forgiving fatherly love of God for repentant sinners.

The same can be said for the perenially disputed book of Jonah. When Jonah is classified as a parable or as a midrash, as it is by many modern authors, the purpose of the author is even clearer than if put in an historical category. As is the case with the parables of Christ, the doctrine taught in Jonah is unequivocal, whether the reader considers the book strict history as many did in the past, or as a simple parable as many authors do at present. In either case, the main point of the book — the love of God for *all* men — is clear. The fine point that has been missed by many is the realization — patent in the parabolic interpretation — that Jonah is a caricature of the narrow-minded, intolerant Jews of the postexilic period, who refused to believe that God could love anyone but themselves, the chosen, covenanted people.

When the books of Tobit, Judith, and Esther are judged according to the knowledge we now have of the haggadic midrash, a literary form popular in postexilic times, most of the historical difficulties in these books disappear. The haggadic midrash was a popular literary form that drew upon ancient traditions or personages for its historical or doctrinal nucleus and then freely elaborated that nucleus with fictitious details in order to edify or instruct the reader according to the intention of the author. Since the principal purpose of the midrash was either religious instruction or spiritual edification, historical events were considered relatively unimportant and used merely to provide background for the story. Since the edifying story had to be interesting in order to attract the reader, the author had his characters appear and speak in a manner arranged by design to keep the story moving and dramatic. Everything was subordinated to the teaching purpose.

If, as most authors hold now, Tobit, Esther, and Judith were written according to the norms for haggadic midrash, it is obviously pointless to belabor the historical inconsistencies in the books; the authors included such detail merely as literary background for their edifying or didactic stories. The value of recognizing the literary form of these books is that it enhances the already obvious teaching of the books and at the same time does away with the serious historical difficulties charged against them by those who insist on classifying and interpreting them as professional historical treatises.

The Church and the study of literary forms

In his encyclical *Divino Afflante Spiritu,* Pius XII not only approves the study of literary forms but urges the Catholic scripture scholar to "make prudent use of this aid." He declares, moreover, that the scripture scholar should "try to discover how . . . the literary form . . . can result in a true and precise interpretation" and that he should be "convinced that he cannot neglect this part of his work without great harm to Catholic scripture study."

> Let the interpreter then, with all care and without neglecting any light derived from recent research, endeavor to determine the peculiar character and circumstances of the sacred writer, the age in which he lived, the sources written or oral to which he had recourse and the forms of expression he employed (DAS par. 33).

The Holy Father is careful to enunciate not only the importance of the sacred writer's purpose for understanding what he has written, but the importance of the literary form as a means for determining the purpose of the author. "There is no one indeed," he says "but knows that the supreme rule of interpretation is to discover and define what the writer intended to express. . . ." (DAS par. 34). Concerning the importance of the literary form for determining the purpose of the author, the Holy Father wrote:

> What is the literal sense of a passage is not always as obvious in the speeches and writings of the ancient authors of the East as it is in the works of our own time. For what they wished to express is not to be determined by the rules of grammar and philology alone, nor solely by the context; the interpreter must, as it were, go back wholly in spirit to those remote centuries of the East and with the aid of history, archeology, ethnology, and other sciences, accurately determine what *modes of writing*, so to speak, the authors of that ancient period would be likely to use, and in fact did use (DAS par. 35; italics by author).

We have stated that what is theoretically true of modern literary forms is equally true of ancient literary forms. We have tried to show, moreover, that while the principles for the study of literary forms, whether modern or ancient, remain the same, the literary forms themselves do not. Different ages and different cultures originate and use different methods of expression. One cannot automatically apply the norms of a specific modern literary procedure to a specific ancient literary procedure unless it can be established that the procedures (forms) are identical. One cannot, for example, apply all of the norms for modern research history to the historical books of the Bible. The ancients used some literary forms which are still in use today, e.g., parables (or stories with a point) and allegories. Other ancient literary forms, e.g., the apocalyptic forms, are never used today. Still other ancient literary forms, e.g., historical and poetical forms, are substantially the same but by no means identical in all details as their modern counterparts. It is of vital importance, therefore, that one determine the precise nature of the ancient literary form and not confuse it with a similar, current style unaware of its divergent characteristics.

> The ancient peoples of the East, in order to express their ideas, did not always employ those forms or kinds of speech which we use today; but

rather those used by the men of their times and countries. What those exactly were, the commentator cannot determine as it were in advance, but only after a careful examination of the ancient literature of the East (DAS par. 37).

If it would be a mistake to confuse ancient literary styles with better known modern ones, it would be equally a mistake to rule out the possibility of certain ancient literary forms just because they differ from modern literary methodology and strike our sophisticated twentieth century mentality as imperfect, strange, or disconcerting.

> Nevertheless no one, who has a correct idea of biblical inspiration will be surprised to find, even in the Sacred Writers, as in other ancient authors, certain fixed ways of expounding and narrating, certain definite idioms, especially of a kind peculiar to the Semitic tongues, so-called approximations, and certain hyperbolical modes of expression, nay, at times, even paradoxical, which even help to impress the ideas more deeply on the mind. For of the modes of expression which, among ancient peoples, and especially those of the East, human language used to express its thought, none is excluded from the Sacred Books, provided the way of speaking adopted in no wise contradicts the holiness and truth of God, as, with his customary wisdom, the Angelic Doctor already observed in these words: 'In Scripture divine things are presented to us in the manner which is in common use amongst men.' For as the substantial Word of God became like to men in all things, 'except sin', so the words of God, expressed in human language, are made like to human speech in every respect, except error (DAS par. 37).

The importance of judging the message and measure of truth in biblical narratives according to the purpose of the author as known from his literary form is discussed briefly in the concluding remarks of Pius XII concerning literary forms.

> Not infrequently — to mention only one instance — when some persons reproachfully charge the Sacred Writers with some historical error or inaccuracy in the recording of facts, on closer examination it turns out to be nothing else than those *customary modes of expression and narration peculiar to the ancients,* which used to be employed in the mutual dealings of social life and which in fact were sanctioned by common usage (author's italics).
>
> When then such modes of expression are met with in the sacred text, which, being meant for men, is couched in human language, justice demands that they be no more taxed with error than when they occur in the ordinary intercourse of daily life. By this knowledge and exact appreciation of the modes of speaking and writing in use among the ancients can be solved many difficulties which are raised against the veracity and historical value of the Divine Scriptures, and no less efficaciously does this study contribute to a fuller and more luminous understanding of the mind of the Sacred Writer (DAS par. 38-39).

The application of the literary forms must eventually be made to all of the books of the Bible if we are to attain to that "fuller and more luminous understanding of the mind of the Sacred Writer" spoken of by Pius XII. This application will be made as the individual books are treated. For the present it is important that the student use his knowledge of literary forms as a help in the solution of the "many difficulties which are raised against the veracity and historical value of the Divine Scriptures."

It is safe to say that no books of the Bible have occasioned more difficulties for the modern exegete than the historical writings. At the same time it is equally safe to say that no study has done more to achieve a fuller and more luminous understanding of these books and to solve their difficulties than the study of the many styles of writing used in the Bible. We shall explain briefly, then, some of the styles involving history employed in ancient times and attempt to show where they can be found in the Bible and with what qualifications.

Among the literary forms utilized by biblical authors, according to the judgment of modern scripture scholars, to narrate history are the following: popular traditions or folklore; narratives written without exhaustive and accurate investigation of sources (as done also by Greeks, Romans, Americans); avowedly religious history; ideal history; and free history or haggadic midrash.

Popular traditions or folklore

By popular traditions are meant those facts concerning the origin and early history of a people which were transmitted orally for a long time, assimilating in the transmission imaginative and legendary embellishment which remained entwined with the objective historical nucleus when put into writing, embellishment which can be distinguished from the historical nucleus only by the guidance of divine revelation and the assistance of a refined literary criticism.

It would appear that the greater part of the Yahwist and Elohist sagas are based on popular traditions. In saying this, however, it must be emphasized that the ancients cultivated the memorization of names and events to a degree undreamed of by moderns and, as a result of their highly developed memories, handed down faithfully and in detail innumerable historical facts that would otherwise have been forgotten in the passage of the centuries.

It must be admitted that professional historians in ancient days wrote their histories with a freedom that would not be tolerated in modern research theses. They did not always make a complete and accurate investigation of the facts, nor did they insist upon contemporary accounts, eyewitness testimony, and authenticated documents with the same passion for exactitude as modern historians. They did not consider the writing of history a science after the manner of moderns, but as an art, whose aim was to narrate the facts as far as possible but to narrate them in an artistic and pleasing manner. As a consequence they arranged their material for the sake of effect, utilized a great deal of direct discourse to give animation to their accounts and even composed and put into the mouths of their historical characters speeches they never actually gave, and in general embellished their accounts in a manner not only to instruct but to please their readers.

One may observe, however, that even at the present time the net result of professional historical research writing at times approaches uncomfortably close to the deprecated unscientific compositions of the ancients — witness the plethora of *scientifically written* histories of religious communities, of national textbooks, of fraternal organizations. Philosophically evaluated, all historical compositions are in some degree tendentious.

With regard to biblical historians there is no doubt they were men of their age subject to the same spirit and outlook as the profane historians of their time. A variant outlook, even imperfections from the modern viewpoint, do not, however, constitute formal error, and must not be equated with formal error. When the inspired writers made formal judgments concerning the historicity of events they were protected by the Holy Spirit from all error. It is to inspiration, therefore, that we must point according to Pius XII as the reason for the superiority of Israel's historians.

> The same inquiry [into ancient literary forms] has also clearly shown the special preeminence of the people of Israel among all the other ancient nations of the East in their mode of compiling history, both by reason of its antiquity and by reason of the faithful record of the events — qualities which may well be attributed to the gift of divine inspiration and to the peculiar religious purpose of biblical history (DAS par. 36).

Religious history

Religious history is history recounted for a moral or doctrinal purpose rather than for itself. Unlike the profane historian, the religious historian does not compose his history merely to leave a record of past events. He writes in order to instruct or inspire his readers. For him history is a means, not an end. As a result he takes liberties with the events of the past which would not be justified if he purposed merely to leave a record of the past. From the mass of material at his disposal he chooses what will serve his purpose, and omits what will not. He recounts objective historical events even to details but with a freedom and elaboration that would not be considered proper in a modern historian. His history is very often incomplete but it is not false. Joshua, Judges, Samuel, Kings, 1 and 2 Chronicles, Ezra and Nehemiah, and 1 Maccabees are religious histories written after this manner. There are subtle differences in all of these histories according to the precise purpose of their authors, but in as much as they all utilize history for a doctrinal or moral purpose, they may be classified under the same general category of religious history. When an author, such as the author of Chronicles, presents only one side in an historical narrative, omitting entirely anything that would detract from his doctrinal purpose and elaborating to an extensive degree those aspects of his history which best serve his purpose, some modern exegetes are inclined to categorize his history as ideal history. There is some justification for a special name for this type of composition, but it could likewise be classified as religious history.

Free history or haggadic midrash

Haggadic midrash will be treated at greater length later (cf. p. 480). For the present it will suffice to say that there existed in postexilic times a literary form that fell only a step short of the later popular literary form known as parable. In the parable a completely fictitious story is used to inculcate a doctrinal or moral truth. In the haggadic midrash a story with a basic historical nucleus of more or less amplitude was freely and generously elaborated with fictitious details in order to edify or instruct the reader according to the precise purpose of the author. In the haggadic midrash, history is not used as a proof or even as a support. It is a facade, a background of no importance except as a frame for the story. Nevertheless, it is based upon historical events and for this reason may be considered in a wide sense an historical literary form. Critics are generally agreed that Tobit, Judith, Esther, Jonah, and Ruth belong to this literary form.

Objections and difficulties

It may be objected to the proponents of the literary form studies that their conclusions make it appear that we had to wait until modern times to find out what the Bible really means, and that the Fathers of the Church were wrong in their interpretations of such books as Jonah, Tobit, Judith, Esther, and parts of Genesis which they seem to consider strictly historical.

These objections are so natural that Pius XII was careful to anticipate and answer them himself in his encyclical *Divino Afflante Spiritu.* In his introduction to the discussion of the literary forms the Holy Father makes the following observations.

> We may rightly and deservedly hope that our time also can contribute something towards the deeper and more accurate interpretation of Sacred Scripture. For not a few things, especially in matters pertaining to history, were scarcely at all or not fully explained by the commentators of past ages, since they lacked almost all the information which was needed for their clearer exposition. How difficult for the Fathers themselves, and indeed well nigh unintelligible, were certain passages is shown, among other things, by the oft-repeated efforts of many of them to explain the first chapters of Genesis. . . (DAS par. 31).

With regard to difficulties, one might object that the investigation of literary forms, an admittedly involved and complicated study, has only made the Bible more difficult than ever to understand. The objection is well taken if it means that one can get little out of the Bible without a study and appreciation of its literary forms. This, however, is far from the truth. The Bible has been read by educated and ignorant alike for thousands of years with great benefit spiritually and culturally. And it has benefited all because the essentials of communication between human beings remain ever the same. Immediately and without great difficulty the main points and principal teachings of the Bible have always been fairly obvious to everybody, even without an explicit knowledge of the more abstruse implications of literary styles. The literary forms, therefore, must not be looked upon as a key without which one cannot even open the Bible, but as a bright and probing light which enables the reader to pierce to the very depths of the biblical author's mind and so understand his message not only in its main points but precisely and in all its amplitude and depth.

It may be hoped that the day will come when the general reader will appreciate the Biblical literary forms as well as he now understands the style in which the sports page of his daily newspaper is cast. It does not seem, however, that the day is near. In the meantime, therefore, it should be remembered that the study is still in flux, that conclusions are being established slowly and painstakingly as evidence accumulates, that despite definite progress made, more evidence has yet to be found, sifted, and evaluated. One cannot easily determine the precise implications of a mode of expression proper to an ancient and as yet imperfectly known culture.

Nevertheless, the reader must never forget that this study is basically literary. It will give him a more accurate understanding and a more profound appreciation of the inspired Word of God, but it will not and cannot change essentially any teaching of the Church concerning faith and morals. As an illuminating parallel and guiding principle in the investigation of the literary forms, the student should keep in mind the theologumenon of Pius XII: "As the substantial Word of God became like to men in all things, 'except sin', so the words of God, expressed in human language, are made like to human speech in every respect, except error" (DAS par. 37). As deeper theological studies about the sacred humanity of Christ in no way change our faith in His divinity, in like manner a more penetrating literary analysis of the revealed Word of God in no way changes our belief in the divine character and absolute inerrancy of the inspired Word of Sacred Scripture.

3

Psalms Related to the Pentateuchal History

1. The Book of Psalms

As indicated in the preface, the psalms will be studied on the basis of their relationship to books of the Bible already treated in the text. We shall begin with a brief introduction to the book of Psalms, taking in order: the formation of the book; the enumeration and titles of the psalms; the elements of Hebrew poetry and poetic style; some suggestions on how to study the psalms.[1] Then, in conjunction with a number of psalms related to the Pentateuchal history, we shall study the nature, the format, and the characteristics of three categories of psalms: hymns, didactic psalms, and thanksgiving psalms. Other categories, e.g., individual and collective supplication psalms; confidence, processional, and messianic psalms will be treated later in conjunction with other books of the Bible.

Formation of the book of Psalms

The book of Psalms, as it exists today, consists of 150 units, divided in imitation of the Pentateuch into five parts Book I: Pss. 1—41; Book II: Pss. 42—72; Book III: Pss. 73—89; Book IV:

[1] Cf. select bibliography on page 575.

Pss. 90–106; Book V: Pss. 107–150), each part ending with a short doxology (cf. Pss. 41:14; 72:18-19).

The book was not composed at one time, but represents the collective writings of many psalmists from the time of Moses in the thirteenth century to perhaps the time of Sirach in the late third century. This is indicated by the existence in the psalter of blocks of psalms by different authors (e.g., Pss. 3–41 in Book I and Pss. 51–65 in Book II, attributed to David; Pss. 41–49 in Book II by the Sons of Korah; Pss. 73–83 in Book III by the Sons of Asaph; Pss. 120–134 in Book V entitled the "Gradual Psalms"), and by the repetition of the same psalm in two different books of the psalter (cf. Ps. 14 in Book I and Ps. 53 in Book II). The change of the name of God from Yahweh to Elohim (the so-called "Elohistic revision"), in Pss. 43-83, is another indication that at one time the psalms existed in small groups or collections. Later these were gathered together into the major collection we now know as the book of Psalms.

Enumeration of the psalms

For those who read translations of the psalms based on the Septuagint version rather than on the Hebrew, a discrepancy in the enumeration of the psalms is immediately evident. Translations following the Hebrew enumeration are frequently one number ahead of those following the Septuagint, e.g., Ps. 22 in the Septuagint is numbered in the Hebrew as Ps. 23. This discrepancy is due to the division into two by the Septuagint of certain psalms which in the Hebrew remain as one psalm, and to the division into two in the Hebrew of other psalms which remain as one in the Septuagint. The difference in enumeration is shown in the following table:

Septuagint							
1–8	9	10-112	113	114–115	116–145	146–147	148–150
Hebrew							
1–8	9–10	11–113	114–115	116	117–146	147	148–150

Titles

Many psalms begin with titles which purport to give one or more of the following points of information concerning the psalm: the author, the nature of the psalm, the mode for singing, the liturgical use, the historical background of the psalm.

Even though the psalm titles are not inspired and are in many ways as unintelligible to us as they were to the Septuagint translators in the second century B.C., they nevertheless have great authority because of the ancient, literary tradition they represent, and in certain cases give valuable information concerning the authors, make-up, and use of the psalms. They show, for instance, that David is by no means the only author of psalms. Other authors mentioned in the titles are: the Sons of Korah, Asaph, Solomon, Moses, Heman, and Ethan. About fifty psalms are anonymous.

The nature or character of certain psalms is indicated in the titles by the words: *mizmor*, a psalm sung to the music of stringed instruments; *shir*, a song or canticle composed for singing; *maskil*, a didactic psalm. *Miktams* and *shiggayons* are mentioned, but the meaning of the terms is uncertain.

The modulation or melody according to which certain psalms were to be sung is indicated in the titles by the word *secundum* (according to) followed by the first word or words of a well known melody or chant, e.g., *sosannim* (lilies) in Ps. 69. Fifty-five psalms have the inscription, *magistro chori* (for the leader), which may mean that the psalm belonged to the choirmaster's collection, or that it was to be sung under his direction.

In a few cases, the title mentions the liturgical use of the psalm, e.g., Ps. 92 for use "on the Sabbath day"; Ps. 30 "for the feast of the Dedication"; Ps. 100 to be used "ad Laudes," perhaps for the thanksgiving sacrifices.

In thirteen psalms, the titles not only give David as the author, but proceed by means of quotations from the books of Samuel to point out the precise historical circumstances in which, or in view of which, the psalm originated. Where the internal evidence of the psalm does not fully agree with the information given in the title, the reader should take into account the fact that not everything about David's life is told in the books of Samuel, and that both additions and adaptations of the psalms were made in the course of time to adapt individual psalms for use in group worship.

Elements of Hebrew poetry

Some elements of Hebrew poetry, such as rhythm and assonance, do not survive in translation. Others, such as strophic structure, the use of refrains, anaphora and epiphora, and especially parallelism show through even in vernacular renditions.

Strophic structure

Division of the psalms into parts or strophes, i.e., into blocks of verses, is done for the most part on the basis of content; e.g., in Ps. 23, the first strophe describes God as the Good Shepherd, the second strophe, as the perfect Host. Sometimes, as in Pss. 42–43 and 107, the recurrence of a refrain sets off the different strophes.

The alphabetic format of some psalms also serves to indicate strophic structure (cf. Ps. 119 where the first eight verses begin with the Hebrew letter *aleph*, the second eight with *beth*, and so on). In other alphabetic psalms the acrostic serves as a mere ornament of style, but does not indicate strophic structure because successive letters of the alphabet introduce individual verses rather than blocks of verses (cf. Pss. 25; 111; 112). Differences in strophic division found in various translations often depend on differences in interpretation.

Anaphora and epiphora

Anaphora means the repetition of the same word or words at the beginning of successive verses. Epiphora means the repetition of the same word or words at the end of successive verses. Ps. 118:6-11 exemplifies both:

Anaphora	*The Lord is with me*; I fear not;
	    What can man do against me?
	The Lord is with me to help me,
	    and I shall look down upon my foes.
	It is better to take refuge in the Lord
	    than to trust in man.
	It is better to take refuge in the Lord
	    than to trust in princes.

Epiphora	All the nations encompassed me;
	    in the name of the Lord I crushed them.
	They encompassed me on every side;
	    in the name of the Lord I crushed them.

Parallelism

Instead of balancing verses or parts of verses by rhyme, the Hebrew poet balances thoughts, a process known as parallelism. In the typical verse, usually consisting of two parts called "stichs," the thought of the first stich is either echoed back in different words in the second stich (synonymous parallelism), or reversed (antithetic parallelism). When the thought of the first stich is developed in the second stich, which explains, demonstrates, or illustrates with a comparison what has been stated in the first stich, the balancing of thoughts is termed, perhaps not too properly, synthetic parallelism. The following examples will illustrate:

Synonymous	He who is throned in heaven laughs;
	the Lord derides them (Ps. 2:4).
Antithetic	He has put down the mighty from their thrones,
	and has exalted the lowly (Luke 1:52).
Synthetic	Happy the man who follows not the counsel of the wicked,
	Nor walks in the way of sinners,
	Nor sits in the company of the insolent (Ps. 1:1).

Parallelism is so basic an element of Hebrew poetry and style that it is found not only in the psalms but in the prophets and wisdom writers as well. Since parallelism often gives the clue to the correct interpretation, the reader is advised always to look carefully at the entire sentence. In addition to parallelism, Hebrew poetry abounds in the figurative language common to all poetry, frequently alludes to events of biblical history (cf. Pss. 78; 105–107; 114; 135–136), and to the geography of Palestine (cf. Ps. 125:4; 133:3). Besides the historical and geographical background, the reader will find the poetry of the Israelites greatly influenced by their pastoral mode of life (cf. Pss. 23; 95), the cruelty of their wars (cf. Pss. 68; 137), their sacred and civil laws and institutions (cf. Pss. 81; 118– 119).

As a result, the best preparation for understanding the psalms is a familiarity with the Bible as a whole. Such a familiarity will show the reader that the psalms are a digest of all that is best in the Bible. "Song like prayer," it has been said, "is forever restating and re-establishing the permanent values." The reader will find that the psalms express precisely the permanent values of the Bible — the values that carry over and find their fullest expression in the New Testament.

How to study the Psalms

Since the psalms are poems, uttered from the heart by eminently religious poets inspired by the Holy Spirit, the reader must from the beginning apply to the psalms what he has learned about poetry in his literary studies. This entails primarily the realization that the message of the poem is more than the words alone and more even than the sum of the ideas. There is, in short, the evocative power of the poem based on human experience, the message of the heart, the touching of intangibles, the reaching for the incomprehensible.

The study of the individual phrases and the evaluation of specific ideas, therefore, will be only the initial work of appreciating the poem. The full appreciation will come when the reader has read and re-read the psalm until his own mind and heart respond to the insights and pulse with the emotions of the psalmist.

It is suggested that the student study the psalms according to types or categories. Since a large number of the psalms fit into certain types or categories, it will be no small advantage to study the nature and format of each particular category of psalms. In this way, when the nature and format of two or three hymns has been studied, it will be easier to recognize and study other hymns of the same type.

For the sake of facilitating the study of the psalms according to the above method, we shall begin with a brief study of three categories of psalms (hymns, didactic psalms, and thanksgiving psalms), each exemplified by a number of psalms related to the Pentateuchal history. Other psalms belonging to each of these categories but not treated in this book will be listed for those who wish to study them privately.

2. Hymns

A hymn is a wholly theocentric psalm in which God is exuberantly praised either in Himself, for His attributes, or for His dealings with His Chosen People. The sentiments expressed in the hymn are the fundamental feelings of joy, veneration, praise, adoration, and religious awe experienced by man in the presence of his Creator and Redeemer. In the hymn, therefore, the psalmist dwells with delight on praising God's omnipotence as manifested in creation, His majesty as manifested in the heavens, the storm, the earthquake, and the phenomena of nature, His providence as manifested in Israel's history.

Structurally, hymns are quite simple, consisting of one, two or three parts: 1. an invitation to praise God, addressed sometimes to the psalmist himself, sometimes to others, sometimes to the nations, sometimes to all creation; 2. the motives for this praise: God's power, goodness, love, solicitous care for His people; 3. a conclusion, usually a repetition of the introductory invitation to praise God, or a prayer to God to accept His worshipper's praise.

The simplest type of hymn, consisting almost entirely of an extensive invitation to praise God, is exemplified in Ps. 148, in which the psalmist calls upon all creation, animate and inanimate, to praise God the Creator.

The more usual form of the hymn, consisting in the invitation to praise God, followed by a motive or motives for this praise, is best exemplified by such psalms as Pss. 117, 150 and 100. Thus Ps. 117:

Invitation Praise the Lord, all you nations;
       glorify him, all you peoples!

Motive   For steadfast is his kindness toward us,
                and the fidelity of the Lord endures forever.

The most elaborate form of the hymn, consisting of invitation, motives, and conclusion, is exemplified in Pss. 103 and 104. In each of these there is an extensive invitation, a long list of motives, and a fairly elaborate conclusion.

In some hymns, the invitation is only implicit, as, for example, in Ps. 8, where the psalmist begins: "O Lord, our Lord, how glorious is your name over all the earth!," and in Ps. 19: "The heavens declare the glory of God." The same is true for the Kingship of Yahweh psalms (93; 95; 99; 47), as for example in Ps. 93: "The Lord is king, in splendor robed." Even in these psalms, however, where the outward structure of invitation, motives, and conclusion is not always evident, the essence of the hymn — praise of God — is abundantly present and is more than sufficient to categorize them as true hymns.

While authors differ in their allocation of psalms to the different categories, most would categorize the following psalms as hymns: 8; 19; 29; 33; 67; 68; 100; 103; 111; 113; 117; 135; 136; 145–150. Pss. 47; 93; 95–99 are hymns, but are treated in a special category entitled the "Kingship of Yahweh Psalms." Pss. 105–106 are hymns in format but are usually categorized as didactic historical psalms.

Psalm 148

Theme	A hymn in which the psalmist calls on all God's creatures to praise their Creator.
Background	The creation account of Gen. 1 (cf. also Job 38—39; Sir. 43:1-35).
Division	1. Praise of God from the creatures of the heavens (vv. 1-6).
	2. Praise of God from the creatures of the earth (vv. 7-14).
N.B.	1. There is a very orderly arrangement in both strophes. The first strophe ranges from the highest animate creatures of the heavens, the angels, to the lowest inanimate; the second strophe, from the lowest inanimate to the highest animate creatures of the earth— men.
	2. The Canticle of the Three Young Men in Dan. 3:38-68 is evidently based on this psalm. Both hymns have as theme the implicit obligation of all creation to praise God the Creator.

v. 1 *from the heavens:* the psalmist begins with a reference to the heavens in general. In v. 1b, *in the heights,* he particularizes according to the Hebrew division of the heavens into three parts: 1. the heights above the highest heavens where God dwells (cf. Ps. 104:3 and 2 Cor. 12:2-4 where St. Paul speaks of this third heaven); 2. *the highest heavens* (v. 4), the heaven of the firmament which divides the waters above from the waters below; 3. the heaven below the firmament, the air or atmospheric heaven.

v. 5 *he commanded:* in the oriental creation myths, the sun, stars, waters, etc., are personified as gods; here, the psalmist puts them in their place as creatures brought into being by God and absolutely obedient to Him.

v. 14 *lifted up the horn:* the author gives a special reason for praising God — because of the great power (symbolized by the "horn," metonomy for the bull, one of the most powerful of beasts) God has given to His Chosen People.

Psalm 93

Theme

A Kingship of Yahweh[1] hymn praising God the absolute King and Lord of the universe.

Background

The description in Gen. 1 of God as Creator and Lord of creation. Also the Marduk-Tiamat creation myth of the Babylonians (cf. McKenzie, *The Two-Edged Sword* 75-82; ANET 66-67; also the numerous biblical texts using imagery from this myth, e.g., Pss. 46:1-4; 65:8; 74:12-14; 89:10; 104:5; Is. 17:12-14; 27:1; 51:9-10; Job 9:13; 17:12; 26:12-13; 38:8-11).

Division

1. God is King and Creator ruling from all eternity (vv. 1-2).
2. The forces of evil are helpless before the all-powerful King (vv. 3-4).
3. The testimonies (revelation and promises) of such a God are worthy of belief; sanctity befits His dwelling place (v. 5).

[1] Cf. p. 468ff.

v. 1 *he has made the world firm:* according to Gen. 1:2, 9-10, the sea at first covered the earth. God separated the two, making bounds for the sea beyond which it could not pass (cf. Job 38:8-11; Ps. 104:5-9). Since God restrains the sea, it is certain that the earth will not be moved.

v. 2 *your throne stands firm:* God's throne, situated in the upper heavens, was established above the firmament (cf. Ps. 104:3; 11:4). Since the firmament itself was considered as resting upon the summits of the great mountains, the waves crashing against the land would threaten to shake the mountains and thereby shake God's throne situated above them on the firmament. By restraining the sea, God sees to it that His "throne stands firm."

v. 3 *floods:* no matter how often the forces of evil, represented by the "waters" or "floods" or "seas" (all symbolic of Tiamat, the primeval principle of evil and disorder in the universe according to the ancient Marduk-Tiamat legend) challenge God, they are helpless before His almighty power.

v. 5 *worthy of trust:* the testimonies (promises and revelation) of so powerful a God are fully worthy of belief under all circumstances. Moreover, holiness, the exclusion of all evil and disorder, the transcendance of good above and in contradistinction to all evil, eminently befits the house of so great and powerful a God (whether the temple be that of the skies or the Temple of Jerusalem).

Psalm 104

Theme	A hymn praising God the Creator whose power and wisdom are manifested in the visible universe.
Background	The psalm is a poetic version of the creation account in Gen. 1 (cf. p. 85ff).
Division	1. Creation of the kingdom of light and the kingdom of the waters (1st and 2nd days; vv. 1-4).
	2. Creation of the kingdom of earth (3rd day; vv. 5-9).
	3. God's loving care for the kingdom of earth (3rd and 6th days; vv. 10-18).

4. Creation of the hosts of heaven: the sun, the moon, and the stars (4th day; vv. 19-23).
5. Creation of the hosts of the seas: fish and reptiles (5th day; vv. 24-26).
6. Dependence of all creatures on God for life and continuance of life (6th day; vv. 27-30).
7. Praise of God who rejoices over the works of His hands (7th day; vv. 31-36).

v. 1 *bless:* the psalm follows the full "hymn" format: begins with an invitation to praise God, gives motives for the praise, and concludes (v. 35c) as it began.

v. 2 *robed in light:* an indirect allusion to the work of the first day, the creation of light. The psalmist pictures God Himself as robed in dazzling light (cf. Gen. 1:3; Is. 6:1-3), and the blue vault of the sky (the firmament, considered solid by the ancients) as the tent cloth of God's pavilion. The firmament is the work of the second day (cf. Gen. 1:6).

v. 3 *palace upon the waters:* the solid firmament was thought to separate the upper from the lower waters (oceans and seas). Above these upper waters God's palace was located. *clouds your chariot* (v. 3b): the clouds poetically are God's chariots, moving back and forth before the entrance to His pavilion so that He can step out upon them and travel as He wills *on the wings of the wind* (cf. Ps. 18:10-11 where God comes down upon a cloud to help David; also the Ras Shamra texts, in which a pagan god is described as "he that rides upon the clouds" — ANET 132).

v. 4 *winds:* the winds are God's messengers just as the clouds are His chariots (the Hebrew *malach* can mean either "messenger" or "angel"). *fire* (v. 4b) probably refers to the lightning which God uses as His servant (cf. Job 38:35).

vv. 5-9 *fixed the earth upon its foundation:* the creation of the kingdom of earth, the work of the third day (cf. Gen. 1:9-13). According to the cosmogony of the ancients, the earth rested on pillars in the midst of the lower waters (the ocean; cf. Job 38:4-6). Covered at first by the waters of the seas (v. 6), the earth, at God's word (v. 7), rose into its present position, and the waters of the sea fled, to be kept forever in place by the shore lines, lest they encroach again on the earth (v. 9; cf. Gen. 1:8-9; Job 38:8-11; and note baptized use of the Marduk-Tiamat legend).

vv. 10-18 *you send forth springs:* in His loving care for the kingdom of earth, God provides water to serve as drink for the cattle (v. 11) and to make the crops (v. 13) and the great trees on the mountains grow (v. 16). The birds and animals mentioned are native to Palestine: the stork (v. 17), the wild goat or chamois (v. 18), and the rock-badger, or hyrax, a small rabbitlike animal sometimes called a coney. The whole section (vv. 10-18) is a digression on water, praising God for Sister Water in an almost Franciscan outburst. The author thus elaborates the work of the third day (cf. Gen. 1:9-13), bringing in by anticipation the work of the sixth day, the creation of the animals (cf. Gen. 1:24-25).

vv. 19-23 *the moon to mark the seasons:* in describing the work of the fourth day, the creation of the hosts of heaven (cf. Gen. 1:14-19), the author subtly attacks the pagans' worship of the sun, stars, and moon by showing them created by God to serve man as timepieces. Thus, the phases of the moon were used to divide the month, and feasts were celebrated at the new moon, and at the full moon. In vv. 20-23, the psalmist shows how beasts and men regulate their lives according to the God-given sun and moon clocks. The reader should compare the psalm with Akhnaton's hymn to Amon-ra and note the basic differences despite certain very superficial similarities (cf. ANET 370-371).

vv. 24-26 *how manifold:* elaborating on the works of creation, the psalmist describes the creation of the hosts of the seas, the work of the fifth day (cf. Gen. 1:20-23), emphasizing the abundance of the living creatures that God in His wisdom has created; the earth is full and the sea also. The LEVIATHAN (v. 26), ordinarily the crocodile, here stands for all the monsters of the deep: whales, sharks, flying fish, etc. In pagan mythology, Leviathan is a monster who battles with the gods after the manner of Tiamat in the Marduk-Tiamat legend. Here the psalmist has him as a creature of God, made to play before Him in the seas (cf. Gen. 1:21; Job 40).

vv. 27-30   *all:* the psalmist emphasizes the dependence of all things on God for creation and conservation (cf. Gen. 1:31, the sixth day of creation), elaborating on the breath of life which comes from God and is taken away by Him. The word "breath" or "spirit" is used in different senses in the Bible. Etymologically, it comes from the Hebrew *ruah* meaning wind (Gen. 1:2), word, breath of life (Gen. 2:7), a special divine influence in a man (note the special power or "spirit" given to Moses, the Judges, Saul, the prophets enabling them to carry out the functions of prophet, judge, and king). Semantically, the meanings of the word probably developed from the observation that the wind brings the clouds, the clouds the rain, the rain the crops, the crops the sustenance of men and beasts. Living creatures breathe. Life, therefore, is connected with breath (cf. Gen. 2:7 where God breathes into man's nostrils and he becomes a living creature). Life and death, then, depend on God's giving of His "spirit" or breath (cf. Ps. 104:29-30; Wis. 1:7; 12:1; Jud. 16:14). In general, one must examine the context to determine the exact meaning of spirit, both in the Old Testament and in the New Testament.[1]

vv. 31-35   *may the Lord be glad:* on the seventh day, God "saw all that he had made was very good" (Gen. 1:31). The psalmist concludes, praising God and recalling God's good pleasure in His creation. He prays that sinners, who mar the harmony of the universe by injecting the only discordant element in all creation, be destroyed.

Psalm 8

Theme   A hymn extolling the majesty of God and the dignity of man.

[1] Cf. Guillet, *Themes of the Bible*, 225-279.

The creation of man in the image and likeness of God,
whereby he becomes by divine decree lord of creation
(Gen. 1:26; 2:19-20; Wis. 13).

1. The majesty of God and the greatness of His creation
make man in comparison seem insignificant (vv. 2-5),
and yet . . .

2. God has made insignificant man the lord of all creation
(vv. 6-10).

v. 2 *your name:* for the Hebrews, lacking philosophical terms
and even a philosophical bent of mind, the "name" stands
for the essence, nature, or even destiny of the person or
thing (cf. Adam Gen. 2:20 naming the animals; 2:23
naming Eve). In this context, the name of God is equivalent to God Himself (cf. Ps. 148:13; change of Abram's
name to Abraham, Simon to Peter — "Rock").

v. 2 *you have exalted . . . above the heavens:* the sun, moon
and stars document the skies with testimony to God's
majesty and power (cf. Wis. 13:1-7; Rom. 1:18-21; Ps.
18).

v. 3 *out of the mouths of babes:* so manifest is the testimony
of the heavens to the majesty of God that even children
perceive it and praise God to the confusion of sinners,
who in their blindness, ignore the testimony of creation
to God's power and majesty (cf. Wis. 13; Rom. 1:18-21;
and Matthew 21:16, where Jesus applies this verse to the
children on Palm Sunday, to the confusion of the embarrassed Pharisees).

v. 4. *when I behold:* struck with awe at the splendor of the
midnight sky aflame with stars and resembling a celestial
tapestry woven by divine fingers, the psalmist is speechless. He contemplates the majesty of God and, conscious
of his own insignificance, wonders how so great a God
could be so good to so insignificant a creature as man.
The apodosis of the sentence, if expressed would probably read, ". . . when I see . . . I think or ask myself:
'what is man?' "

v. 5 *what is man:* the sense of the question is: what is in man
that he should deserve such great love and attention from
the infinite God? The following verses do not so much

answer the question as give the reasons for asking it. They tell of the wonderful power God has given man, making him lord of creation. They do not and cannot, since it is the mystery of divine love, explain why!

v. 6 *little less than the angels:* Hebrew has *'elohim,* God. St. Jerome and others render the phrase: "You have made him little less than God." However, in the Old Testament, the word "god" is used for judges (Ps. 82:6) and for angels (Ps. 97:7c). In either case, the sense is clear: God has made man in His image and likeness, the crown and king of creation (cf. Heb. 2:6-8; 1 Cor. 15:26-28).

v. 7 *rule:* God gave to Adam lordship over creation (Gen. 1:26; 2:19-20), "putting all things under his feet," a common expression for complete domination (cf. Gen. 3:15; Jos. 10:24; Ps. 110:1; 1 Cor. 15:26-27).

Canticle of Moses (Exod. 15)

Theme

A victory hymn celebrating God's power manifested in the deliverance of the Israelites by the opening of the Red Sea and by the destruction of the Egyptians.

Background

Exod. 14—15. Part A written at the time of the Exodus; Parts B and C later.

Division

A. Poetic description of the destruction of Pharaoh's army (vv. 1-10).
B. Transition strophe of praise introducing Part C (vv. 11-13).
C. 1. Report of God's power, manifested in favor of Israel, strikes terror into her enemies during the desert march (14-16).
2. God settles the Israelites in the Promised Land (vv. 17-18).

N.B.

It was customary to celebrate great victories with songs composed soon after the event (cf. Judg. 5:1-31; 16:23-25; 1 Sam. 18:7; 2 Sam. 1:20; Jud. 16; Luke 1—2). These canticles evidently became stereotyped from long use in the liturgy. Later canticles were spoken of as "a new song," indicating that the old songs were not considered adequate to celebrate new manifestations of God's goodness (cf. Is. 42:10; Pss. 33:3; 96:1; 149:1).

v. 3 *the Lord is a warrior:* God is looked upon poetically as a great and powerful warrior. In other books, He is referred to as "Lord of Hosts," i.e., of armies (cf. Exod. 14:14; Ps. 78:65; Num. 21:14). In John 16:32, Christ vindicates this title for Himself in a more refined sense: "In the world you will have affliction, but take courage, I have overcome the world."

v. 6 *your right hand:* it is the right hand that wields the spear, bow, mace — metonymy for God's power (cf. v. 12; Ps. 118:16; Luke 1:51).

v. 17 *on the mountain:* possibly the author speaks of one mountain by metonymy for all the mountains of the Promised Land. On the other hand the author may be speaking of Mount Zion, Jerusalem, the capital city of Judah. If so, the last part of the canticle may have been written after 1000 B.C., the approximate date for the capture of Jerusalem by David.

Psalm 29

Theme

A hymn praising God, the Lord of the storm. In the storm, the psalmist sees a manifestation of God's grandeur and power.

Background

Exod. 19:16-19; Ps. 93.

Division

1. Invitation to the angels of the heavenly court to praise God (vv. 1-2).
2. Description of a great storm, the thunder representing God's voice (vv. 3-9).
3. God, the omnipotent and eternal King, blesses His Chosen People (vv. 10-11).

N.B.

Ps. 29 is one of the oldest in the psalter. Its use of expressions, found in fifteenth century Canaanite poetic texts unearthed at Ugarit, shows that the author was acquainted with such compositions. To appreciate the poetic vigor of the psalm one must, in imagination, stand during a storm on a hillside overlooking the sea, while storm winds raise the whitecaps and shriek through the trees to the accompaniment of stabbing spears of lightning and fearsome thunder. It should be noted too that the thunder as the voice of God witnesses to a widespread, primitive way of thinking.

v. 1 *sons of God:* the psalmist uses this term for the angels of the heavenly court (cf. Pss. 89:6-7; 97; 1 Kings 22:19; Job 1).

v. 2 *in holy attire:* the psalmist likens the angels in the temple of the heavens to the priests clad in sacred vestments in the Temple of Jerusalem (cf. 2 Chr. 20:21; Ps. 96:9).

v. 3 *the voice of the Lord:* the thunder is God's voice (cf. Exod. 9:23-24). It is mentioned seven times because of the sacredness of the number seven. *over the waters:* in its immediate setting, the waters here are not so much the waters of the Mediterranean as the waters above the firmament (Gen. 1:7; 7:11; Jer. 10:13). This interpretation is confirmed by v. 10, where the psalmist sees God seated above the flood, i.e., the upper waters (cf. Ps. 104:3; Ps. 18:14).

v. 6 *he makes . . . leap:* as in Ps. 114, the mountains bound like young bullocks. This can be because of the earthquake, which is conceived to accompany the storm and the lightning, or because of the thunder which often gives the impression of making the earth tremble.
LEBANON — SARION: Sarion is the Phoenician name for Mount Hermon (Deut. 3:9). In ancient times, Mounts Lebanon and Sarion were reputed sacred as dwelling places of the gods. It is not accidental, therefore, that the monotheist author has these mountains bounding in fear before the voice of the true God.

v. 7 *fiery flames:* the lightning. *wilderness of Kadesh* (v. 8): the psalmist pictures the storm moving down from Lebanon and Sarion in the north to Kadesh in the south, the place in the Negeb of Palestine where the Israelites spent the forty years in the desert (cf. Num. 13–20); or perhaps this is a Kadesh in the north.

v. 9 *in his temple:* the conclusion brings us back to the presence of God in the temple of the skies where the angels in awe and astonishment cry "Glory" before the divine power and majesty manifested in the storm (cf. Is. 6:3).

v. 10 *above the flood:* God, the eternal King, sits in the heaven of heavens above the celestial floods. Because He is so powerful, His people confidently expect protection and peace.

Psalm 114

Theme
A hymn praising God who has brought Israel out of Egypt and established her in Palestine as His theocratic kingdom.

Background
Summary of events from Exodus, Joshua, Numbers, and 2 Samuel.

Division
vv. 1-2, the Exodus and the establishment of God's kingdom in Israel.
vv. 3-6, dramatic personification of nature reacting to God's presence.
vv. 7-8, the psalmist calls on all the earth to tremble before the face of God.

N.B.
The Greek and Vulgate make one psalm (Ps. 113) out of two distinct psalms (Pss. 114–115) in the Hebrew. The lyric beauty of Ps. 114, so different from the prosaic language of Ps. 115, would seem to indicate that Ps. 115 is the work of a later author, perhaps of the exile period.

v. 2 *Judah his sanctuary:* while the whole of the Promised Land was regarded as God's sanctuary, it is not unlikely that the author is referring to Jerusalem in Judah, the site of the Temple. *his domain:* after the Exodus, Israel became God's theocratic kingdom.

v. 3 *the sea:* the Red Sea was parted (Exod. 14) and the Jordan river was held back by God for the passage of the Israelites (Jos. 3:12-19). At Sinai (v. 4) the mountains shook when God appeared to Moses (Exod. 19:16-20).

v. 8 *rock into pools:* God provided water from the rock for the thirsty Israelites in the desert (Exod. 17:6; Num. 20:11), showing that nothing can resist His omnipotent power.

Theme	All praise is to be given to God from whom alone comes help.
Back-ground	The exile period (587-539), when the pagans mocked the exiled Jews, claiming their gods had conquered the God of Israel.
Division	1. Implicit prayer for help and deliverance (vv. 1-3). 2. The true God is contrasted with the lifeless idols of the pagans (vv. 4-8). 3. Antiphonal prayer sung by people and priests, expressing their absolute confidence in God (vv. 9-18).

v. 1 *not to us:* an exclamation motivated by an implicit admission that if Israel triumphs over her enemies, it is not due to her own efforts but to God's asssitance.

v. 2 *why . . . say:* another implicit prayer; if God will answer them, the pagans will not be able to say, "Where is their God?," as if He were not able to help His people.

v. 9 *the house of Israel:* all the Israelites; *the house of Aaron:* the priests; *who fear the Lord:* the faithful

Theme	A Kingship of Yahweh hymn inviting the Israelites to praise and obey God.
Back-ground	God the Creator (Gen.); lack of confidence in God manifested during the march through the desert (Exod.; Num.; cf. also Heb. 3:7—4:12).
Division	1. Invitation to praise God because He is Lord of creation (vv. 1-5). 2. Invitation to praise God because He is the shepherd of Israel whom all must obey (vv. 6-11).

v. 3 *a great king:* the subject of the psalmist's praise and his first motive is God, the Father, the King of Creation. *above all gods:* in Hebrew usage, "gods" can refer to the angels, to kings, judges, and to the false gods of the nations. Here the psalmist refers to the false gods of the nations, to whom is contrasted in vv. 4-5 the true God, Creator of all things.

v. 7 *people he shepherds:* the psalmist's second motive is God's care for Israel. Like a shepherd God has led His people out of Egypt through the desert to the promised land (cf. Ps. 23; Ez. 34:31; John 10).

v. 7 *oh, that today:* despite the fact that God is creator and shepherd of Israel, deserving all praise and obedience, Israel has not praised Him, but has instead ungraciously turned a deaf ear to His calls. God, however, is always calling her back. As St. Paul says: "Now is the acceptable day of salvation" (cf. Heb. 3:7–4:12 where St. Paul applies the "today" of this psalm to the people of his time, as we should apply it to ourselves – today).

v. 8f MERIBAH: "contention" (Exod. 17; Num. 20:13) MASSAH: "temptation" (Exod. 17:7). On both occasions the people lost confidence in God as their shepherd and murmured against Him. *where your fathers tempted* (v. 9): by their grumbling and complaining, they questioned God's ability to provide for them and repeatedly showed the weakness of their faith despite the miracles they had witnessed.

v. 10 *forty years:* in the desert for 40 years, the people continued to exhaust God's patience, e.g., at the Red Sea (Exod. 14); at Massah (Exod. 17); at Sinai (Exod. 32); at Kadesh (Num. 12–16); at Meribah (Num. 20); at Baal of Peor (Num. 25). *of erring heart:* sinful and disobedient, *they know not my ways:* in the sense of not knowing efficaciously, since they did not follow the shepherd in the "ways" of observing His divine law.

v. 11 *therefore:* as a result, God is forced to punish them by decreeing they shall not enter the promised land (Num. 14:22-35). N.B. This warning is as much for moderns as for the contemporaries of the psalmist, as St. Paul has stated in Heb. 4:1ff.

Psalm 81

Theme A processional hymn concluding with a plaintive rebuke to Israel for refusing to "hear the voice" of God.

Back-ground	Allusions to events of the Exodus (cf. Ps. 95 and Deut. 32)
Division	Part A. Processional hymn for one of the great feasts (vv 2-6). Part B. Lament for Israel's infidelity to the Sinai pact. 1. Infidelity at the time of the Exodus destroyed God's plans (vv. 7-11). 2. But God is still yearning and ready to pour out His favors on Israel (vv. 12-17).

v. 3 *melody:* instrumental music was added to the singing to enhance the solemnity of the feasts.

v. 4 *at the new moon:* new moon and full moon were two of the occasions when feasts were celebrated (cf. Num. 28:11-15; 10:10).

v. 5 *for it is a statute:* the promulgation of the feast of the Passover (cf. Exod. 12:1-14; Lev. 23:4ff); the feast of Tabernacles (cf. Lev. 23:34).

v. 6 *speech I hear:* the author speaks with emotion of God's fatherly concern for, and compassion toward Israel, in order to point the contrast between God's love and Israel's ungrateful response to that love. Introducing God as speaking (an oracle as in Ps. 95:8), the psalmist contrasts the fatherly voice of God (Exod. 2:24) with the harsh voice of the overseers of the Egyptian oppression. God had spoken to Abraham, Jacob, and Isaac, then was silent for 400 years. At the time of Moses, Israel heard His voice again (Exod. 2:24).

v. 7 *from the basket:* a reference to the hods or baskets for carrying bricks, used by the Israelites during the oppression (cf. Exod. 1:11) until God saved them, spoke to them in "thunder" on Mount Sinai (Exod. 19:16-20) and tried them at Meribah (Exod: 17:7; Num. 20:13).

v. 11 *I . . . am:* emphasis on the first commandment, one God (Exod. 20:2). Infidelity to this commandment by idolatry was a rejection of the Sinai pact. If they will only look to the true God, instead of to the gods of Canaan; if they will only open their mouths, God will be happy to fill them.

v. 14 *if only:* the punch line of the psalm, as in Ps. 95, entreats the people to turn back to God, hear His voice, and walk in His ways instead of in the ways of idolatry. Then God would, without delay, destroy their enemies, forcing from them the constrained homage of enemies (v. 16), while Israel would be filled with the very "best of the wheat" and "honey from the rock," the proverbial milk and honey of the Promised Land (v. 17).

Psalm 135

Theme	A hymn praising God, Lord of creation and protector of His people.
Background	Allusions to historical events in Genesis, Exodus, and Numbers.
Division	Part A. Introduction inviting all present to praise God (vv. 1-4).

Part B. Reasons for this praise:
1. God is the Lord of creation (vv. 5-7).
2. God is the maker of history and the omnipotent protector of Israel (vv. 8-14).
3. To the true God, the psalmist contrasts the pagan gods, who are non-entities, incapable of doing anything for their worshippers (vv. 15-18).

Part C. Conclusion calling on all Israel, priests, laymen, proselytes, to praise God (vv. 19-21).

N.B. The hymn was probably sung antiphonally: vv. 1-4 the chanters; 5-14 one chanter or priest; 15-18 the chanters; 19-21 the whole congregation joining in with the chanters' invitation to "bless the Lord."

v. 1 *praise the name:* the name is praised because, for the Hebrews, the name stands for the person. *you servants of the Lord:* those who stand ready to serve, i.e., Levites, priests, etc. (cf. Ps. 134:1).

v. 4 *for the Lord has chosen:* God's choice of Israel is the great reason for praising Him (cf. Exod. 19:5; Deut. 7:6-9; 14:2; 26:18; and John 15:16: "You have not chosen me. I have chosen you").

v. 8f *the first-born in Egypt:* the tenth plague (cf. Exod. 12:29); *signs and wonders* (v. 9) refer to the plagues (cf. Exod. 7–9).

v. 10ff *he smote many nations:* Israelite victories in Palestine (cf. Num. and Jos.), particularly the victories over Sihon and Og (v. 11), the kings of Transjordan, conquered at the time of the invasion of Canaan (cf. Num. 21:26).

v. 15ff *the idols of the nations:* to the power and protection of the true God who has watched over His people is contrasted the impotence of the pagan gods (cf. same verses in Ps. 115:4-8).

v. 19 *house of Israel:* i.e., all Israel; especially the house of Aaron, the priests, and the house of Levi, the Levites, and lastly all who fear the Lord. All are invited to praise the God who dwells in Jerusalem. The reference to Jerusalem indicates that the psalm was written after the building of the Temple (965 B.C.).

Psalm 136

Theme	A hymn praising and thanking God for His unceasing manifestations of love toward His Chosen People.
Background	The doctrine of love in Deuteronomy, Hosea, and the Bible in general. Historical references to Genesis, Exodus, and Numbers.
Division	1. God's love manifested in creation (vv. 4-9). 2. God's love manifested in His works for Israel during the Exodus (vv. 10-22). 3. God's love manifested in His constant care for Israel (vv. 22-26).
N.B.	1. Psalms 136; 100; and 103 can be taken along with Deuteronomy to show that the doctrine of love at the heart of the Sinai pact did not remain a sterile and lifeless doctrine but entered into the life of the people and was expressed in their prayers. (On the doctrine of love in the Old Testament, cf. Dom Sorg's *Hesed and Hasid in the Psalms.*) 2. It should be noted that the interpretation of Ps. 136

turns on the interpretation of the word "mercy" (Hebrew *ḥesedh*). In the refrain that recurs litany fashion through the psalm, the word "mercy" would better be translated as loving-kindness or charity or grace. No one word can adequately render *ḥesedh*; "mercy," in English, expresses only one of its many implications.

Mercy means pity, forbearance from afflicting punishment, compassionate treatment of the helpless, or of an enemy. The Hebrew word *ḥesedh* means charity, benevolence, kindness, love of a husband for a wife, son for a father, friend for a friend, a love manifested by acts of kindness. In relation to God, *ḥesedh* signifies filial love, piety. When used of God's love for men, *ḥesedh* expresses God's immense inclination to help and save men (cf. Jer. 31:3; Ps. 63:4; Ps. 103:11, and Hosea *passim*).

"*Ḥesedh* describes an attitude of soul and is one of the richest words in the whole vocabulary of the Old Testament, a word here, as often, disguised by the English 'mercy.' It is a form of love, that form of love which Hosea says God prefers to sacrifice (Hosea 6:6). It is the kind of love which is imposed by some relationship between two or more people. It is the proper feeling of a father for a son, a son for a father, a brother for a brother, a wife for a husband, a worshipper for his God and God for His worshippers. . . . The truth is, it is all these and much more. It involves consecration to a personality, a consecration which will manifest itself in practical life. He who has this quality and this attitude to those about him will be in no danger of failing to meet the demand for justice."[1] It is of *ḥesedh* that Jesus spoke when He said: "He who loves me keeps my commandments."

v. 1ff *for:* the refrain, "for his mercy endures forever," became among the Jews a liturgical formula, repeated litany fashion, to express firm faith in God's loving-kindness (cf. 1 Chr. 16:34; 2 Chr. 5:13; 7:3; Ezra 3:11; Pss. 100:5; 106:1; 107:1; 118:1, 30).

Psalm 100

Theme A processional hymn inviting all to praise the good God and serve Him with joy and thanksgiving.

[1] Cf. H. H. Rowley, *The Old Testament and Modern Study* (Oxford: Clarendon Press, 1957) 359.

Deuteronomy: showing Israel's religious life and prayer
was characterized by love and joy rather than by fear
and trepidation.

v. 1 *all you lands:* obviously the author means all men who
are the subjects of the divine King, called upon to praise
Him and serve Him with joy (cf. Is. 56:6-7).

v. 2 *with gladness:* joy, gladness, and song are all proper to
those who love, not to those who fear or who are animated
by strict and cold justice. When the psalmists speak of
"fear of the Lord," it is to be understood in the Hebrew
sense, not as fear opposed to joy, but as that profound
respect, filial devotion, and obedience owed to a good and
loving Father.

v. 3 *know:* the psalmist does not exhort to an intellectual
"knowing" of God. This he presumes. The sense is rather
"acknowledge," i.e., know lovingly by a practical, experi-
mental knowledge that God is our creator and loving
shepherd and acknowledge that loving knowing of God
by worship in praise and joy. *the flock he tends:* we know
from Ps. 23 and Ez. 34 the tender implications of being
able to say: "The Lord is my shepherd." In this psalm, God
is looked upon as shepherd of all men, not just the Chosen
People. Our Lord develops this truth of the one universal
fold and one shepherd in John 10:1-16, though it is already
developed in the Old Testament (cf. Ps. 95:7; 74:1; 79:13;
Ez. 34; Is. 66:20-23).

v. 5 *he is good:* the goodness of God, the constancy of His
love echo in this liturgical formula down through the
centuries in Israel's liturgical life as an acknowledgment
of God's love for His chosen ones (cf. Ps. 136 and *passim*
in the psalms).

v. 5 *his faithfulness:* unchangeable fidelity of God to His
glorious promises. Our constant prayer is "that we may be
made worthy of the promises of Christ." There is no question of God being unfaithful to His promises, only whether
we will show ourselves worthy to have them fulfilled in
our regard.

Theme	A hymn of praise and gratitude to God for the tremendous love He has shown to men.
Background	Deuteronomy and Hosea: the persevering, pardoning love of God for man, substantiating St. John's definition, "God is Love."
Division	1. God's love manifested to the psalmist himself (vv. 1-5).
	2. God's love manifested to the chosen nation (vv. 6-10).
	3. The immensity of God's paternal love and understanding (vv. 11-18).
	4. An invitation to all to praise so great and loving a God (vv. 19-22).

v. 2ff *all his benefits:* doing good for the beloved is a sign of love; in this case the love of one "who pardons . . . heals . . . redeems. . . ." By his use of the present tense (participle in Hebrew), the psalmist expresses the continuousness of these manifestations of love. By his use of different verbs, he shows the many facets of this love and builds to the climax of "crowns . . . fills . . . renews."

v. 5. *like the eagle's:* the eagle, because of its longevity (believed to be a hundred years) was a popular ancient symbol for perennial youth and vigor (cf. Is. 40:31).

v. 7ff *to Moses:* "His ways" made known to Moses are exemplified in v. 8 by a quotation from Exod. 34:6: "The Lord, a merciful and gracious God, slow to anger and rich in kindness and fidelity, continuing His kindness *for a thousand generations* and forgiving wickedness and crime and sin . . . punishing children and grandchildren to the third and fourth generation for their father's wickedness." This text, exemplifying one of the "ways of the Lord," shows God's love triumphing over His justice as one thousand over three.

v. 11f *as the heavens . . . above the earth:* the greatest conceivable height (Is. 55:8-9) in nature is utilized to describe the immensity of God's paternal love (*ḥesedh*). As a result, God casts away our sins as far as "the east is from the west" (v. 12), the greatest imaginable distance (cf. Eph. 3:18

on the love of Christ for us: "That you may be able to comprehend . . . what is the breadth and length and height and depth, and to know Christ's love. . . .").

v. 13 *as a father:* according to Exod. 4:22-23; Hosea 11:1-4, and Jer. 31:20, God loves Israel as a father loves his son; or, as Isaiah tells us (49:14-15), even more than a mother loves her son. In the parable of the prodigal son, our Lord describes perfectly God's fatherly love toward us (Luke 15:11-32).

v. 14ff *he knows:* God knows us and our weakness, a consoling thought. The emphasis on the nothingness of man (v. 14b-16) prepares us for v. 17: one would hardly expect anyone to bother with such a weak creature as man, "but the kindness of the Lord is from eternity to eternity."

v. 19ff *rules over all:* God rules the whole world. The psalmist, therefore, calls upon all creatures to praise Him (v. 20): all angels, all His armies of servants (v. 21), all His works (v. 22) and lastly himself.

3. Thanksgiving Psalms

Thanksgiving psalms as a separate category have a fairly regular format and several identifying characteristics. The format consists in an introductory invitation to join in thanksgiving to God. This is followed by a description of the favor for which the psalmist is thanking God: deliverance usually from some kind of peril (Ps. 116), or sickness (Ps. 30), or attacks of enemies, personal or national (Pss. 118; 124; 129; 138), or captivity (Ps. 107).

The principal characteristic naturally is the expression of joy and gratitude. A special characteristic is the psalmist's vivid reliving of his peril with an expression of how he was practically in Sheol (i.e., practically dead), how he prayed (with an actual ejaculatory prayer inserted), how he vowed a thanksgiving sacrifice if God would save him, and then how he was heard and saved by God. Another characteristic is the frequent reference of the psalmist to his prayers for pardon from sin, because in the popular mind all suffering was regarded as punishment for sin.

The following are categorized as thanksgiving psalms by most authors: Pss. 4; 18; 30; 32; 34; 40; 65; 66; 92; 107; 116; 118; 124; 129; 138; the canticles in general, but especially the Canticle of Hezekiah (Is. 38:10-20), the Magnificat, and the Benedictus.

Theme	The heartfelt thanksgiving of a man saved from great peril.
Back-ground	Lev. 7:11-21: the thanksgiving sacrifice at which a psalm such as Ps. 116 was sung (cf. also 1 Sam. 1:24—2:1-10, Anna's thanksgiving sacrifice and canticle; 1 Sam. 9:11-13; Ps. 66:13-20).
Division	Part A. 1. Metaphorical description of peril (vv. 1-4). 2. Saved from death, the psalmist reflects on God's good-ness (vv. 5-9). Part B. The psalmist, in the Temple, fulfills his promise to offer a thanksgiving sacrifice (vv. 10-19).

v. 1ff *because he has heard:* immediately the psalmist gives the reason for his thanksgiving: God heard his prayer and saved him from the "cords of death" and "the snares of the nether world" (v. 3). The author personifies death as a hunter who lays traps and binds his victims fast, much as we personify death as the "grim reaper" (cf. Cant. 8:6 where love is described as "strong as death" because the monster, death, never lets his victims escape; cf. also Ps. 18:4-6). In the words, "O Lord, save my life!" (v. 4b), the psalmist repeats the prayer he said in his time of peril.

v. 5ff *gracious is the Lord:* the psalmist reflects on the goodness of God who watches over the "little ones," those of un-questioning faith in God, who cannot protect themselves, but put all their confidence in God.

Part B (vv. 10-19)

Saved by God, in whom he put all his trust, the psalmist fulfills the promise he made in the time of peril to offer a thanksgiving sacrifice in the Temple should he be saved. Note the refrain in vv. 13-14 and 17-18, the first referring to the offering of the chalice, the second to the offering of the victim.

v. 10ff *I believed, even when I said:* when the outlook was black-est the psalmist had confidence in God, reminding him-self that though "no man is dependable," in the sense that man's help is never infallible, he nevertheless knew that God could help him no matter how bad matters were. The contrast is between man's help and God's help. Understood is: But God is true to His promise to help those who trust in Him. Therefore — *How shall I make a return?"* The answer is given: thanksgiving and fulfillment of the "vows" he made to offer a sacrifice if and when he was saved (v. 13).

v. 13ff   *the cup of salvation . . . sacrifice of thanksgiving:* these terms refer to the sacrifice in the Temple in fulfillment of the "vows." There, surrounded by his friends, the grateful beneficiary of God's favor explained to his friends what God had done for him (vv. 1-9), offering first the chalice with the libation of wine, and then the victim, one part of which was destroyed on the altar (God's portion). A second portion was given to the priest (the stipend), and the remainder was then eaten by the psalmist and his friends at the sacrificial banquet held in the Temple courts (v. 19) (cf. Lev. 7:11-21; 1 Sam. 1:18-26). Note how the psalm contains the actions of the Last Supper (the Eucharist — thanksgiving): praising God before friends — Christ's discourse before the apostles praising the eternal Father; then the passing of the chalice. . . . Concerning the chalice, cf. Exod. 25:29; 37:16.

v. 15   *precious:* it is because his life is of great price, great value, that God has not let the psalmist die.

v. 16   *the son of your handmaid:* he himself is a servant, i.e., a worshipper of God, and likewise is his mother. He is a true Israelite by origin and by fulfillment of his religious obligations.

v. 19   *in the courts:* his thanksgiving psalm is chanted in the Temple or the Temple courts at Jerusalem (cf. 1 Sam. 1:24—2:1-10 for Anna's sacrifice and thanksgiving psalm in the courts of the Tabernacle at Shiloh).

Psalm 66

Theme   A hymn of thanksgiving to God for redemption from the Babylonian exile.

Background   Lev. 7:11-20, the "sacrifice of praise" (vv. 13-20); with allusions in the first part (vv. 1-12) to the Egyptian and Babylonian exiles.

Division

1. Introduction, calling on all men to praise God (vv. 1-4), followed by reasons for this praise (vv. 5-12).
2. The offering of the thanksgiving sacrifices in the Temple (vv. 13-20).

v. 1 *shout joyfully:* the psalmist invites all men to praise God because of His "tremendous deeds" (v. 3), particularly the deliverance from Egypt in the past (1300 B.C.), and the deliverance from the Babylonian captivity in times more immediate (539 B.C.).

v. 6 *the sea into dry land:* an allusion to the miraculous passage through the Red Sea (cf. Exod. 14), followed by an allusion to the miraculous passage of the Israelites through the Jordan (Jos. 3:9-14) under Joshua.

v. 7 *he rules:* God, the eternal King of the world, watching lest the nations rebel against Him. This is the typical prophetic conception of God as the Maker of history.

v. 10 *you have tested us:* purifying by tribulation, as gold and silver are purified by fire, is a frequent biblical comparison (cf. Ps. 12:7; Is. 1:23; Is. 48:10). Internal evidence from expressions and language used indicate the author refers to the Babylonian exile and return.

v. 12 *you let men ride over:* to tread upon the head of an enemy is a sign of absolute domination (cf. Is. 51:23; Jos. 10:24; Gen. 3:15). "Fire and water" denote great dangers of every kind (cf. Is. 43:2). "Refreshment" refers to the end of the exile.

v. 13 *your house:* the Temple where the "vows" (v. 13b) made in the time of peril are now being fulfilled.

v. 16 *hear now . . . while I declare:* custom required that while fulfilling vows, the worshipper should review for those gathered about in the Temple the circumstances leading to his prayer, promise, and deliverance (cf. Ps. 116:10-19).

v. 18 *wickedness:* the psalmist realizes God hears only the prayer of an upright heart; and since God has heard his prayer, it proves his uprightness and forgiveness.

v. 20 *blessed:* an outburst of praise and thanksgiving to God who has shown toward him His unfailing love.

4. Didactic Historical Psalms

Properly speaking, didactic psalms treat of the law or some aspect of the relations between man and his God as revealed in the law. Pss. 50; 105; 106; 111; 78 and the Canticle of Moses (Deut. 32) treat of the law only indirectly, but they were unquestionably composed to teach – Ps. 50 by a prophetic lesson on the true nature of sacrifice; Pss. 105; 106; 111; 78, and the Canticle of Moses, by means of a commemorative review of Israel's history in such a way that those who said these prayers would draw salutary lessons from the history of their people and apply the lessons to themselves.

The method of these psalmists is similar to that of St. Paul in 1 Cor. 10:1-11; in that passage incidents from Israel's history are described as a warning for the Christians of Corinth, who are reminded "all these things happened to them (the Israelites of the past) as a type, and they were written for our correction, upon whom the final age of the world has come."

The format of the didactic historical psalms varies, but it usually includes some kind of an introduction, followed by a series of incidents from Israel's history from which the psalmist draws a moral for his hearers.

In Ps. 50 the psalmist opposes the delusion of those who believe that God can be propitiated by the mere externals of the cult prescribed in Leviticus without internal dispositions of sincere love, praise, and obedience. In Ps. 105, the psalmist dilates on the fidelity of God in keeping His part of the Sinai promises, implicitly calling upon his hearers to correspond to this fidelity by fidelity to their part of the Sinai pact. Ps. 111 presents the great works of God in behalf of Israel and shows that wisdom consists in contemplation of these works and in worship of their Divine author. Pss. 106 and 78 expressly cite the defections of Israelites in the past as due to a lack of loving trust in God and exhort all to put full trust and confidence in God for the future. In the Canticle of Moses (Deut. 32), the psalmist reviews Israel's history of backsliding and admonishes his hearers to learn from the punishments inflicted on their forefathers to put all their hope for the future in God.

Psalm 50

Theme	A didactic psalm teaching the insufficiency of external cult without corresponding internal dispositions of praise and obedience.
Background	Lev. 1–7 for the external cult; Is. 1:10-20; Hosea 6:6; Mich. 6:6-8; Amos 5:21-24 for the necessity of internal sentiments of religion in cult.

Division

1. God, described with Sinai stage-props, comes to judge His people (vv. 1-6).
2. God does not need or desire purely external cult; He demands sincere praise and obedience to His law (vv. 7-15).
3. Formalism and merely lip worship is excoriated (vv. 16-21).
4. Let them render God true internal worship or suffer the consequences (vv. 22-23).

v. 2ff *from Zion:* using imagery from the Sinai theophany (Exod. 19), the psalmist describes God coming from His Temple on Zion to judge His sinful people (cf. Ps. 18:8-16 and Ps. 76).

v. 8 *not for your sacrifices:* sacrifices are plentiful, but God has no need of material sacrifices. He needs (poetic license), rather, love and praise. God does not say that sacrifices are not good; they are good. It is rather the typical Hebrew way of expressing what is essential as compared to what is accidental (compare St. Paul in 1 Cor. 1:17, "Christ did not send me to baptize but to preach").

v. 10 *for mine are all:* God's complaint is that the people think all He wants are the external offerings. As if He did not own the world and all in it. What he wants is the soul of sacrifice: praise, adoration, love — their private promises to offer up thanksgiving sacrifices, those offerings mentioned in Lev. 7:11-20 requiring ritual purity and sentiments of love and gratitude.

v. 15 *I will rescue you:* this verse shows they are suffering some kind of punishment, and God does not hear their prayer for help because it is not sincere. Verses 7, 21, 22 confirm the fact that the psalmist is writing at a particular time, in a concrete situation, when the people, praying for help and not obtaining it, are carrying out all the externals of worship but without interior sentiments of love and obedience (cf. Is. 1:10-20; and Jer. 7:1-9).

v. 16ff *why do you recite:* they mouth God's commands, but hate His "discipline" (v. 17), i.e., the observance of the moral law, ethical correction. They offer sacrifice, then go out and steal, fornicate, lie and even plot murder against their own brothers (vv. 18-20; cf. Jer. 7:8 11).

Psalm 105

Theme	A didactic historical hymn praising God for the fulfillment of His promises to Israel.
Background	Genesis, Exodus, and Numbers: the joyful mysteries of Israel's history.
Division	1. Joyful invitation to praise God for His wonders in behalf of Israel (vv. 1-7).

Psalm 105

Theme A didactic historical hymn praising God for the fulfillment of His promises to Israel.

Background Genesis, Exodus, and Numbers: the joyful mysteries of Israel's history.

Division
1. Joyful invitation to praise God for His wonders in behalf of Israel (vv. 1-7).
2. The first of these wonders: the covenant with Abraham (vv. 8-11).
3. God's providential protection of the patriarchs (vv. 12-15).
4. Providential history of Joseph (vv. 16-22).
5. Entrance of the Israelites into Egypt (vv. 23-24).
6. Providential call of Moses and Aaron (vv. 25-27).
7. God intervenes against the Egyptians by means of the plagues (vv. 28-38).
8. Miracles of the Exodus in favor of the Israelites (vv. 39-43).
9. Conquest of the promised land fulfills promise made to Abraham (vv. 44-45).

N.B. Probably written during the Babylonian exile (587-539 B.C.), the psalmist's purpose is to remind the people that God has kept His part of the Abrahamitic covenant; now let Israel live up to her part (cf. v. 45).

v. 1ff *give thanks:* note the profusion of verbs of joy. As reasons for this joyful praise, the psalmist will detail the great things God has done for Israel: the call of Abraham, the special care lavished on the patriarchs, the miracles of the exodus, and the conquest.

v. 4 *look to the Lord:* is the Hebrew way of saying, "Seek to please God." God is pictured as watching, smiling when pleased, turning away when displeased.

v. 6 *descendants of Abraham, his servants, sons, chosen ones:* proud titles of the Israelites.

v. 8 *his covenant, oath:* synonyms for the pact made with Abraham (cf. Deut. 7:9; Gen. 17:2; 26:2-6; 28:13; Luke 1:33), promising to them Canaan (v. 11) as their own land and national home.

v. 12 *they were few:* the patriarchal families, small in number, living a nomadic life in a strange land, were protected from enemies by God; e.g., when Abraham went down to Egypt (Gen. 12); to Gerar (Gen. 20); at Shechem (Gen. 34). On these occasions God "rebuked kings" (v. 14) who intended evil (Gen. 12:17; 20:3-7).

v. 15 *my prophets:* the patriarchs were considered prophets because they received visions from God (cf. Gen. 20:7), and "anointed" because as heads of the tribe they were the equivalent of kings who were regularly, along with the priests, anointed with oil.

v. 16 *famine:* the famine predicted by Joseph (Gen. 41:53), which afflicted Palestine as well as Egypt. *he sent:* Joseph had been carried off to Egypt (Gen. 37:38). Note how everything is referred to God as the first and providential cause (cf. Gen. 45:5-7).

v. 18 *fetters:* Putiphar's wife had Joseph thrown in prison. In prison Joseph's prediction (v. 19) about the seven fat and lean years (Gen. 41:12-14) resulted in that the king sent and freed him, making him viceroy of Egypt (Gen. 41:40ff).

v. 23 *Israel came:* the coming of Jacob and his sons to Egypt (Gen. 46:6). "The land of Ham" — the popular name for Egypt.

v. 24 *he greatly increased:* under the patronage of Joseph, with the best of the land in Goshen plus the extraordinary Hebrew fertility, the tribes increased to proportions of a people (Exod. 1:7), so much so that the Egyptians feared them. *stronger than their foes:* anticipation of the inability of the Egyptians to destroy the Hebrews.

v. 25 *whose hearts:* the change in attitude of the Egyptians, particularly that of the Pharaoh, leads to oppression (Exod. 1) and to attempts to decimate the male Hebrews (Exod. 1:10).

v. 26 *he sent Moses:* the providential preparation of Moses in the court of Pharaoh to be the liberator of his people from bondage (Exod. 2–4).

v. 27ff *wonders in the land of Ham:* the plagues (Exod. 7–12). Allusions to the plagues will be made again in Pss. 106 and 78. Note that here as throughout the psalm, the author emphasizes God as the agent, because it is God's wondrous works for Israel that he is presenting as motives for praise and for a return of fidelity.

v. 39ff *he spread a cloud:* the pillar of the cloud by which God guided the Israelites (Exod. 13:21); the quail (Exod. 16), the manna and "the water like a stream" (v. 14), a hyperbolic allusion to the miracle of the water in the desert (Exod. 17), were all wonders of the Exodus period.

v. 42ff *for he remembered:* the psalmist refers all the miracles to the promise made to Abraham, fulfilled in the Exodus from Egypt under Moses and the constitution of Israel as a theocratic nation (cf. Exod. 2:24). Verses 42-45 sum up the psalm.

v. 44 *the lands of the nations:* before the conquest by Joshua, Palestine was inhabited by various peoples: Canaanites, Jebusites, Philistines, etc.

v. 45 *that they might keep:* the purpose of the psalm has been to show how God faithfully kept His part of the covenant. Now it is up to Israel to keep her part — the observance of the divine law given at Sinai (Exod. 19–24).

Psalm 106

Theme   A didactic historical psalm showing how the sorrowful events in Israel's history resulted from their rebellions against God.

Background   Exodus, Numbers, and Judges: the sorrowful mysteries of Israel's history.

Division   Part A. The psalmist invites all to praise God (vv. 1-5).

Part B. The history of Israel's rebellions against God (vv. 6-39).

1. Rebellion at the Red Sea in the time of the Exodus —
   Exod. 14 (vv. 6-12).
2. Murmuring against God, demanding food — Exod. 16;
   Num. 11 (vv. 13-15).
3. Rebellion of Dathan and Abiram — Num. 16 (vv. 16-
   18).
4. Golden calf incident at Sinai — Exod. 32 (vv. 19-23).
5. Revolt on the borders of the Promised Land — Num.
   14 (vv. 24-27).
6. Idolatry and immorality at Baal of Peor — Num. 25 (vv.
   28-31).
7. Demand for water at Kadesh — Num. 20 (vv. 32-33).
8. Disobedience after entering the Promised Land — Judg.
   passim (vv. 34-39).

Part C. Summation and theological schema of the book
of Judges (vv. 40-47).

N.B. Ps. 106 is in the nature of a national confession of sins,
whereby the Israelites of the Babylonian captivity admit
they have sinned as did their fathers (cf. v. 6). In the
name of the nation, the psalmist calls on all to praise God,
pointing out in v. 3 the joy of those who keep God's commands. He does this because in the rest of the psalm he is
going to show how their punishments have been a result
of their not observing God's laws. Implicit is Christ's teaching: "He who has my commands and keeps them, he it is
who loves me" (John 14:21). Verses 5, 27, 47 point to an
author writing either during the Babylonian exile or later
on in the Dispersion.

v. 6 *we have sinned:* the psalmist likens the present generation
to their forefathers. Note how the psalmist comes back
to this idea (vv. 6-7, 13-14, 16, 21, 24, 32). Like St. Paul
(1 Cor. 10:1-11), he uses history to teach his lesson.

v. 7ff *considered not:* ingratitude and rebellion at the Red Sea
(Exod. 14:10), where God worked a miracle for His
people (Exod. 14:21-31), rescuing them from the Egyptians, so that as a result "they sang his praises" (v. 12),
the Canticle of Moses (Exod. 15).

v. 13ff *soon:* this would indicate an event not too long after the
wonders of the Exodus, probably the grumbling at Marah
(Exod. 15:22) and in the desert of Sin (Exod. 16:1ff). As

punishment for this complaining, God sent upon them a plague (v. 15). The psalmist seems to include here a later similar episode mentioned in Num. 11:20.

v. 16 *they envied Moses:* the rebellion of Dathan and Abiram (Num. 16).

v. 19ff *a calf, a molten image:* the golden calf made by Aaron for the Israelites in the desert contrary to the first stipulation of the decalogue (Exod. 20:4; 34:17). *their glory:* the theophanic glory of Sinai where God manifested Himself to the Israelites (v. 20). In place of this, they take the golden calf (cf. Ps. 3:3; Exod. 19; 32). *great deeds* (v. 21): the miracles of the Exodus.

v. 24ff *they despised the desirable land:* the rebellion on the borders of the Promised Land (Num. 14). Pusillanimous and faithless, the people refused to put their trust in God (v. 24b). As a punishment for murmuring against Him and refusing to have confidence in Him, God condemns all over twenty years of age to die in the desert (v. 26).

v. 28ff *Baal of Peor:* idolatry and immorality of the people who took part in the obscene rites connected with the cult of Baal of Peor, the Canaanite god worshipped in Moab (Num. 25).

v. 30 *Phinehas:* the Israelite hero who helped to put an end to the rebellion.

v. 32f MERIBAH: the Israelites complained against God because of the drought (Num. 20), and the place was called the Waters of Contradiction (Meribah). Even Moses and Aaron became guilty of some sin on this occasion. *N.B.* The incident is similar though distinct from Exod. 17, the waters of temptation (Massah), an event which took place at Rephidim in the desert of Sin in the first weeks after the Exodus from Egypt. Here they are at Kadesh.

v. 34ff *they did not exterminate the peoples:* commanded to exterminate the Canaanites after their entrance into the Promised Land (Exod. 23:32-33; 34:12), the Israelites disobeyed. Commanded not to intermarry (v. 35), they intermarried with them (Judg. 3:5). As a result, they were perverted by the Canaanites, worshipped their idols (v.

36), practiced infant sacrifice (v. 37), and in general were unfaithful to their Sinai promises.

v. 40ff *the Lord grew angry:* because of their sins, God leaves His people to the invasions and oppression of pagan neighbors. Vv. 40-45 sum up the teaching of the book of Judges: obedience brings blessings, disobedience brings punishment (cf. Judg. 2 and the theological schema of the author of Judges: sin, punishment, repentance, liberation).

v. 46 *compassion:* despite their falls, rebellions, and ingratitude, God loves His people and never utterly abandons them. Rather, He sees to it that even their very captors and oppressors treat them kindly (cf. the treatment of the deported Jews by the Babylonians, Persians, and later on the Romans).

v. 47 *from among the nations:* a plea to be delivered from exile. Internal evidence points to the origin of the psalm in the period of the Babylonian exile (587-539).

v. 48 *blessed be the Lord:* the doxology added by an editor to bring to an end the fourth book of the Psalter.

Psalm 111

Theme
A didactic hymn praising God for His wonderful works which are to be meditated upon by individuals and commemorated liturgically.

Background
Exodus and Numbers; a digest of Pss. 105–106.

Division
The psalm is alphabetic in form, i.e., each verse in the Hebrew begins with a successive letter of the alphabet (cf. Knox's translation).

v. 2 *exquisite:* God's works are worthy of being studied, investigated, scrutinized by all who love Him. Different translations attempt to bring out the sense of the Hebrew: "Exquisite for all who love him are his works"; "giving pleasure to all who study their purpose"; "satisfying all the desires of the just." In vv. 5-9, the psalmist examines four particular works of God: the manna (v. 5), giving of the Promised Land (v. 6), giving of the law on Sinai (vv. 7-8), liberation from captivity (v. 9).

v. 3 *majesty and glory:* in Hebrew, because of a paucity of adjectives, nouns are used in place of adjectives. Here the psalmist's idea is: "Glorious and majestic is God's work."

v. 4 *renown:* God wants His works remembered and commemorated (cf. Exod. 12:24). Note the same command by our Lord at the Last Supper with regard to the Eucharist: "Do this in commemoration of me" (Matthew 26:26-30; Luke 22:20). The second part of this verse, "gracious and merciful is the Lord," derives from the words of Moses after he received forgiveness for the people at Mount Sinai (Exod. 34:6).

v. 5 *he has given food:* manna in the desert (Exod. 16). Following St. John (ch. 6), the Church accommodates these words to the Eucharist.

v. 5 *his covenant:* the pact promised in Gen. 3:15, initiated in Gen. 15, expanded in Exod. 34:10 was completed at the Last Supper when Jesus said: "This cup is the *new covenant* in my Blood, which shall be shed for you" (Luke 22:26).

v. 6 *he has made known . . . power:* as He had promised (Exod. 34:11-13), God Himself saw to it that the Canaanites were driven from Palestine so that He might give it as a possession to His people.

v. 7 *his precepts:* the laws God gave to Moses, especially the decalogue, but also the law in general, i.e., revelation as a whole.

v. 9 *deliverance:* redemption from bondage in Egypt and Babylon, foreshadowings of our redemption from sin wrought by Christ on Calvary, the true Passover.

v. 10 *the fear of the Lord:* reverence for God, the Hebrew equivalent for our word "religion."

Theme

A didactic historical psalm instructing the faithful to trust unreservedly in God and to learn from the sins of their forefathers, particularly the Ephraimites, not to rebel against God.

Background

The psalmist takes his object lessons from the history contained in Exodus, Numbers, Joshua, Judges, 1 and 2 Samuel and 1 Kings, beginning with the Exodus and ending with the building of the Temple (v. 69).

Division

A prologue explains the author's purpose to make use of historical parables to draw from Israel's history lessons of trust, obedience, and fidelity (vv. 1-8). Six parables follow:

1. Their ancestors' lack of trust in God at the time of the Exodus — Exod. (vv. 9-16).
2. Failure of their ancestors to trust in God to provide for their needs in the desert — cf. Exod. 16—17; Num. 11 and 20 (vv. 17-31).
3. Fickleness and servility of their ancestors in the desert — Num. 14—21 (vv. 32-39).
4. Their ancestors' forgetfulness of God's miraculous interventions against Pharaoh by means of the plagues (Exod. 7—12), and of His bringing them into the Promised Land (vv. 40-55).
5. Rebellions of their ancestors in the time of the Judges, and God's displeasure with the Ephraimites manifested in the destruction of Shiloh — Judg. and Sam. 1—4 (vv. 56-64).
6. God's choice of Judah and David in place of the rebellious Ephraimites — 1 Sam. 5—16 (vv. 65-72).

N.B.

1. The psalmist uses examples from Israel's history to instruct the people of his time just as St. Paul, in 1 Cor. 10:1-10, instructed the Christians of Corinth. For the Jews, as well as for Christians of all times, St. Paul's words concerning Israel's history are true: "All these things happened to them as a type, and they were written for our correction."

2. In Matthew 13:35, Asaph, the author of this psalm, is said to be a figure of Christ. This is to be understood in the sense that in teaching the doctrine of salvation by

means of parables adapted to the intelligence of his hearers, he uses a method which at a later time will be brought to its peak of efficiency in the teaching of Christ.

v. 1 *teaching:* his doctrinal teaching is summed up in vv. 7-8, "that they should put their hope in God," the same doctrine taught by our Lord in the sermon on the Mount: "Be not solicitous. . . ."

v. 2 *in a parable:* Hebrew, *mashal.* The word, *mashal,* has many meanings, most of which can be reduced to a comparison of some kind. In this case, it is an historical comparison, showing the lessons the psalmist sees hidden in the past history of his people.

v. 4 *we will not hide:* the lessons to be drawn from Israel's history are to be passed on, according to the law of Moses (Exod. 12:24-26; Deut. 4:9-11; 6:4-7), to all future ages of the faithful. In a similar manner, Jesus commanded that the Gospel be preached to every creature.

v. 7 *that they should put their hope in God:* the lesson to be imparted by the six historical parables that follow, taken from Israel's sorrowful mysteries.

v. 9 *the sons of Ephraim:* in this section, as throughout, the psalmist is speaking of all the Israelites and not just the Ephraimites, even though the Ephraimites are a prime example. Note that in this and the other strophes, the psalmist begins, as in Ps. 106, with an emphasis on the rebellious spirit of the Israelites (cf. vv. 9-10, 17, 32, 40, 56).

v. 12 *Zoan:* the city on the eastern bank of the Nile near the land of Goshen, where many of the miracles of the Exodus took place.

v. 13 *he cleft the sea:* the passage through the Red Sea (cf. Exod. 14:21; 15:8).

v. 16 *from the crag:* water from the rock in the desert (cf. Exod. 15:24; Num. 20:7-13). In 1 Cor. 10:4 St. Paul associates the "rock" with Christ.

v. 17ff *in the wasteland:* the psalmist points to the failure of the Israelites in the desert to trust in God to provide for them, thus driving home his moral of v. 7. Most of the historical allusions here are from either Exod. 16—17 or Num. 11 and 20.

v. 32ff *they sinned still more:* alluding to incidents recorded in Num. 11—21, such as the revolt of Miriam, Dathan, Abiram, Korah, the burning serpents, etc., the psalmist emphasizes the fickle faith of the Israelites during the long trek from Sinai to the Promised Land. When they turned back to God, their conversion, as the psalmist shows, was only half-hearted, a lip service based on a servile fear rather than firm trust.

v. 43ff *his signs in Egypt:* in vv. 40-55, the psalmist gives a synopsis of the plagues of Egypt (Exod. 7—14), explaining Israel's lack of trust in God as flowing from their forgetfulness of His great display of power there.

v. 55ff *he drove out nations before them:* the conquest under Joshua was followed by Israel's mixing with the Canaanites and practicing idolatry. As a result they were punished (vv. 58-59) by the Philistine oppression (Judg. *passim*) and by the destruction of their sanctuary at Shiloh (1 Sam. 1—4). *his glory* (v. 61) refers to the Ark of the Covenant captured by the Philistines (1 Sam. 4).

v. 63 *fire:* metaphor for war, fire of war, fire of God's anger. Here the author is speaking of the Philistine victory over Israel in the time of Eli (1 Sam. 3—4).

v. 65 *as a champion:* by an unusually bold figure of speech, God in His victory over the Philistines at the time of David is compared to a warrior who, aroused from a drunken torpor, goes out swinging his sword in a frenzy, demolishing enemies on every side (cf. Ps. 110:5-7; 68: 22-24; Is. 63:1-4).

v. 66 *to flight:* literally, the Hebrew reads "he struck his foes back," which could refer to the plague of hemorrhoids suffered by the Philistines in the time of David after their capture of the Ark (1 Sam. 5:6), or to the rout of the Philistine army, fleeing before their enemies who strike at them from behind. In this one line, the psalmist sums up the defeats of the Philistines, who were definitively defeated only in the time of David.

v. 67 *he rejected the tent of Joseph:* one of the "mysteries from of old" (v. 2) which the psalmist through his philosophy of history explains in this psalm is God's rejection of the great and self-reliant Ephraimites (descendants of Joseph) in favor of the humble, unimportant Judean, David. Thus he ends with David, the man after God's own heart, as a positive illustration of one of those who "put their hope in God" (cf. 1 Sam. 16).

v. 69 *his shrine like heaven:* hyperbole to express the greatness of the Temple of Solomon in Jerusalem (1 Kings 5–8). The allusion to the Temple would show the psalm was written after the time of Solomon (965-926) and before the destruction of the Temple in 587 B.C.

The Nash Papyrus, from the second century B.C., giving the Ten Commandments and the Shema 'Yisra' el.

The

Deuteronomist's History

4

The Deuteronomist's History

1. The Deuteronomist's History as a Whole

In the five books of the Pentateuch it is evident that the author is not interested in a general history of ancient times but in the theological history of the Israelite nation. Even in the history of Israel he hews to the line of a principle of selection, choosing for the record events in which the finger of God is manifest in his nation's history. Where this is not so, as for example in the four hundred years in Egypt between Joseph and Moses, the author says little or nothing. If we look for the basic conviction underlying this principle of selection, we find it in the ineradicable belief of the inspired author, based on the revelation made to Moses and the patriarchs, that God has destined Israel to be the instrument by means of which He will bring about the reparation of the primal revolt and the reestablishment of His reign in the world.

The initial indication of this divine plan is given in the protoevangelium (Gen. 3:15), where it is stated that mankind, the seed of the woman, will someday triumph over the forces of evil. In the promise made to Abraham, "I will make a great nation of you . . . in you shall all the nations of the earth be blessed" (Gen. 12:2-3), the identification is made of the instrument through which God will bring about this triumph: it will be through the descendants of Abraham.

In the course of the centuries this group expands, and from its nucleus in the time of Moses a nation is born. From the universal seed of the woman one nation has been selected — a unique theocratic nation — "a kingdom of priests, a holy nation" (Exod. 19:6). With the establishment of this "kingdom of priests," the first broad outline or pattern is drawn. The triumph will be brought about by means of a theocratic kingdom called to imitate the holiness of the all-holy God and led by men, prophets, and eventually kings, who are to be the human vicars of the divine King. The theocratic kingdom might almost be called a church in the proper sense except for its restrictive note of nationalism.

As the Pentateuch comes to an end the question of *how* the triumph of the seed of the woman over the seed of the serpent will be accomplished is still unanswered. There are indications that it will be through the exercise of obedience based upon faith. Abraham, the recipient of the covenant, is called to believe and to obey. The nation in its turn, when the covenant is extended to it, is called to follow in the footsteps of the great patriarch.

The function of the Deuteronomist's history

That the nation fails we know from the testimony of the next group of inspired writings: the Deuteronomist's history, composed of Joshua, Judges, Samuel, and Kings, sometimes referred to as "the Former Prophets." It is the function of these books, however, to relate more than the failure of Israel. They give us new revelation concerning the divine plan for the redemption of mankind. To the promise of triumph through a chosen group, they add the promise of triumph through a dynasty, the Davidic dynasty, from which in the fullness of time will come the Messiah. In him all Israel's hopes for the future will be placed. How he will conquer is not revealed, only that he will certainly conquer, and that through him the promises made to Israel will be extended to mankind. It will be the function of the latter prophets and the Chronicler's history (1 and 2 Chronicles, Ezra and Nehemiah) to focus attention on the Messiah as an individual.

The Former Prophets relate the history of the national theocratic kingdom that failed. The Latter Prophets (Isaiah, Jeremiah, Ezekiel, Daniel, and the twelve minor prophets) tell of him through whom the failure will be swallowed up in victory and the victory extended to all the "seed of the woman." We deal with the Former Prophets first.

The nature of the Deuteronomist's history

The significance of the history narrated in the books of Joshua, Judges, Samuel, and Kings can easily escape the unwary reader. The authors of the source material found in the five parts of the sixth century Deuteronomist's history, all of whom wrote at different times and for different specific reasons, had nevertheless the same general purpose in view: *to give God's viewpoint on Israel's history*. It is because they gave God's inspired judgment on their nation's history that the Jewish exegetes rightly called them prophets, referring to them as the "Former Prophets" in contradistinction to those other prophets, whose words were first preached and later committed to writing, and who are known as the "Latter Prophets."

It would be a mistake, therefore, to look upon the Former Prophets primarily as collectors of facts intent on giving a rounded, detailed, and scientifically documented history. Like the author of the Pentateuch who went before them, they are not interested in a general history of the times nor even in a general factual history of Israel. They are interested in and relate the interventions of God in Israel's history and Israel's response to those interventions.

We cannot say they gave *an* interpretation of Israel's history, because this might imply there could be another, and perhaps better, interpretation. Speaking under inspiration, they gave *the* interpretation: God's revealed explanation of what He expected of His people, what He received in response, and how, despite a pitiful response to His love and guidance, He did not abandon His people but continued patiently to correct their aberrations and lead them in His own way to the fulfillment of their destiny.

The interpretation of Israel's history given by the Former Prophets is not labeled as an interpretation. It is given in an historical form and, though there are frequent explicit formulations of doctrine, the authors for the most part make their message known either by their discreet emphasis on certain facets of Israel's history or by indicating through their choice of episodes the providential arrangement of events to an end predetermined by God.

In Joshua, for example, the author's purpose is to show that God was faithful to His covenant promise of providing a homeland for His people. The author narrates the history of Joshua's conquest of Palestine through which God made good this promise. Implicitly Israel is called upon to be faithful to her part of the covenant.

In Judges, the author shows how the covenant promises made to Israel worked out in practice. In return for fidelity to the covenant, God had promised peace and prosperity; in return for infidelity, oppression and punishment. This teaching is explicitly formulated in Judg. 2, and then exemplified in the history of the twelve judges (Judg. 3–16).

In the books of Samuel, the author's purpose is to show the establishment of the Davidic dynasty and its permanency based upon God's promise to David through the prophet Nathan. To prove these points, the author recounts the institution of the monarchy; the rejection of the first king, Saul, because of his failure to measure up to God's standards; the divine protection accorded David in his days of persecution and in the establishment of his reign over the twelve tribes, coming to his climax in the solemn promise of perpetuity made to David's dynasty by the prophet Nathan (2 Sam. 7).

In Kings, the author's purpose is to explain how the fall of the kingdom resulted from the infidelity of the kings to the covenant. To do this he writes a history showing how, with the exception of three or four kings, all the kings were unfaithful.

While the authors do not positively describe the ideal state of the theocratic kingdom as it is presented in Deuteronomy, it is nevertheless clear that they are dominated by the prophetic teachings enunciated in Deuteronomy; and that the positive picture of the theocratic kingdom in their minds, against which they measure the failings of Israel and the kings, is the picture presented in the book of Deuteronomy.

Since the spirit of the Deuteronomic author pervades the Former Prophets, we can rightly speak of their combined writings as the Deuteronomist's history of Israel. Completed in the middle of the sixth century B.C., the history covers 700 years, from Joshua in the thirteenth century to Jehoiachin, the last king of Judah, in the middle of the sixth.

In its completed form as we have it now, the history is a vast compilation of oral and written accounts including popular narratives, eyewitness biographies, chronicles of the kings, prophetic cycles, documents, inventories and tax reports from the royal archives. Unlike modern authors, the Deuteronomist historian does not fuse his sources into a composed, unified, and freely flowing narrative. For the most part, the sources are taken *en bloc* and arranged in an order sometimes dictated by chronology but more often by the didactic aims of the author. As a result, the reader often finds duplicated narratives. This is particularly evident in 1 Samuel where fragments from different sources have been combined to narrate the origin of the monarchy and the early history of David. It is even more evident in the whole complexus of the Deuteronomist's history in which the final, exilic author-editor repeats on a grand scale, by the arrangement and linking together of Joshua, Judges, Samuel, and Kings, what the individual authors had already done in the compilation of their own more restricted histories.

As a literary work, the Deuteronomist's history is primitive both in its arrangement and in its style. It lacks the order, composition, and continuity of ancient Greek and modern, scientific historical works. Theologically speaking, the Deuteronomist's history is God's view of one nation's history against basic revealed principles valid in their broad outline for all history. If, as Pius XI has defined it, "history is the living tissue of facts, the tissue wherein the thoughts and deeds of man and God unite, mix, cross each other, always with the final result that a marvellous, providential plan is wrought, in which the divine sovereignty dominates all, and the love of God for man is manifest," then the Deuteronomist's history is in its own way, like the Pentateuch, one of the first and most perfect histories ever written.

The basic principles of the Deuteronomist's history

The Deuteronomist's history shows the influence of numerous authors throughout, but of no author so often and so pervasively as the author of Deuteronomy. Upon revealed principles enunciated in their clearest form by him, each of the Former Prophets in one way or the other depends. These principles can be stated succinctly as follows:

1. God is unswervingly faithful to His promises (Deut. 9:1-6; 26:16-19).
2. Observance of the covenant is rewarded, non-observance is punished (Deut. 11:26-32; 28; 20:15-20 and *passim*).
3. God and God alone must be adored (Deut. 4:15; 6:4-19 *passim*).
4. God is to be worshipped only in Jerusalem (Deut. 12:1-14).
5. The prophets are God's spokesmen and must be obeyed (Deut. 18).

The Deuteronomist's history as a whole

Part One / Joshua

Theme	The conquest and division of the Promised Land.
Purpose	To demonstrate God's fidelity in giving His people a homeland in accordance with the Sinai promises, and to inculcate obedience to the covenant on the part of the people.
Division	1—12 The conquest of Canaan. 13—21 The division of the land among the twelve tribes. 22—24 The return of the Transjordan tribes and Joshua's **farewell**.

Part Two / Judges

Theme The exploits of the Judges in saving Israel from destruction.

Purpose To show by examples from the period of the Judges how God punishes betrayal of the covenant and how infallible is His help to save Israel when she repents and returns to Him.

Division
1–3 The incomplete conquest opens the way to corruption of Israel by her pagan neighbors. The author's theological schema.
3–16 The exploits of the judges raised up by God to save repentant Israel from destruction.
17–21 Appendix concerning the tribes of Dan and Benjamin during the disorganized and anarchic period of the judges.

Part Three / Samuel

Theme The institution of the monarchy in Israel and the permanency of the royal power in the dynasty of David.

Purpose To establish the legitimacy of the Davidic dynasty.

Division
1–7 The judgeship of Samuel and the Philistine oppression.
8–15 The institution of the human kings and the rejection of Saul.
16–31 The early history of David, first favored, later persecuted by King Saul.
1–4 David, king over Judah alone after the death of Saul.
5–20 David, king over all Israel; his dynasty assured in perpetuity (ch. 7); his family history (9–20).
21–24 Appendix containing assorted documents about David.

Part Four / Kings

Theme Israel's kings' infidelity to the covenant and Temple.

Purpose To show that the kings' infidelity had brought destruction and that Israel's hope rests now upon the fulfillment of the Nathan oracle in 2 Sam. 7.

Division	1 Kings 1–11 The reign of Solomon (965-926).
	1 Kings 12–2 Kings 17 The division of the kingdom in 926 and a synoptic history of the kings of north and south down to the fall of the northern kingdom in 722.
	2 Kings 18–25 The last kings of Judah, the fall of Jerusalem and the Babylonian exile.

Chronology of the Deuteronomist's history

1250-1225 Joshua's conquest of Canaan (Jos. 1–12).

1225-1025 Period of the Judges (Judg. 3–16).

1025-1005 Institution of the monarchy (1 Sam. 8–12); reign of King Saul (13–31).

1005-965 Reign of King David (2 Sam. 1–1 Kings 2).

965-926 Reign of Solomon (1 Kings 1–11). Writing of David's court history (2 Sam. 9–20 and 1 Kings 1–2).

926-722 From the division of the kingdom of Solomon to the fall of the city of Samaria and the deportation of the citizens of the northern kingdom to Assyria in 722 (1 Kings 12–2 Kings 17). Probably the first editions of Joshua, Judges, Samuel were composed shortly after the fall of the northern kingdom.

926-587 From the division of the kingdom of Solomon to the fall of the southern kingdom to the Babylonians in 587 (1 Kings 12–2 Kings 25).

700-621 Probable time of the composition of Deuteronomy during the last years of Hezekiah (c. 700); and the finding of the book in the Temple (2 Kings 22:8ff) during the reign of Josiah in 621.

562-400 Writing of the books of Kings shortly after 562, the last date mentioned in the book (2 Kings 25:27). Final revision and edition of the Former Prophets, during or after the exile, by an editor greatly influenced by Deuteronomy and Jeremiah.

2. The Geography of Palestine

At the very beginning of the book of Joshua, Yahweh says to Joshua: "Your domain is to be all the land of the Hittites, from the desert and from

Lebanon east to the great river Euphrates and west to the Great Sea" (Jos. 1:4). Since the land of Canaan will be the scene of the vast majority of events narrated in the remainder of the Bible, it will be no small help for the student to study briefly the geography of Palestine before entering the country with Joshua and the Israelites.[1]

Properly speaking biblical geography consists in a description of all the regions in which the events narrated in the Bible took place. This would include Mesopotamia, Egypt, Greece, Cyprus, Turkey, and Persia and would be beyond the scope of this book. It will be sufficient, however, for the present, to concentrate on Palestine: its boundaries, size, division, climate, seasons, products, forests, and peoples.

Boundaries

The ideal boundaries of the Promised Land, realized only during the reigns of David and Solomon, extend on the north from Tyre on the coast inland to Dan. On the east the land is bounded by the desert and on the west by the Mediterranean sea. On the south-east the country is bounded by the river Arnon east of the Dead Sea and on the south by a line that runs from the river of Egypt on the coast inland to Kadesh-barnea and from there to the Arabah, the valley gorge that extends south from the Dead Sea.

Size

In size the Promised Land covers an area totalling about 10,000 square miles, a tiny bit larger than the state of Vermont or just about the size of Lake Erie. In length the distance from Dan on the north to the River of Egypt in the south is approximately 190 miles. In width it is about twenty-five miles from the Lake of Galilee to Acre near Carmel on the coast, and in the south it is about fifty-five miles from the Dead Sea to the Mediterranean.

Divisions of the land

The land can best be described by dividing it into four longitudinal sections: the coastal plain from Byblos on the north to the River of Egypt on the south; the hill country from Mount Lebanon on the north to Beer-sheba on the south; the Jordan valley from the source of the Jordan in the Lebanon mountains near Dan to its terminus in the Dead Sea in the south; and the Transjordan plateau from Bashan in the north to the Arnon River and Edom on the south.

[1] Cf. select bibliography on page 575.

The first of these longitudinal divisions, the coastal plain section, provides a poor coastline for seaports. As a result the inhabitants of Palestine, with the exception of the Phoenicians in the north, turned away from the sea to earn their living off the land by agriculture and husbandry. The Phoenicians, hemmed in by the mountains encroaching almost to the sea, were forced to turn to the sea and despite the limited facilities of their main ports, Byblos, Tyre, and Sidon, became perhaps the most famous mariners of the ancient world. In Palestine proper, the only seaports were Acre a few miles north of Mount Carmel and Joppa, the seaport for Jerusalem, halfway between Carmel and the River of Egypt. Three coastal plains, the plain of Acre north of Carmel, the plain of Sharon between Carmel and Joppa, and the Philistine plain between Joppa and the River of Egypt provided some of the best arable land in Palestine. Between the coastal plains and the mountains of the hill country lay the lowland district of the Shephelah, formed by the broken foothills leading up to the mountain region of Judah, but separated from it by longitudinal valleys. The Shephelah was the first line of defense for Judah on the west.

Hill country

The second of the longitudinal divisions, the hill country, begins only a short distance inland from the coastal plains, rising rapidly to an average height of 2,000 feet above sea level, with mountains running from Syria in the north down the length of Palestine to Beer-sheba and Kadesh-barnea in the south.

In Galilee, the northern section of the hill country, the foothills of the Lebanon range roll gently down to terminate in the flat, fertile valley of Jezreel (Esdraelon), a valley that begins near Carmel on the west and runs in a southeasterly direction almost as far as the Jordan river on the east.

South of the plain of Jezreel, the mountain country of Samaria begins, with the mountains rising from the plain to 1,700 feet above sea level at Mount Gilboa and to 3,000 feet at Mounts Gerizim and Ebal. This hill country continues unbroken from Samaria into Judea, reaching 2,500 feet above sea level at Jerusalem, 3,000 feet at Hebron, and then declining to 1,000 feet at Beer-sheba.

Jordan valley area

The third of the longitudinal sections, the Jordan valley, is part of the great rift or cleft that begins in northern Syria, runs south between Lebanon

16

17

18

19

21

22

23

Nos. 15–26. Megiddo. **15**. Gold-covered bronze statuette from the Late Bronze Age, presumably a representation of Baal. **16**. Zoomorphic vessel from the Early Iron Age, 1200–1100 B.C. **17**. Ivory box with sphinxes and lions in relief; 13th century Megiddo. **18**. Bronze god of war from Canaanite pantheon. **19**. This limestone altar from Megiddo is widely regarded as a cultural type of Canaanite altars of incense; note the four corners or horns. **20**. Axes and adzes of Bronze Age Canaan. **21**. Pottery cooking bowl, brown buff. Well-burnished, red and black decorated, cream-buff pottery jugs. **22**. Reconstructed drawing from an ivory spar from Megiddo, 1350–1150 B.C. **23**. Lamps from the Roman period found at Megiddo. **24**. Reconstructed ivory carved in relief; from Late Bronze II. **25**. The god Reshef brandishing a club; bronze statuette from Early Iron Age, 1200–1100. **26**. Ivory openwork plaque, pupils inlaid with glass; identical in reverse on both sides; Late Bronze II. *Photos courtesy:* Oriental Institute, University of Chicago.

25

26

and Anti-Lebanon down the center of Palestine through the gulf of Aqabah and on into Africa. The Jordan river which flows through half the length of the valley rises at Banias near Caesarea-Philippi (ancient Dan). The river descends rapidly, dropping from 1,000 feet above sea level at Banias to seven feet above sea level at Lake Huleh. In the few miles between the Lakes of Huleh and Galilee the river drops to 675 feet below sea level, then leaving the Lake of Galilee winds down the valley (65 miles as the crow flies, 200 miles on its winding course) to the Dead Sea 1,275 feet below sea level. About ten miles wide, forty-five long, twelve hundred feet deep, the Dead Sea is the deepest body of water below sea level in the world.

Transjordan plateau area

The last of the four longitudinal divisions of Palestine, the plateau of Transjordan, is divided into five sections by four rivers. Thus from north to south, the rivers Yarmuk, Jabbok, Arnon, and Zered divide the plateau into the territories anciently known as Bashan, Gilead, Ammon, Moab, and Edom respectively. From Bashan in the north to Edom in the south the plateau stays an average height of two to three thousand feet above sea level and is so level in sections that it was known and used as a natural highway and called from the earliest times the "King's Highway."

Climate

The climate of Palestine is uneven. Because of its geographical position, thirty degrees to thirty-three and one-half degrees north latitude, the same latitude as southern California, central Georgia, and central Alabama, Palestine is almost a tropical country. The climate, however, varies with the altitude so that a day pleasant in the hill country may be very warm on the coastal plain and unbearably hot in the Jordan valley. Again the west wind from the Mediterranean regularly cools the coast and the mountains in the late afternoon but has no influence on the hot Jordan valley.

Seasons

Palestine has only two seasons, the winter or rainy season from November to April and the dry summer season from May to October. The hottest month is August, the coldest is January. There is no rain between June and September. The first rains, called the early rains, come in October. The heavy seasonal rains fall from December until March. The last rains, called the late rains, fall in April and early May and upon these rains depends the spring harvest between Easter and Pentecost. Failure of these rains for one or two years, or even light rains in place of the usual torrential downpours of the Palestinian winter, has caused famine in the land from the time of Abraham to the present (cf. Gen. 12). Snow is not uncommon in the hill country, and Jerusalem and Bethlehem have been covered with snow several times in recent years. A heavy dew in the morning is frequent in Palestine and greatly appreciated by the people (cf. Deut. 33:28; Ps. 132). After a dewfall the earth in the dry summer may be as wet at dawn as after a light shower.

Fertility and forests

The products of the soil of Palestine spoken of by the Bible include: wheat, barley, grapes, figs, pomegranates, and honey (Deut. 8:8). Undoubtedly many other fruits and vegetables were grown but little is said about them. The land is limited in tillable acreage to the plains of Acre, Sharon, Philistia, Esdraelon, and a few small sections in the hill country. Although in the Bible it is hailed as a land "flowing with milk and honey," which in biblical language means a land provided with an abundance to eat and drink, Palestine is such a paradise only in comparison with the wastelands of the Sinai peninsula and the Negeb, out of which the Israelite nomads had come in the thirteenth century B.C. It is only fertile enough for hard-working farmers to produce sufficient for a comfortable but not easy living.

Never numerous, forests in Palestine are now rare after centuries of cutting without reforestation. At one time, however, there were sizeable forests in Samaria, Bashan, and Edom in addition to the fabled stands of cedar in Lebanon often mentioned in the Bible. All of these have been depleted over the centuries and have begun to be renewed only in modern times.

The people of the land

Biblical authors generally speak of the inhabitants of Palestine either as Amorites or as Canaanites, sometimes applying Amorite to the people of the hill country and Canaanite to the people of the plains (cf. Num. 13:29; Deut. 1:7), but more often using the terms synonymously. These people were Semitic for the most part and spoke a language differing only slightly from the language of the Israelites.

Although the country was in decline in the thirteenth century B.C., its material culture was still impressive and far above that of the semi-nomadic Hebrews. By modern standards their cities were tiny, rarely covering more than five or ten acres, but they were well built with strong fortifications and good drainage; and in larger cities, such as Jerusalem and Megiddo, elaborate tunnels ensured a water supply in the event of a siege. Remains of fine large houses surrounded by hovels indicates a society sharply divided into the very rich and the very poor, with no discernible middle class.

Politically the country was divided into tiny city states, presided over by chieftains who called themselves kings (cf. Jos. 10:1-5) but were for the most part subject to the reigning Pharaoh to whom they paid regular tribute in normal times. Fortunately for Israel, the city states of Palestine were disorganized and helpless in the thirteenth century, due for the most part to an Egyptian foreign policy that kept them purposely disunited and to Egyptian concentration on more urgent affairs at home.

When Israel entered Canaan, the only well organized kingdoms she encountered were the Edomites and the Moabites in Transjordania. These she prudently avoided, preferring with good reason and with eventual success to preserve her strength for the conquest of the hill country. The book of Joshua tells in part the story of that conquest.

3. Joshua

The book of Joshua, the second part of the Deuteronomist's history, is named after its central character somewhat as the name "Caesar" came to be given to Caesar's Gallic Wars. The book takes as its theme the history of the Israelite wars of conquest in Canaan between the years 1250 and 1225 and the subsequent division of the conquered territory among the twelve tribes.[1]

Though written by a different author and at a different time, the action narrated in Joshua links intimately with the last events described in Deuteronomy. Thus in Deut. 34:1-9 the death of Moses and the succession of Joshua is recorded. As the book of Joshua opens, the armies of Israel are camped in the plains of Moab, completing the days of mourning for Moses before advancing to attack Canaan across the Jordan. Joshua, the new leader, is already well known from the Pentateuch. He has been seen there as leader in the war against the Amalekites (Exod. 17), as aide to Moses at Sinai (Exod. 24:13; 32:17), as one of the scouts appointed to reconnoiter the Promised Land (Num. 13:16ff), as the publicly appointed (Num. 27:18) and officially commissioned successor of Moses (Deut. 32:23).

Linked materially by continuity of time, place, and personalities, Joshua is associated formally with Deuteronomy in its purpose which is primarily didactic rather than historical. The author uses the history of the conquest to demonstrate God's fidelity in fulfilling one part of His covenant promises

[1] Cf. CCHS par. 245ff; WHAB 33–39; Bright 117ff; Ricc Hist I par. 279–295; I. Hunt, *The Books of Joshua and Judges*, OTRG, No. 5.

— the promise to the patriarchs (Gen. 15:18ff) and to the nation (Exod. 3:17; 23:23-33; Jos. 1:2ff; 21:41ff; 23:14ff) that He would give them Palestine as their homeland.

Like the author of Deuteronomy in Deut. 7, the author repeats unceasingly the necessity of obedience to God's commands (cf. Jos. 1:6-9; 1:16-18; 6:18; 10:40; 11:15). Moreover, he demonstrates positively that the conquest is the work of God by describing the miracles wrought by God to enable His people to overcome the Canaanites (Jos. 3; 6; 10); and, negatively, by showing that where the armies of Israel fail, it is because of disobedience (cf. Jos. 6:18ff — Achan and the ban; and the Gibeonite alliance, Jos. 9:14ff).

The book of Joshua is divided into three parts: I (1–12) the conquest of Canaan; II (13–21) the division of the Promised Land among the tribes; and III (22–24) the return of the Transjordan tribes and Joshua's farewell address and death.

Significant passages in Joshua

Part One / Jos. 1–12 / The Conquest of Canaan

2:1ff "They went into the house of a harlot named Rahab . . ." Rahab is famous because by her marriage to Salmon, the Judean, she became one of the progenitors of the Messiah (cf. Ruth 4:18-22; Matthew 1:5).

3:1ff The miraculous crossing of the Jordan, predicted in 3:5-13, is described in 3:15-16 as a stoppage of the river at Adamah, 15 miles north of Sittim, and shown to have happened when the Jordan was in flood in 3:15; 4:18 — in the spring therefore. Since we know that on two other occasions in history an overhanging bank collapsed into the Jordan and dammed it up for several hours (for 16 hours in 1276; for 21 hours in 1927), it is not unlikely that a similar cave-in took place providentially at Adamah damming up the river long enough for the Israelite army to pass over to the other side.

6:1-21 The siege and fall of Jericho. Vv. 1-5 relate the unusual military plan for the taking of Jericho; vv. 20-21 the even more unusual success of the plan. Since archeological findings at Jericho tell us nothing about the fall of the city, it is almost impossible to say how the "walls fell down." While it could mean a psychological fall of Jericho's defenses, i.e., surrender, it is more likely that an earthquake (not unusual in the great geological fault of the Jordan valley) aided or brought about the capture of the city.[2]

6:18ff   The prohibition in 6:18 "not to take anything that is under the ban," prepares the reader for the defeat of the Israelites at Ai (7:2-5) as a punishment for Achan's disobedience (7:10-26), and shows negatively that without obedience and without God's help the conquest could not succeed. The "ban" as defined in Num. 18:14 meant the setting aside for destruction of persons, places, or things deemed inimical to the kingdom of God. In Deut. 7:1-4, the Israelites are warned to have nothing to do with the Canaanites lest they compromise their faith and turn to idolatry and the other abominations of the Canaanites. The "ban" or "doom" was one way of preventing this compromise. (For a description of the dangers Israel would encounter in meeting up with Canaanite culture, cf. Num. 25).

9:1-15   Warned in Deut. 7:2 to make no alliances with the Canaanites, the Israelites are tricked into making a treaty with the Gibeonites (Canaanites of the hill country near Jerusalem) and blamed by the inspired author for attempting the alliance "without seeking the advice of the Lord" (9-14).

10:1-27   Besieged by rival Canaanite kings of the Jerusalem hill country, the Gibeonites call on Joshua as a covenanted ally to come to their help (vv. 1-6). Joshua marches his troops up from Gilgal by night and defeats the allied kings. Since it is in the course of this battle that the famous "sun miracle" is supposed to have occurred, it will be helpful for discussion to note that the text contains a prose account (vv. 7-11; 16-27) and a poetic account (vv. 12-15) of the event, and that the sun miracle report is restricted entirely to the poetic section (quoted from the book of Yashar — cf. 10:13).

Whatever the miracle was, it seems clear from both the prose and poetic accounts that Joshua did not need more time. In the poetic description, the sun is over Gibeon, therefore either directly overhead or east of Joshua's position and consequently the hour was no later than noon. The prose report indicates a surprise attack at dawn (v. 9), followed by a great storm (possibly the miraculous heavenly aid poetically described in vv. 12-15; cf. Judg. 5:20), the flight of the kings (v. 16), the end of the battle (vv. 19-20), the kings brought out of the cave (v. 22),

[2] Cf. R. North, "The Walls of Jericho," AER March 1956.

and their execution with their bodies hanged on trees "where they remained hanging until evening" (v. 26) — to all appearances the evening of the same day!

10–11 Ch. 10 relates the conquest of southern Canaan; ch. 11, the conquest of northern Canaan. The description of the conquest completed here is obviously only a brief summary. Realization of this helps toward understanding the principal purpose of the author which was not the narration of all the historical facts but the use of some historical facts to teach a few important truths, namely, the fidelity of God and the necessity of obedience on Israel's part.

Part Two / Jos. 13–21 / The Division of the Land

13:1 ". . . a very large part of the land still remains to be conquered." As indicated here in ch. 13 and in Judg. 1–3, the conquest was by no means complete, and large sections of Canaan (e.g., the Philistine plain, the Canaanite cities along the Phoenician coast, Jerusalem, Megiddo, Beth-shan, and other large cities) held out against the Israelites until the time of David 200 years later.

18:1 The Ark and the Tabernacle are set up in Shiloh, a city in the territory allotted to the tribe of Ephraim some twenty-five miles north of Jerusalem. They remain at Shiloh, which becomes the religious center of Israel (cf. Judg. 21:19 and 1 Sam. 1–3), until the destruction of the city by the Philistines around 1060 (cf. 1 Sam. 4–7).

Part Three / Jos. 22–24 / Joshua's Farewell and Death

22:10ff The building of an altar of their own by the Transjordan tribes is viewed by the other tribes as an act of religious treason. The Transjordan tribesmen explain that the altar is not meant for sacrifices nor as the site of a rival sanctuary, but as a model of the true altar to be used as a means to instruct their children in fidelity to the one true sanctuary beyond the Jordan at Shiloh (vv. 22-29; cf. Deut. 12:4ff).

23:1ff Joshua's final plea to the Israelites is a repetition of the sentiments voiced in Deut. 7:1ff and 32:30ff and, like ch. 1, manifests the influence of the Deuteronomist editor.

24:1ff The solemn ceremony at Shechem is significant not only as a renewal of the Sinai covenant but as the probable means used by the Israelites to amalgamate friendly Canaanites into the covenant kingdom. In relation to the covenant renewal ceremony (cf. p. 24ff) the reader should note the elements characteristic of the Hittite suzerainty pacts upon which the Sinai covenant was patterned: the preamble identifying the author of the covenant in v. 2a, the long historical prologue in vv. 2b-13, the basic stipulation outlawing idolatry in v. 14, the ratification of the covenant in vv. 16-18, 21, 24, the references to witnesses in vv. 22 and 27, and the implicit reference to the deposit of the text of the covenant in the sanctuary in v. 26. In relation to the amalgamation of friendly Canaanites into the covenant kingdom, it is significant that nothing is said in the book of Joshua about the conquest of Shechem. If, as many authors believe, there dwelt in the region around Shechem relatives of the Israelites who remained in Canaan (cf. Gen. 34) when their brethren under Jacob went down to Egypt, then it is not unlikely that these people welcomed the invading Israelites and associated themselves with them. If this hypothesis is sound, the Shechem renewal ceremony suggests the means used by the Israelites to extend the covenant to new tribesmen. Although there is slight evidence to prove it, it seems not unlikely that friendly Canaanites were inducted into the ranks of the Chosen People in the same manner (cf. Bright 122ff; 142ff; J. L. McKenzie, *The World of the Judges*; G. E. Mendenhall, *The Tenth Generation*).

The twelve tribe confederacy

Before closing the book of Joshua, something must be said concerning the organization of Israel into a twelve tribe confederacy or quasi-amphictyony. The word *amphictyony* is derived from the Greek term for a confederacy of city-states bound together by religious ties and by common worship at a central sanctuary defended by the member states. The number of those loosely allied in the amphictyony was usually six or twelve. In Israel it was a loose confederation of twelve tribes united by a common Yahwistic faith, whose cult center was the shrine housing the Ark of the Covenant, located at Shechem or Shiloh in the time of the Judges. Later, in the time of the monarchy, the Ark was located in Jerusalem. At these cult centers regular festivals were celebrated (cf. Judg. 21:19 and 1 Sam. 1–2), and periodically there was a renewal of the covenant (cf. Jos. 24 and Deut. 31:9-13, 24-29). The book of Judges gives abundant testimony to the looseness of the quasi-amphictyonic union, especially in time of war (cf. Judg. 5:14-18).

The book of Joshua closes, as we have seen, with Joshua calling upon the Israelites to make a definite decision to serve either the one true God or the pagan gods (Jos. 24:14-15). It is a decision every generation among the Israelites and their successors, the Christians, the new Israel, will have to make. In the period that follows the death of Joshua, the period of the Judges, many will decide in favor of the gods of the pagans, the Baals of Canaan. In Judges the Deuteronomist will point out the effects of this apostasy for Israel and give us his theological explanation of both the period and the events.

4. Judges

The time of the Judges is a time of transformation for Israel.[1] It can be adequately understood only when taken against the background provided by the book of Joshua and in consideration of the changes a people must undergo when passing from a semi-nomadic to an agricultural life, from a loose confederation to a unified kingdom. The place of Judges in relation to the past and the future can be shown as follows:

Joshua	1250–1225	Period of conquest
Judges	1225–1025	Period of transformation
Samuel	1025– 965	Period of consolidation and expansion

To understand the frequent wars narrated in Judges, the reader must remember that the conquest of Palestine by Joshua was limited in scope, restricted for the most part to the hill country of Judah and Samaria, not even taking in all of that. A reading of Jos. 13:1-7; 17:11-13 and Judg. 2–3 will show that the plains of Acre, Sharon, and Philistia were not conquered. Nor were such cities as Jerusalem, Megiddo, and Beth-shan taken. The plain of Jezreel remained in the hands of the Canaanites and divided the northern from the central tribes; while Jerusalem, Aijalon, and Gezer in the central hill country continued to be held by the Canaanites and thus divided the central tribes from those in the south. As a result, the land allotted to each tribe was theirs in many cases only in theory, since they never succeeded in driving out the people who occupied it. The Danites, for example, could not take over their territory west of Jerusalem to the Mediterranean and were forced as a result to move north to land around the sources of the Jordan (Judg. 18).

[1] Cf. Bright 128–160; J. L. McKenzie, *The World of the Judges*; JBC 149–162.

To understand the social transformation that took place during the period of the Judges, the reader must remember that the generation of Israelites who conquered the hill country around 1225 B.C. had spent almost forty years in the desert, and their conquest of Canaan represented the invasion and conquest of a civilized land by people who were semi-nomads and culturally barbarians. Settling down required a transformation from the semi-nomadic life of the desert to the sedentary agricultural life of Canaan. That these were as a result barbaric times can be seen from some of the incidents related in the book of Judges (cf. 1:7; 8:16; 9:5; 11:31; 19).

Besides the social transformation, there was also a political transformation. Before and during the conquest, the tribes had been led by Moses and Joshua. During the period of the Judges, there was no longer any central authority or centralized apparatus of government. Israel consisted of a loose confederation of tribes, whose only bond was the Sinai pact and its symbol — the Ark of the Covenant, located at Shiloh in the central hill country.

The subjection and oppression of the tribes by neighboring nations during the period of the Judges was a result, therefore, not only of Israel's sins but of her political disunity. Under Samuel, the last of the Judges, the tribes realized the necessity of a central government if they were to survive. This in due time led to the institution of the monarchy in Israel under Samuel and Saul.

The book of Judges is named after its principal protagonists — the twelve Judges. These men are not primarily judicial magistrates. They are military leaders sent by God at critical moments in Israel's history to save the nation or part of the nation from destruction. They are arbitrarily divided into major and minor Judges according to the amount of space they receive in the book. The six allotted the most space are called the major, the others, the minor judges. To the twelve Judges mentioned in the book should be added Heli and Samuel mentioned in 1 Sam. 1–7. Only these last two, it seems, actually ruled the entire nation.

The time of the Judges runs from the death of Joshua (c. 1225) to the anointing of King Saul by Samuel (c. 1025). It should be noted that if all the years mentioned in the book are added together, they amount to over 400 years for the period of the Judges. This would be incorrect, however, not only because the numbers given are often round numbers, but because the Judges for the most part are local not national leaders, and it is quite probable that some of them ruled contemporaneously in different parts of Israel.

As is true of most of the books of the Bible, the primary purpose of the author of Judges is to teach religion rather than to record history. What he proposes to teach his contemporaries and us is that while God cannot brook sin and rebellion and that He invariably punishes the defections of His people, He also always saves them from extinction. Implicit in this teaching is the exalted conception of the sanctity and fidelity God demands from those whom He has chosen in a special way to be His representative people on earth — an idea as valid now as in the time of the author.

Looking for practical demonstrations of his doctrine, the author, who is clearly influenced by the teaching of Deut. 27—28; 32, had at hand from earlier times both written and oral accounts dealing with the period of the Judges. After an introduction in ch. 1 linking Judges with Joshua, he briefly outlines his teaching schema in ch. 2:10-23 and then demonstrates this teaching concretely by means of historical examples (3—16).

This theological purpose of the author, characteristic of the Former Prophets, is evident not only in ch. 2:10-23 but also in the schematic arrangement according to which each of the narratives concerning the Judges is written. It consists of four parts: (a) *sin* (sin of idolatry usually); (b) *punishment* (usually invasion by the surrounding nations); (c) *repentance* (usually expressed by the words "and they cried out to God," implying acknowledgment of sin and prayer for divine intervention); (d) *liberation* (God hears them by sending one of the Judges to save and liberate them from their oppressors). For examples of this cycle in the text, cf. 3:7-11; 3:12-15; 4:14; 6:1-6; 10:6-10.

The book is divided into three parts: I (1—3:6) links with Joshua and the author's theological teaching; II (3:7—16) stories about the Judges, exemplifying the theological objectives; III (17—21) appendices concerning the tribes of Dan (17—18) and Benjamin (19—21).

Significant passages in Judges

Part One / Judg. 1—3:6 / Context and Theological Objectives

1:1 Canaanites not yet completely conquered at the time of Joshua's death (cf. Jos. 13:1-7; Judg. 1:18-36 *passim*).

1:7 ". . . thumbs and big toes cut off." Barbaric times (cf. 8:16; 9:5; 11:31; 19:29).

2:6-9 The death of Joshua, narrated here, shows that the Deuteronomist is summing up the events before and after that event (cf. Jos. 24:29; Judg. 1:1).

2:10-23 Summary of the theological teaching of the author given in schema: sin (vv. 10-13); oppression (vv. 14-16); repentance, followed by liberation through the Judges' charismatic leadership (vv. 18-19).

3:7-11 ". . . serving the Baals and the Asherahs . . .", the male and female fertility gods of the Canaanites, the principal religious stumbling block for the Israelites in their new homeland (cf. Num. 25). Judge: Othoniel; oppressor: Aram Naharaim (possibly Edom).

3:12-30 Aod liberates Israel from oppression by Eglon, king of Moab. Samgar, the third Judge, liberates the Israelites from Philistine oppression (3:31).

4:1ff Deborah and Barak defeat Sisera, the general of Jabin, king of Hazor, the largest city in northern Canaan, located near Lake Huleh. The battle on the western edge of the plain of Jezreel near Megiddo ends in an Israelite victory when a thunderstorm turns the plain to mud and slows the Canaanite chariots to a standstill (4:12-16; 5:19-22). 4:17-22 describes the lethal hospitality of Jahel. The Canticle of Deborah (5:1-31) is one of the best examples of early Israelite poetry.

6—7 Gideon delivers Israel from oppression by the Midianites (vv. 4-5), probably nomads from south of the Negeb. 6:11ff: the call of Gideon (cf. the call of Samson in ch. 16 and the call of Samuel in 1 Sam. 1—2). 6:25-32: the altar to the Baal destroyed by Gideon shows that while many are unfaithful to the covenant, there is, as always throughout Israelite and future history, a hard core of believers, represented here by Gideon, ready to restore the true religion.

8:1ff The jealousy of the Ephraimites, manifested here and in 12:1ff, is a harbinger of the future political rivalry that will exist between Judah and Ephraim in the time of the kingdom, when under the leadership of the Ephraimites the northern tribes will secede from the kingdom of David — twice in the time of David (2 Sam. 15; 20); and irrevocably after the death of Solomon (1 Kings 12). Oreb and Zeeb (7:25) and Zebah and Zalmunna (8:5) are mentioned in Ps. 83.

8:22 The attempt to make Gideon king is the first indication of a pro-monarchist faction in Israel. Gideon's reason for refusing — because "the Lord must rule over you" — is the basic principle of the anti-monarchist faction (cf. 1 Sam. 8—12).

9:1ff Abimelech, the son of Gideon, is not a judge; he is mentioned because of his unsuccessful attempt to establish the monarchy in Israel with himself as the first king.

10:6ff Oppressed by the Ammonites, the people of Transjordan between Bashan on the north and Moab on the south (10:6-18), the Gileadites, a clan of Manasseh, located just south of Bashan, call upon Jephthah, a bandit chief, to lead their forces against the oppressors. Jephthah's vow (11:30) was probably fulfilled literally when he returned victorious over the Ammonites (11:34-39). This episode, along with many others in the book of Judges, shows the barbarous state of affairs during this period and also the strange things that can be done in good faith out of unenlightened theological motives.

12:1-6 The *Shibboleth* incident: another example of the tribal jealousy that will flower into revolt and secession in the time of David and Solomon.

12:8-14 Minor Judges: Ibzan from Bethlehem in Judah; Elon from Zebulon in the north; Abdon an Ephraimite. Along with Tola and Jair mentioned in 10:1-5 and Shamgar in 3:31, these names represent the minor Judges.

13:4-5 Samson, the Danite, is to be a Nazarite, i.e., one dedicated for a time or for life to lead a simple and mortified life, abstaining from alcoholic liquors and refraining from cutting the hair, considered a sign of vitality and, therefore, of a life which belonged to God. Called the great vow, those who took it are the first representatives of those who "take up their cross" in a special way. Other famous Nazarites include Samuel (1 Sam. 1:1), St. John the Baptist (Luke 1:15) and St. Paul (Acts 18:18; 21:23). On the vow, cf. Num. 6:2-8 and R. de Vaux, *op. cit.*, 466-467.

14:4ff The Philistines "had dominion over Israel." Invaders from the northwest, probably from the islands of the Aegean or from Crete, the Philistines were an Indo-European people who invaded Egypt around 1190, were thrown back by Rameses III, settled down along the coast of Canaan fusing with the Canaanites in Phoenicia and setting up a confederation of city states (Gath, Gaza, Ekron, Ashdod, and Ashkelon) in the fertile plain between Joppa and the River of Egypt. By uniting in time of war, the Philistines were able to dominate the Israelites from approximately 1150 down to the time of David (1000 B.C.). In or around 1060, they severely defeated the Israelites and even captured the Ark and destroyed Shiloh (1 Sam. 4–7). Around 1005, they inflicted another defeat on the Israelites in the battle of Mount Gilboa in which Israel's first monarch, King Saul, and his son Jonathan were killed (1 Sam. 28–31).

16:19   The secret of Samson's legendary strength is not in his hair but in what it symbolized: his Nazarite vow. Judging from the amorous life he led, not cutting his hair appears to have been the only part of his vow that he kept. In prison, he repents (16:28) and God restores his fabulous strength.

Part Three / Judg. 17–21 / Dan and Benjamin

17:6   "In those days there was no king in Israel; everyone did what he thought best." These words (repeated in 18:1; 19:1; 21:25) insinuate that if there had been a king to uphold the rights of God, such abuses as those described in these chapters — the entirely human origin of Mikah's sanctuary (17:5), the making of an idol (17:3), the purely arbitrary choice of one of his sons as priest — would not have happened.

19:1ff   The barbarous incident of the levite's concubine is narrated to stress still again the abuses that could take place "when there was no king in Israel." The punishment of the Benjaminites, moreover, is another example of the author's *sin-oppression-repentance-liberation* schema. The repentance of the Benjaminites is perhaps implicit in the remark, "When Benjamin returned at that time . . ." (21:14).

20:27ff   The presence of the Ark at Bethel, with Phinehas, the grandson of Aaron, as highpriest, would appear to indicate a time for these events very early in the period of the Judges.

21:12ff   "Finding among the inhabitants of Jabesh-gilead four hundred young virgins. . . ." The intermarriage between the Benjaminites and the Jabesh-gileadites helps to explain the intervention of King Saul, the Benjaminite, to save the city of Jabesh-gilead from Nahash, the Ammonite, in the early days of the monarchy (1 Sam. 11) and also the courageous act of the Jabesh-gileadites narrated in 1 Sam. 31.

5. Ruth

The book of Ruth does not belong to the Former Prophets collection; it is placed among the Megilloth (the final section) in the Hebrew Bible, indicating perhaps its late composition. Whatever its origin, the book gives us a splendid picture (paralleled by that of Hannah, Elkanah, and Samuel in 1 Sam. 1–3) of pious Israelite family life in the midst of the rude, barbaric age of the Judges. By its genealogy of David (4:18) it also provides a link between the period of the Judges and the period of the monarchy that follows in the books of Samuel. It is the story of David's great grandmother, Ruth the Moabitess — her coming to Bethlehem and her levirate marriage to Boaz, the Judean.

Verified with regard to its minimal historicity by the genealogy of David given in 1 Chr. 2:4-15 and by David's association with the Moabites, mentioned in passing in 1 Sam. 22:3-4, the precise purpose of the author in writing the book is nonetheless obscure. If written merely to give the genealogy of David, why does the author give so much attention to the Moabite origin of Ruth and to the intricacies of the ancient levirate law? If written to explain the working of the levirate law (Deut. 25:5-10), why a special book to explain one relatively unimportant custom?

All things considered — the place of the book in the Hebrew Bible, the neologisms in the language, the explanation of avowedly ancient and outmoded laws and customs, plus the author's apparent intent to show the goodness not only of the Gentile Ruth, who is the heroine, but even of her Gentile sister, Orpah — it appears likely that the book was written by a fifth century author, who, under the influence of Deutero-Isaiah's universalist teaching, put into written form the oral traditions concerning David's great grandmother in order to emphasize the universality of God's call to salvation by showing how even a Gentile like the Moabitess, Ruth, could be called by God to enter the genealogical line of the Messiah (Ruth 4:18; Matthew 1:3-6; Luke 3:31-33).

Significant passages in Ruth

2:1-4 The origin of our liturgical greeting "The Lord be with you."

4:3f The levirate law [1] (Deut. 25:5-10) was one of the four obligations to which a *goel* (kinsman-redeemer) was bound in ancient Israel. Boaz, next after the next of kin to Naomi (2:20), is bound by the law only when the more immediate kinsman cedes his right and obligation (3:12; 4:3-10).

[1] Cf. DeVaux, *op. cit.*, 21-22; 37-38.

The tender overtones of the word "redeemer" (*goel*—kinsman), so often used of God in the Old Testament (Job 19:25; Pss. 19:15; 78:35; Is. 48:17; 59:20; 63:16; Jer. 50:34; Lam. 3:58; Acts 7:35), can best be appreciated by listing what could be expected of the *goel* by his immediate kinsman; in brief, defense of: life (Jos. 20:3-5), liberty (Lev. 25:47-49), name (Deut. 25:5-10 — the levirate law requiring him to raise up an heir for his kinsman so that his name would not die out in Israel), and property (Lev. 25:23-26; Ruth 4:3-4).

4:18   The genealogy of David. From Matthew 1:5, we know that the Salmon mentioned in 4:21 married Rahab, the harlot, mentioned in Jos. 2 (cf. also 1 Chr. 2:4-15; Luke 3:32).

6. 1 and 2 Samuel

The outward form of the kingdom of God changes with the coming of Israel's kings, but the essence remains. This is the basic message of the books of Samuel, to which is added a significant development in the progress of the kingdom toward its climax and completion — the promise that the dynasty of David will be eternal and that through this dynasty God will work out the victory for mankind promised in Gen. 3:15.[1]

In the course of the eleventh century, the last three Judges of Israel, Samson, Eli, and Samuel attempt in vain to liberate their oppressed people from the domination of the Philistines. Toward the beginning of the century, Samson is captured and dies in the ruins of the temple at Gaza. Toward the middle of the century, the Ark of the Covenant is captured by the Philistines. Shiloh is destroyed. Eli dies (1 Sam. 4). In the last half of the century, Samuel — the holiest and most respected of the Judges — is nevertheless unable to throw off completely the Philistine tyranny.

Sick of oppression, envious of the independence of the Moabites and the Edomites with their hereditary kings and standing armies, the Israelites clamor for a king (1 Sam. 8). Convinced that Israel's destiny lies in unswerving fidelity and obedience to God as her only king and that human kings will only serve to entice the people away from God by making them put their trust in "horses and chariots," Samuel is nevertheless constrained against his will to accede and choose a king — Saul the Benjaminite (1 Sam. 9–10).

The victory of the pro-monarchist faction, however, is only apparent.

[1] Cf. Bright 163–208; CCHS par. 268ff; E. Maly, *The Books of Samuel*, OTRG, Nos. 6A, 6B; S. Herzburg, *1–2 Samuel*.

Samuel's basic policy eventually prevails. God remains, as He must in this unique theocratic kingdom, the only true king of Israel. Israel will have her human king as well, but he is not to be like the kings of the nations. He is to be a representative of God, the true King. He is to be the instrument through which God will work out the ultimate destiny of Israel. He must, therefore, be subject to the Mosaic law and to the admonitions and guidance of God's prophets.[1]

Because Saul fails to subject his own ambitions to God's demands, he is rejected (1 Sam. 15) and becomes forever in Israel the example and type of the human monarch who fails to live up to God's expectations and demands. David, on the contrary, Saul's successor, is a man after God's own heart. He understands that God alone is Israel's true king and that he himself, no less than the least citizen of God's kingdom, is subject to God's covenant with Israel; he must, accordingly, be guided by the word of God's inspired prophets. As a reward for his fidelity to this design, God promises to David that his dynasty will be perpetual, that its kings will be adopted by Him as His sons, and that the covenant will now be bound up with David's family (2 Sam. 7).

The eyes of Israel, directed to the future by 2 Sam. and Gen. 3:15; 49:10; Num. 24:17, now focus on each new heir to the Davidic throne. But as each succeeding king fails even to live up to the standards set by David, the founder of the dynasty (cf. the Deuteronomist's history of Kings), the people begin more and more to look to God Himself to effect the triumph predicted, while the prophets, in their turn, assure them that God will indeed intervene by raising up a new David — the ideal king, the Messiah — upon whom will rest Yahwist's spirit — "the spirit of wisdom and understanding, the spirit of counsel and might, the spirit of knowledge and fear of the Lord" (Is. 11:2-3).

It is with such a "philosophy of history" in mind, that the Deuteronomist compiled and edited the books of Samuel. The theme of his history is the institution of the Israelite monarchy and its perpetuity in the dynasty of David, the dynasty from which one day will be born the Messiah.

The climax of the history is reached in 2 Sam. 7, when God solemnly promises perpetuity to the house of David. Everything else is oriented to this climax. The last days of Eli are described (1 Sam. 1–3) because they introduce Samuel. Samuel is described because he institutes the monarchy in Israel. Saul is described because he demonstrates for all time what the Israelite king must not be. David is described (at length and in detail and not without some pride) because like him and from him will come "the desire of the everlasting hills." The ulterior purpose, therefore, of the books of Samuel, as demonstrated by the climactic advance of events

[1] Cf. E. Maly, *The World of Solomon and David.*

up to 2 Sam. 7, is to lay an historical and theological foundation for the monarchy in Israel, for the legitimacy of the Davidic dynasty, and for Israel's faith in the messianic future of that dynasty.

The reader of Samuel will notice immediately certain links with the books of Judges and Ruth, namely, the continuation of the history of the Judges in the descriptions of Eli and Samuel; the establishment of the Ark at Shiloh as indicated in Jos. 18:1 and Judg. 21; the continued oppression of Israel by the Philistines (Judg. 13–16; 1 Sam. 4–7 *passim*); the relation of friendship between Saul, the Benjaminite, and the citizens of Jabesh-gilead (1 Sam. 11) carrying over from the intermarriage between the Benjaminites and the women of Jabesh-gilead described in Judg. 21; the relation of David through Jesse and Obed to his great grandmother, Ruth the Moabitess (Ruth 4:18; 1 Sam. 16:1; 22:3-4).

The reader will also, if he analyses the text, be able to pick out the different sources used by the Deuteronomist in his compilation: (a) ch. 1–3: from the oral traditions about the Judges; (b) ch. 4–7 (plus 2 Sam. 6–7): from a history of the Ark of the Covenant; (c) ch. 8–12: two different versions of the origin of the monarchy; (d) ch. 13–15: two different versions of the rejection of Saul; (e) ch. 16–17: two different versions of David's first meeting with Saul (with the same two sources probably fused in ch. 18–31 as evidenced by the similarity of such episodes as the twofold attempt of Saul to spear David, the two versions of David's flight to Philistia, the twofold sparing of Saul by David); (f) 2 Sam. 9–20: the magnificent court history of David; (g) 2 Sam. 21–24: the collection of miscellaneous narratives and records from the royal chancery. The summaries marking the respective climaxes in the careers of Samuel, Saul, and David (1 Sam. 7:15-17; 1 Sam. 14:49-52; 2 Sam. 8:15-18) are probably the work of the Deuteronomist author.

Originally one homogeneous work, Samuel was early divided into two parts (1 Sam. 1–31; 2 Sam. 1–24). For ease in reading, the books can be divided as follows:

1 Sam. 1–7 The last Judges, Eli and Samuel, and the Philistine oppression.

1 Sam. 8–15 Samuel and Saul, the institution of the monarchy, and Saul's rejection.

1 Sam. 16–31 Saul and David; David befriended at first by Saul, later persecuted.

2 Sam. 1–4 David, king over Judah after the death of Saul.

2 Sam. 5–20 David, king over all Israel and nearby conquered nations.

2 Sam. 21–24 Appendices.

Part One / 1 Sam. 1–7 / Eli and Samuel

1:3 For the custom of celebrating annually at Shiloh, cf. Judg. 21:19; for the references to the sacrificial banquet in 1:4 and 1:18, cf. the ritual explanation in Lev. 7.

1:11 Samuel, like Samson (Judg. 13), is to be dedicated to God by his mother by means of a Nazarite vow (Num. 6). The wholesome, simple devotion and piety of Elkanah and Hannah is characteristic of God's faithful at all times. Note how the story of Samuel follows the literary form used for Gideon and later on for John the Baptist (Luke 1).

2:1-10 Hannah's *Magnificat*, to which Mary's *Magnificat* bears resemblance (Luke 1:46ff), may possibly be original with her, or perhaps is a modification to her own circumstances of a common song of thanksgiving used in the Tabernacle liturgy.

2:12-36 The scandalous example of Eli's sons as well as the far from exemplary example of Samuel's sons (8:1-5) may be cited here by the Deuteronomist to bring out the inherent weakness of any dynasty in which the father may be a saint and the son a degenerate. The same will be true of David's sons, Amnon and Absalom. More likely, however, the chapter is included as an etiological explanation of the destruction of the priestly power of the house of Eli (4:11 and 22:18-19) and its transfer to the house of Sadoc in the time of Solomon (1 Kings 2:27). The humiliating condition of the priestly line of Eli described in 2:36 came to pass as a result of the reform of Josiah around 621 B.C. (2 Kings 23:9); this point may help to date the chapter.

3:1–4:1 The history of Samuel, the Judge, interrupted by 2:12-36, is continued here briefly, then interrupted again by the story of the Ark of the Covenant (4:2–7:2) and terminated in 7:3-17.

4:16–7:2 This section (from a separate source dealing with the history of the Ark and cited again in 2 Sam. 5–6), describing the capture of the Ark and the defeat of the Israelites, is included to emphasize the domination by the Philistines — the state of affairs that led to the demand for a king, described in the next section (ch. 8–12). The capture of the Ark and the destruction of Shiloh (Jer. 7) probably took place about 1060 when Samuel was still a relatively young man. The Ark, though returned to Israelite territory was probably still controlled by the Philistines until the time when it was taken by David from Kiriath-jearim (1 Sam. 7:1; 2 Sam. 6) and brought to Jerusalem.

7:2-14 Note the theological schema typical of accounts in Judges: v. 2 oppression; vv. 3-8 repentance; vv. 9-14 liberation through Samuel.

7:15-17 The Deuteronomist's quick summary of Samuel's career in order to take up the principal theme of the book — the institution of the monarchy (ch. 8—12). These summaries (cf. similar summaries of Saul and David in 1 Sam. 14:47-52 and 2 Sam. 8:13-18) show that the Deuteronomist had no intention of giving a detailed history of the times but only included those events which paved the way for the institution of the monarchy and the promise of the perpetual dynasty to David.

Part Two / 1 Sam. 8—15 / Samuel and Saul

8:1ff In the history of the institution of the monarchy, the Deuteronomist fuses two different versions: the anti-monarchist version (8; 10:17-24; 12) and the pro-monarchist version (9:1—10:16; 11).[1] The author includes both to show that the people's lack of complete trust in God, manifested by their demand for a king, was displeasing to him even though he acceded to their wish. The author, moreover, by expressing the policy of the anti-monarchists that God alone is Israel's true king, prepares the way for the substantial victory of this policy — vindicated as it is by the rejection of Saul (15) and the election of David, who rules not according to the will of the people as did Saul, nor like the surrounding Gentile kings as will Solomon later, but as God's obedient vicar and instrument. The policy of the anti-monarchists is perhaps best expressed in Deut. 17:14ff.

9:1ff In the pro-monarchist version (9:1—10:16 and 11:1-15) good reasons are given for the institution of the monarchy. Saul is then anointed by Samuel, though only privately at first (10:1); and later, after his victory over Nahash the Ammonite (11:1-11), publicly (11:12-15). Saul's intervention in this war is explained by the intermarriage of the Benjaminites with the

[1] Cf. DeVaux, *op cit.*, 94-99.

Jabesh-gileadites (Judg. 21). His action in 11:7 is a significant reminder of the curious episode of the butchered concubine in Judg. 19:29.

12:13-25   Samuel's speech is a resumé of the anti-monarchist stand. The demand for a king has displeased God, but if the king will listen to God's prophet and obey (12:13-25), God will continue to watch over His people (cf. Deut. 17:14-20). This speech prepares the way for the account which follows of Saul's rejection (13-15).

13:3   Jonathan's victory over the Philistine garrison at Gibeah (cf. 14:1-15 for another version of the same event), opens the war with the Philistines. The Philistine garrisons at Gibeah (13:3) and Bethel (10:5) plus the Philistine corner on the iron market (13:19-21) explain clearly enough the nature of the oppression that led the Israelites to demand a king. It also enhances Saul's victory.

13:8-14   Saul's failure to obey God's prophet brings about his rejection, as threatened by Samuel in 12:13-25 (cf. 10:8, Samuel's command to Saul to await him at Gilgal).

14:41   Urim and thummim: the negative and positive lots (probably colored or marked stones) kept in the priest's ephod and used to ascertain God's will in sundry doubtful matters (cf. Num. 27:21).

14:47-51   Summary of Saul at the height of his career, analogous to the summaries of Samuel (7:15-17) and David (2 Sam. 8:15-18) at the height of their careers.

15:10-35   Another version of Saul's disobedience resulting in his rejection and Samuel's declaration of the principle upon which alone human kingship in Israel can survive: "Does the Lord delight in burnt offerings and sacrifices as much as in obedience to the voice of the Lord? Behold, to obey is better than sacrifices and to hearken, than the fat of rams" (15:22).

Part Three / 1 Sam. 16—31 / Saul and David

16—18   David at the court of Saul. Anointed privately by Samuel (16:1-13), David is later summoned to become court musician to Saul (16:14-23). A national hero after his victory over Goliath (17), David rises rapidly to captain (18:5) and then to commander in Saul's army (18:13-16). After his marriage to Michal, Saul's daughter (18:17-27), David is at the pinnacle of success when, without warning, psychotic jealousy turns the king against him (18:28-30).

18—27 David persecuted by Saul. (N.B. It is impossible in this section to give the exact sequence of events because of the different documents used by the Deuteronomist and because of the lack of a strict chronology in the sequence of chapters.) The women's victory song praising David sows the seed of jealousy in Saul's emotionally unstable mind (18:6-8). Saul suggests the dangerous marriage price as a way of getting rid of David (18:20-25). Saul's jealousy mounts as David's popularity with the people increases and he determines to kill David, but Jonathan intercedes (18:28—19:6). In a fit of madness, Saul tries to spear David (19:7-10; cf. the doublet of this episode in 18:10-11). Saved by Michal's strategem, David flees north to Ramah (19:11-18). A second attempt on Jonathan's part (if it is not a doublet of 18:28—19:6) to save David fails (20:28-33). At Nob, David is helped by the priests (21:1ff), who later fall victim to Saul's insane jealousy (22:9-19).

Fleeing to Philistia, David saves himself by feigning insanity (21:10-15). Later he hides out at Adullam where his family and friends rally to his side (22:1-3). From Mizpeh in Moab, David goes to the forest of Hereth in Judah (22:5ff). After defeating the Philistines at Keilah, David remains there until forced by the approach of Saul's army to flee to the desert of Ziph (23:1-14). After barely escaping Saul in the desert of Maon (23:24-27), David hides out at Engedi, where he temporarily has Saul in his power but spares him (24:1ff; cf. possible doublet in 26:7-11). Finally, in despair of escaping Saul's maniacal pursuit, David flees for refuge to Philistia where he becomes a subaltern of Achish, the king of Gath, and dwells in the city of Ziklag until Saul's death two years later (27:1ff).

28—31 When the Philistine armies, around the year 1005 B.C., gather at Shunem in the plain of Jezreel planning to invade the hill country from the north and put down the Israelite rebellion, Saul assembles his army on Mount Gilboa and prepares a counterattack (28:4ff). Before the battle the Philistine commanders, distrusting David's sympathies despite his troubles with Saul, refuse to let him join in the war against the Israelite king (29:1-7). Defeated by the Philistines on Mount Gilboa, Saul's sons die in battle and Saul himself runs on his sword (31:1-6). Later Saul's devoted friends, the Jabesh-gileadites (cf. 1 Sam. 11), risk their lives to give decent burial to the king and his sons (31:11). Thus the first book of Samuel closes as it began — with the Philistines in control, Israel's first king disastrously defeated and his armies dispersed.

Part Four / 2 Sam. 1–4 / David, King of Judah

1:19-27 Rightly considered one of the most beautiful passages in the Bible, David's elegy lamenting the deaths of Jonathan and Saul must be read slowly to be appreciated. On David's friendship with Jonathan, see the first meeting of the friends (18:1-4); Jonathan's intercession with Saul for David (19:1-5; 20:28-34); meeting with David in exile (23:16ff); his death on Mount Gilboa (31:2).

2:1-4 The Judeans secede from Saul's successor Ishbaal, and elect David king of Judah at Hebron, the principal city of their territory.

2:8ff Abner, commander of Saul's army, supports Ishbaal, Saul's son, as king of the remaining tribes, establishing a new capital at Mahanaim in the Transjordan. For approximately seven years, there is internecine war between the adherents of David and Ishbaal, with the house of Saul suffering progressive eclipse (3:1).

3:6-11 Abner breaks with Ishbaal when the new king interprets his espousal of Rizpah, one of Saul's concubines, as an attempt to usurp the kingdom (cf. 2 Sam. 12:8; 16:20-22; 1 Kings 2:17, 21, 22).

3:12-21 Determined to support David, Abner sends secret messengers to David (3:12). To test Abner's intentions, David demands the return of his wife, Michal (3:13-16). Abner rallies the elders to support David (3:17-19), meets with David at Hebron and agrees to bring over to him the northern tribes (3:20-21).

3:26-39 Abner's assassination by Joab, David's general, as blood vengeance for the death of his brother, Asahel (2:22), almost ruins the chance of union between the tribes (3:26-30); but David's genuine sorrow and honorable obsequies for Abner absolve him of any implication in the murder in the eyes of the northern tribes (3:31-39).

4:7ff Ishbaal is assassinated during siesta at Mahanaim by two brothers, Rechab and Baanah, who are subsequently executed by David. With Abner and Ishbaal dead, the opposition to David disappears and the way is open for the house of David to succeed the house of Saul. In his history of the monarchy, the author of Samuel has been very careful to point out that David never used force to become King although on several occasions he could have seized the throne, but became king by the explicit request first of Judah and later of the remaining tribes. The legitimacy of David's dynasty is thus established not only through the will of God (cf. 1 Sam. 16 Samuel's anointing of David) but also through the explicit will of the twelve tribes.

Part Five / 2 Sam. 5–20 / David, King over all Israel

5:1-5 Around 998 B.C., at the age of thirty, David is anointed king of all Israel and reigns with brief interruptions caused by the rebellions of Absalom (2 Sam. 15ff) and Sheba (2 Sam. 20) until 965, when he is succeeded by Solomon.

5:6-9 Taking Jerusalem by stratagem with the help of Joab (cf. 1 Chr. 11:5ff), David makes the ancient Canaanite city his new capital, combining strategic reasons (its impregnability and central location) with political reasons (its location outside of Judah to dispel the jealousy of the sensitive northern tribes and inside Benjamin, to placate the remaining supporters of the Saul dynasty).

5:17-25 The Philistines hold on to the country as long as it continues divided. United under David, the tribes must be put down again. Their attempt is a failure and they are decisively defeated by David, who thereafter even uses Philistine mercenaries in his army.

6:1-19 David, by another stroke of political genius, further consolidates his position by bringing the Ark of the Covenant to Jerusalem, thus making the city the religious as well as the national capital (cf. 1 Chr. 13; 15–16; Pss. 24 and 68).

7:1-16 Nathan's prophecy to David of an eternal dynasty is the climax to the books of Samuel. The occasion of the prophecy is given in vv. 1-3. David, realizing what a disgrace it is that he should live in a palace while the Ark is housed under a tent, decides to build a temple and is encouraged by Nathan. Returning later and speaking under inspiration (vv. 4-10), Nathan tells David he is not to build a temple (cf. 1 Chr. 22:7-8 for reason). God, however, is not displeased with David. In vv. 8-9a, God points out how He has cared for David in the past and, in vv. 9b-10, indicates what He will do for David in the future. In return for the material house David would have built (vv. 11-16), God promises to David a "house," i.e., a royal house, a dynasty which will endure forever.

That "house" and "seed" are to be taken in a collective sense, including Solomon, David's immediate successor, and also all the other successors of David, including the Messiah, is indicated by the context: the emphasis on "forever" (vv. 11d, 13b, 15-16, 19, 25, 29); the contrast with the house of Saul (vv. 15-16); David's amazement expressed in his prayer (vv. 17-29), and his reiterated emphasis on the "eternal" duration of his house (vv. 19, 25, 29). That the promise refers to an eternal dynasty is further confirmed by Isaiah (ch. 9) who writes in the eighth century; by Ps. 89:30-38 (sixth century); and by the New Testament (Luke 1:32ff; Apoc. 11:15).

8:1-14   David's victories over the Philistines, the Moabites, the Syrians, and the Edomites establish him as the ruler of the largest kingdom of the Near East next to Egypt and Assyria, both at this time too weak and torn by internal struggles to contest his rise to power.

8:15-18   A summary of David at the height of his power, similar to the summary of Samuel (1 Sam. 7:15-17) and Saul (1 Sam. 14:49-52), made by the Deuteronomist who compiled the many documents used in the books of Samuel. His hand will be evident again in 20:23-26.

9:1-13   David's kindness to Jonathan's son, Meribbaal (cf. 2 Sam. 4:4-5). *N.B.* The court history of David (ch. 9–20; plus 1 Kings 1–2), a homogeneous, impartial, eyewitness account of David's reign, has been acclaimed by critics as the best written, most dramatic historical document of ancient times, and has merited for its unknown author the title of "Father of History," hitherto given to the Greek historian Herodotus.

Describing the gray years of David's reign, the court history has been included by the Deuteronomist to show that, though the messianic hope of Israel was to be centered in the dynasty of David, David was by no means himself to fulfill that hope. He is a great king, but not the Messiah. His actions revealed in these chapters show him to be far from perfect: he is guilty of adultery and murder; he is too weak to punish those he loves.

As a result of the disillusionment with David and Solomon, the messianic hope raised by 2 Sam. 7, while centered for centuries in the human kings of the Davidic dynasty, gradually shifts to an ideal future king, who will be a combination of all that was great in David and Solomon but without any of their failings.

10–12 The war with Ammon (10:1-19) sets the stage for David's crimes of adultery and murder. While Uriah is in the field with Joab besieging Rabbah, the capital of Ammon, David commits adultery with his wife, Bathsheba (11:1ff), the granddaughter of Ahitophel (2 Sam. 23:24) and the future mother of Solomon (11:26-27). Unable to conceal the adultery because of Uriah's shrewdness (11:5-13), David writes to Joab instructing him to arrange Uriah's death in battle (11:14-25). David then marries Bathsheba (11:26-27). Nathan's parable (12:1ff) brings David to repentance and pardon, but the crimes of adultery and murder bring a promise of punishment. From Nathan, David hears: ". . . the sword shall never depart from your house. . . ." This foreshadowing text sets the tone for the remainder of the court history which describes David's tragic family life.

13:1ff David's family troubles begin with incest between Tamar and Amnon (13:1-20), followed by fratricide — Amnon murdered by Absalom (13:21-36) — and then the exile of Absalom, David's dearest son (13:37-39).

14:1ff Absalom's return from exile is arranged by Joab who will later, despite David's express orders to the contrary, kill him (18:14).

15:1ff In telling the story of Absalom's perfidious revolt against his father (15–18), the author of the court history shows Absalom to be the reversal of all that is good in David. He is cold and calculating (13:21-22), a patient plotter (13:28), physically attractive like his father (14:25), ruthlessly resourceful (14:30), ambitious and suave (15:1-6), thoroughly unscrupulous

(15:14), utterly amoral (16:21-22). He is repaid in the end for his crimes by the same Joab who had brought him back from exile out of compassion for his father who loved him so much (18:9-15).

15:12 Ahitophel, David's Judas, the grandfather of Bathsheba (2 Sam. 23:34) betrays David, perhaps in vengeance for David's murder of his son-in-law, Uriah (11:14-25). When his counsel is rejected by Absalom in favor of Hushai's advice (17:14), he goes home and like Judas commits suicide (17:23).

15:14ff David flees from Jerusalem before the approach of Absalom's rebel army, weeping as he passes over Mount Olivet (15:30); hears that Meribaal, Jonathan's son, has turned against him (16:1-4); and is cursed by Shimei, a Benjaminite (16:5-14).

17:1ff In the meantime, back in Jerusalem, Ahitophel's wise counsel is rejected by Absalom, who listens to Hushai, David's planted agent.

17:24ff David arrives at Mahanaim in Transjordania, the former temporary capital of Saul's son, Ishbaal (2 Sam. 2:8).

18:5 As the army leaves Mahanaim, David gives orders to the troops to spare Absalom, but Joab (18:9-15) deliberately disobeys David's orders and kills him in the course of the battle. When David receives the news of the battle, he forgets the victory in his grief over Absalom (19:1-4), until Joab rebukes him and compels him to go out and see the people (19:5-8).

19:9-10 The northern tribes request David to return and rule them again. Judah, led by Amasa, Absalom's commander-in-chief (17:25), holds back until David promises him the position of commander of the army in place of Joab (19:11-14). David then returns, pardoning Shimei (19:15-23) and Meribaal (19:24-30), rewarding friends like old Barzillai (19:31).

19:40ff Arriving at Gilgal by the Jordan, David is met by representatives of Judah and Israel. When a quarrel breaks out between Judah and the northern tribes, Sheba (a Benjaminite) seizes the opportunity to begin a new revolt against David, perhaps in the hope of reviving the Saul dynasty (20:1-2).

20:4ff When Amasa delays the pursuit of Sheba, Joab and Abishai lead out David's mercenaries to put down the rebellion. Meeting Amasa, Joab treacherously assassinates him as he had Abner (3:27), then continues north and besieges Sheba at Abel-beth-maakah (20:15). The rebellion comes to an end when the Abel-beth-maacahites deliver Sheba's head to Joab (20:22).

20:23-26   Summary similar to the summaries in 1 Sam. 7:15-17; 14:49-51; 2 Sam. 8:15-18 indicates that the Deuteronomist has finished with the court history for the time and wishes to introduce other documents (ch. 21–24). The concluding part of the court history will be used in 1 Kings 1–2 to introduce the reign of Solomon.

Part Six / 2 Sam. 21–24 / Appendices

21:10   Rizpah, Saul's concubine, stands watch heroically over the bodies of her two sons executed by David's order to propitiate the Gibeonites wronged by Saul. The incident dates probably from the early years of David and is alluded to by Shimei in 2 Sam. 16:8.

22:2ff   David's victory psalm, celebrating his deliverance from Saul, is found with slight changes in the psalter as Ps. 18 (cf. p. 248ff).

23:8ff   Ishbaal (v. 8), Eleazar (v. 9), and Shamma (v. 11), the most famous warriors in David's army, known simply as "the Three," risk their lives to get a drink of water for David from the well at Bethlehem (vv. 15-17). The incident demonstrates the intense devotion and stalwart loyalty David inspired in his followers.

24:1ff   Punished by a national epidemic for his pride in taking a census after the manner of the Gentile kings to glory in the greatness of his kingdom (vv. 1-9), David repents (v. 10) and resigns himself to the fatherly hand of God for punishment (v. 14). At the end of the epidemic a special altar is set up for thanksgiving sacrifices on the hill north of Sion, the hill upon which, in the reign of Solomon, the great Temple of Jerusalem will be built (vv. 18-25; cf. 2 Chr. 3:1). The incident is included by the author in accordance with his theme to show that the theocratic king is not to glory in material grandeur but in submission to God, the true King of Israel.

7. 1 and 2 Kings

When the author of Samuel recorded with justifiable pride the origins of the monarchy in Israel and the foundation of the Davidic dynasty, the hopes of Israel in a dynasty so blessed by God and so infallibly guaranteed by His promise of perpetuity were understandably high. With the passage of four centuries, however, the facts of history appeared to give the lie to these hopes.

To begin with, the northern tribes rebelled in 926 and set up a new dynasty and a new kingdom to rival that of Judah.

In 722 B.C., Samaria, the capital of the new northern kingdom, was besieged and captured by Shalmaneser V, and the ten northern tribes were carried off into captivity to Assyria never to return.

In 587 B.C., the southern kingdom fell to the Babylonians led by the great Nebuchadnezzar. The Temple was burned to the ground. Jerusalem was destroyed. The independent rule of the Davidic kings came to a jarring halt.

To all appearances God had deserted His people and had defaulted on His solemn promise to David that his dynasty would last forever. For a secular historian writing after the fall of the kingdom in 587 B.C., this could be the only explanation. For the inspired Deuteronomist, writing sometime after 562 B.C. (the last date mentioned in the book of Kings), the truth runs deeper. It is not God who has been unfaithful. It is His Chosen People. Their infidelity has forced Him to delay at least temporarily the fulfillment of His promises.

Written in exile in Babylon around 560 B.C., the book of Kings is a philosophico-theological history of the kingdom of Israel from 965 to 560 B.C.[1] It is philosophical in the sense that the author's purpose is to point out the root causes of the fall of the kingdom. It is theological because the basic causes for the fall of the kingdom are religious: failure of the kings to observe the monotheism demanded by God in the Sinai covenant and evils resulting from the non-observance of the unity of sanctuary in Jerusalem.

Writing in Babylon for the disillusioned exiles, the Deuteronomist examines the conscience of the nation as a moral person and proves incontrovertably that the catastrophe of 587 followed inexorably as a just punishment for the failure of the majority of the kings both of the north and the south to practice monotheism and observe the unity of sanctuary in Jerusalem demanded by the law. It follows, therefore, that Israel, not God, has been unfaithful. It follows too that if Israel is to resume her God-given mission, she must repent and leave the future to God's unswerving fidelity and to His steadfast love.

The exhortation to repentance is implicit in the history as a whole. The infidelity of the kings is stated much more explicitly. It is explicit in

[1] Cf. Schedl, HOTOT, vol. 3, 277–285; P. Ellis, *First and Second Kings*, OTRG No. 7.

the unfavorable judgment made by the author on the vast majority of the kings, and even more so in the explanations given at the end of each division of the history, at the end of Solomon's reign (1 Kings 11), at the destruction of the northern kingdom (2 Kings 17:7-23), and at the downfall of the southern kingdom (2 Kings 24:1-4).

The careful reader will note that the author uses three principal sources: the acts of Solomon (1 Kings 3–11) giving that king's history from 965 to 926; and the chronicles of the northern kingdom synchronized with the chronicles of the southern kingdom to relate the history of the divided country from 926 down to 587 B.C. (1 Kings 12 to 2 Kings 25).

The author's method in 1 Kings 12 to 2 Kings 17 is to juxtapose excerpts from the respective chronicles of Israel and Judah to present a synoptic view of both kingdoms. His procedure is to complete the narrative of each reign, once begun, then deal with the concurrent reigns in the other kingdom. For each reign the author follows a stereotyped formula: first, the synchronization of the reign under consideration with the reign of the other kingdom; then the length of the reign, the judgment on how the king observed the covenant and the unity of sanctuary, the citation of his sources, something about the death of the king and the name of his successor, and sometimes an additional note about the age of the king and the name of his mother (cf. 1 Kings 15:9-11, 23-24; 15:33-34; 16:5-6). Departures from this stereotyped formula are made wherever the author can give greater attention to his favorite subjects, namely, the Temple (2 Kings 12; 16; 18; 22–23) and the prophets (1 Kings 11; 13; 17–19; 2 Kings 1–8; 18–20).

Initially written as one continuous work, the book of Kings was divided at a later date by translators into two books. The author's work falls into three easily distinguishable parts: I (1–11), the history of Solomon's reign; II (1 Kings 12–2 Kings 17), the synoptic history of the northern and southern parts of Solomon's divided kingdom; III (2 Kings 18–25), the history of the surviving southern kingdom until its downfall in 587.

Chronology of Solomon and the northern kingdom

965-926 The golden age of Solomon ends with the division of the kingdom.

926-907 Jeroboam I, the first king of the northern kingdom, introduces idol worship at Dan and Bethel to prevent the northern Israelites from going south to worship at Jerusalem (1 Kings 11–15).

882-871 Omri founds Samaria, the new capital of the northern kingdom (1 Kings 16).

871-852   Jezebel and Ahab war with Elijah and Elisha for the soul of Israel.

845-781   Jehu's dynasty founded by Elisha destroys Jezebel and the Omrid dynasty (2 Kings 9—15:8).

787-747   Jeroboam II. A time of increasing material prosperity paralleled by moral corruption heralding the end of the northern kingdom (2 Kings 14).

760-750   Amos, the shepherd of Tekoa, preaches in the northern kingdom.

750-730   Hosea, the prophet, makes a final attempt to save the northern kingdom.

747-724   The last kings of Israel: Zechariah, Shallum, Menahem, Pekahiah, Pekah, Hosea, (2 Kings 15—17).

734-732   The Syro-Ephraimitic War. Rezin of Damascus and Pekah of Israel war against Ahaz of Judah; Tiglath-Pileser III of Assyria intervenes.

724-722   Siege and fall of Samaria to Shalmaneser V. Deportation of the northern tribes to Assyria and end of the northern kingdom (2 Kings 17).

Significant passages in the books of Kings

Part One / 1 Kings 1—11 / Solomon

1:1—2:46   1 Kings 1—2 contain the finale of the court history of David (2 Sam. 9—20; 1 Kings 1—2) and cover the story of Solomon's succession to the throne of David. Adonijah, David's oldest son, attempts with the help of Joab and Abiathar to have himself declared David's successor (1:5-10). In the meantime, Nathan the prophet, with the help of Bathsheba, persuades David to nominate Solomon as king (1:11-40). After David's last words and death (2:1-11), the author describes the destruction of the Adonijah faction. Interpreting Adonijah's request to marry Abishag, David's last wife, as a pretension to the throne, Solomon proceeds to destroy him and his followers: v. 25, the death of Adonijah; vv. 28-35, the death of Joab; vv. 36-46, the death of Shimei.

3:5-15   Solomon's wisdom is described in 3:5-15 as a gift of God. It is then exemplified in the story of the rival mothers claiming the same child (3:16-28) and in the description of Solomon's organizing genius (4:1-28). It is completed by a statement concerning the greatness of his reputation as a wise man and as an author of wisdom literature (4:29-34). The description of Solomon as a wise man is resumed and enhanced in 9:15-28 (Solomon's commercial genius) and in ch. 10 (the story of the fabulous Queen of Sheba coming to test for herself Solomon's reputation for wisdom).

5:1—9:14 Solomon's building projects. One of the seven wonders of the ancient world and the first permanent edifice dedicated to the one, true God in His universe was the Temple of Jerusalem. Built by Solomon,[1] with the preliminary help of David (1 Chr. 22; 29), about the year 960, it stood on Araunah's threshing floor (2 Sam. 24:15-25; 1 Chr. 21:18-30) just north of the city of David, where at present is located the Moslem Dome of the Rock. The construction work on the Temple was done by Phoenicians (2 Kings 5:1); it was 90 feet long, 30 wide, 45 high, with an entrance 33 feet high and 15 feet wide. The Temple was renowned not for its size but for its gemlike beauty (white limestone, cyprus and cedar woodwork, gold, silver, and precious fabrics in profusion) and its "mysterious presence" of God above the Ark in the Holy of Holies (later called the "Shekinah"). Size, such as there was, was supplied by the large and elaborate courts through which the worshipper approached the Holy Place. The structure existed until 587, when it was destroyed by the Babylonian army after the fall of Jerusalem.

9:15ff Solomon's further building operations included a royal palace (v. 15); Millo, a fortress mound south of the Temple (v. 15); chariot cities for his numerous chariots (v. 19; cf. 4:26; 10:26); a special palace for his Egyptian wife (v. 24).

9:26ff Solomon's Phoenician-built fleet (9:26-28; 10:11, 22), his mining towns with elaborate smelters at Ezion-geber near the gulf of Aqabah (9:26 and excavations), his horse and chariot trading (10:28-29) make him the first international Jewish merchant and financier.

11:1-10 Solomon's marriages, many of them no doubt political marriages of convenience, lead him to compromise his beliefs and build pagan temples for his foreign wives, even in Jerusalem (vv. 4-8). The author takes this occasion to show that the punishment for Solomon's infidelity will be the division of the king-

[1] Cf. DeVaux, *op. cit.*, 312-322.

dom, the first step toward the final catastrophe of 587 (vv. 11-13).

11:26-43   Jeroboam, an Ephraimite labor foreman, abetted by Ahijah, the prophet, attempts to rebel against Solomon and is thwarted. He flees to Egypt (11:40), returns after Solomon's death (12:2), and becomes the first king of the rebel northern kingdom upon its secession in 926. The author introduces Jeroboam at this point in the narrative to prepare the way for the story of the division of the kingdom which is to follow (1 Kings 12ff).

Part Two / *1 Kings 12—2 Kings 17* / *Synoptic History of the Kings*

In treating the history of the northern kingdom (sometimes called the kingdom of Israel in contradistinction to the kingdom of Judah, the southern kingdom) we shall concentrate in the significant passages on the outstanding kings of the north: Jeroboam I, Omri, Ahab, Jehu and Jeroboam II, leaving the history of the kings of the south to be taken with 2 Chronicles. Along with the kings, we shall concentrate on the outstanding personalities of the northern kingdom: Jezebel, Athaliah, Elijah and Elisha, Amos and Hosea.

The boundaries of Israel, dividing it from Judah, run from Joppa on the Mediterranean to Bethel in the mountains and down to Jericho near the Jordan, including all the territory north of Philistia and Benjamin up to Phoenicia on the coast and Dan north of the Lake of Galilee, plus all of Transjordania from the southern boundary of Moab to the southern tip of the Lake of Galilee. Judah retained, besides the territory of Benjamin, the Negeb and Edom east and west of the southern end of the Dead Sea. In extent, wealth, and manpower the northern kingdom far surpassed the southern, but its position and wealth invited attack and its tribal rivalries left it continually prone to political upheavals.

12:1ff   Rehoboam, Solomon's son, inherits, along with the wealth of his father, the unrest and discontent of his father's subjects and in failing to deal prudently with the discontented northern tribes loses them forever to the dynasty of David. The basic theological cause underlying the catastrophe has been described (11:1-13): *Solomon's idolatry and infidelity to the covenant.* Secondary causes for the division are easy to find: the ancient and ever abiding jealousy of the Ephraimites (Judg.

28

Nos. 27–31. Solomon's Temple, from the Howland-Garber reconstruction model, copyright 1950, 1954, 1967 E. G. Howland.   **27**. Front view of Temple, with the Copper or Molten Sea to left and altar of holocaust to right.   **28**. Temple interior: entrance to right, Holy Place, and Holy of Holies with cherubim to left.   **29**. Detail from Holy Place: candelabrum to right and left, cherubim, etc.   **30**. Twelve oxen holding the Great Molten Sea (see 2 Chron. 4:6; 1 Kings 7:23-26).   **31**. Holy of Holies; note window apertures and Star of David in floor woodwork. *Photos courtesy:* Southeastern Films, Atlanta, Georgia.

29

30

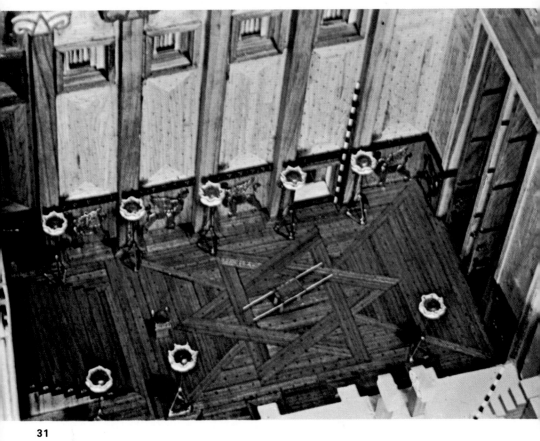

31

8:1ff; 9:1-6; 12:1-7; 2 Sam. 2:9ff; 20:2ff); the heavy taxes imposed by Solomon (1 Kings 12:4ff); forced labor (5:13; 9:21; 11:28) imposed upon the independent and democratic Israelites for the sake of royal projects benefitting for the most part only Judah and the crown domains (1 Kings 11:28; 12:18). Rehoboam's senseless refusal to lighten the taxes (1 Kings 12:12-15) provides the occasion for the rebellion, and Jeroboam's readiness to lead the Israelites provides the final element for the division of the kingdom (12:20).

12:25-33   Jeroboam I, son of Nebat, for political reasons inaugurates calf-worship (the use of golden calves to serve as bearers of the invisible Divinity) at Dan and Bethel, ordains his own priests because the legitimate priests flee south to Jerusalem (2 Chr. 11:13-16), and institutes feast days to rival the great festivals at the Temple in Jerusalem.

Dynasties and kings of the northern kingdom

KINGS		PROPHETS	EVENTS AND PERSONAGES
JEROBOAM I	926-907	AHIJAH	Division of the kingdom (926)
NADAB	907-906		Pharaoh Shishak invades Palestine (918)
BAASHA	906-883		Baasha attacks Judah (1 Kings 15:16-22)
ELAH	883-882		
ZIMRI	882		
OMRI	882-871		Omri founds the city of Samaria (875)
AHAB	871-852	ELIJAH	At Karkar Ahab helps hold back the Assyrians
AHAZIAH	852-851		Athaliah, daughter of Ahab, marries Joram, the crown prince of Judah
JEHORAM	851-845		
JEHU	845-818	ELISHA	Jehu destroys the house of Ahab
JEHOAHAZ	818-802		

KINGS		PROPHETS	EVENTS AND PERSONAGES
JEHOASH	802-787		
JEROBOAM II	787-747	AMOS	
ZECHARIAH	747-746	HOSEA	
SHALLUM	747-746		
MENAHEM	746-737		
PEKAHIAH	736-735	MICAH	
PEKAH	734-733	ISAIAH	Syro-Ephraimitic war (734-733)
HOSHEA	732-724		Tiglath-pileser III invades Palestine
			Siege and Fall of Samaria (724-722)

14:7-11 Ahijah, the prophet who had previously supported Jeroboam (1 Kings 11:29-39), turns against him because of his institution of calf-worship and predicts the destruction of his dynasty. After a twenty-two year reign (14:19-20), Jeroboam dies and is succeeded by his son, Nadab (15:25-31), who is assassinated by Baasha. The author turns in an adverse judgment on both Nadab (15:26) and Baasha (16:2-3).

16:8-23 Baasha's son, Elah, is assassinated by Zimri around 883 B.C., and Zimri, Tibni, and Omri (all generals in the Israelite army) wage internecine war; Omri is finally successful.

16:16ff Omri, acclaimed king by the people, leaves Tirzah and founds the new capital of Samaria (cf. LFAP 154; WHAB 49; 59). Judged unfaithful by the author, nothing more is said about Omri, even though from secular historical records it is known that he was one of Israel's greatest kings. Nothing could better demonstrate the theological purpose of the author than this brief notice about Omri.

16:29-33 Ahab succeeds Omri and marries Jezebel, a Phoenician princess and a crusading apostle of Canaanite Baalism. During the period of the Omrid dynasty (Omri, Ahab, Ahaziah, and Joram), two great crises arise in the history of the true religion: (a) the attempt by Jezebel and Ahab to wipe out the true religion in the north and replace it with Baalism; (b) the near extinction of the Davidic dynasty in Judah by Athaliah, Ahab's daughter (2 Kings 11). Both of these crises are spearheaded by

Jezebel, against whom God sends two of the greatest Old Testament prophets, Elijah and Elisha.

16:30ff Ahab. Severely judged by the author (16:30; 21:20-24), Ahab is nevertheless a brave man (20:11ff; 22:24-36) and perhaps a potentially good one (20:31; 21:27). He is, however, ruined by the wickedest woman in the Bible (21:25). Elijah opposes him because he permits Jezebel to introduce Baalism into the kingdom (18:18) and condones her high-handed murder of Naboth (21:17ff). Ahab wars with Ben-hadad of Syria and is at first successful (20:1-34). In a later war with Syria (22:1ff) assisted by King Jehoshaphat of Judah, whose son Joram had married his daughter Athaliah (2 Kings 8:18), Ahab dies bravely on the field of battle (22:24-26). It is probable that the author of Kings includes these wars only because of the opportunity they afforded him to show Ahab in opposition to the prophets (20:35-42; 22:5-28). A good king according to Deuteronomic standards is one who heeds the admonitions of God's prophets. Ahab follows in the tradition of Saul.

16:31ff Jezebel. A daughter of Ethbaal, king of the Sidonians and priest of the goddess Astarte, Jezebel is an ardent apostle of paganism. She persuades Ahab to build a temple to Baal (16:32), persecutes the followers of the true religion (18:3-5), wages a personal war against Elijah (19:1-3), arranges the liquidation of Naboth with cruel efficiency (21:7-15), dies bravely and flamboyantly at the hands of Jehu, the rebel general of the Israelite army (2 Kings 9:30ff).

17:1ff Elijah. A Gileadite from Tishbeth, Elijah confronts Ahab and predicts a terrible drought as the opening salvo in his war to save the soul of Israel from Jezebel's diabolic influence. He hides from Ahab by the brook Cherith (17:1-7) and later at Zareshath in Phoenicia (17:8-10) where he multiplies food for a widow (17:10-16) to save her son from a starvation death (17:17-24). After three years of famine Elijah confronts Ahab (18:18), confounds the prophets of Baal on Mount Carmel (18:19-39) and has them executed by the brook Kishon (18:40). Threatened with death by Jezebel (19:1-2), Elijah flees for his life to Sinai (19:4-9); there he experiences a mysterious vision of God's spirituality (19:10-14) and is commanded to commission Elisha as his successor and have Hazael brought to power in Damascus and Jehu in Israel (19:15-21).

Back in Israel he threatens Ahab with retribution for his foul condonation of the death of Naboth (21:17-25). And later he calls down fire from heaven upon the messengers of King Ahaziah, Ahab's successor and son (2 Kings 1:1ff). Sometime before 845, he is carried off in a whirlwind (2 Kings 2:11) and is succeeded by Elisha.

19:19-21 Elisha. Called suddenly from his work, like the apostles, Elisha leaves a prosperous farm to follow Elijah and begins a prophetic career that lasts almost 63 years (850–787; cf. 1 Kings 19; 2 Kings 2–13). Unlike Elijah, who was poor and a hermit-type, Elisha is apparently wealthy (twelve yoke of oxen), has a personal servant (2 Kings 4:12 *passim*) and appears to cherish social and community contacts more than Elijah (*passim*). In action Elisha is a wonder-worker whose miracles are remarkably similar to those of Jesus. He cures the waters of Jericho (2:21), calls bears to punish blasphemous boys (2:24), predicts a water supply for the armies (3:20), multiplies oil to support a widow (4:3), rewards the Shunamitess with child (4:16), restores the same child to life (4:35), purifies food for the prophets' meal (4:41), multiplies bread (4:42), cures Naaman's leprosy (5:14; cf. Luke 4:27), restores a lost axe (6:6), and exhibits powers of clairvoyance (6:9; 6:31-33; 8:10).

9:1ff Elisha sends a disciple to anoint Jehu king of Israel, which results in the dissolution of the House of Omri and the slaying of Jezebel. This section (as well as 2 Kings 3:11; 5:8; 6:8; 6:32; 8:6; 13:14) shows the great political influence of Elisha.

9:2ff Jehu, the founder of the fourth dynasty in Israel (Jehu, Jehoahaz, Jehoash, Jeroboam II, Zechariah), is anointed king by a disciple of Elisha (9:2-10) according to the commission of Elijah (1 Kings 19:15). After assassinating Joram, king of Israel, Jezebel's youngest son, and Ahaziah of Judah, Athaliah's son (9:24-29), Jehu drives to Jezreel, orders the execution of Jezebel (9:30-37), executes the remaining members of the royal family (10:1-11), and slaughters the priests of Baal by stratagem. Thus he restores the true religion in Israel and completes the campaign begun by Elijah as early as 870.

10:31-36 Despite the initial reforming zeal of Jehu's revolution (9:22; 10:18-30), the author's judgment on Jehu is negative because eventually he too follows in the steps of Jeroboam I (10:31).

11:1ff Athaliah, daughter of Ahab, Queen-mother in Judah after the death of King Joram, assumes the sceptre of Judah after the assassination of her son by Jehu (9:27-28); she puts to death all her grandsons except Jehoash who is hid in the Temple by his aunt Jehosheba (11:1-2). Six years later (11:4-12), the high priest, Jehoiada, with the help of the army restores Jehoash to his rightful place as king and has Athaliah executed. She, like Jezebel, dies bravely and defiantly (11:13-16).

11:17ff Guided by the high priest, King Jehoash orders the temple of Baal destroyed and the pagan priests executed, thus completing in Judah the work begun in Israel by Jehu of putting an end to the paganism fostered by Jezebel and her family.

14:23-29 Jeroboam II is condemned by the author (14:24) for following in the footsteps of the first king of that name. Nevertheless, he is one of the great kings of Israel. During his forty year reign (787-747), Jeroboam II restores Israel's ancient boundaries from Moab to Hamath north of the Lake of Galilee and brings to Israel a prosperity rivalling that of the Solomonic era. Unfortunately, Israel's apostasy keeps pace with her prosperity, and it is during this period that the prophets Amos and Hosea are sent by God to rebuke king and people and to warn them that God's patience with Israel is being severely tried (cf. Amos 3:9; 4:1ff; 6:3ff; Hosea 4:11ff; 13:1ff). In 747 Jeroboam II dies (14:29). Six months later his son Zechariah is assassinated (15:8) and the dynasty of Jehu comes to an end.

15:8ff With the death of Zechariah, the northern kingdom enters a period of anarchy in government, of blindness and formalism in religion, and of blatant worldliness in society (Amos and Hosea *passim*) that continues until the kingdom is destroyed in 722 by the invading armies of Assyria. Shallum, the assassin of Zechariah (15:8), is himself assassinated after a one month reign by Menahem (15:14), who suffers the first Assyrian assault led by Tiglath-pileser III in 738 (15:19-20). Menahem's son, Pekahiah, is assassinated by Pekah in 735 (15:35). After a two year reign, during which he wages war against Ahaz of Judah (the so-called Syro-Ephraimitic war cf. 2 Kings 16; Is. 7), Pekah is assassinated by Hoshea who then submits to Assyrian domination until 724 B.C.

17:1ff The end of the northern kingdom. Subservient to Shalmaneser V of Assyria in the first years of his reign (17:1-3), Hoshea, depending on Egyptian support, refuses tribute in 725 (17:4). Assyrian retribution is swift. In 724, Shalmeneser begins the siege of Samaria. In 722 Samaria falls, the northern tribes are carried off as captives to Assyria, and their kingdom comes to an inglorious end. *N.B.* Assyria rose to power in northern Mesopotamia during the eleventh century. In the ninth century, her armies were stopped in the course of their advance west at Karkar in Phoenicia by a coalition of kings including Ahab of Israel. Jehu and his successors, however, paid tribute to Assyria from 840 to 800. Internal troubles kept the Assyrian emperors occupied during the reign of Jeroboam II. But in 745 Tiglath-pileser III began a new thrust west. Invited to settle the Syro-Ephraimitic war in 734, Tiglath-pileser put both Israel and Judah under tribute, capturing and deporting Israelites from northern Palestine in 732 (2 Kings 15:29). In 725, Israel refused tribute for the last time and was destroyed.

17:7ff At the end of the second part of his account of Israel's infidelity (1 Kings 12 to 2 Kings 17), the Deuteronomist pauses as he did at the end of Solomon's reign (1 Kings 11) to summarize the melancholy story and to emphasize his teaching that God deserted His people only because they first deserted Him.

17:24-41 The Deuteronomist digresses to record the origin of the Samaritans, their mixed blood and their half idolatrous religion. The Samaritans of later ages (cf. Neh. 4:1-4; New Testament *passim*) were scorned by the Jews because of their tainted origin dating back to this time.

In the third and last part of Kings (2 Kings 18–25) continues the history of the southern kingdom of Judah down to its destruction in 587 by the Babylonians. It should be noted that to this most important period in the history of the kingdom, running from 722 to 587 and embracing the lifetimes of Isaiah and Jeremiah and a half dozen minor prophets, the author of Kings gives a mere eight chapters. It is no accident. It emphasizes once more that the Deuteronomist's primary purpose was *to prove the infidelity of the kings.* Here as in the earlier parts of his history the author gives extra space to those reigns in which the prophets or the Temple are concerned, *viz.*, the reigns of Hezekiah and Josiah. For the others he is content to continue with his stereotyped formula.

In 1 Kings 12 to 2 Kings 17, few Judean kings are of any special importance. The list includes: Rehoboam (1 Kings 12),

Abijam and Asa (1 Kings 15), Jehoshaphat (1 Kings 22:41-53), Joram and Ahaziah (2 Kings 8:16-29), Athaliah and Jehoash (2 Kings 11–12), Amaziah, the contemporary of Jeroboam II (2 Kings 14), Azariah and Jotham (2 Kings 15), and lastly Ahaz (2 Kings 16). These kings, as well as the kings of Judah who ruled after the destruction of the northern kingdom, will be studied with the history of the Davidic dynasty which is treated at length in the Chronicler's account.

8. Amos and Hosea in the Last Years of the Northern Kingdom

In the last years of the northern kingdom, as the Assyrian tidal wave was gathering momentum in the east, a new type of prophet, the "writing prophet," arose among God's Chosen People. Unlike the Former Prophets (the authors of Joshua, Judges, Samuel, and Kings) who wrote but did not preach and the earlier preaching prophets who preached but did not write (Samuel, Nathan, Elijah, and Elisha, etc.), the so-called "Latter Prophets" not only preached but put their sermons in writing for the benefit of posterity. Of these, the first were Amos and Hosea in Israel, to be followed in Judah by Micah, Isaiah, Jeremiah, Ezekiel, and the minor prophets. It is with Amos, therefore, that we find for the first time united in one man the charisms of inspired preaching and inspired writing.

It is with Amos, too, however, that the reader first meets new difficulties in reading the inspired text. He finds, for instance, that whereas the few recorded oracles and sermonettes of the earlier preaching prophets are recounted with historical and psychological context accompanying them (e.g., Moses in Exod. 4–19; Samuel in 1 Sam. 8–15; Nathan in 2 Sam. 7 and 12; Elijah in 1 Kings 17–19; and Elisha in 2 Kings 3–8), the more numerous and more lengthy oracles and sermons of the Latter Prophets are given for the most part devoid of immediate and precise historical context. They are given, in short, in anthological form, one sermon or oracle following another with only a brief inscription at the beginning of the collection to indicate the general period and kingdom in which the prophet preached and the odd scrap of internal evidence in the sermons themselves to indicate precisely where, when, why, and to whom he preached.

Since little or nothing is related in the historical books about any of the prophets with the exception of Isaiah, the reader must content himself for information about the historical context with the meager information given in the introductory inscription to each prophet and with whatever information he can glean from the text itself. This is not much, but in most cases it proves adequate when combined with the additional facts given in the historical books.

Amos

All that we know about Amos, we know from his book of sermons.[1] The inscription (1:1) tells us he was a shepherd from Tekoa, a little town six miles south of Bethlehem; he was a Judean, therefore, and not an Israelite. The incident related in 7:10-17 tells us he was not only a shepherd but a "dresser of sycamore trees." It tells us further that Amos preached at Bethel, one of the two temples founded by Jeroboam I (1 Kings 12:29) to keep the Israelites from journeying south to the Temple of Jerusalem, and that he was opposed there by Amaziah the high priest of the Bethel temple.

The inscription also gives us the historical background of Amos' preaching: "the days of Jeroboam, the son of Jehoash, king of Israel, two years before the earthquake." Amos preached, therefore, in the reign of Jeroboam II (787-747), a time of great material prosperity and corresponding moral corruption (2 Kings 14:23-29 and Amos *passim*). For the crimes that cried to heaven for vengeance and which eventually in 722 brought that vengeance, we have only to read the powerful, colorful, and forthright sermons of Amos — sermons that have earned for him, because of his passionate concern for the oppressed poor, the title of "prophet of social justice."

Of the four great prophets sent to the northern kingdom, Amos is the third in time. He was preceded by Elijah and Elisha and followed by Hosea, the last prophet before the fall of the kingdom. Israelite prophets predominate during this period, because the danger to the true religion is greater in the northern kingdom. Beginning with the sin of Jeroboam I, who set up the idols at Dan and Bethel, Israel slipped more and more into crass idolatry and brazen disobedience to the covenant. Even though Elijah and Elisha had succeeded in staving off the Phoenician spearhead lead by Jezebel, the people continued to turn away from God in the succeeding years (cf. 2 Kings 10:28-32; 13:1-2; 13:10-12; 14:23-24). Idolatry and disobedience reach their peak during the reign of Jeroboam II. The cancer is so general in society that even the preaching of Amos and Hosea is of no avail. Less than thirty years after the preaching of Amos, God is compelled to destroy the northern kingdom.

[1] Cf. JBC 245-252.

The book is divided into three parts: I (1–2), oracles indicting Israel and the surrounding nations for their crimes against the natural law; II (3–6), the "Hear this word" sermons (3:1ff; 4:1ff; 5:1ff), followed by the "Woe to you" sermons (5:16ff; 6:1ff); III (7–9), five visions of the destruction impending on unrepentant Israel (7:1–9:8), followed by a short epilogue on the coming of better days in messianic times (9:9-15).

Significant passages in the book of Amos

Part One / Amos 1–2 / Oracles Against the Nations

1:2ff The words, "Yahweh roars . . . ," keynote the book of Amos. Beginning with an oracle against Damascus (Syria) in vv. 3-5, Amos roars God's displeasure against Philistia, Phoenicia (Tyre), Edom, Ammon, Moab, and Judah, culminating in a devastating indictment of Israel (2:6-16). In each oracle, a set formula is followed:

a) *culpability*: "For the three transgressions. . . ."

b) *threat*: "I will not turn it (threat of destruction) back. . . ."

c) *Specific sin*: "Because they have, e.g., threshed Gilead. . . ."

d) *punishment*: "I will send a fire (destruction). . . ."

Three points should be noted concerning these oracles against the nations: 1. Amos' primary purpose in the oracles is to show that God is ruler of all men and all nations and that He punishes rebellion against His law wherever He finds it. 2. Amos' secondary purpose in castigating the sins of the nations is to highlight the even greater sins of God's chosen ones who, despite their greater gifts and their revealed knowledge of God's will, are no better at times than the ignorant and underprivileged pagans. 3. Beginning with Amos, and for the same reasons, the oracles against the nations become a typical stock-in-trade type of sermon for subsequent prophets (cf. Is. 13–23; Jer. 46–51; Ez. 24–32; Nah. 1-3; Zeph. 2; Hab.).

2:6-16 Following the same formula as in the previous oracles (culpability, threat, specific sin, punishment), Amos concludes with an indictment of Israel. Almost exclusively, he singles out crimes of social injustice: enslaving the poor (2:6); oppressing the weak (2:7); ignoring the covenant laws written to protect the underprivileged (2:8; cf. Exod. 22:20-25; 23:6, 11; Deut.

24:12-13). That such social injustice and oppression of the poor by the rich is widespread in the prosperous reign of Jeroboam II is clear from Amos' consistent return to the same theme (cf. 4:1; 5:11-12; 8:4-6).

2:13-16   Amos' first prediction of the downfall of the northern kingdom—a threat and a prediction that will be repeated many times both by him and by his successor, Hosea.

Part Two / Amos 3–6 / "Hear This Word" Sermons

3:1-15   In. vv. 3-8, Amos the Judean defends his mission as prophet to the northern kingdom (cf. 7:10-17) with a series of rhetorical questions setting up an affirmative answer to all including the last: "When the Lord God speaks, who will not prophesy?" (v. 8). He then goes on to predict the certain destruction of Israel (vv. 9-15).

4:1-13   Second "Hear this word" sermon. Beginning with a violent castigation of the wealthy, luxury-loving women of Samaria ("cows of Bashan"), for whom deportation to Assyria is predicted (vv. 1-3), Amos unmasks the religious formalism and hypocrisy of the northerners (vv. 4-5) and points out to them their stubborn refusal to heed the divine pedagogy of God's medicinal punishments (vv. 6-11). For such crimes and stubborness they are told: "Prepare to meet your God, O Israel" (vv. 11-13).

5:1ff   Third "Hear this word" sermon. Beginning with the dirge, "Fallen never to rise again is the virgin Israel" (v. 1), Amos proceeds to give the reasons for Israel's approaching destruction—her idolatry at Bethel, Gilgal, and Beersheba (vv. 4-5); her oppression of the poor (vv. 6-18); her failure to hate evil and seek good (vv. 14-15). Note that each section has as its keynote either the expression "Seek . . ." (vv. 4, 6, 14), or "Woe . . ." (vv. 7, 18; 6:1). The first "Woe" (v. 7) is directed against Israel's iniquitous law courts where the poor can receive no redress for crimes committed against them by the rich. The second "Woe" (v. 18) is directed to those "who desire the 'Day of the Lord'" (vv. 18-25), an expression introduced by Amos which will later become stereotyped, referring to that time or "day" when God will intervene in Israel's history to punish the wicked and reward the good. While the "day" usually refers to a divine intervention in the forseeable future, in later literature it will refer often to the great "day" when God will realize His plan for the salvation of Israel and the world. It is an expression which will take on eschatological and messianic overtones, although in the time of Amos it has neither the messianic nor the eschatological implications it will later acquire in Isaiah and Jeremiah and in the apocalyptic writers.

The third "Woe" is directed to the idle, luxury-loving rich (6:1-14). Note the scorn for the "beds of ivory" (v. 4), the "best oils" (v. 6), and the "castles" (v. 8; cf. also 3:10, 11, 15). In his references to the wealth of Israel, Amos confirms the brief description of Jeroboam II's reign given in 2 Kings 14:23-28. The sermon concludes with the ominous words: "I am raising up against you, O House of Israel, a nation that shall oppress you . . ." (6:14).

Part Three / Amos 7—9 / Visions of Destruction

7:1-6 Beginning with two visions of destruction (vv. 1-3, a locust plague; and vv. 4-6, a drought) decreed by God but averted by the prayers of the prophet, the sermon relates three more visions of destruction (7:7-9, God with the plumbline of destruction; 8:1-14, the basket of ripe fruit; 9:1-8, God presiding over the destruction of the temple at Bethel). The point of the build-up (visions of destruction averted, followed by visions of destruction that will not be averted) is to show that when God's medicinal punishments are scorned (7:1-6, the locust plague and the drought), there is nothing left for God to do but proceed to total destruction (the visions of God with the plumbline, the basket of ripe fruit, and God presiding over the destruction of the temple at Bethel).

Ch. 7:10-17 interrupts the sequence of visions. Some authors explain this interruption as an explanatory note of an editor on 7:9c. Others claim that Amos' ministry in Israel terminated with his ejection from the northern kingdom after the threat to the king in the third vision and that the incident in 7:10-17 is narrated to bridge the gap between Amos' ministry in the north, summarized in the first three visions, and his ministry in the south summarized in the last two visions.

7:7-9 Third vision, "God with the plumbline." As a builder uses a plumbline in construction, so will God use a plumbline in His methodical destruction of Israel. "I will forgive them no longer" (v. 8) is meant in the sense that God will never again 'spare them', as in Exodus (12:27), where the avenging angel 'passed over' the houses of the Israelites.

8:1-14 Fourth vision, "A basket of ripe fruit." Amos plays on the word *qayits* (ripe), and the word *qaets* (end). As summer fruit comes to maturity and is ripe, so Israel has come to her end, ripe for punishment. The reasons for Israel's punishment (vv. 4-6) are her injustice and oppression of the poor (cf. 2:6-8; 5:11-12).

9:1-8 Fifth vision, "Yahweh presiding over the destruction of the temple at Bethel." Presumably the 'altar' and 'bases' mentioned here are those of the temple at Bethel (cf. 4:4; 7:10), where destruction will begin while the faithless Israelites are gathered there for idolatrous worship. That escape from God's avenging hand is impossible is indicated in the hyperbolical expressions "though they break through to the nether world" (v. 2), "though they hide on the summit of Carmel" (v. 3). The expression, "like the Ethiopians . . ." (v. 7), is God's way of reminding the Israelites that they were no better than any other nation until God chose them. Since they have rejected that choice, God will show them that by themselves they are no different from the Ethiopians — a nation not chosen by God and therefore receiving no special protection (v. 8).

9:9-10 The remnant. As indicated in v. 8, the destruction of Israel will not be absolute — "I will not destroy the house of Jacob completely"; some, therefore, will be saved. Those saved are compared to the pebbles that remain in the sieve after the soil has passed through. (Note the same comparison in the Gospels to signify the separation of the good from the wicked, e.g., Matthew 13:24-29, parable of the weeds; 13:47-50, net and fishes; 25:31-46, sheep and goats.) This doctrine of the "remnant," so frequently mentioned by later prophets, finds its earliest witness in Gen. 18:25-33 (Abraham's search for a remnant in Sodom and Gomorrah); later it is witnessed to in 1 Kings 19:18 (the seven thousand in the time of Elias "who did not bend the knee to Baal"); a final witness is in the Apocalypse (20:5-8). It is this remnant, the small group of faithful in every age, the "Israel of God" according to the expression of St. Paul (Gal. 6:16), that will form the nucleus of the kingdom of God in the Old Testament and, in union with Christ in the New Testament, the nucleus of the Mystical Body, the Church.

9:11-12   "On that day." This is a typical prophetic way of speaking of the "great day," that of God's intervention in history when He will establish the kingdom of the Messiah; when the "fallen hut of David," first ruined by the division of Solomon's kingdom in 926, then partially destroyed in 722, and almost completely annihilated in 587, will be restored and "conquer what is left of Edom and *all the nations*" (its universality).

9:13-15   "Days are coming." Another stereotyped expression for messianic times, followed by the typical metaphorical description of the messianic age as one of fabulous material prosperity (for similar descriptions of the messianic era cf. Hosea 2:21-23; Is. 11:6; 54:1-12; 60; Joel 4:18; Apoc. 22:2).

Hosea

The beginning of the dire end prophesied by Amos for faithless Israel begins to be fulfilled in the days of Hosea, his contemporary and successor in the prophetic office.[1] He preaches during the last chaotic years of Israel's independence, sometime between 750 and 722, though there is no evidence to indicate that he lived to see the actual fulfillment of his own and Amos' fateful predictions.

It is a time of national disintegration. The sermons of Amos to the opulent, luxury-loving Israelites have had no effect. Wealth has increased. Morality, justice, fidelity to the Mosaic covenant have decreased. The people cannot hear, or they ignore, in their single-minded concern for the good life, the approaching tramp of Assyrian troops under the command of the new and vigorous Assyrian king, Tiglath-pileser III (747-727). The apostasy, halted temporarily by Elijah and Elisha battling the inroads of Baalism under Jezebel, moves inexorably to its final stage, leaving the northern kingdom in a state of corruption that can be treated only with the avenging knife of war.

After the death of Jeroboam II (787-747) there are twenty years of nearly continual anarchy (cf. 2 Kings 15:8-31). Jeroboam's son, Zechariah, is assassinated by Shallum. A month later Shallum is assassinated by Menahem, in whose days "Pul, king of Assyria, came against the land" (2 Kings 15:19). Menahem is forced to give Pul (the Babylonian name for Tiglath-

[1] Cf. J. L. McKenzie, "Divine Passion in Osee," *CBQ*, 17 (1955), 167–179; JBC 253–264.

pileser III) a thousand talents of silver. Pekahiah, Menahem's son, reigns two years before he is assassinated by Pekah, who in turn after a two year reign is assassinated by Hoshea, the last king of Israel. Ten years later the northern kingdom is no more.

Of Hosea, the last prophet of the northern kingdom, we know nothing beyond what is told us in the biographical section of his book (1–3), and in the editor's superscription (1:1). Unlike Amos, Hosea is a born Israelite. He preaches at a time when Amos is in retirement writing his prophecies, when Isaiah and Micah have not yet begun their work in the south.

Unlike Amos, the prophet of social justice, Hosea is the prophet of divine love, the Saint John of the Old Testament. Of a nature profound and passionate, all heart, almost excessively emotional, Hosea describes God as a lover beside himself with emotion at the infidelity of his beloved.

To describe God's love, Hosea uses the tragic story of his own unhappy marriage with Gomer. After the marriage and the birth of three children, Gomer leaves Hosea and becomes a sacred prostitute at one of the Baal shrines (cf. Num. 25:1-5; Deut. 23:18-19). Because he still loves her, Hosea takes Gomer back, despite her infidelity.

Later he sees in his own tragic experience with Gomer the parallel of God's experience with Israel. His description of this parallel tragedy is found in ch. 1–3. Here Hosea represents God, Gomer is Israel, the lovers are the Baals with whom Israel was committing adultery by her idolatry; the hire of the harlot constituted the material blessings from God which Israel ascribed to the Baals.

A poorly preserved text, added to Hosea's telegraphic, passionately emotional style, make the book difficult reading. It is divided into two parts: I. the allegory of the marriage (ch. 1–3); II. sermons based on the allegory (ch. 4–14).

Significant passages in the book of Hosea

Part One / Hosea 1–3 / The Allegory of the Marriage

1:2ff *The marriage.* Of the two accounts of Hosea's marriage to Gomer, the first biographical (1:2–3) and the second autobiographical (3:1-3), it is disputed whether the first represents the account of Hosea's first marriage to Gomer and the second the account of his taking her back after her defection; or whether in fact both are accounts of the one and only marriage, the initial marriage of Hosea to Gomer who is already a prostitute when Hosea marries her.

On purely textual grounds it is impossible to determine which is the correct opinion. However, on the working out of the parallel — God's espousals with Israel, Israel's infidelity and rejection, followed by her eventual re-espousal to God after a period of trial— it would appear that the first alternative is more likely. Thus Hosea married Gomer, a woman of a harlotrous bent, who, after the birth of three legitimate children, left her husband (1:2-9). Later, after she had become a sacred prostitute at a Baal shrine, Hosea bought her back from the Baal shrine guardians and following a period of trial of her marital fidelity eventually took her back as wife (3:1-3).

1:3-9 *The children.* The true names of Hosea's and Gomer's children we shall never know. The names given are symbolic. And Hosea's precedent will be followed by Isaiah (cf. Is. 7:3; 7:14; 8:4; 9:5). The children thus become living prophecies as Isaiah will later expressly state with regard to himself and his children: "Look at me and the children whom Yahweh has given me; we are signs and portents in Israel from Yahweh of hosts who dwells on Mount Sion" (Is. 8:18).

2:4ff *Divine pedagogy.* Hosea's words are both a warning that is ignored and a prophecy that is fulfilled within a short time. The words, however, cannot be properly understood unless one realizes that Hosea is dramatizing Israel's history of infidelity from the time of her first encounter with Baalism (Num. 25) down through the days of Jezebel (1 Kings 17ff) to his own day when her apostasy to Baalism has become general and irreversible. His references, moreover, to the crops (vv. 7, 10, 11) and to the "lovers" (vv. 7, 12, 14, 15, 19) must be understood against the background of the Baal fertility cults to which the Israelites had succumbed, putting their confidence for good harvests in the fertility gods rather than in Yahweh (vv. 4-7).

While the adultery spoken of by Hosea is allegorical, representing religious infidelity to Israel's covenant-vowed monotheism, there can be no doubt of Hosea's disgust with and his people's enticement to the orgiastic fertility rites of the Baal shrines (cf. Num. 25:1-5; Deut. 23:18-19; Hosea 2:15; 4:12-18).

The divine pedagogy put in motion to bring Israel to repentance follows three broad steps: 1. the end of her material prosperity (vv. 10-15 plus vv. 8-9); 2. deportation and exile in a foreign land where she is to be purified as she was in the desert after leaving Egypt and before coming into the promised land (vv. 16-17); 3. the rebirth of love (vv. 18-20) and the taking back of Israel as wife by her divine spouse (vv. 21-25).

The reader should note that the following section (3:1-5; 2:1-3) is another version of this same message. It should be noted, moreover, that the "new covenant" theology of Jeremiah (Jer. 31:31-37; 32:36-41; 33) is already implicit in Hosea (2:21-25).

Hosea's use of the marriage relationship will be re-echoed in later prophets (cf. Jer. 2:1-2; 2:20-21; 3:1-5; Ez. 16; 23; Is. 54:4-6; 61:10-11; 62:4-5); and especially in the Canticle of Canticles. It is the New Testament, however, that gives to Hosea's magnificent vision its glorious fulfillment (cf. Matthew 9:15; John 3:29; Eph. 5:25-33; Apoc. 21:1-4; 21:9-10).

Part Two / Hosea 4–14 / Sermons

4:1-3 *The knowledge of God.* In his catalogue of the crimes of Israel, Hosea places in parallelism with "no fidelity, no mercy" the words "no knowledge of God" (v. 1de). Here we have a clear indication of what the word *knowledge* connotes to Hosea: not something purely intellectual and speculative, but something moral and practical. For Hosea, to know God is to love Him, to acknowledge one's relationship to God by doing His will. Thus for Hosea, to know the right is to do the right. The same meaning is clear in 2:22; 5:4d; 6:6.

4:4-11 *Unworthy priests.* Hosea attacks the priests of his time for not fulfilling their duty of teaching the people the law of God (v. 6) and for abetting the sins of the people (v. 8) in order to increase for themselves the portions of the sacrifices for sin (Lev. 6:19-22) and reparation (Lev. 7:7) ordinarily given to them. Thus, instead of manifesting God's holiness (Lev. 10:3) and teaching the people as they had been commissioned by God (Deut. 17:8-13; 33:8-11; Mal. 2:6-7), they have followed the example of the iniquitous priest-sons of Eli (1 Sam. 2:12-17). The point of Hosea's argument is well expressed in the well-known aphorism, *corruptio optimi pessima.* It is taken up by later prophets in similar language (cf. Is. 28:7; Micah 3:11; Jer. 2:8; 6:13; Zeph. 3:4; Mal. 1:6—2:9.

6:1ff *Religious formalism.* Like Amos (4:4-5), Hosea assails the Israelites, as our Lord will later assail the Pharisees (Matthew 23), for putting their confidence in external religious rites divorced from internal dispositions of love and obedience. Like Samuel (1 Sam. 15:22), Hosea exalts love and obedience above sacrifice. His words should not be understood as a rejection of sacrifice, but as a rejection of sacrifice without the requisite internal sentiments of religion, without which all cultic acts are hollow. The opinion of those who hold that the prophets rejected sacrifice entirely is based on a misunderstanding of the Hebrew idiom for emphasis exemplified here (Hosea 6:6) and in Isaiah (1:10ff). The idiomatic meaning of the apparent categoric denial is clear from 1 Cor. 1:17, "For Christ did not send me to baptize but to preach," where St. Paul's meaning is clear from the context. He seems to deny baptism as part of his work, but only to emphasize that his *principal* mission is preaching (cf. also Amos 3:2; Mal. 1:3). Because of the eternal temptation to substitute the easy externals for the difficult internals of religion, Hosea's warning against formalism will be renewed again and again by later prophets and by our Lord (cf. Is. 1:10-17; Micah 6:7-8; Jer. 7:3-11; Ps. 50:8-13; Sir. 34:18-19; Matthew 5:23-24; 23:16-28).

7:8-12 *Foreign alliances.* Hosea attacks foreign alliances because they manifest a lack of faith and confidence in God, who has promised to watch over His people. Jeremiah will be even more direct: "Cursed is the man who trusts in human beings, who seeks his strength in flesh, whose heart turns away from Yahweh" (Jer. 17:5; also Jer. 2:13-19; Is. 7:4-13; 8:5-13; 30:1-16; 31:1).

10:1 *Israel the vine.* The comparison of Israel to a choice vine planted and tended by God is already found in Genesis (49:22); it will be used again by later prophets (cf. Is. 5:1-7; Jer. 2:21; 6:9; 12:10; Ez. 15:1-8; 17:3-10; 19:10-14), by a psalmist (Ps. 80:8ff), and by Jesus in the New Testament (cf. Matthew 21:33-44; John 15:1-8). In most cases there is either implicit or explicit the idea expressed most clearly in Isaiah (ch. 5) and Matthew (ch. 21) that God, having cared so tenderly for Israel, His vine, looks forward to fruits of love and devotion in return.

11:1-9 *Israel, God's beloved son.* The message of ch. 11 is the same in substance as the message of the first three chapters: God's love for Israel — only the metaphor is changed from the love of God as husband loving His unfaithful wife to the love of God loving His ungrateful son (compare Hosea 2:7-8 with 11:1-4; 2:9-13 with 11:5-7; and 2:14-23 with 11:8-9). The metaphor is based upon Exod. 4:22 and is used as well in Deut. 1:31; 32:5ff; Is. 1:2; Ez. 16:5-7. Significant is the expression of God's love in vv. 8-9, comparable in poignancy with Christ's words about Jerusalem on the eve of His passion: "Jerusalem, Jerusalem, how often would I have gathered thy children as a hen gathers her young under her wings, but thou wouldst not" (Matthew 23:37).

Hosea's higher anthropomorphic description of the conflict of emotions in God between His love and His justice, described here as a veritable revulsion of feeling, has no parallel any place in the Bible as an expression of the greatness, tenderness, and genuineness of God's love for His people. It should not, however, blind the reader to the equal greatness and genuineness of God's justice described in ch. 13:2–14:1; in this passage Hosea makes it abundantly clear that God's love cannot be scorned with impunity by His people nor divorced from His justice (cf. J. McKenzie, *loc. cit.*).

14:2-9   *A call to repentance.* By means of a dramatic dialogue, Hosea expresses what God would say to Israel (vv. 5-9) if Israel would heed His call to conversion (vv. 2-3ab) and respond with a cry for forgiveness (vv. 3c-4). It is Hosea's expression of what Ezekiel will more starkly and succinctly state during the Babylonian exile: "Why should you die, O house of Israel? For I have no pleasure in the death of anyone who dies, says the Lord God. Return and live" (Ez. 18:32). It is only in 722 B.C., when Israel has refused to "return and live" and God has punished her with destruction and exile, that the unflinching severity of Amos and the apparent tenderness of Hosea are seen to be equal attributes of the same loving but just God. In Christ's parabolic description of the last judgment (Matthew 25:31-46), the same love and the same justice appear equally clear.

Before continuing with a study of prophetism and a reading of the Chronicler's history and the prophets of Judah, it will be well for the reader to pause for a moment and reflect on the importance of Hosea's vivid description of Yahweh as a God of love. He has already seen God's love described by the Yahwist in his great saga of Israel's beginnings. He has heard the author of Deuteronomy explicitly declare that it was love that motivated God in His dealings with His people. It is, however, the glory of Hosea that he was able by the grace of God to trumpet to the world through his magnificent use of the marriage relationship and the father-son bond between God and Israel, the central position of love in Old Testament religion. It is through Hosea that the dictum of St. John, "God is love," becomes part and parcel of Israel's theological thinking.

For those whose ideas of Old Testament religion is based on a knowledge of the legalistic perversions of the Pharisees described in the Gospels (cf. Matthew 23), Hosea supplies a salutary corrective. His doctrine of love as central in God's dealings with man in the Old Covenant serves to offset the misleading and often slogan-exaggerated impression that in the Old Testament God manifests Himself principally as a God of vengeance with a sadistic eye-for-eye justice. Such slogans unfortunately give an impression of contrast, as if God were a God of justice in the Old Testament and a God of love in the New. Whatever difference there is, is one of comparison, not of contrast. There can be no question of a change in God with regard to His attributes. There can, however, be a change in His manifestation of these attributes, at one time emphasising His justice, at another His love. On this basis, the greatest manifestation of God's love is obviously found in the Incarnation. But the Old Testament knew God very clearly as a God of love as well as of justice, as Hosea so well brings out. The difference, therefore, can only be one of degree and not of kind, since God manifests His love and His justice at all times.

5

Literary Analysis of the Deuteronomist's History

Noth's Theory

Literary analysis of the Deuteronomist's History has been dominated for the last two decades by the work of Martin Noth (*Überlieferungsgeschichtliche Studien*, Darmstadt, 1960). Noth's analysis of the literary evidence led him to the conclusion that a single theologian-author was responsible for the great historical work that runs from Deuteronomy through Joshua, Judges, 1–2 Samuel, and 1–2 Kings. His theory is that the Deuteronomist's History is a work composed during the Babylonian exile from sources selected, organized, and unified by means of transitional additions and strategically placed interpretative discourses and comments (particularly such discourses as Deut. 1–4; Jos. 1; 23; 1 Sam. 12; 1 Kings 8:14ff; 1 Kings 11; 2 Kings 17).

The major sources amalgamated and edited by the Deuteronomist are the following: 1. the seventh century work known as Original Deuteronomy; 2. the conquest traditions found in Joshua 2–11 and passim; 3. the legends of the Judges in Judg. 3–16; 4. the Samuel, Saul, and David traditions in 1–2 Samuel with special dependence on the biographies of David and on the court history of Solomon (2 Sam. 9–20; 1 Kings 1–2); 5. the chronicles of the Kings of Judah and Israel (1–2 Kings passim); 6. a collection of midrashic traditions and legends about the prophets (1–2 Kings passim).

Literary analysis of the work bears out the conclusion that the principal redactional technique of the Deuteronomist was his selection from the abundant sources available to him of those materials which supported the main theses of his theology. Since the source materials did not always make clear to the uninitiated reader the presence of the hand of God in Israel's history, the Deuteronomist complemented his selection of materials by arranging and interpreting his sources to make them intelligible. The literary techniques he used to interpret his sources are the following: explanatory asides (e.g., 1 Kings 11 and 2 Kings 17); explicit theological judgments (e.g., the judgments made on each of the kings of Israel and Judah in the books of Kings); skillfully composed interpretative discourses, put sometimes in the mouth of God (e.g., 1 Kings 9:3-9), but more often in the mouth of a prophet (e.g., 1 Kings 8:23-53; 11:11-13, 31-39; 14:7-16; 2 Kings 20:16-19; 21:11-15; 22:15-19; 23:26-27).

Noth's theory, while not universally accepted (cf. G. Fohrer, *An Introduction to the Old Testament*, pp. 192–195 for a contrary view) has received general and enthusiastic approval accompanied by a criticism of details which does not affect the substance of the theory. In our literary analysis of the Deuteronomist we are much indebted to him.

The Deuteronomist

By means of the first step in his study of the Deuteronomist's history, a familiarity with the text as a whole, the student has seen at least the broad continuity of the work. He has seen the nation constituted at Sinai by the ratification of the Sinai pact take possession of the land of the Canaanites as promised by God (Joshua). He has seen its vicissitudes, religious and political, during the twelfth and eleventh centuries (Judges), its consolidation and expansion after the institution of the monarchy and the promise of a perpetual dynasty made to David (Samuel). In the last part of the history (Kings), he has seen the theocratic kingdom, because of the infidelity of the kings to the covenant, first divided (926) then destroyed, the northern kingdom in 722, the southern kingdom in 587.

In addition to the broad continuity of the Deuteronomist's history, the student, as a result of the principle of selectivity followed by the author, has been aware of the religious interest and purpose of the author. In Joshua he has seen the author's emphasis on God's fidelity to His covenant promises; in Judges his emphasis on God's pedagogy, punishing infidelity inflexibly but pardoning repeatedly whenever His people repented; in Samuel God's experiment with a monarchy and His gratuitous promise of perpetuity to the dynasty of David; in Kings his emphasis on the failure of the monarchy and God's destruction of the kingdom tempered only by the remembrance of His promise to David.

Throughout the length of the Deuteronomist's history, the student has noticed the author's small concern for events of political interest and material greatness. He has seen the conquest of Palestine merely sketched in broad outlines in Joshua. He has seen the events of the 12th-11th centuries summed up in didactic schemas centering on charismatic leaders in Judges. In Samuel he has seen interest focused on Samuel as founder of the monarchy, on Saul as an example of what a king of the theocratic kingdom should not be, on David as the example *par excellence* of what a sovereign of the theocratic kingdom can be. In Kings, he has seen all the kings of the northern kingdom follow in the footsteps of Saul. He has seen kings of great stature politically, such as Omri and Jeroboam II, dismissed with a few lines, but great kings religiously such as Asa, Jehoshaphat, Jehoash, Hezekiah, and Josiah dealt with at length. He has seen in fine an overall emphasis on the covenant, the Temple, and the Davidic dynasty.

A final step remains for the student before he can claim a mastery of the Deuteronomist's history as a whole — an overall appreciation, seeing it as the final author saw it: its purpose, its basic plan, and the execution of that plan. To obtain this overall appreciation will not be easy. The student must examine the sources, put himself in the historical milieu of the final author, see how the final author revised, adapted, and arranged his sources in order to fuse them into a unity subservient to his teaching purpose.

It is clear from the last event narrated in 2 Kings, the raising up of King Jehoiachin by Evil-Merodach, the successor of Nebuchadnezzar in 562, that the Deuteronomist's history must be dated no earlier than 562. Since the author shows no influence on the part of Deutero-Isaiah (*c.* 550-520), and since nothing is said definitely about the end of the exile, it seems most probable that the Deuteronomist himself lived and wrote in exile sometime between 562 and 539. Whether he is the same as the author of Kings, or found Kings along with Deuteronomy, Joshua, Judges, and Samuel ready at hand as source materials, it is clear that he saw in all these works the historical vindication of the major theses of the book of Deuteronomy.

Since these theses were of vast importance for the dispirited and disillusioned exiles, who needed first to be convinced of God's fidelity and their own infidelity to the covenant if they were to do penance and then of God's irrevocable love and unceasing readiness to forgive if they were to hope once again, the Deuteronomist decided to present to them the panorama of their history from the time of their election in the thirteenth century down to the time of their rejection in the sixth.

In that history they would find not only the reasons for the catastrophe of 587 and the resultant exile but the reasons for hoping for better things. If anything was clear from Israel's history it was not only that she had failed her loving Maker and must do penance, but also that He who had punished her had punished as a father, whose hand was extended not only to chastise but to raise up after chastisement. In this history, therefore, the Deuteronomist saw Him who said to Israel, "I Yahweh, your God, am a jealous God, inflicting punishments for their father's wickedness on the children of those who hate me, down to the third and fourth generation, but bestowing mercy down to the thousandth generation on the children of those who love me and keep my commandments" (Deut. 5:9-10). Israel could not forget that God had punished her. It was the Deuteronomist's intention not only that Israel should understand *why* God had punished her, but that she should not forget that God's love and mercy far outran His justice. For in this was Israel's hope.

The sources available to the Deuteronomist for the construction of his pedagogical history were the first edition of Deuteronomy, and at least the main outlines of Joshua, Judges, and Samuel. If Kings is not the work of the Deuteronomist, but was written as many scholars believe at the end of the reign of Josiah (640-609), then he had at least the first edition of Kings as well. It is clear from higher critical discoveries that it was from Deuteronomy that the author took his theological principles and from the Former Prophets his historical facts. It will be of some interest to look briefly at the history of each of these works.

Deuteronomy

It is generally accepted that Original Deuteronomy (ch. 4:44—26:15; 28) came from priestly circles in the northern kingdom. It seems not unlikely that, fortified by the preaching of Elijah, Amos, and Hosea, led to reflection on the law and the teaching of the prophets by the fall of Samaria, and impelled by the introduction of a foreign element into the population in 722 and the following years (cf. 2 Kings 17:25-41), the priests of the northern kingdom compiled from their traditions concerning the law of Moses and from the developments that law had undergone between 1200 and 700 B.C. the written work we know as the Deuteronomic code (ch. 12:2—26:15). Scholars date this compilation to the time between the fall of Samaria in 722 and the finding of the book of the law of the Lord in the Temple in 621, the 18th year of Josiah (cf. 2 Kings 22—23). Indications are that the Deuteronomist's redaction of Deuteronomy was made toward the end of the exile, enriching the existing core by the addition of ch. 1—4:40; 10:6-9; 28:47-68; 29—30; 31:31b-8, 14b, 16-22, 28-30; 32, 34. The final redaction of Deuteronomy is probably the work of the author of the Pentateuch.

Practically all scholars agree that the Former Prophets present a certain unity not only because of their close relationship to the preaching of the prophets, but because the Deuteronomist reedited them in the light of the book of Deuteronomy, inserting at different places in each book his own moral reflections — sparingly in Joshua, less sparingly in Judges, very distinctly in Kings — intending thereby to underline the lesson that infidelity to the covenant had always been pernicious for the Chosen People.

Joshua

The original form of Joshua probably dates to around 900 B.C. One cannot describe the exact state of the book at that time because in its present form it has been reedited. One can see, however, how well the teaching of Joshua concerning God's fidelity to His promises when Israel was faithful to her part of the covenant fitted into the Deuteronomist's theology. Thus retouching was necessary only in ch. 1; 8:30-35; 12; 21:43—22:6; 23; 24:31.

Judges

Critics generally agree in placing the composition of Judges as a literary unit, based upon earlier oral traditions, sometime after the fall of Samaria. After the finding of Deuteronomy in the temple in 621 B.C., the book of Judges along with Joshua was subjected to the Deuteronomist's revision, manifest principally in the moralizing reflections in ch. 2:6—3:6 and 10:6-16, in the formulas for the stories of the Judges, and especially in the introduction to the book (ch. 1:1—2:5). Thus the Deuteronomist found the book a ready made proof for his teaching, and by retouches and reorganization (especially the schema of sin, punishment, repentance, deliverance) emphasized the relevance of this teaching during the exile to prove to his readers that the fall of Jerusalem was a consequence of Israel's infidelity to the covenant, and that God called them to repentance again in view of once more showing His forgiving love as He had in the time of Judges.

Samuel

The source works of the books of Samuel were first put into written form in the reign of Solomon to prove the legitimacy of the dynasty of David and the legitimacy of the succession of Solomon. They were probably reedited during the reign of Hezekiah (715-687 B.C.), and finally revised and retouched by the Deuteronomist. The principal work of revision of the Deuteronomist would appear to be found in the detaching of the last part of the court history (2 Sam. 9—20; 1 Kings 1—2) from 2 Sam. in order to use it for the introduction to the reign of Solomon (1 Kings 1–2), thereby introducing Solomon not so much as the legitimate heir of David but as the first of the bad kings. Thus, while tampering with the arrangements of the original author of Samuel whose purpose in 2 Sam. 9ff was to prove the legitimacy of Solomon's succession (a point no longer at issue in the time of the Deuteronomist), the Deuteronomist retained the book of Samuel as a defense of the Davidic dynasty's legitimacy and perpetuity — theses of no small importance for the encouragement and hopes of the disillusioned exiles of the Babylonian captivity.

Kings

While critics are undecided on the provenance of Kings, a number of texts (1 Kings 4:24; 8:46-53; 9:1-9; 2 Kings 17:19-20; 21:10-15; 22:16-20; 23:26-27; 24:2-4; 25:27-30) indicate that Kings was written after the fall of Jerusalem and probably late in the exile. Those texts which are singled out as indicative of a pre-exilic origin in the time of Josiah (1 Kings 8:8; 2 Kings 8:22; 17-24-34) can be explained as native to the unchanged pre-exilic sources used by the compiler. The exilic view of the origin of Kings has in addition the decided advantage of showing the fall of Jerusalem in 587 as the natural climax of the book and indeed of the whole Deuteronomist's history.

Conclusion

If we have been correct in the analysis of the Deuteronomist's arrangement and retouching of his source works as well as in the origin of his compilation as dating from the end of the exile, then we can be reasonably sure about his over-all purpose. Writing for the exiles, he purposed to present his people with the history of their covenant relations with God in order to prove God's unfailing fidelity to His covenant obligations and their unfailing infidelity to theirs. He intended, moreover, to show that even though the Sinai covenant was abolished, God's continued good will toward His people could not be doubted, not only because of the infinite propensity to forgive manifested by Him, but because of His absolute promise to the dynasty of David. Thus, while the Sinai covenant had failed because of Israel's infidelity, all that was of enduring interest in that covenant had been carried over into a new covenant with the house of David, thereby insuring Israel's future despite her lamentable failures in the past (cf. 1 Kings 8:25; 9:5; 11:32; 36; 15:4; 2 Kings 8:19; also 2 Sam. 7; 1 Kings 3:3; 5:17; 8:17ff; 9:4; 11:4, 6, 33, 38; 14:8; 15:3, 5, 11; 2 Kings 14:3; 16:2; 18:3; 21:7; 22:2).

To achieve this purpose the Deuteronomist took as his basic plan the following steps: 1. the proof of God's fidelity to His part of the Sinai Covenant; 2. the proof that God's punishments are medicinal punishments inflicted in view of inducing Israel to return to her Maker; 3. the proof that God had bound up what was of lasting value in the Sinai covenant with the covenant of a perpetual dynasty made with David; 4. the proof of Israel's infidelity to her part of the Sinai covenant, and the necessity therefore of repentance and return to God. The execution of this plan is evident in the selection and arrangement of events presented in the Deuteronomist's history.

In Deuteronomy, the Deuteronomist lays before the eyes of the exiles the covenant charter of their relationship with God: what God had done for them in history and the nature of the response God expected from them in return.

In Joshua, the author goes out of his way to select those incidents which show God's fidelity to His Sinai promise of giving to Israel her own land.

In Judges, by means of the theological schema of sin, punishment, repentance, deliverance applied to the history of the Judges, he emphasizes not only the purpose of God's medicinal punishments but likewise His unfailing readiness to forgive when Israel repents.

In Samuel, he preserves the account of the legitimacy of the Davidic dynasty and the covenant of a perpetual dynasty in order, before describing the abolition of the Sinai pact and the catastrophe of 587, to lay a firm basis for Israel's future hope.

In Kings, he proves indisputably that Israel, not God, has been responsible for the abolition of the Sinai pact by her infidelity to the monotheism vowed at Sinai and by her neglect of the Temple. In addition, and very significantly, the author goes out of his way to heap up prophetic-prediction fulfillment stories (45 in all). This is done in order to emphasize the teaching that the Word of God is always fulfilled and that as a consequence Israel can look forward confidently to the fulfillment of Nathan's dynastic oracle in 2 Sam. 7, the only prophetic-prediction story as yet unfulfilled.

It is not insignificant, therefore, that the Deuteronomist deals more gently with the Judean kings, and that he ends his history with the encouraging notice in 2 Kings 25:27-29: ". . . . Evil-Merodach, in the year that he became king, summoned Jehoiachin, king of Judah from prison. He spoke kindly to him, and set his throne above the throne of the kings who were with him in Babylon . . . ." Israel in exile was not without hope.

6

Psalms Related to the Deuteronomist's History

In treating the psalms related to the Pentateuchal history, three categories were studied: hymns, thanksgiving psalms, and didactic historical psalms. The nature and structure of the compositions in each category was discussed. A number of psalms were explained and a list of others belonging to the same category was given as an aid to further investigation.

In studying the psalms related to the Deuteronomist's history, the same procedure will be followed. Only the categories will differ: supplication psalms — collective and individual; confidence psalms; processional psalms; and, lastly, messianic psalms.

1. Supplication Psalms

By nature "supplication psalms" are oriented to the person praying, just as hymns or psalms of praise are by nature oriented to God. In the praise-psalms the psalmist's mind is centered upon God, His goodness, greatness, magnificence. In the supplication-psalms, his mind is very much on himself, his needs, his troubles, his enemies. The movement, therefore, in the supplications is from the petitioner to God and back to himself. The needs of the psalmist are primary in these compositions and everything else is secondary.

Structurally, the supplication psalms have at least two parts: (a) the prayer or petition part; (b) the needs of the psalmist, upon which the prayer is based or by which it is occasioned. Frequently, but not always, there is an additional part, peculiarly Hebrew, which is best termed anticipation. In order to express his confidence in God's readiness to hear and answer his prayer, the psalmist expresses what amounts to an *anticipated thanksgiving*. Ps. 54, a simple supplication psalm, will illustrate all three of the elements that enter into the structure of most supplication psalms, whether individual or collective.

Prayer with motives O God, by your name save me,
    (vv. 3-4)   and by your might defend my cause.
               O God, hear my prayer;
                 hearken to the words of my mouth.

     Troubles For haughty men have risen up against me,
occasioning the   and fierce men seek my life;
   prayer (v. 5)   they set not God before their eyes.

Renewed prayer Behold, God is my helper;
   with motives   the Lord sustains my life.
     (vv. 6-7) Turn back the evil upon my foes;
                in your faithfulness destroy them.

  Anticipation Freely will I offer you sacrifice;
    (vv. 8-9)   I will praise your name, O Lord, for its goodness,
             Because from all distress you have rescued me,
               and my eyes look down upon my enemies.

Almost as peculiar as the anticipation is the psalmist's unabashed expression of his own innocence and goodness in contrast to his enemies' wickedness and perversity. What seems boasting on the one hand and hatred for enemies on the other, is only the Hebrew's way of dramatizing his unshakable belief in God's love for what is good and hatred for what is evil. No particular distinction is drawn between hating the sin and loving the sinner, not because the Hebrew psalmist did not believe in God's mercy toward sinners, but because the distinction was simply too sophisticated for him. He knew as we know that the good God hates sin. He is content to state this in his own way without going into abstruse or theological distinctions.

In the final analysis, the apparent boasting and the apparent personal hatred of enemies spring from the psalmist's concern for God's honor. If God does not treat His friends well, His reputation for goodness, power, and fidelity will suffer in the eyes of men. If He does not punish His enemies, His reputation for impartial justice and implacable hatred for evil may be put in question. In either case, His honor is at stake in the eyes of the psalmist. It is the psalmist's concern with God's honor that the student should keep in mind when he reads what might otherwise be interpreted as complete ignorance or forgetfulness of the Old Testament commandment: "Thou shalt love thy neighbor as thyself" (Lev. 19:18).

2. Collective Supplications

Following the normal structure for the literary form of supplication psalms (intermittent petition, description of distress, anticipation of God's response), the collective supplications are distinguished from individual supplications by the following characteristics: (a) the prayer is made in the name of the group or nation; (b) the distress is one that afflicts many, e.g., war, defeat, exile, plague, famine; (c) the anticipation sometimes pictures a world-wide reaction of awe and praise to God's intervention in favor of His people.

The following are generally considered collective supplications: Pss. 12; 83; 80; 60; 108; 79; 74; 90; 102; 77; 44; 123; 126; 129. Some include Pss. 58 and 82. Of these collective supplications, Pss. 83 and 80 are related to the Deuteronomist's history. The remaining psalms will be taken in relation to the Chronicler's history.

Psalm 83

Theme	A collective supplication for help against a confederation of enemies.
Background	There is no certain historical background since the confederation alluded to could have occured in several periods of Israel's history, e.g., 2 Chr. 20; 1 Mach. 5. There are textual allusions to the book of Judges.
Division	1. Israel threatened by a coalition of enemies (vv. 1-9). 2. Prayer for victory and for punishment of God's enemies (vv. 10-19).

v. 2ff   *unmoved:* God appears to be doing nothing even though enemies threaten the existence of His people (note the psalmist's assumption, based upon the covenant relationship between God and Israel, that Israel's enemies are God's enemies; thus, "they who hate you" (v. 3); "against your people" (v. 4). Later, the risen Christ will say to St.

Paul in this same vein: "Saul, Saul, why persecutest thou me?"

v. 6ff *they are allied:* the psalmist lists the members of the confederacy leagued to overthrow God's people. All, with the exception of Assyria, are border-line neighbors of Israel, *viz.,* the Agarenes, a shepherd people from the desert of Ammon and Moab (v. 7); Gebal, a people from the region south of Edom; Amalek, Israel's ancient foe from the region of the Negeb; Philistia and Tyre, from the west and northwest respectively (v. 8); the Assyrians, from the land north and east of the Euphrates (v. 9). It is impossible to say when this federation against Israel took place. It may even be the psalmist's poetic personification of the general conspiracy of evil against God after the manner of the apocalyptic personifications (cf. Ez. 38–39; Joel 4; Zach. 14).

v. 10ff *deal with them:* a prayer that Israel's enemies may be routed as the Midianites were routed by Gideon (Judg. 7:25ff) and as Sisera and Jabin were routed by Deborah and Baraq in the west of the plain of Jezreel near the Kishon river (Judg. 4:7) at Endor, the little town near the site of the battle (Jos. 17:4; 1 Sam. 28:7).

v. 12ff *their nobles:* a prayer that the leaders of the coalition might be defeated as Oreb and Zeeb and Zebah and Zalmunna were defeated by Gideon (Judg. 7).

v. 17ff *that men may seek:* the prayer of the psalmist is not only for the destruction of Israel's and God's enemies (v. 18), but for the enemies' recognition of God as ruler of all the earth (vv. 17 and 19).

Psalm 80

Theme	A collective supplication for the salvation of the northern kingdom.
Background	Probably written during the Assyrian invasion of Israel between 724-722 (2 Kings 16–17).
Division	1. The northern tribes beg God as shepherd of Israel to save them (vv. 2-4).

2. A description of Israel's distress and suffering (vv. 5-8).
3. A recollection of God's love for them in the past when He transplanted them like a vine to the vineyard of Palestine (vv. 9-12).
4. In contrast to the past, He has made them at present a devastated vineyard (vv. 13-16).
5. A prayer for the punishment of Israel's enemies precedes the confident anticipation of God's response and Israel's gratitude (vv. 17-20).

v. 2 *O shepherd of Israel:* God, the shepherd of Israel (cf. Ps. 23 and John 10), is addressed as enthroned above the Ark between the cherubim (cf. Exod. 25).

v. 3 EPHRAIM: the patriarchal heads of the northern tribes, Ephraim and Manasseh, were the sons of Joseph. Joseph and Benjamin were the sons of Rachel (cf. Jos. 16—17; Gen. 30:22; 35:19; 46:19-20).

v. 7 *left us to be fought over:* the spectacle of Israel's neighbors quarelling over the booty to be taken from her and the mockery of Israel's enemies are presented as arguments to obtain divine help; the destruction of His people would reflect unfavorably upon His honor.

v. 9ff *a vine:* the history of the northern kingdom is likened to a fruitful vine (cf. Gen. 49:22, Jacob's blessing of Joseph), transplanted at the time of the Exodus from Egypt to Palestine, where it grew into a great kingdom. *drove away . . . planted . . . cleared:* an allegorical description of God's preparation of Palestine to receive the transplanted vine (cf. Jos.; Judg.; Matthew 21:33-43; Is. 5:1-4).

v. 11f *the cedars of God:* the "vine" grew to such an extent that it covered with its shade the mountains and the great cedars of Lebanon. The phrase "of God," is a Hebrew way of expressing the superlative (cf. Ps. 36:7; Cant. 8:6). *foliage* (v. 12): the psalmist likens the expansion of the kingdom to a vine throwing its branches and runners all the way to the Mediterranean on the west and to the Euphrates on the east. These were the ideal boundaries of Israel (cf. Deut. 11:24).

v. 13ff *broken down:* Israel, battered and scattered by the Assyrian armies, is likened to a ravaged vineyard, whose protecting walls have been demolished, allowing marauders to pillage its fruit, and the "boar from the forest" (a symbolic name for the invading Assyrian) to trample about.

v. 18 *the man of your right hand:* probably the Israelite king (cf. Ps. 110:1; 1 Kings 2:19; Ps. 45:10); possibly the collective nation elsewhere collectively described as God's son (cf. Exod. 4:22; Jer. 31:20; Hosea 11:1).

3. Individual Supplications

Individual supplications are by nature concerned with the plight or distress of the psalmist and follow the normal structure for the literary form of supplications (intermittent petition, description of distress, anticipation of God's response). They have the following characteristics: (a) the distress of the psalmist, which may be from sickness, persecution, ill treatment, slander, or exile, is often described in metaphorical and stereotyped language which makes the precise nature of the distress difficult to determine; (b) the description of the psalmist's distress is often accompanied by a confession of sin or an avowal of innocence, either because he considers his distress the punishment for sin, or because he wants to prove his love for God and the injustice of his enemies; (c) a reference is sometimes made in the anticipation part to the vows (promises made in the time of peril to offer thanksgiving sacrifices in the Temple if the prayer is heard), which the psalmist will fulfill.

The following are generally classified as individual supplications: Pss. 5; 6; 7; 13; 17; 22; 25; 26; 28; 31; 35; 38; 39; 42-43; 51; 55; 56; 57; 59; 61; 63; 64; 69; 70; 71; 86; 88; 109; 120; 140; 141; 142; 143. Pss. 59; 56; 57 will be treated with the Deuteronomist's history.

In studying Pss. 59; 56; 57, the reader will notice in the titles notations taken from the books of Samuel indicating the historical background of the psalms. These historical titles are found in 13 psalms (Pss. 7; 59; 56; 34; 52; 57; 142; 54; 60; 51; 3; 63; 18). They are not inspired, but the Pontifical Biblical Commission (*Decision* 2, May 1, 1910) stated that where the titles agree in th Hebrew, LXX, and other ancient versions, we can rightly conclude that they are more ancient than the LXX version (second century B.C.), and consequently are due, if not directly to the authors of the psalms, at least to very venerable tradition.

32

33

34

Nos. 32–36. Ancient methods of writing.   **32**. Enlarged impression of a stamp seal cut from a piece of black and white banded agate. This fighting cock is one of the earliest representations of a rooster found in Palestine. The script used is that in which Hebrew was written during the sixth century B.C. and reads: "Belonging to Jaazaniah, officer of the king." One of the army captains mentioned in 2 Kings 25:23 was Jaazaniah, who went to Mizpah in 586 to join Gedaliah, the governor appointed by the Babylonians over conquered Judah. *Photo courtesy:* Palestine Institute Museum, Pacific School of Religion, Berkeley, California.   **33**. The other category of seals used to indicate ownership was the cylinder-seal; to the left is pictured the cylinder-seal from which the impression to the right was made, picturing King Darius of Persia in his chariot hunting lions. The inscription gives the king's name in three languages.   **34**. From Nineveh, *ca.* 650 B.C., we have this tablet inscribed with the Assyrian account of the deluge in cuneiform script.   **35**. The Siloam inscription in old Phoenician script from Hezekiah's tunnel; translation below.   **36**. Replica of the Moabite Stone, the longest witness to the Old Hebrew script in existence; from the ninth century before Christ. Nos. 35, 36 *courtesy:* Matson Photo Service, Alhambra, California.

THE SILOAM INSCRIPTION

The tunneling (is finished). Now here is a description of the tunneling. Even while the pick-men were yet swinging the pick, each toward his opposite, and while three cubits still remained to be tunneled, the voice of one calling to the other could be heard, because there was a crack in the rock on the right hand. Then, on the day of tunneling through, the pick-men struck, each to each, pick against pick. And the water flowed from the fountain to the pool, 1200 cubits; and the height of the rock above the heads of the pick-men was 100 cubits (cf. 2 Kings 20:20).

Our procedure in the exegesis of these psalms will be to accept the titles on face value if found in the Hebrew and LXX, weigh the internal evidence (i.e., the agreement of circumstances mentioned in the psalms with events from David's life as we know them from the books of Samuel), taking into account the fact that not everything about David's life is recounted in the books of Samuel and that changes were made in the psalms at a later date to adapt them for liturgical worship.

Psalm 59

Theme An individual supplication for help against bloodthirsty enemies.

Background According to the title, 1 Sam. 19:9-18, when Saul sent his men to assassinate David. Possibly Neh. 3–6, when the Samaritans attempted to impede the rebuilding of Jerusalem's walls.

Division 1. Repeated prayers for help in peril from bloodthirsty enemies (vv. 2-11a).
2. Continued prayers concluding with anticipation of God's help (vv. 11b-18).

v. 2f *rescue me:* the psalmist is in peril from enemies, possibly Saul's soldiers under the circumstances of 1 Sam. 19:9-18, and from "bloodthirsty men," a term equally applicable in similar circumstances.

v. 4 *not for any offense:* the psalmist avows his innocence, not as a boast but as a factor which will win him God's help. David, as a matter of fact, was guilty at this time of no crime deserving of death.

v. 6 *all the nations:* at odds with 1 Sam. 19, these words, along with the same words repeated in v. 9, may be explained as a change from an original "my enemies," in order to adapt the psalm to a time when the peril was from national rather than personal enemies.

v. 7 *each evening they return:* since David fled almost immediately, the metaphorical description of enemies returning nightly and prowling about the "city" is at odds with the circumstances in 1 Sam. 19. It fits better the circumstances described in Neh. 3–6.

v. 8 *blasphemies:* the quotation, "Who is there to listen" (v. 8c), indicates the insults are blasphemies, which would be unlikely in the mouth of Saul's men, but understandable in the mouth of Judah's enemies in the time of Nehemiah.

v. 12 *lest they beguile my people:* based on the theological notion that if God permits the wicked to go unpunished, it will reflect on His justice and power and perhaps lead the simple of mind to doubt God, the prayer to avert such a danger from "my people" does not fit David's circumstances in 1 Sam. 19 as easily as it does the circumstances of Neh. 3–6.

v. 13 *lies . . . under oath:* as in v. 8, such charges would better fit Judah's treacherous enemies in the time of Nehemiah than David's enemies in 1 Sam. 19.

v. 14 *to the ends of the earth:* unless this is a later adaptation, the expression ill agrees with 1 Sam. 19 and fits better as part of a prayer for help against national enemies in the circumstances at the time of Nehemiah.

v. 17 *but I will sing:* the psalmist anticipates God's response to his prayer and confidently speaks of praising and thanking God for having saved him.

The internal evidence against the title may be summed up as follows: (a) David was not in fear of the Gentiles (vv. 6 and 9); (b) his enemies did not menace the city as in this psalm (vv. 7 and 15) but only his home; (c) David's enemies came openly against him without lies or deception, whereas the enemies of the psalmist are described as blasphemers, liars, and detractors (vv. 8-13); (d) simple soldiers carrying out the commands of Saul would not merit the curses hurled upon them by the psalmist in vv. 6c and 14.

If the title is ignored, the internal evidence would perhaps better indicate an historical background in the time of Nehemiah (ch. 3–6), when the Israelites were trying to rebuild the walls of Jerusalem in spite of Samaritan harassment. Such a background would explain better the references to the Gentiles (vv. 6 and 9), and the maledictions hurled upon the psalmist's enemies (vv. 6 and 14). Most of these difficulties, however, may simply be the result of changes in the psalm to adapt it to other circumstances.

Theme   The individual supplication of a man driven into exile by implacable enemies.

Background   According to the title, either 1 Sam. 21:10 or 1 Sam. 27ff, when David fled for safety to Philistia. Certainly the author is in exile (v. 9).

Division   1. Prayer, persecution, expression of confidence (vv. 2-5).
2. Persecution, prayer, confidence (vv. 6-12).
3. Anticipation of God's response to his prayer (vv 13-14).

v. 5   *promise:* possibly the promise made to David that he would be king (1 Sam. 16:3), but equally possible that it refers to the constant promise made by God to protect His people.

v. 8   *the peoples:* if this word is original, the psalmist is in exile outside of Palestine and the enemies are the pagans rather than Saul. It could be, however, that the word is adapted from "them," referring originally to Saul and his men, changed later to "peoples" to fit other circumstances.

v. 9   *my wanderings:* if David, the exile is in Philistia. Some refer it to an Israelite in the exile of the dispersion. *in your flask:* a metaphorical way of saying that God is concerned about the psalmist's sufferings; *in your book:* the same (cf. Mal. 3:16; Pss. 69:29; 139:16).

v. 13   *by vows:* the psalmist anticipates the fulfillment of the vows he made while in peril (cf. Ps. 116:18).

While the title can stand on condition that the expression "peoples" be considered a later adaptation, good authors do not hesitate to consider the psalm postexilic, written either by a Jew of the dispersion persecuted by those around him, or by a Jew in Palestine persecuted by the surrounding nations (as at the time of Nehemiah), or by overlord governors.

Psalm 57

Theme   An individual supplication in time of persecution.

| Back-ground | According to the title, written when David was hiding out from Saul in one of the many caves of Palestine (cf. 1 Sam. 22:1-5; 24:1-3). |

Division

1. Prayers mixed with expressions of confidence and a description of persecution by savage enemies (vv. 2-6).
2. Description of persecution and expressions of confidence, concluding with a firm anticipation of God's response and help (vv. 7-12).

v. 2 *in the shadow of your wings:* an expression of confidence based on a metaphor which pictures God as a protecting eagle watching over its little ones (cf. Deut. 32:11; Pss. 17:8; 36:8; Matthew 23:37).

v. 5 *in the midst of lions:* the lion is a common metaphor for a savage enemy (cf. Ps. 22:14). The reference to "their tongue" (5d) could refer to the Ziphites (1 Sam. 23:19) or to Doeg (1 Sam. 22:9-10).

v. 7 *a net:* a common metaphor for persecution, in which the psalmist likens himself to a hunted deer threatened by a rope trap or a pit covered over with foliage.

v. 10 *I will chant your praise:* anticipation leads the psalmist to speak of the time when he will praise God for having heard him (salvation is implicit). "Among the peoples," referring to the Gentiles, along with "among the nations," may be adaptations of the original readings to postexilic circumstances, when the Jews became more conscious of the universal mission God had confided to them.

Psalm 18

Theme A thanksgiving psalm for protection in persecution and for other favors.

Back-ground According to the title and internal evidence, the psalm was written by David to express his thanksgiving for protection from Saul and for other benefits, particularly that of kingship (cf. 2 Sam. 22).

Division Part A 1. Introduction (vv. 3-4).
2. Description of danger (vv. 5-7).

3. Poetic theophany describing God's coming to help David (vv. 8-20).

4. Retribution theology and the law of talion (vv. 21-31).

Part B God's goodness to David (vv. 32-46).

Part C Concluding sentiments of praise and thanksgiving (vv. 47-51).

vv. 2-3 *my strength:* the psalmist heaps up expressions (rock, fortress, deliverer, shield) showing his boundless confidence in God.

v. 5f *the breakers of death:* roaring waves, swirling waters, ropes of Sheol are all related metaphors for danger of death, based on the popular location of Sheol below the earth in the primeval deep (cf. Pss. 42:8; 57:12; 69:2, 16-17; Jonah 2:2-5). The danger referred to is Saul's relentless persecution (1 Sam. 18—27). "The cords of the netherworld" (v. 6) is a way of personifying death similar to our "grim reaper" (cf. Cant. 8:6). Note that similar language for the abode of the dead is used in the Odyssey (Book XI) and in the Aeneid (Book VI).

v. 7 *from his temple:* since God in the following strophe comes down from the heavens to help David, the reference is to the temple of the third heaven rather than to the Temple of Jerusalem. As usual in a thanksgiving psalm, there is a description of the steps that led up to the thanksgiving: the psalmist's danger (vv. 5-6); his prayer at the time of danger (v. 7); God's answer to his prayer (vv. 8-20).

v. 8ff *swayed:* in the poetic theophany describing God coming to his aid (vv. 8-18), the poet uses the stage-props of the Sinai theophany (cf. Exod. 19:16-18; 24:15-18), which became standard poetic equipment throughout the Bible (cf. Pss. 50:3; 77:17-20; 97:2-5; Is. 24:18-20; 29:6; 30:27-30; 63:19—64:3; 66:15-16; Joel 2:10-11; 4:16; Nah. 1:3-7; Hab. 3:6; Ez. 1). The psalmist describes God descending in anger from the heavens, astride a stormcloud as His chariot, wrapped in darkness through which the sparks of His anger speed like flaming arrows to disperse His foes. Before such an apparition all nature is in turmoil. Mountains leap, oceans roar, the very foundations of the earth are exposed in the troughs of the towering waves. "Smoke from his nostrils" (v. 9) is a description of God's anger in the heroic style (cf. Job 41:18-22). "Mounted a cherub" (v. 11) pictures God in His chariot drawn by cherubim (cf. Ez. 1) or upon His messengers, the winds (cf. Ps. 104:3-4). "His wrap" (v. 12) — God is wrapped in stormclouds as in a cloak (cf. Exod. 19:9; Job 22:13-14). "The Lord thundered" (v. 14) — the thunder is God's voice. "Lightnings" (v. 15) — the lightnings are God's arrows. "Foundations laid bare" (v. 16) — the pillars upon which the earth rests (cf. Hebraic cosmogony) are exposed in the troughs of the waves thrown up by the whistling winds, God's breath.

v. 17ff *he reached out:* God saves David from his enemies. In v. 5, David represented himself as caught in a swirling flood that threatened to sweep him down to Sheol. Now, he pictures God plucking him from the waters of death and leading him to safety in open spaces; after the death of Saul has put an end to his life as a fugitive, he is free to go where he pleases.

v. 21ff *the Lord rewarded me:* the theology of retribution expressed in vv. 21-31, extolling God's justice and protection of those who love Him (vv. 21-25), and in general the application of the law of talion (Exod. 21:23), illustrative of God's impartial justice toward good and wicked alike (vv. 26-31), is characteristic of individual supplications.

v. 29 *light to my lamp:* in the Bible "light" frequently denotes a state of happiness and prosperity, while "darkness" denotes danger and tribulation (cf. Is. 8:23—9:1),

v. 33ff *girded me with strength:* in vv. 32-35, David thanks God for the prowess He has given him as a warrior — for speed afoot, so necessary to a warrior in ancient days when fighting was done on foot (cf. Abner and Asahel in 2 Sam. 2:18ff; and the Iliad, Book XXII, where Hector is pursued three times around the walls of Troy by Achilles), and for skill to bend a bow (v. 35).

v. 36ff *your saving shield:* the psalmist thanks God for protecting and assisting him in battle (vv. 36-43; David, as far as we know, never lost a battle — cf. 2 Sam. 8; 10 *passim*).

v. 44ff *from the strife of the people:* the civil war after Saul's death ended when the northern tribes accepted David as king (cf. 2 Sam. 2–5). Not long after, David became "head over nations" when he conquered the Philistines, Moabites, Ammonites, and Edomites (vv. 44b-46; cf. 2 Sam. 8 and 10).

v. 47ff *the Lord live:* David concludes with a prayer of praise and thanksgiving for all God has done for him, particularly for saving him from his "enemies" (v. 49a) and from a specific "violent man" (v. 49c), who is probably Saul. The psalm concludes with a reference to David's "posterity" (v. 51c), the Davidic dynasty, to which has been promised perpetuity (cf. 2 Sam. 7:15).

4. Confidence Psalms

Confidence psalms are a subdivision of the supplication psalms. Structurally they have the same three parts: (a) prayer of petition; (b) description of distress (at least implied, though always very secondary in the confidence psalms); (c) confident anticipation of God's favorable response.

There is, however, a subtle difference between the supplication and the confidence psalms. By nature the supplication psalms are self-centered, and the elements of petition and description of distress predominate. The movement is from the psalmist to God and quickly back to the psalmist again. Attention is centered on the psalmist, his needs, his petitions, and the description of his distress. It is of the nature of the confidence psalms that the anticipation and not the petition predominates and that the attention of the psalmist is shifted away from himself to rest serenely on God. It is this subtle shift from self to God that distinguishes the confidence from the supplication psalms.

In classifying the confidence psalms as distinct from the supplication psalms, it is not always easy to make a clearcut distinction. It is best made on the degree of the psalmist's detachment from himself with consequent attention to God. On this basis almost all authors categorize Pss. 62; 23; 46; 131 as confidence psalms. Pss. 3; 4; 11; 16; 121 show the psalmist more centered on God than on himself. Pss. 41; 125; 127; 130; 27; 123 are frequently classified as supplications, but the element of confident waiting upon God predominates over the psalmist's attention to his own troubles. Ps. 62 will illustrate the structure and the tone of the confidence psalms.

Confidence in God (vv. 2-3)
  Refrain:

> Only in God is my soul at rest;
>   from him comes my salvation.
> He only is my rock and my salvation,
>   my stronghold; I shall not be disturbed at all.

Distress (vv. 4-5)

> How long will you set upon a man and all together beat him
>   down as though he were a sagging fence, a battered wall?
> Truly from my place on high they plan to dislodge me;
>   they delight in lies;
> They bless with their mouths,
>   but inwardly they curse.

Confidence in God (vv. 6-9)
  Refrain:

> Only in God be at rest, my soul,
>   for from him comes my hope.
> He only is my rock and my salvation,
>   my stronghold; I shall not be disturbed.
> With God is my safety and my glory,
>   he is the rock of my strength; my refuge is in God.
> Trust in him at all times, O my people!
> Pour out your hearts before him; God is our refuge!

God's power to punish, goodness to reward (vv. 10-13)

> Only a breath are mortal men;
>   an illusion are men of rank;
> In a balance they prove lighter,
>   all together, than a breath.
> Trust not in extortion; in plunder take no empty pride;
>   though wealth abound, set not your heart upon it.
> One thing God said; these two things which I heard:
>   that power belongs to God, and yours, O Lord, is kindness;
>   and that you render to everyone according to his deeds.

Psalm 23

Theme   A confidence psalm expressing serene trust in God the
good shepherd and beneficent host of His faithful ones.

The shepherd theme runs through Sacred Scripture from Abraham to Christ. Abraham, Jacob and his twelve sons, Moses, and David were all shepherds. The psalmists speak of Israel as God's flock (Pss. 73:1; 79:2; 94:7; 99:3). The prophets speak of God and His Messiah as the shepherd of Israel (Jer. 23:4; Ez. 34:11ff; Is. 40:11). In the New Testament Christ is the good shepherd of His people (Matthew 9:36; 10:6; 18:12; 25:13; John 10:1-18; Heb. 13:20; 1 Peter 2:25; 5:4). The psalm fits psychologically into David's life after he had been shepherded safely through the years of Saul's persecution (1 Sam. 18—31) and enthroned as king of all Israel (2 Sam. 5).

Division

1. God is the psalmist's good shepherd (vv. 1-4).
2. God is the psalmist's generous host (vv. 5-6).

v. 1f *the Lord is my shepherd:* the allegory of God shepherding the psalmist takes its colors and details from pastoral life in Palestine. Thus the "good" shepherd was one who knew where to find green pastures and dependable water-holes, both rare in semi-arid Palestine (v. 2).

v. 3 *he guides me:* in Palestine the shepherd goes before his sheep and, if he is a good shepherd devoted to his flock, leads them by the shortest and easiest ways in order to conserve their strength. God does this "for his name's sake" because His name stands for His person. God so tends His sheep because of what He is: kind, loving, watchful, with all the tender concern for the psalmist that characterizes the best of shepherds.

v. 4 *in the dark valley:* in times of drought the shepherd must seek out water and pasture in otherwise lonely and unfrequented ravines, where wolves, bears, and even lions (not uncommon in Palestine in biblical times) menace any intruder (cf. 1 Sam. 17:34-37). At such times the thought of God's protection consoles the psalmist as the sight of the shepherd's "rod" and "staff" consoles the sheep. The "rod" a wooden staff about six feet long and the trademark of the shepherd, was used as a walking stick, as a support to lean upon when tired, and as an instrument for keeping the sheep and goats in order. At nightfall, when the shepherd led the flock into the sheepfold, the sheep passed under the rod and in passing were counted and examined by the shepherd for bruises and injuries (cf. Lev. 27:32; Ez. 20:37). The "staff," a cane-like club of heavy wood and about three feet long with a hook to attach it to the belt, was used for defense.

v. 5 *the table:* the allegory of God the bountiful host takes its colors and details from banquet customs in Palestine. At banquets the heads of the guests were anointed with oil or precious ointment (cf. Mark 14:3-4; Luke 7:46; 22:30), their feet were washed by a servant (cf. Luke 7:38, 44), and the host himself tendered to each guest a cup of wine. *my cup:* the mention of the cup in the allegory is more than a reference to a banquet amenity. In Sacred Scripture, the "cup" or "chalice" is used as a figure for one's destiny (cf. Pss. 75:7-9; 60:5). Thus in Matthew 26:39 Jesus prays: "Father, if it be possible, let this chalice pass from me" (cf. also Matthew 20:22 and Jer. 25:15-29).

v. 6 *goodness and kindness:* with God as his host, the psalmist anticipates the continuance of divine goodness and kindness all the days of his life.

5. Processional Psalms

Pss. 15; 24; 68; 81; 95; 100; 118 seem to have been used either in actual liturgical processions or at least as part of an "entrance liturgy." Characteristic of these psalms is either an explicit call to take part in divine worship (e.g., Pss. 81; 95; 100) or an examination of conscience implicitly inviting the faithful to prepare themselves for participation in the liturgy (e.g., Pss. 15 and 24). In some cases there is evidence of dialogue chanted back and forth between alternate choirs of people and leader (a priest or levite — Pss. 24; 81; 118). The emphasis in several of these psalms upon observance of the commandments with a blessing for observance and a malediction for non-observance (Pss. 15:5; 24:1-6; 81:9-11; 95:7-11) suggests they may have been utilized in the covenant renewal ceremonies or some such similar liturgical service (cf. Jos. 8:30-35; 24:1-28).

Although only Pss. 24; 68; and 118 are clearly processional psalms, the others have been grouped here because of their liturgical tone and because of their apparent association with an "entrance liturgy." Pss. 81; 95; 100;

118 are treated elsewhere. Pss. 24 and 68 will be explained here. Ps. 15 will serve as a simple introductory example:

Interrogation of participants (v. 1)

> O Lord, who shall sojourn in your tent?
> Who shall dwell on your holy mountain?

Qualities of participants (vv. 2-5)

> He who walks blamelessly and does justice;
> who thinks the truth in his heart
> and slanders not with his tongue;
> Who harms not his fellow man,
> nor takes up a reproach against his neighbor;
> By whom the reprobate is despised,
> while he honors those who fear the Lord;
> Who, though it be to his loss, changes not his pledged word;
> who lends not his money at usury
> and accepts no bribe against the innocent.

Blessing on the observant (v. 5cd)

> He who does these things
> shall never be disturbed.

Psalm 24

Theme A processional hymn in honor of God the warrior entering Jerusalem.

Background The solemn entrance of the Ark of the Covenant into Jerusalem (cf. 2 Sam. 6) or some such similar ceremony after the construction of the Temple.

Division
1. The greatness of God the creator who is to be worshipped (vv. 1-2).
2. The qualities required of participants in the liturgy (vv. 3-6).
3. The hymn chanted to honor God the king entering Jerusalem (vv. 7-10).

vv. 1-2 *the Lord's are the earth:* in stressing the greatness of God, creator and sustainer of the universe, the psalmist prepares the way for the examination of conscience that follows in the second strophe by implicitly asking: "Who then can be worthy to stand before so great a God?" A

similar association of thoughts, likewise without connect-
ing conjunction, is found in Ps. 8:4-5. *upon the seas:* according to Hebrew cosmogony the earth floats on the
primeval sea which is the source of its springs and rivers
(cf. Gen. 7:11; Exod. 20:4).

v. 3 *who can ascend:* since Jerusalem is in the mountains of
Judea and Mount Sion itself is the oldest of the hills upon which the city was founded, the Bible regularly speaks
of "going up" to Jerusalem (cf. Luke 2:22, 42; John 7:8).
The references to the "mountain of the Lord" and to "his
holy place" indicate that the psalmist wrote these words
after Jerusalem had come to be known as God's mountain
and the Temple as His holy place.

v. 4ff *he whose hands are sinless:* as in Ps. 15 there is an enumeration of the qualities required of those who would
participate in the sacred liturgy. "Sinless hands" (cf.
Deut. 21:6-9; Is. 1:15) and "a clean heart" betoken respectively external actions and internal dispositions. Such
a man will be blessed by the Lord and rewarded (cf.
Deut. 28:1-14; Josh. 8:33).

v. 7 *lift up, O gates:* most commentators consider the third
strophe a triumphal processional hymn composed by David for the transposition of the Ark to Jerusalem after the
capture of the city from the Jebusites (cf. 2 Sam. 5–6).
lintels: possibly the reference is to the lintels of the ancient gates of Jerusalem, but since the gates are apos-
trophized, the idea is more likely that the gates themselves are too small for the entrance of so great a king.
For such a king, the gates must be raised up bodily. *you
ancient portals:* the gates of Jebusite Jerusalem were ancient even in the time of David (*c.* 1000), since there is
good reason to believe that the Salem of Melchizedek
(Gen. 14) from the nineteenth century B.C. is the same
as Jerusalem of the Jebusites and David. The Tel-Amarna
letters testify that "Urushalaim" [*sic*] was a flourishing
Canaanite city in the fourteenth century B.C.

v. 8ff *the Lord, strong and mighty:* the Israelites looked upon
God as the leader of their armies (cf. the reference in
Num. 21:14 to "The Book of Yahweh's Wars," also Exod.
15:3; Num. 10:35; 1 Sam. 18:17; 25:28; 2 Sam. 5:23-24).

Since Yahweh was the leader in all Israelite wars, the solemn taking possession of the captured city of Jerusalem was His privilege. The dialogued question and answer concerning the "king of glory" was no doubt antiphonally by choirs standing before the ancient gates of Jebusite Jerusalem.

Psalm 68

Theme

A processional hymn celebrating the triumphal march of God the warrior from Mount Sinai to Mount Zion.

Background

The first part of the psalm (vv. 1-28) makes allusions to the Exodus, the conquest, and the entrance of Yahweh into Jerusalem. The second part (vv. 29-36) is a prayer that God assert His power over all nations, but particularly over Egypt and Ethiopia (v. 32). The psalm is admittedly very ancient, but the emphasis on the choice of Mount Sion (vv. 16-19) and the references to the Temple (vv. 30 and 36) plus the references to Egypt and Ethiopia place it at the earliest in the time of Roboam (921), when Pharaoh Shishak invaded Palestine (1 Kings 14:25). W. F. Albright considers the psalm a collection of ancient "incipits."

Division

1. Intonation of the processional (vv. 2-4).
2. The march through the desert from Egypt to Sinai (vv. 5-7).
3. The Sinai theophany and God's care for His people (vv. 8-11).
4. The conquest of Canaan (vv. 12-15).
5. God's choice of Mount Zion to be His dwelling place (vv. 16-19).
6. Thanksgiving to God for destroying His people's enemies (vv. 20-24).
7. The triumphal entry of God the warrior into Jerusalem (vv. 25-28).
8. A prayer that God intervene for His people against Egypt and Ethiopia (vv. 29-32).
9. An invitation to all nations to praise and obey the God of Israel (vv. 33-36).

v. 2 *God arises:* the psalm opens with the call to march from Num. 10:35; "And when the Ark was lifted up Moses said: 'Arise, Yahweh, and let your enemies be scattered.'" The words summarize the whole psalm, which describes God's triumphal march in the past and ends with the prayer in the time of the psalmist: "Show forth, O God, your power; the power, O God, with which you took our part" (v. 29ff). References to God the warrior enthroned above the Ark recur in vv. 5, 8, 18, 19, 25-28.

v. 5bff *lay a road for him:* He who leads His people is not only the great King for whom one makes straight the way through the desert (cf. Is. 40:3), but Father and protector of His people as well (v. 6; cf. Deut. 32:8-14; 33:2-5). *God gives a home:* the "home" God prepared for the "prisoners led forth to prosperity" is the promised land of Palestine. *only rebels remain:* the rebels are those who refused to follow God unreservedly as did Caleb and as a consequence were compelled to die in the desert (cf. Num. 14 and 16).

v. 9ff *the earth quaked:* the psalmist hearkens back to the Sinai theophany (Exod. 19:16-19) where God solemnly reaffirmed His promise to give Israel the land of Canaan. *a bountiful rain:* the rain could refer to the rain of manna and quail (Exod. 16), but is more likely a description of the abundant rainfall of Canaan, which is in contrast to the "parched land" of v. 7c. *upon your inheritance* (v. 10): in Sacred Scripture both the people of Israel and the land of Palestine are referred to as "God's hereditary portion." In the context, "your inheritance" refers to the promised land (cf. v. 11: "Your flock settled in it").

v. 12f *the Lord gives the word:* these words sum up the period of the conquest and of the Judges. When God gave the word, Israel conquered (cf. Joshua *passim*; Judg. 4; 6; 14). The whole strophe is based upon Deborah's victory over the Canaanites (Judg. 4–5). The women bearing the "glad tidings" (v. 12b) is a reference to those who announced the victory over Sisera. The "kings . . . are fleeing" is the message they announced (cf. 1 Sam. 18:6; 2 Sam. 1:20).

v. 14 *though you rested:* the line is taken from the canticle of Deborah (Judg. 5:15-17), where it is a rebuke to the Transjordan tribes who refused to answer Deborah's call for volunteers in the war against the Canaanites. *the wings of the dove:* the "dove" probably represents Israel covered with the glory of victory and loaded down with spoils (cf. allusions to Israel as the "dove" in Ps. 74:19-20; Hosea 7:11; 11:11; Zeph. 3:1; Cant. 2:10-14). According to Podechard, the "dove" is a Canaanite trophy captured by the Israelites.

v. 15 *on Zalmon:* the reference is obscure. It could refer to snow-covered Mount Hermon or to the little Mount Zalmon mentioned in Judg. 9:48. The idea is equally obscure. Either it was snowing on nearby Mount Zalmon, or there is some hyperbolical allusion to the Canaanites falling in battle like the snowflakes that fall on the mountains.

v. 16f *mountains of Bashan:* the author personifies the lofty mountains of Bashan in the region northeast of Galilee as jealous because God has chosen to dwell on little Mount Zion instead of on one of them (cf. Pss. 48:2-3; 87:1; 24:3; Is. 14:13-14).

v. 18 *chariots are myriad:* God, accompanied by myriads of angelic hosts, comes "from Sinai to the sanctuary." The "sanctuary" could refer to the Promised Land, but in the context it more likely refers to Mount Zion which becomes God's chosen abode. The angelic hosts surrounding God are common in the Bible (cf. 1 Kings 22:19; Is. 6:1-3; Dan. 7:10; Matthew 26:53).

v. 19 *You have ascended on high:* in the light of the context, the words describe God's conquest of Jerusalem (cf. Ps. 24:7-10; 2 Sam. 5—6). The "captives" and the men "received as gifts — even rebels" is probably a reference to the Jebusites, who held Jerusalem until the time of David (cf. 2 Sam. 5:6-8; 1 Chr. 11:5).

v. 20ff *blessed be the Lord:* before describing the triumphal procession of God the warrior into Jerusalem in vv. 25-28, the psalmist pauses to call upon his people to thank God for the conquests. He has won for them. Thus the psalmist reminds his people that it is God who "bears our burdens" (v. 20b), "is a saving God" (v. 21a), "crushes the heads of his enemies" (v. 22a).

v. 23f *I will fetch them back from Bashan:* the power of God is so great that even if Israel's enemies flee to the heights of Bashan or to the depths of the sea, God will bring them back (cf. Amos 9:3). *you will bathe your feet:* a description by metonymy of a bloody victory (cf. Ps. 110:5-6; Is. 63:1-6; 2 Kings 9:36).

v. 25ff *they view your progress:* in vv. 18-19 the psalmist described the conquest of Jerusalem by God the warrior. In vv. 25-28 he describes the triumphal entrance of God the conqueror into the city (cf. Ps. 24:7-10; 2 Sam. 6). In v. 26 he describes the liturgical procession. In v. 27 he quotes from a hymn sung in the procession. In v. 28 he cites the observation of an onlooker as the royal princes of Israel pass by in the cortege. Benjamin and Judah from the south and Zebulun and Naphtali from the north are mentioned, though probably all the tribes were represented.

v. 29ff *show forth, O God, your power:* the psalmist's prayer follows naturally upon his record of what God has done for Israel. What He has done in the past, He can do again in the present. That gifts be brought for the Temple is given as an added reason why God should assist His people. The mention of the Temple in v. 30 and the Egyptians in vv. 31 and 32 date the psalm to after 965 and possibly to the invasion of Shishak in the time of Rehoboam (1 Kings 14:25). *the wild beasts of the reeds:* the psalmist uses a metaphorical name for Egypt, whose symbol was the sacred crocodile, "the beast of the reeds" of the Nile (cf. Ez. 29:3). In the equally metaphorical language of the "herd of strong bulls and the bullocks," the "bulls" represent the leaders, the "bullocks" the infantry, of the Egyptian army (cf. Jer. 46:20).

v. 33ff *you kingdoms of the earth:* the psalmist calls upon all nations to praise the Lord "who rides on the heights." "He who rides through the heavens" is a title given to the god of storm in ancient Phoenician poetry. Its usage is another indication of the antiquity of the psalm (cf. v. 5;

Pss. 18:11; 104:3; Deut. 33:26; Hab. 3:8; Is. 19:1). *in his sanctuary* (v. 36): since the psalmist is speaking of God who "rides the clouds," whose "voice is the thunder" (v. 34ab), whose "power is in the clouds" (v. 35c), "the holy place" referred to is more likely God's dwelling place in the heavens (cf. Ps. 104:1-3) than the Temple of Jerusalem.

6. Messianic Psalms

Messianic psalms are grouped on the basis of subject matter rather than on the basis of literary form. On the basis of literary form there is hardly a single category of psalms which does not include a psalm that is messianic at least in the widest sense, e.g., Pss. 2 and 110 are prophetic oracles; Ps. 8 is a hymn; Ps. 16, a didactic psalm; Ps. 20, a simple prayer for the king's success in battle; Ps. 21, a prayer of thanksgiving for the king's success in war; Ps. 22, an individual supplication; Ps. 45, a nuptial psalm composed to celebrate the marriage of a Davidic king; Pss. 72 and 132 are elaborate prayers for the king; and Ps. 89 is a collective supplication for the restoration of the Davidic dynasty.

The common denominator of the messianic psalms is their relation to Israel's expectation of a personal Messiah. The degree of this relationship with regard to individual psalms is a matter of debate among scholars. The existence of truly messianic psalms, however, is not a question open to debate. In the New Testament our Lord explicitly declares that the psalms speak about Him (Luke 24:27, 44) and in some few cases (Pss. 118:22; 110:1). He refers to psalms which have found their accomplishment in Himself (cf. Matthew 21:42; 22:44). In their apologetic sermons and letters the apostles appeal to forty different psalms and cite seventy verses from these psalms as proofs of Christ's claim to the title of Messiah. When the Modernists denied the existence of messianic psalms at the end of the last century, the Pontifical Biblical Commission issued in question form the following decision, dated May 1, 1910:

> Whether, judging by the repeated testimonies of the books of the New Testament, the unanimous consent of the Fathers, in agreement, too, with Jewish writers, we must hold that some psalms are to be recognized as prophetic and messianic, i.e., as foretelling the coming of a future Redeemer, His kingdom, His priesthood, His Passion, death, and resurrection. And whether we must in consequence, reject the opinion of those who, perverting the prophetic and messianic character of the psalms, limit these oracles, concerning Christ, to mere predictions

of the future lot of the Chosen People. *Answer:* In the affirmative to both questions.

In the interpretation of this decision, the reader should note that the Commission states only that *some* psalms must be recognized as messianic. It does not say how many, nor in what sense, nor does it go into the question of the re-reading in a direct messianic sense of psalms which in their original meaning may have been only typically messianic or not messianic at all.

Authors are generally agreed on the messianic character of the following psalms: Pss. 2; 16; 22; 45; 72; 89; 110; 132. There is less general agreement about the messianic character of Pss. 8; 20; 21; 41; 69; 118. The same may be said for Pss. 46; 48; 76; 87 which deal with the messianic kingdom directly and with the messianic king only by implication.

In dealing with the messianic psalms the reader must remember that they reflect Israel's messianic hopes. As these hopes progressed from the general to the particular, so Israel's psalmists reflected this progression in their psalms. Three stages can be ascertained in the progressive development of Israel's hopes: (a) the origin of Israel's hope in the promises made to the patriarchs and confirmed by the Exodus and the Sinai covenant; (b) the concentration of this hope in the Davidic dynasty initiated by the oracle to David in 2 Sam. 7; (c) the further limiting of this hope to an individual, future, Davidic king, who is properly entitled the "Messiah" (cf. ch. 10).

To understand the messianic psalms the reader must keep in mind two facts: first, that the majority of the messianic psalms (specifically Pss. 2; 45; 72; 89; 110; 132) were written in the period of Israel's dynastic hope (from the time of David to the fall of Judah in 587) and reflect Israel's hope in the dynasty as a whole; second, that these same psalms were seen to have a deeper and fuller meaning in the period of personal messianism (from 587 to the coming of Christ), and were as a consequence re-read and re-interpreted in the light of Israel's expectation of a personal, Davidic Messiah. The personal messianic interpretation of these psalms, therefore, in the New Testament, must be understood not only in the light of the original Davidic kings about whom they were written and who were types of the future Messiah, but in the light of Israel's re-reading and re-interpretation of these psalms as personally messianic in the period of her personal messianic hope (see p. 365ff).

To understand the messianic psalms in their historical and doctrinal context, the reader is urged to study first Pss. 89 and 132 (cf. pp. 440ff), which testify to Israel's belief in the perpetuity of the Davidic dynasty. With these psalms and the dynastic promise of 2 Sam. 7 as a background, he will be able to understand better the original dynastic messianic background of Pss. 110; 2; and 72, as well as their later re-reading and use in a direct, personal sense during the period of personal messianism (cf. J. L. McKenzie, "Royal Messianism," *CBQ* 19 (1957).

Psalm 110

Theme A prophetic oracle extolling the Davidic prince as king, priest, and conqueror.

Background By installing the Ark of the Covenant in Jebusite Jerusalem (2 Sam. 6; Pss. 24:7-10; 68:1-19), David made Jerusalem, one of the oldest and most famous religious shrines in Canaan (cf. Gen. 14, Melchizedek, priest and king of Jerusalem, the city of the high god, El Elyon), the religious capital of Israel. In return and in reward for his desire to build a temple in Jerusalem (2 Sam. 7:1-2), God gave to David not only the royal and priestly prerogatives of Melchizedek (Ps. 110:1-4), but the promise of an eternal dynasty as well (2 Sam. 7:8-16). It is not improbable that soon after this event or on its anniversary or for the inauguration of Solomon's reign, a court poet composed Ps. 110, extolling his sovereign as king and priest of Jerusalem and as conqueror of his enemies by divine asssitance.

Division
1. By divine decree the Davidic king rules from Jerusalem (vv. 1-3).
2. Like Melchizedek before him, he is priest as well as king (v. 4).
3. With Yahweh's assistance he will conquer and rule the nations (vv. 5-7).

Ps. 110 follows the literary form of the prophetic oracle, a type liberally exemplified in biblical sources (Pss. 2; 60; 83; Gen. 11:3; 2 Sam. 7:8-16; 1 Kings 22:5-23; Is. 7:1-9; Mich. 4:11) and in extra-biblical sources (cf. ANET 449-451). The most significant extra-biblical example is found in Ninlil's prophetic oracle to Ashurbanipal (ANET 451):

This is the word of Ninlil herself for the king: Fear not, O Ashurbanipal . . . over the people of the four languages, and over the armament of the princes you will exercise sovereignty. The kings of the countries confer together saying: The kings of the lands I shall overthrow, place under the yoke, bind their feet in strong fetters . . . I shall arise, break the thorns, open up widely my way through the briers, fill it with lamentation and wailing . . . Ninlil is his mother. Fear not! The mistress of

Arbela bore him. Fear not! As she that bears for her child, so I care for you . . . fear not my son, whom I have raised!

Common to most examples of the prophetic oracle, both biblical and extra-biblical, are: (a) the occasion (a time of war or insurrection against the king); (b) an expression in direct discourse of the rebellious sentiments of the king's enemies (cf. Pss. 2:3; 83:5); (c) the divine adoption of the king as son (cf. Ps. 2:7; 2 Sam. 7:14); (d) the divine avowal to take up arms and destroy the king's enemies (cf. Ps. 110:5-7), or the equivalent (cf. Ps. 2:8-9).

v. 1 *the Lord said:* the words are a translation of the Hebrew, *Ne'um Yahweh,* an expression used to announce the oracle received from God by His prophet (cf. 1 Sam. 2: 30; Amos 3:10-13; Jer. 23:31). The psalmist repeats this oracle to the king: *to my Lord* (Hebrew, *Adoni*): the title of deference used by an inferior to a superior (cf. Gen. 33:8; 1 Sam. 22:12; 25:25). *sit at my right hand:* the right hand was the place of honor (cf. 1 Kings 2:19). It is possible, since the Temple faced east and was situated on the hill north of the royal palace, that the expression, "at my right hand," is a reference to the palace located on the right of God dwelling in the Temple. *your footstool:* the expression indicates complete submission (cf. Josh. 10:24).

v. 2 *the scepter of your power:* the king receives his royal power from God dwelling on Mount Zion and from there he will dominate in the midst of his enemies (David conquered all the nations surrounding him, namely, Philistia to the west, Edom to the south, Moab and Ammon to the east, and Syria to the northeast).

v. 3 *yours is princely power:* based upon 2 Sam. 7:14, "I will be a father to him, and he shall be a son to me," these lines express the adoptive-son relationship established by God with the kings of the Davidic dynasty (cf. Ps. 2:7; and Ninlil to Ashurbanipal: "Fear not, my son whom I have raised"). The text of the new Roman psalter, based on the Septuagint translation (3rd-2nd century B.C.), represents, in the light of later revelation concerning the coming of a personal Messiah, a re-reading of a much disputed original Hebrew text variously translated, e.g., Kissane: "With thee was princely rank in the day of thy birth, in the holy mountains; from the womb princely rank was thine, from the night thou wert begotten"; Podechard: "On the day of your birth you were chosen, consecrated upon issuing from the womb; from the dawn there comes to you a dew of youth." The Roman Psalter note on this verse reflects the messianic interpretation proper to it during the period of personal messianism and voiced by Jesus Himself (cf. Matthew 22:44).

v. 4 *according to the order of Melchizedek:* the Davidic prince will not only be king of Jerusalem but, like Melchizedek of old (Gen. 14:18), priest as well (cf. 2 Sam. 24:25; 1 Kings 3:4).

v. 5 *the Lord is at your right hand:* in v. 1 God promises to make the king's enemies the footstool of his feet. In vv. 5-7 the psalmist describes how God will fulfill His promise, going forth at the right hand of the king, the place of assistance (cf. Pss. 16:8; 109:31; 142:5), to destroy his enemies. So gory a description of Yahweh as the God of battle is not unprecedented in the Bible (cf. Pss. 78:65-66; 68:22-24; Is. 63:1-6; also the descriptions of Yahweh the Warrior in the Canticles of Moses and Habakkuk, in Ps. 24:7-10, and in Is. 59:15-17). Extrabiblical parallels in prophetic oracles are cast in the same vein, e.g., "Ishtar, the Lady of Battle, who likes me to be her high priest, stood at my side breaking their bows, scattering their orderly battle array" (ANET 289); Ishtar to Ashurbanipal: "She held the bow in her hand and a sharp sword was drawn to do battle . . . to the conquest of your enemies she will march forth at your side" (ANET 451); an Egyptian psalm in praise of the god Horus: "Regard ye Horus, he weareth his crown . . . he strideth far and wide o'er the land . . . he hath crushed the heads of his foes. . . ." Both Podechard and Kissane correct the Hebrew text to *Adoni* and read "lord" as referring to the king. The Masoretic text, however, has *Adonai*, the proper Hebrew spelling for God; in the light of the above parallels, biblical and extra-biblical, there seems no good reason for correcting the text.

v. 7 *by the wayside:* in view of the Ugaritic meaning of "way" as "dominion," P. Nober (VD 1948, 351ff) reads v. 7:

"He (God) will make him (the king) ruler (literally — "possessor of dominion"), therefore He (God) will raise up his (the king's) head." The reading is linguistically justified (cf. TS, 1954, 627ff) and provides, in addition to perfect parallelism of members, a conclusion which expresses a fulfillment of the promise of dominion made to the king in v. 1.

The above interpretation sees the psalm in its original setting at a time when revelation concerning a personal Messiah-King had not yet been made. When this revelation was made, the psalm was re-read as a description of the future Messiah. In the New Testament the psalm is understood in relation to the person and mission of Christ (cf. Matthew 22:44; Acts 2:34; 1 Cor. 15:25; Eph. 1:20-23; Col. 3:1; Heb. 1:3, 5, 13).

Psalm 2

Theme A prophetic oracle in which the Davidic prince promulgates to his enemies the prerogatives of power and domination promised to him by God.

Background The enthronement or anniversary of enthronement of a Davidic king (cf. 2 Sam. 7 and 1 Kings 1).

Division

1. Rebellion against God and His king is futile (vv. 1-3).
2. Laughter in heaven at the futility of such rebellion (vv. 4-6).
3. The king promulgates the divine promise establishing his power (vv. 7-9).
4. The king commands his vassals to obey (vv. 10-12). The literary form of Ps. 2 is the same as that of Ps. 110.

v. 1 *why:* the sense of the question is, "What good can it do you?," not, "For what purpose do you plot?," because v. 3 states clearly the purpose of the plotting. Since the death of the reigning monarch and the inauguration of a new king was not infrequently the occasion for a rebellion of vassal kings (cf. 1 Kings 1—2; 11 and the numerous examples of rebellions on similar occasions in biblical and extra-biblical history), it is not unlikely that the psalm expresses the sentiments of a new king on his inauguration day, possibly Solomon's (cf. 1 Kings 1—2).

v. 2 *anointed:* deriving from the custom of anointing kings with oil (cf. 1 Sam. 9:16; 16:12), the term "anointed" originally referred to any king (cf. Ps. 132:10, 17) and sometimes to priests who were anointed for their office (Lev. 8:12; Num. 3:3). In the period of Israel's expectation of a personal, ideal, Davidic king (after 587 B.C.), the term came to be applied to this future king and thus became the New Testament technical term embodying Israel's messianic expectations.

v. 3 *let us break:* the expression in direct discourse of the rebellious intentions of the king's enemies is characteristic of the prophetic oracle (cf. Ps. 83:5, 13, and Ninlil to Ashurbanipal: "The kings of the countries confer together, saying: Come, let us rise against Ashurbanipal" (ANET 451).

v. 4 *laughs:* laughter is the divine reaction to the rebellion of the king's enemies. This is followed by a reminder to these enemies that God has established the Davidic dynasty in Jerusalem "on Zion," the small southern spur of the hill which was the city's original site.

v. 7 *I will proclaim:* the king explains to his enemies the origin of his power based upon the divine promise and divine adoption (cf. 2 Sam. 7:14). In the Code of Hammurabi (ANET 170) the words, "You are my son," constitute the formula for adoption (cf. also Hosea 1:4; 2:1; John 19:25-27). *this day I have begotten you:* on the day that the Davidic prince became king, he became as well, due to the promise of 2 Sam. 7:14, the adopted son of God.

v. 8 *the ends of the earth:* the expression means at least the ideal boundaries of the Promised Land (cf. Deut. 33:17; Pss. 18:44 48; 72:8). With the divine assistance, the Davidic king will rule the subject kings as with a rod of iron, i.e., a scepter, the primeval symbol of a ruler (cf. Ps. 110:5-7).

v. 11 *serve the Lord:* while the term "serve" is ordinarily used in a religious sense, it is also found in the Bible in the political sense, i.e., obey, be subject to (cf. Ps. 72:11). By refraining from rebellion against Yahweh's anointed, the kings "obey" God. The contrary will bring destruction (v. 12; cf. Ps. 110:5-7).

Originally composed in the period of Israel's dynastic, messianic hope, the psalm, as a result of fuller revelation in the period of Israel's personal, messianic hope (after 587 B.C.), came to carry judgments proper to the ideal Davidic king of the future, who would be God's instrument and lieutenant in the extension of His rule to the whole world. It was in this sense that the psalm was understood by the Jews in the three centuries preceding the coming of Christ; later still, with Christ's advent and the revelation of His nature, this message too became part and parcel of the reflections made upon the text (cf. Acts 4:25-28; Rom. 1:4; Heb. 1:5; 5:5; Apoc. 12:5; 19:15). Thus, expressions, which at an earlier stage of messianic revelation were meant and understood according to the tenor of the prevailing, exaggerated "court-style" (cf. vv. 8-10), carried a more profound content in the light of Israel's fuller messianic revelation proper to a later period.

Psalm 72

Theme An elaborate prayer beseeching a beneficent and glorious reign for a new Davidic king.

Background The psalm, like Pss. 20 and 21, is a prayer for a contemporary Davidic king and gives every indication of having been written for the king's inauguration. He is envisioned, however, not as a merely secular monarch but as the representative of that dynasty to which God had promised perpetuity (2 Sam. 7) and through which He has determined to extend His rule to the world.

Division 1. May the king's reign be just and peaceful (vv. 1-4).
2. May it be long and beneficent (vv. 5-7).
3. May it extend to embrace the world (vv. 8-11).
4. May the king be interested in and considerate of the poor (vv. 12-14).
5. May his reign be prosperous and glorious (vv. 15-17).

Since the king is the representative of Israel's covenanted King-God, the psalmist expects from him an ideal reign of peace, justice, and prosperity. He expects as well that the king's rule, like the rule of God, will extend to the ends of the earth. Originally written for an historical king in the period of Israel's dynastic messianic hope, it is probable that the psalm was re-read in a direct messianic sense during the period of Israel's personal messianic hope, and that vv. 8, 10, 11, 15a, 17 were added to enhance this message. Originally the verbs were probably jussive, later future.

v. 1f *the king . . . the king's son:* the two terms, as the parallelism shows, refer to the same person. In the second stich he is called "the king's son" to assure all of his status as son of the previous king and therefore a legitimate successor. *your people:* the psalmist does not say "his" (the king's) people, but "your" (God's) people, since the king is the representative of God, Israel's only true king.

v. 3f *the mountains shall yield:* the mountains and the hills in parallelism represent the whole country, and the hyperbolical wish envisions peace and justice as inherent in the nations very soil. Under such circumstances it follows that the poor will be saved and the oppressor destroyed (vv. 4, 12-17), Isaiah (9:6) and Deutero-Isaiah (Is. 42:1-4) envision the messianic kingdom in similiar fashion.

v. 5ff *may he endure:* the wish is hyperbolical and typical of court-style language. It has behind it, however, the dynastic promise of 2 Sam. 7. *like rain coming down:* the rain is a common biblical symbol for blessing (cf. Deut. 32:2; Job 29:23; Is. 32:2) and aptly illustrates the effect of a wise and just rule.

v. 8ff *from sea to sea:* of themselves the terms of v. 8 do not necessarily extend beyond the ideal limits of the Promised Land (cf. Exod. 23:31). Taken, however, in context with v. 11, which is probably a later addition to the psalm, the terms look rather to that universal reign of the messianic king envisioned by Zechariah (9:10), Micah (7:12), and Ps. 87. *the kings of Tarshish . . . the kings of Arabia and Seba* v. 10): dependent on Is. 60:5-9, in which the context is concerned with the submission of the nations to the messianic kingdom centered in Jerusalem, these verses were probably added to further enhance the universality of the messianic king's rule.

v. 12ff *for he shall rescue the poor man:* the king whose reign is like that of God will be especially considerate of the poor and the downtrodden (cf. Is. 9:6; 42:3; 57:15), will liberate them from oppression, and value their blood, i.e., their lives, as precious (vv. 13-14).

v. 15ff *may he live:* the conjunction relates vv. 15-17 to vv. 12-14. Because of the king's consideration for the poor and the downtrodden, they will bring to him "the gold of Arabia," pray for him, and bless him continually. It is probable that v. 15a, like vv. 8, 10, 11, 17, is an interpolation, added to enhance the universality of the messianic king's rule.

v. 18f *blessed be the Lord:* these verses do not belong to the psalm. They are the doxology with which the editor of the psalms brings the second book of psalms to a close.

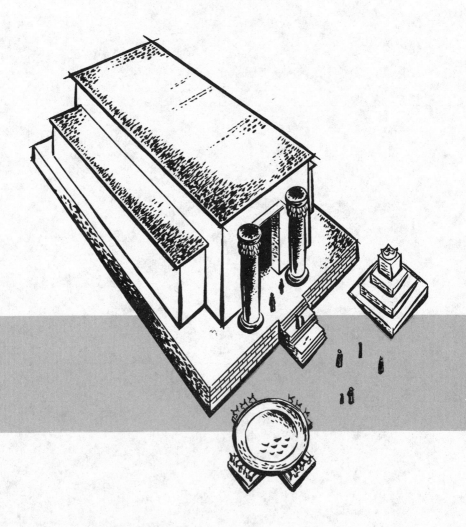

PART THREE

The Chronicler's History

and the

Prophets of Judah

7

The Chronicler's History

1. The Chronicler's History as a Whole

In the Pentateuchal history, the reader has been given an outline of the foundation of God's kingdom on earth. He has been shown how God from the beginning of time providentially planned and prepared a specific people to be the first citizens of His kingdom (Gen.). He has seen the actual foundation of the kingdom (Exod.). He has been told of its "holy" nature (Lev.), its organization (Num.), its spirit of love and obedience (Deut.).

In the Deuteronomist's history, the reader followed Israel into the Promised Land (Josh.), saw her insecurity and need for a king in the troubled centuries after the conquest (Judg.), witnessed the inauguration of the monarchy under Saul and David (Sam.), followed by the division of the kingdom in the time of Rehoboam, the destruction of the northern kingdom in 722, and of the southern in 587 (Kings).

As the reader puts down the book of Kings after reading about the destruction of Jerusalem in 587 and the deportation of the Jews into Babylon, he feels that the thoroughness of the Babylonian victory and the depressing history of the infidelity of the kings as recorded in the books of Kings should have blasted beyond repair the hopes of Israel for a glorious future. Yet he finds it is not so. Against all expectation Israel still has hope. And there is good reason.

In the course of the last centuries of Judah's history, a new flame of undying hope has been kindled. Israel believes — because it has been revealed — that another Davidic king will reign in Judah and over the world, a king who will compensate for all the shortcomings of David and his successors and ensure the permanency promised the dynasty through Nathan. Israel believes because God has promised it through the prophets and God's promise cannot fail — "All flesh is grass . . . . but the word of our God shall stand forever" (Is. 40:6-7). There is hope, therefore, in the midst of desolation.

The function of the Chronicler's history

In the books that take form after the exile (587-539), the reader will find both the reasons behind Israel's hope and the testimony to its survival down the dismal centuries that followed the exile. In the Chronicler's history (1–2 Chr.; Ezra–Neh.), he will find that even in the late fifth century, 150 years after the reign of the last independent king of Judah, Israel still looked to the Davidic dynasty as the source of her hope for a glorious future. In the sermons of the prophets of Judah, preached in the years between 740 and 400, and collected into books during and after the exile, he will find the reasons for that hope. It will be the function of the Chronicler's history to focus our attention on the two sources of Israel's undying hope: (a) the Temple in her midst in which God has taken up His abode; (b) the Messiah who is to come and fulfill all the promises made to the patriarchs and prophets of old.

Since the Chronicler deals almost exclusively with the Davidic kings, we shall begin with his history. The reader will then be able to follow the Chronicler down through the reigns of the Davidic kings, stopping along the way to listen to the sermons of the Judean prophets as they appear in the course of the story.

The nature of the Chronicler's history

It should be noted from the beginning that the Chronicler does not write history as history is written today. What is more important, he never intended to, and it is his intention we must understand if we are to interpret his narrative correctly.

To begin with, it is more than obvious that his attention is directed to the Davidic dynasty and to the Temple. In 1 Chr. 1–9, all of Israel's history from Adam to Saul is summed up in a series of genealogies. In ch.

10–29 the death of Saul is mentioned (ch. 10), but only as a prelude to the career of David with whom the remainder of 1 Chr. is concerned.

In 2 Chr. the author ignores the northern kingdom and devotes himself almost exclusively to the kings of David's house. Throughout, the emphasis is not only on David and his dynasty but on the relationship of the Davidic kings to the Temple of Jerusalem. 2 Chr. 2–7 are given over to a minute description of the building and dedication of Solomon's Temple. In 2 Chr. 10–36, the kings to whom the author allots the lion's share of space are precisely those who concerned themselves in a particular way with the Temple and its personnel.

If the reader looks more closely, he will see from a comparison with parallel accounts in the Books of Samuel and Kings that the Chronicler not only selects his material but carefully edits it, sifting from it whatever might depict David in any but the kindest light. David's sins, the revolts of his people against him, his weakness in the government of his family and his people are all discreetly passed over. He is presented, in a manner quite unlike the impartial portrayal of the books of Samuel, as the ideal king!

To discover the motive behind such a presentation, the reader must look to the midrash, a literary form popular in the centuries that followed the exile. Since a more detailed study of midrash will be given later with the introduction to the books of Jonah, Tobit, and Esther, it will suffice for the present to define a midrash. A midrash is a loosely historical narrative having as its aim an elaboration of ancient texts and traditions in order to edify, teach, or explain some doctrinal or moral question of importance at the time of the writer. It is of the essence of midrash to use history only as a starting point for the development of a religious theme, the author being guided, of course, by the deposit of tradition and by the realization that Israel's history and institutions are not the product of chance but of divine foreknowledge and dynamic development.

The Chronicler's history is midrashic. He uses historical data and to this degree he is an historian. But he selects, emphasizes, and imaginatively embroiders the facts at his disposal, and to this degree he is a midrashic author. The reader, if he wishes to appreciate the Chronicler's teaching, must keep both the historical and midrashic element in mind.[1]

The Chronicler's history as a whole

Part One / 1–2 Chronicles

| Theme | A history of the Davidic dynasty and of the Temple until the fall of Jerusalem. |

[1] Cf. J. Goldingay, "The Chronicler as a Theologian," *Biblical Theology Bulletin* 5 (June 1975) 99–126.

Purpose	To focus attention on Israel's hope — the Davidic dynasty, and on Israel's glory — the Temple of the true God on earth.
Division	I. 1 Chr. 1–9 A summary of Israel's history from Adam to David by means of genealogies.
	II. 1 Chr. 10–29 David's solicitude for the Temple.
	III. 2 Chr. 1–9 Solomon and the building of the Temple.
	IV. 2 Chr. 10–36 The Davidic kings and their association with the Temple.

Part Two / Ezra-Nehemiah

Theme	The religious and political reorganization of Judah after the return from the Babylonian exile.[1]
Purpose	To focus attention on the importance of the Temple and religious reforms for the conservation of the Jewish state.
Division	I. Ezra 1–6 The return of the first exiles in 537, followed by the rebuilding of the altar in 536 and of the Temple in 516.
	II. Ezra 7–10 The return of a second group of exiles in 458 (or 428) led by Ezra, and the marriage reforms introduced by him.
	III. Neh. 1–7 The return of Nehemiah and the rebuilding of the walls of Jerusalem in 445.
	IV. Neh. 8–13 The religious reforms and the renewal of the covenant instituted by Ezra and Nehemiah.

Chronology of the kings and prophets of Judah

998-990 David brings the Ark of the Covenant to Jerusalem.

965-926 Solomon succeeds David and builds the Temple.

926-910 Rehoboam, first king of Judah after the division of the kingdom.

910-908 Abijah.

908-872 Asa, a king especially devoted to the Temple.

872-852 Jehoshaphat, a holy king contemporary with Ahab of Israel.

852-845 Jehoram, king married to Athaliah, daughter of Ahab.

[1] For the relation of Ezra-Nehemiah to 1-2 Chronicles, the reader should consult the introduction to Ezra-Nehemiah, p. 397.

845-844 Ahaziah, son of Athaliah, assassinated by Jehu of Israel.
844-839 Athaliah, Queen-mother in Judah, usurps the throne after the death of Ahaziah at Jezreel.
839-800 Jehoash
800-785 Amaziah.
784-742 Uzziah, contemporary of Jeroboam II in Israel.
760-730 Preaching of Amos and Hosea in the northern kingdom.
758-735 Jotham, regent with Uzziah, then king (742-735).
742-700 Preaching of Micah and Isaiah.
735-715 Ahaz, king at the time of the Immanuel prophecies and the Syro-Ephraimitic war.
715-687 Hezekiah, reformer king and friend of Isaiah.
687-640 Manasseh (687-642) and Amon (642-640).
640-609 Josiah, reformer king and patron of the Temple.
630-587 Preaching of Zephaniah, Jeremiah, Nahum, Habakkuk.
609-598 Jehoahaz (3 months), Joakim (609-598).
597-587 Jehoiachin (3 month), Zedekiah (597-587).
587-539 The fall of Jerusalem and the Babylonian exile. Preaching of Ezekiel and Deutero-Isaiah.
537-516 Return from the exile and rebuilding of the Temple. Preaching of Haggai, Zechariah, Trito-Isaiah, Obadiah.
470-458 Preaching of Malachi. Return of Ezra in 458 (428).
445-433 Nehemiah rebuilds the walls of Jerusalem and institutes religious reforms.
400-300 Probable period during which the Chronicler's history was written.

2. 1 and 2 Chronicles

When the author of Kings compiled his history during the Babylonian captivity, he took as his purpose to prove to his fellow exiles that the fall of the sister kingdoms of Israel and Judah had been richly deserved on account of their infidelity to the covenant and their neglect of the Temple.

When the author of Chronicles wrote, the purpose of the author of Kings had been substantially achieved. With the help of the exile prophets Ezekiel and Deutero-Isaiah, the doctrine of strict monotheism demanded by the Sinai covenant had become the central dogma of Judaism in fact as well as in theory. The Temple, moreover, so often neglected and so frequently deserted for Baalistic shrines before the exile, had become in the postexilic period the center of Jewish life and worship.

Only one element of Israel's ideal was lacking — an independent Davidic dynasty. Instead of a temporal state, Israel, during the 150 years between the end of the exile and the writing of Chronicles, had existed as a church-state, ruled no longer by Davidic kings but by high priests and a council, subject in temporalities to the reigning kings of Persia and their successors, the Seleucids.

When the author of Chronicles wrote, Israel's factual history had for the most part already been written. The Chronicler had before him not only the Pentateuch with its classic description of what the theocratic nation was intended by God to be but the Deuteronomist's history as well with its melancholy record of the rise and fall of kingship in Israel and the rejection of the celebrated Sinai covenant by all but the "remnant" of the Chosen People. Under the circumstances, there was no need for him to write a history of Israel. And yet he did — a history that begins with Adam and comes down by genealogies to his own time in the fourth century B.C. The purpose of this history is revealed as much by its omissions as by its affirmations. It is this purpose we must discover if we are to understand his narrative.

As already indicated, the Chronicler's history is a composite work broken up into parts in the course of the centuries in the same manner as the books of Samuel and Kings. In the division given above (1 Chr. 1–9: Adam to David; 10–29: David and the Temple; 2 Chr. 1–9: Solomon and the Temple; 10–36: the Davidic kings and the Temple), what is significant is the author's attention to David and his dynasty to the exclusion of almost everything else except the Temple.

In 1 Chr. 1–9, Israel's history from Adam to Saul is telescoped into a series of genealogies, but significantly 100 verses are given to the genealogies of Judah and David (ch. 2–4), 120 verses to the priests, the levites, and the other Temple personnel (ch. 6 and 9), 40 verses to the tribe of Benjamin, the tribe most intimately associated with Judah, and only 85 verses to all the other tribes!

In 1 Chr. 10–29, Saul is mentioned only as an introduction to David's reign, which is then described with significant emphasis on the king's liturgical achievements: his transfer of the Ark to Jerusalem (ch. 15–16), his desire to build the Temple (ch. 17), his preparations for the Temple's construction and its liturgical personnel (ch. 21–28).

In 2 Chr. 1–9, the major part of the text (ch. 2–7) is given to matters liturgical: the preparation, building, and dedication of the Temple.

In 2 Chr. 10–36, it is again significant that, while the Chronicler borrows heavily from 1 and 2 Kings for his history of the kings of Judah as he did from 1 and 2 Samuel for his account of David, it is to the kings who lavished time and attention upon the Temple and its worship that he devotes the major part of his text: Asa (ch. 14–16), Jehoshaphat (ch. 17–21), Hezekiah (ch. 29–32), Josiah (ch. 34–35).

From the amount of space given to the Temple, Temple worship, and the Temple personnel, it is obvious that the Chronicler's purpose was to write what we would today call an ecclesiastical history. From the amount of space given to David and his dynasty to the exclusion of almost all others, it would appear equally obvious, considering the circumstances under which the Chronicler wrote in the fourth century, that his principal purpose was to emphasize the messianic and liturgical significance of David and the outstanding part that the Temple was meant to play in the life of Israel.

The book may be described consequently as an ecclesiastical history of midrashic nature composed by compiling existing written documents and oral traditions (proper no doubt to the priests and levites) with the intention of emphasizing the messianic hopes of Israel (based on the promise made to David in 2 Sam. 7) and the ecclesiastical nature of the nation (based on the continuance of Temple worship from the time of David down to the time of the Chronicler himself in the early fourth century).

Since important events in the life of David have already been pointed out in the books of Samuel, and since the significance of the Chronicler's emphasis on the Davidic dynasty and the Temple have been indicated in this introduction to 1 and 2 Chronicles, it will not be necessary to single out significant passages in the books of Chronicles. The reader is advised instead to advert to the ecclesiastical tone of the books, comparing them with the parallel narratives in Samuel and Kings. He is also advised to use the books of Chronicles as a guide to the history of the southern kingdom in contradistinction to the history of the northern kingdom emphasized in the books of Kings (1 Kings 12–2 Kings 17).

By reading 1 and 2 Chronicles down to 2 Chr. 27, the reader will cover the history of the Davidic dynasty until the time of King Ahaz. The rest of the Chronicler's history from 2 Chr. 28 to the end will serve as background for the preaching of the great Judean prophets, Isaiah, Micah, Zephaniah, Jeremiah, Nahum, Habakkuk, Ezekiel, Deutero-Isaiah, Haggai, Zechariah, Trito-Isaiah, Obadiah, Malachi, and Joel.

More is needed, however, than the historical background of the prophets. The reader should know something about the men themselves, their message, the way they received their message, and the way they transmitted it. A study of prophetism will provide no small help toward supplying this knowledge.

3. Prophetism

Modern readers of the prophets are frequently prejudiced by the antecedent impression that the prophets were men whose words were for the most part either predictions of future destruction or revelations about the coming Messiah and his kingdom. On the contrary, as the reader will quickly perceive, the principal concern of the prophets was the current situation: the events, the vicissitudes, the challenges to the religious life of their immediate contemporaries.[1]

That the prophets spoke about the future and made true predictions is incontrovertible. But for the most part they spoke about the future related to and flowing from events contemporary to themselves and their audience. Their attention and their words were directed as a consequence to the audience in front of them, not to future, unknown peoples of another era and another dispensation. This is more than obvious in the preaching of the first of the great prophets, Moses. It is equally true of the later prophets. It should never be forgotten.

The prophet as an individual

No better beginning can be made for an appreciation of the prophets than an attentive reading of Amos and Hosea and a calm reflection on what it was like for the average Israelite to listen to these men. The reader will soon realize that the prophets, like our modern home missionaries, were men who preached to the people the basic truths about God. They were not apostolic missionaries whose mission is to announce the truths of salvation and revelation to people who have never heard them before. Nor were they like the ordinary Sunday preacher whose aim is to instruct, persuade, and inspire to better Christian living. For this the Israelites had their priests in the Temple and, later on, their rabbis in the synagogues. The prophets were rather of the nature of extraordinary preachers, men who came rarely, preached dramatically, on subjects of fundamental religious importance, at times of religious crisis.

A realistic approach to the prophets, therefore, must be based on what we know of them from their writings and from their place in Israel's religious history and not upon what we might like to see or hope to see. It is a mistake to expect too much in the prophets. But disappointment over not finding what is expected should not be permitted to obscure their great contributions to revealed religion.

[1] Cf. select bibliography on p. 575.

From the customary expression used by so many of the prophets, "The word of the Lord," and from the commission to Aaron, Moses' mouthpiece, in Exod. 7:1, "See, I make you a god to Pharoah, and your brother Aaron shall serve as your spokesman," it is clear that the simplest definition of a prophet is a man who speaks for God, God's mouthpiece. The definition is amply exemplified in the lives of the prophets already seen, Moses, Samuel, Nathan, Amos, Hosea. They were men conscious of speaking not their own message but the message God inspired them to speak. Likewise they were men conscious of being called by God, as is clear from the vocations of Moses (Exod. 3:7, 22; 4:1-15), Amos (7:14-16, Isaiah (6:1-13); Jeremiah (1:2-10), and Ezekiel (1:2ff). As messengers sent to Israel by Israel's covenant King, they spoke with the words of Yahweh Himself.

Distinguishing the true from the false prophet

When the reader finds mention of "bands of prophets" (1 Sam. 10:5), "prophets of the Lord" (1 Kings 18:4), "prophets of Baal" (1 Kings 18:19), "sons of the prophets" (2 Kings 2:3), and "prophets who prophecy false-hood" (Jer. 5:31), he may wonder on what basis and with what precise meaning so many and so different men can be grouped under the title of prophets.

Obviously the word prophet is a broad term in the Old Testament, one having a proper and a derived sense, somewhat like our term "saint" today, which at one moment may be used to designate a duly canonized individual and at another anyone who appears saintly or is reputed to be holy "like a saint." It was not greatly different in the Old Testament. There were individuals both inside and outside of Israel who were reputed to be prophets by the people or who claimed to be prophets, e.g., Balaam, the Canaanite (Num. 22:5-8), and Hananiah, the Temple prophet who opposed Jeremiah (Jer. 28). There were in addition bands of religious enthusiasts, men who were called "prophets of Baal" (1 Kings 18:19) when dedicated to the service of the Canaanite Baals, and others who were called "prophets of Yahweh" (1 Kings 18:4) or "sons of the prophets" (2 Kings 2:3) when dedicated to the service of the God of Israel.

What these men had in common was the claim, if not always the call, to speak to the people as God's messengers. For the people there was no great problem in recognizing the falsity of the claims of the Canaanite prophets; though at times, as in the dramatic confrontation between Elijah and the prophets of Jezebel (1 Kings 18), a demonstration was not entirely unnecessary. Nor was there serious difficulty in distinguishing between the "bands of the prophets" or "sons of the prophets" (the Hebrew idiom for expressing the idea of "discipleship") and the true prophets, since the former were recognized either as ordinary religious enthusiasts or as religious followers of the true prophets (cf. 2 Kings 2:3-18; 4:38-44).

There was, however, a real need and often genuine difficulty in distinguishing between those who were truly called and those who falsely claimed to have been called to be God's messengers. As is evident from the description of the vocations of Moses (Exod. 3:7-22; 4:1-15), Amos (7:14-16), Isaiah (6:1-13), Jeremiah (1:2-10), and Ezekiel (1:2ff), no one could claim the right to speak to the people as God's messenger unless he had been truly called by God. Unfortunately, there were individuals in Israel who claimed to be prophets but had received no true call from God. As Jeremiah says, speaking for God: "I did not send these prophets, yet they ran; I did not speak to them, yet they prophesied" (23:21).

We sometimes take it for granted that the prophets were such extraordinary individuals that their claim to inspiration was recognized without difficulty and accepted without demur by their contemporaries. The account of Micaiah's reception by Ahab (1 Kings 22:6-28), of Jeremiah's encounter with Hananiah (Jer. 28), and the jibe of the people about the prophets as recorded by Jeremiah, "No evil shall befall us, neither sword nor famine shall we see. The prophets have become wind, and the word is not in them. May their threats be carried out against themselves" (5:12-13), should give us pause. Then as now the true supernatural and the false were not as simply distinguished as black from white. There was a grey area and very often only faith could see the real difference.

For the most part, the true prophet was distinguished from the false by the integrity and holiness of his life, by the agreement of his teaching with the traditional Mosaic doctrine, and occasionally, but by no means always or even as a rule, by the testimony of miracles or prophecies fulfilled within his own lifetime (e.g., Is. 38:1-8; Jer. 28:15-17). It seems not unlikely that the final popular distinction between the true and the false prophets was accomplished only by the 'canonization' of time.

Whatever the difficulties of the people in recognizing the true prophet, the prophet himself had the certitude of his own inner experience of God's call to assure him. This is particularly evident in the vocations of Amos (7:14-16), Isaiah (6:1-13) and Jeremiah (20:7-10). As St. Theresa of Avila, St. John of the Cross, and St. Margaret Mary Alacoque testify, the certitude of such experiences is overwhelming for the recipient.

The background of Israel's prophetism in pagan prophetism

To understand the dependence of Israelite prophetism upon pagan prophetism it is advisable to recall the incarnational principle enunciated by Pius XII: "Just as the Son of God became man, in all things like to man except sin, so the Word of God became like to human speech in all things except error."

In dealing with Israel as well as with men in general, the principle takes for granted that God does not ordinarily invent something new; rather, He adapts. He inspired Israel's leaders and founders to adapt from the Canaanites and from the cultural accomplishments of the times not only a great deal of her legal and wisdom literature but even such institutions as her priesthood, liturgy, feasts, Temple construction and appurtenances, her monarchical system, her early mythological way of thinking, and even her literary formats for expressing her covenant theology. The salient example for the latter is of course Israel's use of the Hittite suzerainty pact format.

The incarnaional principle suggests the possibility that Israel's prophetism may have been adapted from pagan prophetism. It suggests as well that we may learn a good deal about the precise function of a prophet in Israel by considering the function of prophets in the pagan religions that existed before and during the time of Israel's prophetic age. We know the function of Israel's kings, priests, wisdom teachers, and legislators. We can supply a job description for them and wtih reasonable accuracy reconstruct the self-image they had of themselves. A study of prophetism outside of and before Israel will help us do the same for Israel's prophets.

To appreciate the incarnational dependence of Israelite prophetism upon pagan prophetism we shall have to approach the problem by three steps: (a) the life situation of the messenger in ancient times and particularly in the preliterary ages; (b) the mythmakers' transfer to the world of the gods of such ideas as: the kings, the king's council (sod), and the king's messenger; (c) Israel's demythologizing and retheologizing of the mythmakers' thinking about the gods, the council or sod, and the sending of messengers by the gods to other gods and to men.

The life situation of the messenger

To understand the life situation of the messenger in the preliterary age (prior to 4000 B.C.), it should be remembered there *was* a preliterary age and in that age as in every age it was necessary at times to communicate over a distance with accuracy and authenticity. Since it was impossible to write a letter, it was necessary in the preliterary age to send 'living letters,' i.e., *messengers* — men who memorized the message of the sender, physically bridged the distance between the sender and the addressee, and ultimately delivered *orally* to the addressee the message of the sender.

Simply expressed, the messenger served as the *alter ego* of the sender and when delivering his message would say: "The King . . . has sent me. The word of the King: 'I, the king, say to you . . .'"

In such a situation it is understandable that the most important messages would be those sent by a king following upon a meeting with his advisers, who formed what came to be known in Hebrew as the *sod* or council of the king. The messenger who communicated the king's messages to the people combined the functions of messenger and herald.

The mythmakers' transfer of these ideas to the world of the gods

When the mythmakers attempted to visualize the life of the gods, they could do so only by transferring to the world of the gods all that was most impressive in the world of royal society as they knew it. As a result, the mythmakers patterned the gods' way of life after the way of life among kings on earth. Since one king was usually more important than others, the mythmakers conceived the world of the gods as made up of many gods among whom the high god was more important than the lesser gods. When the high god gathered his council, or *sod*, to discuss matters of some import, he was pictured, like a king on earth, as one who, following the meeting of his *sod*, sent messages to other gods by means of 'living letters' or messengers. The *sod* of the gods is described in the *Enuma Elis* myth (*ANET* 63B, 66A, 68A). The sending of a 'living letter' following the *sod* is described in the same myth where the high god Anshar sends his vizier, Gaga, a lesser god, as messenger to two other gods, Lahmu and Lahamu (*ANET* 64B and 65A).

Israel's demythologizing and retheologizing of these concepts

When Israel's writers spoke about Yahweh and His dealings with men, they adapted the language of the mythmakers. The adaptation is graphic in the prophet Micaiah's description of the court and *sod* of Yahweh in 1 Kings 22:19-23, in Isaiah's description of his inaugural vision (Is. 6:1-12) and in Job's description of the *sod* of Yahweh (Job 1–2). The plural of Gen. 1:26, "Let *us* make man in *our* image and likeness . . .", may well reflect this same situation.

It should be noted that Israelite theologians did not take over the mythmakers' conceptualizations lock, stock, and barrel. They demythologized and retheologized. In Israel's conception of Yahweh, the king, with His council or *sod*, no other gods can be present. The lesser gods of the myths become, in the language of Israel's writers, the "sons of god" or, as they were commonly called, the "angels" (*malachim*—the Hebrew word for "messengers"). The angels of the Bible would appear to be a "spin-off" product of this retheologization of the *sod*. This conceptualization process, however, in no way casts doubt upon the objective existence of angels any more than it jeopardizes the actuality of Yahweh's existence.

Since Israelite writers found it as unbecoming to conceive Yahweh running His own messages as they would for a human king to run his own messages, they regularly pictured God as transmitting His messages to men through the lesser gods now transformed into angels. Thus, we find angels sent by God to bring a message to Abraham (Gen. 18–19); to Gideon (Judg. 6:11-24); to Mary at the Annunciation (Luke 1–2); to St. John in the Apocalypse (Apoc. 17:1ff and passim). Prophetism was born when God chose to use men to serve as His messengers or "living letters" to His covenanted people, Israel.

The prophet's function and self-image

That Israel borrowed her idea of a prophet's function from pagan society and that there is an historical dependence of Israel's prophetism upon pagan prophetism might have been suspected from a perceptive analysis of the little tract on prophetism in Deut. 18:9ff, from Israel's early acceptance of Balaam as a prophet (Num. 22–24), and from Israel's acceptance of the name prophet for the false prophets of Baal described in 1 Kings 18–19.

More recently, evidence has accumulated from extrabiblical documents to indicate that Israel derived her concept of a prophet and even the literary format of the prophets' message from her pagan predecessors. The following documents are particularly persuasive: 'The Wen-Amon Story' (*ANET* 25–29); 'The Moabite Stone Inscription' (*ANET* 230–231); 'The Baalshamaiyam Text (*ANET* 501); 'The Mari Letters' (cf. H. B. Huffmon, "Prophecy in the Mari Letters," *The Biblical Archaeologist*, 31 [Jan. 1969] 101–124). Huffmon's conclusion deserves consideration:

> Although doubts have been expressed, as in H.M. Orlinsky's insistence that "prophecy is a uniquely Israelite phenomenon" and that "it is divination and not prophecy that finds its parallels in the Mari . . . documents" (Orlinsky, *Oriens Antiquus* IV [1965], 170), these doubts obviously do not take the newest texts into consideration. The Mari phenomena include what surely is cultic prophecy as well as prophecy by non-cultic persons and illustrate a wide range of content. . . . In view of the close ties in institutions between the peoples portrayed in the Mari letters—in this case ranging from Aleppo to Sippar—and the forerunners of Israel as well as later Israel, the picture of the development of Israelite prophecy will need reexamination. . . . The

prophets Gad and Nathan, who must have been attached to David's court, represent a continuity with the official prophets of the Mari letters. . . . And the cultic prophets, now well-known within Israel, also have their forerunners in the Mari letters (*art.cit.* 123–125).[1]

The evidence suggests that the elementary function of a prophet was to serve as Yahweh's messenger to His covenanted people. The prophet's self-image accordingly would involve seeing himself as carrying out the same 'living letter' (messenger) function as the messenger angels — the difference being that, in the case of the prophet, God would be sending a human messenger instead of a quasi-divine messenger like the demythologized "sons of god" from the *sod* of the high god in the myths.

It now seems quite possible (though not all would agree[2]) that Israel adapted from her pagan neighbors not only her cult, ritual, and priesthood, her law, and even her literary forms and ritual for expressing her covenant theology, but her conception of a prophet. The same evidence suggests she borrowed not only her conception of Yahweh's use of prophets as messengers but even the literary form in which the divine message was expressed.

The basic forms of prophetic speech

The study of pagan prophecy in the ancient Near East helps toward understanding the prophetic literature as a literature by suggesting that the major part of the prophetic literature may well have developed from the fundamental literary form used by the most ancient messenger-prophets — the messenger formula. Since the earliest announcements of judgment were made against individuals rather than against the nation as a whole and since the later announcements of judgment against Israel and the nations represent a development of the earlier forms of speech against individuals, it will be adviseable to begin with the judgment against an individual. An understanding of the judgment against an individual will contribute to an understanding of the judgment speeches against the nations.

The judgment speech against an individual [3]

Judgments against individuals predominate in the early narrative portions of the Bible. Judgments against the nations begin with Amos and

---

[1] Cf. also W. L. Moran, "New Evidence from Mari on the History of Prophecy" *Biblica* 50 (1969) 15-56; and A. Malamat, "Mari," *Biblical Archaeologist*, 34 (Feb. 1971), 20-21.

[2] Cf. S. D. Walters, "Prophecy in Mari and Israel" *JBL* 89 (March 1970) 78-81.

[3] Cf. C. Westermann, *Basic Forms of Prophetic Speech*, 90-198.

predominate from Amos to the end of the age of prophecy. Two examples, both imbedded in historical narratives (1 Kings 21:18-19 and 2 Kings 1:3-4), show the structure, the form, and the parts of the early judgment speeches against individuals:

The structure:
a) The commissioning of the messenger
b) The accusation
c) The messenger formula
d) The judgment

The form — based on the court trial of an individual:
a) Deals with an individual
b) Adduces evidence of the crime committed
c) The crime is against the covenant law of Israel
d) The guilty party is condemned and liable to covenant curses

Parts of the judgment speech as a whole:
a) The introduction: commissioning of the messenger, e.g., "Go . . ."
b) The accusation: either a direct statement or an accusing question with a causal connection expressed by "because you" or the equivalent.
c) The messenger formula: "The Lord says. . . ."
d) The announcement of judgment, which may have the following parts:
  1. the precise punishment demanded by the crime;
  2. a special punishment flowing from the nature of the king's office;
  3. a correspondence between the judgment and the accusation (cf., for examples, 1 Sam. 15:23; 2 Sam. 12:7, 10-11);
  4. a review of God's saving acts in favor of the king (cf., for examples, the judgment speeches in 2 Sam. 7 and 12);
  5. the giving of a sign (cf., for examples, 2 Sam. 12:14; Is. 7:14).

The judgment speech against the nation [1]

The judgment speech against the nation is similar to the judgment speech against an individual in structure but dissimilar in situation. The situation deals with many crimes, individual and collective, and with accompanying extensive evidence of infidelity to the covenant. The horizon of accusation will be correspondingly broad, and the time between the judgment and the execution of the judgment will necessarily be protracted; e.g., Amos' announcements of destruction precede by thirty years or more the destruction of Samaria, and Isaiah's announcement of

---

[1] Cf. C. Westermann, *op. cit.*, 169-198; J. H. Hayes, "The Usage of Oracles against Foreign Nations in Ancient Israel" *JBL* 87 (March 1968).

destruction for Jerusalem antedates the event by one hundred years at least.

The following outline indicates the common denominators of all prophetic speeches along with a comparison of the situations which account for the dissimilarities in the judgment speech against an individual compared with the judgment speech against a nation.

COMMON DENOMINATORS	AGAINST INDIVIDUAL	AGAINST NATION
Messenger formula	*Situation*: Simple—	*Situation*: complex—
Accusations	a) individual crimes	a) crimes of collectivity
Announcements of judgment	b) against specific covenant laws	b) against covenant as a whole
Inaugural vision	c) horizon low	c) horizon broad
The *sod*	d) evidence obvious	d) evidence— extensive
The *rib*	e) time between judgment and execution—brief	e) time between judgment and execution—protracted
Review of 'saving acts'		
Metaphorical descriptions of punishment	*Form*: Simple— a) messenger formula	*Form*: complicated a) messenger formula
'Sign' related to the punishment	b) brief accusation	b) lengthy accusation
Dramatization of the message	c) curt announcement of judgment	c) broad announcement of judgment
Relation of accusation to the covenant	d) little dramatization	d) extensive dramatization
Relation of accusation to saving history	e) simple legal accusation against covenant law	e) extensive judicial procedure as in *rib*
Relation of message to the kingdom of God		

The inaugural vision

The inaugural vision is an outgrowth of the first part of the messenger formula—the commission of the prophet by Yahweh. Its significance hinges on the importance of the prophet's convincing his audience he is an *authentic* messenger from the *sod* of the covenant King. If his words are not the words of Yahweh, but his own, then they are as ineffective and false as the words of the prophets of Baal.

In addition to authenticating the prophet as Yahweh's messenger, the inaugural visions of Isaiah, Jeremiah, Ezekiel, and Deutero-Isaiah, serve as a summary of the prophet's message.

The best examples of inaugural visions are in Is. 6; Jer. 1; Ez. 1–3; Is. 40:1-8. Amos does not properly describe an inaugural vision but his words in 3:3-8 and 7:14-15 serve the same purpose. The equivalent for Elijah may perhaps be found in his contest with the Baal prophets in 1 Kings 18:21-30, and for Elisha in 2 Kings 2:1-14.[1]

In Is. 6 the prophet claims (equivalently) that he has been admitted to stand before the *sod* of Yahweh and that Yahweh, after consulting with His *sod*, has decided to send Isaiah with a message of judgment against Israel. The scene is unmistakable. The King is surrounded by His angelic court. He consults His *sod* in the question: "Who will go for *us*?" And in the words "Go and say to this people," we have Yahweh commissioning Isaiah as His messenger from the *sod*.

The significance of being present at the *sod* is brought out by Jeremiah in his oracle against the false prophets: "I *have not sent* those prophets, yet they are running; I *have not spoken to them*, yet they are prophesying. Have they been *present at my council (sod)*? If so, let them proclaim my words to my people and turn them from their evil way and from the wickedness of their deeds!" (Jer. 23:21-22). The tenor of the argument here and in Jer. 23:9ff passim, as well as in Jeremiah's dispute with the false prophet, Hananiah (Jer. 28), is that the only authentic prophet is the one who can claim to have been present at the *sod* of Yahweh.

The rib or lawsuit

The *rib* or lawsuit, or 'controversy' as it is sometimes called, is connected with the second and third parts of the basic form of prophetic speech — the accusations and announcement of judgment — just as the inaugural vision is connected with the first part — the messenger formula or commissioning of the messenger.

As a literary device the *rib* is an adaptation of Israel's court trials and trial procedures by the prophets in order to dramatize the accusations and judgments of Israel's covenant suzerain and judge against His unfaithful vassal kingdom, Israel.[2]

[1] Something similar to the inaugural vision may underlie the Gospel accounts of the voice from heaven and the 'spirit descending as a dove' in Mark 1; Matthew 3; Luke 3; and John 1:19ff. The same may be said in a general way for Paul's vision at Damascus (Acts 9; 22; 26).

[2] Cf. B. Gemser, "The *Rib* — or Controversy — Pattern in Hebrew Mentality" in *Wisdom in Israel and in the Ancient Near East* (Vetus Testamentum, 1960, 120-137).

The first chapter of Isaiah illustrates the use of the *rib* form to present Israel haled into court by Yahweh to account for her crimes against the covenant and to be judged guilty by Yahweh. In Is. 1:1-31 Isaiah presents Himself as Yahweh's messenger who has been sent out from the court of Yahweh following the *rib*, or accusation, and the judgment which has been enacted in the *sod* of the covenant king. Read as follows, the chapter shows the importance of the basic form of prophetic speech (the commissioning of the messenger, the accusation, the judgment) as well as the *rib*'s significance in establishing the unity of the prophetic speech.[1]

1. v. 2a   Summoning of witnesses against Israel
                 (*mountains* as in the Hittite pacts).
2. vv. 2b-3   Covenant king's complaint in form of *accusation*.
3. vv. 4-9, 10-14 Further *accusations, interrogations,* and threats in
                 rib form.
4. vv. 16-20   An *appeal* from the covenant judge.
5. vv. 21-23   A final *complaint.*
6. vv. 24-31   The covenant king's *announcement of judgment.*

The *rib* or trial procedure lent itself to many forms and variations. Isaiah's 'Song of the vineyard owner' (Is. 5:1-7) in which Yahweh complains that Israel, His vineyard, has produced only 'sour grapes' is actually a *rib* in poetic form.

In a wider sense the Deuteronomist's History in 1–2 Kings can be understood as a form of *rib*. The book recounts the history of Israel's infidelity to the covenant by concentrating on the infidelity of the kings. The author gives a judgment on every king (the vast majority are adjudged guilty of covenant infidelity) and so describes the three great catastrophes that have fallen upon Israel (the division of Israel in the aftermath of Solomon's death in 922; the fall of Samaria and the Northern Kingdom in 722; and the fall of Jerusalem in 587) that they are seen as the fulfilment of the *curses* called down by the covenant king upon those guilty of infidelity to the covenant.

The most elaborate use of the *rib* as a literary device is found in the book of Job where the *rib* is used as background for the literary form of the book as a whole. The book opens with Yahweh in the *sod* acting as Job's defense lawyer against the prosecuting attorney, the Satan. While Job's case is argued in the *sod* by Yahweh, Job himself is represented on earth arguing his case against a battery of prosecuting attorneys — Bildad,

[1] H. B. Huffmon, "The Covenant Lawsuit in the Prophets," *Journal of Biblical Literature,* (Dec. 1959); R. Clements, *Prophecy and Covenant,* 78ff; B. Anderson and W. Harrelson (edd.), *Israel's Prophetic Heritage,* 26ff. For the semantics of the *rib*, cf. Gemser (*op. cit.,* 122-125); for the terminology of the *rib* in the psalms (*ibid.,* 127f); for the use of the *rib* by the prophets (*ibid.,* 128ff).

Eliphaz, and Zophar, who insist Job's sufferings are indisputable proof of his guilt. Eventually Job claims that if it were possible he would hale Yahweh Himself into court as his witness and Yahweh would have to testify to his innocence. The trial ends with the voice of Yahweh from the 'whirlwind' brushing aside the accusations of Job's accusers, giving judgment in favor of Job against Bildad, Eliphaz, and Zophar, and administering a well-deserved rebuke to 'innocent' Job.

Ez. 17:11-21 provides an example of a profane *rib*, i.e., a suzerainty-pact lawsuit between a human king and his vassal kingdom. It cites the 'lawsuit' controversy between Nebuchadnezzar, the suzerain king of the Babylonian Empire, and King Zedekiah the vassal king of Judah. In the *rib*, Ezekiel finds Judah guilty not only of infidelity to Yahweh but of infidelity to Nebuchadnezzar, who had made a suzerainty pact with Judah following the siege and fall of Jerusalem in 597 B.C.

Covenant theology — the basis of the prophets' theologizing and speeches [1]

It is important to remember that the forms of prophetic speech, the concepts of "messenger," "*sod*," "*rib*" and the inaugural vision deal with the prophets *on the level of the media* they used to express their message.

With covenant theology, we deal with the prophets *on the level of the message* they communicated by means of these media. The prophets are as concerned about the covenant as the Yahwist, the "D" theologian, the Elohist, and the Priestly theologian-author of the Pentateuch. They differ not in the centrality of their interest in the covenant but in their function and their literary presentation. The salvation history theologians emphasize *what God has done for Israel*. The prophets' primary concern is with *Israel's response or lack of response to her covenant suzerain*.

The underlying covenant theology context of the prophetic speeches is consequently of vital importance for understanding the prophetic message and theology. It will be important, therefore, to keep in mind: (a) the history and development of covenant theology; (b) the situation of each prophet in the perspective of Israel's history.

History and development of covenant theology

1) c. 1800   The promises to Abraham which are partially confirmed by the Exodus events, continued in the Davidic covenant, and fulfilled by the New Covenant.

[1] Cf. R. E. Clements, *Prophecy and Covenant*; *Abraham and David*; S. Mowinckel, *He That Cometh.*

2) c. 1250 The making of the conditional Sinai covenant whose end is announced first by Amos (for Israel of the North) and then by the other prophets, and comes to pass in 587 with the destruction of Jerusalem and the deportation of the Jews to Babylon.

3) c. 950 The Yahwist's Sinaitic and Davidic covenant theology.

4) c. 850 The Elohist's saga structured toward the Sinai covenant.

5) 850-780 Elijah and Elisha and the Sinai covenant in the northern kingdom.

6) 750-722 Amos and Hosea — the end of the Sinai covenant for the northern kingdom. But Hosea predicts a new covenant in the analogy of the "new marriage".

7) 700-621 The Deuteronomic school and the "D" theologian of Original Deuteronomy attempt to save the covenant by urging a response of love and obedience to Israel's suzerain King.

8) 732-687 Isaiah and Micah focus attention on the Davidic covenant.

9) 605-582 Jeremiah announces the imminent end of the Sinai covenant and the hopes for the reigning Davidic kings and predicts in place of them a new covenant and a new David.

10) 592-570 Ezekiel repeats the basic message of Jeremiah and speaks of a new Temple, a new Jerusalem, a new covenant, a new David, and a new Spirit.

11) 560-550 The Deuteronomist theologian justifies Yahweh's termination of the Sinai covenant but at the same time focuses attention on the Davidic covenant as the foundation of Israel's hopes for the future.

12) 550-520 Deutero-Isaiah predicts a new Exodus, a new Jerusalem, a new marriage and a new Creation.

13) 550-500 The Priestly theologian of the Pentateuch retains the Yahwist's Davidic covenant theology and, with Hosea, Jeremiah, Ezekiel, and Deutero-Isaiah, looks for a new covenant based on the unconditional promises made to Abraham and David.

14) 400-300 The Chronicler amalgamates the new covenant worshipping community of the Priestly author's theology with the promise of perpetuity to the Davidic dynasty.

The prophets in the perspective of Israel's history

Israel had prophets before and after the period of the kingdom (1020-587 B.C.), but the vast majority of the prophets are associated with the kings of Israel and Judah in the five centuries that elapsed between King Saul, the first king of Israel, and King Jehoiachin, who died in exile in Babylon around 550 B.C. Undoubtedly the historical association of king and prophet outside as well as inside Israel goes a long way toward explaining this phenomenon. Apart from Moses and a few others mentioned as prophets in pre-monarchical times, the majority of the prophets are associated in one way or another with the monarchy. In the perspective of Israel's history, they are generally associated with periods of either religious or political crisis.[1]

Period of the United Kingdom

1000 Monarchy of Saul and David — Samuel and Nathan
922 Monarchy and Solomon — Ahijah

Northern Kingdom — Israel		Southern Kingdom — Judah		
Ahab and Jezebel 850	Elijah and Elisha	Saul	1025	Samuel
Jeroboam II 750	Amos and Hosea	David	1000	Nathan
Fall of Samaria 722		Solomon	962-922	Ahijah

Ahaziah	734	Isaiah and Micah
Hezekiah	701	Isaiah and Micah
Last kings	626-587	Jeremiah, Zephaniah, Habakkuk Nahum
Exile	597-539	Ezekiel and Dt-Is.
Return	550-518	Dt-Is., Haggai, Zechariah
	ca. 460	Malachy
	ca. 300	Joel

Prophetism as an institution in Israel

As the roster of prophets shows, God's call to the vocation of prophet was not restricted to any particular type or group of men. Elisha was a farmer,

---

[1] It should be noted that the early prophets are for the most part simply messengers. The later prophets, in their greater concern for the realization of God's effective reign over his people and the world, become gradually more theological, more pastoral (e.g., Jeremiah and Ezekiel), and more visionary (e.g., Ezekiel and Deutero-Isaiah).

Amos a shepherd, Isaiah a nobleman, Jeremiah and Ezekiel priests. Several women, e.g., Miriam, Deborah, Hulda, appear to have been recognized as true prophetesses.

As the roster also shows, there was a fairly continuous line of prophets from Moses in the thirteenth century B.C., down to Malachi and Joel in the fifth. Prophetism, therefore, appears to have been as much an established institution in Israel as the priesthood or the kingship, even though the legitimacy of the individual prophets was certified by their particular call rather than by descent as in the case of the priesthood and the kingship. Indeed, as the author of Deuteronomy would show in his little treatise on prophetism (ch. 18), the institution of prophetism was as much of divine institution as the priesthood or the kingship.

The purpose of the institution and the authority of the prophets is underlined by the author of Deuteronomy (18:9-22). Israel, because of the danger of syncretism with the Canaanite religion in the early centuries of her history, and in the later centuries because of the failure of the kings and the priests, was in continual need of an authoritative voice to keep alive the enduring message of the Mosaic covenant and to warn the people against the perpetual temptation to aberrations in matters of worship, morality, and national purpose.

One need only read the struggle of Elijah and Elisha against the inroads of Jezebel's Baalism in the ninth century (1 Kings 18—2 Kings 10) to appreciate the need for men of courage and authority in order to preserve the true faith from perversion or oblivion. One need only read the sermons of Amos to appreciate the need for an authoritative voice in matters of morality and the sermons of Hosea to appreciate the need for an authoritative voice in matters of worship. While the failure of the kings and the priests is already manifest in the time of Elijah, Elisha, Amos, and Hosea, it is especially evident in the time of Jeremiah. Without his clarion voice to condemn the aberrations of kings, priests, and people and to reiterate the national purpose, it is doubtful, humanly speaking, if the nation buried in exile by the Babylonian avalanche of 587 could ever have risen again.

It is in relation to Israel's national purpose, moreover, that the prophets became the bearers of Israel's messianic hope. They, far more than the kings and the priests, kept alive in Israel's bosom the messianic hope kindled by the Sinai pact and brought to a flame by the promise to David of a perpetual dynasty. Amos spoke of the day when God would "raise up the fallen hut of David" (9:11). Hosea spoke of a new marriage between God and His people. Isaiah foresaw Immanuel, the shoot from the stock of David, who would rule with all the best qualities of Abraham, David, and Solomon and restore the world to its primitive paradise state (ch. 7—11). Micah spoke of a day when a new David would come out of

Bethlehem (5:1-4). And Jeremiah heralded a new and everlasting covenant in days to come (31:31-34).

In the long run, despite numerous setbacks, the prophets did succeed. Israel never succumbed wholly to idolatry. Never did all of her people degenerate to empty formalism in worship. Never did the nation as a whole completely forget its Mosaic past and its messianic future. There was always and at every period of Israel's history a hard core of dedicated faithful, a remnant indeed, but a true people of God, a spiritual Israel. These were the fruit of the prophets' otherwise futile efforts. They were a seed-bearing group as well, the group from whom would come those Jews of the time of Christ who would be the bridge between the old Israel of the Mosaic covenant and the new Israel of the Christian dispensation.

The mechanics of prophecy

It has been said that the prophets were essentially messenger-preachers, but inspired preachers, men whose words were not their own, but words of God. The problem that presents itself, therefore, is not so much how the prophets communicated to their audiences the words of God, but how the words of God were communicated to his prophets. The mechanics of inspiration, as we know, do not require anything so gross as divine dictation. Its essence is rather a subtle divine influence upon the will and the intellect of the prophet inclining him to speak those things and those things only which God wills to be communicated.

The impact of this influence is so unobtrusive, we might almost say so supernaturally natural, that the personality of the prophet suffers no change. They speak as they would speak even if they were not inspired. Thus we have no difficulty in penetrating to the distinctive personality of each prophet from a study of his words. As Jesus said, "Out of the abundance of the heart the mouth speaks," (Matthew 12:34). It is for this reason that we can so readily distinguish and delight in the extraordinary personalities of men such as Hosea, Jeremiah, Ezekiel, and Deutero-Isaiah.

Since there is no reason to believe that the inspired writers as a rule realized that they were writing under inspiration, we might be inclined on the basis of this general rule to consider the prophets as no different in their work of preaching. Yet, there is evidence to indicate that, unlike the generality of inspired writers, the prophets were to a certain limited extent conscious of God's influence upon them. Moses, Amos, Isaiah, Jeremiah, and Ezekiel speak of visions they have received from God. Unlike the later literary visions of Zechariah and Daniel, these visions give every indication of being genuine mystical experiences by which God made His presence and His message experientially manifest to His prophets. Theologians distinguish between external, sensibly perceived visions, visions impressed on the imagination and through the imagination reaching the mind, and visions directly impressed on the intellect. Whichever type of vision it may be in any particular case, the important thing is that it is the actual vital experience of a finite human being receiving a direct divine contact and communication.

In no place perhaps is the consciousness of the divine influence more strikingly expressed than in the famous confessions of Jeremiah, particularly in ch. 15:16-21 and 20:7-11. One can only marvel at the intrinsic truth in Jeremiah's description of his inability, despite his disgust and aversion for the life of a prophet, to withdraw himself from the overpowering influence of God in his soul virtually compelling him to preach: "You duped me, O Lord, and I let myself be duped; you were too strong for me, and you triumphed. All the day I am an object of laughter; everyone mocks me. Whenever I speak, I must cry out, violence and outrage is my message; the word of the Lord has brought me derision and reproach all the day. I say to myself, I will not mention him, I will speak his name no more. But then it becomes like fire burning in my heart, imprisoned in my bones; I grow weary holding it in, I cannot endure it" (20:7-9).

Apart from visions, it would appear that some conscious experience of divine communication lies behind the frequent use of the expressions, "The word of the Lord," and, "Thus says the Lord." A final testimony to such conscious experience may be drawn from Jeremiah's ten day wait for a divine communication concerning the course of action to be followed by himself and others after the fall of Jerusalem (cf. Jer. 44:7-22).

It will perhaps not be out of place to point out that, despite the visions and the other conscious experiences of divine communications, the prophets in most cases spoke without any consciousness of being under inspiration. In this they would be like the majority of inspired writers whose consciousness extended only to the fact that they were writing things pertaining to God, but not to the actual influence of inspiration on their faculties. Since most of their sermon matter was common knowledge derived either from Mosaic tradition with regard to doctrine or from observations with regard to contemporary events, they would be conscious for the most part only of fulfilling their divine mission by preaching the things of God, but not necessarily of the divine influence under which they preached. Thus their experience of inspiration would probably extend only to those occasions, rare on the whole, when they received a vision or a revelation of some points which could have been known in no other way except through a direct divine communication. To these categories would belong the inaugural visions of the prophets and such occasions when they received messages concerning future contingent events, e.g., Jeremiah's prediction concerning the death of Hananiah (Jer. 28:15-17). Since most messianic statements of the prophets can be shown to flow by deduction either from the Yahwist's saga or from the great dynastic prophecy of Nathan (2 Sam. 7), only those messianic prophecies that added something distinctively new would require direct revelation.

How to read the prophets

The reader has been warned of the textual and psychological difficulties in reading the latter prophets,[1] and he has already experienced them to some degree in reading the sermons of Amos and Hosea. It is only fair to point out now the characteristics that would facilitate an understanding of their words.

The first of these characteristics is the fact that the prophets are as a rule "traditionalists." The vast majority of their sermons reiterate what is "old," i.e., what is traditional doctrine contained either explicitly or implicitly in the Mosaic covenant and already committed to writing for the most part in the Yahwistic and Elohistic sagas.

What appears new is frequently only traditional doctrine expressed in a new way or with a peculiar emphasis attributable either to the personality of the particular prophet or to the needs of his times. Thus God's desire for social justice and charity toward the poor is part of the Code of the Covenant (Exod. 21–23). It is the complete breakdown of justice and charity toward the poor in the time of Amos that compels the prophet to emphasize this old doctrine. The same is true of God's love and holiness, each of which is clearly taught in the covenant theology but dramatized in a new way and with unforgettable vividness in the preaching of Hosea and Isaiah respectively. One might take as weak parallels the new and vivid emphasis given to evangelical poverty, to Christ's example of meekness and gentleness and childlike love as exemplified and propounded by St. Francis of Assisi, St. Francis de Sales, and St. Therese of Lisieux respectively.

What is truly new, on the contrary, is usually easy to single out. Thus specific prophecies concerning individuals, or the people as a whole, or the "New Covenant," or the Messiah, take up a proportionately small part of the prophetic preaching, but are quite clear in broad outlines if not in detail.

A second characteristic of the prophets is the fact that they generally do not argue points. They are not minded to "prove" their teaching. They do not engage in dialectics or apologetics. They take their teaching for granted because it voices the traditional religion. And they present it forcefully,

[1] Cf. p. 281.

directly, almost "kerygmatically." Their aim is to apply the traditional doctrine and whatever direct revelations they have received in such a way as to persuade their hearers to repent and return to God. Like our Lord they continually insist: ". . . unless you repent, you will all likewise perish . . ." (Luke 13:3).

The reader, therefore, should not look for close reasoning, scholastic precision, documented theses. He will find instead that belief in God, the authority of His law, the reasonableness of His demands, and the obligation to observe His covenant are as a general rule taken for granted. In a word, therefore, the prophets should not be read as if they were apologists, theologians, or dialecticians. Their theology is a theology in the raw, the theology of a living tradition which is meant to animate the lives of their hearers, as the living tradition of the apostolic preachers was meant to animate the lives of the first Christians.

A third characteristic of the prophets making them easier to understand than it might appear from one's first acquaintance with them is their basic oneness with preachers of all ages. When they preach, their principal aim is to persuade to action, to move their audience not only to believe but to live their belief. To attain this end, they use all the means customarily allowed to preachers and sometimes referred to as oratorical tricks. They exhort, rebuke, threaten, cajole, entice. They attempt to storm the will by means of the imagination, employing all the persuasive and moving power of concrete words, similes, metaphors, parables, allegories, paradoxes, hyperbole, and even puns. Like all preachers they make the most of that expansive liberty of expression conventionally allowed to those whose principal aim is persuasion and not instruction or the narration of the bare facts.

If the reader remembers this he will not demand of the prophet more than he demands of any other preacher. He will certainly not require the prophet to be as precise as a philosopher or as pretentious as a professional historian. He will not restrict his words to meanings listed in a dictionary. Nor will he cavil if the prophet appears to exaggerate for the sake of effect, or if he treats only one side of an issue (usually God's side) because he considers that aspect alone as truly important. He will on the contrary take the prophet for what he is — a messenger and a preacher — with the realization that if he is taken as anything else — a philosopher, a sociologist, a scientist — he will most certainly be misunderstood.

A fourth and most important characteristic of the prophets is their dependence, doctrinal as well as literary, on the inspired writers and preachers who went before them. As a result, not only is the doctrinal tradition continued, but the literary tradition as well. This can be seen from the recurrence of easily recognizable traditional themes and from the use and re-use of standardized formulas and stereotyped expressions. One would expect and one actually does find among the prophets the same kind of doctrinal unanimity with regard to the Mosaic teaching as one does among the Fathers of the Church with regard to the teaching of Christ in the Gospels.

If the reader will study a few lines of these themes as they occur in Amos and Hosea, he will not only recognize them when they reappear in later prophets, but he will find his understanding of succeeding prophets progressively better and his work of exegesis proportionately easier. Where the motif is known, the variations are more easily recognized and appreciated. The following motifs or themes are presented, therefore, not in the order of doctrinal importance, but in the order in which they appear in the first two writing prophets, Amos and Hosea. In the course of time these themes become common coin well worn and sometimes newly minted by other prophets.

a) Amos 1–2 *Oracles against the nations.* Similar oracles against the nations become a stock in trade literary form of later prophets sometimes developed at unusual length (cf. Is. 13–23; Jer. 46–51; Ez. 25–32; Nah.; Hab. 3).

b) Amos 3:2 *Special favor implies special obligations.* Our Lord's words, "Unto whom much is given, much shall be required" (Luke 12:48), summarize this common prophetic theme (cf. Amos 9:7; Hosea 13:4-8; Is. 5:1-6; Jer. 2:4-13; 18:13-18; Matthew 21:33-44).

c) Amos 4:4-5 *Formalism in worship is hateful to God.* Most of the prophets in one way or another will castigate in their people that hollow formalism in worship which consists in practice of the externals of religion without sincere internal dispositions of love and obedience (cf. Amos 5:21-26; Hosea 6:6; It. 1:10-19; 29:13-14; 58:2-14; Mich. 6:6-8; Jer. 6:20; 7:3-15; Matthew 6:1-18; 23:23-28).

d) Amos 4:6-13 *Medicinal punishments.* God's punishments (war, famine, plague, exile, pestilence), the prophets insist, are inflicted on His people primarily for the purpose of bringing them to their senses, of inducing reflection, repentance, and reformation (cf. Amos 5:1-9; Hosea 2:4-17; Is. 6:9-13; Jer. 5:3; Haggai 2:15-19).

e) Amos 5:18 *The Day of the Lord.* The intervention of God in history to judge and punish either Israel or Israel's enemies, to bring about the messianic age, or to judge the world at the end of time will be expressed in varying ways by the prophets as the "Day of the Lord" (cf. Amos 8:9; 9:11; Is. 2:10-19; 11:10; 13:6-13; Jer. 4:23ff; Zeph. 1:15-16; Joel 1:15; 2:1ff; 3:1ff).

f) Amos 7–9 *Visions.* The visions described by the prophets are sometimes genuine mystical experiences (e.g., Is. 6; Ez. 1), sometimes purely literary descriptions used as rhetorical devices after the manner of parables, allegories, metaphors, etc., (e.g., 1 Kings 22:19-23; Zech. 1–8 *passim*; Dan. 2, 4; 7–12 *passim*). It is not always easy to distinguish between a genuine vision and a vision composed as a rhetorical device (e.g., Amos 7–9 *passim*; Ez. 8–11; 40–48). In any case, the important thing is what the prophet teaches by means of the vision.

g) Amos 9:8-10 *The remnant.* The prophets teach that Israel can never be utterly destroyed because of the divine promises; there will always be at least a hard core of faithful souls in Israel which in messianic times will become the foundation group of a new Israel (cf. Is. 4:2-6; 6-13; 7-3; 10:21; 28:5-6; Micah 2:12; 5:6-8; Zeph. 2:7, 9; 3:11-20; Jer. 3:14-18; 23:3; 29:14; Haggai 1:12; Zech. 8:6).

h) Amos 9:11 *The messianic kingdom.* The hope of Israel in the Davidic family, based on the Nathan oracle in 2 Samuel and on the Yahwist's salvation history, is reflected in many of the prophets (cf. Is. 7:14-15; 9:1-5; 11:1-5; Micah 5:1-5; Jer. 23:5; 33:14-18; Ez. 17:22; 34:23-24; Zech. 9:9-10).

i) Amos 9:13-15 *The new paradise.* Descriptions of the messianic era in terms of the conditions in paradise (Gen. 2–3), based on the Yahwist's salvation history, occur frequently in the prophets (cf. Amos 9:11-15; Hosea 2:19-24; 14:5-8; Is. 11:1-9; Ez. 47; Is. 54:1-12; 60; 65:17-25; Zech. 8-12; Joel 4:18; Apoc. 22:2).

j) Hosea 1–3 *The marriage theme.* The covenant between God and His people and His love for His Chosen People is frequently expressed in terms of human marriage not only by Hosea and other Old Testament writers but by New Testament authors as well (cf. Jer. 2:1-2; 2:20-21; 3:1-5; Ez. 16; 23; Is. 54:4-6; 61:10-11; 62:4-5; John 3:29; Eph. 5:25-33; Apoc. 21:1-2).

k) Hosea 2:16-25 *The new exodus.* The ultimate realization of Israel's messianic hopes is pictured by the prophets as a new exodus from physical and spiritual captivity to a new life characterized by personal joy, intimate love for God, and unswerving fidelity to His will (cf. Hosea 2:1-3; Is. 11:10-16; Micah 2:12; 7:11-12; Jer. 23:7-8; 30:8-10; 31:1-14; Ez. 11:17-20; 20:33-38; 36:24-29; Is. 35; 40—55 *passim*; cf. also 1 Cor. 10:1-11).

l) Hosea 5:11-14 *The futility of dependence on human aid as opposed to dependence on God.* As a covenanted nation, brought into existence by God and kept in existence by His love, Israel must put her faith and confidence in God first and last (cf. Hosea 7:8-16; Is. 7:4, 16; 8:5-17; 28:16; 30:1-22; Micah 7:7; Jer. 2:13-19; 17:5-13; cf. also Matthew 6:25-34).

m) Hosea 11:1-4 *Israel is God's beloved son.* God's great love for His people, likened to that of a father for his child, an early metaphor in the Bible (cf. Exod. 4:22-23; Deut. 14:1-2; 32:4ff), becomes a favorite theme of the prophets (cf. Is. 1:2; 30:1-9; Jer. 3:4, 14, 19; 31:20; Is. 46:3; 49:14-15; 63:9; 64:7; 66:13; Mal. 1:6; cf. also Luke 11:2-13; 1 John 3:12; 4:8).

Much more could be said about prophetism. But the proof of the prophets is in the reading. We shall begin then with Isaiah in the last half of the eighth century and follow the prophets of Judah down the centuries to Malachi in the middle of the fifth century. We shall take Joel and Daniel with the apocalyptic literature and Jonah with the midrashic literature.

8

Judean Prophets during the Eighth Century Assyrian Menace

1. The Isaian, Assyrian Period

In the Assyrian flood that swept through Palestine during the last decades of the eighth century, the northern kingdom was torn up by the roots and carried away. The southern kingdom fared better. It lost independence but escaped destruction.

In both kingdoms the spirit of God spoke through the prophets, in the north through Amos and Hosea, in the south through Isaiah and Micah. We shall begin with the chronology and historical background of the Isaian, Assyrian period and then study Isaiah and Micah, the first of the great writing prophets of Judah.

In interpreting the prophets, the reader is urged to attend to the following basic rules: (a) determine the historical background of the prophet's sermon and interpret in the context of that background; (b) distinguish what is new from what is traditional; (c) distinguish the symbolic from the real and interpret the symbolic according to the rules for symbolic language; (d) in interpreting messianic utterances remember that the prophets speak about the future in symbolic language, without temporal perspective and without complete and detailed knowledge.

784-742 King Uzziah of Judah, contemporary of Jeroboam II of Israel.
768-687 Approximate dates of Isaiah, called around 742.
742-735 Jotham, regent until Uzziah's death, then king.
745-727 Tiglath-pileser III, begins Assyrian advance west in 738.
735-715 Ahaz, king at the time of the Immanuel prophecies.
735-732 Syro-Ephraimitic war: Damascus and Israel against Judah.
727-722 Shalmaneser V, opens siege of Samaria in 724, destroys Samaria in 722 and deports the northern tribes to Assyria.
722-705 Sargon II.
715-687 Hezekiah, reformer king and friend of Isaiah.
711-706 Hezekiah's sickness and the treaty with Merodach-Baladan of Babylon.
705-681 Sennacherib, scourge of Judah, repulsed at Jerusalem in 701.
687-642 Manasseh, the worst of all Judah's kings.

Historical background

Assyria in the eighth century before Christ was to Palestine and the Near East what Germany and Russia have been to Europe in the twentieth century. The reader must be familiar with Assyrian history and policy, therefore, if he is to understand the sermons of Isaiah.

Historians have called the Assyrians the "Nazis" of the ancient world. The title is well deserved. The Assyrians were obsessed by a mania for war and were infamous for brutal efficiency and unrestrained cruelty. The capital of the nation was at Nineveh on the Tigris, but Assyria took her culture for the most part from the old Babylonian empire of the great Hammurabi. She began to assert hegemony in Mesopotamia in the thirteenth century and by the ninth century was ruling most of the former Babylonian empire. Under Tiglath-pileser III, Shalmaneser V, Sargon II, and Sennacherib during the eighth century she reached the height of her power.

Because of her geographical position in north-central Mesopotamia, without natural frontiers and surrounded by enemies on every side, Assyria developed naturally into a nation of warriors. By the beginning of the ninth century she had become the first purely military empire in history. The speed of her armies, the efficiency of her siege machinery, and the frightful cruelty of her soldiers made her the scourge of the Fertile Crescent for the best part of the ninth to seventh centuries. In her march to power she dealt summarily with her enemies, giving them a choice of surrender or destruction. Those who surrendered retained a nominal independence but paid a heavy annual tribute. Nations that resisted were invaded, their cities destroyed, their citizens frightfully tortured. Future resistance was forestalled by deporting all influential citizens to distant parts of the empire. During this period Assyria was symbolized in ancient writings as the "wolf" or the "tiger," and the ferocity and cruelty of her armies made her name a synonym for terror.

Stopped temporarily at Karkar in 854, in a battle to which Ahab of Israel brought 10,000 foot-soldiers and 2,000 chariots, Assyria was nevertheless able by 842 to reduce most of the Palestinian states, including Israel under King Jehu, to the condition of tributary satellites. Internal troubles kept her armies at home during the first half of the eighth century, but during the second half, under Tiglath-pileser III (745-727), the Assyrian "wolf" raised her head and again moved west. Between 738-732, Tiglath-pileser conquered most of Syria and Palestine. When Damascus and Israel warred against Judah (the Syro-Ephraimitic war mentioned in Is. 7) in 735-732, Tiglath-pileser came, at the call of Ahaz of Judah, destroyed Damascus and reduced both Israel and Judah to abject vassalage (Is. 7—8; 2 Kings 16; 2 Chr. 28:16-27).

Shalmaneser V succeeded Tiglath-pileser in 727, and when the northern kingdom rebelled again in 724, his armies besieged Samaria. He died in 722, soon after he had completed the siege, destroyed Samaria, and deported the northern tribes into Assyria, bringing to an ignominious end that dissident kingdom (2 Kings 17—18). He was succeeded by Sargon II (722-705).

When Sargon II died in 705, ambitious satellites in Palestine, including King Hezekiah of Judah, saw a chance to throw off the Assyrian yoke. The story of their failure provides some of the more interesting reading in Judah's history (2 Kings 18—19; Is. 36—38; 2 Chr. 32). In 703, Sennacherib (705-681) moved west and put down one rebellious state after another. In 701, he besieged Jerusalem but miraculously, as Isaiah had foretold, failed to take it.

Weakened by luxury and beset by the fanatical hatred of her numerous and bitter subject states, Assyria fell in 612 when Nabopolassar, king of Babylon and father of the great Nebuchadnezzar, in league with Assyria's bitterest enemies, besieged Nineveh and destroyed it utterly. The book of Nahum describes the downfall of Nineveh and Assyria in vivid phrases.

It is with Assyria in the late eighth century, however, that we are concerned. For it was then, when Assyria was at the height of her power under the great monarchs Tiglath-pileser III, Shalmaneser V, Sargon II, and Sennacherib that Isaiah and Micah preached in Judah.

2. Isaiah

A statesman saint, Isaiah [1] is the Thomas More of the Old Testament. Like More he is a family man, a counsellor of kings, a skilled writer, an ardent defender of God's rights against royal self-will, and in the end a martyr for the faith at the hands of his king. His response to his call (6:8) shows a generous, spontaneous, and naturally courageous nature in contrast to Moses (Exod. 3:11f) and Jeremiah (1:6-8). His poetry and preaching reflect a soul sensitive and refined and endowed with extraordinary power of expression.

Isaiah was born during the prosperous but immoral reign of King Uzziah (784-742). He was a contemporary of Amos and Hosea in the northern kingdom and of Micah in Judah. He preached during the reigns of Kings Jotham, Ahaz, and Hezekiah (1:1). His position as counselor to Ahaz (7:3-17) and Hezekiah (39:1-8), his knowledge of political affairs, his poetic language and exquisite Hebrew style, all indicate a cultured nobleman of high rank in the royal court. Married and the father of two sons with prophetic names, Shear-yashub (7:3) and Maher-shallal-hash-baz (8:3-4), he appears to have done most of his preaching in Jerusalem. According to Hebrew legend he died a martyr for the faith around 687, when, by order of the infamous King Manasseh, he was placed in a hollow tree and sawn in half. His feast day in the Church's calendar of saints is celebrated on July 6 and his Mass is that of a martyr.

While manifesting many of the characteristics of Amos, the prophet of divine justice, and Hosea, the prophet of divine love, Isaiah is preeminently the prophet of holiness. Just as St. Paul's emphasis on the doctrine of the Mystical Body may be traced to the words he heard from Christ at the time of his vision on the Damascus road, "Saul, Saul, why persecutest thou Me?," so the emphasis given by Isaiah to the doctrine of holiness can be traced to the words he heard chanted by the seraphim at the time of his call: "Holy, holy, holy is Yahweh of hosts! All the earth is filled with his glory."

It is in the light of this vision of God's holiness that Isaiah's major ideas can best be appreciated. He is dominated first by an overwhelming realization of the sanctity of God (6:1-4; 1:4; 5:19, 24; 10:17, 20). In contrast to this holiness, he is filled with dismay at the corruption of his people (6:9-13; 1:4-24, 28-31; 2:12-17; 3:16-26; 7:17-20). In view of the fact that the nation has been called to be holy (Leviticus *passim*) and has failed miserably in fulfilling her goal of imitating the holy God, God gives him to realize the necessity and inevitability of chastisement to purge away

[1] Cf. Bright 251-287; E. Kissane, *The Book of Isaiah*, (Dublin: Browne and Nolan, 1963) 2 vols; B. Vawter, *Introduction to the Prophetical Books*, OTRG No. 14; M. McNamara, Isaiah 1–39; OTRG No. 16.

this corruption. Assyria, he is given to understand, will be the instrument used by God to punish and purge his people (10:5-9 *passim*). Out of the destruction (6:9-13), however, will come a purged "remnant" (6:13; 10:20) from which will eventually come the Messiah (9:6-7; 11:1-5; 11:10) and the nucleus of the messianic kingdom (2:1-4; 4:2-6; 9:7; 11:6-9).

The mind of Isaiah may be expressed as follows. Because Israel has forgotten her God, treated the covenant with contempt, and revelled in immorality and idolatry, she will be chastised by the very nations to whom she has betrayed her trust in God. Her chastisement, however, will not be to the death, because the divine promises are without recall. A restoration, therefore, of at least a part of Israel, a "remnant," is certain. The "remnant" will necessarily have to be holy like the God of the prophet's vision, "the Holy One of Israel." Isaiah's doctrine is best summarized in ch. 6, in which is described his inaugural vision and mission.

The book of Isaiah as we know it is an anthology. Part I (ch. 1–39) is in the main the work of the eighth century prophet himself. Part II (ch. 40–55) is the work of an unknown prophet who preached during the Babylonian exile and is referred to by scholars as "Deutero-Isaiah." Part III (ch. 56–66), frequently called "Trito-Isaiah," dates from the years immediately following the return of the Jews to Jerusalem after the Babylonian exile.

Internal evidence, such as the three distinct introductions (1:1; 2:1; 6:1ff), the borrowing of chapters 36–39 from the books of Kings (composed sometime after 562), and the exilic and postexilic references in chapters 40–66, indicate that the book as it stands is the work of a compiler who put it together in its present form sometime after the exile.

Since Deutero-Isaiah and Trito-Isaiah will be treated after Ezekiel and in the context of the Babylonian exile and the return to Jerusalem of the repatriated exiles, it will be sufficient for the present to give the division of the first part of the book which is substantially the work of the eighth century Isaiah. It can be divided into seven parts:

I. Indictment of Israel and Judah (1–5).

II. The Immanuel prophecies (6–12).

III. Oracles against the pagan nations (13–23).

IV. The little "apocalypse" of Isaiah (24–27), probably the work of a disciple in the postexilic period.

V. Yahweh alone is Judah's salvation (28–33).

VI. Yahweh is Zion's avenger (34–35), probably the work of Deutero-Isaiah.

VII. Historical appendix (36–39), taken from 2 Kings 18–20.

Since the greatest difficulties in reading the prophets are found in distinguishing where one sermon ends and the next begins, and in placing each sermon in its proper historical background where alone it can be properly appreciated, we shall try to divide the text into coherent sermons or parts of sermons, and at the same time put each sermon into its proper historical background.

The reader should remember that he is reading not a collection of complete sermons but an anthology of the more significant sayings of Isaiah, collected and arranged in a loose chronological order by editors who lived as much as 200 years after the prophet. This may help to explain the sudden changes of subject and historical background found in different sections of even one chapter. Finally, the reader should study and meditate upon each saying or section of a sermon as a unit, remembering that a synthesis of the prophet's teaching, like a synthesis of any collection of sermons, must be made by collating parallel sections from different sermons dealing with the same topic.

6:1-13   Placed by the final editors with the collection of Immanuel prophecies (7—12), for which it provided a powerful introduction, the inaugural vision of Isaiah should, nevertheless, be taken first. Dating from 742, before the coming of the Assyrians and at a time when there was still peace and prosperity in Judah, the chapter describes Isaiah's vision of God, the Holy One of Israel (1-7), his vocation (8), and his mission (9-13).

1:2-31   Dating to the last years of Hezekiah (after 701) when Judah was reeling from one assault after another by the surrounding Gentile nations (2 Kings 15:37; 2 Chr. 28:5-8, 16-18), the prophet assails his people for ingratitude (2-3), infidelity (4), and hardness of heart (5-9), and inveighs against that formalism in religion so detested by God and so often excoriated by the prophets (cf. Am. 4:4-5; 5:21-27; Hosea 6:4-6; Ps. 50). In 1:20 there is the first prediction of the destruction that would come upon Judah as foretold in the inaugural vision (6:11). The conclusion (vv. 21-31) contains an indictment of Israel (21-23), ending with a declaration (parallel to 6:11-13) of God's redemptive plan for Israel (24-31).

Nos. 37–45. **37**. Camels, as domesticated animals, enter history with the Midianites and their raids on Canaan at the time of Gideon. **38**. Although the Nile is associated with the production of papyrus during most of the Bronze Age, papyrus did grow at other places, for instance, around Lake Merom, Galilee, as here pictured. **39**. Cedars still grow on Lebanon three milllennia after Solomon. **40**. Oases in the Sinai Peninsula provide more than a watering spot for the weary caravan — lush clusters of dates, for instance. **41**. The precious olive is picked with tender care. **42**. The almond tree and its fruit is called *the awakening one, shaked,* quite probably because it is the first to blossom in spring and gladden the eye with its white or roseate flowers. **43**. "A vast army of locusts covers the land; it is a terrible army too numerous to count, with teeth as sharp as those of lions!" (Joel 1:6). **44**. Method of harvesting grain until the inventions of Deere and McCormick in the nineteenth century A.D. **45**. Inspiration for Psalm 23, "The Lord is my Shepherd." *Photos courtesy:* Matson Photo Service, Alhambra, California.

2:1-5 The heading in v. 1 indicates that at one time ch. 2—5 probably constituted a separate collection. The messianic oracle concerning the place of the house of God in the future messianic kingdom probably dates to the same time as the other messianic oracles in ch. 4; 7; 9 and 11.

2:6-22 Another indictment of Israel for her idolatry and materialism (6-9), followed by a threatening description, reminiscent of Amos (5:18ff), of the coming "Day of Yahweh" (10-22).

3:1—4:1 Dating probably to 735, when the period of prosperity in Judah under Jotham was ending, and the chastisement of Judah decreed by God (6:11-13) had begun with a series of wars waged by the surrounding states (cf. 2 Chr. 28:5-7, 16-19), Isaiah describes the anarchy into which these reversals throw the government (1-8), the iniquities that occasion the disasters (9-15), and the consequences of the disasters for the delicate, luxury-loving women of Jerusalem (3:16—4:1).

4:2-6 Like 2:2-5, a messianic prophecy, these verses predict the future glory of Jerusalem and the sanctity of the "remnant." They date probably from the same time as the other messianic prophecies in ch. 2; 7; 9 and 11.

5:1-7 A classic parable likening ungrateful and irresponsive Israel to a carefully tended but inexplicably unfruitful vineyard. (Cf. for the same: Hosea 10:1; Jer. 2:21; 5:10; 6:9; 12:10; Ez. 15:1-8; Mark 12:1-12).

5:8-30 Probably delivered sometime during the last years of Judah's prosperous period, between 742 and 735, the sermon, very similar to Amos 5:16ff, threatens "woe" on Israel for her crimes against social justice and for her materialism and indifference (vv. 8-23), concluding with a prediction of her approaching punishment (vv. 24-30).

Prophecies of Isaiah during the reign of Ahaz (735-715)

When Ahaz came to the throne of Judah in 735, he found the kingdom in a desperate position. A coalition of small nations led by Israel and Damascus had decided to rebel against Assyria. When Ahaz refused to join the coalition, he was attacked on every side. Israel and Damascus attacked on the north (2 Kings 16:5-6; Is. 7:1-2), the Edomites on the south (2 Kings 16:6; 2 Chr. 28:17), the Philistines on the west (2 Chr. 28:18). Rezin, the king of Damascus, and Pekah ben Remaliah, king of Israel, made it clear that they would not only force Judah into the coalition but would depose Ahaz and inaugurate a new line of kings in Jerusalem (Is. 7:6). Not only the nation, therefore, but the Davidic dynasty as well was in peril.

In the war that ensued, called the Syro-Ephraimitic war because the principal members of the coalition against Judah were Syria and Israel, Ahaz, against the solemn advice and warning of Isaiah, called for the help of Tiglath-pileser, the king of Assyria. Tiglath-pileser's armies swept through Israel in 734, deporting to Assyria many of the inhabitants of northern Israel, particularly those in the area around the Lake of Galilee (cf. 2 Kings 15:29; Is. 8:23). Only the death of Pekah ben Remaliah, assassinated by Hoshea ben Elah (2 Kings 15:30), saved Israel from complete destruction. In 732 Tiglath-pileser ravaged Damascus, executed Rezin, deported many of the citizens and organized the conquered country into four Assyrian provinces (2 Kings 16:9; Is. 17).

In Judah the results of the intervention of Tiglath-pileser were mixed. The nation and the dynasty were saved, but Ahaz was forced to pay a huge price both in money (2 Kings 16:8) and in prestige (2 Kings 16:10-18). In addition, and it was for this reason that Isaiah warned against the Assyrian alliance (cf. Is. 8:11-15), Ahaz was forced to introduce Assyrian worship into the Temple of Jerusalem. Whether the force was physical or moral, we do not know, but from the subsequent cultivation of syncretism by Ahaz described in 2 Kings 16:2-4, it is clear that Ahaz was a man of little or no faith in the God of Israel. It is against this background that the book of Immanuel (Is. 6–12) is to be read. It begins with Isaiah's description of his inaugural vision (ch. 6), continues with a description of the outbreak of the Syro-Ephraimitic war (ch. 7) and gives selected oracles from some of the Isaian sermons occasioned by the war and some of the messianic prophecies evoked by the prophet's disgust with the faithless Ahaz.

7:1-25 The beginning of the Syro-Ephraimitic war is the historical background as Isaiah goes out to meet Ahaz at the highway by the fuller's field (cf. Is. 7:1-2; 36:3, 11). Isaiah advises against appealing to Assyria for help (v. 4), promises absolutely that the kingdom will not be conquered (v. 8), and insists further that the throne will be firm only if the king's faith is firm (v. 9). To strengthen Ahaz's faith, Isaiah offers to work any sign that the king would propose (v. 10). When Ahaz contemptuously refuses such a miracle from God (because he lacks faith and is resolved to spurn the prophet's advice and seek assistance from Tiglath-pileser), Isaiah counters with the "sign" of the dissolution of his house and kingdom in punishment for his infidelity and contemptuous spirit: "the virgin will be with child and bear a son and name him Immanuel" (i.e., *God with us*, v. 14; cf. Is. 8:8; 8:10; 9-1-6; 11:1-5; Matthew 1:23), but *before* this child reaches the mentioned age, the land of Syria and Israel will be devastated (v. 16), while "upon you (Ahaz) and upon your (Ahaz's) people, and upon your (Ahaz's) father's house, Yahweh will bring such (calamitously evil) days" as had not heretofore been recorded (v. 17; the "evil days" are then described at length in vv. 18-25).

The Immanuel prophecy has been variously interpreted: directly messianic, i.e., referring directly to Christ and to no one else; indirectly or typically messianic, i.e., referring directly to the birth of Hezekiah, indirectly to Christ, of whom Hezekiah, who will save Judah, reform religion in the kingdom and exemplify in general the ideal king of the theocratic kingdom, will be a type. Against the above and against all other opinions presented up to the present objections can be advanced. There is no universally accepted solution at the present time (cf. p. 331ff).

8:1-10 The promise and warning given to Ahaz more or less privately is now given publicly to all the people, and again a child, this time the infant son of Isaiah, is used as a sign (vv. 1-4). As in ch. 7, Isaiah joins a prediction that Syria and Israel will not prevail in their war against Judah (cf. 7:7-9; 7:16) to a prediction of Judah's invasion by Assyrian armies (vv. 5-8). As in ch. 7 (the reference to Immanuel) Isaiah includes a word of hope — the Assyrian flood will engulf Judah to the neck, but her plan to crush Judah will not succeed because of "Immanuel" (vv. 9-10). "Immanuel" is the pledge of Judah's ultimate salvation.

8:11-20 Despite Isaiah's warnings, King Ahaz puts his trust in man instead of God and makes an alliance with Tiglath-pileser of Assyria (vv. 11-15; cf. 2 Kings 16:7ff). Confident that his predictions will be fulfilled, Isaiah consigns his writings to his disciples and waits for God to vindicate him.

8:23—9:6 At least a year has passed since the events and sermons of ch. 7—8. In the meantime, Tiglath-pileser, called in by Ahaz, has invaded northern Israel and deported to Assyria many of the Israelites from the territory of Zebulun and Naphtali, the region of Galilee (cf. 2 Kings 15:29; Is. 8:23a). To raise the spirits of the people, shocked by the loss of at least two of the original twelve tribes, Isaiah points to an extraordinarily joyous event, the birth of a Davidic prince (9:1-6).

The names given to this child (which like the names Shear-yashub, Maher-shalal-hash-baz, and Immanuel, are symbolic names) have led many to consider the words directly messianic (cf. Matthew 4:15ff). Some, on the other hand, refer these words along with Is. 7:14-15 only indirectly to Christ and directly to Hezekiah, the crown prince of Judah born *perhaps* at this time (734, approximately one year after the promise to Ahaz in ch. 7). According to this latter opinion, Hezekiah is Immanuel, a type of the Messiah, and as such is addressed not only in court style but in words colored by messianic expectations flowing from the promise made to the Davidic dynasty in 2 Sam. 7.

9:7–10:4 Directed against the northern kingdom, sometime before 722, the theme of this sermon is the perversity of the Israelites, who will not learn from the calamities already visited upon them. The refrain in vv. 11, 16, 20, and 10:4 is found in 5:25 and has led many authors to place 5:25-30 after 10:4. The reference in 9:20 to the war of Israel against Judah dates this sermon after 735, the time of the Syro-Ephraimitic war. The reference in 10:3 to the approaching storm indicates a time before 722, when Israel fell never to rise again. Undoubtedly the sermon is meant as a lesson for the Judeans who are in danger of similar treatment. There is a limit to God's patience.

28:1-6 Isaiah's last words on Israel to the north are words of woe and probably date to the fateful days between 724 and 722 when the armies of Assyria under Shalmaneser V besieged and conquered Samaria, and reduced the northern kingdom to just one more province of the Assyrian empire (cf. 2 Kings 17).

During the remaining days of Ahaz's reign, it would appear that Isaiah had little to say. Indications are he remained in relative seclusion after his failure with Ahaz in 735 and gave his time to private teaching (cf. Is. 8:16-20). Ahaz in the meantime had introduced into the Temple not only the Assyrian cult (cf. 2 Kings 16:10-18) but the abominable practices of the Canaanite Baal worship as well (cf. 2 Kings 16:2-4).

In the north, when Tiglath-pileser III died in 727 and was succeeded by his son Shalmaneser V, Hoshea of Israel revolted. Shalmaneser commenced a three year siege of Samaria in 724, and in 722 the city fell (cf. 2 Kings 17; Is. 28:1-6; Micah 1:2-7).

When Shalmaneser V died in 722 and was succeeded by Sargon II, Babylon under Merodach-Baladan rebelled and remained independent from 721-710. Hamath, Damascus, Gaza, and Egypt rebelled as well, but Sargon's armies moved west in 720 and defeated the Syrian kings at Karkar and the Philistines and Egyptians at Raphia (ANET 285).

Isaiah's prophecies during the reign of Hezekiah (715-687)

In 715 Ahaz died and was succeeded by his son, Hezekiah, the best intentioned king of Judah since David. Invited at the very outset of his reign to join with Philistia and Egypt in a revolt against Assyria, Hezekiah under the tutelage of Isaiah (Is. 20) resisted the temptation to join the rebels (cf. Is. 14:28-32) and was spared when the revolt was crushed in 711 (cf. ANET 286f).

Instead of engaging in anti-Assyrian revolts, Hezekiah organized a vigorous religious reform, sweeping away the pagan cults introduced by Ahaz (cf. 2 Kings 18:2-6; 2 Chr. 29—31), even going so far as to invite the remaining Israelites of the conquered north to return their religious allegiance to Jerusalem (2 Chr. 30:1-12). The attempt was not successful, but it gave evidence of that dream of a united Israel that persisted even when a national reunion became impossible and only a religious reunion could be envisioned.

Later, around 705, when Sargon II died and was succeeded by Sennacherib, Merodach-Baladan of Babylon, looking for allies to help him in a revolt against Assyria, sent ambassadors to Hezekiah and succeeded in embroiling him, contrary to the wishes of Isaiah, in a coalition against Assyria (cf. Is. 39; 2 Kings 20:12-19). Merodach-Baladan revolted in 703. About the same time Judah refused tribute (2 Kings 18:7), and Hezekiah prepared for a siege (2 Chr. 32:3ff; 2 Kings 20:20).

The revolt was a dismal failure. In 702, Assyrian armies crushed Merodach-Baladan's Babylonian armies. In 701, when Sennacherib appeared with his armies at the Mediterranean and captured Tyre, many of the rebel states hastened to switch their allegiance back to Assyria. Ascalon, Ekron, Judah, and Egypt refused. Sennacherib attacked and defeated the Philistine city states, paused briefly to defeat an Egyptian army at Elteqa (near Ekron), and then proceeded to besiege and devastate one Judean town after another. Late in 701, only Jerusalem had not yet capitulated. Ensuing events as described by the author of Kings (2 Kings 18–19; Is. 36–37) are not perfectly clear. Two things, however, are certain: Hezekiah paid a heavy tribute to Assyria (cf. 2 Kings 18:13-16); Sennacherib's armies suffered a devastating setback and were forced to raise the siege and retire to Assyria (cf. 2 Kings 19:32-37; Is. 37:33-38). Whether these two events pertain to the same invasion or to separate ones at different times is disputed (cf. Bright 282ff, ANET 288).

20:1-6   Isaiah succeeds, by his symbolic portrayal of the fate of the conquered, in persuading Judah from joining the anti-Assyrian coalition of 714-711 (cf. 14:28-32; 18:1-7).

38—39   Authors agree in placing the sickness of Hezekiah and the visit of Merodach-Baladan's ambassadors before the siege of Sennacherib because after the siege of 701, Hezekiah possessed no wealth to show visiting legates, nor was he in a position to make the alliance with Merodach-Baladan, discreetly insinuated in ch. 39. Originally, therefore, the events in ch. 38—39 preceded the events of ch. 36—37. Probably a later editor rearranged the chapters so that Isaiah's prophecy concerning the Babylonian captivity (39:5-8) would immediately precede the second part of the book (ch. 40–66) which deals with the preaching of Deutero-Isaiah in Babylon. The reader should note that in discouraging the alliance with Merodach-Baladan (Is. 39:3-7), Isaiah acts consistently with the policy of dependence on God and avoidance of alliances with pagan nations, a policy he had advocated already under Ahaz in 735 (cf. 7:1-9; 30:15). Unfortunately for Judah, Hezekiah, like Ahaz, does not follow the prophet's advice. The alliance with Merodach-Baladan (39:1-7) is followed by alliances with Egypt and Tyre and some of the Philistine states. War breaks out between 703-701, and the anti-Assyrian coalition is crushed. Ch. 36—37 describe the results of this ill-starred rebellion.

30:1-7   One of Isaiah's warnings to Hezekiah and the leaders of Judah against the ill-fated alliance with Egypt, c. 703 (cf. also. 31:1-3).

29:1-16   Isaiah apostrophizes Jerusalem under the symbolic name *Ariel* (lion of God) shortly before the siege of Sennacherib in 701 (cf. also 32:9-14; 22:1-25; Mich. 1:10-16).

36—37   The dramatic account of Sennacherib's invasion of Judah and siege of Jerusalem in 701 is described in the Bible and in Sennacherib's annals (ANET 288; cf. also Herodotus' Persian Wars,

II, 141). The raising of the siege following the prediction of Isaiah left in Jewish minds the indelible impression that Jerusalem was impregnable and indestructible because of God dwelling in its midst (cf. Pss. 46; 48; 76; Jer. 7:1-10).

10:5-34 Isaiah outlines the use God makes of the Gentile nations to bring to fulfillment His plans for the course of history (cf. 14:24-27; 17:12-14; 30:27-33; 31:4-9).

11:1-9 Isaiah predicts the birth of a Davidic king who will be filled with the spirit of God, with wisdom and understanding like to that of Solomon, counsel and foresight like to that of David, knowledge and the fear of the Lord like to that of Abraham (vv. 1-3a). He will be a king who will recognize and establish the rights of the good and punish the wicked (vv. 3b-5), so that in his day there will be a return to the reign of peace that existed in paradise (vv. 6-9), a peace symbolized parabolically by the picture of beasts of prey (the lion, the leopard, and the bear) cohabiting peacefully with beasts usually preyed upon (the lamb, the kid, and the cow). N.B. 11:10-16 and 12:1-6 represent the work of one of Isaiah's literary disciples during the period of the Babylonian captivity.

Whether 11:1-9 dates to the same period as 7:1-25; 8:1-10; 9:1-6 (735-734), or to a later period in Isaiah's preaching, such as that assigned to it here (c. 701), is a matter of dispute. It is equally disputed whether the text is directly messianic or typically messianic, referring directly to Hezekiah described in the light of the glorious future predicted of the Davidic dynasty (2 Sam. 7) and indirectly to the future Messiah typified by Hezekiah. If the prophecy could be solidly established as dating to 701, a time when little could be expected of Hezekiah, the case for this text as the first clearly direct and personal messianic prophecy would be greatly strengthened. N.B. Ch. 32-35 contain a number of original Isaian prophecies dating from the Assyrian period but liberally glossed by disciples during and after the Babylonian exile.

30:8-18 Possibly the prophet's last will and testament to his disciples (similar to his testament in the time of Ahaz given in 8:16-18).

Little is known of the fate of Isaiah after the death of Hezekiah in 687. Of the Jewish legend that he was martyred by King Manasseh, the son and successor of Hezekiah, all one can say is that it is not improbable. In the years that followed, all the reforms of Hezekiah were reversed by his impious son, who reigned from 687 to 642, re-introduced the abominations of the Canaanites, and persecuted those faithful to the true religion (2 Kings 21:1-9). The stark words of the author of Kings, "Furthermore Manasseh shed very much innocent blood until he had filled Jerusalem from one end to the other" (2 Kings 21:16), leave no doubt that a male counterpart to Jezebel of Israel was at work during these years in the kingdom of Judah. Before dealing with the last prophets of the southern kingdom, Zephaniah, Jeremiah, Nahum, Habakkuk, and Obadiah, we shall pause briefly to read the sermons of Isaiah's contemporary, Micah.

3. Micah

Micah speaks of himself only twice in the course of his prophecies. In 3:8 he says of himself: "But as for me, I am filled with power, with the spirit of the Lord, with authority and with might — to declare to Jacob his crimes and to Israel his sins." In 7:7 he says: "But as for me, I will look to the Lord, I will put my trust in God my savior, my God will hear me!"

In addition to these autobiographical remarks betraying a strong and resolute character, we are given two biographical notices. The first is by the editor of the book who tells us that Micah preached during the reigns of Jotham, Ahaz, and Hezekiah (1:1) — sometime therefore between 742 and 687, contemporaneously with Hosea in the north and Isaiah in the south. We are told in addition that Micah came from Moresheth, a little town southwest of Jerusalem in the Shephelah not far from the Philistine city of Gath.

The second biographical notice (Jer. 26:18-20) tells us that Micah's threat against Jerusalem and the Temple (3:12) was instrumental in bringing about the reform of Hezekiah between 715 and 701 (2 Kings 18:3-6; 2 Chr. 29:8-11).

From the recorded sayings of Micah it is clear that he was for Judah what Amos had been for Israel — a man who saw the oppression of the poor by the rich as a crime crying out to heaven for vengeance (Micah 2–3; 6:9-11). Micah, however, goes beyond Amos by looking to the future beyond the day of punishment to the day when the expected Messiah would come in person and rule not only Judah but all the nations of the world (Micah 4–5). Perhaps his most quoted words are the words with which he defines true religion: "You have been told, O man, what is good, and what the Lord requires of you: Only to do the right, and to love goodness, and to walk humbly with your God" (6:8).

The book of Micah is divided into three parts: I. Judgment of Israel and Judah (ch. 1–3); II. Israel in the messianic age (ch. 4–5); III. Accusations and judgments (ch. 6–7). Scant internal evidence and a number of exilic glosses and additions make it difficult to date accurately the selections chosen by the editor as representative of the prophet's preaching.

Significant passages in Micah

Part One / Micah 1–3 / Judgment of Israel and Judah

1:2-7 By means of a literary theophany (cf. Pss. 50; 75; Canticle of Habakkuk), Micah dramatically portrays God announcing the destruction of Samaria (v. 6) as a judgment for her infidelity to the covenant (v. 7), expressed after the manner of Hosea (1–3) as prostitution.

1:8-16 By means of a lament (for which vv. 8-9 provide the introduction, vv. 10-15 the actual lament, and v. 16 the conclusion), Micah both warns and threatens Jerusalem. Since most of the cities mentioned in vv. 10-15 lie to the southwest of Jerusalem in the area devastated by Sennacherib during his campaign in 701, it would appear that the lament can be dated with some probability to Sennacherib's siege of Jerusalem in 701 (cf. Is. 36–37). Isaiah has a similar warning in 10:28-32.

2:1-11 The oppression of the poor by the rich, scathingly denounced by Amos in the north (Amos 2:6-8; 5:11-12; 8:4-6), is here singled out by Micah as one of the crimes for which Judah in her turn will be punished. Vv. 12-13 are generally held by the critics to be an exile addition.

3:1-12 In a threefold denunciation (rulers vv. 1-4, false prophets vv. 5-7, and rulers again vv. 9-10), Micah points the finger to those on account of whom "Zion shall be plowed as a field, and Jerusalem reduced to rubble" (v. 12). According to Jeremiah (26:17ff), these words of Micah were uttered during the reign of King Hezekiah and were instrumental in bringing about a reform (cf. 2 Kings 18:3-6; 2 Chr. 29:8-11).

Part Two / Micah 4–5 / Future Glory of Jerusalem

4:1ff The thought of "Zion plowed as a field, and Jerusalem reduced to rubble" (3:12) might lead his audience to despair. Micah, therefore, raises the hopes and the spirits of his hearers by looking beyond the present. To the era of infidelity and punishment (ch. 3) there will succeed "in days to come" an era of peace when all nations shall come to be taught by God in Jerusalem (vv. 1-5). "On that day" God will bring back to Zion a remnant of His people preserved from the general destruction (cf. Is. 1:25-26; 6:13; 10:20; 11:11; 29:17-24) and there rule over them (vv. 6-10). The enemies of Israel, on the other hand, will be punished (vv. 11-13).

Some authors attribute 4:1-5 (cf. Is. 2:1-5) to the exilic author of Is. 60 because of the similarity of tone and teaching. Similarly critics attribute v. 10 to an exilic author because of the reference to Babylon.

4:14ff The "now" (v. 14), the time of siege for Jerusalem and ignominy for her king, is probably the time of the siege of Sennacherib in 701 (cf. 2 Kings 18—19; Is. 36—37), a time of great distress for Judah and her king, Hezekiah. To Bat-gader (a title for Jerusalem) there is contrasted the little town of Bethlehem, the ancestral home of the Davidic dynasty, from which one day will come forth "one who is to be ruler in Israel." The reference to the ruler in this context would appear to go beyond dynastic messianism. The reference to his "origin from of old, from ancient times" refers in all probability to the antiquity of the Davidic dynasty dating back to the very infancy of the kingdom in the late eleventh century B.C. The allusion in 5:2 to the prophecy of Isaiah concerning the mother of the Messiah (Is. 7:14), if it is not a later gloss reflecting the messianic interpretation of Is. 7:14 at the time of the glossator, would indicate that, during the lifetime of Isaiah himself, the prophecy was interpreted as referring to a future and not a contemporary Davidic king (see p. 363f).

Part Three / Micah 6–7 / Accusation and Condemnation

6:1-8 In a dramatic trial scene, Micah portrays God arraigning and convicting His people of base ingratitude. The poignant "*My people, what have I done to you?*" (of the Good Friday liturgy) takes its inspiration from vv. 3-5. In vv. 6-8 Micah gives his classic definition of true religion in contradistinction to mere formal religion: "To do the right (basic theme of Amos) and to love goodness (basic theme of Hosea) and to walk humbly with your God" (basic theme of Isaiah).

6:9ff Accusations similar to those in 2:1-11 and 3:1-12 decrying the oppression of the poor (vv. 9-16) are concluded by the prophet's lament for the almost universal sin of his people (7:1-4) and his final announcement of the approaching "day" of punishment. It seems quite probable that the book ends with 7:7. Two psalms have been appended to the book, both it would seem from the context of exilic times: 7:8-10, a psalm of confidence with close ties to the poetry of Deutero-Isaiah; 7:11-20, another psalm of confidence in the midst of distress.

9

Judean Prophets during the Last Hundred Years of the Kingdom

In the last years of the northern kingdom, two prophets, Amos and Hosea, raised their voices in a vain attempt to halt the onrush to national disaster. In the last years of the southern kingdom, two more voices, Zephaniah and Jeremiah, will be raised in an equally vain attempt. Despite their efforts, Judah will follow her northern sister into exile.

The exile, however, will not be in Assyria but in Babylon. Assyria will fall before the onslaughts of the Medes and the Babylonians, and when Nineveh capitulates in 612, the prophet Nahum will sing a song of triumph to express the joy of the oppressed satellite nations at the intervention of the just God in bringing about the downfall of a hated tyrant.

When Babylon under Nebuchadnezzar comes to fill the place held by Assyria, and like Assyria oppresses the subject nations, the prophet Habakkuk will search his soul and speak in wondering accents of the apparent injustice of God in allowing Babylon, in 605, to take over the reins of empire and punish unfaithful Judah.

When Judah falls in 587 before the armies of Nebuchadnezzar, a mourner will come back to the site of the ruined city of God and pour out his heart in the Lamentations. At the same time, the prophet Obadiah will excoriate

Judah's sister nation, Edom, for her treacherous cooperation with Babylon in effecting Judah's humiliation.

To gather into proper focus all the events surrounding the tragic fall of the southern kingdom in 587, and to unify all the voices in one chorus, we must follow as far as possible a chronological order of the events and the men involved in the tragedy. We shall begin, therefore, with the chronology of events, take briefly the historical background of each prophet, and then against this background read the dialogue between God and His people as given in the inspired words of His prophets.

Chronology of the last hundred years of Judah

687-640 Reigns of Manasseh and Amon, Judah's worst kings.

640-621 Preaching of the prophet Zephaniah.

640-609 Josiah introduces a religious reform in 627 and renews the covenant.

626-580 Call of Jeremiah in 626; he preaches till about 580.

621-609 Josiah's reform is spurred on by the finding of a book of the Law in the Temple.

615-612 Preaching of Nahum, fall of Nineveh to the Babylonians in 612.

609-597 After a three month reign, Jehoahaz is deposed by Pharaoh Necho, who then enthrones as king, Jehoiakim, the mortal enemy of Jeremiah.

605-562 Nebuchadnezzar becomes king of Babylon following upon his victory over Pharaoh Necho at Carchemish in 605. Preaching of Habakkuk about the year 600.

597-587 Jehoiachin (three month reign), Zedekiah (597-587).

597 First invasion by Nebuchadnezzar and first deportation.

587 Second invasion, destruction of city and Temple, second deportation.

587-539 Begun in 587, the Babylonian captivity ends in 539, when Cyrus the Great, king of Persia, conquers Babylon and allows the Jews to return to Jerusalem.

1. Zephaniah

In the years that elapse between Isaiah and Zephaniah and between Hezekiah and Josiah, two infamous kings reign in Judah. Manasseh, the worst of all Judah's kings, succeeds Hezekiah and almost immediately introduces into the Temple the abominations of the Canaanites: infant sacrifice, idol worship, sacred prostitution, sorcery, and divination (2 Chr. 33; 2 Kings 21). Better than any other explanation of the absence of prophets during his long reign is the statement in 2 Kings 21:16: "Manasseh shed very much innocent blood until he had filled Jerusalem from one end to the other."

Manasseh is succeeded in 642 by his son Amon, who continues the idolatrous policies of his father, but mercifully reigns only two years and is succeeded by the saintly Josiah (2 Chr. 33:21-25; 2 Kings 21:19-26).

When the bloody and depraved reigns of Manasseh and Amon end in 640, the remnant of Judah still faithful to God emerges from hiding and sets about the work of once more bringing Judah back to God. Leading the way, while Josiah is too young to act for himself and Jeremiah awaits his call, is the trumpet-voiced prophet, Zephaniah.

About Zephaniah personally we know only that he preached during the reign of Josiah (and almost certainly during the early years of that king) and that he could perhaps trace his ancestry back to King Hezekiah (1:1). He is a prophet of justice in the line of Amos and prepares the way for Jeremiah, as John the Baptist later prepares the way for Christ.

His message is a harsh and resounding proclamation of the coming "Day of Yahweh" for Judah and for the surrounding pagan nations. Under the circumstances, with the religious life of Judah gangrened almost to the death, no other message would be adequate. That his preaching had some effect is perhaps indicated by the reformation of religion and morals under Josiah. That it proved ineffective in the long run is attested by its repetition and its ultimate and almost literal fulfillment in the last years of Jeremiah, when the "Day of Yahweh" for Judah arrived in all its fury with the coming of the Babylonian armies.

The book is divided according to chapters. Ch. 1: an apocalyptic description of the approaching "Day of Yahweh" for Judah; ch. 2: the "Day of Yahweh" for the surrounding nations; ch. 3: a further indictment of Judah and Jerusalem (vv. 1-8), followed by a hymn of joy sung by the returned remnant and a description of the future world-wide fame of Judah (9-20).

2. Jeremiah in the Reign of Josiah

Of priestly descent, Jeremiah was born at Anathoth, a little village three miles north of Jerusalem, around 650, during the reign of Manasseh. After his call in 626, the thirteenth year of Josiah's reign (1:2; 25:3), Jeremiah prophecies until about 580, for the most part in Jerusalem, for a few years at the end in Egypt. He remains a bachelor at God's command (16:2) and suffers immensely from the bitter opposition of his fellow townsmen, his family, and compatriots from the time of Josiah's death in 609 down to the time of his own death in Egypt, where, according to Hebrew legend, he was stoned to death.

Jeremiah the man is a case of the mystic in the marketplace. Quiet, meek, peace-loving, he is sent by God, against his inclinations, to rebuke royalty, thunder warnings in the ears of the populace, and draw upon himself in consequence the scorn, contempt, and homicidal hatred of everyone, even his own relatives.

To begin with, he does not even want to be a prophet (1:4-8). Once a prophet, no one will listen to him, neither people nor kings (5:10-13; 6:10; 7:21-27), and his own relatives and fellow-townsmen try to assassinate him (11:18-19; 12:5-6; 18:18). Contradicted on every side, he begins to wonder if even God has deserted him (15:10-18). He is beaten and imprisoned (20:1-2; 32:1-3; 37:11-16; 38:1-12). The people, enraged by his preaching, want to put him to death (26:7-9). Disheartened, he accuses God of having seduced him into accepting the prophetic office (20:7-10). Almost in despair, he curses the day in which he was born (20:15-18).

Jeremiah speaks his heart freely. But despite his agonized complaints he knows that God is with him (1:10, 18; 16:19; 20:11-13) and that better days are coming for God's chosen ones (30–33). Despite the opposition to his preaching, despite his sufferings from the time of Jehoiakim (609-597) through the heign of Zedekiah (597-587) and even after the fall of Jerusalem when he is carried off unwillingly to Egypt by his fellow-countrymen, he never ceases to beg his people to repent and return to God. Only the stones from the hands of his murderers close that mouth that never gives up crying out to an unhearing people: "Hearken ye unto the voice of the Lord."

Like Job and St. Paul, Jeremiah is a man of great soul, with a gift for speaking what is in his heart (cf. the "Confessions" of Jeremiah: 11:18–12:6; 15:10-21; 17:12-18; 18:18-23; 20:7-18). The insight into his heart that he gives us in the face of the perversity of his people helps us understand how Jesus felt in the face of the perversity of that same people six hundred years later.

Still considered a great prophet by the Jews centuries later, our Lord was asked if He was Jeremiah come back from the dead (Matthew 16:14). The Fathers regarded Jeremiah as the type *par excellence* of the suffering Savior. From the human viewpoint, Jeremiah, like our Lord, seems to have been a total failure. Like our Lord he is put to death by those to whom he came to preach. In the end, the tragedy of Jeremiah, Jerusalem, the

Temple, and the Babylonians parallels with amazing exactness the tragedy of Jesus, Jerusalem, the Temple, and the Romans. In each case the heart of the tragedy lies in the inevitable catastrophe that falls upon a people who will not accept the salvation so lovingly and continuously placed before them.

Dominant ideas of Jeremiah

Though resembling the prophets before him in preaching on the love of God, on the desire of God for justice and holiness, on the divine preparation of a remnant and the advent of the Messiah, Jeremiah differs in his emphasis on the practice of religion in spirit and truth (3:16; 7:1-15; 29:10-14; 31:19ff) and on the making of a future new covenant between God and Israel to replace the broken Sinai covenant (30:18-24; 31:31ff; 32:40). Moreover, better than anyone else in the Bible, he spells out in the parable of the potter (ch. 18) the conditional nature of God's threats and the freedom of man's will.

It is perhaps too much to say with Renan that "without this extraordinary man, the religious history of humanity would have taken another course." It is not too much to say, however, that without Jeremiah the mystical side of man's nature and the unfathomable capacity of the human heart for unselfish suffering might have lain hidden until the coming of Christ. The theology he lived more than the theology he preached influenced the ages that followed him and produced in them psalmists and wisdom writers who, under the guidance of the Holy Spirit, sounded the depths of Jeremiah's heart. His life more than his teaching was a ferment and a fire that permeated the bones of Israel after the exile and prepared the way for Him who came to cast a similar fire on earth and see it kindled in the lives of innumerable saints.

Division and explanation of chronological disorder

Chronological confusion in the book of Jeremiah becomes evident even to the casual reader when he finds the siege of Jerusalem (588-587) mentioned during the reign of Zedekiah in the 21st chapter and then reads further and in the 25th chapter finds himself back in the reign of Zedekiah's predecessor, King Jehoiakim, in the year 605.

The best explanation of this confusion is that there were several collections of Jeremiah's sermons plus biographical sketches of his life. These were placed end to end for the most part instead of being edited into one chronologically ordered whole. The division of the book will give some idea of the different individual collections which were arranged by a post-exilic editor to give us the book as we now have it.

1—25 Many sermons against Judah, little narrative. Probably composed in 604 and dictated to Baruch as described in 36:1-4. 25:3-14 is the original conclusion of this collection. Ch. 1—6 from the time of Josiah; ch. 7—20 from the time of Jehoiakim. Ch. 21—24 contain separate collections from a later time.

26—35 Probably by Baruch, mainly narrative. The summary and brief repetition in ch. 26 of the Temple address, given more fully in ch. 7, brings out the difference between part I (1—25) which is a collection of sermons and part II (26—35) which is basically narrative but with excerpts from sermons.

36—45 Biographical narrative in third person almost entirely taken up with Jeremiah. Probably written by Baruch after the fall of Jerusalem in order to tell the story of Jeremiah's sufferings against the background of besieged and dying Jerusalem.

46—51 A collection of Jeremiah's oracles against the nations after the manner of Amos 1; Zeph. 2; Is. 13-23.

52 Taken from 2 Kings to show the fulfillment of Jeremiah's prophecies, after the manner of Is. 36—39. The work of the postexilic editor.

While this division should be kept in mind by one who reads the book as a whole, we shall try to be more precise and, as far as possible, relive the last days of Jerusalem with Jeremiah by regrouping events, sermons, and prophecies according to the chronological order in which they took place.

Significant events and sermons from the reign of Josiah

The best of all of David's successors, Josiah becomes king at the tender age of eight, following the assassination of his father, Amon, in 640. During the thirty-one years he reigns (640-609), he attempts to make Judah, in fact as well as in theory, a true theocracy. In 627, the twenty-year old king institutes a religious reform, purging Judah and Jerusalem of the idols and idolatrous practices that had taken root in the reigns of Manasseh and Amon. In 621, the reform is aided by the finding in the Temple of an old book of the law (probably Deuteronomy or a part of that book). The covenant is solemnly renewed, and the Passover is celebrated with memorable pomp and ceremony (2 Kings 22—23; 2 Chr. 34—35).

The reform, however, is only skin deep on the part of the people. After Josiah's death in battle with Pharaoh Necho at Megiddo in 609 (2 Kings 23:29), the people revert under Jehoiakim to the abominations and apostasy of the time of Manasseh, and the kingdom begins to roll with relentless and quickening speed toward disaster.

Toward the end of Josiah's reign, in 612, Nineveh falls to the Babylonians, and the prophet Nahum chants the joy of Assyria's long-suffering victims at the sight of the oppressor's downfall. Jeremiah's call and some of his preaching date from the halcyon years of this fairest and most promising of all David's successors.

1:4-10   Called in 626, Jeremiah, like Moses before him, is unwilling and afraid because of the burdens of the prophetic office and accepts only under compulsion.

1:11-19   Visions connected with Jeremiah's vocation. Vv. 11-12, the vision of the "watching-tree" represents God watching over His word to bring it to realization; vv. 13-19, the vision of the boiling cauldron from the north represents the Babylonian armies which will one day come down from the north to besiege and destroy Jerusalem.

2:1—4:4   Excerpts from sermons explaining the reasons for the coming of the boiling cauldron of trouble from the north: the idolatry and perversity of Judah and Jerusalem (probably before 621).

4:5—6:30   Excerpts from sermons describing the destructive and punitive power of the boiling cauldron from the north, i.e., the invading armies of Babylon (probably before 621).

11:1-17   A brief summary of Jeremiah's preaching on the covenant. Around 621, sometime after the beginning of the reformation of religion and morals undertaken by Josiah, an ancient book of the law (probably Deuteronomy) is found in the Temple occasioning a solemn renewal of the Sinai covenant throughout Judah (cf. 2 Kings 22:3, 8; 2 Chr. 34:8ff; Deut. 27—29).

11:18—   First attempts on Jeremiah's life by his fellow townsmen of Ana-
12:6   thoth and even by members of his own family, either because his preaching is a scandal to them, or because his insistence on centralization of worship in Jerusalem according to Deut. 12:5 (2 Kings 23:5-15) is depriving the men of Anathoth of their prerogatives as priests.

3. Nahum

During the last years of Josiah's reign, the power of Assyria begins to wane. After the death of the great Ashurbanipal in 625, a coalition of Medes and Babylonians succeeds in destroying the empire. Besieged by Babylonian and Median armies, Nineveh falls in 612. In 609 the last Assyrian armies are crushed at Haran in Syria by Nabopolassar, the father of Nebuchadnezzar.

Nahum of Elkosh, writing shortly before 612, sees in these events God's moral government of the world and His punishment of Assyria for misusing the great power given to her.[1]

In ch. 1, using the Sinai stage-props, Nahum describes God coming to judge the wicked (vv. 2-6). In 1:7-8, the basis of this judgment is given: "Yahweh is good . . . he takes care of those who have recourse to him . . . he makes an end of his opponents, and his enemies he pursues with darkness." The rest of the book develops this thought in the prediction and description of Nineveh's imminent destruction.

Nahum's whole book is an oracle against one nation — Assyria. His voice is raised under inspiration to describe the fate of those who misuse their God-given power, abuse nations, destroy peoples, and heap up injustice like a tower of Babel against the God of history.

Those who read the words of St. Paul about Sacred Scripture, "Whatsoever things were written, were written for our instruction, that through the patience and consolation afforded by the Scriptures, we may have hope," may wonder what instruction we receive from Nahum. What hope does he give us, what consolation? In the mechanistic world of today, it would be enough if Nahum only reminded us, as he does, that God and not man is the maker of history. But he does more. He reminds us as well that nations are judged, and rewarded or punished according to that judgment. He tells us abuse of power, perhaps unpunishable by man, will be punished by God. He gives hope to those in totalitarian countries, teaching them to trust in God as the avenger of evil and as the source of security and peace for those who love Him.

4. Jeremiah in the Reign of Jehoiakim

After the fall of Nineveh, Josiah lives only three years, dying in battle at Megiddo in 609 in a futile attempt to prevent Pharaoh Necho from helping the beleaguered Assyrian armies making a last stand against the Babylo-

---

[1] Cf. CCHS par. 568ff; G. Montague, *Nahum*, OTRG No. 19; Bright 288–294.

nians at Haran in Syria. He leaves behind him three sons: Jehoahaz, Jehoiakim, and Zedekiah. Jehoahaz succeeds him for three months. In the late summer of 609 Pharaoh Necho returns from the battle at Haran, deposes Jehoahaz, and establishes Jehoiakim as king of Judah (2 Kings 23: 29-37; 2 Chr. 36:1-4).

Jehoiakim reigns for eleven years (609-597). Unfortunately for Judah, he is a cynical, godless butcher in the tradition of Manasseh and Amon, murdering prophets, oppressing the faithful, and re-establishing the Baalistic cults abolished by Josiah (2 Kings 24:1-6; 2 Chr. 36:5-8; Jer. 26:20; 36:15-26).

When Nebuchadnezzar takes over Judah after defeating the Egyptians at Carchemish in 605, Jehoiakim is forced to submit to a new master. But Egyptian ties are strong, and Jehoiakim rebels against his Babylonian overlord in 598. Just before Nebuchadnezzar's siege of Jerusalem opens, Jehoiakim dies (Jer. 22:18-19; 2 Chr. 36:6). It is during his eleven year reign that Jeremiah dictates to Baruch the first and second editions of his sermons (Jer. 36), and that the book of Habakkuk is written.

Significant passages

7:1-15   In the early years of Jehoiakim's reign, Jeremiah appears at the Temple and excoriates the Jerusalemites for their formalism in morals and their superstitious belief in the protective power of the Temple (cf. Is. 36–37; Pss. 46–48). The consequences of this sermon for Jeremiah are told in ch. 26, the first part of Baruch's biography of Jeremiah. After a brief summary of the Temple address (26:1-6), Baruch tells how Jeremiah is prosecuted for blasphemy against the Temple (26:7-11), how he defends himself (26:12-15) and is acquitted (26:16-24). The execution of the prophet Uriah is mentioned to indicate what might have happened to Jeremiah if his friends had not interceded for him.

13:1-11   The parable of the "linen loincloth" (representing Judah) buried in exile by the Euphrates represents what happens to Judah when she separates from God and is perhaps Jeremiah's first clear intimation of the Babylonian exile. The parable probably dates to 605, the year Nebuchadnezzar's armies crushed the Egyptians at Carchemish (Jer. 46). It is difficult to say whether this is a literary parable or a parable in action.

18:1-12   In the parable of the "potter" (cf. Sir. 38:29-31; Rom. 9:20-23), God, the potter, is represented in complete and absolute control of men and nations (the clay). Israel, therefore, is entirely in God's power; but men are free. Their fate is in their own hands (vv. 7-10). Consequently, Israel can still change and thus avert her impending destruction (vv. 11-12), though, as God tells Jeremiah, and as Christ later on tells His apostles (Matthew 23:37ff), she will not. The point of the parable is that God's dealings with men depend on men. His threats are conditional. If there is repentance, the threats will be withdrawn (cf. Is. 1:19-20; also Jonah).

19:1-13   The parable of the smashed "potter's flask" dramatizes symbolically the approaching destruction of Jerusalem. Entering a Baal shrine in the valley of Ben-hinnom, southwest of the city, Jeremiah excoriates the Jews who are assembled there to take part in the Canaanite rites of sacred prostitution and child sacrifice (Num. 25; Jer. 7:30—8:3), shattering before their eyes the flask which he tells them symbolizes Jerusalem. It is probable that 19:14—20:6, describing Jeremiah's first imprisonment, gives the consequences for Jeremiah of this courageous sermon. His discouragement and despair upon being imprisoned for preaching the word of God is plaintively described in the following verses (20:7-18).

25:1-14   Jeremiah's dramatic prophecy of the Babylonian invasion and the seventy years of exile in store for Judah is probably occasioned by Nebuchadnezzar's victory over the Egyptians at Carchemish (Jer. 46) in the year 605. This date is confirmed by ch. 36, in which Baruch tells how Jeremiah dictated a summary of his sermons to him, the last of which would appear to be the sermon given here (cf. 36:28-32).

25:15-26   The sermon on the wine-cup of God's wrath to be drunk by Jerusalem and the surrounding nations is probably the introduction to Jeremiah's oracles against the nations, given in full in ch. 46—51. The Septuagint translation was made from a Hebrew manuscript in which Jeremiah's oracles against the nations followed immediately upon 25:15-26. Thus it is probable that the original position of the oracles was here rather than at the end of the book.

36:1-32   Jeremiah, in hiding for fear of Jehoiakim (36:6, 19, 26), dictates to Baruch the first edition of his collected sermons. When the manuscript is read before Jehoiakim, he has it burned in the brazier (36:20-27). In the following year (604), Jeremiah dictates a second, fuller edition (36:28-32). The purpose of his writing apostolate is stated in 36:3: "Perhaps when the house of Israel hears of all the evil that I am planning to bring upon them, they will turn each from his evil way, and will receive my pardon for their guilt and their sin."

35:1-19   Jeremiah and the Rechabites. The time is approximately 598, just before the death of Jehoiakim and the fall of Jerusalem to the Babylonians in 597. The Rechabites, a reactionary sect founded by Jonathan ben Rechab in the ninth century and dedicated to the semi-nomadic way of life of Israel's earliest days (2 Kings 10:15-24), had come to Jerusalem to escape the approaching Babylonian armies. Jeremiah uses them as an object lesson, contrasting their obedience to the laws laid down for them by their human founder Jonadab with the disobedience of the Judeans to the covenant enjoined upon them by their divine founder and creator.

21:11ff   Jeremiah's opinion of Jehoiakim is found in the collection of his prophecies against the kings of Judah gathered together and placed near the end of part I (ch. 1–25). 21:11–22:9 may be directed against the kings in general, but it is more likely that Jeremiah had either Jehoiakim or Zedekiah in mind. 22:10-12 is an oracle concerning Jehoahaz. 22:13-19 is against Jehoiakim (also called Eliakim). 22:20-30 is Jeremiah's bitter oracle against Jehoiachin (also known as Jeconiah, Conia, and Joachin). Having expressed his disgust with Judah's kings of the present, Jeremiah looks to the future to the coming of a Davidic king who "shall reign as king with success, doing justice and righteousness in the land" (23:1-8; cf. pp. 364ff on the messianic interpretation of this oracle). 23:9-40 is a collection of oracles against the false prophets.

The last days of Jehoiakim's reign are described in 2 Kings 24:1-7 and 2 Chr. 36:1-8. Nebuchadnezzar's armies besiege Jerusalem in 598 shortly before which Jehoiakim dies. When the siege ends in March of 597 Nebuchadnezzar deposes the young King Jehoiachin, carries him off as a hostage to Babylon and replaces him with his uncle Zedekiah, the last and weakest of Josiah's sons. Before reading Jeremiah's sermons and history during the reign of Zedekiah, the minor prophet, Habakkuk should be read.

5. Habakkuk

When Nebuchadnezzar rose to power after his victory at Carchemish in 605 (Jer. 46), Jeremiah immediately realized who would constitute the "cauldron from the north" (1:13-15) and the "wind from the desert heights" (4:11). At the same time another prophet, Habakkuk,[1] more philosophical about the impending punishment of Judah, wondered just how God's justice could be served by a nation as wicked as Babylon.

Reference to the coming of the Babylonians (Hab. 1:6), without any allusion to the capture of Jerusalem in 597, places the composition of the book of Habakkuk sometime between 605 and 597, Since Judah became subject to Babylon definitively around 601, and the invasion of the Babylonian armies began when Judah revolted three years later (2 Kings 24: 1-2), the most probable historical background of Hakakkuk lies somewhere around 599-598, when the Babylonian invasions had begun, and it was more than evident that Judah would be punished by the foreigners from the Euphrates.

Contemplating such a paradoxical situation, Habakkuk begs God to explain the apparent injustice of Judah the sinful being punished by the still more sinful Babylon. Ch. 1 poses the question dramatically by means of a dialogue between God and the prophet: in vv. 2-4, Habakkuk asks how long will sinfulness go unpunished. In vv. 5-11, God answers that the Babylonians will come and punish Judah. In vv. 12-17, Habakkuk poses the question that troubles him: where is the justice in a sinful nation being punished by a still more sinful nation, itself deserving of punishment?

In ch. 2:2-4, we have the key to the book in God's answer to Habakkuk. God tells Habakkuk in a vision, upon which the rest of ch. 2 and 3 are based, that "the rash man has no integrity, but the just man, because of his faith, shall live." This is sufficient for Habakkuk who then goes on in vv. 5-20 to predict the eventual downfall of Babylon and in ch. 3 to describe in magnificent poetry the coming of God the Warrior (Is. 59; 63; Ps. 76) along the old Exodus route from Sinai to Palestine to Babylon to destroy the enemy Babylon and save His people and their anointed one.

In the development of the doctrine of the future life. Habakkuk holds an important place. He poses the question of the problem of evil, already alluded to in Jer. 12, later to be discussed at length and with literary grandeur in the book of Job, and finally adequately answered only in the book of Wisdom and in the New Testament.

---

[1] Cf. Vawter, *The Conscience of Israel*, 225–231; CCHS par. 570.

6. Jeremiah in the Reign of Zedekiah

The invasion that occasioned the book of Habakkuk ended in the year 597, when Jerusalem fell to the Babylonians. Jehoiachin, who had succeeded his father Jehoiakim at the beginning of the siege, was carried off to Babylon after only three months as king. In Babylon he remained a captive until 562 when, upon the accession of a new king, Evil-Merodach, he was restored to royal honors, but not permitted to return to Judah (2 Chr. 36:1-10; 2 Kings 24:10-17; 25:27).

Back in Judah, Jehoiachin's uncle, Zedekiah, the last of Josiah's three sons, is placed on the throne as puppet king by Nebuchadnezzar. Unfortunately for Judah, Zedekiah is weak and vacillating. Despite the warnings of Jeremiah, he sides with the Egyptophile faction at court and joins a coalition of nations in revolt against Babylon. This time the Babylonian juggernaut rolls on Judah for the last time. After disposing of an Egyptian army sent to help Judah, and after an eighteen month siege, Nebuchadnezzar's generals breach the walls of Jerusalem in July of 587. Zedekiah is captured. His sons are executed before his eyes. He himself is blinded and carried captive to Babylon. In the following months the city is utterly destroyed. Houses and Temple are burnt to the ground. The walls are overthrown and the cream of the population is carried off in death marches to Babylon. It should be and is, to all appearances at least, the end of the kingdom of Judah (2 Chr. 36:11ff; 2 Kings 24:18—25:21; Jer. 52).

Significant passages

24:1-10   In the parable of the two baskets of figs (the good figs representing Jehoiachin and the exiles in Babylon, the bad figs Zedekiah and the remaining Jews in Judah), Jeremiah dramatically foretells the future of his people. The bad figs will be wiped out (24:8-10). The good figs will remain to become the remnant out of which a new Israel will be born.

27:1-15   Ch. 27—29 form a unit detailing Jeremiah's patriotic efforts diplomatically, orally, and by letter, to avert the suicidal policy of resistance to Babylon which is contrary to God's explicit directives, since the Babylonian domination is a divine punishment which Judah must accept with patience and humility. Jeremiah, wearing a yoke symbolic of the Babylonian domination, appears before the ambassadors of the satellite kings gathered in council at Jerusalem to discuss with Zedekiah their revolt against Nebuchadnezzar. Jeremiah appeals to the ambassadors (27:3ff), to Zedekiah (27:12ff), and to the priests and people (27:16ff) to submit to Nebuchadnezzar. According to Jer. 28:1 these events take place in 593, only four years after the fall of Jerusalem. It is in this same year that a new Pharaoh rules in Egypt, Psammetichus II, son of Necho (593–588).

28:1-17 Following upon his plea to the ambassadors, Jeremiah engages in public debate with the false prophet, Hananiah, who takes the yoke from Jeremiah's shoulders and breaks it, declaring: "Thus will the Lord break the yoke of Nebuchadnezzar." (On the false prophets, cf. Jer. 23:9-40.)

29:1-32 Taking advantage of an official legation to the Babylonian court around 592, either to pay tribute or perhaps to allay Nebuchadnezzar's suspicions after the meeting of the ambassadors at Jerusalem, Jeremiah sends a letter to the exiles of 597 encouraging them to be good subjects of Nebuchadnezzar (vv. 4-9) and to await the end of seventy years of exile after which God will restore them (vv. 10-14). At the same time, Jeremiah predicts the destruction of those remaining in Jerusalem (vv. 16-20), referring to them as the "bad figs" (Jer. 24). An exchange of letters and threats between Jeremiah and some false prophets in Babylon is recorded at the end of the chapter.

Jeremiah during the last days of the kingdom of Judah

Four years after the meeting of the ambassadors in Jerusalem (ch. 27), in the year 588, Judah in league with Egypt and other smaller nations revolts against Babylon. The story of the ill-starred revolt is told briefly and laconically in 2 Kings 25; 2 Chr. 36:13-21; Jer. 52. Fortunately, however, for posterity Baruch keeps a record of Jeremiah's activity during the days of the siege, and it is through the eyes of Baruch and Jeremiah that we witness the final days of Jerusalem.

21:1-10 In January 588, Nebuchadnezzar invades Judah and opens the siege of Jerusalem. Consulted by Zedekiah, who secretly believes in him, Jeremiah predicts certain disaster for king, city, and citizens (vv. 1-7). He urges the people to desert to the Babylonians if they wish to save their lives. Jerusalem, he says is irrevocably doomed (vv. 8-10).

34:1-7 In the course of the siege, Jeremiah warns Zedekiah a second time that Jerusalem will certainly fall (vv. 1-4). In the following verses (vv. 6-7), mention is made of two fortress cities still holding out, Lachish and Azekah, indicating that the noose around Jerusalem is drawing tight (cf. LFAP 192ff on the "Lachish Letters," military dispatches found in the ruins of Lachish).

34:8-22 Jeremiah's sermon on the broken pledge to the slaves informs us that the promised Egyptian army has arrived and temporarily raised the siege of Jerusalem (vv. 21-22).

37:1-10 Encouraged by the intervention of the Egyptian army, Zedekiah consults Jeremiah again, hoping for good news (vv. 1-6). For the third time Jeremiah repeats that Jerusalem is doomed, blasting unequivocally any hopes Egyptian intervention might have raised (vv. 7-10).

37:11-21 During the break in the siege, Jeremiah, attempting to go home to Anathoth to settle some property matters, is arrested by his enemies as a deserter and thrown into prison (vv. 11-16). Called secretly to the palace for fear of the Egyptophile nobles, Jeremiah is again consulted by Zedekiah and reiterates for the fourth time the inevitable doom not only of the city but of Zedekiah himself (v. 17). Pleading with the king not to send him back to prison in the house of Jonathan the secretary, Jeremiah is consigned to prison in the guard-court (vv. 18-21). The following episode seems to be linked with this one.

32:1-15 In the guard-court and unable to go to Anathoth, Jeremiah is visited in prison by his counsin Hanamel who has come to settle the real estate affair earlier attempted by Jeremiah (37:11-16). With the Egyptians defeated and the siege reopened (32: 24-25), the property is obviously valueless. Nevertheless, Jeremiah seizes the opportunity to profess his faith in the restoration of Israel by buying the worthless property and sealing the transaction with great solemnity (vv. 6-15). The significance of this action is explained at length in the rest of the chapter, showing Jeremiah's mission is not only "to wreck and to ruin" but "to build and to plant" (1:10). In a long prayer (vv. 16-44) Jeremiah details the history of Israel's ingratitude (vv. 16-25), the reasons for the present invasion and destruction (vv. 26-36), the promise of eventual restoration (vv. 37-39), and finally the promise of the new covenant to be written in men's hearts (vv. 40-44). The new covenant is treated also in 31:27-34.

33:1-26 Further solemn promises of restoration made by Jeremiah while in prison in the guard-court, with special emphasis on the restoration of the Davidic dynasty (vv. 14-26; cf. 23:5-8).

38:1ff In the last days of the siege, Jeremiah's enemies throw him into a cistern to die (1-6), but he is saved by Ebed-melech, a palace eunuch (7-13). In desperation, Zedekiah sends again for Jeremiah, hoping against hope for deliverance. For the last time and unsuccessfully, Jeremiah warns the weak and vacillating king that the city is doomed, and that he can save himself only by surrendering to the Babylonians (14-28).

39:1-10 In the last days of July 587, the final act in the tragedy of Jerusalem is played to the finish. Baruch summarizes briefly the events: the breaching of the walls, the capture and blinding of Zedekiah and the nobles, the burning of the city, the demolishing of the walls, the deportation of the citizens. (Cf. Jer. 52 for a fuller description taken from 2 Kings 24:18—25:30 and appended by the final editor after the exile to show that Jeremiah's prophecies had been fulfilled to the letter.)

The last days of Jeremiah

40:1-6 In the confusion attendant upon the fall of Jerusalem, Jeremiah is led off in chains to a concentration camp at Ramah to await, along with the other captives, deportation to Babylon. Discovered there by Nebuzaradan, he is released according to the personal order of Nebuchadnezzar (cf. 39:11-12) and goes to Mizpah to join the Jews who have been allowed to remain in Judah under the governorship of Gedaliah. Baruch does not mention any of Jeremiah's sermons from this time, but the reference in 31:15 to Ramah (cf. 40:1) suggests that some of his sermons of consolation may date from his days in the concentration camp at Ramah. Ch. 30—33 is a collection of Jeremiah's sermons of consolation. Of these ch. 32—33 are clearly dated to 588-587, the time of the siege. Ch. 30-31 contain earlier oracles, perhaps uttered in relation to the remnants of the northern kingdom in the time of Josiah. Later, however, they were revised and directed to all Israel but especially to Judah. After the sermon on the healing of the wound (ch. 30), Jeremiah proceeds in ch. 31 to speak of the new covenant. The reader should note the climactic arrangement: the promise of restoration (vv. 1-9),

B.C.	Personalities	Events	In the Neighborhood	Literature
800	Amaziah—Jehoash Uzziah—Jeroboam II —Zechariah AMOS—Shallum HOSEA—Menahem Jotham—Pekahiah ISAIAH—Pekah AHAZ—Hosea	Amos and Hosea threaten the destruction of Israel for infidelity to the covenant Syro-Ephraemitic war and the Immanuel prophecies of Isaiah Siege and fall of Samaria to Shalmaneser V in 722 Reform of Hezekiah Isaiah predicts the raising of the siege of Sennacherib in 701	Tiglath-Pileser III invades Palestine (c. 734–732) Shalmaneser V invades Palestine (725–722) Sargon II invades Palestine to put down Philistine rebellion (c. 711)	Elohist's synthesis of patriarchal and exodus traditions in north First (?) edition of Deuteronomy (Deut. 12–26) Fusion of J and E traditions in south by Judean editor Collection of Solomonic proverbs Holiness Law (Lev. 17–26)
	HEZEKIAH MICAH	Micah's Bethlehem prophecy	Sennacherib besieges Jerusalem but fails to take it (701)	
700	Manasseh Amon Zephaniah JOSIAH JEREMIAH Nahum Jehoahaz Jehoiakim Habakkuk	Period of persecution of Yahwism in Judah under Manasseh and Amon Deuteronomic reform Finding of Deuteronomy in the Temple Death of Josiah at under Josiah (626–609) Megiddo	Manasseh becomes a vassal of Assyria Esarhaddon succeeds Sennacherib Fall of Nineveh Nebuchadnezzar defeats the Egyptians at Carchemish (605)	Collection of Isaiah's and Micah's sermons and prophecies First (?) edition of the Deuteronomist's history NAHUM First edition of Jeremiah's prophecies (605–604)
600				

the canticle to be sung by the returned exiles (vv. 10-14), the new thing, "the woman who must encompass the man with devotion," (vv. 15-22; cf. Hosea 1–3; Jer. 3:1-10), and finally the new covenant (vv. 27-34; cf. 32:26-44).

40:7ff When the Babylonian armies leave, Israelites who had escaped the city before its fall return and associate themselves with Gedaliah, the governor appointed by Nebuchadnezzar (vv. 7-12). Although warned, Gedaliah refuses to believe that Jewish reactionaries are plotting to take his life (vv. 13-16). Not long after, Ishmael and a band of zealots murder the high-minded Gedaliah along with some Babylonian troops and a group of eighty pilgrims, and lead away to Ammon the refugees who had gathered around Gedaliah at Mizpah (41:1-10).

41:11ff An army leader named Johanan pursues and rescues the little group (vv. 11-18). Against Jeremiah's advice (ch. 42), Johanan leads the little band into Egypt (42:1-7). There Jeremiah preaches his last sermons (42:7–44:30). It is in Egypt according to Jewish tradition that Jeremiah dies, stoned to death by his own people.

45:1ff Baruch ends his memoirs of Jeremiah (ch. 36–44) with the prophecy of good fortune made for him by the prophet "when he wrote in a book the prophecies that Jeremiah dictated in the fourth year of Jehoiakim, son of Josiah, king of Judah."

7. The Influence of Jeremiah

There is no simple measuring of the influence of Jeremiah. In time his words, like a two-edged sword, penetrated the very marrow and spirit of Israel, stirred the heart of the nation in exile, and reverberated through sacred writ, even into the books of the New Testament.

Like Moses before him and Christ after him, Jeremiah lived at a turning point in his people's history and bridged the gap between the old and the new. In his inaugural vision he was set over "nations and over kingdoms, to root up and to tear down, to destroy and to demolish, to build and to plant." He fulfilled his mission to the letter. He saw Assyria disappear from the stage of history and the new empire of Babylon tread heavily in from the wings to take over center stage. He preached the funeral oration on the defunct kingdom of Judah and the abrogated Sinai covenant, and at the same time he declared the continuity of God's kingdom and predicted the institution of a new covenant. He declared the Davidic kings rejected, but heralded the coming of a new David.

Of Jeremiah it can be said, no man did more for his nation and was treated worse. The mystery, however, is not his passion and death; rather, the resurrection of the nation that died and was buried in Babylon in fulfillment of his prophecies.

Israel's resurrection from national death in Babylon is one of the wondrous works of God. But God works through men. And of all the men who worked for Israel's resurrection, none did more than Jeremiah. When he came on the scene in 626, there was hardly an Israelite alive who would admit that the city of Jerusalem could be taken and the Temple destroyed.

In the popular mind God was bound to Jerusalem and to the Davidic kings, and the city of His choice, Jerusalem, was inviolable because He had chosen it. The defeat of Sennacherib in the time of Isaiah had only confirmed the average Israelite in this false theology. More than anything else it explains the senseless revolts against Babylon and the childish expectation even in the last months of the siege that God would intervene and destroy Nebuchadnezzar as He had Sennacherib.

Jeremiah's thankless task was the destruction of this false theology. He reminded the people in his Temple address that God was not bound to the Temple, that He could and would destroy it as He had destroyed Shiloh in times past. He insisted repeatedly that Jerusalem would be destroyed by the Babylonians, that the nation was as a piece of clay in the hands of the Divine potter, that the kings, though they might be as the signet ring on God's finger, could nevertheless be taken off and cast away.

He tried to make the Jews understand that Babylon was God's servant, that the fall of Jerusalem would not be the work of Babylon, but the work of God using Babylon as His juggernaut. He was derided, mocked, scorned. His enemies, the false prophets, carried the day.

But when the Day of Yahweh came for Jerusalem, for the nation, and for the kings, there were those who remembered. Then the parables of the loin cloth and the potter and the broken flask were seen in a new light. Then the Temple address was seen to make sense. The false prophets were proved false, the childish optimism groundless, the popular theology a trap.

If that had been all that the people learned from Jeremiah's preaching, it would have been enough to vindicate the prophet, but at the terrible price of national despair. There was more, however, and in exile the people remembered the good as well as the bad. They remembered that Jeremiah had spoken of the "good figs" who would some day return to Judah, to whom the Lord had said: "Only after seventy years have elapsed for

Babylon will I visit you and fulfill for you my promise to bring you back to this place" (25:10). They remembered his sermons of consolation (30–31), his buying of property in the last days of the siege and his promise from God: "Houses and fields and vineyards shall again be bought in this land" (32:1-15). They remembered most of all his promise of a new covenant for Israel (31:31-34; 32:40) and his promise of a new David in days to come (33:14-26; 23:5-6).

The downfall of Jerusalem, the Temple, and the kings came as Jeremiah had predicted it would come. But when it came, some at least were prepared to understand it as it should have been understood — in the light of the covenant between God and His people according to which all the nation's future depended on her loyalty or disloyalty to the stipulations agreed to on Sinai. For these at least, the tragedy was explicable and explicable in terms of the faith by which Israel lived. Amongst these too that faith continued to live, through the dreadful days of siege and destruction and through the days and years of the exile. It was the link that joined the Israel of old to the new Israel that arose from the grave of the exile to become a nation again in 539. And it was Jeremiah who forged the link.

The fateful events of the summer of 587 had a profound influence on the development of Israel's theology. They forced Israel's thinkers to look deeper into their covenant theology and to reassess their messianic expectations. The results for Israel's covenant theology are patent in the Pentateuchal and Deuteronomic histories, which achieved substantially their present arrangement during or shortly after the exile, and which may be considered in a broad sense as historical commentaries on the covenant. The results are not so patent with regard to Israel's messianic expectations. Before closing the last hundred years of Judah, therefore, we shall attempt to explain Israel's messianic theology.

10

Messianism

1. The Meaning of Messianism

The study of messianism, like the study of covenant theology, serves the all important purpose of focusing the student's attention on the divine plan for the salvation of the world, opening to his eyes the progressive revelation and realization of this plan against an historical perspective of two thousand years. It serves as well, though on a less important plane, as a preparation for the science of apologetics.

Before entering on a study of messianism, a note of caution is necessary. The student will almost certainly have preconceived opinions concerning the meaning of the word messianism, the texts which are messianic, and perhaps even the precise interpretation of these texts. These opinions he will find have been, if not wrong, at least uncritical. The same may be said for arguments from authority which invoke too easily the teaching of the Church or the unanimous interpretation of the Fathers. In the encyclical, "Divino Afflante Spiritu," Pius XII issues a warning to the uncritical:

Let them (those who are not scripture scholars) bear in mind above all that in the rules and laws promulgated by the Church there is question of doctrine regarding faith and morals; and that in the immense matter contained in the Sacred Books — legislative, historical, sapiential and prophetical — there are but few texts whose sense has been defined by the authority of the Church, nor are those more numerous about which the teaching of the holy Fathers is unanimous.

Perhaps the greatest misconception concerning messianism is the meaning of the term itself. As the student will find, not every text that is messianic refers to the Messiah. Some refer simply to the messianic hope of Israel with no further involvement. Others refer to a messianic kingdom or a messianic dynasty, and here the thought or implication of a personal Messiah would or could be present only because of the impossibility of projecting a kingdom or a dynasty without its king. Still other passages will refer to the Messiah, but in a typical rather than a literal sense.

In considering the messianic texts, the student will often labor under the misconception of considering all of these texts the result of direct revelation. He will find on the contrary that the majority are indirectly revealed, i.e., the prophets and the inspired writers come to the belief in a messianic kingdom and a personal Messiah not as a result of direct revelation but as a result of reasoning under inspiration on the acts of God in the past in favor of Israel, arriving thereby at new conclusions for the future.

In addition to the difficulties occasioned by these common preconceptions, the student will meet difficulties with the texts themselves. Since the books of the Bible were written over the course of a thousand years and more, he will often find that a messianic revelation, whether direct or indirect, is not written down until long after the historical period in which it took birth. Moreover, later messianic revelation is sometimes projected into the past by a literary fiction, with the result that neither the date of the book nor the period indicated by the book for the messianic revelation objectively designates the actual time of the revelation.

What has been said about the difficulties of studying messianism has not been said without reason. It has been said to persuade the student of the complexity of the problem, to dissuade him from relying on the simple but deceptive proof-text method. It has been said, moreover, with the conviction that a more critical historical approach to the study of messianism will not only be more convincing but will be infinitely more rewarding both for theology and for apologetics.

Our method will embrace the following five steps: 1. a definition of messianism; 2. an outline of the progressive stages of messianic revelation; 3. the dating and interpretation of individual messianic texts in the light of their ideological and historical background; 4. the significance of later "rereading" of messianic texts; 5. the fulfillment of the messianic prophecies.

2. A Definition of Messianism

Messianism may be defined in the broadest sense of the word as Israel's expectation, based on revelation, of a great and glorious destiny. More narrowly, messianism may be defined as Israel's divinely founded and firm expectation of a reign of God over Israel in which Israel will enjoy spiritual regeneration, complete freedom, and continual happiness, and be the vehicle for the same for the rest of humanity.

Nothing is explicitly said in either of these definitions about a personal Messiah because messianism existed before and involved more than a personal Messiah. When Israel finally learned to look forward to the coming of a personal Messiah, she looked forward to him not so much as the object of her expectations but as the one through whom her expectations would be brought to fulfillment. For Israel the messianic kingdom was always the kingdom of God rather than the kingdom of the Messiah. The Messiah was to be God's agent. When God became man and Messiah, fulfillment for Israel dwarfed expectation.

3. The Progressive Stages of Messianism

One of the most important lessons we learn from a study of Israel's history from the time of the patriarchs to the time of Christ is the revelation, step by step, of God's plan for the salvation of the world and for the effective realization of His reign over the minds and hearts of men.

Israel did not learn at one fell swoop the full intent of God for her future. When she was a child, she was treated as a child. As she grew up, God saw to it that she increased not only in age but in "wisdom and grace before God and men." In the fullness of time, He came Himself in the flesh to complete her education in the things of God and to flood with light all obscurities in the lessons of the past.

With the eyes of faith, the student can look back and see in Israel the child the fullness to which she would eventually mature with the advent of Christ. For the sake of apologetics, however, and for the sake of a more reasoned study of God's plan as revealed in the history of Israel and written down in the Bible, it will be advisable to proceed by the historical method.

We shall begin, therefore, with the origin of Israel's hope in the promises made to the patriarchs and confirmed by the Exodus and the Sinai covenant, continue with the development of Israel's hope in the dynastic period initiated by the oracle of Nathan to David in 2 Sam. 7, and conclude with the predictions cast in a more personal form during the period of the latter prophets.

Over the course of two thousand years of history, the student will see that Israel's hope remains constant. What changes is not the basic hope but Israel's knowledge of the object of that hope: her deeper and purer appreciation of the kingdom of God, of what it means to be members of that kingdom, and of how it will be brought to fulfillment.

The period of soteriological messianism

Soteriological messianism (from the Greek *sōtēria*, salvation) is a technical expression used to describe that period of Israel's hope when she looked for salvation from her spiritual and human ills through the intervention of God. It has its historical beginning for the people of Israel in the promises made to Abraham and repeated to Isaac and Jacob.

In the earlier chapters of Genesis (1–11), this hope is projected into the past (Gen. 3:15). The student must remember, however, that these chapters contain an elaboration rather than a remembrance of Israel's past, and the facts attested to therein are accepted on faith, not on historical evidence.

Israel's remembered past, carried down the centuries by the living memory of her tradition, begins with the call of Abraham from Mesopotamia and with the promises made to him by God that from him would come a great people, that to this people would be given a homeland (Canaan), and that through his seed (the people Israel) there would be mediated to the world great blessings. The historical evidence for the reality of these promises is based upon the unanimous testimony of all four witnesses to Israel's earliest history (cf. the Yahwist tradition in Gen. 12:1-3, 7; 18:17-19; the Elohist tradition in Gen. 15:5-7, 13-20; the Deuteronomic tradition in Deut. 6:10; 26:5-10; the Priestly tradition in Gen. 17:1-14). It is attested as well in those parts of Exodus and Joshua which appeal to or summarize Israel's past history as the basis for her future hope (cf. Exod. 2:24; 3:6, 15-16; 6:2-8; Jos. 24:1-4).

The student should note that the mighty acts of God whereby He intervened in the history of the Israelites to deliver them from the slavery of Egypt (Exod. 1–14) and to constitute them His holy covenanted kingdom (Exod. 19–24) are performed as partial fulfillment of the promises made to Abraham. Israel's hope, therefore, is *confirmed, not originated,* by the miracle of the Exodus and the institution of the Sinai covenant. It is further fulfilled and confirmed by the conquest of Canaan in the time of Joshua.

By these interventions Israel's faith becomes established and her expectations increased. She is assured that she has indeed been chosen by

God for a great destiny and for a glorious future. What that future will be in detail she does not know, but the horizons of her hope are broadened immeasurably by her knowledge of the goodness, the power, and the fidelity of the God who has chosen her. She is assured, moreover, that as a nation she has a very definite part to play in the plan of God for the salvation of all mankind, and that He who intervened in the past will intervene again in the future to bring about the fulfillment of that plan. Israel in Palestine, therefore, from the thirteenth to the eleventh century B.C., is not as the rest of nations. As a consequence of God's promises to Abraham, partially confirmed by the Exodus and the Sinai covenant, Israel is a nation that looks to the future. What God will do, how He will accomplish His plan, she does not fully perceive. But she waits, not without expectation.

The period of dynastic messianism

Dynastic messianism is the term generally used to describe that period in Israel's history when she came to look to the Davidic dynasty as the divinely ordained vehicle through which her expectations would be fulfilled. The period begins in the tenth century with the revelation made to David through the prophet Nathan that his dynasty will be eternal. The historical testimony to the origin of this revelation in the time of David is found principally in three places: 2 Sam. 7:8-16; 1 Chr. 17:7-14; Ps. 89:20-38.[1]

The significance of the dynastic oracle can best be appreciated by understanding what it implied for Israel. Substantially it meant that, from the time of David on, the fulfillment of her hopes became inextricably and eternally imbedded in the Davidic family. With the Nathan oracle the covenant between God and Israel made at Sinai becomes individualized in the covenant between God and the house of David which from this time on represents the nation and becomes the mediator of the covenant. The kingship of Yahweh is to be exercised through kings of David's blood. There exists between God and the kings the same father-son relationship that existed between God and Israel as a result of the Sinai covenant (cf. Exod. 4:22; 2 Sam. 7:14; Ps. 89:27). The obligations of the covenant formerly imposed upon the nation are now imposed upon the kings as representatives of the nation (cf. Deut. 17:18-19).

The extent to which the Sinai covenant became one with the dynastic covenant can be best appreciated from the argumentation used by the author of Kings to prove that Israel had been unfaithful to the covenant. His argumentation is based upon the non-observance of the covenant by

[1] Cf. J. McKenzie, "The Dynastic Oracle: 2 Samuel 7," *Theological Studies* 8, 187ff.

the majority of the Davidic kings. Because the kings have been unfaithful, Israel has been unfaithful!

It is difficult to assess the full effect of the dynastic oracle on the messianic expectations of Israel. It is reasonably certain that in the beginning and for at least two centuries it focussed Israel's attention on the dynasty as a whole. Precisely because the Davidic kings were the lieutenants of Israel's covenanted King-God, Israel expected from them as a group and as individuals a godly reign of peace, justice, and prosperity. Since her God was the maker and ruler of the whole world, Israel expected as well that the rule of the Davidic kings would eventually embrace the world. These hopes are expressed in the psalms (cf. Pss. 2; 45; 72; 89; 110; 132). They are also expressed in the Yahwist's saga of the history of Israel.

What the Yahwist testifies to is the existence in Israel of a unique hope, based on the promises to the patriarchs, the Exodus experience, and the dynastic oracle, involving a plan of God that embraced not only the kingdom of Israel but all humanity. What the Yahwist expected from the Davidic dynasty was a universal, spiritual, earthly kingdom, in this world yet not of this world, enjoying peace and union with God and peace, justice, and prosperity among men.

This can be shown from the Yahwist's reconstruction of Israel's history according to a schema of promise, election, and covenant. As demonstrated from Gen. 2–3 and from his saga as a whole, the kingdom of the future toward which Israel tends is essentially the restoration of the reign of God that existed before the fall of Adam. The victory promised to mankind in Gen. 3:15 is the Yahwist's clearest testimony to the spiritual nature of the kingdom of the future, since this future victory will reverse the defeat sustained by Adam and mankind in the original encounter with the tempter.

For the Yahwist, then, who writes from the standpoint of the Exodus experience and the dynastic oracle, the Davidic dynasty is to play a major role in the re-establishment of God's rule over the world. How the dynasty would fulfill this role, the Yahwist does not tell us. He probably believed that the dynasty would produce a succession of ideal kings, whose fidelity to the spirit and stipulations of the Sinai covenant would win for Israel and the world a return to paradisaical holiness and bliss. He is generally believed to have written around 950 B.C. in the golden age of the Davidic dynasty. If he lived much longer and witnessed the decline and fall of Solomon from grace, he must certainly have been disillusioned.

The kings, though the Yahwist did not know it, would not be faithful either as a group or as individuals and would not bring about the fulfillment of the divine plan of salvation. Solomon fell into idolatry. Even David had not been without serious sin. And the books of Kings and the preaching of the prophets make abundantly clear the failure of the majority of the kings.

For the prophets the Sinai covenant was basic. Underlying the preaching of Elijah, Elisha, Amos, Hosea, Isaiah, Jeremiah and the prophets in general is the solid core of covenant theology, which they repeatedly insist must be the basic charter of the royal rule. When the kings make alliances with pagan nations or permit idolatry, the prophets make it clear that they are going directly counter to the very first stipulations of the Sinai suzerainty pact with Yahweh. When they permit the rich to oppress the poor, when they wink at the injustices in the law courts, when they countenance the general breakdown of morality in the kingdom, they are in the eyes of the prophets not just failing as kings, but as covenanted kings, since they fail to enjoin the observance of the secondary stipulations of the Sinai suzerainty pact which governed the relations between all of Yahweh's subjects.

At the root of the opposition and tension between prophet and king was the prophetic concern for the kingship of Yahweh. The prophets insisted that Israel must never place so much hope in her royal institutions and political power that she will lose faith in her true king who is God and her true kingdom which is essentially the reign of God Himself over her. The prophets, as W. F. Albright emphatically declares, "were, first and last, religious reformers . . . their task was not to teach a new . . . theology, but rather to demand a return to the purer faith of their forefathers" (Journal of Bible and Religion, VIII (1940, 131).

It is difficult to determine when the prophets became so disillusioned with the kings that they gave up all hope in them as the means for fulfilling Israel's hopes. Elijah becomes disgusted with Ahab, but his disciple Elisha hopes to make a new beginning with Jehu. Amos and Hosea see no hope for Israel in the northern kings, but there is no evidence that they gave up all hope in the house of David. Isaiah is utterly disgusted with Ahaz, but his relationship with Hezekiah is quite different. Only Jeremiah clearly abandons hope in the Davidic kings as a group and looks forward to a special act of God to ensure the fulfillment of Israel's destiny.

With Jeremiah, therefore, hope in the dynasty as a whole ceases and hope in a specific individual as the Messiah definitely is present. Whether Israel as a people had learned at an earlier time that her messianic hopes would not be fulfilled by the Davidic dynasty as a whole but by one extraordinary Davidic king is a question that still awaits its final clarification.

The period of personal messianism

Whatever one holds about the origin of Israel's belief in a personal Messiah as opposed to a messianic dynasty, there was certainly a period in her history when she looked for the fulfillment of her hopes to the dynasty as a whole. It is certain as well that Israel's theologians considered absolute and unconditional the promise to the dynasty. Unlike the conditional Sinai covenant and the conditional part of the oracle to David concerning the punishment of individual erring kings, the covenant with the dynasty as a whole was considered as absolute and irreversible as that made with Abraham. These two covenants remained, therefore, even when both the Sinai pact and the rule of the Davidic kings came to an end in 587 B.C. with the fall of Jerusalem to the Babylonians and the deportation of the Davidic ruling family to Babylon. Since by divine promise the dynasty was to be eternal, there had to be a restoration of the dynasty. It is upon this foundation that a belief in a personal Messiah is ultimately based.

During the period of the monarchy, from the oracle of Nathan in the tenth century down to the violent overthrow of the Davidic dynasty in the early sixth, there existed side by side in the Israelite consciousness two discordant facts, one a fact of faith — the unconditional promise of perpetuity to the Davidic house, the other a fact of experience — the proven inability and even incapacity of the Davidic kings as a group to bring about the realization of the divine plan for the salvation of Israel and the world. It is from the tension between this fact of faith and this fact of experience that is born a new fact of faith — the belief in the coming of a unique Davidic king, who will be filled with the spirit and the power of Yahweh and will successfully bring to fulfillment the reign of God over Israel and the world.

Whether this belief in a personal Messiah is the result of a direct revelation or the rational conclusion of Israel's theologians reasoning under the guidance of inspiration upon the absolute promises made to Abraham and to the Davidic dynasty is a matter of debate. In either case belief in a personal Messiah after the year 587 B.C. is certain.

By the first quarter of the sixth century B.C., it had become abundantly clear to the prophet Jeremiah that the Sinai covenant and the divine experiment with monarchy in Israel had been abysmal failures (Jer. 31:31-34; 22:20-30). Thoroughly disillusioned with the Davidic kings as a group and convinced by the approaching downfall of Jerusalem and the destruction of the Temple that the Sinai covenant had been repudiated by God, Jeremiah looked to the future and, on the basis of the absolute promises made to Abraham and to David, predicted not only a new covenant (Jer. 31:31-34) but a new David who would rule with success (Jer. 23:1-6; 30:8-9, 21). In prophecies that date from roughly the same time, Ezekiel predicts or confirms the same (Ez. 16:60; 36:25-38; 17:22-24; 21:32; 34:23-24; 37:24-27).

Whatever the extent of Jeremiah's inspired knowledge about the future "righteous shoot to David," who as king will "reign and govern wisely" (Jer. 23:5), whether he believed him to be merely the founder of a new and successful Davidic line of kings or a superhuman king who would inaugurate a period of unending fidelity to God and thereby fulfill the divine plan for Israel and the world, Jeremiah's oracle is basic to Israel's belief in a personal Messiah. The vicissitudes of this belief in the last five centuries of the Old Testament can be traced in the writings of the Chronicler, in the prophecies of Deutero-Isaiah, Zechariah, Malachi, and Daniel, and in the re-reading of many of the ancient texts. The belief is certain. The date of its fulfillment remains unknown until the Samaritan woman says to Christ: "I know that the Messiah is coming, and when he comes he will tell us all things." And she hears the reply, "I who speak with thee am he" (John 4:24-26).

4. Dating and Interpretation of the Messianic Texts

Due to the fluid state of present studies on messianism, it is impossible to give a definitive dating and interpretation of all the messianic prophecies. For the same reasons and also for lack of space, it is neither possible nor feasible to give an exhaustive explanation of each text. The most that can be done is to suggest the more probable dating and the more likely interpretation of each text in the context of its ideological and historical background and for further information refer the student to the commentaries.

The order in which the texts are listed here represents the author's opinion concerning the chronological order of the texts in their present, not in their original state, thus allowing for the re-reading and development of earlier texts in the light of later messianic revelation. The student is reminded, moreover, that messianic revelation as we have it now was not written down, as a general rule, until long after the historical period in which it occurred. He is also reminded of the Israelite practice of projecting later messianic revelation into the past by means of a literary fiction, with the result that neither the date of origin of the book in which it is contained nor the period indicated by the book itself objectively designates the actual time of the revelation.

Genesis 12:1-3

The origin of Israel's messianic hopes can be dated sometime during the nineteenth-eighteenth centuries before Christ when the promises were made to Abraham. The promises look to the future to a people (Israel, the posterity of Abraham), a land (Canaan), and a blessing (good things for the people and through them for all mankind).

The historicity of these promises is well attested by Israel's living memory — her tradition. Against the argument that the promises represent not historical fact but a projection backward of later belief, there is in addition to the unanimity of Israel's four documented traditions (Gen. 12:1-3, 7; 18:17-19; 26:2-4; 28:13-15 in the Yahwist tradition, Gen. 15:5-7, 13-20; Exod. 3:6, 15-16 in the Elohist tradition, Deut. 6:10; 26:5 in the Deuteronomic tradition, and Gen. 17:1-14; 35:11-12; Exod. 2:24; 6:2-8 in the Priestly tradition), the recourse of Moses to the patriarchal promises at the time of the Exodus (cf. Exod. 2:24; 3:6, 15-16; 6:2-8) and the two versions of Israel's cultic credo found in Deuteronomy (26:5ff) and Joshua (24:1ff). For a fuller discussion and critical defense of the historicity of the promises made to the patriarchs, the student should read the chapter on the patriarchs in Bright's, *A History of Israel* (61ff, especially 86-93).

2 Samuel 7:11-16

The birth of the nation Israel under Moses and the conquest of Canaan under Joshua did not assuage but increased Israel's expectations. As the kingdom of God on earth, whose king was God Himself, there was no limit to what Israel might expect. How she would become great, however, was another question. In the late eleventh century, with the institution of a monarchy in Israel, it was thought the answer was at hand — Israel would be great through her kings. God would rule Israel and extend His rule from Israel to the world through the kings. For four hundred years and more (1000-587), the theocratic nation experimented with that arrangement. The experiment failed, and the failure was clear in 587; but out of the experiment had come something positive — the assurance that someday God would raise up a successful king from the line of David and through him fulfill his plans for Israel and the world. The foundation for this belief is found already in Nathan's oracle to David.

Indirect testimony to the oracle of Nathan is found in many places in the Old Testament. Direct testimony is found in three places: 2 Sam. 7:8-16, 1 Chr. 17:7-14, and Ps. 89:20-38. Fr. John McKenzie has shown that the text of Ps. 89:20-38 most nearly approximates that of the original oracle.[1] The historicity of the oracle is testified to not only by the disparate sources (original Samuel dating to about the year 700, Chronicles to as

[1] Cf. McKenzie, *op. cit.*, 187ff; also J. L. McKenzie, "Royal Messianism," *CBQ* 19 (1957) 25ff.

late as 300, and Ps. 89 to approximately 587) but by the circumstances in which each of these sources reached its final state. Thus the books of Samuel were incorporated into the Deuteronomist's history no earlier than the late seventh century and more probably during the exile after the fall of the "eternal" dynasty. Chronicles was written at a time when there were excellent reasons to doubt the "eternity" of the Davidic dynasty, since no Davidic king had reigned for two centuries prior to the writing of the book. And Ps. 89, written at a time when the dynasty was in imminent danger of destruction, makes no sense unless the author was convinced that a promise of perpetuity had been made to the house of David at an earlier period.

The circumstances under which the oracle was given are described in 2 Sam. 7. Considering it a disgrace that he should live in a palace while the Ark of the Covenant is housed in a tent, David decides to build a temple and is encouraged by Nathan (vv. 1-3). Returning later and speaking under inspiration, Nathan tells David that he is not to build a temple (cf. 1 Chr. 22:7-8 for the reason). God, however, is not displeased with David. He has done much for David in the past and will do far more in the future (vv. 4-10).

In the oracle that follows, God promises perpetuity to the house of David and adopts David as His son just as He had adopted Israel as His son at Sinai (cf. Exod. 4:22). In return for the material house David would have built for God, God promises to David a royal "house" i.e., a dynasty, which will endure forever. That "house" and "seed" are to be taken in a collective sense including the successors of David is clear from the context: the emphasis on "forever" (vv. 11d, 13b, 15-16, 19, 25, 29), the contrast with the house of Saul (vv. 15-16), and the amazement attributed to David in his prayer (vv. 17-29).

The full significance of the oracle, however, depends on the meaning of the term "forever." In Hebrew "forever" ('adh 'olam) is ambiguous. It can mean a long time, indefinitely long but not forever (cf. 1 Sam. 1:23; 27:12), or forever in the full sense of without end. That the latter is the meaning in the oracle is clear from the emphasis on the term throughout, from David's evident amazement (vv. 17-29), and from the contrast expressed between the short-lived dynasty of Saul and that to be David's (vv. 15-16). The same implication is present in the distinction between the conditional nature of the promise as applied to the individual kings and the absolute nature of the promise as applied to the dynasty (vv. 14-16).

It is now almost universally agreed among exegetes that the oracle of Nathan is the root and foundation of dynastic or royal messianism in Israel. The development of the expectations to which it gave rise can be seen in the psalms (Pss. 2; 45; 72; 89; 110) and in the royal messianism of the prophets, especially Isaiah and Micah. Before treating dynastic messianism in the prophets, however, it will be rewarding to see how the author of the Yahwist saga projected dynastic messianism into the past in Gen. 3:15 and 49:8-12 in order to bring out the place of the Davidic dynasty in the divine plan.

Genesis 3:15

The solution proposed here for the interpretation of Gen. 3:15 can be summarized as follows. 1. The text belongs to that part of the Yahwist's saga which contains not the remembered past of Israel but the past as reconstructed by the Yahwist. 2. Gen. 3:15, like Gen. 12:1-3 and 49:8-12, is one of those texts in which the author uses the storyteller's device of foreshadowing the future in order to arouse suspense and at the same time prepare his audience to look for an interconnection of the parts of his story with the whole. 3. The meaning of the terms in the text, purposely vague so as not to destroy the element of suspense for the audience, is quite clear to the mind of the author: the serpent is a symbol taken from the Canaanite fertility cults of the author's day and used to represent the nature worship of the Canaanites; the seed of the serpent represents the devotees of the fertility cults; the seed of the woman represents the Davidic dynasty through which God will bring to fulfillment His plan for the conquest of Satan and the salvation of the world; the woman who is associated with the dynasty in the work of conquest and salvation is the Queen-mother of the Davidic king.

The divinely established enmity

The meaning of the enmity between the serpent and the woman, the seed of the serpent and the seed of the woman, the seed of the woman and the serpent is reasonably clear from Gen. 2:4b—3, 24, the literary unit which constitutes the immediate context of Gen. 3:15. The enmity which will eventually culminate in the crushing of the serpent's head by the seed of the woman is an enmity which will reverse the victory of the serpent over the woman. Since that victory consisted in deceiving the woman into turning away from God and placing her confidence in the serpent, the predicted victory of the woman's seed will bring about a rejection of the serpent, a return to God, and a restoration of relations with God as they were before the fall.

The meaning of the remaining terms in Gen. 3:15 is not equally clear from the context. However, when the meaning of terms is not clear from either text or context, the exegete has no recourse but to look to the wider literary context of the passage in question and to the historical and ideological background of the author. If it is remembered that Gen. 2:4b–3:24 has no historical background in the proper sense because it belongs not to Israel's remembered past but to her past as symbolized by the Yahwist, it will be evident that the wider literary context of Gen. 3:15 is the Yahwist's saga. A review, therefore, of the historical and ideological background of the Yahwist and a partial analysis of his saga should throw additional light on the meaning of the remaining terms in Gen. 3:15.

The historical milieu of the Yahwist according to most authors is the reign of Solomon. It is the time consequently of Israel's greatest glory as a nation. It is a time also of danger to Israel's faith. Solomon, like Saul, is forgetting the place of the monarchy in God's plan for Israel. The kingship of men is becoming more important than the kingship of God. In the last decades of his reign, as a consequence of his marriages with Canaanite women and of his building Canaanite shrines even in Jerusalem, Solomon has not only given bad example to his people but has allowed Canaanite religion to threaten the true faith as it would a century later in the time of Ahab and Jezebel (1 Kings 11:1-10, 31-39; 18—22). If the threat is to be countered, the Yahwist must dramatize for his readers the dangers of Canaanite fertility worship for the theocracy and at the same time show the relevancy of Israel's ancient traditions to the immediate situation.

The ideological background upon which the Yahwist bases his saga is relatively simple. There are three fundamental articles in his creed: the promises to the patriarchs, the Sinai covenant and the kingship of God, the promise of perpetuity to the dynasty of David. It is upon the vitality of these truths in Israel's life that the theocracy depends for the fulfillment of its destiny.

The whole of the Yahwist's saga has not been preserved in the Pentateuch. Enough has been preserved, however, to show that the Yahwist's purpose was to establish the place of the theocratic kingdom and the Davidic dynasty in the divine plan for the salvation of the world, and at the same time to show Israel and the kings that there must be an undying enmity between them and Canaanite religion, which like the serpent in Genesis threatens to deceive Israel and undermine her fidelity to God. If this analysis of the Yahwist's intentions is correct, then the Yahwist continues the line of Nathan and Samuel and is a predecessor of Elijah and the great prophets in his teaching concerning the relationship between monarchy and theocracy in Israel. It is against this background that we interpret the meaning of the serpent and his seed, the woman and her seed.

The serpent

Recent exegetical studies have shown that the author of Gen. 2–3 used the serpent as a symbol because it was the popular symbol for life in the fertility worship of his time. The serpent, therefore, represents the Canaanite fertility religion in the time of the author. In the summary-conclusion of his article on "Sin in Paradise" (*CBQ* 20 ('58) 26-40). L. Hartman, C.SS.R., makes the following remarks pertinent to the identity of the serpent:

> The author wishes to explain the presence of moral and physical evil in a world which God had made good as being the result of man's sin. According to the Israelite principle that the ancestor of any group had the characteristics of that group, he made the sin of the first parents of all mankind consist in the basic sin of all mankind *as he knew mankind in his day*. This sin was *nature worship*, the ascribing to creatures what belongs to God alone. For him all the abominable rites which were practiced among the pagans and among his own people in as far as they were unfaithful to the worship of the Lord, in order to placate the nature gods and thereby ensure fertility in man and beast, in field and plant, were sinful magic, *the symbol and personification of which was the serpent*. Only the Lord can give the true fruit of the tree of life (author's italics).

The seed of the serpent

If the above line of exegesis is correct and the serpent is a symbol for the nature worship of the author's day, then it is reasonable to expect that the Yahwist's audience would see in the seed of the serpent the Canaanites of their day who were the devotees of the nature worship of which the serpent was the symbol. This conclusion is borne out by the Yahwist's repeated attacks upon nature worship and the Canaanites in his narrative.

Thus, for seeking through nature worship of the serpent that fertility and life which only God can grant, the man is punished by loss of life (Gen. 3:22), the woman by bearing children in pain (Gen. 3:16), the land by a loss of fertility (Gen. 3:17-19). The first murderer is Cain the "tiller of the soil" (the Canaanites were predominantly an agricultural people), who is also the founder of the first city (the Canaanites were city dwellers in contrast to the semi-nomadic Israelite herdsmen). Noah plants a vineyard like the Canaanites and gets drunk (drunkenness was one of the many Canaanite vices). Only Ham looks upon Noah in his nakedness and for this, *Ham's son, Canaan,* is cursed in terms that re-echo the curse of the serpent (cf. Gen. 9:25 and Gen. 3:14). In the patriarchal history Sodom and Gomorrah are destroyed for the unnatural crimes that the Canaanites have made a part of their religion (Gen. 18:1ff). The incestuous origin

of the Moabites and Ammonites is recorded (Gen. 19:30-38). The patriarchs show their repugnance for the intermarriage of their sons with the
Canaanite women (cf. Gen. 24:3; 27:46; 28:1, 6-9 and the long trips undertaken to find non-Canaanite wives for Isaac and Jacob). In the scandalous
story of Judah and Tamar (Gen. 38) intermarriage with a Canaanite
woman results in death for Judah's sons, the unnatural sin of Onan, and
the incest of Judah with Tamar — all object lessons for those who would
attempt to condone intermarriage with the Canaanites by appealing to
the example of the great patriarch Judah.

From the Yahwist's repeated attacks upon the Canaanites and their
vices it would appear one can safely identify the seed of the serpent as
the devotees of the Canaanite fertility cults. The importance of this identification lies in the clue it gives for the identification of the seed of the
woman. If the Yahwist has gone out of his way to identify the seed of
the serpent, one can reasonably expect that he will identify the seed of the
woman as well. It is when one is looking for this identification that
the elimination of peoples-process in Genesis takes on a new significance.[1]

The seed of the woman

Almost all exegetes are agreed that the Yahwist (later followed by the
Priestly author) used genealogies to prove to his readers that from
the very beginning of history God had singled out a special line of men
(Adam, Seth, Noah, Shem, Abraham, Isaac, Jacob and his sons) from which
would come His Chosen People. Although the conclusion of the Yahwist's
saga has not been kept by the final editor of the Pentateuch, it is reasonably
certain from the emphasis upon Judah (Gen. 37:26; 38; 43:1-12; 44:14-34;
46:28; 49:8-12) and from the historical and ideological background of the
author that the process of elimination would have continued through the
clans of Judah to Perez, Hezron, Ram, Amminadab, Nahshon, Salmon,
Boaz, Obed, Jesse to culminate in David (cf. Gen. 38:27-30; Num. 26:19ff;
Ruth 4:18-22).

If this is true, then the Yahwist used his genealogical device not only
to single out the Israelites as a nation but to single out of Israel itself
one special family — the family of David. Since the Yahwist begins with
Eve, the mother of all the living (Gen. 2:24), and divides her seed by
genealogies into those who are chosen and those who are not, opposing
to those who are chosen (the Israelites) one group (the Canaanites)
among those who are not chosen, it would appear reasonably certain that

[1] Cf. pp. 7; 94ff.

from the beginning the Yahwist had in mind as the "seed of the woman" the dynasty of David and as the "seed of the serpent" the devotees of the Canaanite nature worship.

One may cite in confirmation of this identification the Yahwist's use of foreshadowing in Gen. 3:15. Thus the announcement of the enmity between the seed of the woman and the seed of the serpent prepares the audience in advance for the enmity between the Chosen People and the Canaanites. The announcement that the seed of the woman will crush the head of the serpent prepares the audience in advance for the ultimate destruction of Canaanite nature worship and all that it entails by the Davidic dynasty. The same foreshadowing device is used in Gen. 12:1-3 as the author prepares to narrow the seed of Abraham to the seed of Israel and in Gen. 49:8-12 as he prepares the audience for the rise of the Davidic dynasty.

From the broad context of the whole of the Yahwist's saga, it would appear then that the "seed of the woman" is narrowed by the genealogical process of elimination until by a narrowing of the focus from Gen. 3:15 to Gen. 12:1-3 to Gen. 49:8-12 to 2 Sam. 7:8-16 it eventually reaches as terminus "the seed of David." It would appear too that the "seed of the serpent" does not represent the rest of mankind eliminated by the genealogical process, but only one part of it — the Canaanites, who continue toward Israel the enmity of the serpent-deceiver in paradise.

The woman

If the "seed of the woman" has been correctly identified as the Davidic dynasty, it is a simple step to the identification of the woman as the Queen-mother in the Davidic dynasty. This identification can only be made on the basis of the broader literary context of the Yahwist's history. In the immediate context of Gen. 3:15 the woman is open to three different interpretations. She could be Eve as in Gen. 2:25; or woman in general as in Gen. 2:23-24; or some future woman, since the prophecy looks to the future. The use of the definite article does not resolve the ambiguity any more than the context, because grammatically the article can be used to determine the woman as an individual, present or future, or as a species.

Leaving the ambiguous context of Gen. 3:15 for the broader context of the Yahwist's historical background, there is abundant evidence to show that the Queen-mother, or *gebirah* (powerful lady) as she was called, enjoyed extraordinary prestige and influence not only in Egypt, Mesopotamia, Hatti, Ugarit, and Persia (cf. Dan. 5:10-12) but in Judah as well.

In the late eleventh century, Israel asked Samuel: "Set up for us a king to judge us like all the nations" (2 Sam. 8:5). Subsequently under

David, Israel became in externals at least "like all the nations." Under Solomon who literally cultivated kingship, it is notable that Bathsheba, following the pattern of the Queen-mother in other kingdoms of the time, occupies the role of *gebirah*. Her importance at court is brought out clearly in the court historian's account of the *coup d' état* that put Solomon on the throne (cf. 1 Kings 1:11-31) and in his description of Solomon's deferential reception of her when she came to ask a favor of him (cf. 1 Kings 2:19-20 and Ps. 110:1).

The importance of the Queen-mother in the subsequent history of the Davidic dynasty is testified to by the care of the author of Kings to record her name as he introduces each new king (cf. 1 Kings 14:21; 15:2; 22:42; 2 Kings 8:26; 12:2; 14:1; 15:2; 18:2; 21:1; 22:1; 23:31), and by the remark of Jeremiah about the Queen-mother, like the king, wearing a diadem (cf. Jer. 13:18). The autocratic behavior of the Queen-mother Athaliah, who took over the throne of Judah after the death of her son Ahaziah and ruled for six years until deposed by the high priest Jehoiada in favor of King Jehoash, is perhaps the clearest indication of the official power and influence of the Queen-mother.[1]

Exegetically there is no revelation concerning the part of woman in the fulfillment of Israel's hopes comparable to the revelation made to David (2 Sam. 7) which would explain the prominence given by the Yahwist to the Queen-mother. Yet it is nonetheless true that the Yahwist pays extraordinary attention to the place of women in Israel's history. He is careful at the very beginning of his saga to establish the dignity of woman by showing her to be, like man, made in the image and likeness of God (Gen. 2:18-25). She is eminently fit, therefore, to cooperate with man in any great mission God might choose for her. The Yahwist goes on to show that in Israel's history women did indeed cooperate with men in a singular way (Sarah, Rebecca, Rachel). He points out, moreover, that although each of these women suffered the curse of barrenness (cf. Gen. 11:30; 25:21; 29:31), they did not seek fertility from the nature gods but waited and by the power of God eventually conceived.

We conclude, therefore, from the emphasis given to womankind in Gen. 2–3, from the Yahwist's concern for detailing the significant part played by women in the exploits of Israel's greatest men, and from the importance of the Queen-mother known from extra-biblical and biblical sources other than the Yahwist's saga that the woman of Gen. 3:15 is the Queen-mother of the Davidic king.

We conclude as well that the Yahwist envisaged a truly active part for

[1] Cf. B. Ahern, "The Mother of the Messiah," *Marian Studies* 12 (1961, 46ff; S. Rowe, "An Exegetical Approach to Genesis 3:15," *ibid.* 49ff; DeVaux, *op. cit.*, 117-119.

the Queen-mother in the defeat of the serpent and his seed and that this active role of the woman was as much a part of the divine plan as the active role of the woman's seed. The Yahwist placed Israel's hopes for the future in the kings and queen-mothers of the Davidic dynasty. There is no good reason to believe that his prophetic glance saw beyond the dynasty to an individual messianic king nor beyond the role of Queen-mother to the Immaculate Virgin Mother of the Messiah. But in associating the Queen-mother with the messianic king, he has done more than enough to merit the title of the first mariologist. Later on the final Priestly editor will treat the Yahwist's saga afresh and will re-read Gen. 3:15; 12:3; 49:8-12 in a personal messianic sense (cf. p. 366ff).

Genesis 49:8-12

Critics are agreed, on the basis of internal evidence and a comparison with Deut. 33, that the promises of Jacob in Gen. 49:1-28 do not originate with the great patriarch but are the poetic creation of an Israelite author in the period of the Judges (cf. CCHS par. 172). The author's use of the promises as a literary device to foreshadow the future is obvious from the reference of Jacob to himself as a people (cf. 49:7, also 49:16, 28) and from the geographical descriptions of the different tribes which correspond to their location in the time of the Judges (cf. 49:7, 11, 13, 15).

Critics are likewise agreed, on the basis of the geographical descriptions and the lack of allusion to the division of the kingdom in 965 or to the rise of Saul to kingship in 1020 or to the change in the status of the Levites between the time of the Judges and the monarchy (compare Gen. 49:5-7 and Deut. 33:8-11), that the poem was composed early in the period of the Judges at a time when "Israelite poets were dependent on a young literary tradition that leaned heavily on Canaanite models."[1]

The only verses in the poem which do not accord well with a date early in the period of the Judges are the verses which deal with the tribe of Judah (vv. 8-12). Critics generally agree that these verses are the interpolation of a later author, probably the Yahwist, who retouched the original text to make it foreshadow the rise of the Davidic dynasty in Israel.

Since it is characteristic of the poet to liken the different tribes to animals (cf. vv. 14, 17, 21, 27) and to make an allusion to the location of the tribes (cf. vv. 7, 13, 17, 20), it is likely that the original texts of the poem dealing with Judah are found in vv. 9, 11, 12. In these verses Judah is likened to a lion or lioness, probably because of her conquest of the southern Canaanite shrine of the lion-goddess, Asherah (cf. Vawter

[1] Cf. B. Vawter, "The Canaanite Background of Gen. 49," *CBQ* 17 (1955) 1ff.

ibid., 5-6), and her geographical location is indicated by the allusion to vineyards and wine (vv. 11-12).

The allusions in v. 8 to Judah's hegemony over the other tribes and in v. 10 to her conquest of the surrounding nations presuppose the election of David as king of all Israel described in 2 Sam. 5:1-5 and his subsequent conquest of the surrounding nations described in 2 Sam. 8:1-8 and 10:1-19. It is because of these obvious allusions that critics date the retouching of the poem to the time of David or Solomon.

If this explanation of the literary form of the poem and of the later interpolation of vv. 8 and 10 by the Yahwist is correct, then the predictions, like the prediction in Gen. 3:15, are not prophecies in the proper sense of the word but rather retrospective foreshadowings introduced into the poem by the Yahwist to more clearly foreshadow the rise of the Davidic dynasty.

It should be noted that the "until" in v. 10c does not imply that Judah's hegemony will cease when there comes the "obedience of the nations" (cf. Gen. 28:15; Ps. 110:1). The meaning is rather that royal power will perdure in Judah. Substantially, therefore, v. 10 restates the permanency promised the Davidic dynasty in the oracle of Nathan.

Since v. 10ab presupposes the existence of royal power in Judah, v. 10c either refers to David the founder of the dynasty, the one "to whom it belongs," or, as seems more probable, the Hebrew *shilo* of the text should be translated "tribute to him." This translation, as W. Moran shows, not only leaves the original text absolutely intact, but restores to it perfect parallelism of members. Moran translates the text: "Until there is brought to him tribute, and to him the obedience of the peoples." He concludes: "In our understanding of the blessing, Judah is referred to throughout, but Judah exists in David, whose history with its triumphs, is not only his own, but in the thought patterns of the time, also predicable of his ancestor."[1]

If, as some critics hold, v. 10 is postexilic, then it is probable that the *shilo* of v. 10c should be read, "to whom it belongs," and be interpreted as a re-reading of the original text in the light of personal messianism and the text of Ez. 21:32.

Numbers 24:7 and 17

These texts which allude to the rise of the monarchy in Israel should be interpreted after the manner of Gen. 3:15 and Gen. 49:8, 10 as later re-readings by the Yahwist. As in Genesis, the Yahwist retouches earlier texts to make them foreshadow the rise of the Davidic dynasty.

[1] W. Moran, S.J., "Gen. 49:10 and Ez. 21:32," *Biblica* 39 (1958) 405, 416.

In the centuries that followed the Yahwist, Israelite writers, particularly the psalmists and Isaiah, exploited the dynastic promise in different ways. The author of Samuel recorded the oracle and alluded to it in the last words of David (2 Sam. 23:1-5). The psalmists extolled the king on the occasion of his inauguration (Pss. 2; 72; 110) and on the occasion of his marriage (Ps. 45).

Since the Davidic king was God's anointed and God's adopted son, there is little doubt but that the people in general held high hopes for the reign of each new king (cf. Ps. 72). There is little doubt too but that an ideal of kingship based on the divine kingship and on the best that Israel saw in David and Solomon gradually developed.

That Israel however restricted these hopes for the ideal king to an ideal king of the distant future and not to each successive king of the Davidic dynasty as he came along is not evident from the texts. The people had reason to be disappointed in many of the Davidic kings, but there is no evidence to indicate that they lost hope in the dynasty as a whole. With the advent of each new king Israel's hopes flamed anew.

Although there is no evidence from the text to prove it, it is reasonable to suppose that Israel's faith in the eternal dynasty was severely tested by the usurpation of the throne by the Queen-mother Athaliah and the near extinction of the dynasty. It is equally reasonable to suppose that with the deposition of Athaliah and the enthronement of Jehoash, the Davidic prince, there was a renewal and strengthening of Judah's faith in the perpetuity of the dynasty.

The rise and fall of the different dynasties in the dissident kingdom of the north no doubt contributed as well to the strengthening of this faith. In the time of Isaiah the dynasty successfully hurdled two more crises that threatened its existence, the threat in the time of Ahaz (734-732) and the threat in the time of Sennacherib's invasion (701). It is not surprising, therefore, that in the time of Isaiah we should have further testimony to Israel's faith in the perpetuity of the Davidic dynasty. It is with this testimony, from Isaiah principally, but also from Micah that we must deal.

It has generally been believed that at the time of Isaiah and through Isaiah Judah's hopes were transferred from the dynasty as a whole and focussed upon a coming Davidic king who would be king and savior *par excellence*. Since this opinion is no longer commonly advanced by scholars, it is in place to review the position currently in vogue, namely, that Isaiah did not go beyond dynastic messianism. The Isaian texts are important, it is first of all maintained, not only because they are truly messianic in that they reinvigorate the dynastic messianic hopes of Judah and add immeasurably to Israel's concept of the ideal king, but because they point the way to the catalyst (dissatisfaction with the kings as individuals and as a group) which in the time of Jeremiah gives rise to Judah's belief in the coming of an ideal future king — the personal Messiah in the proper sense of the word.

Of the messianic texts in Isaiah (Is. 4:2; 7:10-17; 8:8b, 10b; 9:1-6; 11:1-9; 11:10; 16:5; 32:1-8; 55:3f), critics generally agree on attributing to Proto-Isaiah only 7:10-17; 8:8b, 10b; 9:1-6. The remaining texts are attributed, though with less certainty, either to Proto-Isaiah, Deutero-Isaiah, or disciples of the Isaian school. Leaving to the critics and to time the evaluation of the other texts, we shall concentrate upon Is. 7:10-17; 8:8b, 10b; 9:1-6; 11:1-9 and Micah 4:14—5:5.

Isaiah 7:10-17

An increasing number of exegetes consider both Is. 7:14 and Is. 9:1-6 to be concerned directly with a Davidic crown prince (the future King Hezekiah) and with his mother (the 'almah of 7:14), Abi (cf. 2 Kings 18:2). It is impossible to elaborate all the pros and cons for this opinion. The line of argumentation is as follows.

To begin with, the sign given by Isaiah, if it is to corroborate his prediction that Judah will not fall to Israel and Syria, must be a sign recognizable by Ahaz. Since Israel and Syria plan to put an outsider, Tabeel, on the throne of Judah (Is. 7:6), and since Ahaz has sacrificed his son to the fertility gods (cf. 2 Kings 16:3; 2 Chr. 28:3), the dynasty as a consequence is in danger of extinction, and the birth of a crown prince, either already conceived or about to be conceived, is of considerable import at the moment.

The prophet, moreover, speaks of the childhood of the predicted infant in relation to the defeat of Israel and Syria and the invasion of the Assyrians (7:15-25). Both of these events take place in the immediate not the distant future, the one c. 732 (cf. 2 Kings 16:9 and 17:1ff), the other periodically between 732-701 (cf. 2 Kings 16—19).

A further argument for the contemporaneity of the child predicted as a sign for the king is the birth of Isaiah's son, given as a sign to the people in 8:1-8. Ch. 7 and 8 are parallel and present similar signs to corroborate the same predictions. Thus the son of Isaiah, whose birth is followed by the defeat of Israel and Syria and the invasion of the Assyrians, and who, like the son of the 'almah, is given a symbolic name related to the same events, is intimately linked with the child of 7:14. In both cases, moreover, Assyria's failure to completely destroy Judah is attributed to the child of 7:14 (cf. 8:8, 10).

With regard to the announcement-of-birth-formula used in 7:14, it is sometimes stated that the solemnity of the announcement presages something extraordinary and that therefore the meaning of each word is to be stretched to the utmost. There is, however, no indication from the formula that this will be an extraordinary birth either in the sense that the child will be divine (the inference sometimes made from the name *Immanuel* meaning "God with us"), or in the sense that the mother will remain a virgin even in conceiving (the inference sometimes made from the word *'almah* meaning a young maiden of marriageable age and presumably a virgin and from the fact that the mother names the child and nothing is said about a father). The same formula is found in more ancient texts, both biblical and non-biblical, and there is consequently no reason for pressing the meaning of each word in the formula. Thus in Gen. 16:11 the formula is identical except for the words *'almah* and *Immanuel*. Hagar conceives Ishmael through Abraham and herself names the child. In Judg. 13:5, 7, 24 the formula is used to announce the birth of Samson and the mother names the child. 1 Sam. 1:20 states: "Anna bore a son and called his name Samuel." In non-biblical literature the exact announcement-of-birth-formula, even including the word *'almah* is found in a Ugaritic text from "The Wedding of Nikkal and the Moon God": "Behold, an *'almah* shall bear a son."[1]

As we have indicated above the Hebrew word *'almah* means a young woman of marriageable age. The word does not specify but it does imply virginity just as our modern usage of the words girl, maid, maiden, young lady imply but do not specify virginity. The technical term in Hebrew corresponding to our technical term "virgin" is *bethulah*. Presumably Isaiah speaks of *the* maiden (*ha 'almah*) because she is someone well known to Ahaz. If this definite *'almah* is not a contemporary of Ahaz, but as some exegetes claim, an *'almah* of the distant future, then we must presume from the allusory nature of Isaiah's statement that the king already knows from some other source about this *'almah* of the future. If this is true we must presume previous revelation of such an *'almah*. But there is no testimony elsewhere that Israel knew of her. On the contrary, the importance of the Queen-mother, already discussed in relation to the exegesis of Gen. 3:15, is more than sufficient reason for Isaiah to single out the particular wife of Ahaz who through the birth of the Davidic crown prince would be in line eventually to bear this august title.

An evaluation of the above commonly propounded exegesis of Is. 7:10f would not gloss over the following observations.

1. In the situation Isaiah found himself after being rebuffed contemptuously by the impious Ahaz who had scoffed away the one only occasion

[1] Cf. B. Vawter, "The Ugaritic Use of GLMT," *CBQ* 14 (1952) 319-323.

in salvation-history when an individual could have named a miracle anywhere from heaven's height to sheol and God would have performed it, who had, if one may so phrase it, "politely spit in the face of a prophet and his Lord" (v. 13) after that prophet had perseveringly attempted a second audience to gain the king's good will — such a situation psychologically and according to the demands of divine justice would exclude the promise of blessing to the grossly disobedient individual, namely, the promise of the blessing of a king-son to be born to him. Rather, the spirit and actions of Ahaz would demand sentence of punishment. Since, therefore, Ahaz had haughtily refused a beneficent sign or miracle (which would have implied his conversion to Isaian policy and Yahwistic morality had he accepted the offer), he would be given a "sign" appropriate to his evil conduct, namely, "such (evil) days as have not come since the day Ephraim parted from Judah" (v. 17); how evil those days could be is described in detail (vv. 18-25).

2. Verse 14, accordingly, would be incidental; the Davidic dynasty will, of course, continue; "Immanuel" will be born (which no one can doubt), but BEFORE God's blessing again descends upon Judah through His Immanuel on the throne, the devastation of the House of David will have taken place. Note: according to v. 13 the principal recipient of the sign is the "House of David"; according to the principle of solidarity, so solemnly invoked by scholars, it need not be pressed whether or not Ahaz personally was or was not taken into captivity; v. 17 spells out the punishment as "upon you, upon your people, and upon your father's house."

3. These observations on the nature of the sign do not by any means imply that Isaiah was "looking into the far distant future," much less that he implied or predicated divinity for the child, or virginity for its mother. Immanuel could well still be the incarnation of messianic hopes according to prevailing notions of the eighth century B.C. Reference to him is simply made as a *terminus ante quem*, i.e., before God will raise him up on the throne, the throne of Ahaz will have suffered severe humiliation. It was not long before Ahaz actually did experience the heavy hand of Assyria, thereby receiving his sign. Isaiah had no intimation of the length of time it would take before the ideal king, Immanuel, would arise and continue the Davidic dynasty.

With regard to the opinion of S. Mowinckel that Isaiah uses the mythical theme of the "supernatural woman who would bear a son whose birth would be an omen of a great and happy transformation," one must be more cautious. The opinion cannot be ruled out of court peremptorily, especially in view of the remarkable similarity between the birth formula of Is. 7:14 and the birth formula from "The Wedding of Nikkal and the Moon God." However, in the monotheistic circles of the prophets, ever at war with the Canaanite fertility cults, the use of such a myth at such a moment in Israel's history is difficult to conceive. The use of the birth formula is more realistically explained on the supposition that it had long been naturalized in Israelite literature, as evidenced in Gen. 16:11; Judg. 13:5, 7, 24; 1 Sam. 1:20, and that thus its pagan overtones had from constant usage disappeared. One might add that it is almost inconceivable that Isaiah the monotheist would have used a pagan myth which suggested a consort for Yahweh — a thought that would be anathema to any orthodox Yahwist.[1]

Isaiah 9:1-6

The announcement of the birth of a child who is clearly a Davidic prince (cf. Is. 9:6) is associated with the devastation of northern Israel by the Assyrians in 734-732 (cf. Is. 8:23 and 2 Kings 15:29). It should be noted that grammatically the announcement could hail a crown prince who has just been born as well as a prince who will be born in the future (v. 5). In the throne names given the child (v. 5cd) there is nothing that cannot be explained against the background of Nathan's oracle, the exuberant language of Pss. 2; 72; and 110, and Israel's conception of the ideal Davidic king. The passage as a consequence could find a natural explanation in the actual birth of the crown prince predicted in Is. 7:14. This exegesis presumes the validity of the more common explanation to Is. 7:10ff as its background and likewise labors under its defects.

Isaiah 11:1-9 and Micah 4:14—5:5

Is. 37:35 suggests that this prophecy may be dated to 701 B.C., when the kingdom of Judah was overrun and the royal house almost demolished by Sennacherib. At this point Isaiah again hails the eternal dynasty and predicts it will continue even though it has been cut down almost to the roots by Sennacherib.

It is probably this event, the divine intervention saving Judah and the Davidic dynasty from the destruction threatened by Sennacherib, that occasions the prophecy of Micah 4:14—5:5. The reference in v. 2cd to the dispersion of the Jews suggests that this text as a whole (including therefore the allusion to Is. 7:14 in v. 2ab) is a gloss on the original text of Micah. When read without v. 2, Micah's oracle amounts to a repetition on the part of Micah of the expectations voiced by Isaiah in Is. 9:1-6 and 11:1-9. If, however, it should be definitively proved that personal mes-

[1] Cf. S. Mowinckel, *He That Cometh* (Oxford: Basil Blackwell, 1956) 113ff.

sianism does begin with Isaiah, its date of origin will more likely be found here in these texts from 701, than in the time of Ahaz. At present the evidence is not compelling.

Jeremiah 23:5-6

Jeremiah's prediction of "a righteous shoot to David" is probably the turning point in Israelite messianic expectations. From this time on she no longer looks to the historical kings and the dynasty as a dynasty to fulfill her messianic hopes but to a future, divinely raised up Davidic king who, unlike the historical kings of the past, will "reign and govern wisely" and "do what is just and right in the land."

Jeremiah's prediction is unambiguous and speaks for itself. Commentators do not question the meaning of the text, only its authenticity. For those who believe that Israel's belief in the coming of a personal Messiah arose after the exile, the prediction is considered the redaction of postexilic editors who added the oracle to the original collection of oracles against the kings in order to soften the impact of the oracle against Jehoiachin (Jer. 22:28-30). It is also argued that in 17:24-25 and 22:4 Jeremiah does not contemplate a break in the dynastic succession.

The arguments, however, in favor of authenticity are imposing. To begin with, it is true that in his earlier years Jeremiah did not contemplate a break in the dynastic succession. The same is not true in the last years of his life. Once Jeremiah realized the fall of Jerusalem was inevitable, he began to look to the future. The turning point is clear in his prophecies concerning the exile (cf. 25:11; 29:10; 24:11ff; 32:10-15; 31:31-34). In these texts Jeremiah shows that he puts his hopes in the "good figs" in exile in Babylon since 597 and destined to remain there for a long time. In his prophecy concerning the new covenant (31:31-34) Jeremiah implicitly professes his belief in the abrogation of the old covenant and of the historical kings who were its mediators. In his oracle against Jechoniah (22:20-30), he makes it clear that not only has the era of the old covenant come to an end but the era of the old kings as well. Both have failed — covenant and dynasty. Under such circumstances nothing is more likely than that Jeremiah should link with the new covenant a new David as different from the old Davidic kings as the new covenant would be different from the old. Indeed just as the new covenant will be in practice what the old never was except in theory, so the new David will be in practice what the historical kings never were except in ideal.

Additional arguments for authenticity can be found in the poetic form of vv. 5-6 and in the play on the name of Zedekiah. In the collection of oracles against the kings in 21:11ff, the original oracles are in poetic form, the commentary in prose. In 23:1-6, vv. 1-4 are in prose and have the marks of a postexilic redaction. Since vv. 5-6 are in poetic form, they are in all likelihood as authentic as the preceding oracles concerning Joachaz, Joakim, Jehoiachin, and Zedekiah. The play on words contrasting the name of Zedekiah (in Hebrew, *sidqi-yahu* meaning "my justice is Yahweh") with the symbolic name to be given the new David (in Hebrew, *Yahweh-sid-qenu* meaning "Yahweh is our justice") is eminently likely in the time of Zedekiah, the reigning king in the last days of Judah's independence.

It is sometimes argued that Jeremiah's expression, "a righteous shoot," (23:5b) is dependent on Zech. 3:8; 6:10-13. The term, however, hardly originated with Zechariah. "The rightful shoot" (Hebrew, *semah sedek*) had already been used in Phoenician to designate the legitimate heir to the throne and is found even earlier in the prologue of the code of Hammurabi where Hammurabi refers to himself as Zer-sar-ru-tim meaning "the royal branch or shoot."

Of no small weight for proving the authenticity of Jeremiah's oracle in 23:5-6 are the parallel oracles of Ezechiel. In 17:22-24, Ezechiel contrasts the future Messiah with Zedekiah in a manner reminiscent of Jer. 23:5-6. And in 34:23-24 and 37:25-26, he associates the new David, as does Jeremiah, with the return from the exile and the new covenant.

In the years that follow the exile, Israel's hopes for a new David fluctuate but never die. They are attested by Deutero-Isaiah toward the end of the exile (Is. 55:3), by Haggai (2:21ff) and Zechariah (3:8; 6:9-14) around 520. The canticle of the suffering servant in Is. 53 has royal overtones. The oracles of Deutero-Zechariah (Zech. 9:9-10; 12:1—13:6) and the enthusiasm of the Chronicler for the Davidic dynasty show that the expectation of the Messiah was still strong in Judah as late as the year 400.

It is true that in the last three centuries before Christ, Israel's expectations were centered more on the coming of the kingdom of God and on the kingship of Yahweh (cf. the kingship of Yahweh psalms) than on the Davidic Messiah, but the enigmatic figure "coming on the clouds of heaven" in Daniel (7:13) and the intense preoccupation of the Jews with the coming of the Messiah in the time of Christ show that Israel's hopes for the advent of the new David never died. The surest sign that these hopes lived on can be found in Israel's "re-reading" of the ancient Scriptures in the light of her new expectations.

5. Re-reading of Messianic Texts

Re-reading means the reading into ancient texts by later authors of new meanings and new evaluations based upon fuller revelation. It is a fact, testified to by the Septuagint translation of the Old Testament, by the tradition of the Jews, and by the usage of the New Testament authors, that Israel's teachers not only re-read the ancient texts in the light of their contemporary knowledge of revelation but even at times "retouched" or changed the original texts to make them testify to their current doctrinal beliefs.

In most examples of re-reading, the old texts are not changed verbally but a richer message is injected into the original words (cf. Matthew 22:41 and Ps. 110:1; Matthew 2:15 and Hosea 11:1). In some cases, however, the original texts are changed or "retouched" to elicit from them and express more clearly the new understanding given them in the light of further revelation. If the student will compare the massoretic text of Gen. 3:15; Num. 24:17, and Is. 7:14 with the corresponding Septuagintal translation of these texts, he will immediately notice that these texts have been "retouched" to make them express Israel's belief in the coming of a personal Messiah.

The link between the original meaning and the new, more developed message is found in Israel's conception of God as the Lord of history who plans all things from the beginning toward a predetermined end — the coming of the Messiah and the actualization of the kingdom of God. As each step in a journey leads to the end of the journey and is determined in direction by the goal of the journey, so for the Israelite writers each stage in the development of God's plan for Israel was seen to lead onward toward the fulfillment of the plan and to find its full significance not so much in itself as in its relation to the plan as a whole. The Yahwist was perhaps the first to realize this and the first to retouch and re-read ancient texts to make them bear witness to new revelation (cf. Gen. 49:8-12; Num. 24:17). But he was not the last. The editor of the Deuteronomist's history, the editors of the prophets, and the translators of the Septuagint followed in his footsteps. The greatest re-reader of all was our Lord Himself (cf. Luke 4:14-22 and Is. 61:1-2).

Thus, while the original author of a text or book may have seen only the immediate significance of a particular event as the work of God in behalf of His people, a later author with fuller knowledge of the divine plan will see the past event not only in itself but in relation to the unfolding plan of God that has been made known to him. We know as a result that Moses had a fuller knowledge of the significance of the call of Abraham than Abraham himself, and the prophets a fuller knowledge of the significance of the Exodus events than Moses. When in the fullness of time Christ came "not to destroy but to fulfill" (Matthew 6:17), the New Testament writers, in possession of the fullness of God's redemptive plan, were able to look back, as men who have climbed to the top of a peak can view the tortuous route that led upward from the valley below, and see the unilinear direction and advance of the divine plan from its inception to its completion. In a very true sense, then, one can speak of the New Testament as the definitive re-reading of the Old as centered in Christ, the continuation in the flesh of Israel and the one in whom all her messianic hopes are fulfilled.

For an example of simple re-reading, the student may consult the original meaning of Deut. 18:5 and compare it with the judgment read into it in New Testament times (cf. John 1:45; 4:25; 5:46; 6:14; 7:40; Acts 3:22; 7:37). For an example of re-reading and retouching the student may consult the original meaning of Ps. 110 and then compare the massoretic text of v. 3 with its translation in the Septuagint (probably retouched in the light of 2 Sam. 7 or Dan. 7:13). If the student will then read Matthew 22:41, he will see that the Jews in the time of Christ had come to re-read the psalm not only as if originally written by David himself, but as if directed by him to the personal future Messiah. What was originally written of David or Solomon, therefore, has been given a more significant meaning as a result of Israel's belief not only in the perpetuity of the Davidic dynasty but as a result of her belief in the coming from that dynasty of a future, personal Messiah (cf. also Acts 2:30-35; 4:25; 13:33-37; Rom. 1:2-4; 1 Cor. 15:24-27; Heb. 1:3, 5, 13; 10:12-13).

The significance of Israel's re-reading of ancient texts lies in its testimony to her understanding of written revelation in relation to tradition. She looked upon written revelation not as a static, lifeless record of the past, but as something dynamic in itself, oriented to the future for completion, ready as a consequence for further loading. As she learned more about God's plan for her and the world's salvation, she saw more and more the unity and rectilinear direction of revelation from the seed of the woman, to the seed of Abraham, to the seed of David, to the Messiah himself. New revelation never undid the old. It showed in it hitherto unplumbed depths and unsuspected fullness.

It was on the basis therefore of tradition, the living magisterial understanding of revelation, that Israel's teachers not only re-read but retouched the ancient texts. The surest sign that such an attitude toward the text was inherited and put to use by the Church, the new Israel, is the re-reading of the Old Testament by New Testament writers and the Church's subsequent use of the Sacred Scriptures in the liturgy, where the old texts are re-read with a wealth of meaning undreamed of by their original inspired authors.

6. The Fulfillment of the Messianic Prophecies

It is impossible to understand the fulfillment of the messianic prophecies unless one realizes that Israel's expectations, great as they were, fell far short of their fulfillment.[1] She expected a scion from the ancient dynasty of David who would be raised up by God to be His vicegerent as ruler over Israel and the world. He would be a superhuman kind of king who would rule wisely, justly, successfully. All nations and all men, as Ps. 87 envisioned, would be born spiritually in Zion and live as citizens of a world-wide Israelite nation. From Zion too would go forth instruction, as Isaiah predicted (2:2-4), so that all men might be instructed in the ways of God and walk in His paths, and so reap the harvest of an everlasting peace.

Greater expectations no nation ever had, but the fulfillment so far surpassed the expectations that the expectations seem pale in comparison. Israel expected the kingdom to extend her boundaries to the ends of the world, but the New Israel, the Church, broke down all boundaries. Israel expected a state of peace between man and God, and Christ fulfilled that dream with a peace "which the world cannot give". She expected a king who would master the world. She received a king who was master of the world because He had created it. She who looked for the fulfillment of the prophetic words she had received, received the Word Himself in the flesh. All her institutions were imperfect and looked to the future for their perfection: her priesthood, prophetism, kingship. When Christ came — the everlasting priest, the prophet of prophets, the king of kings — all were fulfilled at once and in one Person. Israel's cup of expectations was not just filled, it was deluged.

If the question is asked, Did Christ fulfill all the messianic prophecies in detail and exactly?, the answer must be yes and no. Since Israel's messianic expectations were only an imperfect apprehension of what lay in store for her, an equivalently exact fulfillment would demand no more and no less than what was expected. It would mean that the fulfillment be commensurate to the limited and imperfect expectations. Since the boundless fulfillment infinitely surpassed Israel's imperfect expectations, one cannot speak about mathematical equivalence between expectations and fulfillment. One can only speak of that fullness which brings to perfection the hitherto imperfect and educes potentialities hitherto unrecognized.

It is not so much therefore a matter of equivalence as a matter of *identity*. In Christ, Israel's expectations find fulfillment as the boy finds fulfillment

[1] Cf. J. L. McKenzie, "Messianism and the College Teacher of Sacred Doctrine," *Proceedings of the Society of Catholic College Teachers of Sacred Doctrine* (Card. Cushing College, Brookline 46, Mass., 1960) 34-53; A. Gelin, "Messianism," in *Dictionnaire de la Bible: Supplement* (Paris: 1955) V, 1206-1211.

in the grown and perfect man. There is identity but not equivalence. "Jesus is the reality," as Fr. McKenzie says, "which gives fullness to the reality of the Old Testament; He satisfies its desires, realizes its hopes and potentialities, gives it intelligibility. He is the fullness of Israel."[1]

As to mathematical equivalence between prediction and fulfillment, Christ chose to fulfill some predictions mathematically because they were in conformity with the divine plan and would not conflict with the true evaluation of His mission. Others He did not fulfill as Israel expected Him to fulfill them because such fulfillment was not in conformity with His mission and could only have led astray those whom he came to save. Thus He was born a king, but a lowly king, in Bethlehem and in unregal surroundings lest anyone think He had come to be a king after the manner of kings "of this world," or to found an earthly kingdom.

For the same reason He entered Jerusalem on Palm Sunday "meek and seated upon an ass," exactly as Zechariah (9:9) had predicted. Before Pilate he solemnly declared, "I am a king," but just as solemnly He declared, "My kingdom is not of this world." Christ fulfilled Israel's expectation of a king, but He transformed the idea of kingship by showing that He preferred to rule not by the mechanics of political power and conquest but by winning men's hearts and wills and minds to accept Him and acknowledge Him freely as their king.

The theme of the suffering servant (Is. 53) never captivated Israelite hearts as did the theme of the king and the kingdom, but Christ chose to stress this theme precisely because it was through His passion and death, through being the suffering servant, that He would reconcile all mankind to God and win for Himself as risen king the free and loving allegiance of all mankind.

The theme of the Messiah as prophet was never emphasized in the Old Testament, perhaps because it was too closely associated with the paradoxical theme of the suffering servant. But this theme too Christ chose to emphasize — by being the "Word" in the flesh, and by preaching as the prophets had preached. Jeremiah had predicted a new covenant and in fulfilling this prophecy at the Last Supper wherein He spoke explicitly of the chalice as "the new covenant in my blood," Christ chose not only to fulfill the prophecy of Jeremiah but to present Himself as the fulfillment of Israel's institutions of priesthood and sacrifice. For the Jews who had eyes to see, Christ was the one in whom all Israel's hopes were fulfilled, all her institutions completed, in whom all her true personality was expressed. He was in a word "the fullness of Israel."

It has seemed opportune to treat messianism at that point in Israel's

[1] McKenzie, *op. cit.*, 36.

history when she had only her faith in the prophetic word to sustain her in the dreadful catastrophe of 587. It would seem fitting to bring to a close the last hundred years of Judah with a treatment of Baruch, the little book entitled after Jeremiah's secretary. But it is reasonably certain that the book of Baruch is a late pseudonymous work, written long after the time of the historical Baruch, perhaps even as late as the early second century. We close the fateful history of Judah's last one hundred years, therefore, with Jeremiah and the treatise on messianism, and begin a new period in the history of the kingdom of God.

The new period, the time of the Babylonian exile, will be relatively short, 58 years at the most (597-539), 48 years at the least (587-539). It will make up for its brevity, however, by its importance. It will be a period of suffering and reflection, a period of deep spirituality, dynamic doctrinal development, and prolific literary productivity. More than that it will be a period of conversion, for out of it will come the purified "remnant."

The period begins "in the depths" of spiritual despair and apathy and ends on the heights. It will be the mission of the prophet Ezekiel, as we shall see, to raise Israel out of the depths, and the mission of the prophet Deutero-Isaiah to place her once more on the heights.

11

Judean Prophets during the Babylonian Captivity

1. The Exile Period

The significance of the Babylonian captivity may escape the reader if he fails to realize that the route the exiles took to Babylon in 597 was a route leading straight to the nation's conversion. It was, in short, one of the many crooked lines of history with which God wrote remarkably straight. As God Himself expressed it through the mouth of Deutero-Isaiah: "My thoughts are not your thoughts, nor are your ways my ways . . . as high as the heavens are above the earth, so high are my ways above your ways and my thoughts above your thoughts" (Is. 55:8-9).

Long ago God had said through the prophet Hosea: "I am going to persuade her and lead her into the wilderness and speak to her heart" (Hosea 2:14). The wilderness, as Israel was to discover in later years, would be Babylon, and the mouthpieces through whom God was to speak to the heart of Israel would be the prophets of the exile, Ezekiel and Deutero-Isaiah.

The actual reduction of Judah to a wasteland, predicted by Isaiah (6:11-13), did not take place until 587, but the invading armies of Babylon had breached the walls of Jerusalem in 597 and carried off into captivity the first of the Judean exiles. It was among these exiles of 597, strangely enough, and not among the exiles of 587, that the remaining stump of the burned out nation would retain that spark of life which would in God's good time be fanned again into a holy flame (Is. 6:13).

When they had gone into exile in 597, Jeremiah had predicted of them in the parable of the "good figs" (Jer. 24) that they would turn to God with all their heart and would one day be restored to the land of promise. Later he had written urging them to settle down peacefully among their captors and await in patience the day of the return (Jer. 29). Thus it happened that while Jeremiah in Jerusalem was making a last vain attempt to save the "bad figs," the "good figs" in exile in Babylon were undergoing the first phase in the process of the conversion predicted for them by Jeremiah.

The process, as we shall see, will be begun by Ezekiel and completed by Deutero-Isaiah. Before reading these prophets, however, something must be said about the chronology and the background of the exile period.

Chronology

612-609 The fall of Nineveh in 612 and the defeat of the last Assyrian armies at Haran in 609 mark the dissolution of the Assyrian empire.

605-562 Nebuchadnezzar succeeds Nabopolassar after defeating the Egyptians at Carchemish in 605. He reigns until 562.

597-562 The first invasion of Jerusalem and deportation to Babylon of Jews ("the good figs"), including Ezekiel and the young king Jehoiachin. The first harsh phase of the exile ends with the death of Nebuchadnezzar in 562.

592-570 Ezekiel's prophetic career: his call in 592, his last dated prophecy in 570.

587-582 Destruction of Jerusalem followed by the second (587) and third (582) deportations to Babylon. In January 586, a fugitive from the fallen capital brings the news to Ezekiel in Babylon, and a new phase in the prophet's preaching begins.

562-560 Evil-Merodach, favorable to the Jews, succeeds Nebuchadnezzar.

560-556 Neriglissar reigns until 556, succeeded briefly by Labashi-Merodach.

550-540 Conjectural dates for the prophetic career of Deutero-Isaiah.

Historical background

In the midst of the turbulent years between 612 and 539, history records the making and breaking of three great empires: the fall of the Assyrian

47

Nos. 46–50. Assyria.　**46**. Reconstruction of a mural from House K at Khorsabad, *ca.* 705 B.C.　**47**. A calcareous stone, winged bull in high relief, which once flanked a principal entrance to the throne room of Sargon II, 721–705, at Khorsabad (now at the Museum of the Oriental Institute of the University of Chicago); note composite, stylized art-form (man, bird,

bull), employed at a later date by Ezekiel in an immeasurably richer and more profound manner.   **48**. Pharaoh Rameses marched his army along the Dog River east of Beirut and marked his passage with an inscription six centuries before the Assyrian King Shalmaneser (left) followed precedent.   **49**. Ashurbanipal, 668–630, embellished his palace at Nineveh with sculptures in bas-relief; fighting lions on foot and on horseback seems to have been a royal sport.   **50**. Esarhaddon, king of Assyria, 681–669 B.C., commemorated his anointing with this bas-relief in stone; a magical figure, perhaps a priest, dressed with the head and wings of an eagle, served as minister. Nos. 46, 47 *courtesy:* Oriental Institute, University of Chicago; No. 48 *courtesy:* Matson Photo Service, Alhambra, California.

49

50

empire (1300-612), the rise and fall of the Neo-Babylonian empire (605-539), and the beginning of the Persian empire (539-333). What is even more important, history records during these years the Babylonian exile of the Jews (597 [587]-539), a period dominated by Jeremiah in Jerusalem, Ezekiel and Deutero-Isaiah in Babylon, and Nebuchadnezzar in both. It is with these men, the exiles, and the place of exile that we are concerned.[1]

Nebuchadnezzar

The moving spirit of the age is a young Babylonian general Nebuchadnezzar. He succeeds his father, Nabopolassar, in 605, after defeating the Egyptian armies at Carchemish and proceeds in the early decades of the sixth century to dominate the major part of the middle-eastern world from the Persian gulf around the fertile crescent to Egypt.

As the man whose generals destroyed the city of God, burned the Temple, and deported the Chosen People into captivity, it was inevitable that the name of Nebuchadnezzar should be associated in the popular mind with the enemies of God and His people. Religious considerations apart, however, Nebuchadnezzar is one of the titans of history. He is outstanding not only as a brilliant young general but as an able administrator and a prodigious builder. During the 43 years of his reign, he makes Babylon the center of artistic, cultural, and intellectual life in the ancient world. He repairs the famous tower of Babel and the great temple of Marduk, builds the "hanging gardens of Babylon" (one of the seven wonders of the ancient world), and constructs the incomparable Ishtar Gate and the processional boulevard that leads from it to the temple of Merodach. He also expands the irrigation system of Babylon's ancient canals and rebuilds the wall of Babylon to make that city the greatest walled city of the ancient world.

When Nebuchadnezzar dies in 562, after a long and prosperous reign, Babylon has reached her zenith. Under his successors she plunges rapidly to impotence and disintegration, falling eventually to Cyrus the Great and his Persian-Median armies in 539.

Long before the rise of Cyrus, however, Nebuchadnezzar enters the drama of sacred history. It is he, as we have seen, who brings Israel to the grave in 587, extinguishing her national life and threatening her spiritual life as well. It will be the task of Ezekiel to keep the spiritual life of Israel from flickering out in the uncongenial atmosphere of Babylon, and the task of Cyrus to restore to Israel her national life. But first we must consider the condition of the exiles during the Babylonian captivity.

[1] Cf. LFAP 185–192; Bright 323ff; Herodotus, *The Persian Wars*, I 178ff; Schedl, HOTOT, vol. 4, 341–445.

Both in 597 and 587, after foolish rebellions against Nebuchadnezzar, the Jews were gathered in concentration camps outside Jerusalem, bound with chains or ropes, and led off on a 400 mile death-march around the fertile crescent to Babylon. Those who could not stand the heat, the cruelty of the guards, and the exhaustion of the march were left to die. Those who eventually arrived in Babylon were put to work on the civic improvements of Nebuchadnezzar and on the plantations of the rich land-owners. In this way they were separated into colonies throughout the land and although they were certainly treated as hostages and perhaps even as slaves, there is no evidence to show they were oppressed as they had been in the latter part of the Egyptian captivity (cf. 2 Chr. 36:20; Ez. *passim*; Bar. 1:1-10; Dan. 1–3).

On the contrary, as the years of exile went on, many adapted themselves so thoroughly to life in Babylon that when Cyrus gave permission to return to Jerusalem they preferred to remain in Babylon. Others, however, the "good figs," the "remnant," did not succumb to the allurements of pagan Babylon but, purified by the rigors of the early years of captivity and undefiled by the riches and idolatry of Babylon, waited patiently, praying for the day when the prophecies of Jeremiah, Ezekiel, and Deutero-Isaiah would be fulfilled. In the year 539 their prayers were answered. Cyrus took Babylon and decreed the return of the Jews to Jerusalem.

In the meantime the preparation of the "good figs" to carry out the mission foreordained for them by God was not left to chance. It was begun by Ezekiel and completed by Deutero-Isaiah. It is Ezekiel, the prophet of the early years of the exile, whom we shall consider first.

2. Ezekiel

One of the priests deported from Jerusalem to Babylon in the deportation of 597, Ezekiel was called to the prophetic office in 592 (1:2) and preached among the exiles until 570, the year of his last dated sermon (29:17). He was married but lost his wife the same year that Jerusalem fell to Nebuchadnezzar (24:15-19).

Unquestionably one of the most colorful personalities in the Bible, Ezekiel's own people labelled him as "The one who is forever spinning parables" (21:5) and recognized in him an irrepressible pantomimist and actor — a man whose imagination was continually on fire.

In his inaugural vision he sees the weirdest of theophanies (1:4ff).

When he is commissioned a prophet, there is no simple touching of his lips as in the case of Jeremiah and Isaiah. He is given a scroll with the message he is to preach written upon it, told to eat and digest it, and then to preach (2:1ff)!

Like Jeremiah he foretells the siege and fall of Jerusalem, but unlike Jeremiah he acts it out in pantomime (4–5) and mimics the escape of the fugitives from Jerusalem by digging through the wall of his house and fleeing into the night (12). When the time comes for Nebuchadnezzar's armies to march upon Jerusalem, Ezekiel pantomimes the march with a sword, setting up guideposts for the sword to take as it leaves Babylon on its way to Jerusalem (21:14-19). When he preaches, he clenches his fists, stamps his feet and cries "alas" (6:11), or groans heart-rendingly until the exiles out of curiosity beg the reason (21:11-12).

What are we to think of so strange a prophet? As we know from the history of the other prophets, God used prophets as they were, adapting their personalities to suit His purpose. At the beginning of the exile He needed a man who would make a strong and vivid impression on the minds of the doubting and discouraged exiles. Ezekiel fitted the role to perfection. Words are easily forgotten, but actions inspire curiosity, arouse discussion, and endure in the imagination along with their significance. What Ezekiel did was not easily forgotten. While only a few of the embittered exiles came to his home at first to consult and listen to him (8:1; 14:1; 20:1), he succeeded eventually in interesting the crowd by his eccentric behavior, and before long his words and actions were being discussed from house to house and in the streets and lanes (33:30-33).

When Jerusalem fell in 587 the full significance of Ezekiel's behavior became apparent to all, and his position as a true prophet was established. From that time on there was little pantomime, much serious preaching, and elaborate planning for Israel's prophetically assured return and restoration.

Dominant ideas of Ezekiel

Ezekiel repeats such classic prophetical themes as God's punishment of Israel because she has been the special object of His love (16 and 23), God's punishmnt of sin wherever He finds it, even among the pagans (25–32), and God's disgust with idolatry (*passim*). To these classic themes Ezekiel adds the teaching that God always acts for His own glory (20:9, 22; 36:20-22), and that those to whom God gives a ministry have a grave responsibility (3:17-21; 33; 34:1-19). While he does not neglect the principle of retribution in its collective and national sense, unlike anyone before him he emphasizes the principle of individual retribution (3; 14; 18; 33), although he is not specific as to the nature of the retribution. Following the line of Jeremiah, he speaks of a new covenant and a new David (11:14-21; 16:59-63; 17:22-24; 34:23-25).

Division

Unlike the books of Isaiah and Jeremiah, Ezekiel is fairly well ordered both topically and chronologically despite changes and additions by later editors. The style, while strong in places and lofty on occasions, is loaded with symbols and allegories and is perhaps too repetitious for modern tastes. The book is divided into three parts.

I. ch. 1—24 contains for the most part threats against Jerusalem and predictions of her certain destruction, practically all dating before 587.

II. ch. 25—32 contains threats against the nations in which Ezekiel stresses the classic prophetic teaching that God is the maker of history and the punisher of sin wherever He finds it.

III. ch 33—48 contains Ezekiel's encouraging prophecies concerning the national and religious restoration of Israel, almost all dating after 587. Part III can be divided as follows:

33—39 Ezekiel consoles the exiles after the fall of Jerusalem.

40—43 Ezekiel designs an ideal new Temple.

44—46 Ezekiel outlines an elaborate liturgical worship.

47—48 Ezekiel symbolizes the spiritual benefits that will flow from the restored Temple and sketches out a new territorial division of Palestine in relation to the Temple.

Significant passages in Ezekiel

Part One / Ez. 1—24 / Before 587

1—3 Ezekiel's inaugural vision, his audience, his commission and responsibilities as a prophet, the means he is to use to make his stubborn audience listen to him.

1:1-28 The inaugural vision. The symbolism of Ezekiel's unique inaugural vision is directed to the instruction of the exiles and to the strengthening of their faith. The exiles are in danger in Babylon of succumbing to the pagan belief that the true God who dwells in Jerusalem is, like the pagan gods, only a local divinity incapable of exercising dominion outside His own territory and capable of being conquered by a more powerful local divinity. In the light of these false beliefs, the approaching fall of Jerusalem may well be misinterpreted by the pusillanimous exiles. The inaugural vision is designed to offset such beliefs by showing: (a) God is not bound to Jerusalem. He leaves Jerusalem and comes (from the north — the exiles' route from Jerusalem to Babylon) to visit His people in exile. (b) He is a universal God, as powerful in Babylon as in Jerusalem. His universality is symbolized by the multi-winged, multi-wheeled, multi-eyed *sedia gestatoria* capable of moving in any direction without difficulty. (c) The pagan nations are His servants. This is symbolized by the "cherubim" (tutelary divinities of the Babylonians, with the head of a man, body of a lion, wings of an eagle, and limbs of a bull), who are shown in the vision as God's lackeys, bearers of His throne (cf. illustrations of the cherubim in LFAP 217 and ANEP nn. 644, 646, 647).

2:1-8 Ezekiel's audience. God reminds Ezekiel that He is sending him to a people hard-faced and stubborn. These are the "good figs" of Jer. 24, the exiles of 597, but before the fall of Jerusalem they are as unbelieving and unheeding as their fellow citizens back in Judah (vv. 3, 7, 26).

3:1-15 Ezekiel's commission as a prophet. The divine message is written on a scroll which the prophet is to eat, digest, and then preach. God instructs Ezekiel (vv. 16-20) concerning his obligations as a prophet by likening them to those of a sentry guarding a city during wartime (cf. ch. 33). Finally, Ezekiel is told in a metaphorical way (vv. 22-27) not to preach in public until God commands. Until then he is to do pantomimes in order to attract attention and arouse discussion. At the opportune moment God will inspire him to speak.

4–7 In ch. 4 Ezekiel is told to pantomime the siege of Jerusalem, in 5:1-4 the slaughter and dispersal of the Jerusalemites. From 5:5 to 7:27 he preaches, spelling out prosaically the meaning of the pantomimes.

8–11 Carried in vision to Jerusalem in September 591, Ezekiel is shown the depths of idolatry to which his fellow-citizens have descended. It is because of such rampant infidelity that God will proceed to punish the wicked, destroy the city, and abandon His Temple. It should be noted that these chapters restate more emphatically and more dramatically what Ezekiel has already prophesied in pantomime and word in ch. 4–7: Jerusalem is doomed, not because God is being conquered by the invaders but because God is leaving Jerusalem to be punished by the Babylonians, the instruments of His justice.

8:1ff   Idolatry in the Temple. V. 5, Asherah, a Chanaanite idol; v. 10, reptiles and beasts, probably Egyptian deities; v. 14, Tammuz, a Babylonian deity; v. 16, Re, the Egyptian sun-god.

9:1ff   Punishment of the idolaters and sparing of the innocent who are specially marked to be passed over at the time of the slaughter.

10:1ff   Description of God, as seen in the inaugural vision (ch. 1), commanding the destruction of the city and preparing to abandon His Temple.

11:1ff   A vision of God leaving the Temple (vv. 22-23) followed by a denunciation of those who persist in saying God will not destroy Jerusalem (vv. 1-13) and promises of restoration for the exiles already in Babylon (vv. 14-21).

12–14   Ch. 12–14, which should be read as a unit, deal with the mistaken ideas of the exiles.

12:1-20   Ezekiel drives home his prediction of the fall of Jerusalem by pantomiming the flight of the people from the doomed city. 12:21-28 introduces ch. 13.

13:1ff   Ch. 13 is directed against the false prophets, insisting that the prophecies of destruction, at which the people are scoffing because "the days drag on, and no vision ever comes to anything" (12:22), will indeed be fulfilled, while the predictions of the false prophets will be shown up for what they are, "the whitewashing of the flimsy wall of hope raised by the people" (13:10-16). In 13:17-23 Ezekiel excoriates the prophetesses who encourage the people to abide in their delusions (cf. Jer. 28; 29:15ff).

14:1-11   Ezekiel declares there can be no compromise with idolatry. In 14:12-23 he punctures another illusion of the exiles. They believe that at least for the sake of those who are holy in Jerusalem, God will spare the city. Ezekiel replies that the doom is inexorable. The city would not be saved even if men as holy as Noah, Daniel, and Job were to intercede for it.

15–17   The allegories in ch. 15–17 prove the point made in 14:23: "You shall then know that it was not without reason that I did to it what I did."

15:1ff The Vine (Israel) is no better in itself than any other tree (nation) of the forest. Only the gratuitous love of God manifested in the Sinai covenant has made them any different. Since they have rejected the covenant, they are fit, like any other wood of the forest, for the fire.

16:1ff Ezekiel elaborates Hosea's allegory of Israel the adulterous wife (cf. Hosea 1–3; Is. 1:21-26; Jer. 2:2; 3:6-8) to detail Israel's long history of infidelity (cf. ch. 23 where Ezekiel applies the same allegory to the two sister kingdoms of Israel and Judah, both of whom have been unfaithful to their divine spouse). Note the promise of restoration and the new covenant in 16:53ff.

17:1ff Allegory of the eagles (foreign powers) and the kings of Judah (tip of a cedar, vine) Jehoiachin and Zedekiah, concluded with a reference to God's planting of a "tender shoot" from the crest of the cedar which "shall become a majestic cedar" under which shall nestle birds of every feather — Ezekiel's metaphorical description of the Messiah and his universal kingdom (vv. 22-24; cf. Jer. 23:5-6).

18–20 God's way of dealing with Israel in the past has led to some confusion and to some false hopes. Ezekiel explains God's way of dealing with individuals as individuals (ch. 18), his sorrow over Israel's fate (ch. 19), the dominant place that God's honor holds in His government of Israel's fate down through history (ch. 20).

18:1ff Ezekiel begins by puncturing a fatal delusion of the exiles. By overemphasizing the principle of collective responsibility, the exiles have been attributing their misfortunes to the sins of their ancestors and deluding themselves into believing that they as individuals are innocent and God as a consequence is unjust (cf. vv. 2, 25, 29). Ezekiel, who has already shown the force and pertinence of the principle of collective responsibility in ch. 16, now concentrates on the principle of individual responsibility (already indicated in passing in ch. 3; 9; 14). Like Jeremiah (16:10-13), Ezekiel must convince the exiles that their personal sins play a part in their misfortunes before he can hope to convert them. Hence, in each case presented — father (vv. 5-9), son (vv. 10-13), grandson (vv. 14-20) — the individual is judged on his own merits (v. 20), and the ultimate judgment is based not on the individual's past but on his present and future personal actions (vv. 21-24). God therefore is by no means unfair (vv.

24-29), and if Israel will only repent, she will be saved (vv. 30-32).

On the origin of the exiles' erroneous thinking, the reader should confer the impact of the collective Sinai covenant and particularly the text of Exod. 20:5; on the belief in individual responsibility before and under the Sinai covenant, Gen. 18:25; 1 Sam. 2:25; 26:23.

The emphasis given to personal responsibility by Ezekiel leads in the following centuries to doubts and speculations about the adequacy of merely earthly retribution (cf. Job and Qoheleth) and becomes a milestone in the development of the doctrine of retribution in the future life, clearly taught for the first time in the second century books of Daniel, 2 Maccabees, and Wisdom.

19:1ff The allegorical lament for the royal princes, Jehoahaz and Jeho-iachin, and for Mother Israel (the vine), gives eloquent expression to the sentiments of God more prosaically expressed in the last verses of ch. 18: "Why should you die, O House of Israel? For I have no pleasure in the death of anyone who dies," is the oracle of the Lord God. "Return and live!"

20:1ff If Israel is as wicked as Ezekiel claims, why has God so often in the past saved her from destruction? To this objection which presumes from God's mercy in the past that He will be merciful to them in their present plight, Ezekiel responds that God has only been restrained from destroying His people by the consideration of His own honor, since, if He had so acted, He might appear unfaithful to His promises and thus give occasion among the nations for the profanation of His name.

21–24 As the day for the destruction of Jerusalem advances, Ezekiel's invectives against the idolatrous capital grow in intensity.

21:1ff He begins, in the "Song of the Sword" (vv. 1-22) by dramatizing the approaching destruction of Jerusalem. He then pantomimes the sword as undecided whether to take the road to Jerusalem or to Rabbah, the capital of Ammon, and has Nebuchadnezzar, the wielder of God's sword, decide after the usual divinatory practices to attack Jerusalem first (vv. 23-28). In vv. 30-32, Ezekiel speaks of the downfall of Zedekiah and the ruinous state of the monarchy which is to last "until he comes who has the claim against the city." If the "he" here is the Messiah of Gen. 49:10, then the "it" is probably the diadem mentioned in

v. 31. Some, however, consider the text a reference to Nebuchadnezzar, who is the one who by God's design has "the claim against the city."

22:1ff Jerusalem is scathingly entitled "the bloody city" and the list of the crimes of the present generation is given in detail.

23:1ff By means of an allegory similar to ch. 16, Ezekiel shows that the guilt of the Israelites of the present generation (ch. 22) has so characterized their history that even after the destruction of the harlot, Oholah (the northern kingdom), Oholibah (the southern kingdom) has not had sense enough to learn a lesson but has continued in unbridled idolatry down to the present.

24:1ff On January 10, 588, Nebuchadnezzar invests Jerusalem and Ezekiel climaxes his preaching by allegorizing Jerusalem as a rusty pot which along with its contents (the people of Jerusalem) is destroyed by the flames (vv. 1-14). In the evening of the same day (vv. 15-24), Ezekiel's wife dies, and he is commanded by God to show none of the usual signs of mourning the better to symbolize the paralyzing shock of the exiles when in turn they receive the news of the fall of Jerusalem and the burning of the Temple. Instead of mourning they are to enter into themselves and concentrate on their sins (v. 23) which have brought about the catastrophe. At the same time God promises Ezekiel he will be relieved of his temporary dumbness on the day a messenger arrives with the news of the fall of Jerusalem (vv. 25-27).

In the first period of his preaching (ch. 1—24), Ezekiel has been at pains to prepare the people for the destruction of Jerusalem so that when the day comes, they will be able to reflect upon the fact that the holy city fell not because God was weak before the onslaught of the Babylonians, but because God Himself had decreed its destruction as a punishment and had summoned the Babylonians to accomplish His decree.

Once the exiles realize this, Ezekiel can hope to convert them. Once they realize that their sins are the cause of its fall, he can call them to repentance, hope, and purification. This will be the purpose of the third part of Ezekiel (ch. 33—48). Ezekiel's mouth will be opened in the sense that now he will be able to speak freely to a people who will no longer scoff at him, but will listen meekly, humbly, and penitently. He will no longer, therefore, have to restrict himself to preaching in and around his own house.

Before the fall of Jerusalem in 587, the exiles were proud and confident, stubbornly insisting Jerusalem could not perish. Ezekiel's preaching as a consequence had been harsh and threatening. After 587, the people are in despair. To all appearances Israel is dead. The exiles are in need now not of threats but of comfort, consolation, hope, confidence. Ezekiel's preaching in ch. 33—48 reflects this need

33:1ff With the fall of Jerusalem, Ezekiel's prophecies are confirmed and his reputation as a prophet assured. Once more, as at the beginning of his prophetic career (3:16-21), God impresses upon him his responsibility as spiritual watchman of Israel (vv. 1-9). To assure the discouraged exiles that God's mercy awaits them if they will only repent, Ezekiel recapitulates the main points of ch. 18, concerning the responsibility of each individual to return to God (vv. 10-20). He then tells how the news of the fall of Jerusalem was brought to him by a fugitive in January 586 (vv. 21-22), and how God commanded him to blast the illusion of those who put their hope in the few Jews remaining in the ravaged homeland (vv. 23-29; cf. Jer. 40—44). Finally, God assures Ezekiel that though the exiles look upon him at present only as an entertainer, they will soon (when the news of the fall of Jerusalem spreads among the people) know him as a true prophet (vv. 30-33).

34—37 By means of a series of contrasts, involving the leaders, the land, and the people, Ezekiel paints for the exiles the picture of a happy future in which God will shepherd them, the land will be prosperous, and the people will rise from the tomb of exile to exist once more as a unified nation.

34:1ff Ezekiel contrasts Israel's last kings, the bad shepherds (vv. 2-10) with the Good Shepherd, God, who will lead His flock (vv. 11-22; cf. John 10:11-16; Ps. 23) and set up for them one shepherd, the Messiah (vv. 23-31; cf. 37:22-24; Is. 11:1-9; Jer. 23:1-6).

35—36 Ezekiel contrasts the dire future in store for Mount Seir and the Edomites (ch. 35) with the prosperous messianic future in store for the mountains of Israel (ch. 36). The reader should note the similarity of ch. 35 to Obadiah; and of ch. 36:27 to Jer. 31:31-34 concerning the new covenant (cf. Ez. 37:26-27).

37:1ff Ezekiel first contrasts the dismal present (the dry bones of Israel buried in exile in Babylon) with the glorious future when God will once more breathe life into the dead nation resurrecting it from the tomb of exile (vv. 1-14; cf. Is. 26:11-19). He then continues in the allegory of the two sticks (one representing the northern kingdom, the other the southern kingdom) to describe the reunion of the two kingdoms under the Messiah, and the everlasting new covenant that God will make with His people (vv. 15-28).

38—39 In the apocalyptic allegory of Gog and his mob, Ezekiel consoles the pessimistic exiles by showing the rallying of the forces of anti-God to try to destroy the restored exiles (ch. 38) and the cataclysmic defeat inflicted upon them by God (ch. 39). It is Ezekiel's way of saying what Christ would say more simply (John 16:33), "In the world you will have affliction. But take courage, I have overcome the world." The same teaching will be found in Isaiah (24—26), Zechariah, Joel, Daniel, 1 and 2 Thessalonians, and the Apocalypse of St. John. These passages are all in the apocalyptic style, which will be treated more at length with the book of Daniel.

40—48 In ch. 8—11, Ezekiel described the abominations that had forced God to abandon the Old Temple. In his consoling vision of the new Temple (40—42), the return of God to the Temple (43:1-4), the re-organization of Temple worship (43—46), the special blessings proceeding from the new Temple (47:1-12), and the new division of the land around the new Temple (48:13-35), Ezekiel reverses the shameful events of ch. 8-11 and sketches for the remnant the ideal theocratic state.

The date of the Temple vision is 572, fourteen years after the fall of Jerusalem. The exiles have evidently begun to look ahead. Ezekiel does the same, but he keeps an eye out on the past. In his plan for the future he removes the palace of the prince far from the Temple and curtails previous royal privileges (43:7-9; 46:1-18). He sets up an elaborate series of gates and courts (40—42) to screen out the unworthy and the aliens (44:5-9) and legislates a more exact liturgical worship (43—46 *passim*). These prescriptions are intended to correct the aberrations in worship brought about in the past by the king's control of the Temple and by the promiscuous entrance of non-Israelites into the Temple of God.

Ezekial's work, for all practical purposes, ends with his last dated discourse in 570 (29:17). But his influence continues. His vision of the ideal theocratic state influences the Jews of the following centuries and earns for him the title "Father of Judaism." His apocalyptic vision of Gog and his army (38–39) influences the apocalyptic writers and earns for him the title "Father of apocalyptic." More important still, his work brings the first part of the exile period to a close with the formation of "the good figs," the remnant, who will keep alive the true religion in Babylon until the return to Judah in 538.

Out of this remnant will come the writers of the literature of reflection on Israel's past: the author of Lamentations, the author of Kings (written or at least re-edited sometime after 562), the authors of many psalms (cf. Pss. 79; 74; 89; 77; 102; 123; 125; 129; 130), and especially the author of Is. 40–55, the great prophet of the last part of the exile known as Deutero-Isaiah. Before treating the deeply theological writings of Deutero-Isaiah, the reader is urged to read the books of Lamentations and Obadiah and the psalms of the exile period mentioned above.

3. Lamentations

For some God's medicinal punishment is only the occasion for outraged cries of rebellion. For others it is the occasion for an honest examination of conscience and gentle tears of repentance, softened by the realization that God's punishing hand is the hand of a father always outstretched to welcome back a repentant son. In the Lamentations,[1] Judah preserved the expression in poetry of one of her finest hours — the hour of honest admission of guilt and sincere return to God, the hour Jeremiah had preached so long to effect and succeeded in achieving only after his death.

Sometime after the fall of Jerusalem or on the return from the exile, a sensitive religious poet went back to the burnt and devastated city, sat solitary on the rubble and meditated upon the scene around him. Out of these melancholy meditations came the five short elegies known as the Lamentations, describing in poignant and moving poetry the ruin of the city of God and the heartrending misery of its desolate citizens.

In his elegies the poet uses an alphabetic structure, a favorite Hebraic poetic form in which each strophe or verse begins with a successive letter of the Hebrew alphabet (cf. Pss. 111; 112; 119 and Knox's translation of the Lamentations).

In the Lamentations the author not only describes the catastrophe that has overtaken Jerusalem but points out clearly that Judah's punishment

[1] Cf. CCHS par. 501ff; G. Montague, *Lamentations*, OTRG No. 19.

is not from chance but from the hand of God, the Maker of history, the first cause, using Babylon as His instrument (cf. 1:5, 12-15; 2:1-8; 2:17, 22; 3:2-16). The reason for the catastrophe is not merely Judah's sins but her continual apostasy (cf. 1:5, 14, 18; 3:42, 4:6; 5:16). The purpose of the punishment is medicinal, calling for penance (cf. 3:19, 40 *passim*). There is reason for hope and confidence because of God's goodness (cf. 1:21; 2:20; 4:22; 3:19-24; 3:31-33; 4:23; 5:1ff; 5:19-22).

In the Lamentations the dominant ideas of the author are sentiments of sorrow, amendment, and conversion — all the sentiments Jeremiah and Ezekiel sought to inspire in the hearts of their recalcitrant countrymen. The punishment, the author assures us, has not been in vain. It has been a healing medicine (cf. Jer. 30:1-17).

4. Obadiah

For the reader who remembers the little book of Nahum, whose sole theme was the downfall of Nineveh in punishment for crimes against the Lord and Maker of history, it will come as no surprise to meet another minor prophet, Obadiah, whose whole book consists in nothing more than a single oracle against one nation — Edom.[1]

Unlike Nahum, which can be dated with some certainty to the years immediately preceding the destruction of Nineveh in 612, the book of Obadiah gives no certain evidence of when it was composed. It looks back to the time of the fall of Jerusalem and forward to the time of Edom's downfall and Judah's triumph. It may be dated as late as the fourth century, but for reasons of convenience it is best treated in conjunction with the fall of Jerusalem (cf. vv. 10-14).

The reader should recall before reading Obadiah that the enmity between Judah and Edom had ancient roots. Despite the fact that the Edomites were descended from Jacob's brother, Esau, they had nevertheless refused passage through their country to the Israelites on their way to the Promised Land (Num. 20:18ff). David had subdued the Edomites in the tenth century (2 Sam. 8:13). Joram did the same in the ninth century (2 Kings 3:20-22). Not only Obadiah, but Amos (1:11-12), Jeremiah (49:7-22), Ezekiel (24:12-14; 35:1-15), the author of Lamentations (4:21-23), and a psalmist (Ps. 137) inveighed against them.

Obadiah begins with a prediction of Edom's downfall and a condemnation of her pride (vv. 2-9); then, with glances at the fateful summer of 587, he explains the reason for Edom's downfall. He reminds the Edomites of their guilt in exulting over and assisting in the destruction of Judah

[1] Cf. JBC 443–445.

by the Babylonians (vv. 10-14). For this crime against their brother nation the Day of the Lord is coming upon them (vv. 15-16). Judah on the other hand will be restored, and Yahweh will again reign as King on Mount Zion (vv. 17-21).

The theme of Obadiah is simple, yet it gives rise to profound questions concerning the relations God expects to exist between nations. It presumes the principle of solidarity and consequent collective punishment. It presumes also the existence of obligations on the part of one nation toward another and the just anger and retribution of God when these obligations are not fulfilled. In these days of the United Nations and the captive satellite countries, the theological implications of the book of Obadiah must give reason for reflection to all.

5. The Last Years of the Exile

When Ezekiel died sometime after 570, he left behind him a people who were still enslaved, still discouraged, still weak in the faith. But he did not leave them deceived. He had told them that Jerusalem would fall and he had explained to them the theological reasons that made its fall a foregone conclusion. When his predictions were fulfilled in 587, even the roots of the exiles' self-deception were destroyed.

On such uncluttered soil, Ezekiel had planted new seeds of hope, promising the exiles that though the nation might lie dead and buried in Babylon, as lifeless as dead bones on the surface of the soil, the day would come when the wind of God would sweep through the valley of death, put a new spirit and a new heart into the dry bones, and bring the nation out of the tomb into the land of the living once more (Ez. 37). He sowed other seeds as well, seeds of national and religious reconstruction that would put forth shoots in the second spring of Israel's history that followed the exile (Ez. 40-48).

Ezekiel had planted. Another prophet, Deutero-Isaiah, would water the seeds, and in 539 God Himself, through His servant, Cyrus, would give the increase. Keeping the seed and the sprout alive, however, until the harvest, would require patience, hope, and an iron faith. These were the virtues of Deutero-Isaiah and the virtues he inspired in the discouraged and indifferent exiles during the last trying years of the exile.

Chronology of the last years of the Babylonian exile

592-570 Ezekiel clears the ground and plants the seed.

562-560 Evil-Merodach, favorable to the Jews, succeeds Nebuchadnezzar.

560-556 Neriglissar reigns until 556, is succeeded briefly by Labashi-
Merodach.

550-540 Conjectural dates for the prophetic career of Deutero-Isaiah.

559-530 Cyrus becomes prince of Anshan in 559, captures Ecbatana and
becomes king of the Medes and the Persians in 549, beginning
his meteoric rise to world domination.
Nabonidus and Belshazzar, the Crown Prince, Babylon's last
kings.

546-539 Cyrus conquers Croesus, king of Lydia, in 546, takes Babylon
in 539, becomes master of the Middle East before his death in
530. In 539, he sends the Jews back to Palestine.

Historical background

When Nebuchadnezzar died in 562, the heartbeat of the Babylonian
empire ceased. Babylon continued for another twenty-three years like a
dead knight held up by his armor. Evil-Merodach, Neriglissar, Labashi-
Merodach, Nabonidus and Belshazzar inherited a great empire but not the
genius for administering it. Under their inept direction the empire dis-
integrated from within. When the end came, it came swiftly.

Cyrus and the exiles

Shortly after the death of Nebuchadnezzar in 562, a new star had begun
to rise in Persia, a few hundred miles east of Babylon. Rallying the Persian
tribes in 559, Cyrus, the son of Cambyses, the Achaemenid, became king of
Persia. In 549 he conquered Media and acclaimed himself king of the
Persians and the Medes. In Babylon, Nabonidus was only mildly alarmed.
But in 546 the alarm turned to panic when Cyrus marched his armies
across northern Syria and conquered Croesus, the fabulously wealthy
king of Lydia (modern Turkey) at the Halys river and at Sardis.

Among the exiles in Babylon meanwhile, a new prophet had arisen to
succeed Ezekiel — Deutero-Isaiah — who saw in Cyrus God's servant-
instrument who would destroy Babylon, send the Jews back to Palestine,
and thus fulfill the ancient prophecies. His predictions would soon become
reality.

Cyrus' victorious campaigns continued. In 539 his general, Gobryas, took

Babylon without a battle. Not long after, Cyrus decreed the return of the Jews to Palestine; the prophecies of Jeremiah, Ezekiel, and Deutero-Isaiah were vindicated.

With regard to the exiles, it is true that when Nebuchadnezzar died their condition was greatly improved. The new king, Evil-Merodach released Jehoiachin from prison and granted him the privileges of hostage-royalty (2 Kings 25:27). Many of the exiles became free and gathered in their own towns and settlements. Some became business men — records found by archeologists tell of one Jewish family, Murashu and Sons, having commercial transactions not only with the Babylonians but with the Persians, Medes, and Arameans. Others took government positions in which they quickly rose to prominence as we learn from the success of Daniel and his three friends. It is true, too, that as the years went on, many among the exiles got along so well and adapted themselves so thoroughly to life in Babylon that when Cyrus gave permission to return to Jerusalem, they preferred to remain in pagan Babylon.

The others, however, the "good figs," the "remnant," did not succumb to the allurements of the great capital but persevered and returned to Jerusalem. That they persevered was due to many factors, not the least of which was the white hot rhetoric of Deutero-Isaiah. When he appeared upon the scene after the death of Ezekiel, many of the exiles had been already purified by the rigors of the early part of the captivity and were as yet untainted by the riches and idolatry of Babylon. But they were discouraged and confused. They could see no escape from the might of Babylon and they were in danger of forgetting their place in God's plan for the world. They knew that the Sinai covenant was finished but they were unable to look back to the absolute promise made to Abraham nor far enough into the future to visualize the reality of the new covenant promised by Jeremiah and Ezekiel. It was at this critical moment in Israel's destinies that Deutero-Isaiah began to preach.

6. Deutero-Isaiah (Is. 40—55)

We know nothing about Deutero-Isaiah beyond the few details that can be gleaned from autobiographical remarks in his work;[1] and even these are doubtful, though most authors consider 61:1-3 (4-11) as certainly, and 50:4-11, as possibly, autobiographical. Internal evidence in ch. 40—55 indicates that he preached in Babylon between 550 and 540. Indications in ch. 56—66 point to an apostolate back in Jerusalem after the exile

[1] Cf. E. Kissane, The Book of Isaiah, II; Bright 335–344; C. Stuhlmueller, Isaiah 40–66, OTRG No. 20.

but authors are divided on whether these chapters are the work of Deutero-Isaiah or some other postexilic prophet.

Like the author of the Iliad, Deutero-Isaiah is a poet whose writing stirred the ordinary man and inspired the intellectuals. He is the Dante of the Old Testament, the poet *par excellence* of the Bible. He moves consistently on the lyric heights, in turn rhapsodical when contemplating the great things God has in store for Israel in the future and tragic when faced with the exiles' stubborn resistance to that vision in the present.

Authenticity

Until a century ago it was popularly believed that all 66 chapters of the book of Isaiah had been written by the great Judean prophet of the late eighth century.[1] It was, of course, nonetheless obvious that in ch. 40—66 the prophet was addressing himself to the Jews in exile and not to the Jews in Jerusalem of his own time, but it was always taken for granted that the prophet who could predict the Babylonian exile in his rebuke to King Hezekiah (Is. 39:5-7) in 705 could just as easily project himself 150 years into the future and speak to the Jews in exile as if he were living amongst them.

In an uncritical age such a belief went unchallenged. In the last century, however, more critical readers discovered innumerable reasons for denying to Proto-Isaiah the last 26 chapters of his book, postulating in his place a prophet living in Babylon during the exile.

The arguments in favor of a distinct exilic Isaiah are now quite convincing. Besides the difference in style and theological emphasis, the following points can be singled out: (a) nothing whatever is said about events in Jerusalem at the time of Hezekiah; (b) the prophet addresses himself exclusively to the exiles in Babylon; (c) the captivity and the destruction of Jerusalem are past, not future, events (cf. 40:1-2; 47:6; 48:20); (d) the prophet is concerned with the end of the exile and the return to Jerusalem; (e) Cyrus is spoken of as a contemporary (cf. 44:28; 45:1); (f) neither Jeremiah nor Ezekiel mentions the prophecies of Is. 40—66, though these prophecies would have been telling arguments for them in their preaching about the end of the exile.

Division

The division of these chapters has long been, and still remains, largely conjectural. The similarity in style and thought content with earlier chap-

[1] Cf. EB nn. 291–295; CCHS par. 476ff; JBC 366–386; C. Stuhlmueller, *Isaiah 40–66*, OTRG No. 20.

ters in Part I of Isaiah would seem to indicate that a number of chapters in Part I have been written by the author or authors of Part II. In light of the conflicting views on the subject, it seems best to posit a school of Isaian authors (the disciples of the first Isaiah, cf. Is. 8:16; 50:10; 51:7), whose works, because of their relation by way of style and content, were all embraced under the one volume entitled Isaiah, edited some time after the exile, possibly as late as the middle of the third century.

Whether such an explanation is adequate or not, the whole book of Isaiah can be divided on the basis of style, content, and historical background as follows:

PROTO-ISAIAH   ch. 1–11; 15–20; 22–23; 28–33. (Ch. 36–39 from 2 Kings after 562).

DEUTERO-ISAIAH ch. 40–55; Servant canticles: 42:1-4; 49:1-6; 50:4-9; 52:13–53:12. Parts of 56–66.

TRITO-ISAIAH   ch. 11:10-16; 13–14; 21; 24–27; 34–35; 56–66; Servant Canticles (?).

In reading Is. 40–55, the reader must not only put himself in Babylon in the sixth century, he must remember that the purpose of the author is to console, encourage, and inspire the disillusioned, faint-hearted exiles who see no hope of returning to Jerusalem and are in danger of being won over to the pagan idolatry of Babylon. While Deutero-Isaiah addresses himself for the most part to this large group who are wavering between abandoning hope or putting their trust in God and His prophet, there are indications throughout of two other groups in Isaiah's audience: his disciples and his enemies.

To encourage and inspire the dispirited exiles, Deutero-Isaiah repeatedly stresses the following truths:

a) God is omnipotent and eternal; all flesh (human power) is nothing in comparison.

d) God is creator of the universe; saving Israel is a simple matter for Him.

c) God alone has foretold the future in the past; as a consequence His promises of restoration in the immediate future can be believed with confidence.

d) The gods of Babylon are non-entities; the God of Israel alone is truly God.

e) God will save Israel because He has a mission for her: to make Him known to the whole world.

f) God will use the vicarious suffering of the Servant to save the whole world.

Since critical opinion on the Servant Canticles is divided roughly into two views, (a) the collective (the Remnant as the Ideal Israel); (b) the individual (the servant as a concrete individual of the present or an ideal individual of the future), we shall treat the collective interpretation first in the course of chapters 40—55, and then all the canticles taken as a separate work interpolated into 40—55 at a later date but originally written about one ideal individual, the Messiah of Israel and the world.

Significant passages in Deutero-Isaiah

40:1-5 Announcement of the end of the bondage in Babylon and the beginning of the new exodus. Vv. 1-11 represent the inaugural vision and mission of Deutero-Isaiah.

6-8 No need for the exiles to fear the might of Babylon; it is grass.

9-11 Let Jerusalem, the capital, announce to her daughter cities that God is leading back the exiles as a shepherd leads his flock.

12-25 God's omnipotent power contrasted with the helplessness of Babylon's lifeless idols should encourage the exiles to trust in their God. Is. 41:6-7 belongs between 40:20 and 40:21.

26-31 The God who watches over every star in the sky will not forget His chosen nation. There is no reason for Israel to be discouraged.

41:1-4 A judgment scene in which it is shown that God alone has predicted the rise and conquests of Cyrus (cf. 41:25; 44:26-28; 45:1-7).

5-12 The nations fear Cyrus, but Israel need not fear because God is with her and Cyrus is merely God's servant (cf. 44:28; 45:1).

13-20 God encourages Israel promising an end to her difficulties and a renewal of the ancient miracles in a new exodus.

21-29 Again God reminds the exiles that He alone, in contrast to the senseless idols, was able to foretell the victories of Cyrus.

42:1-4 FIRST SERVANT CANTICLE: Israel is God's servant and will fulfill her mission to the Gentiles with God's help. Authors are divided on the interpretation of 42:1-4. Some refer it directly to the Messiah, either in a direct Christological sense, or in a direct but ideal sense. Others refer it to the ideal Israel. In corroboration of this latter interpretation, cf. 41:8-9, 10, 13; 42:5-9; 43:7, 10, 21; 44:1-8; 44:21-22.

5-9   Israel by leading the nations out of darkness will fulfill God's designs for her (note parallel between 42:6-7 and 49:5-8).

10-12   Let the exiles sing a new canticle in praise of God who is about to begin the conquest of Babylon.

42:13-17   God will lead out the exiles but destroy the apostates.

18-25   Israel has been blind to her divine mission and God as a result has been forced to punish her.

43:1-8   But God loves them nonetheless and will redeem those who have been formed and made for His glory.

9-13   No one among the nations could ever have foretold that this people, blind and deaf to God's call, would nevertheless become God's witness (v. 10) through whom the nations would come to know and believe in God.

14-21   For this reason God will destroy Babylon (v. 14) and make His chosen people forget the old Exodus by effecting a new and more miraculous one from the bondage of Babylon.

22ff   In the past Israel sinned against Him, but now God is ready to forgive (22—28) and to renew them in spirit (44:1-5). 44:6-20: the folly of idolatry.

44:21-23   Let Israel remember God has forgiven her. Let her praise Him for He is about to reveal to her again His redeeming love.

44—46   God the Maker of history will use the pagan Cyrus as His serv-
44:24-28   ant-instrument to lead Israel out of exile. Israel will then be able to bring God's revelation to the whole world.

God's promise to restore Jerusalem by means of Cyrus.

45:1-8   The call and mission of Cyrus.

9-13   No one can thwart God's plans since all creatures are as clay in His hands.

14-25   The salvation of the world through Israel: all nations will worship the God of Israel (14-17). God's plan for the world was revealed to Israel and to no one else (18-21); therefore let all nations turn to the one true God (22-25).

46:1-13   A rebuke to the rebellious Israelites. Let them contrast the true God with the idols of Babylon (1-7). As God in the past foretold events to come, so now He foretells the coming of Cyrus to bring about the restoration of Israel (8-13).

47:1-15   Babylon will be widowed for her treatment of Israel (1-7). All her wisdom and wise men will be of no avail (8-15).

48:1-16   As God foretold to Israel her destruction (1-6), so He now foretells to them despite their obstinacy the coming of Cyrus to destroy Babylon (7-16).

48:17-21   God tells them what might have been their fate if they had obeyed in the past (17-19). Despite the past, they will get another chance. Let them go forth therefore from Babylon (20-22).

49:1-6   SECOND SERVANT CANTICLE: Israel, God's servant, has thus far failed in her mission, but now it is God's plan not only to restore the survivors of Israel but to make them the source of salvation for the world (cf. 42:1, 6; 45:4-6, 14-25; 51:4-8).

49:7-23   Israel, despised by the nations, will cause kings and princes to look on in amazement when they see God reverse her fortunes and lead her back in triumph from bondage to freedom (7-13; cf. 52:13-15; 55:5; 60:1-14). To the despondent God promises the rebuilding and repopulation of their ravaged homeland (14-23).

49:24ff   To their doubt whether the prey (Israel) can be taken from the warrior (Babylon), God tells them not to fear (24-26). Nor are they rejected. God has taken back the writ of divorce (50:1-3; cf. 54:1ff; Jer. 3:1).

50:4-11   THIRD SERVANT CANTICLE: The Servant speaking for himself cites his own positive suffering, borne with absolute trust in God, as an example for the other exiles to imitate. Jewish exegetes, St. Thomas, and a number of modern exegetes refer this canticle to Deutero-Isaiah personally. Others refer it to the ideal Israel or to the ideal Messiah (cf. 61:1ff in the same vein).

51:1-8   Let the exiles learn from the example of Abraham, to whom God both promised and fulfilled His promises.

51:9ff   The prophet reminds them of God's power to save them (9-16) and of the fact that they have already done penance for their sins (17-23). He urges them to prepare, because the time for the new exodus has arrived (52:1-12). Note the crescendo leading to the fourth Servant Canticle (51:9, 17; 52:1).

52:13ff   FOURTH SERVANT CANTICLE: Like the previous Servant Canticles, 52:13—53:12 can be interpreted as referring to the Ideal Israel, i.e., to that little group in Israel, the "good figs," the "remnant," who are suffering innocently in exile because of their faith and their refusal to apostatize (cf. 49:5-9; 50:10-11; 51:7; 65:8-15; 66:5). The following parallel passages can be adduced in confirmation of this interpretation: for the group described as an individual, cf. Is. 1:5-6; 54:1-8; Ps. 129; for the parallel of 52:13-15, cf. 45:14-16; 49:7, 23; 55:5; 60:1-14; for the resurrection of the Servant as the resurrection of the nation, cf. Is. 26:16-19; Ez. 37; for a description of Israel enslaved, cf. 41:14; 42:6-7, 21-25; 47:5-6; 49:7; 50:5-7, 51:7, 13, 17, 22-23; for vicarious suffering, cf. 55:6-9; for the posterity promised to Israel, cf. 49:17-21; 54:1-6. From start to finish of Is. 40—66 the mission of Israel has been stated to be the salvation of the nations (cf. 42:4-6; 43:8-10, 12; 45:4-6, 14-15, 21-24; 51:4-5; 52:10; 55:3-5; 56:1-8; 60:12-14; 66:15-19).

54—55   Ch. 54 describes the New Zion idealized as the barren wife rejected for a time but then taken back by God to become the bountiful mother of a new Israel. Ch. 55 describes the blessings of the citizens of the New Zion.

The identification of the "Servant"

In the few remarks made about the Servant Canticles (Is. 42:1-4; 49:1-6; 50:4-10; 52:13—53:12), we have done nothing more than indicate the exegetical approach of those who propose a collective interpretation of the Servant either as the ideal Israel or as that group within Israel who represent the "remnant." Whether this interpretation looks to an idealized Israel of the future or to that remnant or hard core of faithful Israelites that always existed and will continue to exist, it is an interpretation in line with the thought of the prophet and in harmony with the prophetic and historical background of the nation. In addition it is an interpretation worthy of intensive thought and meditation, for it is a compelling and provocative portraiture of the New Israel, the Mystical Body of Christ.[1]

The interpretation which sees in the Servant an individual either from Israel's past (Moses, Jeremiah) or present (Jehoiachin, Deutero-Isaiah, Zerubbabel) or future (either Christ directly foreseen and presented or the future Messiah ideally described) has a long and continuous history. It would be beyond our scope to propose and defend adequately any of these interpretations. To do so would be neither possible nor practical at the present time, since, if there is anything certain, it is that there is no unanimity of opinion among even the best exegetes concerning the precise identity of the Servant.

On the other hand, one can speak of unanimity of opinion with regard to the messianic character of the Servant. Catholic authors agree, and they are joined by many non-Catholic authors, that the Servant looks either directly or as a type to the future Messiah. This opinion is supported by pre-Christian Jewish tradition,[2] by the unanimous tradition of the Fathers of the Church, by the almost miraculous fulfillment of the Servant Canticles in the life of Christ, and especially by the interpretation of the New Testament authors (cf. Matthew 8:17; 12:17-21; Mark 8:31; 9:12; 14:21; 14:49; Luke 18:31; 24:44; Acts 2:23; 3:18; 4:28; 7:52; 8:26-35; 13:27-29; 26:22; 1 Cor. 15:3; 1 Peter 2:21-25).

Considering all the interpretations, the one that appears closest to the mind of the prophet is the interpretation that sees in the Servant a future individual who will sum up in himself all that is best in Israel and will himself, by his preaching, his vicarious death and suffering, fulfill Israel's divinely appointed mission. Deutero-Isaiah beholds him who is to come and describes him ideally as the incarnation of all that God desires of Israel and has destined her to accomplish.[3]

[1] Cf. H. W. Robinson, *The Cross in the Old Testament* (Philadelphia: Westminster, 1955) 58-114.

[2] Cf. W. Zimmerli and J. Jeremias, *The Servant of God* (Naperville, Ill.: Allenson, 1957) 53-78.

[3] Cf. C. North, *The Suffering Servant in Deutero-Isaiah* (London: Oxford University Press, 1956) 214-219.

12

The Return from the Exile and the Postexilic Prophets

What Jeremiah foretold from afar, what Ezekiel envisioned from the depths and Deutero-Isaiah described on the horizon became fact in 539 when Cyrus the Great defeated the Babylonians, established the Persian Empire, and decreed the return and reestablishment of the Jews in the Holy Land.

The history of the return and the reestablishment is told in Ezra-Nehemiah, the last part of the Chronicler's ecclesiastical history of Israel. It is, however, almost the last gasp of Israel's historians. Both Ezra and Nehemiah are sketchy and incomplete, covering only the outstanding events in the century that followed the return from the exile. While the prophetical books of Haggai, Zechariah, and Trito-Isaiah fill in some of the history between 520-516, and Malachi gives some idea of the conditions prevailing around 460-450, there are long gaps about which we know nothing; of these the shortest runs from 537 to 520, the longest from 516 to 458. What happened in the years following Nehemiah's second trip to Jerusalem in 433, we can only conjecture. There is historical silence down to the time of the Maccabees in the early second century.

The information such as it is shows the returned exiles dropped from the lyric heights of Deutero-Isaiah to the stark reality of a poor and devastated homeland, bristling with economic and political problems and surrounded by hostile Samaritans to the north and unfriendly Edomites to the south. It also shows us Judaism isolating itself from the world and developing that monastic exclusiveness outlined by Ezekiel (40–48), objected to in vain by the author of Jonah, and ultimately erected into a quasi-dogma by the legalistic Scribes and Pharisees just before the coming of Christ.

Chronology of the postexilic period

539-333 Persian period – from the conquest of Babylon by Cyrus to the conquest of Persia by Alexander (Cyrus the Great, 539-530; Cambyses, 530-522).

538-537 Return of first exiles to Palestine.

536-516 Foundations of the Temple laid in 536, completion interrupted until 516. Preaching of Haggai, Zechariah, and Trito-Isaiah.

522-485 Darius I (repulsed by the Greeks at Marathon in 490).

485-465 Xerxes I (defeated by the Greeks at Thermopylae and Salamis).

480-350 The Golden Age of Greece. Aeschylus (525-456), Sophocles (496-406), Euripedes (480-406), Aristophanes (448-380); Themistocles (527-460), Pericles (480-429); Socrates (470-399), Plato (423-348), Aristotle (384-322); Herodotus (484-425), Thucydides (471-400), Xenophon (434-355); Alexander the Great (356-323).

460-450 Preaching of Malachi. Time of apathy and despair; priesthood corrupt, society ravaged by intermarriage with pagans.

465-424 Artaxerxes I, patron of Ezra and Nehemiah.

458-428 Ezra leads a second group of exiles from Babylon to Jerusalem.

445-433 Nehemiah rebuilds the walls of Jerusalem and institutes reforms.

433-175 Historical silence in Judah. Jonah, Tobit, Esther, and some Wisdom books written during this period.

356-323 Alexander the Great conquers Persia in 333, dies in Babylon 323.

1. Ezra — Nehemiah and Ezra 1—6

Ezra-Nehemiah constitute the last part of the Chronicler's ecclesiastical history of Israel. Like its first part, 1 and 2 Chronicles, Ezra-Nehemiah show a great interest in genealogies, the Temple, the Temple personnel, religious reforms, and the Davidic dynasty. For this last part of his history the Chronicler no longer had such copious sources as Samuel and Kings, but he was able to use the memoirs of Ezra and Nehemiah, genealogical lists from the Temple archives, and documents from the Persian state archives. Originally one with 1 and 2 Chronicles, Ezra-Nehemiah were eventually separated from the first half of the Chronicler's history and entitled Ezra. Later on this title gave way to the present division.

The theme of Ezra-Nehemiah is the history of the return from the exile and the political and religious reorganization of the postexilic Jewish state.[1] To understand the condition of the Jewish state during the century that followed the exile, three points must be taken into consideration: the general benevolence of the Persian emperors, the economic prostration of the land of Palestine, and the persistent hostility of the Samaritans.

The benevolence of Cyrus the Great permitted the initial return in 538. Darius I (522-485) sanctioned the rebuilding of the Temple in 520-516. And Artaxerxes I (465-424) promoted the return of Ezra in 458 (or perhaps 428) and the return of Nehemiah in 445 and 433.

The economic prostration of the land after the exile explains the discouragement of the repatriated exiles as depicted in Haggai, Zechariah, and Trito-Isaiah, and no doubt had a part in leading to the disillusionment and loss of fervor so manifest in the sermons of Malachi. It also explains to some extent the twenty year delay in rebuilding the Temple.

The hostility and guerrilla warfare of the Samaritans explain not only the slow economic recovery of the nation (cf. Ezra 4:1-6; Neh. 4–6) but also the inability of the repatriates to rebuild the walls of Jerusalem until the arrival of Nehemiah in 445, almost a century after the initial return.

Not to be disregarded, moreover, is the disillusionment of the people when the idealistic promises of Deutero-Isaiah failed to be fulfilled immediately after the return and had to be reinterpreted as referring to a more distant future. Hard as it was for the repatriates to understand, in the inscrutable designs of God the time was not yet ripe for the realization of the messianic promises, and 500 years had yet to pass before the coming of the king and his promised universal kingdom. As the books stand, they should be divided into four parts:

I. Ezra 1–6   The return of the first exiles in 538, followed by the rebuilding of the altar in 536 and the Temple in 516. (Haggai, Proto-Zechariah, and Trito-Isaiah should be read in conjunction with Ezra 5–6).

II. Ezra 7–10   Describing events that occurred at least 58 years later than the events of Part I, Ezra 7–10 describes the return in 458 (428) of a second group of exiles under Ezra the Scribe and gives

---

[1] Cf. F. Moriarty, *Ezra and Nehemiah*, OTRG No. 11; Schedl, HOTOT, vol. 5, 187–206; Bright 341–386; Herodotus, *The Persian Wars* I, 107ff.

a brief account of his marriage reforms. (Malachi should be read as an introduction to Ezra 7—10 and Neh. 1—13.)

III. Neh. 1—7 — The return of Nehemiah in 445 and the rebuilding of the walls of Jerusalem.

IV. Neh. 8—13 — The religious reforms and the renewal of the covenant forced through by Nehemiah and Ezra.

If, as is not improbable, the events of Ezra-Nehemiah are not in chronological order, it is perhaps more likely that Ezra's work followed that of Nehemiah. In this hypothesis, the books would be divided: Ezra 1—6; Neh. 1—13; Ezra 7—10; and the return of Ezra would be dated either to the 37th year of Artaxerxes I (428), or to the 7th year of Artaxerxes II (398).

Significant passages in Ezra 1—6

1:1-11 Cyrus decrees the liberation of the exiles around 538, and they return under the leadership of Sheshbazzar and Zerubbabel, princes of Judah, and Joshua, the high priest.

3:1-10 The altar is set up. The feast of Booths is celebrated. The foundation of the new Temple is laid in 536 but completion is delayed until 516 (cf. Ezra 5—6).

4:1-5 The proffered help of the Samaritans is refused and their animosity is aroused. The reader should note that the chapter contains a dossier on Samaritan attempts to thwart Israelite efforts at reconstruction. Vv. 1-4, 24 refer to the time of Darius I, vv. 6-23 to the reigns of Xerxes and Artaxerxes I.

5:1ff Spurred on by the prophets Haggai and Zechariah, the people complete the Temple under the direction of Zerubbabel and Joshua in 516, the sixth year of Darius I.

Since, as the text of Ezra 6:14 tells us, "The elders of the Jews built and prospered through the prophyesying of Haggai, the prophet, and Zechariah, the son of Iddo," it is fitting that the sermons of these two minor prophets as well as those of Trito-Isaiah be read here before continuing with the second part of Ezra (7—10), which describes events at least 58 years after the time of these prophets.

2. Haggai

Haggai preaches in 520, the second year of Darius I (522-485). His message is blunt: God wishes the Temple rebuilt without further delay. As is evident from his words, the times are difficult, money is short, and there is need of much sacrifice to complete the Temple.

The book is divided into five short sermons: an exhortation to rebuild the Temple (1:1-15); an encouraging prophecy of the glory of the new Temple in messianic times (2:1-9); a rebuke to the people for their uncleanness, either because of their association with pagans or because they have not rebuilt the devastated Temple (2:10-14); a promise of blessings that will accompany the work of rebuilding (2:15-19); and finally a consoling promise of God to Zerubbabel, the crown prince of Judah, to show God has not forgotten the Davidic dynasty (2:20-23).

Significant passages in Haggai

2:7-9   The future glory of the new Temple to which will be brought in messianic times the tribute of the Gentiles (cf. Is. 60:1-14).

2:21-24   Zerubbabel, grandson of King Jeconiah (cf. 1 Chr. 3:19), is declared by Haggai to be as dear to God as the signet ring on his finger, which is never to be taken off. Thus, at a time when the dynasty of David had little to offer, God reverses His curse of Jeconiah (Jer. 22:24) and reiterates His promise of perpetuity to the Davidic dynasty.

3. Proto-Zechariah (Zech. 1—8)

A contemporary of Haggai and like him credited with bringing the Temple reconstruction to a happy conclusion (Ezra 5:1; 6:14), Zechariah takes as his theme the rebuilding of the Temple and the encouragement of his fellow Israelites by assuring them of God's favor in the present and by pointing out to them the glories of the messianic age in the future.[1]

The historical background of Zechariah is the same as that of Haggai. It is the year 520. The people are discouraged because of the depressing economic outlook and the continued hostility of the Samaritans. The allusions to peace throughout the earth appear to refer to the end of the turbulent period in the Persian empire which followed upon the death of King Cambyses (530-522), when two rival claimants, Gaumata the Magus and Darius the son of Hystaspes, fought for the throne of Persia with Darius I winning around 520.

The book is divided into two parts: I. (1—8), a series of eight visions and

[1] Cf. G. Denzer, *Zechariah*, OTRG No. 21.

their accompanying sermons preached in 520 to encourage the people to rebuild the Temple; and II. (9–14), a collection of prophecies dealing with messianic times.

It should be noted that, while there is no question concerning the authenticity of Zech. 1–8, there is serious doubt about the authenticity of Zech. 9–14. The style and subject matter of Zech. 9–14 is so different that many authors posit a Deutero-Zechariah, while others consider the whole section, along with the book of Malachi which immediately follows it, a collection of fragments of unknown authorship appended, for that reason, to the end of the minor prophets' collection. As of now, the question of the provenance of Zech. 9–14 is still open, and no completely satisfactory solution has been proposed.

Significant passages in Proto-Zechariah 1—8

After a call to repentance (1:2-6), Zechariah delivers himself of a series of eight flamboyantly symbolic visions reminiscent of Amos 7–9 and Ez. 8–11; 40–48. The visions are most likely literary, i.e., fictional visions used by the prophet, the way Jesus used parables and Ezekiel used pantomimes, to dramatize certain fairly simple ideas.

While the purpose of the visions is the same as the purpose of Haggai's more prosaic sermons, i.e., to encourage the people, the reader should note the emphasis on the visual, which is proper to apocalyptic writers, in contradistinction to the emphasis on the "word of Yahweh," which is characteristic of the earlier prophets. A study of these visions and an analysis of the symbols used will be a valuable aid to understanding the difficult apocalyptic literary form which can be seen in the process of development in Zechariah and in a more advanced form in Daniel and the Apocalypse of St. John.

1:8-17   *The four horsemen.* One for each corner of the earth, the four horsemen symbolize graphically the watchful control and providence of the God of history over the affairs of the earth. "The earth resting peacefully" probably indicates that the wars for the control of the Persian empire are over, and Jerusalem has nothing to fear (cf. Apoc. 6:1-8).

1:18-21   *The four horns and the four blacksmiths.* Symbolizing power, the horn is a common symbol throughout the Bible (cf. Deut. 33:17; 1 Sam. 2:10; Dan. 7:7-9; Luke 1:69). The number four symbolizes here, as the four horsemen above and the four cherubim in Ez. 1, the idea of universality. The powers (horns) to be destroyed by the blacksmiths represent the nations that were responsible for the fall of Judah.

2:1-6 *The man with the measuring line.* Since the plumbline is an obvious symbol for a builder, Zechariah uses it to symbolize the rebuilding of the Temple and Jerusalem (cf. Ez. 40:3; Apoc. 21:15). On the repopulation of Jerusalem and the presence of God within her, cf. Is. 54:2-3; 60:20; Apoc. 21:22-26.

2:7-17 Since the defeat of Israel's enemies (1:21) is the prelude to the messianic era, a summons to the exiles to return to Mother Zion logically follows. As in Is. 45:22, all nations turn to God on that day, and Jerusalem becomes the religious metropolis of the universe (cf. Zech. 8:23; Is. 2:2-4; 60; Ps. 87). The reason for this is given in 2:14-17: God once more returns to His Temple in Jerusalem.

3:1-10 *The metamorphosis of the high priest.* Joshua, arraigned before the heavenly tribunal, probably represents the Jewish people at the end of the exile when they are vindicated by God (vv. 1-5). In vv. 6-10, Joshua represents the priesthood, which is now promised a much greater intimacy with God. In relation to this is mentioned the coming of the Messiah — "the Branch," a messianic title taken from Jer. 23:5.

4:1-14 *The lampstand* represents the restored community (cf. Apoc. 1:20 for a similar use of this symbol). The two *olive trees* symbolize Zerubbabel, the governor, and Joshua, the high priest, the spiritual and temporal powers in the Jewish state (cf. Jer. 33:14-18).

5:1-4 *The flying scroll.* Like the scroll in Ez. 2:9, only much larger, the flying scroll is covered with curses and dramatically symbolizes by its action the uprooting of evildoers from the people of God. Following Leviticus, Proto-Isaiah, and Ezekiel (40–48), Zechariah here and in 5:5-11 emphasizes the holiness that must be a mark of God's people.

5:5-11 *The woman in the bushel-basket.* The wickedness of Judah uprooted by the flying scroll must be put far from God's people. Symbolized by a woman, it is covered over and transported to Shinar (the ancient name for Babylon), the symbolic center of the forces that oppose God, where a temple will be built for it (cf. Apoc. 17, where this vision is elaborated at length to describe the great harlot, Babylon-Rome).

6:1-8 *The four chariots.* In Babylonian mythology, two mountains of copper guard the entrance to the dwelling place of the gods in the far mountains of the north (cf. Is. 2:2-4; 14:13; Ps. 48:1-2). Like the four horsemen, the four chariots patrol the four corners of the earth executing God's watchful providence and justice. Verse 8 is probably a reference to peace in the Persian empire in the year 520 (cf. Zech. 1:11).

6:9-15 *The symbolic crowning* of Zerubbabel emphasizes the messianic significance of the Davidic prince who, although only governor under the Persian king, is nevertheless a scion of that dynasty from which one day will be born the Messiah (cf. 3:8; 4:1-14).

8:18-23 *The coming of the nations* to the kingdom of God announced by Zechariah reiterates the doctrine of Is. 2:2-4; 60:1-14; Haggai 2:7.

4. Trito-Isaiah (Is. 56—66)

There is a subtle change in tone and orientation as one passes from Is. 40—55 to Is. 56—66. There is the feeling that one is no longer in Babylon awaiting the return from captivity but back in Palestine experiencing the hardship, frustrations, and pessimism of the returned exiles. The atmosphere is similar to that of the books of Haggai, Zechariah, Ezra-Nehemiah, and even Malachi.[1]

The prophet says nothing about Cyrus or Babylon. Geographical allusions, such as there are, are indicative of the hills and valleys of Palestine rather than the flat, canal-irrigated plains of Babylon; and when the prophet speaks about exiles, he seems to have in mind the Israelite brethren who have not yet returned from the exile (cf. 57:5-7; 58:12; 61:3-4; 62:6-7; 66:18-21).

The prophet still looks to the future for Israel's glorification (cf. 57:14-19; 60—62; 66:18-24), but he is forced to explain to his listeners that their sins have delayed it; and the impression one gets (that is all one can call it) is that the prophet is speaking to Israelites who returned to Palestine with high hopes and have seen their hopes shattered by the grim realities of life in postexilic Judah.

There are a number of references to the Temple but they are tantalizingly ambiguous. At times the Temple seems already rebuilt (cf. 56:5-8; 58:2; 62:9; 66:6, 20). At other times, as in Haggai and Zechariah, the prophet appears to be concerned with the actual rebuilding of the Temple

[1] Cf. Kissane, *The Book of Isaiah*, II xlvi lv; 213-328; C. Stuhlmueller, *Isaiah 40–66*, OTRG No. 20.

or at least with refurbishing it so that it will be a fitting dwelling place for Yahweh (cf. 60:7, 13; 66:1). The prophet's concern for the observance of the Sabbath, the keeping of fasts, and the offering of acceptable sacrifices (56:6-7; 58:1-8; 61:1-6) reflects the concerns for cult and ritual characteristic of Ezra, Nehemiah, and Malachi. Lastly, when the prophet shows himself incensed at the conduct of Israelites who take part in pagan rites, the rites described are typical of those practiced in Palestine by the Canaanites of old (57:3-13; 65:1-7, 11-12) and suggest the religion of those who remained in the land during the exile and became as pagan as their Canaanite neighbors.

Critics are divided on the identity of the prophet whose oracles are preserved in Is. 56—66. There is general agreement upon referring to him as Trito-Isaiah, but the name is as much for the sake of reference to the third part of the book of Isaiah as it is to the unknown prophet. Those who consider him a prophet distinct from Deutero-Isaiah and Proto-Isaiah date him sometime between the years immediately following the return from the exile down to as late as the year 400. Those who consider him Deutero-Isaiah returned from the exile date him naturally to the decades immediately following the return.

Whoever the prophet is, his message is clear. Israel's messianic future is assured, but it is still in the future. The Temple must be a house of prayer. The Israelites must be holy with a holiness that is genuine and a charity that is sincere. The dismal days of the return will pass and Israel will persevere. But in the trials of the present there is no substitute for confident faith and genuine piety.

The division of Trito-Isaiah is a matter of conjecture, since there are few clear dividing lines in the text. 56:1-8 contains an instruction on conditions necessary to belong to Israel. The references to the Temple date the passage to after 516. 56:9—57:21 is a prophetic rebuke to Israel's wicked leaders (56:9—57:13a) to whom are contrasted the humble of spirit (57:13b-21) and should be dated after the time of Zerubbabel and Joshua. 58:1-14 on fasting presumes the Temple rebuilt (v. 2) and should be dated after 516. 59:1-15a is the prophet's explanation of why Israel's messianic expectations have not been fulfilled — her sins are the cause. 59:15b-20 is probably the introduction to the apocalyptic passage continued in 63:1-6. It is impossible to date but it savors of the same feelings toward Edom manifested in Ez. 35, Obadiah, and Ps. 137. 60—62, although possibly exilic, seem to presume the Temple has been rebuilt but is lacking in the splendor befitting God (vv. 7 and 13; cf. Haggai 2:1-9). If the author is not Deutero-Isaiah himself, he shows here that he is a true disciple of the great exile prophet. 63:7—64:11 contains a lamentation for the devastated Temple, apparently before 520. 65—66 contain encouraging words for the disconsolate Israelites and like such earlier chapters as Is. 24–27 and Is. 34–35 are strongly apocalyptic in tone and imagery.

5. Malachi

Malachi's preaching is an attack on the low religious morals of the priests and the people of his time — the priests for their loss of zeal in caring for purity of worship and religious instruction, the people for their moral laxity and pessimism, manifested by contempt for the Mosaic marriage laws and failure to support the Temple and the priesthood.[1]

The historical background in Malachi makes it clear that the days of zeal and fervor that rebuilt the Temple in 516 are long past and dead. A spirit of routine and weariness has set in. The decreasing fervor of the repatriates has led to disgraceful negligence on the part of the priests in carrying out the liturgical services of the Temple (1:6–2:9) and to increasing pessimism on the part of the people (1:2-5; 2:17; 3:13-18).

A comparison of texts shows that the evils attacked by Malachi become the object of the reforms introduced by Ezra and Nehemiah, e.g., corrupt priesthood (Mal. 1:6–2:9 cf. Neh. 13:1-10, 29); mixed marriages (Mal. 2:1-11; cf. Ezra 10:1-12; Neh. 13:23ff); refusal to support the Temple worship (Mal. 3:8-9; cf. Neh. 10:32ff; 13:10-22). As in the time of Ezra and Nehemiah, the people are discouraged by famine and locust plagues (Mal. 3:10-11; cf. Neh. 5:3) and cynical about the quality of God's justice (Mal. 2:17; 3:13-15; cf. Neh. 5:1-5).

It is clear that Malachi's preaching led the way for the reforms of Ezra and Nehemiah in the same way that the preaching of Micah and Isaiah prepared the way for the religious reforms introduced by Hezekiah (2 Chr. 29–31) and the preaching of Zephaniah led the way for the reform under Josiah (2 Chr. 34–35). What the prophet attacked, the reformers attempted to correct. It is on this basis that Malachi is dated by almost all scholars to the years immediately preceding the reforms of Ezra and Nehemiah (460-445), a good half century and more after the time of Haggai and Zechariah and the rebuilding of the Temple.

Malachi's preaching, which should be read before Ezra 7–10 and Neh. 1–13, is divided into two parts: I. (1:1–2:16), the sins of the people and the priests; II. (2:17–3:24), the coming of God to judge, to punish, and to reward.

Significant passages in Malachi

1:2-5 Malachi defends God's love against the pessimism of the people (cf. Neh. 5:1-6). The reader should note the peculiar dia-

[1] Cf. G. Denzer, *Malachi*, OTRG No. 21.

logue style of the prophet's preaching. He states the objections of his audience and then refutes them.

1:6-14 The contempt of the priests for the sacrifices leads God to reject them and promise a new universal sacrifice, a clean oblation to be offered everywhere among the nations (cf. Neh. 13:1-14).

2:1-9 A biting criticism of the tepid priests who neglect their duty to teach the people the law of God (on the alliance with Levi, v. 4, cf. Deut. 18:1-8; 33:8-11).

2:10-16 A protest against intermarriage with pagans and against divorce, even though permitted by the law of Moses (cf. Ezra 9:1-2; 10:14-44; Neh. 10:28-30; 13:23-31).

2:17ff To the cynical complaint, "Where is the just God?," Malachi retorts: ". . . suddenly there will come to the Temple the Lord whom you seek," to judge the wicked (3:2-15) and reward the good (3:16-18). He will, moreover, be preceded by His messenger who, it is said in 3:23, will be Elijah the prophet (cf. Matthew 3:11; Luke 12:49; but note that although Elijah is mentioned by name, our Lord expressly states that John the Baptist, coming in the "spirit of Elijah," fulfills the prophecy. Thus Matthew 11:14; 17:9-13; Luke 1:17, 76; 7:27; Mark 1:2).

6. Ezra 7—10 and Nehemiah 1—13

A reading now of the second part of Ezra (ch. 7—10) and all of Nehemiah will fill out the history of the return from the exile and the political and religious reorganization of the Jewish state and show how the evils attacked by Malachi became the object of the reforms of Ezra and Nehemiah in the years following 458.

Significant passages in Ezra 7—10

7:1-10 After 58 years (the time separating the events described in Ezra 1—6 from those described in 7—10), Ezra in 458 or perhaps 428 (depending on whether he is to be dated to the 7th or the 37th years of Artaxerxes I), leads a caravan from Babylon to Jerusalem, consisting for the most part of Temple personnel (vv. 6-7).

7:25-26 Artaxerxes delegates to Ezra sweeping powers of jurisdiction.

8:15ff The caravan gathers at the river Ahava, fasts, and beseeches a safe journey to Jerusalem.

9:1-2 Intermarriage with the pagans of Palestine (perhaps necessary because more men than women returned) threatens both the faith of the Israelites (v. 1) and their racial purity (v. 2). Intermarriage with pagans had been interdicted in Deut. 7:1-4; 23:4-9, but the law is probably late since mixed marriages were not uncommon in earlier Israelite history (cf. Ruth; 2 Sam. 3:3; the marriages of David and Solomon).

10:1-4 The drastic decision is made to divorce all foreign wives and is enforced stringently (v. 44). On divorce, cf. Mal. 2:10-16; Neh. 10:28-30; 13:23-27).

Significant passages in Nehemiah

2:1ff Nehemiah tells how Artaxerxes sent him to Palestine in 445 with authority to govern and to rebuild the walls of Jerusalem (vv. 1-10); how, secretly and by night, he inspected the dilapidated walls (vv. 11-16) and with the cooperation of the people began the work of reconstruction (3:1ff).

4:1-9 The Samaritans conspire to prevent the rebuilding of the walls but the Jews continue the work with weapons near at hand in case of attack (vv. 15-23).

5:1-12 A brief digression explaining how Nehemiah dealt with the oppression and enslavement of poor Israelites by their wealthier brethren.

6:1-19 Samaritan attempts to assassinate (v. 3) or at least compromise Nehemiah fail because of his shrewdness (vv. 10-13).

8:1-8 Ezra reads the law of Moses to the assembled Jews every day during the octave of the feast of Booths (cf. Deut. 31:10-13; Lev. 23:33-43).

9:38 After the reading, the people sign a covenant agreeing to follow the law of Moses.

11:1-2 Jerusalem is repopulated and thus assured of defenders by means of volunteers and others chosen by lots.

12:27ff The dedication of the wall of Jerusalem with a double procession meeting in front of the Temple (v. 40).

13:6-7 Nehemiah's second trip from Babylon to Jerusalem in 433, followed by reforms affecting the support of the levites (vv. 10-14), the observance of the Sabbath (vv. 15-22), and the marriage laws (vv. 23-27; cf. Ezra 10:1-4; Mal. 2:10-16).

7. Deutero-Zechariah (Zech. 9—14)

In Deutero-Zechariah the age of the rebuilding of the Temple is past. Nothing is said about Zerubbabel and Joshua. Nothing is said about the Persian empire. The center of interest is no longer restricted to the struggling little postexilic community but embraces the broader scene of Israel and the world and the end of time. Instead of prose oracles clearly dated and definitely attributed to Zechariah, there is a collection of dateless, anonymous oracles for the most part in poetry.[1]

No definite date can be given for Deutero-Zechariah, but the references to the exile (9:11-12; 10:6-9) would favor a date after 539, and the strong apocalyptic tone plus the emphasis on eschatology would favor a date perhaps as late as the third century.

"A burden," the word with which each of the two parts (ch. 9—11; ch. 12—14) opens (the same as the first word of Malachi), is probably the addition of an editor and does not militate against the unity of authorship. Whatever the date of the book, the message of the prophet is eschatological. He looks to the great day at the end of an epoch when God will directly intervene to judge the world, bring glory to His people and punishment to all evildoers.

Significant passages in Deutero-Zechariah

9:9-10 The humility of the messianic king and his rule of peace over the nations (cf. Matthew 21:5; Mark 11:1; Luke 19:29; John 12:14; also Gen. 49:11 and Judg. 5:10).

11:4-17 The prophet, taking God's place as the good shepherd, is rejected by the leaders of the people. When he asks for his wages, they give him the wage of a slave — 30 pieces of silver (cf. Exod. 21:32; Matthew 26:15; 27:9). 13:7-9 should probably be read after 11:17.

12:10 "They shall look on him whom they have thrust through. . . . " No clue is given to the identity of the person described, but the anthological style of the author makes it not improbable that he

[1] Cf. CCHS par. 579–581.

refers to the Servant of Yahweh in Is. 52:13–53:12. St. John sees this prophecy fulfilled in the piercing of the side of Christ on Calvary (19:37).

13:1-7 "... a fountain to purity from sin and uncleanness" (v. 1) strikes an anthological note from Is. 12:3 and Ez. 47:1. "What are these wounds" (v. 6), a reference to the self-inflicted wounds of the false prophets, is accommodated to the wounds of Christ in the liturgy. "Strike the shepherd that the sheep may be dispersed" (v. 7): since the words refer literally to the foolish shepherd, it is obvious that the application of the text to our Lord by St. Matthew (26:31) is by way of accommodation.

14:1-21 "Lo, a day shall come for the Lord. . . ." The description of the "coming day" that follows is cast in apocalyptic imagery and shows dependence on Ezekiel (38–39).

It would seem advisable to close the Chronicler's history with the study of the book of Joel. Joel, however, will be treated with the apocalyptic literature. Instead we shall close with the Canticle of Canticles. The Canticle is usually treated with the Wisdom books. It is not, however, properly a Wisdom book. Neither is it an historical nor a prophetical book. It is, as we shall see, a type of dramatic, didactic poetry with allegorical overtones. Since these overtones reflect the fervent anticipation and continual frustration characteristic of the early postexilic period, we shall take the Canticle against the background of Ezra-Nehemiah and the postexilic period in general. We shall then conclude the Chronicler's history with a literary analysis of this book and a study of the psalms related to the history under consideration.

8. The Canticle of Canticles

The title "Canticle of Canticles" like "Holy of Holies" and "King of Kings" is a Hebrew form of the superlative. The title is well deserved not only because of the exquisite poetry of the Canticle but because of its theme: the love of God for His people and His people for their God.[1]

Hebrew regard for the Canticle was expressed by the Rabbi Aqiba at the Synod of Jamnia (90 A.D.): "All the scriptures are sacred," he said, "but the Canticle is the most sacred of all." Later the Rabbi Aquila hyperbol-

---

[1] Cf. R. Murphy, *Introduction to the Wisdom Literature of the Old Testament*, OTRG No. 22.

ically declared: "The world itself is not worth the day on which this book was given to Israel."

Among Christians, the Canticle was always held in the highest esteem. It was the favorite book of St. Bernard who wrote eighty-six sermons explaining it. It was a commentary on the Canticle that engaged St. Thomas Aquinas in the last days of his life. St. John of the Cross used the theme and format of the Canticle to express his highest mystical teachings. And St. Alphonsus returned again and again to the text of the Canticle in the loftiest sections of his great ascetical works.

The allegorizing parable interpretation

The exegete in search of a thoroughly satisfying interpretation of the Canticle is like a retreating soldier in search of a defensive position. Each new position seems at first sight defensible. Before long, however, he sees it is open to attack on several sides. He then moves on. So far no exegete has found an impregnable position.

The allegorizing parable interpretation, although open to attack, seems the best interpretation of the Canticle. The literal interpretation of the Canticle as a series of poems extolling the singleness, bliss, and indissolubility of human love and marriage is certainly worthy of consideration. The marriage union, which is praised in its institution in the Old Testament (Gen. 2:18-25) and raised to the dignity of a sacrament in the New (Eph. 5:21-33), is by no means a suspect subject for an inspired author. Nevertheless, the literary tradition among both Jews and Christians has always been in favor of either an allegorical or a parabolical interpretation.

The difficulty with a purely allegorical interpretation is that it may become too forced and far-fetched. An allegory is an extended metaphor, but not all exegetes remember that not every detail carries a specific transferred meaning (cf. the allegory of the vineyard in Is. 5). To find a transferred meaning for some of the people, places, and events described in the Canticle is not difficult. To do it with the reserve required in interpreting an allegory reasonably is not easy.

In a simple parable on the other hand the words are taken in their proper literal sense but the story or comparison as a whole conveys a lesson or a meaning in another order. It is an extended comparison in which the central feature, but not the details, illustrates the teaching intended by the author. The details are embellishment, added to bring out more clearly the overall picture, or to fill in the story, or most often simply for the sake of literary art. To discover the message of a parable, therefore, one looks for the single point of comparison and ignores the details (cf. the parables of the Good Samaritan and the Prodigal Son in Luke 10 and 15 respectively).

Antecedently, a straight parabolic interpretation of the Canticle has much to commend it. The comparison of God's love for His Chosen People to the love of a husband for his wife has a long history in the Bible beginning with Hosea and ending with the Apocalypse (cf. Hosea 1–3; Jer. 3:1-10, 20; Ez. 16; 23; Is. 54:4-8; 61:10—62:5; John 3:29; Eph. 5:21-33; Apoc. 21:1-10). The interpretation, therefore, which sees in the bride and the groom of the Canticle and the description of their mutual love an implied comparison with the love of God for His Chosen People, rests upon a figurative way of speaking that is both ancient and well-known in the literary milieu of the Bible.

In the Canticle, moreover, as in a parable, one is not surprised to find many details based upon Hebrew marriage customs. They are part of the Canticle, not because they are meant to have a transferred sense as in an allegory, but because the author gives free rein to his literary genius in filling out the details of the overall comparison. Some of these customs can be paralleled by examples in the Bible, others by Egyptian poetry, still others by marriage customs of ancient origin still practiced in the rural areas of modern Syria.

Thus the Bible itself speaks of the marriage price or *mohar* (cf. Gen. 29:18; 1 Sam. 18:25; Cant. 8:8-12), the friends of the bridegroom (cf. Judg. 14:11; John 3:29; Cant. 3:7-8), the woman attendants of the bride (Matthew 25:1-13; Cant. 1:4; 2:7; 3:5), and the bringing of the bride in procession to the home of the groom (cf. 1 Mac. 9:37-41; Cant. 3:6-11; 8:5).

The custom of the groom referring to his bride as "sister" is common in Egyptian love songs from the biblical period. For example: "Seven days to yesterday I have not seen the sister. And a sickness has invaded me. . . . more beneficial to me is the sister than any remedies . . . when I embrace her, she drives evil away from me — but she has gone forth from me for seven days!" (ANET 468-469; cf. Cant. 4:9; 4:12; 5:1). Common likewise to both Egyptian love songs and to the Canticle are the themes of love-sickness, absence of the beloved, and the association of the springtime season with love (cf. Cant. 2:5; 2:8-13; 3:1-5; 7:13).

From the rural areas of modern Syria come other customs reflected in the Canticle. Just as at the time of Jacob (Gen. 29:17-28) and Samson the married couple celebrates a week of festivities. During this time they are regaled as king and queen (cf. Cant. 3:7, 9; 7:2). A throne is set up for them and villagers sing songs before them celebrating their happiness. Prominent among these songs is the *wasf*, a poetical description of the physical beauty of the bride and groom (cf. Cant. 4:1ff; 5:10ff; 6:4-10). A special *wasf* sung by the bride as she dances brandishing a sword in her hand may have some relation to the dance of the two companies mentioned in the Canticle (7:1-2).

Even a brief survey such as this shows the author's use of customs and literary modes to embellish and lend verisimilitude to his parable. We have called the Canticle an allegorizing parable, however, and the qualification should be explained.

An allegorizing parable is a parable in which the author adds, over and above his basic comparison, certain details which have a transferred meaning as in an allegory. Thus, in the allegorizing parable found in Matthew 21:33-42, allegorical overtones are audible in the descriptions of the servants (prophets) beaten by the vine-dressers, and of the Son (Christ Himself) seized, cast out of the vineyard, and put to death.

Of their very nature, allegorizing overtones are difficult to catch since they depend so much on traditions and history peculiar to a particular audience. As a result, many of the allegorical overtones of the Canticle, perceptible without strain to the author's contemporaries, are completely lost to moderns. Some few, however, stand out clearly enough for those who have read the earlier books of the Bible.

The titles of the bridegroom, for example, shepherd (1:7; 2:16; 6:2-3), king (1:4, 12), spouse (*passim*), were familiar names for God both in the psalms and in the prophetical books, and especially in the exilic and post-exilic prophets (for the title, shepherd, cf. Pss. 23 and 95; Jer. 23:1-3; 31:10; Ez. 34:11-16; Is. 40:11; for the title, king, cf. Pss. 95–100; Is. 6:1-2; 24:23; 33:22; 41:21; Zech. 14:9; Mal. 1:14; for the title, spouse or husband, cf. Hosea 1–3; Jer. 3:1-5; Ez. 16; 23; Is. 54:4-8; 62:5).

When the bride is spoken of as a vineyard (1:6; 8:12) or garden (4:12; 5:1; 6:2; 8:13), the audience is already familiar with the theme of Israel as God's vineyard (cf. Hosea 2:14; Is. 5:1-7; Jer. 12:10; Ps. 80) and with the idea of the new Israel as a renewed garden of paradise (cf. Hosea 14:6-7; Ez. 36:35; Is 35; 51:3; 58:11; 61:11).

Additional allegorical allusions may be intended in what appears to be the bride's reference to the Babylonians and the exile (1:6), her fear of wandering away after the Gentile nations rather than after her true shepherd (1:7-8, cf. Jer. 31:21; 50:6-17; Ez. 34; Is. 53:6), her willingness to keep vigil until the bridegroom awakes and spontaneously brings to an end her waiting (2:7; 3:5; 5:2; 8:4-5, cf. Hosea 2:18; Is. 51:17; 52:1-2), the enigmatic descriptions of the bridegroom by allusion to the Temple (5:10-16; cf. 1 Kings 6–7; 2 Chr. 3) and of the bride by allusion to the land of Israel (7:2-10). Assuredly other allegorical allusions can be discovered, but they require a perceptive eye and delicate literary vivisection. Lacking these, the easiest way to an appreciative understanding of the Canticle lies in knowing its literary, psychological, and historical background.

The broad literary background of the Canticle is certainly to be found in those texts comparing the covenant relations between God and His people to the relations between a husband and his wife (cf. Hosea 1–3; Jer. 3:1-6; 31:21-37; Ez. 16; 23; Is. 54:4-8; 61:10—62:5).

The more immediate background, however, is found in those marriage texts which speak of a new marriage between Israel and her God. The initiative is taken by Hosea who foretells a day when God will lead Israel into the desert, speak to her heart, convert her, and then espouse her forever in a new covenant of right and justice, love and mercy (Hosea 2:16-25).

Jeremiah then develops this prophecy of Hosea in his idealistic description of the return of Israel from the exile (Jer. 31:1ff, particularly vv. 4, 21-22, 31-34).

Toward the end of the exile, Deutero-Isaiah takes up the same theme and speaks in glowing accents of the new marriage, in which God will espouse Israel "as a young man marries a virgin. . . . as a bridegroom rejoices in his bride" (Is. 62:5 cf. Is. 54:4-8; 61:10—62:5).

In the Canticle, we are given the crowning poetic development of the ideas first enunciated by Hosea (2:16-22). Unlike Ezekiel, who allegorically describes the Sinai covenant as a marriage between God and Israel that ends in divorce because of Israel's repeated infidelities (Ez. 16), the author of the Canticle prescinds from the unsuccessful first marriage and concentrates on the new marriage. His procedure, therefore, is the opposite of Ezekiel. He takes Israel in her state of penance and purification after God has led her into the desert, spoken to her heart, captured her enduring love, and brought about the miracle of conversion described by Jeremiah: "Yahweh has created a new thing upon the earth: the woman must encompass the man with devotion" (31:22).

All the theology of conversion brought out in Hosea is repeated in the Canticle, namely, a period of punishment, a period of reflection, new initiatives of grace and love, testing of reawakened love, acceptance of the bride by the bridegroom as if nothing had ever happened to break up the first marriage (Hosea 2:16-22; 3:3-5).

At this point, according to the predictions of Hosea, Jeremiah, and Isaiah, the second and eternal marriage should take place. But here it is that the author of the Canticle shows not only his originality but his profound knowledge of the prophets and his piercing insight into the history of Israel, both past and present. According to Hosea and Jeremiah, Israel's conversion is apparently a simple matter. The author of the Canticle, however, shows the great return taking place slowly, little by little, in response to the divine advances, by a spontaneous and completely free decision, at the price of hard knocks which serve to rid Israel of some tenacious illusions. It is only at the end of this long psychological journey that the omnipotent power of God steps in to bring about what Israel hopes will be the definitive conversion and the final happy marriage.

The immediate historical background of the Canticle is not easy to determine. But if there is any key to the solution of this problem, it is the situation of the bride as described in the Canticle. The winter of the exile is over (Cant. 2:8ff), the bridegroom is intermittently speaking to the bride, the bride is continually searching for the bridegroom, repeatedly finding him, but only for a short time. As often as she finds him, she loses him, and the search begins anew. It would appear that the bride's love is being tested. Her desires are ardent. Her love is sincere. But her frustrations are continual. The bridegroom alone decides when he will visit her, where she will find him, how long he will remain with her, when and under what circumstances he will espouse her definitively.

The situation of the bride is the situation of Israel after the exile. The exiles returned from Babylon chastened, purified, expectant. The magnificent promises of Deutero-Isaiah, however, were not fulfilled. The new marriage predicted by the prophets did not take place. Palestine, far from being a new garden of Eden was a desolate and ravaged land. Instead of a messianic age, there was a long and bitter period of economic prostration on the one hand and Samaritan oppression and harassment on the other. It was a time of great expectations but little realization. It was a time as well of renewed love, ardent faith, dogged patience. It is precisely the faith, the hope, the love, and the patience of Israel in this period that are mirrored in the sentiments of the bride. If this surmise is correct, the Canticle was written some time after the exile, probably in the period following the reforms of Ezra and Nehemiah (c. 400-350). Late Hebrew forms of expression, frequent Aramaisms, and occasional Persian loan words (e.g., *pardes*, garden or paradise in 4:13, and *egoz*, walnut tree in 6:11) lend confirmation to this surmise.

Literary form and division

The Canticle is a series of poetic dialogues, carried on for the most part between the bride and the bridegroom, occasionally between the bride and the daughters of Jerusalem. The daughters have a very small part and appear to have been introduced, after the manner of the wives of Tobit and Job, as foils to provide the bride with opportunities for praising her beloved.

Authors have spoken of the Canticle as a drama, but the Canticle lacks both the form and the action required for a drama in the classical sense of the term. There is no real conflict, no clear dramatic action, no strict unity beyond that of subject. There are on the contrary frequent and abrupt transitions both of speakers and of place. The presence of the same lyrical feeling throughout, the recurrence of the same ornate metaphors, and the reappearance of the same characters testify to the literary but not the dramatic unity of the Canticle.

One may, however, speak of the Canticle as dramatic poetry. In each of the poems there is some action, at least psychological. Either the bride searches for the bridegroom and finds him, or the bridegroom comes to the bride and rejoices with her. Though the bride longs to be united indissolubly with the bridegroom, this happy event never takes place within the Canticle. On the contrary, the same series of motifs recur: searching, frustration, joyful discovery, blissful possession. It is not clear that 8:5-6 describe a definitive blissful possession.

The literary origin of the poetry is probably found in the allusions of Jeremiah to the love songs sung at Israelite weddings: "There shall be heard again the sound of mirth and the sound of gladness, the voice of the bridegroom and the voice of the bride" (Jer. 33:11; cf. also 7:33; 16:5-9; 25:10).

It seems not unlikely that the author has collected and unified some of the finest of Israel's nuptial songs to express that divine colloquy of love between God and His people foretold by Hosea: "So I will allure her; I will lead her into the desert and *speak to her heart . . . she shall respond* there as in the days of her youth, when she came up from the land of Egypt" (2:16f). It is precisely this colloquy that we have in the Canticle.

The author, however, does more than dramatize the response of Israel "as in the days of her youth." He arranges his poems to bring out the significance of those other words of Hosea so fateful for Israel's future:

> Many days you shall wait for me;
>   you shall not play the harlot
> Or belong to any man;
>   I in turn will wait for you.
> For the people of Israel shall remain many days
>   without king or prince,
> Without sacrifice or sacred pillar,
>   without ephod or household idols.
> Then the people of Israel shall turn back
>   and seek Yahweh, their God,
>   and David their king;
> They shall come trembling to Yahweh
>   and to his bounty, in the last days (Hosea 3:3-5).

The Canticle can be divided in different ways. The following division into five sections has met the approval of most exegetes:

1:1-4 Prologue introducing theme and principal characters.
I. 1:5–2:7 The bride's apologia, search, discovery, colloquies.
II. 2:8–3:5 The bridegroom comes, departs, is sought for and found again.
III. 3:6–5:1 The bridegroom comes and extolls the beauty of the bride.
IV. 5:2–6:3 The bridegroom comes but the bride is not ready for him. She searches for him, extolling his beauty to the daughters.
V. 6:4–8:7 Final colloquies of the bride and bridegroom.
8:8-14 Appendix concerning the bride and her brothers.

Significant passsages in the Canticle

The following passages have been selected on the basis of their allegorical meaning. No attempt is made to explain all the allegorical elements, nor even to explain fully the passages chosen. Such explanation requires copious reading and comparison of parallel texts. The Canticle as a whole should be interpreted as a parable as explained in the introduction.

1:4ff *Draw me.* The fulfillment of the prophecy of Jeremiah, "Yahweh has created a new thing upon the earth: the woman must encompass the man with devotion" (31:22), is evident from the beginning of the Canticle to its end. The bride, Israel, makes most of the overtures of love, calling upon the groom to draw her, seeking him on all occasions, praising him, rejoicing in his love. The bridegroom on the contrary comes when he likes, leaving the bride entirely dependent on his whim as Hosea had predicted: "Many days you must dwell as mine; you must not play the harlot, nor have a husband, nor will I myself come near you" (Hosea 3:3). The "maidens" who join with the bride, saying, "We will follow you eagerly," refer allegorically to the cities of Judah, after the manner of speaking of Hosea (cf. Hosea 2:4) and the common prophetic reference to cities as virgin daughters (cf. Is. 1:8; 23:12; Jer. 31:4). It is possible as well that the daughters represent the Gentile nations (cf. Is. 47:1; Jer. 14:17), whose conversion to the true faith was predicted by the prophets (cf. Is. 2:2-4; 42:4; 51:5; Zech. 8:22-23).

1:5-9 *I am dark but beautiful.* Israel, in exile in the vineyards of her brothers, the Babylonians, is dark from the sun (v. 6c; cf. Lam. 4:7-8), but still beautiful in the eyes of God. She admits she did not care for her vineyard, herself (v. 6e; cf. Is. 5:1-7; 27:2-4; Jer. 2:7, 20-21; Ps. 80). Fearful that she might lose her divine Shepherd (cf. Ps. 23; Ez. 34:11-31; Is. 40:11) and wander off again after the pagan nations as she had before the exile, Israel asks God to show her where He pastures His flock (v. 7). The daughters answer and advise her to follow the tracks of the flock, an allusion to the words of Jeremiah (31:21). Suddenly, the groom speaks likening his bride to the elaborately caparisoned horses of Pharaoh, an allusion to the servitude of Israel in Egypt (v. 9). In the colloquy that follows, God speaks to Israel's heart, and Israel responds "as in the days of her youth" (Hosea 2:16-17; cf. Jer. 31:2-6).

2:8ff *Hark! My lover.* God comes to Israel in Babylon and bids her "arise and come" for the winter of the exile is over (vv. 8-13, cf. Is. 40:1-4; 52:1-7) and the messianic springtime has arrived (cf. Hosea 14:6-8; Is. 35:1-10). The enigmatic reference to "the little foxes that damage the vineyards" may be an allusion to the Samaritans, Ammonites, and others who occupied Palestine during the exile and harassed the returning Israelites (v. 15; cf. Jer. 12:7-11; Is. 56:9; Ezra 4:4; Neh. 4:3, 7-8).

3:1ff *On my bed at night I sought him.* Paradoxically, the bridegroom has disappeared and the bride must search for him again in order to bring him back to "the home of her mother," most likely a reference to the Temple (v. 4; cf. 1:4, 17; 5:10-16). The adjuration to the daughters (v. 5) indicates that the bride realizes she must patiently await God's good pleasure for the realization of the definitive nuptials (cf. 2:7; 8:4; Hosea 3:5; Jer. 29:13).

3:6ff *Coming up from the desert.* If the first poem (1:5–2:7) has been rightly interpreted as alluding to the time of the exile, and the second (2:8–3:5) as alluding to the end of the exile, the third (3:6–5:1) might be expected to contain allusions to the return of the exiles to Palestine. Parallels with the Exodus from Egypt in the "column of smoke" (cf. Exod. 13:19-20) and with the descriptions of Deutero-Isaiah speaking of the return from the exile (40:3-5; 43:16-19; 49:8-12; 61:10–62:5) would indicate that in vv. 6-11 the author is alluding to the messianic fervor of the Jews returning to Palestine in 537-515 B.C. (cf. Haggai 2:23; Zech. 3:8-9; 6:12-13).

5:2ff *My heart kept vigil.* Still waiting, still being tested by her divine lover, the bride is visited by God but found not yet perfectly

B.C.	Personalities	Events	In the Neighborhood	Literature
600	Jehoiachin	597: first deportation to Babylon		*Lachis letters*
	ZEDEKIAH	587: Babylonian captivity		Baruch's recollections of Jeremiah
	EZEKIEL	Jeremiah predicts a "New Covenant" and a "new David"		
	DEUTERO-ISAIAH	Ezekiel's visions of restoration and the new Temple	Cyrus united the Medes and the Persians (c. 549)	First (?) edition of the Deuteronomist's history, Additions to Deuteronomy
		Deutero-Isaiah announces the victories of Cyrus and exodus of Israel from Babylon	Cyrus defeats Croesus of Lydia (546), Fall of Babylon to Cyrus	LAMENTATIONS, Poems and Canticles of Deutero-Isaiah
	Sheshbazzar	First exiles return to Judah		
	Zerubbabel, Joshua	Building of the Temple (520–516)	Darius I defeats Gaumata (520)	HAGGAI
	Trito-Isaiah			PROTO-ZECHARIAH
	Haggai			KINGSHIP OF YAHWEH
	Proto-Zechariah			PSALMS
500	*Obadiah*	The universal sacrifice (Mal. 1:11)	Xerxes I (485–465) wars with Greece	Apocalypse of Isaiah (Is. 24–27 Persian period (?))
	Malachi	Nehemiah rebuilds the walls of Jerusalem (445). Reforms of Ezra-Nehemiah	Artaxerxes I (465–424)	JOB, JONAH, RUTH, *Elephantine papyri* (495–401)
	EZRA			Memoirs of Ezra
	NEHEMIAH			Memoirs of Nehemiah, SONG OF SONGS, JEDP SYNTHESIS forms the Pentateuch
400				

detached. The disposition of the bride in this poem corresponds well with the condition of the postexilic community as described by Trito-Isaiah (56–66) and in Ezra-Nehemiah — one part devout, one part hesitant and pessimistic (vv. 2-6). Though it is night, the daughters are conveniently present (vv. 8-9). In response to their question concerning the bridegroom, the bride recites a *wasf*, in which the laudatory description of the bridegroom is studded with allusions to the Temple of Jerusalem, e.g., "head of pure gold" refers to the Holy of Holies (cf. 1 Kings 6:20-21); "locks like palm fronds" refers to the palm fronds used in the Temple as a decorative motif (cf. 1 Kings 6:29, 32); body, "a work of ivory," refers to the white limestone of the Temple (cf. 1 Kings 6:7); "stature like the trees of Lebanon, imposing as the cedars" refers to the abundant cedar wood used in the construction of the Temple (cf. 1 Kings 6:9–10:18).

6:4ff   *Beautiful as Tirzah.* The bridegroom recites a *wasf* in praise of his bride (vv. 4-10), stressing the uniqueness of Israel as compared to the Gentile nations (vv. 8-9; cf. Deut. 7:6-8; 32:8-9; Is. 60). Then the daughters recite a *wasf* in praise of the bride (7:2-6) describing her in a manner that appears to contain allusions to the geography of Palestine, e.g., the navel (v. 3) corresponds to Jerusalem (cf. Ez. 38:12); the breasts (v. 4) to Ebal and Gerizim; the nose (v. 5c) to Mount Lebanon; the head (v. 6) to Carmel. The description of the Bride as the land of Israel corresponds to the allegorical description of the bridegroom as the Temple (5:10-16).

8:6-7   *Set me as a seal on your heart.* The encomium on love sums up the feeling behind all the poems of the Canticle and re-echoes the words of God through Jeremiah, "With age-old love I have loved you, so I have kept my mercy toward you" (Jer. 31:3). It is on this enduring divine love that Israel, the bride, depends for the fulfillment of all her expectations.

13

Literary Analysis of the Chronicler's History

When the student comes to the end of the Chronicler's history, he is conscious of having passed successively from the promising morning light of David to the dazzling noonday splendor of Solomon and then down the long afternoon of Israel's history to the evening of the exile and the somber twilight of the time of Ezra and Nehemiah. As he enters historical darkness following the last events in the memoirs of Nehemiah, he is aware that the light from David's reign still glows in the surrounding darkness to brighten the years ahead. It is this light and the light from the Temple that the Chronicler intended to keep burning by means of his history.

In the Pentateuchal history the student has followed the saga of the institution of God's kingdom on earth with its essentially churchlike charter making it "a kingdom of priests, a holy nation" (Exod. 19:6). In the Deuteronomist's history he has seen an exile historian detail the sorry story of Israel's covenant relations with God, the fidelity of God and the infidelity of Israel, the unfailing love of God and the unabashed abandonment of covenant and Temple by Israel's kings — whose political interests led them to undermine the theocratic state and force God to begin all over again in the bondage of Babylon.

When the student reads the Chronicler's record of Israel's ecclesiastical history, it is as if the pentateuchal historian's "kingdom of priests and holy nation" had almost but not quite been realized under David and Solomon and the best of their successors, and as if the Deuteronomist's history were only a bad dream to be suppressed and forgotten, lest it prejudice the expectation of better things to come. If indeed this is the impression the student takes away from the Chronicler's history, it is no accident. It was precisely what the Chronicler planned: to impress upon his readers that the covenant charter has been reaffirmed in and through the promise made to the Davidic dynasty, that this promise was absolute in nature, eternal in duration, and by no means annulled because of the unfortunate conduct of the Davidic kings as a group, and that, therefore, Israel should look forward confidently to the fulfillment of this promise in the future.

To state this is easy, but to see the Chronicler's history as the Chronicler himself saw it — its purpose, its basic plan, and the execution of that plan — is far from easy. As with the Pentateuchal and Deuteronomical histories, the student must examine the sources, put himself in the historical milieu of the Chronicler, and see how the Chronicler revised, adapted, and arranged his sources in order to fuse them into a unity subservient to his teaching purpose. It will not be easy because the historical milieu of the Chronicler falls in the most obscure period of Israel's history (400-300 B.C.), and because the Chronicler has chosen a very subtle and roundabout method to achieve his aim.

To begin with, the Chronicler uses his sources selectively to highlight the two great phases of the establishment of the kingdom of God in Israel, emphasizing in (a) 1 and 2 Chronicles the place of the dynasty of David in God's plan for His kingdom, and (b) in Ezra-Nehemiah the restoration of the kingdom of God after the exile through the efforts of the two great reformers, the final effects of whose reforms — failure or success — are not declared, unlike the failure of the reforms of Jehoshaphat, Hezekiah, and Josiah.

In the first phase there can be no question but that by God's plan the Davidic kings were to be His representatives on earth whose principal function was to lead the people of His kingdom to worship and obey Him according to the moral and cultic requirements of the Sinai covenant which had been amalgamated with the covenant divinely made with the Davidic dynasty. Neither can there be question but that the Davidic kings, with the exception of David, Jehoshaphat, Hezekiah, and Josiah, had been unfaithful to their commission and had brought down on themselves and their people the catastrophe of 587.

This is the message of 1 and 2 Chronicles. But significantly the Chronicler ends 2 Chronicles with the notice that "In the first year of Cyrus, king of the

Persians, *to fulfil the word of Yahweh, which he had spoken by the mouth of Jeremiah*, Yahweh stirred up the heart of Cyrus, king of the Persians, who commanded it to be proclaimed through all his kingdom, and by writing also, saying: Thus saith Cyrus, king of the Persians: All the kingdoms of the earth hath Yahweh, the God of heaven, given to me; and he hath charged me to build him a house in Jerusalem, which is in Judea. Who is there among you of all his people? Yahweh, his God, be with him, and let him go up" (2 Chr. 36:22-23).

What is significant is the emphasis laid upon the fulfillment of God's word "spoken by the mouth of Jeremiah." Jeremiah clearly foretold not only the return of God's people from Babylon (Jer. 32:36-42), but the rise of a new David to fulfill the absolute promise of a perpetual dynasty made to the first David (2 Sam. 7), a king "who shall do justice and righteousness in the land . . ." (Jer. 32:14-26; cf. 23:5-8; 30:9). In Jeremiah's prediction, moreover, is summed up the predictions of Amos (9:11), Hosea (3:5), Isaiah (9; 11), Micah (5:1-4), and Ezekiel (34:23; 37:24).

The significance of the reference to the fulfillment of Jeremiah's predictions is fortified by the Chronicler's own insistence on the absolute nature of the promise made to David (cf. 1 Chr. 17:10-14; 28:4-7; 2 Chr. 13:4-8; 21:5-7; 6:1-42). Neither is it by accident that the Chronicler closes Solomon's prayer for the dedication of the Temple (1 Kings 8:12-53; 2 Chr. 6:1-42) by adding in his version vv. 8-10 of Ps. 132 (cf. 2 Chr. 6:41-42), a psalm dating from the last years of the kingdom and calling upon God not to abandon His Davidic king precisely because He has made an eternal covenant with the Davidic dynasty and has even ratified this covenant with an oath (Ps. 132:11-18)!

In the first part of his history (1 and 2 Chr.), therefore, the Chronicler has established two points: 1. the Davidic dynasty is an essential element in the divine plan for the theocratic kingdom; 2. this dynasty is assured by God, all indications to the contrary notwithstanding, of perpetual stability.

Surprisingly, in the second part of his history (Ezra-Nehemiah), the Chronicler has nothing to say explicitly about the Davidic dynasty and the perpetuity promised to that dynasty. He describes on the contrary the fulfillment of the predictions of Jeremiah concerning the restoration, but not the fulfillment of Jeremiah's predictions concerning the Davidic dynasty. The people have returned. The Temple has been rebuilt. Through the reforms of Ezra and Nehemiah the "new heart" and the "new spirit" predicted by Jeremiah (32:39) and Ezekiel (36:26) have presumably begun to be formed. For those who have eyes to see and even to those who do not have eyes, it is more than obvious that the only thing lacking to the restored kingdom is the expected king, the "one shepherd" predicted by Ezekiel (34:23), "the righteous shoot" predicted by Jeremiah (23:5), "the child born to us" predicted by Isaiah (9:6), "the ruler in Israel whose origin is from of old" predicted by Micah (5:1).

By the use of his sources, the Chronicler has established the place of the dynasty of David in God's plan for His kingdom. He has shown as well that the predictions of the prophets have all been fulfilled save one. It remained, therefore, for Israel to look forward prayerfully and confidently to the coming of the Messiah promised by the prophets.

The occasion that gave rise to the writing of the Chronicler's history is difficult to determine. If the Chronicler wrote shortly after the reforms of Ezra and Nehemiah, it is not unlikely that he wrote in order to second their reforms. If, as is more likely, the Chronicler wrote about the year 300, it is not improbable that the building of the Samaritan temple on Mount Gerizim and the Samaritans' claim to be the true Israel of God prompted the Chronicler to write. Such an occasion would explain a number of the more subtle aspects of the Chronicler's history.

It would explain the extraordinary attention paid to the Temple and the Temple personnel as an indirect refutation of any claims the Samaritans might make for their temple and priesthood.

It would explain the practical exclusion of all except Judah and the dynasty of David from the divine plan for the kingdom as an indirect method of eliminating any claims the Samaritans might make to be the true Israel of God. It would explain too the emphasis placed on pedigree in the genealogies.

It would explain the apparent neglect of the Chronicler to emphasize the great part played by Moses and the Sinai pact in God's plan, as well as his care to show that the Sinai covenant was swallowed up in the covenant made with the house of David. By such procedures, the Chronicler may well have intended to refute indirectly the Samaritan claim that only the Pentateuch was inspired and that upon the Pentateuch alone could the true faith be based.

If we are correct in these surmises, then the Chronicler's history is an apologia against the Samaritans, stressing as the essentials of the true religion not only the possession of the true Temple, true priesthood, and legitimate liturgy, but above all the fact that the true kingdom of God included not only the Temple and the liturgy but the Davidic dynasty as well. Though the dynasty was in decline at the time of the Chronicler, and the Samaritans may well have used this against the Jews, the Chronicler could boast of the absolute promise of perpetuity made to the dynasty of David, a promise which could not be annulled by any human power or even any human failing and which must be fulfilled some day in the family of David and the tribe of Judah (cf. John 4:19-26).

If such was the background of the Chronicler's work, then his purpose becomes even more clear and his plan more efficient. Thus in 1 Chr. 1–9, the reduction of all Israel's history prior to David to mere genealogies highlights in an unmistakeable way the paramount importance of the covenant with David over against the covenant with Moses detailed in the Pentateuch.

1 Chr. 10–29 not only establishes David as the legitimate king of God's kingdom and his dynasty as the only legitimate one, but establishes him as the power behind the Temple and as the true successor to Moses as liturgical legislator.

In 2 Chronicles, without ever detracting for a moment from the promise of perpetuity made to the Davidic dynasty, the Chronicler shows, nevertheless, that only a few of the Davidic kings were faithful to their trust and that as a result of the infidelity of the majority, the kingdom was destroyed. The book, however, ends up on a note of hope — the fulfillment of the prophecies of Jeremiah through the decree of Cyrus.

Ezra-Nehemiah demonstrate the fulfillment of the promises made by Jeremiah, pointing specifically to the rebuilding of the Temple and the reestablishment of the cult and to the exclusion of the Samaritans from both. Nothing is said about the Davidic dynasty because at the time of the Chronicler there was no immediate prospect of its reestablishment. All that could be said had been said in 1 and 2 Chronicles, where the emphasis on the promise to David by that God whose word endures forever was sufficient to make all the years following the exile, even the most dismal, pregnant with the expectation of the coming Messiah. It was this expectation, in a great part kept alive by the Chronicler's history, that led the disciples of John the Baptist some three hundred years later to ask of Jesus: "Art thou he who is to come, or shall we look for another?" (Matthew 11:3).

With the close of Ezra-Nehemiah, the Chronicler rings down the curtain on his history of Israel, bringing the reader no further than the last years of the fifth century. What happens in the years that follow, we can only conjecture from a study of the books of Tobit, Esther, and certain sections of Daniel, and from an analysis of the Jewish state as it is described in the year 175 in the two books of Maccabees.

The most significant development during this "dark-age" period of Israelite history is the increasing importance of the "Diaspora," i.e., the term used to designate Israelites who lived outside of the Holy Land. As is already evident from a reading of Ezra-Nehemiah, not all the exiles returned from Babylon. Many preferred to remain, and they made up the largest portion of the Jews of the Diaspora. Other groups gathered in the course of time in Alexandria, Antioch, and Rome. What characterized them and set them apart from the peoples among whom they lived, and by whom as a result they were more and more persecuted, was their religious separatism. They were conscious of their religious superiority and when strong showed it. In a Gentile world of crass idolatry and basic materialism they shone as the stars in the heavens. Gentile reactions varied between two extremes — admiration and resentment. Admiration sometimes led to conversion. Resentment led to persecution.

As the years rolled on, the Jews of the Dispersion became more numerous than the Jews of the homeland. Their importance grew with their numbers, and it is not surprising, therefore, that some of the inspired books of the Old Testament should be written by Jews of the Dispersion. While it is not certain, it seems not unlikely that such books as Esther, Judith, and some of the Wisdom books come from authors who were not living in Palestine.

Our next block of material, therefore, will deal with these works and others like them. Since some of them represent new literary forms proper to the age, we will study them in the light of these new approaches. We will begin with Jonah, the parable excoriating the narrow individualism of many of the Palestinian Jews, and continue with the para-historical books of Tobit, Esther, and Baruch. But first the reader is invited to study the psalms related to the Chronicler's history.

14

Psalms related to the Chronicler's History

In relation to the Pentateuchal history the student has studied hymns, thanksgiving psalms, and didactic historical psalms. In relation to the Deuteronomist's history he has studied individual and collective supplication psalms, confidence psalms, processional psalms, and messianic psalms.

In dealing with psalms related to the Chronicler's history, three new categories will be introduced: (a) the individual supplications of the sick; (b) the Jerusalem-Temple psalms; (c) the Kingship of Yahweh psalms.

In addition to some sample supplications of the sick (the Canticle of Hezekiah and Pss. 6; 88; 30), some sample Jerusalem-Temple psalms (Pss. 48; 46; 76) and some sample Kingship of Yahweh psalms (Pss. 47; 96), a number of psalms belonging to various categories and for the most part from the exilic and postexilic period will be treated, namely, a group of collective supplications (Pss. 79; 74; 89; 77; 102); a group of thanksgiving psalms (Pss. 107-118); a group of Jerusalem-Temple psalms (Pss. 137; 84; 87); lastly, all the Gradual psalms (Pss. 120–134).

1. Individual Supplications of the Sick

In dealing with individual supplications, it has already been pointed out that they are by nature very personal prayers in which the psalmist begs God for help in trouble, surcease from sickness, deliverance from persecution or exile. Their structure, as already indicated, consists usually of three parts: (a) a plea for help with motives; (b) a description, usually highly figurative and hyperbolical, of the besetting troubles; (c) an expression of confident anticipation that the plea will be heard.

Individual supplications of the sick do not constitute a new category of psalms, but rather a group of psalms under this general category, one in which emphasis is placed on a specific kind of trouble, sickness. They are best studied as a group because of the recurrence in them of certain ideas dealing with suffering and retribution which are surprising to our developed Christian way of thinking about these subjects.

Thus, besides the hyperbolical and figurative descriptions of suffering peculiar to these psalms, the reader will notice: (a) references to sin, either advertent or inadvertent, as the implied cause of all suffering; (b) expressions implying that if the psalmist dies he will no longer be able to worship and praise God; (c) references to enemies who persecute him, who tempt him to blaspheme God and to join them in apostasy, and requests for a cure precisely in order to rout these enemies.

As a background for these psalms, we shall begin with the sickness and prayer of King Hezekiah described in Is. 38. We shall then take the exegesis of Pss. 6; 88; 30. The reader can study the other psalms of the sick at his leisure. In some of these compositions the psalmists have already been cured or relieved of their sufferings and they combine with a description of their sufferings an expression of thanksgiving, e.g., the canticle of Hezekiah and Pss. 22; 30; 40. In others the psalmists are still suffering but hoping for deliverance, e.g., Pss. 6; 31; 38; 39; 41; 69; 88; 102.

Canticle of Hezekiah (Is. 38:10-20)

Theme	Thanksgiving of a man upon recovering his health after a serious illness.
Background	The sickness of King Hezekiah described in Is. 38.
Division	1. Reflections and spirit of a dying man (vv. 10-14). 2. Thanksgiving of the sick man after his recovery (vv. 15-20).
N.B.	The psalm need not have been composed by Hezekiah. It may have been a well known psalm adapted by the sick king or attributed to him by the author.

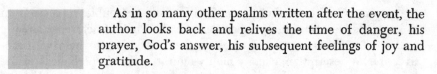

As in so many other psalms written after the event, the author looks back and relives the time of danger, his prayer, God's answer, his subsequent feelings of joy and gratitude.

v. 10 *in the noontime of life,* i.e., prematurely (cf. Ps. 55:24). Hezekiah was between 25 and 35 years old at the time of his sickness. *the gates of the nether world:* to go to the gates of Sheol is to be almost dead. Sheol, the dwelling-place of the dead, was the habitat of the deceased, perhaps a shadowy, passive kind of existence but from which there was no return to the land of the living.

v. 11 *I shall see the Lord no more:* the expression means to come to the Temple and participate in the worship of God. It comes either from the expression "to regard the face of (one's master or one's God)" in the sense of serving, i.e., as a servant who watches the face of his master to be ready to serve him; or to serve before the face of the idols representing gods in the pagan temples. The psalmist laments that he will no longer be able to worship God in the Temple (cf. Pss. 11:7; 17:15).

v. 12 *like a tent:* the transitoriness of life is compared to a shepherd's tent put up for the night and taken away in the morning, leaving no trace of the shepherd's brief stay. *folded up, like a weaver:* man's life is like the roll of cloth the weaver weaves. As long as the thread is fed into the machine, the cloth can be woven and rolled up by the weaver. When God cuts off the supply of thread (life), the weaving and life is over.

v. 13 *I cry out . . . like a lion . . . like a swallow . . . like a dove:* a hyperbolical description of his terrible sufferings, during which he looks prayerfully to God for help until his eyes grow weak (v. 14).

v. 15 *what am I to say:* cured of his sickness, he thanks God in the Temple (cf. v. 20; Ps. 116; Ps. 22:23-31).

v. 17 *behind your back all my sins:* since sin, either "defiant" sin or inadvertent sin (cf. Num. 15:22-24, 27-31; Lev.

4:2; Ps. 19:13), was considered the ultimate cause underlying any punishment or sickness with which a man was afflicted, the psalmist declares, since he has been cured, that God has forgiven him his sins. In John 9, our Lord corrects the popular notion that all sickness and sufferings must be accounted for either by reason of the sin of the sufferer himself or of his parents (cf. Sir. 38:15 and Job *passim*).

v. 18 *not the nether world:* the psalmist exults that, unlike the dead who cannot worship and praise God with solemen cult in the Temple, he can now by reason of his cure continue to worship God and "sing psalms all the days of his life in the house of the Lord" (v. 20).

Psalm 6

Theme Individual supplication of a sick man on his bed of pain.

Back-ground Textual: similar to canticle of Hezekiah (Is. 38:10-20).

Division
1. Prayer with motives (vv. 2-4).
2. Prayer with motives (vv. 5-6).
3. Description of suffering (vv. 7-8).
4. Confident anticipation that God will hear him (vv. 9-11).

v. 1 *in your anger:* the mention of divine wrath is an implicit acknowledgment that the psalmist is being punished for his sins, either "defiant" or "inadvertent" (cf. Num. 15:27-31).

v. 3 *for I am languishing:* the "for" (repeated in vv. 3b and 6a) introduces the reason why God should hear and heal the psalmist, e.g., v. 3: because of his sufferings; v. 6: because if God does not heal him, he will not be able to praise him in the Temple; in vv. 7-8, the "for" is implicit or goes back to 6a: because of his repentance, since God always hears the repentant sinner.

v. 6 *among the dead no one:* those who are dead and in Sheol can no longer praise God with solemn worship in the Temple (cf. Pss. 30:9; 88:10-12).

v. 7 *with weeping:* the exaggerated description of floods of tears is typical oriental hyperbole (cf. Jer. 9:1; 14:7). The tears are probably the result of repentance rather than of suffering.

v. 9 *depart from me:* confident that God will hear his prayer, he calls upon sinners to depart from him. They will no longer have occasion to gloat over him. The sinners are either his enemies who rejoice in seeing him suffer or the wicked in general who rejoice at the apparent downfall of the good. Whether the expression, "the Lord has heard," is one of confident anticipation before the event or the expression of what has actually occurred is not certain. It may be that the psalmist is giving thanks in the Temple after his cure (cf. Pss. 22:23ff; 31:20-25; Is. 38:15-20).

Psalm 88

Theme	Individual supplication of a man desperately ill.
Background	Textual: Is. 38:10-20; Pss. 6; 38; 39.
Division	1. The psalmist's desperate condition (vv. 2-9).
	2. In the tomb he will not be able to worship God (vv. 10-13).
	3. He pleads the length and bitterness of his suffering (vv. 14-19).
N.B.	The evidence of the text (vv. 9 and 19), plus the stark and longstanding suffering described, suggest the psalmist may have been a leper. Like Job, he is severely afflicted, abandoned by all, and practically dead. But unlike Job, the psalmist ends his prayer without any mention of or even anticipation of surcease to his suffering.

Psalm 30

Theme	Thanksgiving psalm of a sick man returned to health.

Back-ground	Similar to the canticle of Hezekiah (Is. 38:10-20) and Pss. 31; 32; 40; 116; 66.
Division	A. Act of thanksgiving and description of how God heard his prayer (vv. 3-6).
	B. (a) Retrospective description of his fall from prosperity to sickness (vv. 7-8).
	(b) The prayer he said while sick (vv. 9-11).
	(c) His joy when his prayer was heard (vv. 12-13).
N.B.	The mood of the psalmist is best recaptured by picturing him in the Temple joyfully making his thanksgiving sacrifice (as in Pss. 66 and 116) and recounting to his friends the story of what happened: how he became sick, his prayer, God's answer, his present joy. It is evident from the composition of the psalm (the sudden changes in vv. 7, 9, 12) that the psalm was written after the psalmist's cure to be used during a thanksgiving sacrifice in the Temple.

v. 2 *I will extoll you:* act of thanksgiving (cf. Ps. 40:6). *my enemies:* those who rejoiced at seeing him suffer and who mocked at his trust in God.

v. 5 *faithful ones:* the faithful who surround him during his thanksgiving sacrifice in the Temple are called upon to join him in praising God (cf. Ps. 22:23-31).

v. 6 *but a moment:* an indication perhaps that his sickness was of short duration. *his anger:* the mention of God's wrath is an implicit acknowledgment on the part of the psalmist that he had sinned.

v. 7 *in my security:* in retrospect the psalmist declares he sinned by pride and excessive confidence in himself (cf. Deut. 8:11-20). *I shall never be disturbed:* as if his prosperity depended on himself and not on God.

v. 10 *what gain:* God will get nothing from his death since the dead are no longer able to worship and praise Him in the Temple (cf. Ps. 6:6; Is. 38:18).

v. 12 *sackcloth:* sackcloth was worn in time of mourning and fasting (cf. Is. 3:24; 61:3; Ps. 35:13).

INDIVIDUAL SUPPLICATIONS OF THE SICK 431

2. Jerusalem-Temple Psalms

The presence of God among His chosen ones has always been a part of the true faith. The Ark, the footstool of His invisible throne, was the permanent sign of His presence during the period between Sinai and the building of Solomon's Temple. After David and Solomon, Jerusalem became the city of God and the Temple the house of God.

With the coming of Christ, God dwelt amongst His own in human form, and just as Christ was the true Temple of the Godhead because of the hypostatic union, so each Christian became a Temple of God because of the divine Indwelling (cf. John 14:23; 1 Cor. 3:16-17; 6:19; 2 Cor. 6:16).

It was inevitable in ancient times that the place in which God chose to dwell should be regarded with special reverence and by some even with superstitious awe. Thus the Ark was considered a kind of talisman in the time of the Judges (1 Sam. 4), and neither the destruction of Shiloh nor the capture of the Ark by the Philistines destroyed Israelitic reverence and awe for the place wherein God dwelt.

When Jerusalem became the city of God in the time of David and the Temple the house of God in the time of Solomon, Israel's psalmists took as special subjects for their hymns both the city of God (Pss. 68:10-19; 132:13-17) and the Temple in which He had taken up His abode (Pss. 84; 122). In the time of Isaiah, only Jerusalem withstood the assault of Sennacherib, and Israel's psalmists waxed loud in their praise of the Holy City (cf. Pss. 46; 48; 76).

So great in later years was popular belief in the inviolability of Jerusalem that Jeremiah was accused of blasphemy when he foretold its downfall and the destruction of the Temple (Jer. 7:1-11; 26:1ff); and Ezekiel was forced to preach at length to persuade the exiles that the destruction of the Temple was the work of God and not the conquest of God by Babylonian gods (cf. Ez. 8–11).

By the time the Temple of Zerubbabel was completed, Israel's concept of God's dwelling place had been purified and her psalmists and prophets were raising their eyes to the new Jerusalem, the spiritual capital of all men (cf. Ez. 40–48; Is. 60; 62; 65:17-25; 66:7-24; Pss. 137; 87).

Soon after the fullness of time arrived, the earthly Temple of Jerusalem was destroyed. But He who said, "Destroy this temple, and in three days I will raise it up," (John 2:19) became Himself the temple of the new covenant and the light of the new Jerusalem (Apoc. 21–22). It is in this vein that the Church today sings the Jerusalem-Temple psalms in the Mass and the breviary, praising Him who dwells not only in temples built by man but in the hearts of the faithful as well. It is in this vein that the author of the hymn for the dedication of a church sings:

Theme	Collective supplication lamenting the apparent unconcern of God for His ruined Temple and His desolate people.
Back-ground	Either Babylonia or Palestine twenty or thirty years after the destruction of the Temple and the deportation of the people.
Division	1. A lament for the ruin and profanation of the Temple (vv. 1-11).
	2. The psalmist excites confidence by recalling God's power in the past and begs Him to intervene now in favor of His people (vv. 12-23).

v. 1 *forever:* the emphasis on a long time, here and in vv. 3, 9, 10, 19, 23, indicates that the psalmist writes twenty years or more after the fall of Jerusalem in 587.

v. 2 *remember:* the psalmist's prayer for God's intervention in the present is strengthened by his references to God's interventions in the past. Thus he asks God to remember the little flock, Abraham and his family; the tribe which He made His own at the time of the Exodus; the city, Jerusalem, which He had chosen in the time of David to be His dwelling-place.

vv. 3-7 *the utter ruins:* after speaking of God's interventions in the past, the psalmist now begs God to direct His steps to the ruined Temple, where His enemies, the Babylonians, have set up their military standards as a testimony to their conquest after burning the Temple to the ground and thus profaning the house of God (cf. Jer. 52:13; 2 Chr. 36:19).

v. 8 *all the shrines:* the reference is probably to such ancient sanctuaries as Shiloh, Bethel, Gibeon, and Gilgal destroyed along with Jerusalem by Nebuchadnezzar's armies in 587.

v. 9 *deeds:* in this context, the signs are not military standards as in v. 4 but the interventions or miracles that God had worked for His people in the past, sadly missed at this time. To this is added the lack of a prophet who might reassure them as in times past that God would soon intervene. If the psalm was written, as the evidence indicates, long after the destruction of Jerusalem, the psalmist could well say, "There is no prophet now," since Jeremiah and Ezekiel were certainly dead by the year 560 at least, and Deutero-Isaiah was as yet either unknown or unacknowledged as a prophet. If written in Palestine, there is all the more reason for saying, "There is no prophet now."

vv. 12-18 *my king from of old:* in language borrowed from the Marduk-Tiamat legend (cf. Job 7:12; 9:13; 26:12; Is. 27:1; 51:9; Pss. 89:10-11; 104:7), the psalmist describes God's awesome power in creation, implying that as God had destroyed the powers of evil in the past (personified by Leviathan, the sea monster—cf. Is. 27:1), so He can destroy His enemies at the present time. Thus, in v. 18, the psalmist reminds God that His enemy, presumably Babylon, insults and derides Him.

vv. 19-23 *give not to the vulture:* the psalmist concludes by begging God not to hand over to the vulture, Babylon, the life of His "dove," a metaphorical name for Israel (cf. Cant. 2:10-14; Hosea 7:11; 11:11; Ps. 68:14), and by begging Him to arise and take in hand His cause (Israel's plight), lest His unconcern permit His enemies (the Babylonians) to continue insulting Him.

Psalm 89

Theme	A collective supplication lamenting the apparent failure of the divine promise granting perpetuity to the royal house of David (cf. p. 439).
Background	Nathan's oracle to David concerning the perpetuity of his dynasty (2 Sam. 7) and its apparent dissolution after 587.
Division	1. The psalmist solemnly recalls God's promise to David (2 Sam. 7) (vv. 2-5).
	2. The psalmist digresses on God's omnipotence either as a *captatio benevolentiae* or to reassure himself that God can fulfill His promise (vv. 6-19).
	3. A detailed elaboration of the promise emphasizing its perpetuity (vv. 20-38).
	4. The apparent failure of the promise after 587 (vv. 39-46).

5. The psalmist's impassioned prayer for his people and his king (vv. 47-53).

N.B. The psalmist's state of mind is similar to that of the apostles at the time of our Lord's passion and death. Just as the apostles could not believe that Christ would die on the Cross and end their glorious expectations, so the psalmist, in 587, seeing the Davidic king carried into exile by Nebuchadnezzar, the Temple burned to the ground, Jerusalem in ruins and the Chosen People dispersed, could not believe that God would cancel out His promise. His faith is strong but sore pressed by events. Therefore, he forces himself, as it were, to strengthen his trust in God.

vv. 2-5 *the favors of the Lord:* the psalmist opens with the two motifs that will run through his psalm: God's love (*hesedh*), the source of His promise to David in Nathan's oracle (2 Sam. 7), and His fidelity (*'emunah*), the assurance that He will fulfill the promise (cf. Exod. 23:6). The psalmist repeats these loaded words regularly throughout the psalm (cf. vv. 2, 3, 6, 9, 15, 25, 29, 34, 50). The strophe concludes (vv. 3-5) with a solemn statement of the promise made to David.

vv. 6-19 *the heavens proclaim your wonders:* in vv. 6-9, the psalmist describes God's power in the heavens; in vv. 10-15, His power on earth; in vv. 11-19, the good fortune of the people and the king who have God for their protector. The language is hymnic, and some authors consider the verses (6-19) an independent psalm added here by an editor. The unity of the psalm, however, is clear from the characteristic emphasis on "favors and faithfulness" found here (vv. 6, 9, 15) as well as throughout the whole psalm (vv. 2, 3, 25, 34, 50); from the natural transition in v. 19 (emphasizing the king) to v. 20, the beginning of the elaboration of the promise made to the dynasty; and from the psychological state of the psalmist, requiring reassurance of God's power to fulfill His promise as a bolster to his faith.

v. 6 *the holy ones:* the angelic hosts, referred to in v. 7 as the "sons of God" and in v. 8 as the "council of the holy ones" surrounding God (cf. Is. 6:3; 1 Kings 22:19; Dan. 7:10). It is quite probable that in this section (vv.

6-15) the psalmist is drawing for his imagery upon the Babylonian myth of Marduk in the council of the gods receiving his commission to engage in mortal combat the monster goddess, Tiamat, the personification of the forces of evil. Thus, the reference in v. 10 to the "surging of the sea" shows the sea personified as the enemy of God, crushed by him at the beginning of creation; and in v. 11 the psalmist uses "Rahab," a popular name for the mythological Tiamat (cf. Pss. 74:13-14; 93:3-4; Job 9:13; 26:12; Is. 51:9-10).

v. 19 *to the Lord our shield:* "our shield" and "our king" are equivalent terms. The psalmist declares that the king is in the hands of this all powerful God. This declaration serves as transition from the digression on God's power back to the king and the promise made to David, the main theme of the psalm.

vv. 20-38 *once you spoke:* elaborating the promises made through Samuel and Nathan, the psalmist extolls David, the great warrior, the man divinely chosen through Samuel (cf. 1 Sam. 16:12), the obedient servant of God unlike Saul, the man anointed by Samuel (cf. 1 Sam. 16:1-13). In vv. 22-26, the psalmist paraphrases 2 Sam. 7:9-13. In v. 26, he describes the limits of the Davidic kingdom (the sea — the Mediterranean; the rivers — the Euphrates, cf. Pss. 72:8; 80:12; Deut. 1:7; 11:26). In vv. 27-38, every group of four verses ends with a repeated emphasis on the perpetuity of the promise made to David (cf. vv. 30, 34, 38).

vv. 31-34 *if his sons forsake my law:* "The condition enunciated here was fulfilled at the time of the destruction of Jerusalem; wherefore, at that time God punished with rod and stripes (v. 33); the "grace," however, which He does not withdraw, is the duration of the Davidic kingdom, which He will restore and conserve under another, higher form, namely, the kingdom of Christ the King, born of the Davidic line. Thus the prophecy is fulfilled, even though the terrestrial kingdom of the Davidic line falls. In a non-literal but more eminent, higher way, God heard the prayer of the psalmist, who, without distinguishing between the absolute and the conditional fulfillment of the promise, lamented and besought a remedy for the prostrate kingdom of David. This more eminent, though non-literal way, was by way of the Davidic kingdom restored in Christ" (Note on vv. 31-34, LP 182).

vv. 39-46 *yet you have rejected:* to the certitude of the promise, the psalmist now opposes the apparent failure of the promise occasioned by the cessation of the dynasty in 587. In vv. 41-42, the psalmist compares the kingdom to a devastated vineyard (cf. Ps. 80; Is. 5:1-7). In v. 46, the statement, "You have shortened," is probably a reference to the 400 year old Davidic dynasty rather than to the young king, Jehoiachin. Four centuries is a long time, but it is only the period of youth for a kingdom to which was promised perpetuity.

vv. 47-52 *how long, O Lord?:* The psalmist concludes with the prayer that has been implicit throughout the psalm: How long will God permit the faith of His people to be tested? More directly he asks: "Where are your ancient favors, O Lord, which you pledged to David by your faithfulness?" In vv. 51-52, he implicitly appeals to God's honor, reminding Him that his people and his king are derided (in captivity in Babylon) by the Gentiles, who have apparently given the lie to the divine promises.

Psalm 77

Theme	A collective supplication beseeching redemption from captivity.
Background	Internal evidence suggests the time of the Babylonian exile.
Division	1. The psalmist's anguished prayer and meditation during a time of great calamity (vv. 2-13). 2. His recollection of the first Exodus encourages him to hope for a new one (vv. 14-21).

vv. 1-5 *aloud to God I cry:* oppressed by some great calamity (probably the Babylonian exile), the psalmist seeks consolation in unceasing prayer.

vv. 6-13 *I consider the days of old:* meditating on God's merciful dealings with Israel in the past, the psalmist asks himself the burning question of the exile: has God forgotten Israel (v. 8), has He utterly rejected His people, forgotten His covenant? In v. 11, *the right hand . . . is changed,* — the psalmist touches the nadir of discouragement: God, it appears, has changed His merciful way of dealing with His people. With this terrible thought, the psalmist cannot be reconciled. In vv. 12-13, he reanimates himself with more cheerful thoughts, the remembrance of the Exodus and its miracles.

vv. 14-21 *O God, your way is holy:* — continuing the line of thought in vv. 12-13, the psalmist recalls God's mighty power to deliver His people manifested in the plagues and in the Exodus from Egypt whereby He made known His power among the Egyptians (vv. 15-16; cf. Exod. 7–10; 14). In the remainder of the psalm (vv. 17-21), the psalmist describes the intervention of God at the time of the Exodus in conventional theophany language (cf. Exod. 19; Hab. 3; Ps. 114:1-4). The lesson and hope to be drawn from this ancient intervention of God is implicit but clear: the God who could save Israel from Egypt in the past can with equal power save Israel now from the bondage of the Babylonians (for the same type of implicit argumentation, cf. Is. 42:14ff; 43:1ff; 43:16ff).

Psalm 102

Theme	An individual supplication begging God to end the exile and restore Jerusalem.
Background	In Babylonia after long years of exile.
Division	1. The prayer and the lament of the psalmist suffering in exile (vv. 1-12).
	2. The psalmist's prayer for and anticipation of Jerusalem's restoration (vv. 13-23).
	3. The contrast between God's eternity and the brief span of man's life (vv. 24-29).
N.B.	The language of the psalm is simple and conventional. The argumentation, however, is subtle. After describing his

own protracted sufferings in exile (the conventional language masks the real nature of the sufferings) and the shortness of man's brief span of life (vv. 4-12), the psalmist suddenly contrasts man's brief span to God's eternity (v. 13), and then begins to pray passionately for the restoration of Zion (vv. 14-23). In v. 24, he returns to the contrast between the brevity of man's life and the eternity of God. The implicit argumentation of the psalmist in favor of God's hearing his prayer seems to be that God is eternal and time means nothing to Him, but to finite man time does mean a great deal. Let God, therefore, hear and help quickly (cf. v. 3d, "answer me speedily," and v. 14b, "it is time").

The psalm, very similar in background and argumentation to Ps. 90, is addressed to God in the singular, but it is not unlikely that it is a collective singular (cf. Is. 53–54; Ps. 22) and that as a result the psalm is a collective rather than individual supplication.

Psalm 107

Theme A thanksgiving psalm praising God for liberating Israel from exile.

Background Not long after the return in 538. The psalmist echoes Deutero-Isaiah.

Division *Introduction:* an invitation to thank God for redeeming Israel (vv. 1-3).
Part A. four metaphors or allegories of Israel redeemed from exile (vv. 4-32).
　　　　1. Israel, a caravan lost in the desert (vv. 4-9).
　　　　2. Israel, a prisoner in chains (vv. 10-16).
　　　　3. Israel, sick unto death (vv. 17-22).
　　　　4. Israel, a ship in a storm (vv. 23-32).
Part B. The land and the people before and after the exile (vv. 33-43).

vv. 2-3 *the redeemed:* the principal reason for the praise is God's love manifested to those who have been redeemed from exile, those whom God brought back from Assyria, Media, Persia, Babylonia, and Egypt, all the lands to which they had been deported in the great deportations of 721 and 587. When Cyrus' decree of liberation went out in

539, they returned to Israel "from the east and the west, from the north and the south" (cf. Is. 49:12).

vv. 4-9 *they went astray in the desert wilderness:* Israel in captivity is likened to a caravan lost in the desert. The reader should note the refrain (vv. 6 and 8), which though substantially the same in each of the four allegories (cf. vv. 13 and 15; 19 and 21; 28 and 31) is nevertheless modified slightly in the intervening verses (e.g., vv. 7 and 9; 14 and 16; 20 and 22; 29 and 32) to adapt it to the motif of each allegory.

vv. 10-16 *they dwelt in darkness:* Israel in captivity is likened to a prisoner in chains (cf. Is. 42:9; 49:9). The reason for her bondage is given "They had rebelled" (v. 11). Because of this rebellion, God humbled them (v. 12; cf. Is. 51: 17-20).

vv. 17-22 *stricken:* the comparison of Israel to a man sick unto death who is suddenly cured corresponds to the apparent end of Israel's hopes when she was buried in Babylon (cf. Ez. 37) and to her miraculous release under Cyrus. *because of their wicked ways:* as in v. 11, the psalmist shows the sickness and sufferings were not accidental but the punishment for sin. *he sent forth his word:* God's word is His decision to act — in this case His decision to end the exile (cf. Is. 55:10-11; Ps. 148:15, 18; Wis. 16: 22).

vv. 23-32 *they who sailed in ships:* Israel at sea is perhaps an allegory likening the final years of Judah to a tempest in which the ship of state is sunk in Babylon (cf. Is. 54:11; Jer. 51:34, 44; Ez. 27:19-21). It is possible that the comparison is similar to Ps. 46:3-4, where the attack of the Assyrian armies is likened to a great storm. *trading on the deep waters:* — perhaps this is an ironic reference to Israel's attempt to make herself a great power in the ancient world rather than obey God's plan for her as made known by Isaiah and Jeremiah.

vv. 33-41 *he changed rivers into desert:* the absence of the refrain and the lack of explicit thanksgiving in vv. 33-41 make it possible that these verses are an addition to the psalm, which appears to end with v. 32. However, the theme is the same—return from the exile, and the tone of thanksgiving is at least implicit. Moreover, the language as in other parts of the psalm reechoes Deutero-Isaiah, and the psalmist uses the same metaphorical language as Deutero-Isaiah in his description of the reestablishment of the people in the Promised Land (cf. Is. 35:1-7; 41:17-20; 42:15; 50:2). Out of many possible interpretations, the following seems the best: vv. 33-38 describe the ravaged *land* of Palestine made fertile once more at the time of Israel's return from exile. Thus vv. 33-34 refer to the punishment of Israel in 587 when the land was turned into a desert by the Babylonians (cf. Is. 42:15; 50:2); vv. 35-38 refer to the restoration of the land from desert to fertile and habitable land again at the time of the return (cf. Is. 35:1-7; 41:17-20). In vv. 39-41, on the other hand, the psalmist describes the restoration of the *people*. Thus v. 39 refers to the people decimated by invasions and captivity; vv. 40-41 refer to the return of the people and the rebirth of the nation (cf. Is. 54).

vv. 42-43 *the upright see:* the psalmist describes the joy of the returned exiles, particularly those who scrutinize spiritually the providence of God and see in it the "favors of the Lord" (cf. vv. 8, 15, 21, 31). The question, "Who is wise enough" (v. 43), is taken from Hosea 14:10 and is similar to Is. 41:20. The thought is: he is a wise man who sees these events of history as part of God's plan, a plan in which the agony of the exile and the joy of the return are manifestations of God's steadfast love for Israel.

Psalm 118

Theme	A psalm of thanksgiving sung in procession on a feast day.
Background	Internal evidence suggests some great occasion after the return from the exile (cf. Ezra 3; 6:13-18; Neh. 9:9-18; 12:27ff).
Division	A. An introduction calling on all Israelites to thank God (vv. 1-4).
	B. 1. Prayer and confidence in time of tribulation (vv. 5-9).

2. Surrounded by foes the psalmist conquers by the help of God (vv. 10-14).
3. Cries of thanksgiving of those gathered for the feast (vv. 15-18).
C. 1. Colloquy between leader, priests, and people arriving at the Temple for the thanksgiving sacrifice (vv. 19-25).
2. Entrance of the procession into the Temple and blessing of the priests (vv. 26-29).

vv. 1-4 *give thanks:* the psalm begins with a call upon all to thank God, inviting in turn the whole nation or "house of Israel," the priests or "house of Aaron," and the proselytes "who fear the Lord."

vv. 5-9 *in my straits:* as usual in thanksgiving psalms, there is some description of the danger from which God saved the psalmist. Here, since the psalmist speaks for the whole people, the danger or tribulation referred to is probably the exile or the guerrilla warfare of the Samaritans following the return to Palestine (cf. Ezra 4–6; Neh. 2:4ff). *better . . . in the Lord:* while the returned exiles received some help from the Persian kings, the psalmist nevertheless re-echoes the warnings of Isaiah and Jeremiah that Israel's real source of help is from God and not from man.

vv. 10-14 *all the nations:* after the return from the exile the Israelites were harassed continuously by the Samaritans, Edomites, Moabites, and others who opposed the re-establishment of the Jewish state (cf. Ezra 4–6; Neh. 2:4ff). *I was hard pressed* (v. 13): the psalmist probably refers to the continuous attacks of Israel's enemies, first by slanderous letters to the Persian emperor (cf. Ezra 4), later physically (cf. Neh. 2–6) when marauding bands tried to prevent the rebuilding of Jerusalem's walls so that the Jews were compelled to work with their weapons always at hand.

vv. 15-18 *the joyful shout:* the reference to cries of thanksgiving "in the tents of the just" inclines many commentators to believe the psalm was composed for the celebration of the feast of Tabernacles (cf. Neh. 8:14-17; Lev. 23:40ff). The allusions to salvation from death (vv. 17-18) may very well express the sentiments of the returned exiles who realized the exile had been a chastisement but not unto death (cf. Ez. 37).

vv. 19-25 *open to me:* the change of subject and the antiphonal character of the lines suggest some kind of an entrance ceremony as the procession arrives at the Temple gates. Perhaps as in Pss. 15 and 24 there was an interrogation to remind the worshippers that only the worthy might enter in. The different parts may have been distributed somewhat as follows: v. 19, the leader speaks for those in the procession and requests entrance; v. 20, the priests inside point out that only the just may enter in; v. 21, the leader or all in procession respond to the priests and chant a brief hymn of thanksgiving.

v. 22 *the stone:* the stone represents Israel, whom the Gentiles (the builders) rejected in the time of the exile, but whom God now has brought forth back from exile and made once more the "cornerstone" nation of the world. The reference is either to the cornerstone (cf. Jer. 51:26), the stone first laid and upon which all measurements for the building are based, or the keystone (the center stone, cf. Zech. 4:7) uniting the two sides of an arch. N.B., Stone, a key word joining the Old Testament and the New Testament, is used in various ways — in Is. 28:16 the stone is confident faith in God; in Dan. 2:34 the stone "hewn from the mountain" is the messianic kingdom; in Matthew 21:42 Christ refers it to Himself quoting Ps. 118:22, cf. Matthew 16:18; Eph. 2:12-22; Rom. 9:33, 1 Peter 2:6ff). *by the Lord has this been done* (v. 23): bringing Israel back from exile and making her the cornerstone is the work of God, a miracle of divine providence.

vv. 26-29 *blessed is he who comes:* the high priest or priests as a group bless the leader of the procession and those with him in response to their acclamations in vv. 24-25 (cf. Matthew 21:9 where these words are used by the crowd on Palm Sunday to hail Jesus as the Messiah). The priests invite the people (v. 27b) to "join in procession with leafy boughs (cf. 2 Mac. 10:7; Neh. 8:15; Mark 11:8) up to the horns of the altar." The psalm concludes in vv. 28-29 with a final triumphant expression of thanksgiving.

Theme   A Jerusalem-Temple psalm expressing the passionate love of the exiles for the city of God.

Background   Memories of the exile. Probably written soon after the return, recalling their devotion while in exile to the city of God.

Division
1. Their sorrow while in exile (vv. 1-3).
2. Their refusal to sing while Jerusalem was in ruins (vv. 4-6).
3. A passionate plea for punishment of all who sought to destroy the city of God (vv. 7-9).

v. 1   *by the streams:* in their dwellings by the canals of the Euphrates (cf. Ezekiel dwelling by the Chebar canal), the exiles sat and wept for Jerusalem. The reference is perhaps to the places where the exiles held their liturgical meetings, usually near water because of the ritual purifications (cf. Acts 16:13).

v. 2   *on the aspens:* hanging their lyres on the aspen trees is a metaphorical way of expressing their refusal to sing while Jerusalem was in ruins.

v. 3   *the songs of Zion:* the Babylonians wanted them to sing their psalms about Zion (perhaps such as Pss. 122 and 126). But to respond is unthinkable for those who love Zion.

v. 4   *how could we sing:* how could one who loved Jerusalem sing the inspired psalms in the midst of pagan Babylon! Perhaps there was even question of singing them as part of pagan worship.

v. 5   *if I forget you:* the psalmist declares he would rather lose his right arm and have his tongue become paralyzed in his mouth than sing the sacred psalms in Babylon. This impassioned declaration of love and devotion for the city of God should be the attitude of all who truly love the Church.

v. 7   *against the children of Edom:* the Jews never forgot the treachery of Edom in siding with the destroyers of the

Holy City (cf. Is. 34:5-15; Ez. 25:12ff; Jer. 49:7-22; Obadiah).

v. 9 *little ones against the rock:* one of the customary horrors of ancient warfare was the barbarous destruction of children (cf. Is. 13:16). The allusion, therefore, to the killing of the infants is only the poet's way of saying: "As you have done to us, so may God in His justice do to you." The poet has nothing against children. His expectation of the destruction of Babylon is shared by Isaiah (47:1-9) and Jeremiah (51:24ff).

Psalms 42—43

Theme
An individual supplication expressing the longing of an exiled priest or levite for the Temple and the city of God.

Background
The psalmist is in exile outside Palestine.

Division
The repetition of the same refrain (vv. 6; 12; 42:5), the unity of the theme throughout, and the absence of any title in Ps. 43 show that Pss. 42—43 are really one psalm.
1. The ardent longing of the exile to return and take part once more in the Temple liturgy (vv. 1-6).
2. His misery in exile is tempered only by his confidence in God (vv. 7-12).
3. His prayer for deliverance and his anticipation of once more going up to the altar of God (Ps. 43:1-5).

vv. 2-3 *as the hind:* comparing his longing for the Temple to the pitiful condition of a deer in time of drought (cf. Joel 1:20), he thirsts for the day when he will be able to take part once more in the Temple liturgy, literally "behold the face of God" (a baptized idolatrous expression — seeing the face of an idol — used by the psalmist without scruple to express his desire to see "the living God" in contradistinction to the lifeless idols of the pagans).

vv. 4-5 *my tears are my food:* living an existence in exile in which tears have become his daily bread, constantly taunted by the pagans with the question, "Where is your God?" as if God had abandoned him, his only solace is in the remembrance of the happy days in Jerusalem when he used to take part in the Temple festivities (cf. Pss. 24:7-10; 68:25ff; 81; 118).

v. 6 *why are you so downcast:* the refrain, repeated in v. 12 and in 43:5, supplies the expression of confident anticipation typical of supplication psalms.

v. 7 *from the land of the Jordan and of Hermon:* it is not clear whether the psalmist in exile is remembering the land of the Jordan, Mount Hermon, and Mizar (either the little town of Zaorath near the sources of the Jordan, or more probably little Mount Zion; cf. Pss. 43:3; 68:17), or is actually exiled in the land of the sources of the Jordan.

vv. 8-11 *deep calls unto deep:* the reference to the torrents and the waves is the stereotyped Hebrew figure of the "waters" to describe a sorrow or sickness so serious the psalmist considers himself on the way to Sheol in the depths of the abyss (cf. Pss. 18:5; 69:1; 88:8; Jonah 2:4). The crushing of "bones" (v. 11) is another stereotyped Hebrew expression to describe trouble, whether sickness (cf. Is. 38:13) or persecution (cf. Ps. 31:11; 102:4).

42:1-5 *do me justice:* the psalmist prays for redress against his oppressors (perhaps the Babylonians), and against one particular individual (unless the word "man" is to be taken in the collective sense), whose identity is unknown. *send forth your light:* with the help of God's light (His judgment making known the truth) and the assurance of His fidelity, the exile is confident he will someday return to Jerusalem and the Temple, where again he will be able to visit God's altar.

Psalm 84

Theme	A Jerusalem-Temple psalm expressing the passionate love of the pilgrim-Israelites for the House of God.
Background	Probably written to be sung by the pilgrims going up to Jerusalem for the great feast days (cf. Pss. 122 and 125).
Division	1. The burning desire of the psalmist to go up to the Temple of God (vv. 2-4).

2. The privilege of those who live near the Temple or who can go up to the Temple in pilgrimage (vv. 5-8).

3. A prayer for Yahweh's anointed and a final expression of the happiness of those who dwell in His courts (vv. 9-13).

vv. 3-4 *my soul yearns and pines:* his longing for the Temple (cf. Pss. 42:1; 61:5) makes him envy the privileged birds that nest in the Temple and leads him to express elliptically his wish that the Temple might be his home. Simple as this is, it is in harmony with vv. 2 and 11.

vv. 6-8 *pilgrimage:* for the man who has it in his heart to make a pilgrimage to the Temple, passing through the arid valley (the trek up to Jerusalem) is as nothing. Indeed the thought of going up to Jerusalem clothes the arid valley with greenery as after the first rains (v. 7). Moreover, journeying along, *they go from strength to strength:* the thought of soon arriving at the Temple makes them feel stronger by the mile. A longed-for destination always makes the road easier and the way shorter.

v. 10 *our shield:* some authors put "shield" in apposition with "God"; but it is more correctly read in apposition with "anointed." In either version, "your anointed" represents the king if the psalm is pre-exilic (cf. Pss. 89:19; 132:1), the high priest if the psalm is postexilic (cf. Lev. 4:3; 6:9; Dan. 9:26).

Psalm 87

Theme

A Jerusalem-Temple psalm extolling Jerusalem as the spiritual mother of all men. A prophetic vision of messianic Sion.

Background

Is. 2:2-4; 42:5-6; 45:14-25; 49:5-6; 54; 60; 62; 66:19; Ez. 37:28 — prophecies about Zion verified in the New Testament (cf. Gal. 4:26 and Apoc. 21).

Division

After declaring God's love for Zion and the great things that lie in store for her (vv. 1-3), the psalmist predicts that all men will find a spiritual metropolis and mother in

Zion (vv. 4-6) and that all will rejoice in the blessings that come from her (v. 7).

v. 3 *glorious things are said of you*: not only are material blessings promised to Zion (cf. Pss. 122 and 132) but messianic glories (cf. Is. 2:2-4; 4:2-6; 11:1-9; 54; 60, 62; 66:10-24). The promises of Christ, for which we pray, are precisely these glories of Jerusalem, the city of God spoken of by Isaiah (Is. 60 *passim*) and by St. John in the Apocalypse (Apoc. 21—22) as the eternal Jerusalem descending from heaven as a bride for the Lamb.

v. 4 *I tell of*: God makes a list of the people whom He will call to the faith, a book of life from which sinners are excluded (cf. Ps. 139:16). In this list are included men from all the four corners of the earth who will worship God; thus Egypt represents the people of the south; Babylon, the people of the east; Philistia and Tyre, the people of the west and northwest; Ethiopia, the people of the far southeast, Africa, and the then known ends of the earth.

v. 5 *one and all*: all are born spiritually in Zion by faith and obedience to the law of God who has founded this city as the spiritual metropolis of the world (cf. St. Cyprian, "No one can have God for his father if he does not have the Church for his mother.")

v. 6 *they shall note*: in His book of the people who belong to Him, God marks down the names of those who are born in Zion. Thus all men besides their national allegiance are to have a single religious allegiance. They are to belong to one spiritual city, Zion of God. As Pius XI happily expressed it: "We are all Semites spiritually."

v. 7 *and all shall sing*: the inhabitants of spiritual Zion will sing out in praise of their mother: "My home is within you."

3. The Gradual Psalms

Ps. 120 is the first of the "Gradual Psalms" (Pss. 120—134), psalms so-called either because sung by the faithful "going up" in pilgrimage to the

Temple for the three great feasts of the liturgical year (Exod. 23:17; Deut. 16:12) or because they were sung by the Israelites "coming up" or returning from the exile.

Most of the gradual psalms betray an exilic or postexilic background, some reflecting the hope of the anguished exiles (Pss. 123 and 130), some the sentiments of the returning exiles (Pss. 121; 124; 126; 129), some the conditions in Palestine after the return from the exile in the time of Ezra and Nehemiah (Pss. 122; 125; 127; 133).

For the most part the gradual psalms are a collection of short lyric poems expressing the spirit of the children of God in every age, a spirit of dependence, trust, and joy in the Lord — the spirit described by Jesus in the Sermon on the Mount when He said: "Blessed are you, poor in spirit . . . be not solicitous . . . seek ye first the kingdom of God and all things else will be added to you." The reader should remember that what is necessary to appreciate these psalms is not so much study as meditation.

Psalm 120

Theme
An individual supplication pleading for help against evil tongues.

Background
The psalmist lives in a place where he and his people are subjected to continual lying slander. The time of the exile or the time of Ezra and Nehemiah, when the Jews were surrounded by envious and hostile Samaritans and Edomites who wrote lying letters to the Persian court, would fit the sentiments of the psalm (cf. Ezra 4:6; Neh. 6).

Division
1. Prayer (vv. 1-2).
2. Threat (vv. 3-4).
3. Lament (vv. 5-7).

v. 1 *in my distress:* in the past when in distress the psalmist prayed and God heard him. Therefore he prays now with confidence: "O Lord, deliver me. . . ."

v. 3 *what will he inflict on you:* the psalmist plays on the words of the lying oaths taken by his slanderers. A person taking an oath would say: "May God do this and add that . . . if I do not do as I have promised" (cf. 1 Sam. 3:17; 14:44; 25:22). He tells the slanderers that God will give them more than they have bargained for.

v. 4 *sharp arrows:* a common metaphor for punishment and afflictions (cf. Ps. 38:2 where sickness is described as "arrows fixed in the flesh," and Ps. 64:4 where the words of a slanderer are described as "poisonous arrows"). Here there is added to the piercing arrows of a mighty warrior fiery coals of the broomwood — a wood noted for making the best charcoal — perhaps hendiadys for "burning arrows."

v. 5 MESHECH: a barbarous country between the Black and Caspian seas (cf. Gen. 10:2; Ez. 27:13). KEDAR: a region in the Syro-Arabian desert (cf. Gen. 25:13; Ez. 32:26-27). Reference to these places is the author's way of saying that those around him are like barbarians, people who love fighting and seem to hate peace (v. 6). Of his enemies, he can say as he would say of barbarians: "When I speak of peace, they are ready for war."

Psalm 121

Theme	A confidence psalm. God is the guardian and protector of His people.
Background	Perhaps the sentiments of the exiles in Babylon, perhaps the sentiments of the pilgrims on their way to Jerusalem (cf. Ezra 8:21-23).
Division	1. Help comes from God (vv. 1-2). 2. Help comes faithfully (vv. 3-4). 3. God is ready to help day or night (vv. 5-6). 4. God is ready to help always and everywhere (vv. 7-8).

v. 1 *toward the mountains:* he looks to the mountains where Jerusalem the city of God is located (cf. Pss. 125; 87; Is. 2).

v. 3 *who guards you:* the repetition of "guards" (six times in 6 verses) may reflect the bad times after the exile when the pilgrims going up from remote villages were in danger of being attacked by the Samaritans.

v. 6 *the sun:* they knew the dangers of sunstroke (cf. 2 Kings 4:19; Jud. 8:3). *the moon:* popular belief attributed certain diseases to the moon. But perhaps the meaning here, as in Gen. 31:40, is nothing more than an addition to "the sun will not hurt you by day" of "nor the moon by night," meaning the cold of the night — God will protect them both day and night.

v. 8 *your coming and your going:* a Hebraism to designate universality — everything a man does (cf. 2 Sam. 3:25; Deut. 28:6).

Psalm 122

Theme A Jerusalem-Temple psalm expressing the sentiments of joy and confidence experienced by the pilgrims upon arriving at the gates of Jerusalem.

Background The sentiments are inspired by Is. 2:2-4, but the psalm could have been written any time after the building of the Temple of Solomon in 965 or the Temple of Zerubbabel in 516 (cf. Pss. 87; 125).

Division
1. Joy of the pilgrims arriving at Jerusalem (vv. 1-3).
2. It is the seat of divine worship and the site of the Davidic palace (vv. 4-5).
3. A prayer for Jerusalem and for all who put their trust in her (vv. 6-9).

vv. 1-3 *I rejoiced:* the pilgrim recalls the joy he felt when summoned to go in pilgrimage to the house of the Lord. *and now . . . within your gates:* arrived before the gates of Jerusalem, he expresses his admiration for the great city. To him, a pilgrim from a small town, Jerusalem is "built as a city" (v. 3), presenting an appearance of great strength and solidity.

vv. 4-5 *to it the tribes go up:* according to the law of Moses (Deut. 12:4-12; 16:16), every male Israelite was to appear yearly to worship God in the Temple (cf. Luke 2:41). *judgment seats:* being the capital, Jerusalem is the seat of the law courts and the site of the royal palace.

vv. 6-9 *pray for the peace of Jerusalem:* the reader should recall that for an Israelite "peace" (*shalom*) meant not merely the absence of war but the possession of all good things, in a sense the kind of peace "the world cannot give." *be-*

cause of my relatives: the pilgrim's prayer for Jerusalem is based on two motives: the fact that Jerusalem means so much spiritually to himself and his companions, and because in Jerusalem is the house of God (v. 9).

Psalm 123

Theme   A collective supplication of oppressed Israelites waiting with perfect resignation for God to come to their help.

Background   The exile or any of the other numerous occasions when the Israelites were oppressed by enemies.

Division   1. Israel looks to God, ready like a slave to heed the slightest beck of her master (vv. 1-2).
2. Israel's prayer for surcease from oppression (vv. 3-4).

vv. 1-2   *I lift up my eyes:* with eyes lifted in prayer and resignation, Israel stands like a slave, her gaze upon the Lord; a word is not necessary, a mere flick of the Master's finger will suffice. Thus perhaps the Jews in exile awaited the word of God to send them back to Jerusalem. The description of suffering usually found in supplications is only implicit here. Confidence in God, while not expressed by the usual formula of anticipation, suffuses the entire psalm.

vv. 3-4   *have pity on us:* the Israelites humbled by chastisement and oppressed by their masters pray God to have mercy on them.

Psalm 124

Theme   A psalm of thanksgiving for liberation from some great peril.

Background   Most likely the peril referred to is the Babylonian captivity.

Division   1. Escape from peril (vv. 1-5).
2. Gratitude to God for this deliverance (vv. 6-8).

v. 1   *let Israel say:* let Israel admit with all humility and truth that without God's help and intervention she was lost.

v. 3 *swallowed us alive:* in Prov. 1:12 death is described as a swallowing up: "Let us swallow him up alive and sound in health, as sheol swallows up those who go down to the pit" (cf. Ps. 107:23; Jer. 51:34).

v. 4 *the waters . . . the torrent:* the stereotyped Hebrew metaphor of the waters through which one passed on the way to sheol in the depths of the abyss is used to express the danger of death (cf. Pss. 18:17-18; 69:1-2).

v. 6 *a prey to their teeth:* Israel's enemies are compared to lions or beasts of prey (cf. Ps. 22:13-14, 17).

v. 7 *rescued from the snare:* they had been trapped as birds by the fowler, but God opened the trap and released them (cf. Prov. 6:5).

Psalm 125

Theme

A psalm of confidence expressing Israel's serene expectation of God's help.

Background

Internal evidence (vv. 3-5) suggests a time when Israel was in the power of foreigners and when there was a cleavage in the Jewish community between the faithful and the apostates, a situation true of many periods but particularly true during the exile and during the time of Ezra and Nehemiah.

Division

1. God's protection of Israel is compared to the security of Jerusalem surrounded by impregnable mountains (vv. 1-2).
2. Such confidence inspires hope of God's intervention (v. 3).
3. Prayer for justice toward good and wicked apostates alike (vv. 4-5).

v. 1 *like Mount Zion:* surrounded on almost every side by hills, Jerusalem in the mountains of Judea was in an impregnable position.

v. 3 *lest the just put forth:* since oppression by the wicked easily leads to the defection of those weak in the faith, the psalmist confidently anticipates that God will remove the temptation by removing the oppression.

v. 5 *such as turn aside:* for the apostates in Israel, who are contrasted with the "upright of heart," the psalmist foresees a sorry fate. *peace:* his prayer for Israel is repeated by St. Paul (Gal. 6:16): "Whoever follow this rule, peace and mercy upon them, even upon the Israel of God."

Psalm 126

Theme

A collective supplication for the fulfillment of Israel's messianic hopes aroused during the exile and unfulfilled upon the return.

Background

Probably the difficult years following the return of the exiles from the Babylonian captivity (cf. Ezra 3–6; Haggai 1:6-11; 2:15-17; Ps. 85).

Division

1. (*Then*) their delirious joy upon return from the exile (vv. 1-3).
2. (*Now*) their disillusionment in the time of Ezra and Nehemiah and their prayer for better times (vv. 4-6).

v. 1 *like men dreaming:* could mean that the return from the exile was a dream come true; or, they were so happy that all the bitterness of the exile seemed a dream; or, they thought when they returned from the exile that all their troubles would be over, but that was only a dream.

v. 2 *then:* their sentiments when they heard the decree of Cyrus permitting the return from the exile, so wonderful an event that even the Gentiles were forced to admit that Yahweh had done great things for them.

v. 4 *our fortunes:* the present in contrast to what they had dreamed is disillusioning. Deutero-Isaiah had perhaps painted the glories of the return so brilliantly that they expected the inception of the messianic age. Instead they found new hardships and continuous strife with the Samaritans. *like the torrents:* in the autumn with the first rains the dry wadies swell with water and turn the arid Negeb into a garden spot. The change is sudden and dramatic. The psalmist prays for a similar change in Israel's fortunes.

v. 5 *in tears:* the psalmist uses an old proverb to show his confidence that present tears will end in joy just as the farmer who sows with much labor reaps with happiness.

Psalm 127

Theme

A wisdom psalm teaching that "God's blessings make men rich."

Background

Doctrinal: without God's blessings man's striving is vain (cf. Prov. 10:22).

Division

1. The labors of man are fruitless without the help of God (vv. 1-2).
2. Without the blessing of God a man cannot have a happy and numerous family (vv. 3-5).

v. 1 *the house:* most likely any house since the psalmist is voicing a general truth. The same is true of any city.

v. 2 *put off your rest:* to work long and late is useless unless God blesses the work. For those whom He loves, God gives even without excessive industry, i.e., while they sleep.

v. 3 *sons:* God's blessing is necessary for house, for city, for man's labor, but it is especially necessary for God's greatest benefit — a numerous family.

v. 4 *like arrows:* a popular metaphor for a strong son. Even today Arabs refer to a trustworthy son as "The best arrow in my quiver" (cf. Is. 49:2).

v. 5 *at the gate:* in disputes held at the city gate, it was no small comfort for a father to be surrounded by a number of vigorous sons.

Psalm 128

Theme

A wisdom psalm teaching that a happy family is the reward of virtue.

Background

A general wisdom truth.

1. God blesses the labors, the wife, and the children of the virtuous man (vv. 1-4).
2. Prayer for a long and happy life (vv. 5-6).

vv. 1-2 *who fear the Lord:* Hebraism for reverence, worship of God. *you shall eat the fruit of your handiwork:* the virtuous man will not be defrauded of the fruits of his labor.

v. 3 *like a fruitful vine:* hyperbolical for a fruitful spouse, who remains in the home as a good wife should in contrast to the foolish woman (cf. Prov. 9:13-17).

Psalm 129

Theme

A collective supplication in which Israel, perennially oppressed and repeatedly saved, begs God to confound her enemies.

Background

Because of the long persecutions mentioned (v. 2) and the release from persecution (v. 4), most authors consider the psalm postexilic (cf. Ps. 137).

Division

1. The psalmist reviews Israel's past when, although greatly oppressed, she was never, because of God's protection, destroyed (vv. 1-4).
2. Israel begs God to confound her enemies (vv. 5-8).

v. 1 *from my youth:* enslaved in Egypt at the beginning of her history, Israel was later oppressed by the Philistines, Assyrians, and Babylonians. Repeating this thought in v. 2, the psalmist adds with a note of triumph: "Yet they have not prevailed against me."

v. 3 *upon my back:* Israel's oppressors plowed her like a field (cf. Micah 3:12, "Zion shall be plowed like a field"), but God in His mercy cut the ropes binding the oxen to the plow, thus ending the plowing of Israel by her enemies.

v. 5 *may all be put to shame:* a prayer for the confusion of her enemies (either the Babylonians as in Ps. 137, or the Samaritans of the time of Ezra and Nehemiah, who, despite the decrees of Cyrus and Artaxerxes, continued to harass the returned exiles).

v. 6 *like grass on the housetops:* he prays that Israel's enemies may be like the weeds that spring up after the rains on the flat, mud-covered roofs and then quickly wilt when the hot sun beats down on them.

Psalm 130

Theme
A psalm of confidence expressing Israel's unwavering expectation of God's merciful forgiveness.

Background
It is impossible to be precise. However, Israel in exile was "in the depths," and the psalmist's reference to Israel waiting on the Lord for redemption (vv. 7b-8) hints at the time of the exile.

v. 1 *out of the depths:* the depths are the waters leading to sheol (cf. Pss. 18:5; 69:1; Jonah 2). Israel in exile suffered for her national and her personal sins. The psalmist realizes that it was her sins that brought her to the depths.

v. 3 *if you . . . mark iniquities:* the question demands an emphatically negative answer. God does not remember our sins. He is too merciful (Ez. 33:11; Is. 43:25; Ps. 103:10).

v. 4 *that you may be revered:* the more one is forgiven, the more one loves and serves God in gratitude (cf. Luke 7:47).

v. 6 *waits:* the longing of Israel for redemption is compared to the patient longing of a sentry on night watch waiting for the dawn.

v. 8 *he will redeem Israel:* the messianic promises made to Israel (cf. Jer. 31:21; Ez. 11:17-20; 37) leave no doubt that God will redeem Israel.

Psalm 140

Theme
A psalm of confidence expressing absolute resignation and childlike repose in God. "Unless you become as little children . . ." (Matthew 18:3).

Background
No certain background can be determined, but the psalmist would appear to be speaking for Israel (v. 3), declaring she has put an end to her proud and presumptuous efforts

to become a great power and has finally realized that her greatness is to be found in God and God alone. If this interpretation is correct, the psalm is certainly exilic or postexilic.

v. 1 *nor are my eyes haughty:* he will not be haughty as the proud man who holds his head high and looks down in disdain on others (cf. Ps. 101:5; Jer. 45:5; Sir. 3:18ff). *great things:* in the past Israel had attempted to vie with the great powers, pitting her strength against Assyria and Babylon, unmindful that her greatness lay not in material but in spiritual strength. Isaiah and Jeremiah repeatedly preached to Israel that her salvation lay in God and not in her armies. Israel did not listen. In exile, however, she meditated on her mistake, learned humility and the necessity of being like a child utterly dependent on God.

v. 2 *like a weaned child:* greater security than that felt by a child at its mother's bosom cannot be imagined. This, the psalmist realizes, is the kind of security Israel can find in God. Perhaps he has meditated on the words of Deutero-Isaiah: "You shall be carried at the breasts and upon the knees; as one whom the mother caresseth, so will I comfort you" (Is. 66:12-13; cf. also Prov. 9:4: "Whosoever is a little one, let him come to me"; and Hosea 11:4; Matthew 18:3).

v. 3 *O Israel, hope in the Lord:* let Israel so trust in God and not in material things or in human power.

Psalm 132

Theme
A prayer for the king, adducing in favor of a propitious reply David's solicitude for God's worship and God's corresponding promise of a perpetual dynasty in reward for this solicitude (cf. Ps. 89).

Background
David's solicitude and God's promise (2 Sam. 7) and the bringing of the Ark to Jerusalem (2 Sam. 6).

Division
A. David's solicitude: 1. His desire to build a Temple (vv. 1-5).
2. He brings the Ark to Jerusalem (vv. 6-10).

B. God's response: 1. The promise of a perpetual dynasty (vv. 11-13).
2. Blessings on the Holy City (vv. 14-18).

N.B. Some consider the psalm a poetical recapitulation of 2 Sam. 7, showing God rewarding David's solicitude as Jesus rewarded St. Peter's profession of faith in Matthew 16:17: "Thou art the Christ . . . Thou art Peter and. . . ."

Others consider the psalm a prayer for the king when the dynasty was in danger of destruction at the time of the Babylonian conquest in 587. The psalmist would be urging God to come to the aid of the dynasty, basing his plea on the record of David's solicitude and on God's promise of perpetuity to the dynasty, which would apparently be nullified if the dynasty were to fall.

Internal evidence, the reference to a reigning king in vv. 10 and 17 and to the Temple in v. 14, in addition to the lack of lamentations which characterize exilic and post-exilic psalms would seem to indicate a pre-exilic date for the psalm anytime from 965 to 587 B.C. It became part of the gradual psalms collection because of its references to Jerusalem.

v. 1 *his anxious care:* David's solicitude for the interests of God was manifested in his bringing of the Ark to Jerusalem (2 Sam. 6), his desire to build the Temple (2 Sam. 7), and his preparation of materials for the future edifice (1 Chr. 22—26).

v. 2 *how he swore:* either a hyperbolical expression of David's earnest desire to build the Temple, or an actual oath sworn by David but not mentioned in 2 Sam. 7 (cf. Acts 23:21; Prov. 6:4). *the Mighty One of Jacob:* a name used for God the powerful protector of Israel (cf. Gen. 49:24; Is. 49:26; 60:16). In vv. 3-5 the author gives the words of David's oath.

In part A, vv. 1, 2, 10 are the words of the psalmist; vv. 3-6 are the words of David; vv. 6-9 are the words of the people in procession.

v. 6 *we heard of it:* ambiguous but most likely the reference is to the Ark. *in Ephrata:* it is not certain whether the psalmist refers to Bethlehem in Ephrata, David's native city (cf. Ruth 4:11 and Micah 5:2), or if Ephrata is a defective reading for Ephraim of the Hebrew locative "Ephratha." JAAR is short for Kiriath-jearim (forest-town) where the Ark was kept after its return from Philistia (1 Sam. 4), until brought by David to Jerusalem.

v. 7 *let us enter:* the people's desire to worship God. *his dwelling:* either the tabernacle in which the Ark was kept or the Temple. *his footstool:* the Ark was considered God's footstool (cf. Pss. 80:2; 99:5).

v. 8 *advance, O Lord:* vv. 8-9 are taken from Solomon's prayer at the dedication of the Temple (cf. 2 Chr. 6:41-42; 1 Kings 8). *your resting place:* the Temple, the permanent resting place for God in place of the portable tabernacle. *you and the ark:* is a reference to God invisibly present above the Ark (cf. Num. 7:89). *your faithful ones:* refers to the Levites whose office it was to carry the Ark (1 Chr. 15:2).

v. 10 *your anointed:* the psalmist's prayer for the king connects v. 10 with vv. 1-2. The intervening lines are put on the lips of David and the people.

v. 11 *the Lord swore:* the psalmist paraphrases God's response to David through the prophet Nathan (cf. 2 Sam. 7:8-16). In v. 11 he gives the absolute promise made to the dynasty; in v. 12 the conditional promise regarding the individual kings (cf. 1 Kings 8:25; Ps. 89:31-38).

v. 13 ZION: another reason why God should answer the psalmist's prayer is the fact that God Himself chose Zion, the city captured by David from the Jebusites, to which the Ark had been brought, and (vv. 14-16) upon which God bestowed His richest blessings (cf. Pss. 68:17; 87; Is. 2:1-4).

v. 17 *I will make to sprout:* the Messiah is called "shoot" (*ṣemaḥ*) in Jer. 23:5; 33:15; Zech. 3:8; 6:12. *a lamp:* metaphor for a son, in the sense that he is the light continuing the life of the dynasty (cf. Job 18:6; 21:17; 1 Kings 11:36; 15:4).

v. 18 *upon him my crown:* Jewish and Christian tradition agree in referring these words to the messianic king.

Psalm 133

Theme A wisdom psalm describing the happiness of brethren gathered together.

Background A general principle true of any harmonious religious gathering.

v. 1 *dwell at one:* in several places (Gen. 13:16; 36:7; Deut. 25:5) the expression is used of the dwelling together of family groups suggesting the psalm is meant to describe the happy family life of a clan or patriarchal-type family. Kissane suggests the happy reunion of scattered brethren "sitting down together" (another meaning of the expression) at the family sacrificial banquet on the occasion of a feast-day in Jerusalem.

v. 2 *as when the precious ointment:* the anointing of heads with perfumed oil was customary at Jewish banquets (cf. Luke 7:46; Matthew 26:6-7). The psalmist likens the joy of such a reunion to the abundant and exquisite oil used to anoint the high priest (cf. Exod. 30:23-33), so abundant that it ran down upon his beard and from there on down to the priestly vestments; equally overflowing is the joy of united brethren.

v. 3 *a dew like that of Hermon:* dew in dry Palestine is a delightful natural gift of God. According to the psalmist, the joy of united brethren is as refreshing and abundant as the copious dew descending from perennially snow-covered Mount Hermon. It is where brethren are gathered together that God grants His blessing (cf. Matthew 18:20 "Where two or three are gathered together. . . .").

Psalm 134

Theme An invitation to the priests to praise God at night in the Temple.

Perhaps recited in the Temple at evening when the night
watch of priests came to take over. The group leaving
would exhort those arriving to praise God through the
night. Those taking over would bless the others as they
left. Some think vv. 1-2 were addressed by the departing
pilgrims to the priests and levites; v. 3 would be the
blessing of the priests on the departing pilgrims.

v. 1 *you servants of the Lord:* the psalmist refers to the priests
and levites (Deut. 10:8). In the Scriptures "to stand"
often has the sense of "to stand and serve" as does a
servant; thus the priests and levites are the Lord's servants (cf. 1 Chr. 23:30). *during the hours of night:* noc-
turnal services in the Temple are mentioned by Isaiah
(30:29), and Josephus testifies to the fact that the priests
passed the night in the Temple on the occasion of great
feasts.

4. The Kingship of Yahweh Psalms

The Israelite conception of God as the King of Israel is found very early in
sacred history (cf. Exod. 15:18; Num. 23:21; Deut. 33:5; Judg. 8:22; 1 Sam.
8:7). It would appear to have been a natural consequence of the Sinaitic
pact, particularly when viewed against the background supplied by the
Hittite suzerainty pacts. The Ark of the Covenant, the visible sacred sign
of God's presence among His people, was unquestionably looked upon as
the footstool of the throne of God the King and as such helped to keep alive
and vivid the idea of His kingship (cf. Pss. 24:7-10; 68:25-28; 99:1).

That the kingship of the Davidic dynasty never completely obscured the
divine kingship may be gathered from the inaugural vision of Isaiah in
which the prophet sees God enthroned in the Temple as the all holy king
of Israel (Is. 6:1ff). It should also be evident from the Jerusalem-Temple
psalms, particularly Ps. 48 in which the psalmist praises God as the "Great
King," the conqueror of Sennacherib and protector of Israel (cf. Is. 33:5,
22; 37:21-37).

During the exile and in the years that follow the return, the preaching of
Ezekiel, Deutero-Isaiah, Zechariah, Malachi, and Daniel enlarge and
deepen Israel's concept of Yahweh's kingship. There is no longer that narrow outlook that sees God only as King of Israel. He is the Lord of the
world, the king of the nations, the creator of all, the ruler of all. He who is
king by right of physical creation will come to establish His moral rule

over the universe. When He comes, He will rule not only Israel but the pagan nations as well. When His rule is established, all nature will rejoice and Israel and the nations will sing a "new canticle" to celebrate the glorious event.

Thus in the years that follow the exile, there is a notable emphasis on the advent of God Himself to rule Israel and the nations. The coming of a Davidic Messiah is not forgotten, but it takes a lesser place in Israel's vision of the future. There is a double expectation — the expectation of a Messiah who will reestablish the Davidic dynasty, and the expectation of God Himself who will come as king by right of creation and reestablish His moral rule over the universe. What few could have suspected was the fulfillment of both expectations with the Incarnation of the Second Person of the Blessed Trinity.

What is significant about the Kingship of Yahweh psalms (Pss. 47; 93; 95–100; 150) and puts them in a category by themselves is their joyful anticipation of God's coming as king to rule all nations and to restore the primeval relation of subjection to His rule of all creation. These compositions are all hymns, psalms of praise, and follow the structure of hymns, namely, an invitation to praise God (in some cases only an implicit invitation), motives for praising God (because He is king, creator, saviour), concluding with a repetition of the introductory invitation to praise God.

The student will find it helpful to note the recurrence of the following motifs in the Kingship of Yahweh psalms and the dependence of the psalmists on Deutero-Isaiah not only for the basic ideas but in many cases even for the very words with which the ideas are expressed: 1. God is entitled king, or His reign is acclaimed: Pss. 47:7-8; 93:1-2; 96:10, 13; 97:1; 98:6, 9; 99:1, 150:2 (cf. Is. 24:23; 41:21; 43:15; 52:7).

2. God will establish His rule over the nations: Pss. 47:8-10; 93:1; 95:10, 14; 97:1, 9; 98:2, 9; 99:2, 9; 99:1-2 (cf. Is. 45:22-24; 51:4-5; 52:10).

3. God's rule is based on His right as creator: Pss. 93:2; 96:5 (cf. Is. 40:21-22; 42:5; 45:9-12; 48:12-13).

4. The pagan nations will come to know and serve God: Pss. 96:1-3; 98:2-3 (cf. Is. 2:2-4; 41:1; 42:10-12; 45:23-24; 60:1-7).

5. Even inanimate nature will rejoice at the coming of God the king to establish His rule: Pss. 96:11-13; 98:7-9 (cf. Is. 35:1; 44:23; 49:13; 55:12).

Psalm 47

Theme	A kingship of Yahweh hymn praising God as king of all nations.

Back-ground	Possibly occasioned by the defeat of Sennacherib in 701, but more probably an eschatological psalm based on Deutero-Isaiah's teaching about the appearance of God the king to rule all nations.
Division	1. God subjects all nations to His rule: let all praise Him (vv. 2-5). 2. Having subjected the nations, God ascends to heaven (vv. 6-7). 3. Let all praise God, the king of all the earth (vv. 8-10).

v. 2 *all you peoples:* not only the Jews but all peoples are called upon to rejoice at the establishment of God's rule (cf. vv. 3b, 8a, 9-10). This note of universalism is characteristic of the kingship of Yahweh psalms.

v. 4 *he brings peoples under us:* God subjects all nations to Israel, His messianic kingdom. In Deutero-Isaiah and in Daniel, it is to Israel as God's chosen nation that the peoples of the world must come to enter the messianic kingdom.

v. 6 *God mounts:* after establishing His kingdom on earth, God ascends to His heavenly throne. The picture in the psalmist's mind is probably similar to that in Ps. 18:10ff or in Is. 63:1-6. Some authors see here a part of the ritual for one of Israel's feasts, namely. the enthronement of God as ruler. The "shouts of joy" and the "trumpet blasts" would refer to the participation of the people in this ceremony. In v. 9, the psalmist refers directly to the "throne of God" (cf. Pss. 93:2; 97:2; 99:1, 5, 9).

Psalm 96

Theme	A kingship of Yahweh hymn praising God the King of all the earth.
Back-ground	Deutero-Isaiah, *passim.*
Division	1. An invitation to all nations to praise God (vv. 1-3). 2. This praise is motivated by God's majesty, power, and splendor (vv. 4-6).

3. All nations are called upon to adore God and acknowledge His benign rule (vv. 7-10).
4. Even inanimate nature is called upon to praise God the ruler of all the earth (vv. 11-13).

v. 1 *a new song:* for so great an occasion, an old canticle would be inadequate (cf. Is. 42:10; Jud. 16:13; Ps. 98:1). *all you lands:* universalism characteristic of the kingship of Yahweh psalms is expressed here as well as in vv. 3b, 9b, 10c, 13.

v. 2. *announce his salvation:* the news to be announced is God's intervention to save, His glory (v. 3a), and His wondrous doings (v. 3b). In Is. 40–55, "salvation" and "glory" have an eschatological value, i.e., they refer to the coming of God in the last days to rule the world.

v. 10 *the Lord is king:* this is the great news: God will rule from this time on.

PART FOUR

The Didactic Literature

and the

History of The Maccabees

15

The Midrashic Literature

In the centuries following the exile, literary activity flourished in Israel as never before. The Pentateuch was put into final form. The writings of the prophets were gathered and edited into complete books. The numerous collections of psalms were brought together to form the book of psalms as we know it now.[1]

In addition new inspired books were written. Sometime in the sixth or fifth century an Israelite author dramatized the eternal problem of evil by means of poetic dialogues between Job and his friends. In the fifth century a poet dramatized in the Canticle of Canticles the undying love of God for His people. In the fourth century a learned priest wrote the midrashic ecclesiastical history known as Chronicles-Ezra-Nehemiah.

Still other authors developed new literary forms to teach and encourage the people of God. One wrote a satire (Jonah) to remind the narrow-minded Jews of the postexilic period that God loved all men and that the missionary vocation of Israel, so insistently inculcated by Deutero-Isaiah, might not be abandoned without displeasing God. Another reflected on the teaching of Moses and drew up a picture of the ideal Israelite (Tobit). Others seized on parts of Ezekiel (ch. 38–39),

[1] Cf. select bibliography, p. 575.

Isaiah (ch. 24—27), and Zechariah and developed the literary form known as apocalypse which reached its perfection in the Old Testament in Daniel and in the New Testament in the Apocalypse of St. John.

In the profusion of literary forms developed during these centuries, none was more surprising or more open to later misunderstanding than the para-historical form known as haggadic midrash — a form of didactic literature in which an historical nucleus is elaborated with fictitious details, prayers, and speeches in order to instruct, encourage, or edify a particular audience.

As the centuries passed and the true understanding of haggadic midrash was lost, the para-historical books came to be looked upon as strict history. As long, however, as their historical background remained in darkness, there was no great critical outcry against them. Jerome wondered but could not make up his mind. Luther and the reformers doubted and discarded them. Catholic authors found them a source of embarrassment but clung to them with a conviction born of faith. This state of affairs lasted until recently.

In modern times a better knowledge of ancient history plus a more accurate understanding of biblical literary forms has relieved Catholic faith of its embarrassment by restoring these books to their legitimate literary family. Before dealing with the inspired para-historical books, we shall study the meaning of the word "midrash," the characteristics, origins, development of the midrashic literary forms, and finally the para-historical or haggadic midrash. We shall then apply our knowledge of the haggadic midrash to the books of Jonah, Tobit, Esther, and Baruch.

1. The Midrashic Literary Forms

The practice of reading aloud the Scriptures and interpreting them for the faithful is attested by the Chronicler as early as the time of Ezra (cf. Neh. 8:1-13). Whether it began with Ezra in the fifth century or had been instituted earlier, it was a practice that was to have a great future not only in Judaism but in Christianity as well.

In Judaism the public reading of the Scriptures followed by a commentary became the central rite of the synagogue service (cf. Luke 4:14-30; Acts 13:15; 17:2-3) and gave rise in the course of the centuries to a rabbinic literature more vast than the Bible itself.

In the early Church the reading of the Scriptures followed by a homily was taken over from the synagogue and became the central rite of the Foremass (cf. 1 Tim. 4:13; Acts 20:7-12), giving rise in the course of time to a patristic literature not entirely unlike the rabbinic commentaries and in extent just as vast. The homiletic commentaries of the Fathers are not given any special name. The homiletic commentaries of the rabbis are generally known as midrash or (in the plural) midrashim.

The meaning of the word midrash

The Hebrew verb *darash* means to investigate, search for or into, scrutinize. The noun *midrash* means an investigation or searching for, whence the meaning "commentary." The verb is used many times in Sacred Scripture, very frequently in the sense of search into, study, or scrutinize (cf. Pss. 111:2; 119:45, 94, 155; 1 Chr. 28:8; Ezra 7:10). The noun is used only three times. The Chronicler speaks of the Midrash of the Prophet Addo (2 Chr. 13:22) and the Midrash of the Book of Kings (2 Chr. 24:27). Sirach speaks of his school as a "house of midrash" (Sir. 51:23), presumably a school of exegesis where the Scriptures were studied and expounded.

In rabbinic literature both the verb and the noun are used extensively, so much so that the name Midrashim was commonly given to the homiletic commentaries of the rabbinic authors. The extent to which midrashic studies were pursued in some quarters may be gauged from a requirement found in one of the Dead Sea Scrolls:

> And in whatever place the ten are, there shall not cease to be a man who expounds the Torah day and night continually, expounding orally each to his fellow. And let the many keep awake in Community a third of all the nights of the year in order to read aloud from the Book and to expound laws and to bless in Community" (*Dead Sea Manual of Discipline*, VI, 6ff).

Technically the term midrash means a commentary or explanation of the Scriptures. In rabbinic circles a distinction was made between *peshat* and *midrash*, the former referring to an explanation of the literal sense of the Scriptures, the latter to an explanation that went beyond the literal sense to search out the more profound and less obvious sense of the inspired word.

Characteristics of the midrashic literature

The midrashic literature, which flourished from the second century B.C. to the sixth century A.D., has four distinctive characteristics: (a) it is essentially a literature about a literature, consisting in a reflection on, meditation of, and searching into the Sacred Text; (b) it pursued the study of the Bible in the light of the Bible, based upon the rabbinic conviction that the

Bible is a unity and that consequently "the Bible best explains the Bible"; (c) it is of a homiletic character, i.e., an explanation of the Sacred Text following its reading in the synagogue (cf. Luke 4:14-30); (d) it is a practical rather than speculative literature in that it seeks to adapt the sense and teaching of the Sacred Text to the immediate spiritual needs of the audience. Like St. Paul and the Fathers of the Church, the rabbis were convinced that "the word of God is living and efficient and keener than any two-edged sword . . . a discerner of the thoughts and intentions of the heart" (Heb. 4:12).

Types of midrash

Depending on the nature of the Biblical Text studied and expounded, rabbinic commentary can be divided into three types: halakhic, haggadic, and pesher midrash.

The commentaries which expounded the legal portions of the Bible were called halakhic midrash. The rabbis studied the law of Moses, drew up principles of interpretation, and sought to draw from the Mosaic code new precepts and regulations for different times and altered circumstances. The extent to which some of them could go is graphically described in the Gospels (cf. Mark 7:9-13). Halakhic interpretations, which were passed down orally for centuries, were eventually collected into the Mishnah and the Talmud. The Mishnah, which contains halakhic commentaries up to the second century A.D., is the work of Rabbi Judah ha-Nasi. Halakhic commentaries from the third to the sixth century A.D. are contained in the Talmud, which exists in two forms: the Jerusalem Talmud and the Babylonian Talmud. The divorce disputation in Matthew 19:3-12 has all the earmarks of an halakhic commentary.

The commentaries which dealt with the non-juridical narrative portions of the Scriptures were called haggadic midrash. The rabbis sought to interpret Israel's history and draw from it salutary lessons and examples for the spiritual life of the faithful. No single corpus of collected haggadic midrashim was ever compiled, but extensive portions of haggadic midrash can be found in the Jewish apocryphal writings, in the works of Josephus, in Pseudo-Philo (a first century A.D. haggadic commentary on the Old Testament historical books), and in the Dead Sea Scrolls. Certain ancient versions of the Scriptures (e.g., the Septuagint and the Peshitto), the New Testament, and the writings of St. Clement of Alexandria, Origen, Eusebius of Caesarea, and St. Ephraem allude to haggadic literature. In the Old Testament the best example of haggadic midrash is found in Wisdom 10–19. The books of Jonah, Tobit, Esther, Baruch, and Daniel 1–6; 13–14 are generally held to be early examples of haggadic midrash.

Commentaries on the prophets which sought to interpret the words of the prophets in the light of contemporary events and make them relevant to contemporary audiences were known as pesher midrash. There is no collection of pesher midrash but chapter 9 of Daniel and the Dead Sea Habakkuk scroll provide excellent examples of pesher. In the New Testament Matthew, St. Paul in Romans and Hebrews, and St. John in the Apocalypse make use of pesher midrash.

The terms halakhic, haggadic, and pesher are not used of Christian exegesis, but the New Testament writers were in the main rabbinic authors brought up on the exegesis of the synagogue and adept in rabbinic exegetical methods and as a consequence followed the same general lines in their explanation of the Old Testament. The Church Fathers did the same, adapting Old Testament laws to Christian life, Old Testament history for edification and instruction, and the prophecies of the Old Testament prophets for apologetic purposes. After the manner of the rabbis and for the same reasons, the New Testament writers and the Fathers used the Bible to explain the Bible. In the course of time, however, and under the influence of Greek thought the explanation of the Bible by the Bible decreased and explanation by means of reason increased. When the happy mean between Scripture and reason was reached and passed is a matter of debate, but it marks the point of departure from a biblically orientated to a rationally orientated theology, to the detriment of both.

Origins of the midrashic literature

Three factors in the history of Israel contributed to the origin and evolution of the midrashic literature: the Babylonian exile, the gradual fixation of the canon of Sacred Scripture, and the rise of the learned priests and scribes.

In the exile Israel was stripped of all her material possessions and was thrown back for comfort upon her spiritual patrimony — her written and unwritten traditions. On these she focused all her attention, examining her laws, her history, and her prophetic writings to find the explanation of her present unhappy plight and the revealed principles upon which she might be guided to a more happy future.

During the exile and in the centuries following the exile the ancient writings of Israel's historians, prophets, and psalmists were gradually gathered together, edited, and stamped by the approval of living tradition as "the word of God." It is probable that by the time of Ezra the Pentateuch was accepted as canonical (cf. Neh. 8:1-9). In the course of the Persian period most of the remaining books of the Old Testament achieved the status of canonicity. From this time on, Israel became "the people of the Book."

The work of editing the inspired writings, in conjunction with the need for men to read and explain them in the synagogue services[1] which became popular in the centuries following the exile, gave rise to the learned priests and scribes (cf. Ezra 7:6, 10). These men devoted their lives to the study and explanation of the Scriptures and in the course of time produced the homilies and the commentaries which comprise the bulk of the midrashic literature.

In addition to historical factors, three psychological factors help to explain the origin of the midrashic literature: 1. Israel's belief in the inspiration of the Scriptures; 2. her firm conviction that the Scriptures contain all God's secrets and lessons for every occasion; 3. her persuasion that individual texts find their full meaning not in themselves but against the background of all the Scriptures and tradition. It was in the light of these beliefs that Israel's teachers scrutinized the Scriptures, searching them for parallels, analogies, and similarities, balancing one text against another, one book against another, confident that in the end the Scriptures would yield divine solutions to her daily problems and divine direction for her national life.

Development of midrashic literary forms

The constant scrutiny of the Scriptures in order to draw from them spiritual nourishment and practical norms of behaviour for daily life gave rise in the course of the centuries to a huge and varied literature. It had its beginning, however, very early in Israel's history. One can say indeed that the midrashic tendency was always alive in Israel. It is testified to by the inspired writers themselves. The author of Deuteronomy adapted for the people of his day earlier writings (the covenant renewal recitations) which testify to even more ancient attempts to make the covenant and the covenant laws relevant to Israelites of an earlier period. Isaiah shows his dependence on Amos, Jeremiah on Hosea, Ezekiel on Amos, Hosea, Isaiah, and Jeremiah. Deutero-Isaiah shows his dependence on Hosea and Isaiah.

After the exile the golden chain of tradition becomes more intimately linked with the earlier Scriptures. New inspired writers depend ever more closely on earlier writers, paraphrasing and quoting them freely, multiplying references to them to such an extent that some postexilic books resemble tissues of quotations from earlier books. This is particularly true of the wisdom books. Proverbs 1–9 contains a tissue of quotations from Deuteronomy, Isaiah, and Jeremiah. Sirach 24 depends on Proverbs 8.

[1] Cf. De Vaux, 343-345.

Wisdom 10–19 paraphrases and expands the Exodus narrative. The practice testifies not only to a great love and veneration for the inspired Scriptures but to the insistence of the living voice of tradition on using the inspired words for its contemporary expression of Israel's teaching.

But postexilic authors did more than use the words and explain the meaning of the earlier inspired authors. Relying on tradition, they developed what was implicit in the earlier texts, re-reading them in the light of new revelation and new conditions. Thus Ezekiel used Hosea's metaphor of the unfaithful wife to give an expanded allegorical history of Israel from the time of the patriarchs down to his own time (cf. Ez. 16 and 23). The author of the Canticle of Canticles did the same to adapt the teaching of Hosea to the conditions of the postexilic period. The Chronicler adapted the Priestly document of the Pentateuch and the Former Prophets to show the relevancy of the Temple and the Davidic dynasty to Israel's destiny in the last part of the fourth century. The authors of Daniel and Judith adapted portions of Amos, Ezekiel, and Zechariah in their use of the apocalyptic midrashic literary form.

In the New Testament Matthew uses midrashic procedures regularly (cf. Matthew 2:13-15 and Hosea 11:1; Matthew 2:16-18 and Jer. 31:15; Matthew 27:3-10 and Zech. 11:12-13). Luke gives examples of midrashic style in the Magnificat and Benedictus, and in the sermons of Peter, Stephen, and Paul in Acts. St. Paul adapts midrashic procedures in Gal. 3–4; Rom. 4; 9–11; 1 Cor. 10; 2 Cor. 3:7-18; Heb. 7. The Apocalypse provides a midrashic (pesher) interpretation of many Old Testament texts particularly Isaiah, Zechariah, and Daniel.

The para-historical midrash

The para-historical midrash is properly called haggadic midrash and consists in a commentary on the narrative portions of the Scriptures for homiletic purposes. Among the rabbis haggadic midrash was the term used to designate any kind of a non-juridical commentary on the Scriptures directed to the spiritual formation of the faithful.

The main purpose of this type of commentary was instruction or edification. The question the writer or preacher proposed to himself was: "How can I make the word of God yield its wealth of doctrine and edification for the spiritual nourishment of my audience?" To accomplish his aim, which might consist in the explanation of one of Israel's liturgical feasts, or an exhortation to right living, or the exposition of a particular doctrine, the author was allowed great latitude. He might give a simple explanation of some text or texts, or a paraphrase, or an expanded version. He could even, if he desired, compose a story based on the text or narrative in order to bring out its full import and make it relevant in contemporary language for his audience.

In the midrashic stories of Jonah, Tobit, Esther, and Baruch, it is this last method that the commentators have used to make the Word of God relevant to the needs of their audience. Thus the story of Jonah is composed to inculcate graphically the love of God for all men even the pagans, Tobit to illustrate the saintly life God expects of every good Israelite, Esther to explain in a memorable manner the institution of the feast of Purim, and Baruch to inculcate the sentiments with which Israelites should make their annual pilgrimage to Jerusalem.

The type of haggidic midrash under which we have categorized Jonah, Tobit, Esther, and Baruch may be defined as a literary form which freely elaborates for didactic purposes an historical nucleus of more or less amplitude. Since the literary form mixes history and fiction, it is in most cases impossible to determine where the one begins and the other ends. In some cases, as for example, in Wis. 10–19, one can separate the history from the didactic elaboration by a simple comparison with basically historical descriptions of the same events in other books. Where the same or similar events are not narrated in other books of the Bible, as is the case with Jonah, Tobit, Esther, Baruch, and Daniel, it is extremely difficult to determine what is basically historical and what is elaboration of the basically historical. However, it is not important, because the author's purpose was not to narrate history but to instruct or to edify.

Haggadic midrash has the following characteristics: (a) religious edification or instruction is the object envisioned by the author; (b) characters appear and speak in a way arranged by design to keep the story moving and dramatic; (c) the prayers and speeches of the principal characters usually serve as vehicles for the expression of the author's teaching; (d) the historical nucleus upon which the story is based is relatively unimportant. Historical events are used by the author to provide background for his story and characters. As a result he does not bother to integrate his story with the general history of the times. Nor does he make a distinction between the primary and secondary characters of history. For him the secondary characters are primary, religiously speaking. Esther, for example, is represented as the principal wife and queen of Xerxes, though she was probably only one of several wives of the great king.

For reasons that are easy to understand, the term midrash has contracted a pejorative nuance. Unlike the parable which is completely fiction, and into which the question of history does not enter, the haggadic midrash is part history and part fiction and the question of history (especially in modern times) is very much to the fore. For those who were brought up to accept such books as Jonah, Tobit, Esther, and Baruch as strict objective history, it comes as a shock to discover they are perhaps more fiction than history, more didactic than historical in nature. For some the discovery has resulted in an attitude of distrust, as if the midrashic authors set out to deceive their readers by representing as historical such events as have no foundation in fact. It is this pejorative nuance attached to the word midrash that we have tried to face squarely by referring to the haggadic midrash as a para-historical narrative. In all truth that is what it is—a narrative that appears historical but is partly fiction.

It must be understood, however, that deception was the farthest thing from the midrashic author's mind. In his mind and in the understanding of his audience, the doctrinal illustration or the edifying example was the important matter, not the historical content of the story. The audience delighted in the literary fiction in the same manner that modern audiences delight in the literary fictions in plays and moving pictures; in the same manner our Lord's audiences made allowances for and loved the fictitious parables He composed for doctrinal purposes. Authors are to be judged by their purpose. The midrashic authors sought to instruct and edify, not to act as professional historians.

2. Jonah

Asked to choose which is history and which fiction, the average reader of the Bible will probably choose the parable of the Good Samaritan as fiction and the book of Jonah as history. The reason for the choice, however, will probably be that the reader has *heard* that the Good Samaritan is a parable and Jonah history. If he were reading both for the first time with an unprejudiced mind, his initial judgment would more likely be the opposite. Since such a reader is rare, we shall list the reasons both for and against the historicity of Jonah and let the reader see why the majority of modern commentators consider Jonah didactic fiction rather than strict history.

To begin with, both Jewish and Christian tradition have commonly considered Jonah historical. A prophet named Jonah really existed in the time of Jeroboam II (2 Kings 14:25) in the eighth century B.C. Our Lord referred to Jonah as a sign of His resurrection (Matthew 12:39-42), coupling his reference to Jonah with a reference to the historical Queen of Sheba. Nineveh, as the excavations show, was truly a very great city. Both the sperm whale and the great shark are capable of swallowing a man whole. When in mourning, the Assyrians actually did extend the fast and sackcloth even to their animals as mentioned in Jonah (3:7). Moreover, one can argue that a later writer would hardly have made a hateful character out of a prophet if he had not been exactly as portrayed in the book. Finally, the visit of the prophet to a foreign country is not unprecedented. Elijah went to Phoenicia, Elisha to Syria. And if one objects to the extraordinary miracles in Jonah, why not object to the Gospel miracles since the same power is required for every miracle?

These are reasons of some weight in favor of the historicity of Jonah, and yet they did not convince St. Jerome. Nor did they deter St. Gregory Nazianzen (alone among the Fathers in this interpretation) from explicitly interpreting the story as a parable. Why he embraced this interpretation we do not know. Modern authors base their interpretation on a number of reasons. None of these reasons is convincing by itself. All however, taken together, give a cumulative weight to the interpretation (didactic fiction) sufficient to establish it as the accepted modern position.

As in a parable, there is no effort expended in Jonah to state names and specify times. Nor is there any attempt to pursue the story beyond the main events. Significantly the pagans are the heroes of the book (cf. 1:5; 1:10; 1:13; 1:16; 3:5; 3:10); Jonah is the villain (cf. 1:3; 1:5-6; 4:1-4; 4:10-11). There is no explanation of how Jonah or the author knew about the events in 1:16. There is no explanation of how Jonah made himself understood in preaching to people of a different language. As in the parable of the Good Samaritan, the use of Israel's hated enemy in the role of hero enhances the effect of the teaching. Of all the nations God could be expected to love, or who could be expected to do penance immediately upon the word of a Hebrew prophet, the last one the Jews would expect would be hated Assyria.

Equally significant is the fact that the language of the book is fifth century Hebrew rather than the eighth century Hebrew of the time of the historical Jonah. Jonah is placed in the Hebrew Bible with the didactic books rather than with the historical books. It is a matter of fact, moreover, that after the exile it was the Jewish practice to present teaching under the form of para-historical narrative as already noted.

Finally, the book is studded with an accumulation of unlikely though not impossible happenings. Never in Israelite history did a prophet have a mission like Jonah. Never in all history has a great city like Nineveh been converted by one short mission, given by one missionary, who spoke for a foreign God in a foreign language, and who did not want to convert his hearers anyway.

Granting that the book is a parable, or at least didactic fiction, what is its purpose? As in Nathan's parable to David (2 Sam. 12), as in the play within the play in Hamlet, as in the New Testament parable of the vinedressers (Matthew 21:33-46), the purpose of the book of Jonah is to provide a mirror for its readers to see themselves as they really are—petty, selfish, unreasonable men, unwilling to admit that God's love extends to all men and not only to chosen Israel, and that God's threats against the Gentiles can be revoked by repentance as surely as His threats against Israel as taught by Jeremiah (18:8ff).

In this interpretation, Jonah is a satire on the narrow nationalism and malignant intolerance of the fifth century Jews who were pushing Ezekiel's monastic concept of Israel to unreasonable lengths. It is the Old Testament version of the doctrine "outside the Church no salvation," understood without qualification and so excluding even those who are joined to the Church at least in desire. It is, moreover, the author's protest against Israel's refusal to take up the mission to be "a light to the Gentiles" urged on her by Deutero-Isaiah (cf. Is. 41—42; 49:6).

The basic theme and teaching of the book is God's love and care for all men, Gentiles and Jews. This doctrine is clear from the beginning of the Old Testament but becomes obscured by the jealousy of the Chosen People. In Gen. 3:15 hope is offered to all men. In Gen. 12:3 God promises Abraham, "In you all nations shall be blessed." In Is. 2:3 and Micah 4:1—4, the prophets see all nations ascending the mountain of God to learn God's ways. Pss. 72; 87; 117, and others show the universality of the kingdom of God and God's love for all men.

In its insistence on God's love and care for all mankind, Jonah is another proto-evangelium. In the Gospels, other Jews, the apostles, after they have been enlightened by the Holy Spirit (Acts 10), will do graciously and enthusiastically what the narrow-minded Jews of the fifth century refused to do—bring God's revelation to the Gentiles by preaching the Gospel to every creature.

Significant passages in Jonah

1:2 Told to go east to Nineveh, Jonah sails west to Tarshish (for reason, cf. 4:1-3).

1:5ff The good dispositions of the pagans are emphasized: they immediately cry out to their gods for help while Jonah sleeps and has to be awakened by their pagan captain and told to pray. In v. 10, the pagan sailors are horrified at Jonah's disobedience. In vv. 13-14, they row hard to save Jonah and only with great reluctance cast him into the sea (for the irony of this see Jonah's attitude toward the pagans in 4:1-3; cf. also Jer. 26).

1:16 "The men feared and sacrificed": for the fourth time the author brings out the good dispositions of the pagans. (If the book were historical, one might ask how the author found out what went on after Jonah was thrown overboard.)

2:1 "Great fish": the purpose of the fish is to save Jonah so that he will in turn be able to save Nineveh. The psalm that follows (vv. 2-9) is one of thanksgiving.

3:4 Jonah has to go through only one third of the city. The pagans heed the word of God immediately and do penance (compare the reception received by Isaiah and Jeremiah to appreciate the irony of this description).

3:7-10 Like the pagan sailors in ch. 1, the Ninevites are most God-fearing and their repentance (following God's promise in Jer. 18:7-8) brings immediate reversal of the punishment threatened in 3:4.

4:1-3 Key lines. Jonah refused to go to Nineveh in the first place precisely because he despised the pagans and feared that God, because of His great goodness and mercy, would forgive them. He would rather die than see the hated Ninevites forgiven!

4:5ff As Jonah sits outside the city avidly hoping for its destruction, God teaches him a lesson. He provides shade for him by a miraculously fast-growing vine, then produces a worm to destroy the vine. Jonah is angry because the destruction of the vine affects his comfort. If Jonah has so much concern for something in no way belonging to him, should not God be concerned with the fate of all those He has created — even the despised Gentiles?

3. Tobit

The reader of Tobit is filled with admiration for the charity and patience of the elder Tobit, the filial piety of the younger Tobiah, the chastity of both Sarah and young Tobiah, and the marvellous providence of God in watching over and caring for all of them. This is as it should be. More important still, it is precisely what the author of Tobit hoped to achieve in writing his story.

Like our Lord in His parables of the Good Samaritan and the Prodigal Son, the inspired author of Tobit is not content with stating that we must love our neighbor and put our trust in God as a loving Father. He gives us a story in which these truths are lived, and lived to perfection. He chooses a story to put across his message because we are all moved to practice virtue more by example than by words.

Whatever the actual facts may have been in the story of Tobit, the author goes far beyond them and embodies in his hero, Tobiah, the virtues of the ideal Israelite and in the angel Raphael the providence of God watching over His loved ones.

The literary form the author uses is that of the haggadic midrash — a type of writing that consisted in freely elaborating and building upon some historical event or character in such a way as to provide instruction or edification for the reader. The freedom with which the author of Tobit arranges his story to gain interest and suspense (cf. ch. 3; 6; 12), the detailed description of the virtues of the elder Tobit (ch. 1–2), and the frequency of the moral and dogmatic instructions placed upon the lips of the principal characters (cf. 3:2-6; 3:13-23; 4:2-23; 6:16-22; 8:7-10; 12:6-15; 13; 14:6-13), give more than enough indication that the author is writing haggadic midrash.

In reading Tobit, therefore, according to the inspired author's intention, we are to learn the kind of life God desires His loved ones to live and we are given an inspiring example to follow. We are to ask ourselves the question we ask when reading or hearing the Gospel parables: What is the doctrinal or moral truth that I am to learn from this story? And, at least implicitly, the author says to us what Jesus said to His audience at the end of the parable of the Good Samaritan: "Go thou and do likewise!"

Like any good story teller, the author lays his scene, develops his plot, sustaining suspense and interest to the last moment, and then concludes. On this basis we can divide the book into three parts.

I. (Ch. 1– 3) *The setting*. Tobit's loss of sight and dire poverty. Sarah's loss of seven husbands. The prayers of Tobit and Sarah in different places heard simultaneously by God.

II. (Ch. 4–11) *The plot*. The angel Raphael (the providence of God) guides young Tobiah to Media, saves him from a devouring fish, whose entrails are instrumental in driving off the devil that plagues Sarah and in curing the blindness that afflicts the elder Tobit.

III. (Ch. 12–14) *Conclusion*. The angel reveals his identity. Tobit recites a canticle of praise and thanksgiving. All concerned live happily and blessedly for long years after.

4. Esther

God's watchful providence in saving His people from destruction is the theme of the book of Esther. The author wrote some time during the Persian period, or shortly thereafter, to impress upon his readers the care of God for His people and to recount for them the origin of the happy feast of Purim.[1]

Like Tobit, the book of Esther is a midrash. The author writes to edify and encourage his readers. To do this he seizes upon an otherwise unrecorded event in Israelite history — a massive pogrom against the Jews of the dispersion that failed because of the intervention of a woman — and elaborates it freely and dramatically.

The historian does not know how much objective historical fact can be salvaged from the book of Esther because the author's primary interest was religious edification rather than professional historiography. However, it is assumed from the nature of the midrash, which usually began with an historical nucleus, and from the verisimilitude of the situation and the character of the Persian king, that the book of Esther is historical in substance and perhaps even in many of its particulars. As such the book is of some interest to historians.

The author's purpose, however, is not historical but didactic, and it is in his portrayal of God's care for his people that we find his intended message. To dramatize this consoling truth, the author uses all the techniques of the skilled story-teller: contrasts between the petulant Vashti and the serene Esther, between the dedicated and humble Mordecai and the ambitious and proud Haman; passing remarks about seemingly insignificant events which at the end of the story are seen in their true significance; the gradual heightening of suspense by means of the apparent success of Haman's plot; the ironic use of the gibbet prepared for Mordecai for the execution of Haman; the destruction of the enemies of the Jews on the very eve of the day determined by Haman for the destruction of the Jewish people. Until the telling of the story of the Prodigal Son, no better story-teller arose in Israel.

The Hebrew text of Esther is somewhat shorter than the Greek text. In the Greek there are additions which make the book almost one third longer than the Hebrew. While the Jews and the Protestants reject these additions as uninspired, the Church has accepted them as equally inspired with the rest of the book. No one can determine where precisely the additions came from, whether they belonged to the original book and became detached from it by design or accident, or whether they are, as most Cath-

[1] Cf. T. Wahl, *Judith and Esther*, OTRG No. 25; De Vaux, 514–517.

olic authors consider them, inspired additions to the original text of Esther. The book can be divided into four parts:

I. (Ch. 1–2) The setting of the scene in the court of Assuerus with the deposition of Vashti and the exaltation of Esther the Jewess.

II. (Ch. 3–7) The development of the plot. Haman, because of Mordecai, plots the destruction of the Jews (ch. 3). Mordecai urges Esther to intercede with Ahasuerus (ch. 4). While Haman prepares a gibbet for Mordecai, Esther, unknown to him, prepares his downfall (ch. 5). By happy chance Ahasuerus reads of Mordecai's unrequited service to him in revealing an assassination plot and rewards him (ch. 6). Esther reveals Haman's plot against the Jews and brings about his execution on the gibbet prepared for Mordecai (ch. 7).

III. (Ch. 8–10) Mordecai becomes chancellor and Haman's letters decreeing the destruction of the Jews are reversed (ch. 8). The Jews are allowed to destroy their enemies, and in remembrance of their preservation from Haman's machinations, the feast of Purim is instituted (ch. 9–10).

IV. (Ch. 11-16) Deutero-canonical additions to the book found only in the Greek.

5. Baruch and the letter of Jeremiah

However surprising to modern literary sensibilities, there is no question but that a strange and apparently deceptive literary form known as pseudepigrapha was not only popular but extensively used in the last centuries of Jewish history.[1]

Books written according to this literary form fictitiously claim as author an ancient sage, prophet, or patriarch who then speaks in place of the real author. Most examples of pseudepigrapha are found among the apocryphal books. Among others, the following may be mentioned as examples: the Psalms of Solomon, the Assumption of Moses, the Apocalypse of Baruch, the Testaments of the Twelve Patriarchs, the Book of Adam and Eve, the Testament of Job. In all of these, the authors pose as personages living in ancient times and speaking with the authority of these established biblical personalities.

[1] Cf. C. Stuhlmueller, *Baruch*, OTRG No. 17.

The popularity of this literary form became so great and was so well established that inspired authors also made use of it. Thus, most commentators would agree that the Canticle of Canticles, Qoheleth, Proverbs, and Wisdom, all of which are attributed to Solomon, are in reality pseudepigrapha. Most commentators would agree as well that Daniel, Baruch, and the Letter of Jeremiah fall into this same category. It is on this basis, therefore, that we treat Baruch and the Letter of Jeremiah as pseudepigrapha.

The book of Baruch was probably compiled by a Jew of the dispersion around the beginning of the second century B.C. Posing as the famous secretary of Jeremiah (cf. Jer. 32; 36; 45), the author's purpose is to instruct and encourage his readers and in particular to inculcate the sentiments with which the Israelites are to make the annual pilgrimage to Jerusalem. His book can be divided into three parts:

I. (Ch. 1:1–3:8) The solicitude of the exiles in Babylon for the continuance of Temple worship in Jerusalem (1:1-12) and their long penitential prayer (1:13–3:8).

II. (Ch. 3:9–4:4) The nature of true wisdom which comes from God alone and is found in His holy law.

III. (Ch. 4:5–5:9) A penitential psalm (4:5-29) culminating in a magnificent apostrophe to Jerusalem (based on Is. 60–62) to prepare for the happy return of the exiles and for her own future messianic glory (4:30–5:9).

The Letter of Jeremiah, which follows as ch. 6 of Baruch, is a distinct work, written sometime in the Greek period when Alexander and his successors gave new life to the cult of the ancient Babylonian idols. The author, posing as the prophet Jeremiah who during the exile had written letters to the exiles in Babylon (cf. Jer. 29), calls upon his readers to beware the idolatry of the pagans (6:1-6). He then satirizes at length the impotence and inanity of the idols, borrowing from Is. 44:9-20 and Jer. 10:1-16 to amass a colorful and sometimes humorous diatribe against idol worshippers (6:7-72). The splendor of monotheism shines here as no place else in the Bible.

16

The Wisdom Literature

1. Wisdom Literature and the Wisdom Teachers

The reader who jumps from the historical or prophetical books to the wisdom books finds himself in a different world. There is no more invective against idolatry, no more talk about covenant relations, little about God, little about the Temple and divine worship, much about man, his character, his conduct, his foibles, and his failings.

The reader feels he has left the theocentric world of the prophets and the priests and entered an anthropocentric world in which man and the "good life" claim the center of the stage. This illusion is very real despite the fact that it is truly an illusion. For that reason the reader should know well the background of the wisdom literature, its growth in Israel, the nature, purpose, and methods of the wisdom teachers, and the nature of the wisdom Israel's sages taught.[1]

The background of the wisdom literature

The wisdom movement and its literature grew on Israel's soil and were nourished by Israel's faith. It is certain, however, that the roots of the movement came from outside. There is no doubt that a flourishing wisdom literature antedating that of Israel existed not only in Egypt but in Arabia and in Mesopotamia.

[1] Cf. select bibliography, p. 575.

When Stephen in his discourse before the Sanhedrin said of Moses that he "was instructed in all the wisdom of the Egyptians" (Acts 7:22), he made reference to no small volume of wisdom literature. There was, for example, the instruction of the vizier Ptah-hotep, a collection of wise sayings giving directives for a successful life and dating to about 2450 B.C., approximately 1100 years before Moses (cf. ANET 412ff). There is also the instruction for King-Meri-ka-re (about 2200 B.C.), advice given by a king to his son and successor on how to rule successfully. There are similar collections of instructions for King Amen-em-het (about 1960 B.C.), for Prince Hor-dedef (about 2700 B.C.), and for Amen-em-opet (about 1000 B.C.). That Israel knew the existence of this literature is attested by the statement of Kings: "Solomon surpassed all the Cedemites and all the Egyptians in wisdom" (1 Kings 5:10).

A further statement of the author of Kings, "He was wiser than all other men — than Ethan the Ezrahite, or Heman, Chalcol, and Darda, the musicians" (1 Kings 5:11), testifies to Israel's acquaintance with these Arabian or perhaps Canaanite sages. Even more significant is the fact that the author of Job chooses for his hero a wise man who is not an Israelite at all but either an Edomite or an Arabian. The same can be said for Job's friends, Eliphaz from Teman, Bildad from Shuh, and Zophar from Naamath.

There is little direct reference in the Bible to Mesopotamian wisdom literature, but the book of Tobit mentions Ahiqar and Nadab, the two principals of a wisdom story from Assyrian literature (ANET 427ff), and the theme of the suffering just man so magnificently developed in the book of Job is found even earlier in the Babylonian poem, "I Will Praise the Lord of Wisdom."

Wisdom literature in Israel

Wisdom literature entered Israel with the importation of Egyptian scribes by David to fill administrative positions in his new kingdom. It grew under the patronage of Solomon, who was probably educated by an Egyptian, is known to have married an Egyptian princess, and is reputed by the author of Kings to have written "three thousand proverbs, and his songs numbered a thousand and five" (1 Kings 5:12). So great was Solomon's reputation that in later centuries he came to be for wisdom what Moses was for the law and David for the psalms.

The remark of Jeremiah's enemies, "Come, let us contrive a plot against Jeremiah. It will not mean the loss of instruction from the priests, nor of counsel from the wise, nor of messages from the prophets," shows that the sages in the last years before the exile ranked as one of three classes of communal leaders, the others being the priests and the prophets. Another clear indication of the activity of the sages before the exile comes from a remark in Proverbs attributing to the men of Hezekiah, king of Judah, the transmission of the proverbs of Solomon contained in ch. 25–29 (cf. Prov. 25:1).

After the exile, when prophecy was on the wane, wisdom literature in Israel entered its golden age. The maxims and sayings of Solomon, Agur, Lemuel, and some anonymous sages were gathered together in the book we know as Proverbs sometime in the 6th-3rd centuries B.C. and provided the broad basis for the longer and more elaborate wisdom teachings of Jesus, ben Sirach, in the early second century B.C. The wisdom literature dealing with the great problem of retribution was initiated by the author of Job in the 6th-5th century B.C., continued by Qoheleth, the author of Ecclesiastes, in the 4th-3rd centuries, and brought to a happy conclusion toward the middle of the first century B.C. by the author of the book of Wisdom. Tobit, Baruch, and Daniel, all postexilic books, as well as a number of psalms betray close affinities with the wisdom literature.

What is most significant about the growth of the wisdom literature in Israel after its transplanting from Egypt, Mesopotamia, and Arabia is the subtle change it undergoes. In form and content, it remains much the same. In tone and underlying spirit, it differs drastically. The use of proverbs and maxims and the literary fiction of a king addressing his subjects, or a father counselling his son, remains as in the Egyptian wisdom literature. The content too does not differ radically: how to comport oneself, how to live well, how to make the most of life in this world. The tone, however, and the underlying spirit are completely different. Wisdom in Israel is religious, not secular. Unlike the indifferently ethical wisdom of the Gentile nations, Israelite wisdom is adamantly ethical and moral. It begins and ends with "the fear of the Lord," and without the fear of the Lord (religion), there is no wisdom. What Moses had done for the common law and the common cult of the ancient near east, what David and the Israelite psalmists had done for the common music and psalmody of the ancient near east, the Israelite sages did for Wisdom. It is a striking example of grace building upon nature.

Since the apparent secular nature of the inspired wisdom literature (a genetic resemblance reducible to its Gentile roots) is often a stumbling block for the unwitting reader, the student should note clearly from the very beginning that the wisdom writers repeatedly affirm in no uncertain terms that there is no wisdom without "fear of the Lord," i.e., without religion or ordination of the individual to God by love and obedience. What appears, therefore, in their words to be merely mundane wisdom or worldly wise prudence—the art of living well, knowing the practical solutions of life's problems, political sagacity, artistic skill, common prudence, and even such trivial matters as good table manners, the training of children, and mannerly comportment in public — must be understood as the fruits of the supernatural gift of wisdom (cf. Prov. 1:7; Job 28:28; Qoh. 12:13-14; Sir. 1:9-18; 6:37; 15:1-10; 19:17-26; 39:1-11; Ps. 119:97-104). Purely mundane wisdom is compatible with sin. The divinely infused wisdom of the sages, commensurate with the fear of the Lord, comes and goes with the acquisition or loss of sanctifying grace (cf. Sir. 1:22-29; 2:12-18; 19:17-20).

The wisdom teachers

The patience of Job, the pessimism of Qoheleth, the moderation of Sirach — all of these are proverbial. But what kind of men were the authors who wrote these books? Of the three classes of communal leaders mentioned by Jeremiah (18:18), the priests, the prophets, and the wise men, only the wise men have been truly difficult for moderns to categorize. They have been labelled the philosophers, the intellectuals, the humanists, the individualists of Israel. In one way they are all of these and more. In another way they are not. The labels are convenient. But they are not accurate.

The priests, concerned with affairs of worship and the interpretation of law, moved in the incense-laden atmosphere of the Temple. The prophets, concerned with the relations between God and His people and the declaration of God's will to His people, moved in the rarified atmosphere of revelation. The sages, on the contrary, had little to say about the Temple worship and less about revelation. They kept their feet very much on the ground and breathed the same prosaic atmosphere as the rest of men. They were the school-masters of Israel, the prudent counsellors, the experienced elders, the learned scribes. They broke down fine the lofty message of revelation and the prosaic lessons of experience and spoon-fed them to their students.

The ministry of the sages was to reprove, correct, and instruct. And their subject matter covered the whole realm of human behavior. They studied man as man in the light of reason, revelation, and experience; and to this degree they can be called philosophers. They had great respect for the acquisition of knowledge about God and man; and to this degree they can be called intellectuals. They were concerned with the whole sphere of man's life and behavior, the human as well as the divine in man's life; and to this degree they can be called humanists. They have been called individualists because they apparently thought things out for themselves, gave their own opinions on a multitude of matters and rarely appealed either to the authority of divine revelation or to the authority of other learned sages.

Nevertheless, they never gave to reason the preeminence given to it by philosophers, nor to mere knowledge the adulation given to it by the intellectuals. The human side of man's life was important to them, but it never overshadowed the importance of the divine. And though they taught as if theirs was the last word on matters of human behaviour, they would have been the first to insist that God's word was both first and last; indeed, that "the beginning of wisdom is the fear of the Lord."

Like St. Paul they taught their students "whether you eat or drink, or whatever you do, do all to the glory of God" (1 Cor. 10:31). Their purpose, therefore, was not knowledge for the sake of knowledge, but knowledge for the sake of godliness. They taught their students the art of excellence in all things and not just in the things of God, so that there might be said of them what was later said of one "greater than Solomon": "He has done all things well" (Mark 7:37). They became "all things to all men" (1 Cor. 9:22) after the manner of St. Paul, because they were convinced that all things came from God and were destined through man to be returned to God. Religion concerned all of man's life and involved a total commitment. It was their purpose to see to it that their students made this commitment and extended it to every area of their lives (cf. Prov. 1:2-7).

To accomplish this purpose the sages sought in their own lives for an ever increasing knowledge of God and God's will with respect to men. They studied the Scriptures (cf. the foreword to Sirach). They meditated on the manifestations of God's power and glory in the works of His hand, the physical universe and the marvellous make-up of man, His most illustrious creation. From the nature of man, and from experience of his way of acting, they reasoned to the blueprint for a moral universe. And from the conclusions of the wisdom writers who had gone before them, both Jew and Gentile, they gathered that deposit of distilled wisdom that comes only from the time-tested experience of generations of sages. Sirach says of the wisdom teacher as he conceived him: "He explores the wisdom of the men of old . . . he studies obscure parables . . . he is in attendance on the great . . . he travels among the peoples of foreign lands . . . if it pleases the Lord Almighty . . . he will pour forth his words of wisdom. . . . While he lives, he is one out of a thousand, and when he dies his renown will not cease" (Sir. 39:1-11).

The wisdom writers have the following characteristics. First, they teach by *mashals*, i.e., pointed comparisons loaded with practical wisdom. These comparisons or mashals can be in the form of parables, allegories, riddles, but usually they are in the form of proverbs, i.e., maxims expressed in poetic diction, rhythm, and parallelism, and concerned with moral instruction. The figurative and sometimes enigmatic way of presenting the instruction demanded of the reader a certain amount of thought and reflection in order to penetrate its meaning. It was their way of teaching just as the syllogistic method was the way of the scholastics.

Secondly, the sages cultivate truth in its dual aspects of reason and revelation. Their teaching consequently differs from that of the priests and the prophets in that it is more universal in scope and much less nationalistic. It is for all men and not just for the Jews. Because of their great respect for reason and experience, they have been called the humanists of the Bible (cf. Wis. 7:17-22).

Thirdly, they stress the fact that religion is not only doctrine but a mode of existence. They show how God and His law, positive and natural, enter into every last prosaic detail of life. And they emphasize the necessity of not restricting religion to any special time or place, but making it inform all that man does all of the time.

According to the wisdom teachers, the sources of wisdom are: revelation, tradition, divine infusion, experience, reason. The means of acquiring wisdom are: study, instruction, discipline, reflection, meditation, counsel. Synonyms for a wise man are: prudent, perceptive, discrete, sensible, understanding. One who hates wisdom is: a fool, sinner, simpleton, simple, ignorant, obstinate, proud, scoffer, wicked, senseless.

The wisdom writers may be defined as teachers who used mashals to convey their message, and who wrote with the aim of praising, describing, and teaching whatever wisdom they had themselves acquired from their study of God's revelation as found in the law and the prophets or as discovered by their own meditation on and experience of the created universe and the nature, affairs, and destiny of man. The message they imparted to their students may be summed up in the word of St. Paul: "Whatthings are true, whatever honorable, whatever just, whatever holy, whatever lovable, whatever of good repute, if there be any virtue, if anything worthy of praise, think upon these things. And what you have learned and received and heard and seen in me, these things practice (Phil. 4:8-9); whether you eat or drink, or do anything else, do all for the glory of God" (1 Cor. 10:31).

The wisdom of the wisdom teachers

Anyone in ancient times who possessed a special knowledge of things enabling him to act skillfully and with success was considered a wise man. Wisdom as a consequence was considered primarily a practical not a speculative kind of knowledge.

Joseph's success in interpreting Pharaoh's dream gained for him the reputation of a wise man (Gen. 41:39). The success of the wise woman of Tekoa in maneuvering David to return Absalom to Jerusalem was typicai of the practical results expected from wisdom (2 Sam. 14:1-23). Solomon's knowledge of the human heart which enabled him to distinguish the true from the false mother by ordering the child cut in two was considered an excellent illustration of the great king's wisdom (1 Kings 3:16-28).

Throughout the Wisdom books it is not so much great intellectual ability as the ability to order one's life well that is the mark of the wise man. Essentially the wise man is a man who succeeds. Whether he is an architect who builds well, or a king who rules well, or a king's counsellor who gives successful advice, it is in the success that attends the practical application of his knowledge that the wise man is known.

Since wisdom was so precious a commodity it was presumed that the gods possessed it in abundance. Indeed it was by wisdom that the gods as wise architects had created the world, and as wise rulers ruled it. "El," as a Ugaritic text of the fourteenth century B.C., declares, "created me (wisdom) at the beginning of his dominion." And in the Baal epic of Ugarit, it is El who is all-wise: "Thy command, O El, is wise, thy wisdom lasts forever. A life of good fortune is thy command."

In Israel it is no different. No one is wise as God (Job 9:4-10; 12:13; 21:22). In God and in God alone is all wisdom found (Job 28:12-27; Bar. 3:15-38). If man has wisdom, it is because he has received it from God. "With him," as Job says, "are wisdom and might; his are counsel and understanding" (Job 12:13). "Immense is the wisdom of the Lord," says Sirach, "he is mighty in power, and all seeing. The eyes of God see all he has made; he understands man's every deed" (Sir. 15:18-19). "There is but one, wise and truly awe-inspiring, seated upon his throne; it is the Lord" (Sir. 1:6).

From what has been said it might be thought that in Israel and in the pagan nations of old the concept of wisdom was the same: preeminently a practical knowledge, preeminently the possession of the divinity. There was a difference, however, and a very important difference. Since the pagan gods were indifferently ethical and disturbingly arbitrary with regard to what constituted good and evil, pagan wisdom could be conceived independent of an objective moral order. In Israel such a wisdom was unthinkable. No one could be wise who was not also good. No man could be wise who did not avoid sin and hate evil. In Israel, wisdom declared: "Wickedness my lips abhor . . . pride, arrogance, the evil way, and the perverse mouth I hate" (Prov. 8:7, 13). Sirach emphatically states: "Worthless men will not attain to her, haughty men will not behold her. Far from the impious is she, not to be spoken of by liars" (Sir. 15:7-8). "The knowledge of wickedness is not wisdom, nor is there prudence in the counsel of sinners. . . . There are those with little understanding who fear God, and those of great intelligence who violate the law" (Sir. 19:18-20).

On the contrary, wisdom is preeminently "fear of the Lord," i.e., religion, knowing, loving, and serving God. So important is fear of the Lord that it is called by Sirach, the "beginning of wisdom," "the fullness of wisdom," "wisdom's garland," "the root of wisdom" (Sir. 1:9-18). Lest there be any doubt about what "fear of the Lord" means, Sirach explains: "Those who fear the Lord disobey not his words; those who love him keep his ways. Those who fear the Lord seek to please him, those who love him are filled with his law" (Sir. 2:15-16; cf. also Sir. 4:14; 7:29, 30; Wis. 6:8; 7:22-28).

The wisdom of the wisdom teachers, therefore, is only in appearance similar to pagan wisdom. Since it comes from God and is a reflection of His wisdom, it consists essentially in knowing and loving all things as God knows them and loves them. It is sacred because it sees all things in relation to God (Wis. 13:1-9; Prov. 8:22-23). It is supernatural, since it can come from God alone (Sir. 1:1; Prov. 2:6; Wis. 8:21). It is practical rather than theoretical, since it embraces not only knowledge but practice, making it impossible to be truly wise unless one not only knows but does. A sinner, therefore, is automatically a fool, no matter how great his knowledge, because knowledge divorced from life and conduct is not wisdom at all, but the clearest proof of folly. Finally, in the sense that the wisdom teachers do not receive direct revelation from God as the prophets, the wisdom they describe is more human than divine. It is based more on practical theological reasoning than on direct revelation.

Since the wisdom writers repeatedly affirm that there is no wisdom without fear of the Lord, which is equivalent to that ordination of the individual to God by love and obedience which we call religion, we know that basically they are speaking of supernatural wisdom, that wisdom that accompanies and flows from sanctifying grace. What appears in their words to be merely human wisdom — the art of living well, knowing the practical solutions of life's problems, great and small, political sagacity, artistic skill, common prudence, and even such trivial matters as good table manners, the training of children, and comportment in public — must be understood as the fruits of the gift of wisdom. Such wisdom not only resides in the intellect which is illumined by God's grace, but overflows to the will, so that the recipient knows things in relation to their ultimate cause, loves them, and acts according to the dictates of that love. Natural wisdom is compatible with sin; supernatural wisdom comes and departs with the acquisition or loss of sanctifying grace.

Divine or uncreated wisdom may be defined as that divine attribute (manifested to men through revelation and through the works of creation) by which God, acting by means of His perfect knowledge and comprehension of the nature and capacities of created things, purposes, plans, and effects all things, adapting means to ends in the best possible way.

Besides describing wisdom as an attribute of God, the sages sometimes go further and personify divine wisdom as if it were distinct from God, proceeding from Him, and having as it were a personal character. This personification of divine wisdom is so striking and has provoked so much discussion and dispute, that it must be treated in a special way.

To begin with, divine wisdom is personified in the wisdom books in varying degrees. In some texts the personification is simple (cf. Prov. 1:20-23; Sir. 4:11-19; 14:20-14; 10; Wis. 1:4-8; 6:12-22 and *passim*); in others it is quite extravagant (cf. Prov. 8:22-31; 9:1-6; Sir. 24:1-29; Wis. 7:7—8:16). To put these texts in true perspective, the reader must take into consideration: (a) the Old Testament practice of personifying divine attributes; (b) the extraordinary esteem of the sages for wisdom as the queen of God's attributes; (c) the high estimation of the ancients for a wise counsellor, particularly the counsellor of a king; (d) the precise purpose of the wisdom writers' use of personification.

It is clear from the psalms that the Old Testament practice of personifying divine attributes is not restricted to wisdom. In Ps. 85:11-14, a number of God's attributes are personified, e.g., "Kindness and truth shall meet; justice and peace shall kiss." In Ps. 89:15, the psalmist speaks in a similar manner, e.g., "Justice and judgment are the foundation of your throne; kindness and truth go before you" (cf. also Ps. 79:8; Is. 55:11; Hab. 3:5).

The reason for the more frequent and more extravagant personification of wisdom is obviously the great esteem of the wisdom writers for wisdom as the queen of the divine attributes. Apparently they could not praise wisdom too much. This is evident even apart from the use of personification (cf. Prov. 3:13-24; Sir. 6:18-27). This esteem for wisdom, moreover, and even the personification of wisdom is not peculiar to Israelite wisdom writers. The Baal epic from Ugarit (about 1400 B.C.) contains a parallel to Prov. 8:22, differing only in the divine name: "El (the high god of the Ugaritic pantheon) created me (wisdom) the beginning of his ways." In the "Words of Ahiqar," a seventh century Assyrian didactic work, the author speaks the following extravagant words about wisdom: "To gods also she is dear. For all time the kingdom is hers. In heaven is she established, for the lord of holy ones has exalted her" (ANET 428).

Particularly significant for the interpretation of the personification texts is the close connection of wisdom with the counsel of the counsellor. The counsellor in ancient times was the adviser of the king. He might be a learned scribe, or an experienced elder statesman, or even at times the Queen-mother. He was looked upon as a wise man, and his counsel or advice was equated with wisdom. A few texts will demonstrate the ancients' association of wise counsel with wisdom. In Deuteronomy we read: "They are a nation without counsel, and without wisdom. O that they would be wise and would understand, and would provide for their last end" (32:28-29). Jeremiah asks: "Is there no more wisdom in Teman, has counsel perished from the prudent, has their wisdom become corrupt" (49:7)? The parallelism clearly indicates the identity of counsel with wisdom. The importance of counsellors and their counsel is many times brought out in the Bible (cf. Exod. 18:19; 2 Sam. 15:12, 34; 16:20; 17:7, 14; 1 Kings 1:11-14; 12:6-11; Is. 1:26; 3:1-3; 11:2; 16:3; 47:13; Jer. 18:18; Ez. 7:26; Micah 4:9-12; Job 12:13; Dan. 5:7-16; Ezra 4:5; 7:28; 10:3). These passages indicate that wise counsel is the guarantee of salvation, security, victory. It is a decision given by an authorized person and cannot be ignored without dire consequences. The counsellors are usually attached to the king's household and assist him in making his decisions.

Finally, the sages personify wisdom in order to dramatize for their students the supreme value and importance of wisdom. This is particularly obvious in the introduction to Proverbs. The author begins by stating that he is presenting the proverbs of Solomon "that men may appreciate wisdom, may understand words of intelligence." He continues extolling wisdom in different ways (ch. 1–7), climaxing his praise by the personification of wisdom (8:22-31). He then concludes logically in the following verses: "So now O children, listen to me; instruction and wisdom do not reject . . ." (8:32-36).

If the reader will now examine carefully the personification texts, he will see that wisdom is personified in a very particular way – as the divine "counsellor," that important member of the royal court to whom the king turned for enlightenment and advice before acting or making decisions.[1] God is the great king, the king *par excellence*. It is, therefore, fitting that he have the counsellor *par excellence*. This counsellor is wisdom herself. If, as the sages indicate by this personification, even God does not act without consulting wisdom, His counsellor, it follows that it would be the height of foolishness for man to act without consulting this same counsellor.

Several observations lend weight to this interpretation. First, it is clear from numerous texts of the Bible that the Hebrews did represent God after the manner of an earthly king surrounded by his counsellors and courtiers (cf. Is. 6:1-3; 1 Kings 22:19-23; Job 1:6-7; Ps. 89:8).

[1] Cf. P. A. H. de Boer, "The Counsellor," in Vetus Testamentum, III, *Wisdom in Israel and in the Ancient Near East* (Leiden: E. J. Brill, 1960).

Secondly, the texts, when read closely, show wisdom speaking and acting after the manner of a counsellor. It is certainly the elder counsellor or the Queen-mother counsellor who can say: "I, wisdom, dwell with experience, and judicious knowledge I attain. . . . Mine are counsel and advice. . . . By me kings reign" (Prov. 8:12-15). She is a member of the court of God: "In the assembly of the most high she opens her mouth, in the presence of his hosts she declares her worth" (Sir. 24:2). She ministers to God after the manner of a royal counsellor: "In the holy tent I ministered before him, and in Sion I fixed my abode" (Sir. 24:10).

Thirdly, since wisdom, the divine counsellor, is so essential even for God, it is not surprising that He should never be without her; indeed that she should be the firstborn of His creation: "The Lord begot me the firstborn of his ways" (Prov. 8:22). When building the universe, God consults wisdom, His architect-counsellor: "Then was I beside him as his craftsman" (Prov. 8:30). Following immediately upon this personification of wisdom as God's counsellor comes the sage's very obvious and pointed moral: "So now, O children, listen to me; instruction and wisdom do not reject" (Prov. 8:32ff).

Lastly, it might be observed that the personification of wisdom in Prov. 8:22-31; Sir. 24 and Wis. 7–8 is so vivid and personal that wisdom seems to be represented as another divine being, proceeding from God, co-eternal with Him. Such a representation, however, by a Hebrew writer is inconceivable. If he had even suspected that his readers might take from his words the suggestion that there was a duality of persons in God, which would have been the equivalent to the people of his generation of a duality of gods, he certainly would not have used such language. If, on the contrary, as has been suggested, the people were accustomed to an anthropomorphic description of God surrounded like a human king by courtiers and counsellors; if the personification of wisdom as a being distinct from God was so common that it was found even in pagan wisdom literature, then the danger of an apparently heretical interpretation is avoided and the language is readily conceivable.

Since all evidence, and particularly a comparison with Canaanite-Phoenician didactic sources, points to the greater antiquity of Prov. 8–9, the personification texts of Sirach and Wisdom are best interpreted as developments of the line of thought initiated by the author of Proverbs.

If there was no danger of misinterpretation of the personification texts at the time of the wisdom writers, the same cannot be said for interpreters who read these texts after the Incarnation of the Second Person of the Blessed Trinity. The personification is so strong that it has lead many to believe the wisdom writers were favored with a pre-incarnation revelation of the existence of the Second Person of the Blessed Trinity. The more

57

58

59

60

61

62

64

65

66

Nos. 57–67. The kingdom of Darius and Xerxes.   **57**. Ahuramazda symbol on the north jamb of the east doorway to the tripylon at Persepolis.   **58**. East staircase of the Apadana; palace of Darius at Persepolis in the background.   **59**. Gate of Xerxes.   **60**. South stairway of the winter palace of Darius at Persepolis.   **61**. King Darius enthroned, with his son, the crown prince Xerxes, standing behind him; behind the prince are two court officials followed by two guards.   **62**. A section of the Apadana stairway with lower left corner showing Phoenicians bringing tribute to Xerxes.   **63**. Aerial view of the palace complex of the Persian kings at Persepolis; to the left, Nos. 58 and 60 are easily discernible; on the site of the ancient harem, quarters for the archaeologists were constructed (lower right).   **64**. Ten-ton black limestone bull's head from the main portico of the Throne Hall.   **65**. A sphinx figure from the palace of Darius at Persepolis.   **66**. A gold rounded applique with a winged lion from the Achaemenid period.   **67**. From an Achaemenid grave at Nippur, Iraq, a pottery figurine of a man riding a horse. *Photos courtesy:* Oriental Institute, University of Chicago.

reasonable interpretation, we believe, is that the wisdom writers received no such revelation. Their extraordinary descriptions of God's wisdom, however, did provide an excellent background for the explanation of the procession of the Son from the Father given at a later time by St. John, St. Paul, and the Fathers of the Church. But it was only background, not revelation, that the wisdom writers provided. Their mind and the meaning of their words is determined more accurately from the background of the wisdom movement than by the injection of New Testament revelation into Old Testament writings. As our Lord Himself said, it is dangerous to put new wine into old bottles (Mark 2:22). The old wine, however, could and did give a taste for the new!

2. Proverbs

All that has been said about the wisdom literature, its roots and background outside of Israel, its growth in Israelite soil, the nature, purpose, and methods of the wisdom teachers, the nature of wisdom and its personification, is exemplified in the books of Proverbs and Sirach.[1]

Unlike Job, Qoheleth, and Wisdom, Proverbs and Sirach are not restricted to particular problems but cover a broad conspectus of human affairs and teach a multitude of particular wisdom lessons. The two books portray the same general condition of society and teach many of the same lessons. It is certain that Sirach knew the book of Proverbs, but their similarity is due more to a common wisdom tradition and to a common purpose than to any direct dependence of one upon the other.

Proverbs is entitled *Mishle Shelomoh* from its first words meaning the proverbs of Solomon. It shows its indebtedness to Egyptian wisdom literature from the very beginning by using the literary fiction of a father addressing instructions to his son: "Hear, my son, your father's instruction . . ." (1:8ff), and later on in a series of proverbs modelled upon the maxims of Amen-em-Ope (22:19ff). Its indebtedness to Arabian wisemen is acknowledged in the collections attributed to Agur and Lemuel, wisdom teachers from Massa in northern Arabia (30:1; 31:1).

The growth of the wisdom movement in Israel is testified to in Proverbs by the large collections of proverbs attributed to Israelite authors (10:1–22:16 and 25:1–29:27 by Solomon; 24:23-34; 30:15-33; 31:10-31; 1–9 by anonymous but probably Israelite authors), by the religious tone that prevails throughout the book (cf. 5:21; 15:3-11; 20:1-24 and *passim*), and by

[1] Cf. E. Lussier, *Proverbs and Sirach*, OTRG No. 24; P. W. Skehan, "The Seven Columns of Wisdom's House in Proverbs 1–9," *CBQ* 9 (1947) 190–198, and "A Single Editor for the Whole Book of Proverbs," *CBQ* 10, (1948) 115–130.

the repeated emphasis on "fear of the Lord" as "the beginning of wisdom" (cf. 1:7, 18, 29; 9:10; 15:33; 16:6; 22:4).

In the manner characteristic of wisdom teachers the author of Proverbs has little to say about the externals of religion and less to say about theoretical ethics. What appears on the surface to be utilitarianism in the author's very much down to earth advice is rather the typical concentration of the wisdom teacher on the practical. He gives a practical demonstration of the profit to be gained from living according to the dictates of wisdom and opposes to it a practical demonstration of the fateful consequences of living a life of folly. The means he uses to teach his readers is almost exclusively the piquant, thought-provoking, two stich proverb. Occasionally he uses allegory (cf. 1:20-33; 8:1-36; 9:1-6, 13-18).

In the manner peculiar to Israelite sages he manifests throughout his work the influence of revelation. But the influence is subtle. On the surface he is a man of the world and his proverbs for the most part are not the product of revelation but of experience and reason. Like all the sages he urges his readers to commit themselves to a life guided by wisdom (1:2-7) and to seek out wisdom by means of study, instruction, discipline, reflection, meditation, and counsel.

Proverbs is not the unified product of a single author's mind. It is a compilation, like the book of psalms, of a number of separate collections of proverbs, put together by an editor and prefaced by a long introduction (1–9). The age of the different collections cannot be accurately determined, but it is generally agreed that the majority are pre-exilic. Of the pre-exilic collections two go back, at least in part, to the time of Solomon (10:1–22:16; 25:1–29:27). The introduction (1–9) is the work of the editor and the compilation was probably completed by him sometime around the end of the fourth century before Christ. The book may be divided as follows:

I. The editor's introduction lauding the value of wisdom (1:1–9:18).
II. The first collection of Solomonic proverbs (10:1–22:16).
III. A collection entitled, "The Sayings of the Wise" (22:17–24:22)
IV. Another collection entitled, "Sayings of the Wise" (24:23-34).
V. A second collection of Solomonic proverbs (24:5–29:27).
VI. A collection entitled, "The Words of Agur" (30:1-14).
VII. A collection of numerical proverbs (30:15-33).
VIII. A collection entitled, "The Words of Lemuel, king of Massa" (31:1-9).
IX. Praise of the ideal wife (31:10-31).

As the distilled wisdom of centuries of experience and reflection, the individual proverbs contain much in little. The reader is advised against reading them on the run or at length. They are to be sampled, savored, and digested slowly.

3. Sirach

The editor of Proverbs would have been proud of his illustrious pupil, Jesus Ben Sirach, whose book on wisdom teaching, entitled "Ecclesiasticus" in the Vulgate and Douay versions and "Sirach" in the New American Bible, shows the kind of man a serious student of Proverbs could become.[1]

As the numerous biographical references in his book reveal, Sirach was a member of the scribal class, a student of the Scriptures from his youth, a world traveller who had mixed with high society and had been employed at court, a man who settled in Jerusalem in his old age and opened a school for the scriptural and moral instruction of his younger compatriots (cf. the Prologue; 34:9-12; 38:24; 39:1-6; 50:27; 51:1-23).

Sirach's work for all its dependence on Proverbs and similarity to it in content has its own distinctive characteristics. It is not a compilation of other men's work but the product of one man's lifetime of meditation on the Scriptures, on life in general, and on his own broad experience. Sirach not only does not follow the strictly universal outlook on Wisdom characteristic of Proverbs, but glories in the wisdom teaching proper to Israel and in the heroes of Israel's past who were led by wisdom to do great things for their people. Unlike Proverbs which consists for the most part of unrelated proverbs, many of Sirach's proverbs are gathered in groups on individual themes and sometimes a whole chapter is given to one theme.

Although originally written in Hebrew and known in the Hebrew by St. Jerome, Sirach's work came down in Greek and was not known in Hebrew by moderns until the discovery in 1896 in a Cairo geniza (a storeroom for old and unusable biblical manuscripts) of about two thirds of the Hebrew text. The New American Bible version of Sirach is based on this Hebrew text corrected by means of the ancient versions.

Sirach is one of the few books of the Old Testament that can be dated with any accuracy. The dating is based upon the testimony of Sirach's grandson, who translated his grandfather's book into Greek. In the preface to his translation he mentions that he came to Egypt in the year 132 and began his translation soon after. In his book (50:1ff), Sirach speaks of the

[1] Cf. Murphy, *Seven Books of Wisdom*, 104–126; CCHS par. 438ff; L. Hartman, "Sirach in Hebrew and Greek," *CBQ* 23 (1961) 443-451.

high priest Simon II (219-196). On the basis of this twofold testimony Sirach is dated around the year 180. The book can be divided as follows:

I. Practical moral instructions for all (1–43).
II. A eulogy of the great men of Israel's past (44:1–50:24), followed by an epilogue containing biographical details and several canticles (50:25–51:30).

4. Job

Along with Qoheleth and Wisdom, Job belongs to the problem type of wisdom literature. Unlike Proverbs and Sirach, Job's author is not concerned with broad generalities nor with a multitude of particular wisdom lessons. He attacks one problem — the insoluble enigma of the suffering of the innocent.[1]

His work has been called the greatest poem of ancient or modern times, the most wonderful poem of any age or language, one of the grandest things ever written with pen. The author himself has been ranked with Homer, Dante, and Shakespeare, and his language and theme have fascinated and stimulated readers down the centuries.

Nevertheless, the book is not easy reading and the swift reader will find neither fascination nor stimulation. Job's author abominated superficialities and scorned the easy solution. The book therefore must be pondered. A study of the literary form of the book, the theological background of Job's problem, and the format of his masterpiece will provide no small help for the reader who encounters Job for the first time.

The literary form of Job

The patience of Job, like the charity of the Good Samaritan, has become so proverbial that it is often taken for granted that the book is a biography of a definite historical character. On the contrary, the book is a poetic, psychological drama in which the author uses as protagonist a legendary hero of ancient times. Proof that Job once existed is based on Ez. 14:14, 20, where he is placed on a par with Noah, the hero of the flood story, and Daniel, a legendary Ugaritic king, who lived sometime before 1400 B.C. It is clear, however, from the construction and tone of the book that the author has no intention of recounting the story of Job's life. Rather than an historical character, Job is used by the author as a type of the suffering just man. He

[1] Cf. Murphy, *Seven Books of Wisdom*, 53-66; Guillet, *Themes of the Bible*, 147-170; CCHS par. 360ff; P. W. Skehan, "Strophic Patterns in the Book of Job," *CBQ* 23 (1961) 125-142.

also uses him as his mouthpiece and provides the three friends and Elihu as opposition in order to give edge and vivacity to his discussion of the problem of suffering.

The book bears manifest signs of poetic fiction and license: the round numbers of the prologue and epilogue, the scenes in the prologue with the Satan coming before God, the dramatic efficiency of the messengers in the prologue (only one escapes in each case in order to bring news of the calamity to Job), the storm-theophany of God at the end of the dialogues, and the clearest sign of all — the same magnificent and unmistakeable poetic style and diction for each of the characters.

It is generally agreed that a drama must have a generous amount of external action. Since the action of Job is almost entirely internal, many refuse to consider the book a drama. It is certainly not a drama in the conventional meaning of the term. However, the heart of good drama lies in the unfolding of the character of the protagonist in response to the particular crisis around which the dramatic action revolves. In Job, this unfolding of Job's character is brought about in response to the problem of suffering. In the dialogues, in which the heart of the book is contained, there is abundant internal action. It is on this basis that we can consider Job a psychological drama.

The background of Job's problem

The theme around which the whole book of Job revolves is the mystery inherent in the unmerited suffering of the just man. How can a just God permit an innocent man to suffer? Since nothing can happen independent of the will and knowledge of God, how can it be that a man who has committed no sin should nevertheless be compelled to undergo severe and prolonged suffering?

In the early days of Israel's history men were satisfied with the simple assurance of God's justice and goodness. The explanation, taken for granted by the Deuteronomist and by most ancient writers, that God punished the wicked by means of physical ailments and an early death and rewarded the good by means of a long and happy life on earth was accepted generally and rarely questioned (cf. Gen. 15:15; 49:25; Exod. 20:12; Deut. 7:12-15; 8:6-18; 27–30).

The inadequacy of this explanation when applied to individual cases rather than to men in general does not seem to have perturbed Israel's thinkers until the time of Jeremiah in the late seventh century. Jeremiah could not help noticing that the wicked sometimes prospered and the innocent suffered. Very humbly he presented his difficulty: "You would be in the right, O Lord, if I should dispute with you; even so, I must discuss the case with you. Why does the way of the godless prosper, why live all the treacherous in contentment" (Jer. 12:1ff)?

Not long after Jeremiah, the prophet Habakkuk raised the question in a similar way: "Too pure are your eyes to look upon evil, and the sight of misery you cannot endure. Why, then, do you gaze on the faithless in silence while the wicked man devours one more just than himself" (Hab. 1:13)?

During the captivity in Babylon, some of the more cynical among the exiles complained that God was punishing them, not for their own sins, but for the sins of their ancestors. "The fathers have eaten green grapes," they said, "thus their children's teeth are on edge" (Ez. 18:1ff). In attempting to refute this accusation against God's justice and to prove to the exiles that they were being punished for their own sins, Ezekiel went out of his way to emphasize personal responsibility for sins. "Only the one who sins shall die," he said (Ez. 18:20).

Ezekiel, of course, was simply making very explicit the meaning of the general truth that God punishes the wicked and rewards the good. His words, however, focused attention on the individual. And while it was true that in general sinners were punished and the good rewarded, it was more than obvious that there were exceptions to this general truth. Innocent men suffered. Why? This was the question Jeremiah had timidly raised a generation earlier and almost immediately dropped. Ezekiel's emphasis on personal responsibility made it a burning question for Israel's thinkers.

Toward the end of the exile, Deutero-Isaiah gave a partial answer to the question in his famous fifty-third chapter. The suffering servant was indeed sinless. Nevertheless, God punished him unmercifully. Why? Deutero-Isaiah's answer was vicarious suffering: "He was pierced for our offenses, crushed for our sins; upon him was the chastisement that makes us whole, by his stripes we were healed . . . the Lord laid upon him the guilt of us all" (Is. 53:5-6). It was a good if not an adequate answer to the question that plagued the author of Job. But Job never says anything the equivalent of St. Paul's avowal of vicarious suffering: "I rejoice now in the sufferings I bear for your sake; and what is lacking of the sufferings of Christ I fill up in my flesh for his body, which is the Church . . ." (Col. 1:24). Why not? Either because he did not know the teaching of Deutero-Isaiah, or because he did not consider vicarious suffering an adequate solution to the problem.

Neither did Job know the existence of an after-life in which the scales of justice left unbalanced for some during this life are balanced once and for all by God Himself. The well-known passage of Job 19:25ff, which is textually corrupt, cannot be made to mean that Job expresses his faith in a future resurrection. The truly adequate solution of reward and punishment beyond the grave, a doctrine that became common knowledge in Israel only during the Maccabean period (after 168 B.C.; cf. Dan. 12:2-3; 2 Mac. 6–7; Wis. 1–5), was not part of the deposit of faith in the time of Job.

The author of Job had only the basic statement of Israel's faith in God's justice to guide him. God, that faith assured him, is a God of love and a God of justice. He rewards good and punishes evil. The Israelite believed that man continued after death in some kind of an after-life. But he knew nothing about that after-life. As far as he knew, it was the same for saint and sinner alike (cf. Job 3:13-19; 7:7-11; 14:10-15; 30:23). Rewards and punishments, therefore, had to be meted out in this life, here on earth. Ordinarily life, with long years, material good things, many children, and an honorable name was considered the just lot of the good man. Death was the lot of the wicked. It meant primarily a short life, loss of the good things of life at an early age, no posterity, a name burdened with disgrace (cf. Job 15:20-35; 18:5-21).

This doctrine of material rewards and punishments sufficed for centuries with regard to the nation as a whole, particularly in view of the principle of solidarity. It was gradually realized to be inadequate when applied to individuals. It could explain the generality of men's lives, for many of the good did prosper, and many of the wicked were indeed cut off by death. But when applied to every individual case, it was found sadly inadequate. It could not explain the death of so good and pious a king as Josiah. It became pitiable when applied to the life of a suffering saint like Jeremiah.

The reader must always remember, therefore, that for Job the solution of suffering given by Christ on the Cross and by the parable of Dives and Lazarus was unknown. If Job had known what we know about the theology of rewards and punishments, most of his protestations would have been pointless. On the contrary, he was faced with the awesome task of defending God's justice in a world where it was manifest for all with eyes to see that not all the wicked were punished and at least some who were certainly just nevertheless suffered and suffered intensely.

The final solution the author of Job gives us is that the question is too big for man. Man cannot comprehend God's purpose in inflicting suffering on the just man. Man cannot penetrate the secrets of God's providence. He must adore the divine wisdom even when he does not understand it. Therefore, until God chooses to explain why the just suffer, and the wicked prosper, man must trust in God's goodness and justice and not claim the right to know what God does not choose to reveal. Man must have something of the awe and humility of the psalmist in Ps. 8, plus the realization of the truth expressed by Isaiah: "My thoughts are not your thoughts, nor are your ways my ways, says Yahweh. As high as the heavens are above the earth, so high are my ways above your ways and my thoughts above your thoughts" (Is. 55:8-9). Job's words after his encounter with God, "Behold,

I am of little account; what can I answer you? I put my hand over my mouth. Though I have spoken once, I will not do so again; though twice, I will do so no more" (40:4-5), prove that he has come through his ordeal and learned from it that man's wisdom consists in serving God, not in being equal to God in the knowledge of His providence.

Despite this basically negative solution, the book of Job does definitely and positively establish that there is no necessary connection between sin and suffering or between virtue and prosperity. Since this conclusion is so forthrightly established by the author, one might think that it would lead him unerringly to the solution of sanctions in the future life. Why the author does not make this further step is a mystery of God's providence. It must be remembered, however, that no pre-Christian philosopher reasoned to the existence of a future life on the basis that it must exist since there was no adequate justice in this life. Buddhists, with their doctrine of nirvana for the good and annihilation for the wicked, came closest to it. It remained for later books of the Bible, Daniel, 2 Maccabees, and Wisdom, to bring this revelation to Israel.

The book is not without other solutions to the problem, but they are all shown to be either false or inadequate. The contention of Job's friends that sin is the cause of suffering is far from false, but their insistence that all sufferers are sinners is erroneous. The main purpose of the debates is to disprove this thesis. God's rebuke to Eliphaz and his friends, "I am angry with you (Eliphaz) and your two friends; for you have not spoken rightly concerning me, as has my servant Job" (42:7), is certainly directed against the infamous extremes to which the argument was pushed. However, as the question in John 9:2 shows, "Rabbi, who has sinned, this man or his parents, that he should be born blind," the old error weathered both the withering arguments of Job and the devastating rebuke of God.

The other solutions urged by Job's friends and by Elihu, namely, that chastisements serve as a corrective to lead a man to live a better life, that they try, purify, and increase man's virtue and consequently his reward, are certainly true. But none of these solutions, nor for that matter any solution known to man, completely solves the problem of the suffering of the just. Ultimately there is no completely satisfying answer to Job's problem and the author probably realized this even before he wrote his book. In the long run, it is safe to say that the author's practical solution, once he has shown up the error of his friends, gets down to another expression of the basic tenet of the wisdom literature: "The beginning of wisdom is the fear of the Lord." Man's reasonable search for solutions must never infringe on the divine liberty. God may be besought, even importuned. He may never be forced.

If this approach is correct, it may help to determine the origin of the book. Critics generally agree that Job was written after the time of Jeremiah (cf. Jer. 20:14-18; Job 3:1-10). On the other hand, the book's undeveloped doctrine of the future life places it before the time of Daniel and Wisdom (164-60 B.C.). Authors, therefore, admitting the great difficulty of dating the work with any real accuracy, place it anywhere between 587 and 200 B.C., preferably in the latter part of the fifth century.

If this conjecture is correct, it is not unlikely that the author wrote at the time of the prophet Malachi. The book would be an answer to those who cynically asked: "Where is the just God? . . . It is vain to serve God, and what do we profit by keeping his command?" (cf. Mal. 2:17; 3:14).

The format of the Book of Job

The book consists of a prologue in prose followed by a long debate between Job and his friends. There are three cycles of speeches in the debate, Job answering each of his friends in each cycle. At the end of the debate between Job and his three friends, a new character, Elihu, enters and takes up the debate against Job. The book concludes with God's two speeches followed by an epilogue in prose corresponding to the prologue. It may be divided as follows: I. Prologue (1:1–2:13); II. First cycle of speeches (3:1–14:22); III. Second cycle of speeches (15:1–21:34); IV. Third cycle of speeches (22:1–28:28); V. Job's final summary of his case (29:1–31:37); VI. Elihu's speeches (32:1–37:24); VII. Yahweh's speeches (38:1–42:6); VIII. Epilogue (42:7-17).

It should be noted that the speech of Elihu is generally considered an addition to the book, since he contributes nothing positive to the argument and is not mentioned in the epilogue. Also it is generally agreed that the third cycle of speeches is in disorder, since Zophar is given no speech. This is probably due to textual corruption. An attempt to restore Zophar's speech would read the text as follows: Eliphaz ch. 22); Job 23–24); Bildad (25: 1-6); Job (27:2-6, 11-12); Zophar (27:7-21); Job (ch. 26 and ch. 28).

Each of the different parts of the drama has a bearing on the development of the theme. A short analysis of each may help to put the whole in focus.

The prologue

The prologue in prose (as well as the epilogue) is generally considered to be from an ancient folk tale. The author, however, has certainly told the tale in his own words. He has arranged the prologue as a double scene, one part in heaven, one part on earth, somewhat like the last acts of the operas Aida and Faust.

The purpose of the first scene (1:1-5), as of all the scenes in the prologue, is to establish beyond question Job's absolute innocence. Thus, even before the debate begins, the audience knows Job's friends are wrong in accusing him of sin and, what is more, suffering is certainly not always a consequence of sin. Job's innocence is established first by the direct and repeated statement that Job was "a blameless and upright man . . . who feared God and avoided evil" (cf. 1:1, 8, 9, 22; 2:3, 10). A second assurance of Job's sinlessness is given for the sake of those who might claim he was being punished for the sins of his children or for sins of inadvertence. This is done by describing Job's habit of regularly offering a sacrifice of expiation to atone for any sins his children might have committed and for which he might be held accountable (cf. 1:5 and Num. 15:22-29). A third assurance of Job's sinlessness is provided by the satan (not the devil but a sort of devil's advocate), who in his solicitude for God's honor tests Job's virtue (1:6-12; 2:1-7).

The prologue concludes with the main scene of the drama: Job surrounded by his friends who have come to comfort him. Astonished at Job's affliction, they consider him as good as dead, sit down and wake him for seven days and seven nights, the time of mourning for a dead friend.

The speeches

The first cycle of speeches in the unfolding psychological drama is begun by Job, who shocks his friends by cursing the day he was born (3:1ff, cf. Jer. 20:14-18). By implying that it would have been better if he had never been born at all, Job appears to be insinuating a lack of goodness and justice on the part of God for not taking him out of life. By seemingly impugning God's goodness and justice, Job rouses his friends from their silence.

In the speeches that follow, each friend takes a turn defending God's goodness and justice, and each in turn has his arguments refuted by Job. In the first cycle of speeches, the friends all believe that Job is being punished by God for some sin. Let Job repent, they say, and God will restore him to his former state of prosperity. Their tone is at first conciliatory, but when Job defends his innocence, their charges become more and more vehement. In the second and third cycles of speeches, the friends begin to doubt their former good opinion of Job and begin to consider him a monster of pride and rebellion.

The author's purpose in the debates is to refute the stock arguments of the traditionalists who push the connection between sin and suffering to absurd lengths. The power and poetry of the language in these speeches has always been the delight and the envy of litterateurs.

In reading the debates, it is important to observe not only the physical agony of Job but his mental agony as well. It is in the metamorphosis of his soul, wracked and torn by the apparent injustice of his treatment at the hands of God, that the heart of the drama is concentrated.

The reader should also note that the method of development is not linear, i.e., the solution of the problem is not spun out syllogistically. On the contrary, the author shows us the problem from a dozen different aspects and lets us come to our own conclusion with the help of God's final speeches.

Yahweh's speeches

Job ends his case with the brave words: "This is my final plea; let the Almighty answer me!" (31:27). In ch. 38—41, the Almighty answers. Before the addition of Elihu's words (ch. 32—37), which add nothing specifically new to the debate though they emphasize the disciplinary aspect of suffering (ch. 33), a thought suggested earlier by Eliphaz (5:17), the divine speeches probably followed immediately upon Job's words: "Let the Almighty answer me!"

Out of the storm comes the answer: "Who is this that obscures divine plans with words of ignorance? Gird up your loins now, like a man; I will question you, and you tell me the answers!" (38:1-3). Little Job in his tiny corner of the great universe has presumed to call the Lord of all to the witness stand. The situation is ridiculous. Job is an ant attacking a mountain.

God will not be questioned; but He will question. Standing above the petty details of the presumptuous debate, ignoring both the friends' accusations and Job's defense, the architect of the universe puts Job to the question. The question is meant to daunt not only Job but all who would join with him in questioning the Almighty. Job has questioned God's wisdom in the running of the universe. Now God will test Job's wisdom (38:2ff).

To begin with, Job did not even exist at the creation of the universe. Indeed, he is practically nothing even now. Yet he questions the wisdom of the architect of heaven and earth. The ironic questions pour forth inexorably: "Where were you when I founded the earth? Who shut within doors the sea? Have you ever in your lifetime commanded the morning? Have you entered into the sources of the sea? Which is the way to the dwelling-place of light? Have you entered the storehouse of the snow? Who has laid out a channel for the downpour? Has the rain a father? Have you fitted a curb to the Pleiades or loosened the bonds of Orion?"

There is no waiting for an answer because there is no possibility of an answer, only an avowal of ignorance. When the first divine speech ends with the words, "Will we have arguing with the Almighty by the critic? Let him who would correct God give answer" (40:2), the man who had so recently issued the belligerent challenge, "Let the Almighty answer me," is suitably subdued. "Behold," he says, "I am of little account; what can I answer you? I put my hand over my mouth. Though I have spoken once, I will not do so again, though twice, I will do so no more" (40:4-5).

It should be enough, but Job has questioned God's power as well as his wisdom. Let Job, therefore, give a demonstration of his power! Again the relentless questions pour forth flaying the proud presumption of the insignificant mortal: "Have you an arm like that of God? Can you lead about Leviathan with a hook? Can you play with him, as with a bird?"

Job's final answer is more than an avowal of ignorance. It is a retractation. "I know that you can do all things, and that no purpose of yours can be hindered. I have dealt with great things that I do not understand; things too wonderful for me, which I cannot know. I had heard of you by word of mouth, but now my eye has seen you. Therefore I disown what I have said, repent in dust and ashes" (42:1-6).

The dust has settled and the battle is over. Job is defeated. He realizes now the impertinence of impotent man questioning the Omnipotent. His questions have not been answered and yet he has received an answer. Only the answer cannot be expressed. It can only be experienced. It is not even a rational answer because it cannot be translated into words. It is more the realization of a state of being—the state of a creature in the presence of the Creator. The creature instinctively realizes he is in the presence of mystery. It is not the time for questions. It is the time for faith and humility. It is a time to remember: "The beginning of wisdom is fear of the Lord!"

The epilogue

The epilogue of Job establishes four points: 1. the three friends have not spoken rightly about God (42:7); 2. Job has on the whole spoken rightly concerning God (42:7); 3. Job, the just man, can intercede for the guilty friends (42:8-9); 4. Job is rewarded with great prosperity and a long life.

It should be noted that the epilogue confirms what has been stated in the prologue and in the debates, again affirming Job's innocence and repudiating the doctrine of the friends that suffering is always a consequence of sin.

Modern tastes in drama would prefer to see Job die unrewarded yet justified in his innocence. And critics are inclined to find the epilogue disconcerting because it appears both to support and contradict the explanation of the problem of suffering given by Job's friends. Job has humbled himself and has been given twice what he possessed before his ordeal. This is what the friends claimed God would do if Job repented. But is this not a confirmation of the friends' thesis? And if it is, why have they been rebuked? "I am angry with you and with your two friends," God says to Eliphaz, "for you have not spoken rightly concerning me as has my servant Job" (42:7).

The rewarding of Job by no means destroys his thesis, nor does it confirm the thesis of his friends. The epilogue shows indeed that God in His providence usually does reward His servants. This Job never doubted. The reward, however, does not explain Job's sufferings. Nothing does. And certainly not sin. That was Job's thesis and the epilogue in no way either disproves it or waters it down.

The friends have been rebuked because they have attempted to foist on God their own justification of Job's suffering and indeed of all suffering. They have limited God's providence to the narrow confines of their own theology. They have not allowed Him the liberty to have His own mysterious reasons for inflicting suffering even where there is no sin to provoke it.

Job, on the other hand, has questioned God's reasons for inflicting suffering on the innocent. He has not, however, questioned God's liberty nor restricted the working of His providence. For Job, God is more mysterious, but He is more God. For the friends, God is less mysterious and correspondingly less God. There can be no choice between the two theodicies.

5. Qoheleth

Almost all we know about Qoheleth is told us by an editor in a brief epilogue. "Besides being wise," he tells us, "Qoheleth taught the people knowledge, and weighed, scrutinized and arranged many proverbs. Qoheleth sought to find pleasing sayings, and write down true sayings with precision" (12:9-10). Unfortunately the description fits any wisdom teacher. However, a further remark of the editor, "The sayings of the wise are like goads" (12:11), is particularly pertinent to Qoheleth and probably reflects the editor's personal reaction to the book.[1]

Qoheleth's sayings are goads and more than goads. They torment the spirit, harass the mind, disturb the heart. They unsettle the complacent, shock the orthodox, and trouble even the wise. It is advisable, therefore, before reading the book, to note the concluding words of this remarkable work: "The last word, when all is heard: Fear God and keep his commandments, for this is man's all; because God will bring to judgment every work, with all its hidden qualities, whether good or bad" (12:13-14).

[1] Cf. Murphy, *Seven Books of Wisdom*, 87–103; JBC 534–540.

The reader who does not keep in mind these and other words of Qoheleth (5:1-6; 7:18; 8:12-13; 12:1) may easily misinterpret both the man and his book. He would not be the first to do so. Qoheleth has been labeled among other things: a skeptic, a pessimist, a hedonist, a materialist and, in recent times, the earliest existentialist. He is not any of these for the simple reason that he is a man of faith. He believes in the reality of divine providence (3:11, 14-15; 8:17; 11:5), praises divine wisdom (7:12, 20; 9:13-18), and expects divine judgment (3:17; 11:9; 12:13-14). These things must be remembered if Qoheleth is to be rightly understood.

The name Ecclesiastes is Greek for Qoheleth, a Hebrew word that probably means preacher or leader of the congregation. Possibly he was the head of a group of sages. His remark, "I, Qoheleth, was king over Israel in Jerusalem, and I applied my mind to search and investigate in wisdom all things that are done under the sun" (1:12-13), as well as the title of the book, "The words of David's son, Qoheleth, king in Jerusalem" (1:1), indicate that Qoheleth wished to pose as Solomon, the wise man *par excellence*. It is a poetic fiction as the epilogue clearly indicates (12:9-14). Linguistic indications point to a postexilic origin for the book and most authors would date its composition around 300 B.C.

The theme of the book is the vanity of all things, an expression that means the uselessness, transitoriness, and intrinsic insubstantiality of all things human. A modern author has aptly rendered the expression, "Vanity of vanities," as "the absolute absurdity of it all!" The author pursues this theme relentlessly. All man's labors are vain (1:4-11), wisdom itself only leads to greater perplexity (1:12-18), pleasure brings no enduring satisfaction (2:1-12), the wise man as well as the fool ends up in the grave (2:13-17), the pursuit of wealth is a chase after the wind (2:18-26), the unchanging order of events impresses upon life a lamentable monotony (3:1-13), and the uncertainty of the future places a pall over the present (3:14-22). Thus it goes to the end of the book.

It is a dreary theme for the author. He examines life under the microscope of long experience and finds it unsatisfactory. The realities of life do not correspond to the yearnings of the heart. Man's deepest desires are constantly thwarted by the hard facts of experience, and the timelessness in his heart is frustrated by the time-restricted span of his days. There is a time for everything. And the time for dying sounds a deathknell for his hopes.

It is more than obvious that the author knows nothing about the true nature of the after-life. If he had, he would have said with St. Augustine, "Our hearts are restless, O Lord, until they rest in thee," but he only knows that his heart is restless. He does not know that the timelessness in his heart, the yearning after true satisfaction, the fulfillment of his deepest desires will one day be swallowed up in the timelessness and depthlessness of God.

The basic message of Qoheleth is simple: this world, this life, all its pleasures, all its wonders cannot satisfy the restless heart of man. At bottom, therefore, Qoheleth is concerned with man's happiness as Job is concerned with man's suffering. He can see no lasting, certain, secure happiness in this earthly existence. Even if a man gain the whole world, have all riches, be able to indulge his every desire — even then, Qoheleth would say, he would not be satisfied, he would not be perfectly happy.

The book, therefore, cries out for the revelation of the future life given to the Jews only in the last two centuries before Christ in the books of Daniel (12:2-3), 2 Maccabees (6–7), Wisdom (2–5), and in the Gospels. Ignorant of the solution to his insoluble dilemma and his insatiable yearnings, he is forced to satisfy himself with the act of faith contained in the epilogue of his book: "The last word, when all is heard: Fear God and keep his commandments, for this is man's all" (12:3).

It was enough for justification, for Christ stated: "If you keep my commandments you will abide in my love, as I also have kept my Father's commandments, and abide in his love." But it was not enough to satisfy Qoheleth's tormented heart. Nor was it the last word. The last word, the word Qoheleth would have rejoiced to hear in his lifetime, was spoken by Christ: "In my Father's house there are many mansions. Were it not so, I should have told you, because I go to prepare a place for you. And if I go and prepare a place for you, I am coming again, and I will take you to myself, that where I am, there you also may be" (John 13:2-3).

It is to the lasting glory of Qoheleth that he sensed and expressed with unforgettable clarity the yearnings of man's heart for the mansions of heaven long before God made them a subject of divine revelation. Indeed, his unflinching appraisal of the hard and inescapable realities of life prepared his readers to answer a resounding "Nothing!" to the question of Christ (Matthew 16:26): "What does it profit a man if he gain the whole world and suffer the loss of his soul?"

The reader must not expect rigid order in Qoheleth. The book does not contain a systematic presentation nor a logical demonstration of the vanity of all things human. It is rather a notebook containing the author's reflections. It may even be the notebook of one of his students. In any event, the book is a collection of more or less related observations after the manner of Pascal's "Pensées," and it is to be interpreted accordingly.

Anyone who reflects for a moment will realize that proverbs express general truths of experience. They do not always express universal truths. If it is generally true that "absence makes the heart grow fonder," it is equally true to say "out of sight, out of mind." No one ever understood better the relative value of proverbs than Qoheleth. Thus, where we would use adjectives or adverbs to qualify our statements, Qoheleth qualifies one proverb with another. He will say for instance: "Those now dead, I declare more fortunate in death than are the living to be still alive" (4:2); but in another place he qualifies this pessimistic view with the contrary statement: "Indeed, for any among the living there is hope; a live dog is better off than a dead lion" (9:4). Again Qoheleth declares sorrow better than laughter (7:3). Later, however, he commends mirth (8:15).

It would be a mistake to think Qoheleth is contradicting himself. Rather he is dealing with a most delicate subject — the value of life. He knows very well that for some life is a terrible burden. For others the burden is lighter. But for all there is a lack of balance between the good sought for in life and the effort put into the search. The good is never proportionate to the yearnings of man.

Life is essentially vibrant and cannot be pinned down like a butterfly in a laboratory. Qoheleth, therefore, walks around his subject, looks at it from different angles, reflects on it in varying moods. Sometimes his mood inclines him to see the wintry side of life. At other times, it is the springtime that catches his fancy. Sometimes his restlessness is manifested by a subtle inquietude breaking through his reflections and giving them a kind of haunting melancholy. At other times the emptiness of life that afflicts the modern existentialist with a positive nausea gnaws at Qoheleth's vitals and leaves him only the leap of faith to escape the absolute darkness. The key, therefore, to Qoheleth is not a relentlessly logical analysis of his statements but a subtle balancing and weighing of his remarks on the scale provided by the questions: "What does it profit in relation to the restless and timeless spirit of man? Does it result in a permanent, definitive good?"

If the reader will keep this key in mind, he may indeed come to see in Qoheleth "the earliest existentialist." He will not mistake him for a materialist, a hedonist, a pessimist, a stoic, or an epicurean. In the face of the enigma of life, the leap of faith is not a luxury, it is a necessity. "The last word, when all is heard: Fear God and keep his commandments, for this is man's all; because God will bring to judgment every work, with all its hidden qualities, whether good or bad" (12:13-14). Or, as all the wisdom writers tirelessly teach: "The beginning of wisdom is fear of the Lord."

17

The History
of the
Maccabees

Biblical history between the years 433 and 175 B.C. takes the reader through a long, dark tunnel. He enters the darkness with the closing of the book of Nehemiah and emerges again into historical daylight only with the opening of the books of the Maccabees. In the intervening years great changes have taken place outside the tunnel. Alexander the Great has come and the Persian empire of the time of Nehemiah has gone. It is a new world. The old world has not died, but it breathes a new atmosphere—a wind from the west from Athens. The change for the biblical world and the last books of the Old Testament is no small one. It will considerably influence the books of Maccabees, Daniel, and Wisdom. And even the New Testament, when it comes to be written, will be written for the most part in the language of the cultural conquerors from Greece.

Since an understanding of Hellenistic times will be necessary as a background for the history of the Maccabees and Maccabees for the background of Daniel, we shall treat first the historical background of the Maccabean period and then the books of Maccabees. With Maccabees for a background the reader will be prepared for an introduction to the apocalyptic literary form and to the greatest of the Old Testament apocalypses, the book of Daniel.

1. The Maccabean Period and the Books of the Maccabees

After conquering the Persian empire at Gaugamela in 331 and reaching India by 327, Alexander the Great died at Babylon in 323, leaving unfulfilled his vision of a world empire unified outwardly by the authority of Macedon and inwardly by the leaven of Hellenistic culture.[1] In a short time the unity imposed by conquest dissolved. By 305 the rapidly conquered empire had broken into three parts: Macedonia, Syria-Mesopotamia, and Egypt, governed respectively by Alexander's generals and successors, Perdiccas, Seleucus, and Ptolemy. The leaven of Hellenistic culture, however, remained; and in the last centuries before Christ gradually permeated the major part of the Mediterranean world including Palestine.

During these centuries Palestine shuttled back and forth as a subject state between the Seleucids of Syria and the Ptolemies of Egypt, picking up in the process continual infusions of Hellenistic culture. In due time Greek became the second language of the country. Many cities acquired Greek names. Greek architecture was borrowed for public buildings, Greek philosophy was taught in the schools, and Greek customs became part and parcel of public and private life.

In the meantime Alexander's dream of an empire unified internally by the leaven of Hellenistic culture did not die out among his successors. The Ptolemies, in the periods when they controlled Palestine, habitually tolerated Judaism as a pocket of resistance to the leaven. The Seleucid empire, however, under Antiochus IV did not. In 169 Antiochus pillaged the Temple. A year later, when it became apparent that the religious Jews would not submit voluntarily to Hellenization, he decided on the use of force. A Syrian army partially destroyed Jerusalem. A Syrian garrison was installed on the hill west of the Temple.

Not long after, Antiochus began a systematic persecution aimed at destroying the Jewish faith. Regular sacrifices in the Temple were suspended. Jews were no longer permitted to observe the Sabbath and the traditional feasts. It became a crime to possess a copy of the Law or to circumcise Jewish children. Pagan altars were set up throughout the land and Jews who refused to sacrifice swine's flesh upon these altars were liable to death. In December 167, the cult of Olympian Zeus was instituted in the Temple, an altar to Zeus was set up, and Jews were compelled to take part in the pagan festivities. The first systematic religious persecution in history was in full swing.

In the resistance to Hellenism and to Antiochus' persecution the soul of

[1] Cf. M. Schoenberg, *First and Second Maccabees*, OTRG No. 13; Schedl, HOTOT, vol. 5, 289–368; LFAP 206ff; WHAB 70ff; Plutarch's *Alexander*.

Judaism was tested in the furnace and came out shining. The test, however, will be only half understood if the external source of the fire, the Seleucid persecution, alone is considered. The internal and vital test for Judaism was not on the battlefield, but in the mind and in the heart, in the internal struggle to preserve inviolate the true faith against the attraction and fascination of pagan Hellenism. The ideological struggle between Judaism and Hellenism began long years before and lasted long years after the persecution of Antiochus IV. The Hellenistic culture that had penetrated the ghettoes of the Diaspora in the century after Alexander opened a door in the heart of Judaism itself in the time of the Maccabees. Its spread was rapid and wide, reaching even to the Temple, the priests, and the high priest himself. The author of 2 Mac. describes for us the effect of Hellenism on the high priest, Jason. His words are better than a commentary:

> He willingly established a gymnasium right under the citadel, and he made the finest of the young men wear the Greek hat. And to such a pitch did the cultivation of Greek fashions and the coming in of foreign customs rise, because of the excessive wickedness of this godless Jason, who was no high priest at all, that the priests were no longer earnest about the services of the altar, but disdaining the sanctuary and neglecting the sacrifices, they hurried to take part in the unlawful exercises in the wrestling school, after the summons to the discus-throwing, regarding as worthless the things their forefathers valued, and thinking Greek standards the finest (2 Mac. 4:12-15).

In the ensuing years many Jews apostatized from the faith of their fathers. In contrast to those who apostatized, however, the Seleucid persecution brought out many who remained faithful unto death — the Maccabean martyrs, saints, and warriors, the true Israel of God, the spiritual heirs of the "seven thousand who did not bend the knee to Baal" in the time of Elijah. It is with them that we are concerned, for we in turn are their heirs.

Chronology of the Maccabean period

356-323   Alexander the Great: born at Pella in Macedonia, general at 18, king at 20, conquered Persia at 25, reached India at 29, died in Babylon at 33.

305-281   Seleucus I founds the Seleucid empire which periodically controls Palestine.

187-175   Seleucus IV, the first king mentioned in 2 Mac.

175-164   Antiochus IV Epiphanes, persecutor of the Jews.

170   Assassination of Onias, the high priest.

169-164   Desecration of the Temple begins period of intense persecution.

166-160   Outbreak of the Maccabean resistance movement under Mattathias Hasmoneus and his son, Judas Maccabeus. Victories of Judas, rededication of the Temple in 164, death of Judas in 160.

165-164 Writing of the book of Daniel.
164-161 Antiochus V Eupator succeeds Antiochus IV.
161-150 Demetrius I Soter succeeds Antiochus V.
160-143 Campaigns of Jonathan Maccabeus.
150-145 Alexander Balas succeeds Demetrius I.
145-125 Demetrius II Nicator, Antiochus VI, Trypho, Antiochus VII.
143-134 Simon Maccabeus wins independence for the Jews.
134-104 John Hyrcanus, son of Simon, becomes quasi-king.
     64 The Romans under Pompey annex Judea.

The Books of the Maccabees

The two books of Maccabees deal with substantially the same theme, viz., the glorious history of Israel's resistence under the inspirational leadership of the first Hasmoneans to the religious persecution instigated by Antiochus IV Epiphanes.

Unlike the books of Samuel and the books of Kings, the two books of Maccabees are independent works, written by different authors, in different languages, from different viewpoints, only partially covering the same period: 1 Mac. from 175 to 134, and 2 Mac. from 176 to 160. Both books derive their name from Judas Maccabeus (a name meaning the "Hammer," or perhaps better, the "designated one," cf. Is. 62:2), the most famous of the Maccabees, the five sons of the priest, Mattathias (1 Mac. 2:1-5).

1 and 2 Mac. are to be distinguished from the non-canonical, apocryphal works known as 3 and 4 Mac., which were given the name "Maccabees" by analogy, because they deal with the persecution of the Jews and in places parallel the accounts given in the canonical books of Maccabees.

2. 1 Maccabees

1 Mac. gives the history of the Maccabean wars from 175 to 134 B.C.[1] The book is divided into four parts: a prelude, followed by three sections treating respectively Judas, Jonathan, and Simon Maccabeus.

Part I (ch. 1–2) provides a prelude to the history of the Maccabean wars, moving quickly from the advent of Hellenism into the Near East under Alexander the Great and the Diodochi to the rise of Antiochus IV Epiphanes and the initiation of his program of Hellenization of Judea and consequent religious persecution of the Jews. The prelude concludes with a description of the outbreak of the Jewish rebellion under the priest Mattathias and his five sons, the Maccabees.

[1] Cf. CCHS par. 586ff.

Part II (ch. 3:1–9:22) treats the military exploits of Judas Maccabeus: his victories over Apollonius and Seron in Samaria and at Bethhoron, over Nicanor and Gorgias at Emmaus, and over Lysias at Beth-zur. Following the account of Judas' recapture and rededication of the Temple, the author describes the death of Antiochus IV, the inconclusive battles of Judas against the Syrian army under Lysias and the young king, Antiochus V Eupator, at Bethzur and Bethzacharam (Beth-Zacharia), the death of Lysias and Antiochus V and the rise of a new king to the throne of Syria, Demetrius I. Part II concludes with the account of Judas' victory over Nicanor in 161 B.C. at Adasa, and his defeat and death in battle against Bacchides in the spring of the following year at Laisa (Elasa).

Part III (ch. 9:23–12:54) describes the diplomatic and military victories of Jonathan Maccabeus (160-143 B.C.): his negotiation of a truce with Bacchides, whereby he preserved the battered remnants of Judas' guerrilla army from disintegration, his later alliance with Alexander Balas, a new pretender to the throne of Syria, following whose victory in 152 B.C., Jonathan was named high priest, "friend of the king," and made military and civic governor of Judea. Part III concludes with Jonathan's initial support of Demetrius II, his turn to the side of Tryphon, another pretender, after a quarrel with Demetrius II, and finally his betrayal and capture by Tryphon at Ptolemais in 143 B.C.

Part IV (ch. 13–16) deals with the exploits of Simon (143-134 B.C.), the last of the five Maccabee brothers: his support of Demetrius II against Tryphon for which he received in return almost complete political independence; his initial support of Antiochus VII, the successor of Demetrius II, followed by their quarrel and the defeat of Antiochus' army under Cendebeus by Simon's sons, Judas and John, at Cedron south of Jamnia. Part IV concludes with the treacherous assassination of Simon and his two sons, Judas and Mattathias, by Ptolemy at Doch near Jericho in the year 134 B.C.

Author

Nothing certain is known concerning the identity of the author. His knowledge of Palestinian geography, plus his intimate acquaintance with the politics of the period, the military campaigns, the court intrigues, and the Maccabean chieftains, leads one to believe he was a contemporary of much he has written about and perhaps even the official historiographer of the Hasmonean family. This, however, is only conjecture. His attitude toward the unworthy high priests, Jason and Menelaus, whose names he does not even mention, and Alcimus, whom he mentions but in disparaging terms, his failure to speak of the future life, a doctrine popular among the Pharisees, as well as his tolerant attitude concerning the observance of the Sabbath, suggest he belonged to Sadducean rather than Pharisaic circles. His outstanding characteristic is a genuine admiration for and devotion to the Hasmonean family (cf. 1 Mach. 5:62; 13:3-9).

Although 1 Mac. was certainly written originally in Hebrew, and Jerome and Origen knew of the Hebrew text at their time, only the Greek translation has come down. The Vulgate version is the Old Latin unrevised, made from a better Greek manuscript than our extant manuscripts and consequently of great value.

Sources and date

The author includes in his history twelve letters (5:10ff; 8:22ff; 10:17ff; 10:25ff; 11:30ff; 11:58ff; 12:6ff; 12:20ff; 13:30ff; 14:20ff; 15:2ff; 15:16ff) plus the copy of an inscription honoring Simon Maccabeus (14:25ff). Although some authors consider these documents literary creations, others defend their authenticity. The opinion of authors who consider 14:16 to the end of the book a later addition, on the grounds that Josephus who follows the first part of the book step by step does not utilize the last chapters at all, is no longer seriously considered. 1 Mac. 9:22 would seem to indicate that the author drew upon a "Life of Judas." And 1 Mac. 16:23f may refer to annals in which the official acts of the high priests were recorded.

The book must have been written after the death of Simon Maccabeus in 134 B.C. If 16:23-24 are not from the pen of an editor but belong to the original manuscript, then the book must be dated after the death of John Hyrcanus in 104. Since the author speaks kindly of the Romans in 1 Mac. 8, it is probable that he wrote before the year 63, the year Pompey the Great took Jerusalem and outraged Jewish feelings by entering the Temple and even the Holy of Holies. The book can be dated, therefore, sometime between 104 and 63.

Historical value

The exactitude of the topographical and chronological details, the ease with which the author's presentation of his facts fits into the picture of the contemporaneous history of the Near East, and the honesty of the author in describing the defeats as well as the victories of his heroes, testify convincingly to the genuine historical value of 1 Maccabees. If there be added to these indications the impression one gets that the author was an eyewitness of much that he has described (cf. 6:39; 7:33; 8:19; 9:43ff), one can understand the esteem of modern historians for the historiography of this composition.

The author nonetheless is a man of his times. He is not entirely unbiased, nor is he perfectly objective. Since he writes to glorify the Maccabees as "those men by whom salvation was brought to Israel" (5:62), his viewpoint is that of one who writes history indeed, but the history of a propagandist. After the manner of the ancient Israelite historians, he exaggerates the size of the armies sent against the Maccabees in order to enhance their victories. Although he records defeats as well as victories, he does not hesitate to enhance the victories and minimize the defeats. Nor is he loath, in his hostility to Hellenism as the cause of the apostasy of so many of his compatriots, to describe Alexander the Great as a man bloated with pride, whose victories have loosed a flood of evils on the earth. The Maccabean revolt, moreover, appears in his eyes a world-shaking event, of importance to Rome and Sparta and the pivotal point of Seleucid politics. Despite such imperfections, common to historians, there is no reason to doubt the substantial historicity of the book.

Religious value

The absence of the name of God from the book has led many, who refuse to acknowledge the inspired character of the deutero-canonical book of 1 Maccabees, to consider it a purely secular work devoid of religious value. Although it is true that the author does not use the divine name, no doubt out of that scrupulous reverence for the name of God so common in late postexilic times, he does use numerous paraphrases for God, e.g., "Heaven" (3:18f; 4:10, 40; 9:46; 12:15; 16:3), and the personal pronoun "He" (2:61; 3:22; 16:3). His heroes pray before they go into battle (3:46-54; 4:10f; 7:37f; 9:49; 11:71; 12:11), and the author speaks about God as the saviour of Israel (2:61; 3:19; 4:30; 12:15; 16:3).

Despite the author's emphasis on the human rather than the divine element in history, there is no doubt that he is deeply penetrated with the truth that it is God who is guiding the history and deciding the fate of His Chosen People. Nor is there any doubt but that he wished to impress his readers with that love of God, love of nation, fidelity to the law, and determination at any cost to serve God rather than man manifested by the heroes of the Maccabean resistance. In its implicit invitation to its readers to emulate the zeal and generosity of the Maccabees lies the lasting appeal of the book.

Significant passages in 1 Maccabees

Part One / 1 Mach. 1–2 / Prelude to the Wars

> **1:1ff** Alexander and his successors down to Antiochus IV, the persecutor (vv. 1-11); the pro-hellenistic Jews (vv. 12-16; cf. 6:21-

27; 2 Mac. 4:12-16); systematic religious persecution (vv. 43-64; cf. 2 Mac. 6–7).

2:1ff   Mattathias Hasmoneus and his five sons, John, Simon, Judas, Eleazar, and Jonathan (vv. 1-5); Mattathias slays the king's agents and the Maccabean wars begin (vv. 15-28); the Hasideans, forerunners of the Pharisees, join in the resistance (v. 42; cf. 7:13-17; 2 Mac. 14:6); Mattathias before dying commissions Judas to lead the resistance (vv. 65-70).

Part Two / 1 Mac. 3—9 / Judas Maccabeus (166-160 B.C.)

3:1ff   An appraisal of Judas (vv. 1-9; cf. 3:18-20; 3:58-60; 4:8-11; 4:30-33; 9:7-10; 2 Mac. 8:1-7); Judas' victories over Apollonius and Seron (vv. 10-26); Antiochus IV, before leaving for the east, commissions Lysias to wipe out Judas and his guerrilla armies (vv. 31-36).

4:1ff   Judas defeats Georgias near Emmaus (vv. 1-25); defeats Lysias at Beth-zur forcing the Syrians to retreat to Antioch (vv. 26-35); purifies the Temple in December 164, and celebrates the feast of the Re-dedication (vv. 36-60; cf. 2 Mac. 10:1-8; John 10:22).

5:20-35   Simon, with 3000 troops, rescues the faithful Israelites in Galilee, while Judas with 8000 troops does the same in Gilead.

6:14-17   Antiochus IV dies and is succeeded by Antiochus V Eupator (164-161).

6:42-47   Eleazar Maccabeus dies in battle near Beth-Zacharia.

6:55-63   Lysias and King Antiochus V return to Antioch. There is a brief peace.

7:1-4   Demetrius I slays Lysias and Antiochus V and becomes king of Syria (161-150).

7:26-47   Judas defeats Nicanor, Demetrius' general, at Adasa and there is another brief peace (cf. 2 Mac. 15:25-28).

9:1-22   Judas, defeated by Bacchides at Elasa, dies in battle in the spring of 160.

Part Three / 1 Mac. 9:23–12:53 / Jonathan Maccabeus (160-143)

9:28-31 Jonathan is chosen to lead the resistance after the death of Judas.

9:43-49 Jonathan defeats Bacchides at the Jordan and at Bethbasi (vv. 65-69).

10:1-25 Alexander Epiphanes, the son of Antiochus IV, and Demetrius I, contending for the Syrian throne, vie with each other for the friendship of Jonathan (vv. 1-3; 15-17; 22-25), with Alexander winning out (vv. 46-50), and making peace with Jonathan in 152 (vv. 59-63).

10:67-89 In 147, Demetrius' son, Demetrius II, as a preliminary to obtaining the throne of Syria, wages war against Jonathan and is defeated.

11:8ff Ptolemy of Egypt, Alexander's father-in-law (10:58), enters the war on the side of Demetrius against Alexander and Jonathan (vv. 8-13). In the ensuing war, Demetrius II finally becomes sole king after the deaths of Alexander and Ptolemy (vv. 14-19); Jonathan and Demetrius II become allies for awhile (vv. 32-38), until Demetrius II is deposed by Alexander's young son, Antiochus VI, who is helped to the throne by Trypho, one of Alexander's old generals (vv. 54-57).

12:1ff Jonathan renews the treaty with Rome (1 Mac. 8) and enters a treaty with Sparta (vv. 1-23); he is treacherously captured at Ptolemais by Trypho and later executed (vv. 39-48; 13:23).

Part Four / 1 Mac. 13–16 / Simon Maccabeus (143-134)

13:1ff Simon, acclaimed leader by the people after the capture of Jonathan, rallies an army and continues the resistance (vv. 7-10). Trypho executes Jonathan (vv. 22-24), returns to Syria and becomes king after eliminating Antiochus VI (vv. 31-32). Simon takes possession of the citadel in Jerusalem, held through the years by the Syrian army (vv. 49-51; cf. 1 Mac. 1:35-38).

14:4-15 The peaceful and prosperous reign of Simon from 143-134.

15:29-35 Simon arouses the anger and animosity of Antiochus VII who after deposing Trypho begins war with Simon.

16:1ff Simon's sons defeat Cendebeus, the general of Antiochus VII (vv. 1-10). Simon and his two sons are treacherously assassinated (vv. 15-16). Simon's son, John Hyrcanus, becomes the new leader and high priest of the Jews.

3. 2 Maccabees

2 Maccabees can be divided into three parts.[1] Part I (ch. 1–2) begins with two letters from the Jews of Jerusalem to the Jews of Egypt urging them to take part in the celebration of the new feast instituted by Judas Maccabeus in 164, the feast of the Dedication of the Temple (cf. 1 Mac. 4:59). It ends with the author's preface (2:20-33), explaining the source he has used, the five volume work of Jason of Cyrene, and the principles by which he has been guided in making his epitome.

Part II (3:1—10:9) details a number of events, for the most part relating to the Temple, the priesthood, and the Syrian persecution of the Jews, from the year 176 to 164. The author describes the struggles for the office of high priest (ch. 3–5), the desecration of the Temple and the persecution of the Jews who refused to give up their faith (ch. 6–7), the outbreak of the Jewish rebellion under Judas Maccabeus, and the winning back and re-dedication of the desecrated Temple (8:1—10:9).

Part III (10:10—15:40) concentrates for the most part on the successful military campaigns of Judas Maccabeus in the time of Antiochus V and Demetrius I, concluding with Judas' conquest of Nicanor in 161, and the institution of a new feast, popularly referred to as "Nicanor's Day."

Author

Nothing is known about Jason, the author of the five books epitomized in 2 Mac., except that he was a Jew of the Diaspora from Cyrene in North Africa, where a flourishing Jewish community existed in the last centuries before Christ.

Less is known about the anonymous author who abridged the five volume work of Jason to give us our present 2 Maccabees. Since there is no evidence that the work is a translation, it would appear from the excellent Greek and the flowing, well-balanced periods of both the preface and the body of the Book that both Jason and his epitomist had received a good education in Greek rhetoric and culture. Since the main task of the epitomist was to make a choice of episodes from the longer work of Jason, it is impossible to tell what belongs to the one and what to the other.

[1] Cf. M. Schoenberg, *Second Maccabees*, OTRG No. 13.

Authors generally concede that Jason's main sources were oral. There are, however, a number of letters from the Seleucid kings and from the Jews of Jerusalem, seven in all, which probably came from the archives of the Hasmonean kings (1:1ff; 1:10ff; 9:19ff; 11:16ff; 11:22ff; 11:27ff; 11:34ff).

The last event recorded in 2 Maccabees takes place in the year 161 B.C. How long after this event Jason composed his history is difficult to determine. It would appear, however, from the date of the letter with which the book begins (124 B.C.), that at least the abridgment was made after this date, providing, what is not likely, that the letters were not prefixed to the book by a later editor. Some authors are of the opinion that the letter from the year 124 B.C. was written to accompany the book to its Egyptian readers. If this is true, the abridgment and the five volume work of Jason certainly antedate 124 B.C.

Literary form and historical value

It is clear from a comparison with other histories of the period that 2 Maccabees belongs to a type of historical writing popular in the Hellenistic world and known as "pathetic history," a type of literature that uses every means to appeal to the imagination and the emotions of the reader, e.g., colorful descriptions, rhetorical appeals, exaggerated numbers, prodigious miracles involving celestial manifestations, and a preference in general for the edifying and dramatic in place of a somber detailing of specifics. In a way similar to the author of Chronicles, the author idealizes his story and concentrates on certain aspects of the overall picture to the relative exclusion of others.

In justice to the author, one must not judge 2 Maccabees according to the criteria of modern scientific historical writing. It was not his intention to write scientific history. His intention was to use certain historical events as a means to edify, instruct, and inspire his readers. The substantial historicity of these events can be safely vouched for on the basis of a comparison with 1 Maccabees and with those extra-biblical historical sources which treat of the same period. The discriminating reader, however, will make due allowances for those exaggerations, distortions, and fanciful descriptions proper to the literary form known as "pathetic history."

Purpose

The general purpose of the author is to edify and instruct his Egyptian compatriots. This he accomplishes by extolling the high priest, Onias III, the old man, Eleazar, the seven martyr brothers and their mother, and Judas Maccabeus, and in an inverse way, by excoriating, as examples not to be imitated, such enemies of the Jews as Heliodorus, Antiochus IV, the two wicked high priests, Jason and Menelaus, Nicanor, and the pagans in general.

Besides this general purpose, there are indications that the author had a more immediate and specific purpose in mind. From beginning to end he shows a persistent interest in the Temple, the priesthood, and the Temple feasts. Thus the book begins with two letters inviting the Egyptian Jews to associate with their compatriots in Jerusalem in celebrating the feast of the re-dedication of the Temple. The sacredness of the Temple is emphasized in the Heliodorus incident. The fidelity of the martyrs to their faith, which involved fidelity to the Temple of Jerusalem as the one true house of God on earth, is likewise emphasized. And in the section dealing with Judas Maccabeus (ch. 8–15), the author goes out of his way to show that Antiochus IV, who had desecrated the Temple, and Nicanor, who had blasphemed against the Temple and intended to destroy it, were both punished by defeat and death. In view of the fact that a rival temple to the Temple of Jerusalem had been erected at Leontopolis in Egypt under Onias IV, the son of the Onias extolled in 2 Mac. 3–4, it seems not unlikely that the author of 2 Maccabees aimed to wean the Egyptian Jews away from the temple of Leontopolis and to secure their allegiance to the one legitimate Temple in Jerusalem.

Religious value

Unlike 1 Maccabees, 2 Maccabees not only frequently uses the name of God, but the author visualizes God close at hand, waiting to be prayed to and anxious to answer the prayers of His chosen ones. Throughout the book, the activity and intervention of God in the affairs of His people are constantly highlighted. In addition the author stresses the doctrines of resurrection from the dead (7:9ff; 14:46), the intercession of the saints (15:11-16), and the ability of the living to assist the dead by their prayers and sacrifices (12:39-45). The book is pervaded throughout with the confident faith, optimistic hope, and sincere love of God of the author.

Significant passages in 2 Maccabees

Part One / 2 Mac. 1–2 / Letters and Preface

1:1-9 A letter, dated in the year 124 (v. 9) and sent to the Jews of Egypt, urges them to celebrate the feast of the Dedication.

1:10ff A second letter, dating from the year 164 and incorporating material from an apocryphal book about Jeremiah (2, 1) and an apocryphal book about Nehemiah (2:13), urges the Jews of Egypt to join with their brethren in Palestine in celebrating the re-dedication of the Temple (2:16-18).

2:19-32 The author's preface, explaining the nature of his source, a five volume work by Jason of Cyrene (2:23), and the purpose for which he has made his compendium of this work (2:24-30).

Part Two / *2 Mac. 3:1—10:9* / *The Persecution*

3:1ff Following a disagreement with Onias III, the high priest, Simon, a Temple official, plots against him through Apollonius, the governor of Syria, who goes to the king, Seleucus IV (187-175), and suggests that he appropriate the money banked in the Temple of Jerusalem (vv. 4-8). Seleucus sends Heliodorus to take the money but he is miraculously repulsed (vv. 9-40). The incident is included because of its relation to the Temple and the holy high priest, Onias.

4:1ff Simon accuses Onias of thwarting Heliodorus and Onias goes to Antioch to explain the true state of affairs to the king (vv. 1-6). When Seleucus IV dies and is succeeded by Antiochus IV (175-164), Jason, the brother of Onias and an ardent Hellenist, has himself appointed high priest in place of Onias, and begins a systematic Hellenization of Jerusalem and the Temple (vv. 7-20). This is the first phase of the new king's program of unifying his kingdom by means of the leaven of Hellenistic culture. Its failure leads to persecution. About 171, Menelaus supplants Jason as high priest, returns to Antioch and has Onias murdered (vv. 23-36; cf. Dan. 9:26).

5:5ff While Antiochus IV is at war with Egypt, Jason returns to Jerusalem, slaughters many of his fellow-countrymen, fails to regain power, dies in exile in Greece (vv. 5-10). Antiochus IV, in the meantime, thinking Judea is in revolt, returns from his Egyptian campaign (v. 5:1), massacres many and loots the Temple (vv. 11-17; cf. 1 Mach. 1:16-24). Still incensed, Antiochus sends Apollonius to further punish the Jews (vv. 24-26; cf. 1 Mac. 1:29-33).

6:1-11 In 168, Antiochus IV begins the second phase of Hellenization which consists in the methodical eradication of Judaism. Aiming at the extermination of the true religion, the persecutor concentrates on the Temple, circumcision, the Sabbath, and the Bible, martyring all who support them. On December 15, 167, an altar to Jupiter Olympus (the "Abomination of desolation" of Dan. 9:27; 11:31) is set up before the Sanctum Sanctorum of the Temple (cf. 1 Mac. 1:41-64).

6:12ff The author gives his philosophy of persecution (vv. 12-17). In 6:18—7:42, he describes in detail the tortures undergone by the martyrs. In the statements of these martyrs, several doctrines held at the time are alluded to, namely, immortality and the resurrection of the body (vv. 7, 9, 11, 14, 23, 36), vicarious suffering (v. 38). It should be noted that this mother and her seven sons are the only Old Testament martyrs whose feast day (Aug. 1) is celebrated throughout the universal Church.

In the persecution many died for their faith, many apostatized, many fled to the hills and gathered there under Judas Maccabeus to form the guerilla armies which eventually repulsed the persecutors and re-established the faith in Jerusalem and throughout Palestine. It is with them and their active resistance that the remainder of 2 Maccabees is concerned.

8:1ff Judas gathers an army (vv. 1-7; cf. 1 Mac. 2:27-48; 3:1-9). His victories over Nicanor, Georgias, Timotheus, and Bacchides (vv. 8-36).

9:1ff The death of Antiochus IV (cf. 1 Mac. 6). For dramatic purposes the author of 2 Maccabees narrates first the death of a persecutor, then the institution of a feast, viz., ch. 9: the death of Antiochus; ch. 10: the institution of the feast of the Dedication; 15:25-27: the death of Nicanor; 15:35-36: the institution of the feast of Nicanor's Day.

10:1-8 Judas recaptures Jerusalem, purifies the Temple, institutes the the feast of Hannukah (the Dedication) to be celebrated on December 24th (cf. 1 Mac. 4:36-61).

Part Three / 2 Mac. 10:10—15:40 / Judas Maccabeus after 164

10:10-24 Judas' victories over Gorgias, Timotheus and Lysias (11:1-15) during the reign of Antiochus V and the regency of Lysias (cf. 1 Mac. 4:1-35).

12:39-45 The purgatory text. After a description of Judas' punitive expeditions against the Arabs, Timotheus, and Gorgias (12:1-

B.C.

B.C.	Personalities	Events	In the Neighborhood	Literature
400	Joel	Samaritans build a Temple on Mt. Gerizim (c. 328)	Alexander the Great conquers Persia (331)	CHRONICLER'S HISTORY ESTHER, TOBIT DEUTERO-ZECHARIAH PROVERBS; ECCLESIASTES MINOR PROPHETS' COLLECTION PSALTER in final form
↓ 200	Deutero-Zechariah		Division of Alexander's empire; Casander rules Macedon-Asia-minor Ptolemy rules Egypt; Seleucus rules Syria-Mesopotamia	BARUCH and the LETTER OF JEREMIAH
200			Antiochus, the Great	SEPTUAGINT TRANSLATION OF THE OLD TESTAMENT SIRACH (Ecclesiasticus)
	Onias III Jason Mattathias Hasmoneus	Hellenization of Jerusalem Persecution of Jews by Antiochus IV Maccabean wars	Seleucus IV Antiochus IV	
	JUDAS MACCABEUS JONATHAN MACCABEUS	Rededication of the Temple (164)		DANIEL
↓ 100	SIMON MACCABEUS John Hyrcanus	Jewish independence	Antiochus V Demetrius I	2 MACCABEES 1 MACCABEES
100	Alexander Jannaeus		Roman control over Palestine (63) Julius Caesar	JUDITH WISDOM
	John the Baptist	End of the Old Testament	Augustus Caesar Tiberius Caesar	Qumran Literature

TIME OF CHRIST

37), the author gives details of an encounter with some of the troops of Gorgias. In looting, some soldiers had broken the law of Deut. 7:26 against contact with idols or things used in idol worship. When found with these objects in their possession, they were presumed to have died in a state of sin. Judas takes up a collection to pray for them that they may attain to eternal life. In v. 44, the inspired author explicitly approves this offering showing his belief in prayers for the dead.

13:1-26 The death of Menelaus, the false high priest (vv. 3-8), and Judas' victory over the armies of Antiochus V and Lysias (cf. 1 Mac. 4:26-35).

14:1ff After the accession of Demetrius I (161-150), the new king is persuaded to send an army under Nicanor to quell the rebellion in Judea (vv. 1-14). Judas and Nicanor at first agree to terms of peace (vv. 15-25). But Alcimus convinces Demetrius that Nicanor is being disloyal in befriending Judas, and the friends are alienated (vv. 26-33).

15:1-6 Intercessory prayer text. Before the battle with Nicanor, Judas relates his dream about the heavenly intercession of the holy high priest, Onias (cf. 2 Mac. 4:36), and Jeremiah, the prophet, in favor of his people. Dogmatically, the passage (vv. 12-16) demonstrates the existence of a belief in the power of intercessory prayer and the communion of saints.

15:25ff The author concludes his epitome of Jason of Cyrene's five volume work by recording the victory of Judas over Nicanor (vv. 25-27; cf. 1 Mac. 7:26-27), and the institution of the feast of the "Day of Nicanor," the thirteenth day of Adar, probably March 28th of 161 (vv. 35-36).

Nos. 68–71.   **68**. Coins from the age of the Maccabees. *Top row:* tetra-drachma of Antiochus IV Epiphanes (reverse to right showing actual size); *second row:* Alexander the Great; *third row:* tetradrachma of Antiochus IV Epiphanes; *fourth row:* Mithradates I, 171–138 B.C.; *bottom row:* Antiochus IV Epiphanes; Phoenician drachma from Aradus, struck in 171–170 B.C. **69**. Cave One, Qumran.   **70**. Scroll of the Book of Isaiah found in a cave at Qumran; also found were portions of practically every Old Testament book and of many apocrypha; see front cover. The script used witnesses to the change that had already taken place from Old Hebrew to the Aramaic square type.   **71**. Several hundred Samaritans still living on the slopes of Mounts Ebal and Gerizim retain and honor the Pentateuch only as their Bible. The script is in the tradition of the Old Hebrew alphabet; these Samaritans continue to keep the Passover annually with the ritual as prescribed in Exodus 12. No. 68 *courtesy:* Koninklijk Kabinet van Munten, The Hague, Holland; Nos. 69, 71 *courtesy:* Rev. Josef Nachtmann, Regensburg, Germany; No. 70 *courtesy:* American Schools of Oriental Research, Jerusalem.

18

The Apocalyptic Literature

1. The Apocalyptic Literary Form

In the midst of the great persecution of the Jewish Church by Antiochus IV, an unknown author composed the strange and disconcerting book known under the pseudonym of Daniel, a Jewish sage and "prophet" from the time of the Babylonian captivity. The reader will find the book of Daniel strange because it is written according to the norms of the new and complex literary form known as apocalyptic. He will find it disconcerting because its apocalyptic literary form is almost completely alien to the Greek mentality inherited by the western world.

The understanding of Daniel as a consequence requires of the reader a previous study of the apocalyptic literary form, its psychological origins, its principal characteristics, its literary origins and development. In the light of these the reader will clear up many of the difficulties encountered in the book and at the same time appreciate to the full its magnificent doctrine concerning the coming messianic kingdom and its universal rule.

In the many apocalyptic books, both apocryphal and canonical, written between the second century B.C. and the second century A.D., the psychological state of the authors and their audiences is one induced either by persecution or by the need for assurance that the promises made by God to Israel in the past are trustworthy and certain of eventual fulfillment. This is a conclusion based upon the nature of the writings themselves and on the fact that almost all apocalyptic literature, even its first manifestations, has its origin at a time of crisis for the faith, brought about either by pagan oppression or by religious persecutions.

The first incipient apocalyptic literature, for example, in Amos and Isaiah, dates to the time of the Assyrian crisis; in Ezekiel and Deutero-Isaiah to the gloomy years of the Babylonian captivity; in Zechariah and Joel to the years of disillusionment that followed the return from the exile; in Daniel, to the time of the crusading paganism of Antiochus IV, when materialistic Hellenism threatened to wipe out completely the struggling Jewish Church. Even the Apocalypse of St. John in the New Testament, as will be seen, stemmed from a time of crisis — the persecution initiated by Nero and continued under the subsequent Roman emperors.

Characteristics of apocalyptic literature

A careful reading of apocalyptic literature will disclose such psychological characteristics as a state of suffering combined with an invincible confidence in the eventual intervention of God to reward the faithful and punish the wicked, and a refined appreciation for the exalted superiority of the true faith over the perversions and superstitions of paganism.

From the literary viewpoint, the apocalyptic form will be sharply distinguished from other literary forms by its imaginative descriptions of the cosmological upheavals heralding the coming of the "Day of the Lord" (based for the most part on Amos, the Sinai stageprops, and the plagues of Egypt), its conventional use of symbolic names, numbers, and fantastic beasts, and its introduction of angels, either as interlocutors between God and His prophets, or as supplying the place of secondary causes in God's government of the world (cf. Is. 24:17-23; 34:1-4; Ez. 38:1-8; 40:3-5; Zech. 1:8-21; 6:1-8; 14:6-14; Joel 2:1-2; 2:28-32; 3:9-21; Dan. 7—12 *passim*). In a more general way, the apocalyptic literary form will be characterized by its fondness for systematic presentation, its remarkable outbursts of imagination, and its indestructible faith in the authority of the inspired books.

Perhaps the most unusual characteristic of apocalyptic literature will be its use of pseudonyms. In an age in which wisdom literature is regularly written under the pseudonym of Solomon, the wisdom writer *par excel-*

lence, the apocalyptic authors will pose as ancient prophets or patriarchs (cf. apocryphal apocalypses), in order by this conventional fiction to give greater authority to their writings. Prophesying thus from the historical standpoint of the ancient author, they will reveal and interpret history from his day to their own. Then fortified by this fictitious fulfillment of their prophecies, they will launch into a description of the future, which will see the realization of all that the ancient prophets foretold in the establishment of the messianic kingdom and the destruction of the forces of evil.

In its final stage, therefore, the apocalyptic form will be characterized by the following: pseudonymity, esoteric teaching (i.e., the revelation of secrets which are not to be disclosed until the time of the true author), a motion-picture, deterministic unrolling of history, the intervention of angels, and the use of symbolic language (beasts, horns, mysterious numbers, and cosmological disturbances) to designate the forces of evil and the forces of God in the great struggle from which the forces of God eventually emerge victorious.

The book of Daniel will be found to display most of the above characteristics. However, before studying an almost perfect example of the apocalyptic literary form such as Daniel, it will be of no small help to the reader to follow the development of the form from its first incipient manifestations in Amos and Isaiah through its more developed stages in Ezekiel, Zechariah, and Joel.

Literary origins and development of the apocalyptic literary form

To study adequately the development of any literary form, it is necessary from the beginning to have a sampling of books or literary pieces representative of the form during the period in which it developed. This is possible for most modern literary forms. It is not possible for all ancient literary forms.

It is particularly unfortunate that an adequate sequence of books or literary pieces in the apocalyptic literary form is not available. It makes it impossible to trace the exact development of the form from its initial manifestations to its definitive form in Daniel and the other apocalypses in the intertestamental period. The careful reader, however, can recognize the seed or seeds from which a literary form flowers provided he knows the flower and has at least some idea of what it looked like at some stages of its development. This is the most that can be done for the apocalyptic literary form, but it is enough.

The experienced eye discerns the first manifestations of apocalyptic literature in such early writings as Deut. 28:60-68; Amos 3:14; 5:18ff; Is. 13–14; and in such psalms as Pss. 11; 48; 50; 83; 97; 98. The main stages, however, in the development of the form can be readily recognized in Ezekiel, the father of apocalyptic literature (ch. 38–39; 40–48); in Deutero-Isaiah (ch. 24–27; 34–35); in Zechariah and Joel *passim.*

In its definitive form, attained in the last two centuries before Christ, the form is represented by one canonical apocalypse, the book of Daniel, and a large number of apocryphal apocalypses, among which the book of Henoch, the Assumption of Moses, the Psalms of Solomon, the Apocalypse of Ezra, the Apocalypse of Baruch, and the Jewish Sibyl are of especial importance.

A reading of the following passages selected from various books and dating from different periods will give the reader some idea of the origin of the principal ideas and of the more common symbolic language from which, after a period of several centuries, there developed the mature apocalyptic literary form as represented in Daniel and the Apocalypse of St. John. Although a multitude of texts could be cited, it is hoped that by a reading of these select few a cumulative effect will make up for the lack of more detailed citations.

Exod. 7–12
The plagues. The fact that God had decisively intervened at a time of great crisis for Israel to free her by means of the plagues from the persecution of the pagan Egyptians led to the realization in due time that God could and would, if necessary for the salvation of His people, do the same again. Not only, therefore, do the apocalyptic authors confidently expect God to intervene again against their enemies but they frequently make use of the plagues to describe God's interventions against the forces of anti-God (cf. Deut. 28:58-61; Ez. 38:21-22; Zech. 14:12-15; Joel 2:2-9; Apoc. 9:18).

Exod. 19:16-19
The lightning, thunder, storm clouds, smoke, and trumpet blasts accompanying the great Sinai theophany become stereotyped stageprops used to describe the coming of God to judge, not only by poets (cf. Pss. 18; 50; 76) and prophets (cf. Is. 6; Ez. 1; Micah 1:3-4; Zeph. 1:14-16; Hab. 3:3-6) but by the apocalyptic writers as well (cf. Ez. 38:18-23; Dan. 7:9-10; Apoc. 4:4-5).

Deut. 28
The blessings and curses enumerated here become a literary mine for future prophets and apocalyptic writers. From this and similar passages future writers derive not only their certainty that God will punish the evildoers and particularly the forces of anti-God but much vivid language for describing

the effects of God's inevitable intervention to punish the wicked (cf. Ez. 39; Zech. 14:1-5, 13-15; Apoc. 19:17-19).

Amos 5:18 The "day of the Lord." Although Amos' "day of the Lord" refers primarily to the destruction of Samaria in 722 B.C., the implications of God's intervention to change the course of history at this time as He had at the time of the Exodus lead later writers to adopt the expression, "the Day of the Lord," with its dire effects for the wicked and its blessed effects for the good, to express any great intervention of God in history and particularly that great intervention which would bring about the destruction of the forces of anti-God and the establishment of the reign of God. Thus, when the forces of anti-God appear so powerful that only the intervention of God Himself can save His people, the confident expectation of the "day of the Lord" and the description of its coming become a staple literary mode not only for the prophets (cf. Is. 2:12-22; 4:2-6; 11:10-16; Jer. 4:9-18; 50:27-29; Zeph. 1:14-18; Ez. 30:1-3) but for the apocalyptic writers as well (cf. Ez. 38:18-23; 39:11-16; Is. 13:6-22; 24:21-23; 25:9-12; Zech. 12:3-9; 13:1-4; 14:1-21; Joel 1:15; 2:1-2; in Dan. 7—12 and in the Apocalypse of St. John the day of the Lord is implicit).

Ez. 38—39 The great battle. In what is generally conceded to be the first piece of genuinely apocalyptic literature, Ezekiel portrays for the pessimistic exiles the great battle between the united forces of anti-God (symbolized by Gog and his army) and the forces of God. The prophets had announced that God would make use of the pagan nations to punish His people (Is., Jer., Zeph., Hab. *passim*). Ezekiel points out that when the pagan nations go beyond their commission as avenging agents of God and attempt to destroy His people entirely, they become in effect enemies of God Himself and as such will be entirely destroyed in the day of His anger. Apocalyptic writers, therefore, assure God's people that ultimately God will destroy the forces of anti-God and establish His reign not only over Israel but over all men (cf. Is. 13:4-9; Zech. 2:1-4; 12—14 *passim*; Joel 4:9-21; Dan. 7—12 *passim*; Apoc. 13—20 *passim*).

Ez. 40:3-4 Ezekiel's interlocutor angel, used as intermediate between God and the world, becomes another staple stageprop of apocalyptic literature (cf. Zech. 1:8ff; 2:2; Dan. 8:16; 9:21; 10:5; Apoc. 21:15ff).

Is. 11 In this famous chapter, of which vv. 1-9 are probably from first Isaiah and vv. 10-16 from second Isaiah, the coming of the Messiah and the return of the paradisiacal age of Gen. 2—3 are united with the concept of the "Day of the Lord" paving the way for the frequent unification of these themes in future prophetic and apocalyptic literature (cf. Amos 9:11-15; Is. 65:17-25; Zech. 14:6-11; Joel 4:17-21; Dan. 2:44-45; 7:13-14; 9:24-27; Apoc. 21—22).

Is. 13:10-13 The present form of this Deutero-Isaian oracle against Babylon (ch. 13—14) describes the coming of the "Day of the Lord" for Babylon, Israel's oppressor. To enhance the terrible gloom and darkness of that day, the poet, stretching his imagination in truly apocalyptic fashion, says: "The stars and constellations send forth no light; the sun is dark when it rises, and the light of the moon does not shine" (v. 10). In v. 13, God says: "I will make the heavens tremble and the earth shall be shaken from its place." Such references to cosmic disturbances become, like the imagery of the Sinai theophany, additional stageprops for the apocalyptists' description of the great day of the Lord (cf. Is. 24:17-23; Joel 3:3ff; 4:15; Matthew 24:29-31; Apoc. 6:12-17).

Zech. 1—8 Zechariah amasses much of the symbolic language that will become the clichés of apocalyptic: his horns (1:18-21), representative of power, from a common Old Testament metaphor (cf. Deut. 33:17; 1 Kings 22:11), will be used extensively in Daniel (cf. 7:8; 8:3-8) and in St. John's Apocalypse (cf. 12:3; 13:1). His seven eyes (3:9; 4:10) taken from Ezekiel (1:18) and symbolizing God's omniscience, appear again in Daniel (7:20) and in the Apocalypse (5:6). His four horsemen (1:8-17; 6:1-8), symbolic figures representing God's providential care in the guidance of history, turn up again in the Apocalypse (6:2ff). His woman in the basket (5:5-11), representing wickedness transplanted to Babylon where a temple is built for her, appears again as the great harlot in the Apocalypse (17:5-6). Finally, Zechariah's use of the literary vision (1:7; 2:1; 2:5 *passim*), based probably on Amos 7—9 and used as a means to dramatize his message, finds extensive use in Daniel (2:19; 4:7; 7:1; 8:1; 9:21; 10:7) and in the Apocalypse (9:17).

Job 1—2 Early example of pseudonymity. While in no sense an apocalypse, the book of Job is, nevertheless, an early example (6th-

5th century B.C.) of postexilic authors' use of pseudonyms. Job, as is obvious from the text and from Ezekiel (14:14), was an ancient and famous non-Israelite sage. The author takes advantage of Job's reputation to use him as his mouthpiece. The use of pseudonyms will become common among the wisdom writers, a number of whom unite under the pseudonym of Solomon, and a genuine characteristic of the apocalyptic writers (cf. the Apocalypse of Ezra, the Apocalypse of Baruch, the Assumption of Moses, etc.). The Daniel of the book of Daniel is certainly a pseudonym.

2. Joel

The book of Joel should be read immediately before Daniel for two reasons. First, it is certainly a late book (400-350 B.C.) as indicated by the mention of the Greeks (4:6), the position of the priests and elders as heads of the community (1:13-14; 2:15-17), the absence of any reference either to Jewish kings or to Babylon, and the literary dependence of Joel on such late authors as Ezekiel (47:1ff, cf. Joel 4:18). Obadiah (v. 17, cf. Joel 3:5), and Malachi (3:2, cf. Joel 2:11).

Secondly, the book is clearly intermediate between the old style prophetic literature and the new style prophetico-apocalyptic. Thus Joel is not a pseudonym as most authors' names in mature apocalyptic literature but a genuine prophet of the 5th-4th century B.C. His style, moreover, at least in the first two chapters is that of the old style prophet. He addresses the people, the priests, and the elders directly and calls upon them in forthright language to "return to me with your whole heart, with fasting, and weeping, and mourning" (2:12-13).

On the other hand, in ch. 3—4, Joel moves ahead into the atmosphere and the literary milieu of the apocalyptists. He portrays the messianic "Day of the Lord" (3:1-2) as accompanied by dramatic cosmic disturbances (3:3-4), culminating in the judgment and destruction of the nations in the valley of Jehoshaphat (4:1-3, 9-16), with the consequent exaltation of God's people (4:17) and the advent of the messianic age, described in language from the paradise story (4:18).

The book is divided into two parts. Part I (ch. 1—2) consists of two sermons (1:2-20; 2:1-17), calling upon the elders, the people, and the priests to pray and do penance in order to avert a calamitous locust plague. The reader should note the liturgical background provided in these chapters for the psalms of collective lamentation (cf. Pss. 74; 79; 80). As in the collective lamentations, there is a description of the calamity—the locust plague (1:4-12; 2:1-11), the prayers for surcease (1:14; 2:17), and the anticipation of help based upon a divine oracle (2:18-27). Part II (ch. 3—4) is entirely apocalyptic, describing the great day of the Lord (3:1-5), the destruction of the enemies of God and Israel (4:1-16), and the coming of the reign of God (4:17-21).

The transition of Joel from a particular day of the Lord (the locust plague) in his own time (ch. 1—2) to the future messianic day of the Lord (ch. 3—4) in the distant future is probably to be explained by the different background and different viewpoint of each section. The first part was occasioned by a definite and calamitous locust plague. The second part was probably occasioned by the continual distress of the Israelite community in the late postexilic period. Thus the purpose of the first part is to exhort the people to beseech God by common liturgical prayer and by fasting to avert a particular calamity. In the second part, the prophet's purpose is to encourage the people in a time of distress and perhaps of pessimism to look forward to the time when the messianic prophecies of old, particularly those concerning the outpouring of the spirit of God (Is. 11:1-2; Ez. 36:20-29, cf. Joel 3:1-2), the conquest of God over the enemies of His kingdom (Ez. 38—39, cf. Joel 4:1-16), and the stream of blessings from the Temple (Ez. 47:1-12, cf. Joel 4:18) would be fulfilled.

Significant passages in Joel

1:4ff The locust plague. Joel graphically describes the devastating nature of the locust invasion by showing its effects upon the wine-bibbers (vv. 5-7), the priests (vv. 8-10), and the farmers (vv. 11-12). He concludes by calling all to the Temple to beg surcease from God through prayer and fasting.

2:1ff A vivid and stirring description of the locusts advancing like a mighty army in battle array (vv. 1-11) prefaces God's plea to His people for sincere penance and repentance (vv. 12-14) and Joel's own call to prayer and penance (vv. 15-17). God's answer to the prayers of His people is given by Joel in a prophetic oracle (vv. 18-27). The reader should note that in both sermons the prophet's attention is directed to a particular plague with very real consequences for his contemporaries.

3:1ff The outpouring of the spirit in messianic times. The reader should note that in ch. 3—4 the prophet's attention is directed solely to the future. Following a practice that becomes characteristic of the apocalyptic writers, Joel picks up an old prophetic teaching, the outpouring of the spirit in messianic times (cf. Is. 11:1-2; Jer. 24:7; 31:33; 32:40; Ez. 36:25-27; 37:14; 39:29; Is. 42:1; 44:3; 54:13; 59:21) and repeats it in the context of the great Day of the Lord. When St. Peter quotes these words at Pentecost to declare that the charismatic gifts so characteristic of the apostolic Christian community (cf. 1 Cor. 12 and 14) are the fulfillment of Joel's prophecy (Acts 2:17-21), he is not the least embarrassed because the latter part of the prophecy concerning the cosmic disturbances (vv. 3-4) is not taking place. He knows them to be nothing more than those literary stageprops used throughout the Old Testament, and particularly by the apocalyptists, to describe the Day of the Lord (cf. Exod. 19:16-19; Is. 13:9-10; 24:21-23; Ez. 32:7).

4:1ff The conquest of united heathendom, a feature of the messianic Day of the Lord already described by Ezekiel (38–39) and Zechariah (9:14ff; 14:1-15), is described by Joel as followed by the judgment of the forces of evil in the symbolic valley of Jehoshaphat (vv. 1-12). Likening the destruction to the vintage harvest when the blood of the enemies of God will flow like the wine presses at vintage time (vv. 13-16; cf. Is. 63:1-6), Joel concludes his description of the messianic day of the Lord with a prophecy of the return of the paradisiacal age (vv. 17-21; cf. Amos 9:11-15; Is. 65:17-25; Zech. 14:6-11).

The message of Joel is not new since it is only a repitition of already well established prophecies, but its restatement in a time of distress and doubt to encourage and fortify the despairing is characteristic of apocalyptic literature. The same message expressed in a more bizarre and imaginative way will be at the heart of the book of Daniel.

3. Daniel

The book of Daniel reveals all the characteristics of midrashic and apocalyptic literature.[1] In its first part (ch. 1–6), the author, who writes during the persecution of Antiochus IV (167-164), culls from tradition a number of stories dealing with Daniel and his friends during the Babylonian captivity. In typical midrashic style, he elaborates the stories freely and skillfully in order to encourage the persecuted faithful of his time to resist Antiochus and his pagan culture as Daniel and his friends resisted Ne-

---

[1] Cf. CCHS par. 525ff; K. Sullivan, *The Book of Daniel*, No. 28, OTRG.

buchadnezzar and Babylonian idolatry. Besides this didactic purpose, the stories serve the additional purpose of introducing Daniel, the Jewish sage and prophet from the time of the Babylonian captivity, who will act as the author's alter ego in the apocalyptic section that follows.

In the second part of the book (ch. 7–12) the author, under the pseudonym of Daniel, unreels and interprets by means of visions the history of the great world empires from the time of Nebuchadnezzar down to the time of the reigning persecutor of the Jews, Antiochus IV. On his own from this time on, the pseudo-Daniel foretells the downfall of the persecutor and the advent of the messianic kingdom.

A third part (ch. 13–14), added to the book after the manner of an appendix, contains additional midrashic stories about Daniel and the priests of Bel in Babylon and the unjustly accused Susanna saved from martyrdom by the perspicacity of Daniel.

The theme of the book is clearly the coming of the eternal, universal, and basically spiritual messianic kingdom and its superiority over all merely earthly powers. Written for people suffering actual martyrdom (cf. 2 Mac. 6–7) and unrelenting persecution, the purpose of the book is to encourage the faithful to put their faith in the age-old promises of the prophets and to persevere patiently under the trials of the persecution in the certain expectation of the fulfillment of these promises in the imminent future. That this is the purpose of the book as a whole is confirmed by the identity of purpose in the midrashic (ch. 1–6) and apocalyptic (ch. 7–12) sections of the book. The connection between the dream of Nebuchadnezzar in ch. 2 and the visions in ch. 7–12, both concerned with the history of empires, shows the basic unity of the book.

The difficulties with which the book swarms when interpreted as a strictly historical and traditionally prophetic form of literature disappear for the most part when the book is seen as midrashic and apocalyptic in nature. Such difficulties as the presence of the book among the hagiographa (after Esther in the Hebrew Bible rather than after Ezekiel), the silence of Sirach, written about the year 200 B.C., concerning the very existence of the book of Daniel, and the ignorance of the authors of Job, Ecclesiastes, and Sirach with respect to the teaching of Dan. 12 on the future life, are all invincible enigmas for those who refuse to recognize Daniel as a second century apocalypse.

Interpreted as an apocalypse, written during the persecution of Antiochus IV, the book quite naturally finds its place among the hagiographa, the last formed section of the Hebrew Bible, rather than among the prophets, a section formed before the year 200 B.C.; and the postexilic authors down to the second century B.C. are ignorant of Daniel's existence for the simple reason that it had not as yet been written.

Other difficulties such as the existence of three different languages in the book (Hebrew 1:1–2:4a and ch. 8–12; Aramaic 2:4b–3:23 and 3:91–7:28; Greek 3:34-90, and ch. 13–14) and the apparent confusion of names when treating of such kings as Nabonidus and Darius the Mede are less easy to solve and must await further investigation and perhaps the help of as yet undiscovered historical sources.

The teaching of Daniel assures the faithful that the promises of the ancient prophets are worthy of belief. The messianic kingdom foretold of old will follow and supplant the empires of the ancient world. These empires, Babylon, Media, Persia, and Greece-Syria, are symbolized in ch. 2 by the different metals in Nabuchodonosor's dream statue crushed by the "stone hewn from the mountain without hands" (2:44) and in ch. 7 by the "four great beasts rising from the sea," handed over by God to be burned at the advent of "one like to the Son of Man coming with the clouds of the heavens to receive dominion and glory and kingly power over all peoples and nations and tongues" (7:13-14). Since this kingdom is the kingdom of the saints, it is not only universal but spiritual. In the last years of the following century the King will be born in Bethlehem and, in an obvious reference to the symbolic figure in Dan. 7:13, He will refer to Himself as "the Son of Man."

For the broad historical background of Daniel, embracing the rise and fall of the great empires from the sixth to the second century, the reader is referred to the Books of Kings, Ezra-Nehemiah, and Maccabees. For the immediate foreground of the author, the reader is referred to 1 Mac. 1–4 and 2 Mac. 1–7. The following chronological outline will indicate the principal personages and dates pertinent to the development of the apocalyptic literary form and to the events alluded to in the book of Daniel.

Chronology

605-562   Reign of Nebuchadnezzar. Daniel deported to Babylon in the first year of Nebuchadnezzar. Active period of Ezekiel (the father of apocalyptic literature).

550-540   Active period of Deutero-Isaiah, intermediate form of apocalyptic literature (Is. 24–27).

555-539   Nabonidus (last King of Babylon) and Belshazzar, crown prince and co-regent in the last years of Babylon.

539-530   Cyrus the Great and the Persian empire (539-331).

522-485   Darius I, third emperor of Persia.

520-350   Zechariah and Joel, intermediate stages of apocalyptic literature.

356-323 Alexander the Great. Conquers Persia 331. Empire divided after his death in 323 among his generals. Seleucus originates the Seleucid kingdom (305-63).

175-164 Antiochus IV, persecutor of Judaism, figure of anti-Christ.

170 Onias the high priest assassinated.

170-164 Week of Years of the persecution of Judaism in Maccabean times by Antiochus IV, beginning with the assassination of Onias early in 170 and ending with the capture and re-dedication of the Temple by Judas Maccabeus in December of 164.

167-164 Half Week of Years beginning with the desecration of the Temple in 167, after which sacrifices and offerings ceased while Antiochus IV controlled the Temple and set up the "Abomination of the Desolation." Sometime during these years Daniel was written.

Significant passages in Daniel

Part One / *Dan. 1—6* / *Midrashic Section*

1:1ff Introducing Daniel as a young Jewish nobleman deported to Babylon in 605 (vv. 1-7) to serve as a page in the court of Nebuchadnezzar, ch. 1 not only serves to explain Daniel's rise to prominence in the Babylonian court (vv. 17-21) but gives to the second century Jews in Hellenistic surroundings the edifying example of Daniel and his friends observing their Jewish dietary laws in the midst of a thoroughly pagan milieu. A reading of 1 Mac. 1:41-50; 2 Mac. 6:6-7 will show the cogency of this midrashic element in ch. 1 of Daniel.

2:1ff Nebuchadnezzar's dream of a statue composed of four different kinds of metal, gold, silver, bronze, iron (vv. 24-36), is interpreted by Daniel as symbolic of the four great empires of ancient times: Babylonia, Media, Persia, and Greek-Syria; these are destroyed and replaced by the eternal and universal messianic kingdom, the stone from the mountain (vv. 37-45).

3:1ff The spirit of martyrdom and absolute trust in God manifested by Shadrach, Meshach, and Abednego before the ordeal of the fiery furnace (vv. 16-18) serves as a shining example for the Jews of Maccabean times, forced by the Syrian Hellenists to undergo similar tests of their faith (cf. 1 Mac. 1:44-63; 2:15-18; 2 Mac. 6—7; Jer. 29:2122).

4:1ff The pride of Nebuchadnezzar (vv. 28-30) punished by insanity (vv. 31-33) demonstrates an important principle of the prophetic philosophy of history: the authority and power of kings comes from God and must be referred to God (vv. 34-37). This example has particular cogency in the time of Antiochus IV, who abused the power given him and was punished by God (2 Mac. 9:5ff). N.B. A successor of Nebuchadnezzar, King Nabonidus (558-539), but not Nebuchadnezzar himself, is known from Babylonian records to have spent a mysterious seven years in seclusion at Tema in the Arabian desert (ANET 306). We have either confusion in the transmission of the names or the author is using Nebuchadnezzar as the Babylonian king *par excellence.*

5:1ff Brought in to interpret the mysterious writing on the wall (vv. 1-16), Daniel explains the words as meaning that the number of years of Belshazzar's kingdom has been brought to an end, his rule has been weighed and found wanting, and his kingdom is to be divided among the Medes and the Persians (vv. 17-29). The purpose of the story is to illustrate again, as in ch. 4, the prophetic philosophy of history, according to which God punishes the proud, who misuse God-given power, by taking away from them their power and glory (vv. 17-23). In Maccabean times, the story has its parallel in the blasphemous pride of Antiochus IV. The persecuted faithful can be assured that his kingdom too will be taken from him.

6:1ff In order to destroy Daniel's power, jealous Babylonian politicians have the king pass a law making it unlawful to pray to anyone but to the king for 30 days (vv. 1-8). When Daniel, as expected, continues his private devotions to the true God, he is discovered and condemned to death (vv. 9-16). God, however, delivers Daniel from the mouth of the lions, and when the king discovers this, Daniel's enemies are punished (vv. 17-28). The purpose of the story is to encourage the faithful in Maccabean times to continue the exercise of religion forbidden by Antiochus IV (cf. 1 Mac. 1:41-51 *passim*).

Part Two / Dan. 7—12 / Apocalyptic Section

Written in apocalyptic style, ch. 7—12 have as their theme the coming of the messianic kingdom which, according to the author, will follow in the period after the end of the Syrian persecution. Ch. 2 contains in essence the same message as ch. 7—12. The four metals in Nebuchadnezzar's dream statue representing the kingdoms of earth which are destroyed and replaced by the stone from the mountain representing the messianic kingdom find their parallels in ch. 7–12 with variations in symbolism with the kingdom of the saints as the direct parallel of the stone from the mountain. The repetition of the same message in several different tableaus (e.g., statue in ch. 2, beasts in ch. 7, ram and he-goat in ch. 8, 70 weeks of years in ch. 9, and the conflict of kingdoms in ch. 10–12) is characteristic of apocalyptic literature and is based upon the Hebrew method of developing a theme by means of different complete and independent tableaus, each of which will emphasize a different aspect of the same subject. Thus ch. 7 concentrates on the opposition between the kingdoms of this world and the kingdom of God which supplants them. Ch. 8 describes the persecution and death of the persecutor, Antiochus IV. Ch. 9 concentrates on the time when the messianic kingdom will come. Ch. 10–12 describe at length the history of the Seleucids and the persecution of the Jews by Antiochus IV ending in ch. 12 with the promise of resurrection and eternal life for the martyrs of the persecution.

7:1ff Daniel's vision of the four beasts and the son of man (vv. 2-14; cf. Zech. 1–6 for the first use of visions as a literary device) is explained symbolically as referring to kingdoms and kings (vv. 17-18) and is followed by a more detailed explanation of the fourth beast, the kingdom of Antiochus IV, and his persecution of the saints which will end in victory for the kingdom of the saints (vv. 19-27).

Concerning the symbolic language used by the author it is generally agreed that the beasts (vv. 2-8) represent the Babylonian, Median, Persian, and Graeco-Seleucid kingdoms and their kings (cf. vv. 17, 23) as in ch. 2. The venerable One represents God. The Son of Man (vv. 13-14) represents the collectivity known as the "saints of the most High" (vv. 22, 25, 27), and the king of the collectivity, the Messiah (cf. Jewish and Christian tradition and the interpretation given in Matthew 24:30; 26:64; Mark 14:62; Luke 9:26; Apoc. 1:7; 14:14). The fourth kingdom described more in detail has ten horns which represent the ten kings of the Seleucid dynasty (vv. 19, 20, 24). The little horn with the "mouth speaking arrogantly" and "making war against the holy ones" (vv. 20, 21), "speaking against the Most High," "thinking to change the feast days and the law," and having the holy ones in his power "for a year, two years, and a half-year" (v. 25) certainly represents Antiochus IV who dared to call himself *God Manifest* (cf. 1 Mac. 1:24, 41-51; 2 Mac. 5:21; 9.4; 9:7-11; Dan. 2:42-43; 8:9-14;

8:23-25; 11:21-45; 12:11-12 where this same king is described in greater detail).

The reader should note how the author opposes the kingdom of the holy ones to the kingdoms of the earth. The kingdom of the holy ones is like "a man," the kingdoms of earth like to "beasts." The earthly kingdoms are from below, from the sea, the kingdom of the holy ones is from above (vv. 3, 13). The earthly kingdoms are temporal and restricted (vv. 12, 26); the kingdom of the holy ones is universal and eternal (vv. 14, 27).

8:1ff Repeating the substance of ch. 7, ch. 8 restricts itself to the persecution of the holy ones by the little horn, Antiochus IV (cf. 1 Mac. 1—2; 2 Mac. 4—7). The author describes a vision of a ram and a he-goat (vv. 3-13). These are interpreted by an angel (vv. 15-19) in the following manner: the ram represents Media-Persia; the he-goat with horns represents Alexander and his successors; the little horn represents Antiochus IV, the persecutor who persecutes the holy ones, the faithful of Israel during the Maccabean times, and rises up against God Himself, the "prince of princes" (vv. 20-26). The two thousand three hundred evenings and mornings (vv. 14 and 26) represent the three and one-half years (167-164) during which the morning and evening sacrifices in the Temple were not able to be offered up because of the Temple's desecration.

9:1ff Daniel wonders about the seventy year period mentioned in Jeremiah (25:12; 29:10; 31:38) and prays for enlightenment (vv. 1-19). The angel Gabriel comes (vv. 20-23) and explains the seventy years as seventy weeks of years (vv. 24-27).

By an ingenious manipulation of numbers (like the original seventy years of Jeremiah, however, to be taken as round numbers for the most part), the author repeats the messianic substance of ch. 7—8, concentrating on the last week of years (170-164), the time of the persecution of Antiochus IV, promising at its end the coming of the messianic era (v. 24), when prophecies will be fulfilled and "a Most Holy will be anointed" (cf. 1 Chr. 23:18). The artificial numbers are best understood as follows:

v. 25 a) "from the utterance of the word" (Jer. 25:12)   605
b) "until one anointed (Cyrus) 7 weeks" — 49 years   558
c) "it shall be rebuilt" 62 weeks — 434 years   170

v. 26 a) "anointed (Onias) cut off" after 62 weeks — 434   170
years

c) "city and sanctuary shall destroy" (1 Mac. 1:30)   167
f) "until the end war" (Maccabean wars)   167
v. 27 a) "one week compact with the many" — apostasies   170-164
c) "half the week abolish sacrifice" — Temple dese-   167-164
crated
e) "horrible abomination" (cf. 11:31; 1 Mac. 1:54)   167
f) "until the ruin upon the horror" (1 Mac. 4:37ff)   164

The reader should note that different translations and innumerable variant interpretations of the above passages combined with an amazing coincidence in numbers between some of the possible *termini a quibus* (458 and 445 for the "utterance of the word," for example) and the time of Christ as *terminus ad quem* have made this passage the plaything of interpreters for centuries. The above interpretation has its difficulties, e.g., the reckoning of the 62 weeks of years from 605 instead of from 538, 458, or 445, the total of only 63 weeks of years between 605 and 164, and the fact that the messianic era prophesied in v. 24 does not begin until at least 160 years later. Nevertheless, this interpretation has gained the acceptance of modern Catholic biblical scholars. The principal reasons for this acceptance are the similarity of phraseology in ch. 9 and 11, the parallel in basic plan with ch. 2; 7; 8; 10–12 — all of which run quickly through the period up to the time of Antiochus IV, concentrating in the last place and at length on the reign of this king and his persecution of the Jews in Maccabean times, and lastly the fairly accurate correspondence of the divisions of years with the events of the persecution of Antiochus IV.

10:1ff Ch. 10–12 should be taken as a unit. 10:1–11:1 describes Daniel's meeting with the revealing angel, who then in 11:2-4 tells Daniel facts about the kings of Persia and about Alexander the Great and his successors; 11:5-20 describes the Seleucid kings from Seleucus I (305-281) to Seleucus IV (187-175) down to the history of Antiochus IV (175-164) and his persecution of the Jews; 12:1-13 describes the reward of resurrection and eternal life that awaits those who persevere to the end of the persecution.

11:1ff The kings of Persia (vv. 2-3) are reduced to four after Cyı :
Cambyses, Smerdis (The Usurper), Darius, and Xerxes I, after whom comes Alexander (v. 3) and his successors. The "king of the south" (v. 5) is Ptolemy I (304-285), and "one of his

princes" is Seleucus I (305-281) the founder of the Seleucid dynasty, whose kings are referred to as the "kings of the north." The two kingdoms become "allies" when Bernice, the daughter of Ptolemy II, marries Antiochus II (261-246). The "descendant" of her line is Bernice's brother, Ptolemy III (246-221). The wars conducted by Antiochus III, the Great (223-187), are terminated by "a leader who puts an end to his shameful conduct," i.e., the Roman, Cornelius Scipio, who defeated him at Magnesium in 189 B.C. (vv. 10-19). V. 20 speaks of Seleucus IV (187-175) who sends a "tax collector through the glorious kingdom," i.e., Heliodorus (cf. 2 Mac. 3:7ff). In vv. 21-45, the author describes the reign of Antiochus IV with references to Onias III (v. 22, cf. 2 Mac. 4:33-38), "ships of the Chittim," i.e., the Roman Popilius Laenas, who in 168 B.C. ordered Antiochus IV to get out of Egypt (v. 30), Jewish apostates to Hellenism (v. 32; cf. 1 Mac. 1:11-15; 1:43) the persecution of 167-164 (vv. 33-35), the "horrible abomination" (v. 31, cf. 9:27; 12:11; 1 Mach. 1:58). Concerning the events mentioned in vv. 40-45 we have no extra-biblical record.

12:1ff Mention of the doctrine of the resurrection of the dead (v. 2) is the earliest unequivocal statement of this doctrine in the Old Testament (cf. 2 Mac. 7:9-14, 23-36; 12:43-46). There is no good explanation for the differences in numbers (1290 and 1335) given in vv. 11-12, but both come to about 3½ years, the time during which the Temple was in possession of the pagans (167-164).

Part Three / Dan. 13–14 / Midrashic Section

13:1ff Susanna, a martyr in spirit, prefers to die rather than commit sin (vv. 1-43). Inspired by God, Daniel confounds the lecherous old judges and saves Susanna (vv. 44-64). Like ch. 1–6, the story of Susanna has its historical nucleus, which is here elaborated midrashically to teach the faithful during the persecution of Antiochus IV to be ready to die rather than break the law of God (cf. 1 Mac. 1:41-50, 60-64; 2 Mac. 6–7, and particularly 2 Mac. 6:1ff concerning the licentiousness of the Hellenizers). Emphasis on elders attempting to pervert Susanna may be intended to offset the pernicious example of such men as Jason (cf. 2 Mac. 3–4).

14:1ff The midrashic stories of Daniel and the wily priests of Bel (vv. 1-22) and Daniel and the dragon (vv. 22-42) are related to bring out, as in ch. 1—6, the exalted superiority of the true religion over the puerilities of paganism. Such teaching had a salutary effect on the faithful of Maccabean times, many of whom were drawn to apostatize because of the apparent superiority of the pagan, Hellenistic culture (cf. 1 Mac. 1:11-15; 2 Mac. 4:10-17).

4. Judith

It has become increasingly clear in recent years that the author of Judith never intended to write anything remotely resembling what moderns call history.[1] Nebuchadnezzar was a Babylonian, not an Assyrian. He began to reign in 605 B.C., seven years after Nineveh and the power of the Assyrian empire had been destroyed. He never fought against the Medes, never took Ecbatana.

Arphaxad, king of the Medes, is unknown to history. Holofernes and Bagoas were Persians who lived under Artaxerxes III (358-337) two hundred years after the death of Nebuchadnezzar. Judith herself is unknown in biblical history.

In the book Israel is ruled by a high priest and senate and no mention is made of a Davidic king. In 8:18, Judith declares there is no idolatry in her time as in former ages, a statement incomprehensible in the time of Nebuchadnezzar.

The author, moreover, does not know the topography of northern Samaria, and in 5:22-23 makes clear reference to the return from the Babylonian captivity. His presentation of Nebuchadnezzar, the Babylonian, as king of the Assyrians, waging war against Arphaxad, an unknown Median king, with an army commanded by the Persians, Holofernes and Bagoas, is the equivalent of saying that Peter the Great, the king of England, waged war with Arphaxad, the king of France, with an army led by Generals Eisenhower and MacArthur.

The outrageous arrangement of incompatible events and personages is obviously the author's way of announcing that he intends to write something other than a chronicle of events. But if Judith is not history, what is it? Is it intended to be a parable, or an allegory, or an haggadic midrash, or perhaps an apocalyptic midrash?

The midrashic interpretation

The more common opinion is that Judith is a midrashic history. A midrashic history, as we have seen, is an account based on some semblance of

[1] Cf. T. Wahl, *Judith and Esther*, OTRG No. 25.

an historical nucleus, but freely elaborated for didactic purposes. In Tobit, for example, the didactic purpose of the author is to teach dependence on the loving providence of God; in Esther, to persuade the reader that God protects His chosen nation and will let no enemy destroy it. In the midrashic parts of Daniel (ch. 1–6 and 13–14), the author's purpose is to encourage his brethren, persecuted by Antiochus IV, by assuring them of God's protection in the face of persecution and by pointing out to them for the reassurance of their faith the superiority of the true religion over the puerilities of paganism.

What is the purpose of the midrashic author of Judith? Those who consider the book an haggadic midrash believe the purpose of the book is similar to that of Esther, namely, to assure the faithful that God always protects His Chosen People; to assure them in fact that no matter how great the odds, God can destroy the enemies of His people using even the weakest of means — the hand of a woman.

Those who date the book to the late Persian period hold that the basic historical nucleus of the story comes from an incident in one of the campaigns of Holofernes, a general of the Persian King, Artaxerxes III Ochus (358-338). Holofernes in 350 B.C. passed through Palestine on the way to Egypt. Presumably along the way he stopped to subdue the Jews in order to protect his flank as he moved south. On this occasion the events mentioned in Judith took place. A midrashic author later elaborated these events for didactic purposes.

Authors who date the book to the second century B.C. associate it either with the Syrian persecution under Antiochus IV (175-164) or with the Egyptian persecution under Ptolemy VII in the years following 145 B.C. In either case the Nebuchadnezzar of the book of Judith is a pseudonym for the persecutor, and Judith herself is either a contemporary heroine of the persecution or a new and symbolic Jael (cf. Judg. 4) destroying the enemy of her people.

Much more could be said for the interpretation of Judith as a haggadic midrash. The opinion is so common it would be effrontery to eliminate it as one eliminates the strict historical interpretation. The difficulties one finds with this interpretation, moreover, are not of such tangible importance that they destroy the foundations upon which the interpretation rests. They are rather the almost intangibles that distinguish two closely related literary forms, in this case the different forms and developments of midrash. If it is true that the apocalyptic literary form is an extreme development of the midrashic literary form, then Judith appears to be on the border line between the haggadic midrash and the apocalyptic midrash. The distinction will perhaps best be demonstrated by showing where Judith subtly departs from the haggadic midrash in its lack of concern for homogeneity and verisimilitude of historical background and approaches the apocalyptic midrash in its theme and symbolism.

In Tobit and Esther, for example, the authors restrict themselves to local events described against the background of one pagan empire. Tobit is acted out against the backdrop of Assyrian history in the late eighth century; Esther against the backdrop of Persian history in the fifth century. In Tobit the background is provided merely to establish Tobit as an exile. In Esther, the Persian background enters intimately into the whole story and the events of the story and the background are well integrated. In both stories there is a genuine attempt to establish verisimilitude to real life. Events occur and personages act and react much as in the ordinary interplay of life. Individual characters, moreover, are given some definition and particular places are described with a fair degree of accuracy.

In Judith, on the contrary, the story lacks both homogeneity of historical background and verisimilitude of events. Everything possible seems to have been done to make the historical background vague and confusing. Not one but four great empires are assembled to form the backdrop for the local story of Judith: Assyria, Babylonia, Media, and Persia. The principal personages are either unknown or could not possibly have been contemporaries. Thus Judith has never been heard of anywhere else in the Bible. Nor has Arphaxad, king of the Medes. Nebuchadnezzar, who lived in the first half of the sixth century, is paired with Holofernes who lived in the second half of the fourth century. The place described as Bethulia is a phantom city. Its name is unknown. Its position corresponds exactly to no city in the region in which it is located by the author. Most implausible of all, the city is located in the territory of the Samaritans, the great postexilic enemies of the Jews. Throughout Persian times and up until its conquest by John Hyrcanus in 108 B.C., the hill country fronting on the plain of Esdraelon was occupied and controlled by the Samaritans. In addition, the critical events of the story, the beheading of Holofernes and the defeat of his army, have no attestation whatever outside the book of Judith. The recorded facts, on the contrary, indicate that Holofernes, far from suffering an ignominious death at the hand of a woman, returned safely from his Egyptian campaign and was later honored by his sovereign, Artaxerxes III.

Adding to the lack of verisimilitude are the book's chronological indications, which seem to have been thrown about in a manner calculated to discourage any attempt to pin down the actual date and background of the events narrated. For example, the first date recorded in the book (cf. translations based on the Greek) places Nebuchadnezzar in Nineveh in 592 B.C. (1:5), although Nineveh as a matter of historical fact was utterly destroyed twenty years earlier in 612 and remained a ruin for centuries. The second date in the book is given as 587 B.C. (2:1), the year Jerusalem was taken and the Temple destroyed. Despite this definite dating, the author clearly speaks about the return from the exile in 539 (cf. 5:23), an event forty-five years later. The use of Holofernes, who lived in the fourth century, as the immediate protagonist of Judith completes the chronological confusion and places the local events of the book against a background lacking all homogeneity. As a simple midrash, therefore, Judith would have been most disconcerting to its Jewish readers since it presented little verisimilitude and no homogeneity of historical background.

The case for Judith as an apocalyptic book

Since a lack of homogeneity and verisimilitude of historical background is thoroughly characteristic of apocalyptic midrash, Judith approaches the apocalyptic midrash in the same way that it subtly departs from the haggadic midrash. In addition, the theme, the purpose, and the symbolism of Judith are apocalyptic.

Theme. The basic theme of the apocalyptic literature is the certain victory of God over the forces of anti-God. The victory is the essential thing. The time element, which is entirely indefinite in Ezekiel 38–39, Zechariah 14 and Joel 3–4, and relatively indefinite in Daniel 7–12, is not essential.

In Judith, the basic theme is unquestionably the victory of God over the forces of anti-God. The author makes this clear by showing Nebuchadnezzar in direct opposition to God (cf. translations based on the Greek). He has Nebuchadnezzar speak of himself as "The Great King, the Lord of all the earth" (2:5; Vulgate 2:3). He has Holofernes tell how he "succeeded in destroying all the gods of the country, in order that all the nations should worship Nebuchadnezzar alone, and that all their tongues and tribes should call upon him as god" (3:8; Vulgate 3:13). In ch. 5, after telling how all the other nations of the earth had capitulated to Nebuchadnezzar, the author uses Achior, an Ammonite general, to set the stage for the battle between the forces of anti-God represented by Nebuchadnezzar and the forces of God represented by insignificant little Judah. When Achior warns Holofernes, "Their God will protect them and their God defend them," Holofernes responds with the words that pit Nebuchadnezzar against God: "What god is there except Nebuchadnezzar? He will put forth his strength and destroy them off the face of the earth, and their God will not save them" (6:2-3; Vulgate 5:27-29).

Purpose. In Judith as in all apocalyptic literature the purpose of the author is to encourage and reanimate the confidence of the people. This is more than evident in the speeches of Achior and Judith, in the description of the victory over Holofernes, and in the Canticle of Judith. And it is confidence in God to destroy the forces of anti-God, a sentiment characteristic of apocalyptic literature, that is the concluding sentiment in Judith's prayer just before she goes out to bring about the downfall of Holofernes and with him the powers of anti-God paganism: "Make your whole nation and every tribe to know and understand," Judith prays, "that you are God, the God of all power and might, and that the nation of Israel has no protector but you" (9:14; Vulgate 9:19). This in a word expresses the basic teaching purpose of the apocalyptic literature.

Symbolism. The principal reason for considering Judith an apocalyptic book is the marked resemblance of the symbolism of Judith to the basic symbolism of the apocalyptic literature. There are three points of comparison to be made, each of which brings Judith progressively closer to the camp of the apocalyptists. The three points are: (a) the vast army intent on destroying Israel and making paganism supreme throughout the earth; (b) the symbolic leader of the forces of paganism; (c) the conglomerate of world empires united to form a composite symbol of the forces of paganism opposed to God.

In Zechariah and Joel, the forces of anti-God are represented simply by the armies of the nations attempting to destroy Jerusalem, the city of God. In Ezekiel, the forces of anti-God are not only symbolized by an immense army, but a symbolic leader named Gog is provided as well. In Daniel, the forces of anti-God are symbolized by a conglomerate of world empires (the Babylonian, Median, Persian, and Greek-Seleucid empires) united in the colossus of Nebuchadnezzar's dream (Dan. 2), and by the four beasts who come up from the sea (Dan. 7). In addition, the symbolic leader of the forces of paganism is Nebuchadnezzar in Dan. 1–4 and "the little horn uttering blasphemies against God" in Dan. 7–12.

In Judith we find the vast army, the symbolic leader of the forces of paganism, and the conglomerate of world empires united to form a composite symbol of the forces of paganism opposed to God.

The author emphasizes the size of the army and its purpose in the very first chapters of the book. Nebuchadnezzar commands Holofernes: "When you go from my presence, you must take with you men confident in their strength to the number of a hundred and twenty thousand infantry and twelve thousand mounted men" (2:5; Vulgate 2:5-7). The purpose of the campaign is clearly defined in 3:8: "And Holofernes broke down all their frontier landmarks and cut down their groves, and he succeeded in destroying all the gods of the country, in order that all the nations should worship Nebuchadnezzar alone, and that all their tongues and tribes should call upon him as god" (Vulgate 3:13). The means and the intent of paganism are identical in Ez. 38–39; Dan. 2; 7–12; and in Judith.

The author presents Nebuchadnezzar as the symbolic leader of the forces of paganism by prescinding from him as an individual. He accomplishes this negatively by ignoring Nebuchadnezzar's remarkable feats as king and conqueror and positively by associating him with Holofernes who lived two centuries after him and by describing him as king of the Assyrians, conqueror of the Medes, served by a Persian army. Since it is well known that Nebuchadnezzar became for the Jews in postexilic times the enemy *par excellence* of God because of his destruction of Jerusalem and the Temple in 587, the author of Judith in presenting Nebuchadnezzar as the symbolic leader of the forces of paganism adopts a way of speaking that is definitely *de rigeur* in apocalyptic literature (cf. Zech. 5:5-11; Dan. 1–4; Apoc. 17:3-18).

The third feature of the basic symbolism of Judith that associates the book with the apocalyptic literature is the author's use of four great empires to symbolize the magnitude of the power of anti-God paganism. The four empires are Assyria, Babylon, Media, and Persia in that order. The number four is used because it designates universality (cf. Is. 11:12; Zech. 1:7; 6:5-8; also Gen. 4:10; Jer. 49:36; Mark 13:27; Apoc. 7:1). Thus Zechariah uses "four horns" to symbolize the powers of paganism that have destroyed Jerusalem (Zech. 1:18-21), and the author of Daniel unites four great empires — the Babylonian, Median, Persian, and Greek-Seleucid empires — to constitute the colossus of Nebuchadnezzar's dream (Dan. 2), that symbolizes the forces of anti-God paganism. The four beasts in Daniel 7 are used in the same way.

Readers have always wondered why the book of Judith portrays Nebuchadnezzar, the Babylonian, as king of the Assyrians. They have wondered as well why he is represented as having destroyed Arphaxad, the king of the Medes, and taken over Ecbatana, the capital of Media. Finally they have wondered why the author of Judith represents Nebuchadnezzar as served by a Persian army led by two famous Persian generals. The explanation lies in the use of apocalyptic symbolism similar to that of Daniel (ch. 2 and 7). The author of Judith united the four empires of Assyria, Babylon, Media, and Persia under the leadership of Nebuchadnezzar, the enemy *par excellence* of God, in order to form a composite symbol for the worldwide forces of anti-God. Thus Judith's conquest of Holofernes, the Persian leader of the army of Nebuchadnezzar, the Babylonian king of the Assyrians and conqueror of the Medes, represents God's conquest of the combined forces of anti-God, just as the stone from the mountain crushing the composite colossus of Nebuchadnezzar's dream represents God's conquest of the combined forces of anti-God in Daniel.

Lesser reasons for associating Judith with the apocalyptic literature are the following: (a) the location of the great battle in the plain of Esdraelon not far from Megiddo, where Jael conquered Sisera in the time of Judges, and where St. John in the Apocalypse (16:16) later placed the great battle between the forces of God and the forces of anti-God, the place "that is called in Hebrew Armageddon." (b) The book is not strictly pseudonymous, but Judith ("the Jewess") represents the nation rather than any real person (cf. 16:4; Vulgate 16:6 where Judith identifies herself with the nation). (c) Finally, there are numerous textual contacts of Judith with Daniel, Ezekiel, and Joel (cf. Dan. 1:8 and Jud. 12:2; Dan. 2:38 and Jud. 11:7; Dan. 3:1-5 and Jud. 3:8; Dan. 3:14-18 and Jud. 6:2; Dan. 3:34-36, 43-45 and Jud. 13:5; Dan. 11:28 and Jud. 9:13; Ez. 16; 20 and Jud. 5:5-21; Ez. 38—39 *passim*; Joel 2:17 and Jud. 7:29; Joel 4:1-5 and Jud. 16:17).

All things considered, then, Judith appears to have greater affinities with the apocalyptic midrash than with the haggadic midrash. Unlike Daniel, which is a prophetic apocalypse, Judith is more of a simple narrative or para-historical apocalypse after the manner of Ez. 38—39.

The origin of the Book of Judith

The exact dating of Judith is extremely problematical. The explicit mention of the Persians makes a *terminus a quo around* 350 B.C. reasonably certain. The mentality that would represent a king as aspiring to be god to his subjects takes the story out of Persian times and brings it down to the period following Alexander the Great, the first of the kings after 350 to aspire to divinity. The zeal for the observance of dietary laws and the Sabbath manifested by Judith (8:4-8; 11:12-14; 12:1-4) would appear to indicate a time when the Pharisaic influence was strong, a time therefore either during or after the Maccabean wars of 166-142. Judith's statement in 8:18, "There has not arisen in our age nor is there today a tribe or family or people or town of our stock that worships gods made with hands, as they did in former times. . . ," would point to a date after the Maccabean wars, since there was a good deal of apostasy and at least token idol worship in the time of the Syrian persecution of 167-164. The laying of the scene in the region of Samaria, territory that did not belong to Judah until the conquest of Samaria by John Hyrcanus in the year 108 B.C., appears to indicate a date sometime in the late second or early first century.

Such a late date would help to explain why the book was not included in the Jewish canon and why Josephus made no mention of it. It would also explain the fact that Judith was read on the feast of the Dedication, a feast instituted by Judas Maccabeus in 164 (cf. 1 Mac. 4) to celebrate the purification and re-dedication of the Temple profaned by Antiochus IV in 167.

Since the book appears to have been written to encourage Jews undergoing persecution, it is not improbable that it was written either during the persecution of the Jews by Antiochus IV in the years following 171, or what is more probable, during the persecution of the Jews in Egypt by Ptolemy VII in the years following 145. It is impossible to be more precise.

The original text of Judith has never been found. Peculiarities in the Greek version indicate that the book was originally written in Hebrew. The Vulgate translation of St. Jerome was based on an Aramaic version and took into account the readings of the Vetus Latina. The existing Greek versions are the most trustworthy.

The book is divided into two main parts: Part I (ch. 1–7) sets up the battle between the overpowering forces of paganism and helpless, little Israel. Part II (ch. 8–16) describes the defeat of the forces of paganism by the hand of the woman, Judith.

19

The Book of Wisdom

Written in Egypt around 100 B.C. by an Alexandrian Jew, the book of Wisdom is probably the last book of the Old Testament.[1] It is written in Greek and directed to the author's compatriots of the Egyptian Diaspora. Unlike Proverbs and Sirach, the author of Wisdom is not staid and professorial. He is colorful, enthusiastic, persuasive. He delights in the well chosen word and the memorable phrase. Unlike Job and Qoheleth, he is not weighed down by the problem of suffering or the restless yearning for the undefinable. He is cheerful, optimistic, buoyed up by the grandeur and beauty of his message, and evangelistic in its telling.

As the reader passes from the older wisdom books to the Wisdom of Solomon, he finds that he is still in the synagogue even though he has moved from Palestine to Egypt and from a distinctly Jewish to a distinctly Hellenistic atmosphere. The thought is more abstract, the speculation more philosophical, and the language more technical. The doctrine, nevertheless, is strictly Jewish and strongly biblical.

A brief outline of the book will make clear the author's theme, purpose, and audience, and perhaps indicate as well the period and occasion that gave rise to its composition.

[1] Cf. Murphy, *Seven Books of Wisdom*, 127-142; R. Siebeneck, "The Midrash of Wisdom 10-19," *CBQ* 22 (1960) 176-182.

The author divides his work into three main parts: Part I (ch. 1–5) deals with the vital importance of wisdom in determining the eternal destiny of men; Part II (ch. 6–9) treats of the origin, nature, and activities of wisdom, as well as the means to acquire it; Part III (ch. 10–19) provides a midrashic description of divine wisdom directing the destiny of Israel from Adam to the Exodus from Egypt.

The importance of wisdom

In Part I (ch. 1–5), the author contrasts the philosophy of life (2:1-20) and errors of the wicked (2:21-24) with the happy lot of the just, who are rewarded by God with eternal life (3:1-9; 5:3-5; 5:15-16), while the wicked are punished by God during their earthly life by dishonor and ill-fame (3:10–4:19) and by separation from God in the next life (4:20–5:23).

The author's description of the philosophy of life of the wicked (2:1-20), who are reproached for their "transgressions of the law" and for their "violations of our training" (2:12), suggests he is speaking about reprobate Jews who have succumbed to the allurements of Hellenism and given up their Jewish birthright. His description of the determination of the wicked to put the just to the test by revilement and torture and to condemn them to a shameful death (2:17-20) suggests as well that he writes at a time when faithful Jews are being persecuted. References to the passing away of the just as "an affliction . . . and utter destruction" (3:2-3) perhaps indicate that the persecution involved martyrdom.

The purpose of the author, therefore, in these chapters is to encourage and sustain the just in time of persecution by recalling to them the happy reward that awaits them after death. His doctrine of the future life is more refined than the doctrine of Daniel (12:2-3) and 2 Maccabees (7). "The souls of the just are in the hand of God . . . they are in peace . . . their hope is full of immortality" (3:1-4). The just man "is accounted among the sons of God . . . his lot is with the saints" (5:5). The same ideas are found in the "Manual of Discipline," one of the Dead Sea Scrolls discovered in Cave I in 1947: "Those whom God has chosen he has made an eternal possession, an inheritance in the lot of the holy ones, and he has united their assembly with the sons of heaven . . ." (1QS 11, 7-8).

The nature of wisdom

Part II (ch. 6–9) follows logically upon Part I. Since "justice is immortal" (1:15), and "he who despises wisdom and instruction is doomed" (3:11), it is of paramount importance that men should learn wisdom (6:1-12), because to observe wisdom's laws "is the basis for incorruptibility; and incorruptibility makes one close to God; thus the desire for wisdom leads up to a kingdom" (6:18-19).

Since wisdom is so vitally important, the author speaks first about the necessity of desiring wisdom "for the first step toward discipline is a very earnest desire for her" (6:17). He then goes on, posing as Solomon, the wisdom teacher *par excellence*, to describe wisdom (6:22–8:1).

In enumerating twenty one qualities of wisdom (3 x 7 = 21, the perfect number), the author betrays not only an acquaintance with Greek philosophical terms but a desire to impress upon his audience that there is nothing the philosophers might postulate concerning the world soul, the *nous* or *logos* of Plato, which cannot be found in wisdom, the attribute *par excellence* of the one true God.

The author's condescension to use Greek terminology in describing wisdom, without in any way prejudicing the purity of his monotheistic beliefs, is significant. When taken in context with a number of other statements regarding the pagans, it suggests the author had in mind a pagan as well as a Jewish audience.

Thus, by his use of Greek philosophical language, he shows there is nothing barbaric about Hebrew theological thought. In deference, moreover, to the feelings of pagan readers, he is careful to point out that God has mercy on all men and overlooks the sins of men "that they may repent," because he loves "all things that are" and "loathes nothing that he has made . . ." but rather rebukes "offenders little by little . . . that they may abandon their wickedness and believe" (11:23–12:2; cf. also 12:13-22).

In his little treatise on the foolishness of idolatry (13:1–15:17), he is adamant in his condemnations, but he is careful to suggest that "for these (some of the pagans) the blame is less; for they indeed have gone astray perhaps, though they seek God and wish to find him" (13:6).

There is, moreover, his implicit invitation to the pagans to seek out the Artisan of the universe and his assurance to them that God is good and merciful (13:1-9). All these are subtle indications that the author had in mind, if not the pagans in general, at least those among them who were sympathetic to the true religion and had perhaps become Jewish proselytes.

The author closes his description of wisdom with a brief reflection on the necessity of prayer for attaining so great and necessary a gift (8:17-21), followed by the beautiful prayer of Solomon for wisdom, the spiritual highpoint of the book (9:1-18).

Midrashic description of God's wisdom guiding Israel's history

The last section of the book is introduced by ch. 10, which reviews the dealings of wisdom with the patriarchs as a preparation for the concluding midrashic description of the Exodus miracles. The description is called midrashic because of the license the author takes in describing the events of the Exodus. A superficial comparison with the parallel sections in Exodus (ch. 7–18) and Numbers (ch. 10–21) will show the fantastic lengths to which the author has gone to dramatize the events of the Exodus (already sufficiently dramatic), and to draw from them the lessons he wished to teach his audience.

While such liberties are not congenial to modern tastes, the reader must remember that they are of the very nature of the midrashic literary form, a didactic form of writing developed from the preaching in the synagogues. It must be remembered as well that such license has always been allowed to preachers and has been limited only by the canons of contemporary good taste.

What is significant about the midrashic section of Wisdom is the attention paid to Egypt. The author quickly passes over Israel's history from Adam to Moses in fourteen verses of ch. 10. From 10:15 to the end of the book, he concerns himself almost entirely with Egypt, elaborating the story of the Exodus miracles to contrast God's protection of Israel with His punishment of the Egyptians. It is a sort of demonstration from history of the thesis developed more theoretically in ch. 1–5: "The souls of the just are in the hand of God, and no torment shall touch them" (3:1); the wicked on the contrary, God "shall strike down speechless and prostrate and rock them to their foundations" (4:10). The purpose of the demonstration is not only to show that God is on the side of the just, whom He has chosen and promised to protect, but that the vaunted superiority of the Egyptian, Hellenistic culture is vitiated in its very foundations by a foolish and senseless idolatry, which should be an affront to any thinking man (cf. especially 13:1–15:17).

The origin of the book

If our analysis has been correct, then the author of Wisdom writes to encourage his persecuted brethren in Egypt (ch. 2–3; 10–19), by showing them that true wisdom (ch. 6–9), which ensures real success (ch. 3–5), is found, not in Egyptian, Hellenistic culture, vitiated by idolatry (ch. 13–15), nor in purely material well-being (ch. 2), but in that wisdom which comes from God, is attained by prayer (ch. 6–9), and brings eternal life (ch. 3–5 *passim*).

The allusions to persecution (2:10-20; 5:1; 10:15; 15:14; 16:4; 17:2), in addition to the emphasis on Egyptian idolatry and on the victory of Israel over Egyptian persecution in the time of the Exodus, gives weight to the opinion that the book was occasioned by the persecution of the Egyptian

Jews in the time of Ptolemy VII (145-116) and Ptolemy VIII (116-80). Sometime during this period an unknown wisdom writer composed the book of Wisdom to encourage his persecuted brethren just as at an earlier time and in similar circumstances an unknown apocalyptic writer composed the book of Daniel for a similar end.

Wisdom, the bridge between the testaments

The humanism and the universalism of the book of Wisdom, in addition to its extraordinarily refined personification of wisdom, make the book a natural bridge between the Old and the New Testaments.

When St. John comes to write his Gospel, he will develop themes already opened up by the author of Wisdom: the way of life and the way of death, the continual warfare between the light and the darkness, the ultimate and certain victory of the light despite the apparent success of the darkness. For his Trinitarian teaching he will reach back to Wisdom for many an illustration and many a technical term (cf. John 1:1, 18 and Wis. 8:3; 9:4; John 1:3, 10 and Wis. 7:21; 8:6; 9:1, 9; John 5:20 and Wis. 8:4; 9:9, 10, 11, 17; John 3:16-17 and Wis. 1:6; 7:23; 11:24, 26; John 14:23; 16:27 and Wis. 7:28; John 17:3 and Wis. 15:3).

St. Paul will do the same and for the same purpose (cf. Heb. 1:3 and Wis. 7:26; Col. 1:15 and Wis. 7:26; Rom. 1:18-20 and Wis. 13:3-5; Rom. 1:21-32 and Wis. 14:22-31; Rom. 2:4 and Wis. 11:23, 26; 12:2, 10, 19; Rom. 9:20 and Wis. 12:12; Rom. 9:21 and Wis. 15:7; Eph. 6:14-17 and Wis. 5:17-20).

The reader will realize he has stepped on to the bridge between the testaments when he reads the words of Wisdom: "For to know you well is complete justice, and to know your might is the root of immortality" (Wis. 15:3). He will realize he is over the bridge and on the other side when he reads the words of St. John: "Now this is everlasting life, that they may know thee, the only true God, and him whom thou has sent, Jesus Christ" (John 17:3).

20

Psalms Related to the Didactic Literature

Since the wisdom writers are essentially teachers, intent upon persuading their readers to adopt a way of life regulated by the tenets of wisdom teaching, it is not surprising that they should make use of the psalm form as a didactic vehicle. As practical men dedicated to the art of teaching they could hardly have been ignorant of the pedagogical value of regularly recited prayers. A prayer like a slogan is the subtlest and shortest path to the mind and the heart. It is for this reason that the didactic value of the liturgy has always been immense. It was this didactic value that prompted the wisdom teachers to compose their psalms.

The aim of the wisdom psalmists is not only to teach their readers the art of praising God and living a life that will itself praise God, but to make of their prayers pious works which will themselves praise God. As the name implies, the wisdom or didactic psalms are concerned with teaching. Their contents, like the teaching of the sages, are moralistic and didactic and deal with the practical side of life, not however without the expected emphasis on true wisdom as the fear of God.

The didactic psalms are characterized by a frequent use of exhortations, proverbs, and sayings. But since the wisdom psalmists generally use the different psalm forms already in existence, the student cannot readily use the form or structure of a wisdom psalm to distinguish it from other psalm types.

The distinction is not always easy to make. It can be made, however, on the basis of the didactic tone that runs through the psalm. Whether the wisdom psalm is in the form of a hymn (e.g., Pss. 92 and 105) a thanksgiving psalm (e.g., Ps. 34), or a supplication (e.g., Ps. 14), there is always discernible a didactic tone, which indicates the intent of the psalmist.

In some few cases the didactic intent is stated in the introduction (e.g., Ps. 49 and 78). In several psalms the use of the alphabetic form (beginning each verse or group of verses with successive letters of the Hebrew alphabet) is an indication of didactic intent (e.g., Pss. 34; 111; 112; 119).

For the most part the student will have to determine the didactic nature of the psalm from the subject matter and from the psalmist's subtle invitations to his readers to learn a lesson or lead a life regulated by wisdom.

The didactic psalms are the response of the wisdom teachers to the request, "Teach us to pray," a request made at a later time to the Wisdom Teacher *par excellence* and rewarded by the giving of the most excellent of prayers, the "Our Father" (Luke 11:1-4). The reader must never forget that the wisdom psalms are prayers.

Authors for varying reasons consider the following psalms didactic: Pss. 1; 14; 15; 19; 32; 34; 37; 49; 50; 52; 73; 92; 94; 101; 105; 106; 111; 112; 114; 119; 127; 128; 133; 135; 136; 139; the Canticle of Anna (1 Sam. 2:1-10), the Canticle of Tobit (13:1-9), the Canticle of Judith (16:15-21), the Canticles of Sirach (51:1-12; 51:13-30), the Magnificat (Luke 1:46-55), and the Benedictus (Luke 1:68-79).

For convenience the didactic psalms may be divided into: (a) those that utilize Israel's history for didactic purposes (Pss. 78; 105; 106; 111; 114; 135; 136); (b) those that extol God's law, in the sense of 'teaching' or 'revelation' (Pss. 19; 119); (c) those that deal with religious wisdom after the manner of the books of Proverbs and Sirach in the sense of "fear of the Lord" as defined in Prov. 1:1-4 (Pss. 1; 15; 32; 50; 52; 92; 112; 128; 133); (d) those that deal with the problem of retribution in relation to God's justice after the manner of Job and Qoheleth (Pss. 37; 49; 73); (e) those that utilize the format of the thanksgiving psalms for didactic purposes (Ps. 34, the Canticles of Anna, Tobit, and Judith in the Old Testament, and the Magnificat and the Benedictus in the New Testament).

The psalms utilizing Israel's history for didactic purposes have already been treated (cf. p. 157ff). Pss. 19; 1; 37; 49; 73; 34 will provide sample treatment of the remaining groups of didactic psalms.

Theme	A didactic hymn extolling the glory of God, manifested physically in the heavens, intellectually in the law (divine revelation).
Back-ground	The same combination of themes stressing God the creator and God the revealer is found in Sir. 24:1-31; 43:1-12 and in Pss. 33 and 93.

Division	A. The voiceless heavens sing a song without words in praise of God.
	    1. Day and night pour forth their praise of God (vv. 2-5).
	    2. In its own special way the sun praises God (vv. 6-7).
	B. As the sun illuminates the physical universe, so the law (God's revelation) enlightens the mind and heart of man.
	    1. The perfection of the divine law (vv. 8-11).
	    2. The psalmist's prayer for grace to observe and live by God's law (vv. 12-15).

N.B.	Part A is a perfectly baptized Babylonian hymn to the sun-god, Shamash, to which Part B, a typical wisdom psalm in praise of the law, has been added. Castellino prefers to see the whole psalm as a composition, using earlier pagan psalms, designed to express the idea: "Just as the heavens and creation have a clear language and announce the majesty, power, and wisdom of God, so the 'law' is the other direct language, not typical, explicit, not requiring the will of God, revealing at the same time the other interpretation, which expresses to man the divine thought attributes of wisdom, goodness, majesty, etc." (p. 452).

v. 2 *the heavens declare:* all join in a concert of praise of God their creator, praising Him the way the work of an artist's hands praises the artist. In Ps. 8 these works of creation elicit praise even from infants. Here they are personified as if they themselves were praising God.

v. 3 *day to day . . . night to night:* the concert of praise is ceaseless since each day passes it on to the next and each night to the following night. We might expect the day to pass on the message to the oncoming night, but according to oriental cosmogony night and day had each a special place to which they returned at the end of their daily tenure (cf. Job 38:14). Thus when the day gets to the home for days it passes on the message to the next day, and the night to the next night.

v. 4 *not a word:* the praise is voiceless and yet, paradoxically (v. 5), it is heard throughout the universe. Some translations (e.g., Vg, LXX, Knox, CCD) understand this in the sense: "There is not a word of this message that is not intelligible." This makes good sense but the words of the psalm appear rather to express the intelligibility of the message despite its lack of words. Podechard has the best translation: "Without words or sound . . . their message goes out to the ends of the earth."

v. 5c *there:* i.e., in the heavens, where God has placed a tent for the sun (personified as a bridegroom going forth from his nuptial tent, Shamash, the sun-god in the Babylonian hymn, had a bride named Ai). The sun is described as a giant running his course, because in the Babylonian hymn he is considered a hero who goes forth each day to conquer the darkness and the cold of night, so that as a result nothing escapes his heat (v. 7c).

v. 8 *the law of the Lord:* the law is perfect, steadfast, clear, giving men wisdom, joy, and truth. In the psalm, law means *torah*, the divine teaching and revelation. The author is writing before the Pharisees and the Scribes of New Testament times have made the law of God odious by their burdensome regulations and narrow legalism. To the psalmist the law is something precious, the source of great peace and joy. It is for him what Jesus said of His teaching: "The truth will make you free."

v. 12 *though your servant is careful:* the psalmist professes his zeal for keeping the law of God, but he realizes he cannot be perfect and asks God (v. 13) to forgive him his sins of inadvertance, i.e., ritual sins as in Lev. 4:13-14; 5:17.

v. 14 *from wanton sin:* the great sin, or true sin in our sense, is a turning away of the will from God and is contrasted here with the legal sins of inadvertance (cf. Num. 15: 23-30).

v. 15 *my redeemer:* the psalmist calls on God to be his *Goel* or redeemer as in the book of Ruth (cf. Ruth 4; Is. 41:14; 43:14). The *goel* was that near relative who had special obligations toward his kinsman, e.g., avenging his death or injury, preserving his property rights, keeping his family line intact, and ransoming him from slavery.

Psalm 1

Theme   A didactic religious wisdom psalm describing the happy lot of the just man and the unhappy lot of the wicked.

Back-ground   As in Proverbs (4:10-27) the psalmist has a simple and undisturbed faith in God's justice. The problems of Job and Qoheleth are not considered.

Division   1. The way and the reward of the just man (vv. 1-3).
2. The way and the punishment of the wicked (vv. 4-6).

v. 1 *nor walks in the way of sinners:* "way" is a frequent hebraism to signify a man's mode of living and acting. The just man's avoidance of evil and evil men is described negatively in a gradation: (a) he does not follow their counsel or advice; (b) does not adopt their mode of life; (c) does not settle down with them permanently.

v. 2 *but delights in the law of the Lord:* a positive description of the just man. He finds his delight in God's law and like a wisdom teacher meditates upon it day and night (cf. Sir. 6:37). As in the wisdom books in general, law is not to be understood in the restricted sense of positive law, but in the larger sense of that great law governing and relating all things to God, in a word the wisdom of God given to men.

v. 3 *like a tree:* the simile of the just man as like to a tree planted by running water which insures its growth, fruitfulness, and longevity is based almost word for word on Jer. 17:7-8, but is a popular simile throughout the Scriptures (cf. Ez. 17:3; 19:10; Job 29:19; Wis. 4:35; Pss. 52:8; 92:13).

v. 4 *they are like chaff:* like the chaff or short straw (the light pod or husk inside of which the heavier grain is found and which at threshing time is carried off by the wind while the heavier grain falls to the ground), the life of the wicked is short and transitory in contrast to the life of the just man (cf. Wis. 5:14).

v. 5 *in judgment the wicked shall not stand:* the psalmist simply states his conviction that God who watches over the lot of the just man (v. 6) will judge and punish the wicked man. There is no indication of where or when the judgment will take place, simply that it will take place, that there will be a reckoning. The whole psalm seems to have been written as an encouragement for the just man, who is called "blessed" not so much on the basis of his present state, as on the perfect confidence of the psalmist in the eventual working out of God's justice.

Psalm 37

Theme

A didactic psalm urging the popular solution of the problem of retribution: God in due time rewards the just and punishes the wicked.

Background

The psalmist faces the same problem as Jeremiah (12:1-6) and Job: Why do the wicked prosper? He does not progress beyond the simple faith of Ps. 1, the books of Proverbs and Sirach, and the friends of Job, but he does face up to the problem. What stands out is not the psalmist's solution, but his indomitable faith and heroic patience in the face of so difficult a question. He is convinced of the truth of the beatitude: "Blessed are the meek, for they shall possess the land" (Matthew 5:4).

Division

The psalm is a collection of wisdom sayings in alphabetic form with two verses to each letter of the alphabet, but without clear and fast divisions. Although the break in thought is not always clear, the psalmist appears to treat four aspects of his general theme:

Vv. 1-11 Let the just not envy the wicked, for in due time God will punish them.

Vv. 12-20 Let the just not fear the power of the wicked, for in due time they will be punished.

Vv. 21-31 Let the just remember that in the long run God will reward them and punish the wicked.

Vv. 32-40 Let the just not fear the wicked, for God watches over the good to reward them and save them from the power of the wicked.

v. 1 *be not vexed:* the psalmist fears that the just will be tempted by the prosperity of the wicked to follow their example. He feels compelled to warn against such a mistake (cf. vv. 7c, 8, 16-17; Prov. 3:31; 34:1; Ps. 73:2-3, 10-15).

v. 7 *leave it to the Lord:* the psalmist's practical solution and advice is: "Leave it to the Lord, and wait for him."

v. 12 *the wicked man plots against the just:* the psalmist knows well the hatred of the wicked for the just (cf. vv. 14 and 32; Wis. 2:12-20), but he reminds the just man that God laughs at the wicked (collective throughout), because he sees what the wicked refuse to see — the coming day of judgment (v. 13) and the application of the law of talion (v. 15).

v. 21 *the wicked man borrows:* the idea, similar to that expressed in Deut. 15:6; 28:12; 44, is that the wicked will be so poor they will not be able to pay back what they have borrowed. The just on the contrary will be sufficiently well off to be able to dispense charity to others, because those whom God blesses will possess the land (v. 22).

v. 25 *neither in my youth:* the psalmist's appeal to his own experience would not have convinced Job or Qoheleth, but it is at least generally if not universally true, that even in this life the good are, all things considered, better off than the wicked. The psalmist has seen the just man suffer (v. 24), but he has never seen him really abandoned by God. The remainder of the psalm is repetition.

Psalm 49

Theme A didactic psalm dealing with the enigmatic prosperity of the wicked, which appears to contradict the justice of God.

The psalmist is concerned with the same problem as
Job and Pss. 37 and 73, i.e., the apparent failure of God's
justice. His solution, that death makes the difference,
goes beyond Job and Ps. 37, but it does not reach the
clear solutions of Wis. 1–5 and the New Testament.

Division

An introduction inviting all to hear the solution of an
enigma (vv. 2-5).
1. The wicked, however great their wealth, cannot escape
   death (vv. 6-13).
2. Not only will the wicked die, but their death will be in
   contrast with the fate of the just (vv. 14-20).

v. 5 *my ear is intent upon a proverb:* the proverb or mashal
the author refers to is expressed in the refrain (vv. 13
and 21). The comparison in vv. 13 and 21 with thought-
less beasts describes the state of the wicked rich. A fuller
understanding of the proverb is aimed at in the psalm,
but the psalmist leaves to the reader's sagacity the task of
divining its full truth. *to the music of the harp:* the psalmist mentions the music of the lyre (used at times by the
prophets to attune themselves for inspiration, cf. 1 Sam.
10:5 and 2 Kings 3:15) to indicate he is about to reveal
something new under the influence of inspiration.

v. 6 *why should I fear:* the scandal given by the apparent divine injustice seen in the prosperity of the rich makes the
poor man fear there is no justice (cf. Ps. 73:2-3). The
psalmist's answer in vv. 7-13 is that death, which comes
to all, brings justice.

v. 12 *tombs are their home forever:* the rich are destined for
the tomb even though territories or great estates are
named for them. It is precisely in not seeing this that they
are similar to the dumb beasts (v. 13).

v. 14 *this is the way:* the psalmist contrasts the death of the
wealthy wicked (vv. 14-15) with his own fate (that of
the just). Death therefore changes everything, leading
the wicked to sheol forever (cf. v. 20).

v. 16 *God will redeem:* the good on the contrary will be freed
from sheol and taken up to God. The precise meaning
of the verb "to take up" is not certain from the context.

In Ps. 18:14 it refers to "saving from death." In Gen. 5:24 and 2 Kings 2:9 it refers to the assumption to God respectively of Enoch and Elijah. It is possible that the psalmist is saying that the just will be saved from an early and sudden death. It is also possible that he is saying they will be taken out of sheol by God and that it will not be for them as it will be for the wicked a place where "they will not see the light forever" (v. 20). In favor of the latter interpretation is the promise of something special mentioned in the introduction (vv. 2-5) and the whole thought content of the psalm. The psalmist would otherwise be offering small consolation to the poor, since all men eventually die. Moreover, he in no place explicitly assigns an "early" death to the wicked.

v. 17 *fear not:* In vv. 17-21 the psalmist repeats what he has already said in vv. 6-13.

Psalm 73

Theme	A didactic psalm dealing with the enigmatic prosperity of the wicked, which appears to contradict the justice of God.
Background	The psalmist treats the same problem as Job and Pss. 37 and 49, but his solution is more profound; not this life, but the next in which the wicked will perish and the good will be rewarded by God, decides man's lot.
Division	Introduction: the psalmist believes in God's goodness, but his faith has been severely tested by the prosperity of the wicked (vv. 1-3).

1. The inexplicable prosperity of the wicked and the scandal it occasions for the faithful (vv. 4-12).
2. The psalmist's struggles to solve the problem of retribution (vv. 13-17).
3. The miserable fate of the wicked (vv. 18-22).
4. The glorious destiny of the just (vv. 23-28).

v. 1ff *how good:* before admitting the theoretical doubts he has had concerning God's justice, the psalmist anticipates his solution by professing his firm belief in God's goodness. In vv. 2-3 he admits that the prosperity of the wicked was a temptation for him to lose faith in God's goodness.

v. 4ff *for they are in no pain:* the psalmist describes vividly the god-like existence of the comfortable, independent, and godless rich. They do not know suffering (v. 4a) or troubles (v. 5). They are proud and violent (v. 6). Conscienceless (their hearts are so surrounded by fat that they become hardened and insensible to the voice of conscience), they vaunt whatever capricious desires or thoughts come to their minds without fear of consequences (v. 7). They say whatever pleases them, even going so far as to blaspheme (vv. 8-9).

v. 10ff *so my people:* the poor, seeing wickedness and prosperity going hand in hand, are tempted to lose their fear of divine justice and imitate the apparently unpunished and wicked rich. They are tempted to wonder whether God really knows what is going on in His world (v. 11).

v. 13ff *is it but in vain:* the psalmist rhetorically asks if his innocence is vain. (*washed . . . as an innocent man* is a reference to the washing of hands as a solemn protestation of one's innocence, cf. Deut. 21:6 and Ps. 26:6). If he even thought of speaking as the wicked do (in vv. 8, 9, 11), he would be unfaithful to the way of life of the pious sons of God (v. 15).

v. 16f *though I tried to understand:* Like Jeremiah and Job, he could not fathom the workings of God's providence, and the attempt to reconcile God's justice with the prosperity of the wicked was burdensome to him until he entered into the "counsels of God" and understood the fate of the wicked, thus arriving at the solution (v. 17). In the American Bible note, *till I entered the sanctuary of God* is interpreted to mean "in spirit the psalmist penetrated God's heavenly court." Latest evidence indicates that *the sanctuary* hardly signifies the Temple, but rather the divine counsels which form as it were the intimate sanctuary of God. In any case the psalmist claims to have a solution to his most vexing problem.

v. 18ff *on a slippery road:* the way of the wicked is slippery and God dashes them into a calamitous and sudden fall (cf.

Wis. 4:17—5:15), their life ending as swiftly as a dream (vv. 18-20). The present realization of this makes the psalmist conscious of his ignorant simplicity in the past (vv. 21-22).

v. 23ff *yet with you I shall always be:* in contrast to the downfall of the wicked and their deprivation of God is the glorious destiny of the just man, which is to be always with God (v. 23), to be guided by God's counsel and taken up finally with Him in glory (v. 24).

v. 25ff *·whom else have I in heaven:* the psalmist concludes with a rapturous description of what it means to him to have God as his reward.

Psalm 34

Theme

A didactic thanksgiving psalm describing the rewards God bestows on those who fear Him.

Background

Allusions to Deutero-Isaiah, similarity to Proverbs, and emphasis on wisdom teaching suggest the psalm is the composition of a postexilic wisdom teacher.

Division

1. The psalmist gives thanks to God and invites the faithful to join him (vv. 2-4).
2. A description of how God heard his prayer and saved him in a time of troubles (vv. 5-11).
3. Wisdom's exhortation to her sons to live, and reap the rewards of a good life (vv. 12-23).

v. 3b *the lowly will hear:* the term "humble" is not meant in the Christian sense of humble as opposed to proud, but in the sense of obedient and submissive to the will of God. It is a quasi-technical term co-terminous for the most part with the "poor of the land," i.e., those God-fearing Israelites who suffer patiently the injustice of men while awaiting vindication by a just and loving God. It is of this group that our Lord speaks when He says: "Blessed are the poor in spirit."

v. 5ff *I sought the Lord:* as in the typical thanksgiving psalm (Pss. 115—116; 66:13-20), the psalmist describes how he prayed in time of peril and was heard and saved by God (vv. 5 and 7) and presents his case to his readers for their encouragement (v. 6). The psalmist's own case is immediately seized upon to teach a wisdom lesson, viz., the protection afforded those who "fear the Lord" (vv. 8-11).

v. 12ff *come, children:* after the manner of Proverbs (1:8; 2:1; 5:7), the psalmist addresses his disciples as "sons" and takes as his theme "the fear of the Lord" (cf. Prov. 1:7; 2:5), which will bring life (v. 13), provided they avoid sins of the tongue (v. 14; cf. Prov. 4:24; 13:3, 5; Sir. 28: 13-16), and seek peace by avoiding evil and doing good to their neighbor (v. 15).

v. 16ff *the Lord has eyes:* the practice of good assures happiness because God hears the prayers of the just (v. 16) but turns away from the wicked (v. 17).

v. 18ff *when the just cry out:* the psalmist continues describing God's solicitude for the just. He hears their prayers (v. 18), is near to save them (v. 19), even when they are in the midst of many evils (v. 20).

v. 21ff *he watches:* the psalmist closes by repeating in different words what he has already said, contrasting God's care for the just (v. 21) with the punishment of the wicked (v. 22).

A Select Bibliography

Introduction to the Old Testament

Anderson, B. W. *Understanding the Old Testament.* Englewood Cliffs, New Jersey: Prentice-Hall, 1966.

Bentzen, A. *Introduction to the Old Testament.* 2 vols. Copenhagen. G. E. C. Gad, 1948.

Eissfeldt, O. *The Old Testament: an Introduction.* Nashville: Abingdon Press, 1968.

Fohrer, G. *Introduction to the Old Testament.* Nashville: Abingdon Press, 1968.

Robert, A., and Feuillet, A. (edd.). *Introduction a la Bible.* 2 vols. Tournai: Desclee, 1959.

Weiser, A. *The Old Testament: Its Formation and Development.* New York: Association Press, 1961.

Archaeology

Albright, W. F. *The Archaelogoy of Palestine.* Baltimore: Penguin Books, 1960.

————. *Archaeology and the Religion of Israel.* Baltimore: Johns Hopkins Press, 1953.

Finegan, J. *Light from the Ancient Past.* Princeton: Princeton Univ. Press, 1959.

Kenyon, K. *Archaeology in the Holy Land.* New York: F. A. Praeger, 1960.

Kramer, S. N. *History Begins at Sumer.* Garden City, New York: Doubleday, 1959.

Pritchard, J. *Archaeology and the Old Testament.* Princeton: Princeton Univ. Press, 1958.

Woolley, D. L. *Ur of the Chaldees.* New York: Norton, 1965.

Wright, G. E. *Biblical Archaeology.* Philadelphia: Westminster Press, 1957.

Geography

Baly, D. A. *The Geography of the Bible.* New York: Harper & Row, rev. ed., 1974.

Grollenberg, L. *Shorter Atlas of the Bible.* London: Nelson, 1959.

Smith, G. A. *The Historical Geography of the Holy Land.* London: Collins, 1935, rep. 1966.

Wright, G. E., and Filson, F. V. *The Westminster Historical Atlas to the Bible.* rev. ed.; Philadelphia: Westminster Press, 1956.

History

Albright, W. F. *From the Stone Age to Christianity*. New York: Doubleday Anchor Books, 1957.
Bright, J. *A History of Israel*. Philadelphia: Westminster, 1972.
de Vaux, R. *Ancient Israel*. New York: McGraw-Hill, 1961.
Foerster, W. *From the Exile to Christ*. Philadelphia: Fortress, 1964.
Noth, M. *The History of Israel*. New York: Harper & Row, rev. 1960.
Olmstead, A. T. *History of the Persian Empire*. Chicago: Univ. of Chicago Press, 1948.
Reicke, B. *The New Testament Era*. Philadelphia: Fortress, 1968.
Schedl, C. *History of the Old Testament*. Staten Island: Alba House, 1973.
Tcherikover, V. *Hellenistic Civilization and the Jews*. Philadelphia: Jewish Publication Soc. of America, 1961.

Theology

de Vaux, R. *Ancient Israel*. New York: McGraw-Hill, 1961.
Dentan, R. C. *Preface to Old Testament Theology*. New Haven: Yale Univ. Press, 1950.
Eichrodt, W. *Theology of the Old Testament*. 2 vols. Philadelphia: Westminster, 1961.
McKenzie, J. L. *A Theology of the Old Testament*. New York: Doubleday, 1974.
Robinson, H. W. *The Religious Ideas of the Old Testament*. London: Gerald Duckworth and Co., Ltd., 1956.
_____. *The Cross in the Old Testament*. Philadelphia: Westminster, 1955.
Rowley, H. *The Faith of Israel*. Philadelphia: Westminster, 1957.
Young, E. J. *The Study of Old Testament Theology Today*. Westwood, New Jersey: Fleming H. Revell Co., 1959.
von Rad, G. *Old Testament Theology*. 2 vols. New York: Harper & Row, 1962.
Vriezen, Th. *An Outline of Old Testament Theology*. Oxford: Blackwell, 1958.
Wright, G. E. *The Old Testament against its Environment*. London: SCM Press, 1950.
_____. *God Who Acts*. London: SCM Press, 1952.

Reference Guides

Glanzman, G. S., and Fitzmyer, J. A. *An Introductory Bibliography for the Study of Scripture*. Westminster: Newman, 1961.
Hartman, L. *The Encyclopedic Dictionary of the Bible*. New York: McGraw-Hill, 1964.
McKenzie, J. L. *Dictionary of the Bible*. Milwaukee: Bruce, 1965.
Pritchard, J. B. (ed.). *The Ancient Near Eastern Texts*. Princeton: Princeton Univ. Press, 1965.
_____. *The Ancient Near East in Pictures*. Princeton: Princeton Univ. Press, 1954.

Commentaries in Series

Albright, W. F., and Freedman, D. N. (eds.). *The Anchor Bible*. Garden City, New York: Doubleday & Company, Inc.

Briggs, C. A., Driver, S. R., and Plummer, A. (eds.). *The International Critical Commentary*. New York: Scribner's, 1895-1951.

Brown, R., Fitzmyer, J. A., and Murphy, R. E. (eds.). *The Jerome Biblical Commentary*. Englewood Cliffs: Prentice-Hall, 1968.

Fuller, R. C., Johnston, L., and Kearns, D. (eds.). *A New Catholic Commentary on Holy Scripture*. London: Nelson, 1969.

Heidt, W. G., Stuhlmueller, C., Sullivan, K., and Ahern, B-M. (eds.). *Old Testament Reading Guide*. 31 vols. Collegeville: The Liturgical Press.

Literary Analysis

Ellis, P. F. *The Yahwist: The Bible's First Theologian*. Notre Dame: Fides, 1969. 1-146.

Frank, H. T. and Reed, W. L. (eds.). *Translating and Understanding the Old Testament*. Fest. H. G. May. Nashville: Abingdon, 1970.

Habel, N. *Literary Criticism of the Old Testament*. Philadelphia: Fortress, 1971.

Hahn, H. *The Old Testament in Modern Research*. Philadelphia: Fortress, 1966.

Hayes, J. H. (ed.). *Old Testament Form Criticism*. San Antonio: Trinity Univ. Press, 1974.

Koch, K. *The Growth of Biblical Tradition*. New York: Scribner, 1968.

Rast, W. E. *Tradition History and the Old Testament*. Philadelphia: Fortress, 1972.

Tucker, G. M. *Form Criticism of the Old Testament*. Philadelphia: Fortress, 1971.

The Priestly Theologian

Brueggemann, W. "The Kerygma of the Priestly Writers" ZAW, 84 (1972), 397-414.

Coats, G. W. *Rebellion in the Wilderness*. Nashville: Abingdon, 1968.

Cross, F. M. "The Priestly Tabernacle" *Biblical Archaeologist*, 10 (1947), 45-68.

Elliott, J. H. *The Elect and the Holy: An Exegetical Examination of 1 Peter 2:4-10 and the Phrase basileion hierateuma*. Leiden: Brill, 1966.

Hayes, J. H. (ed.). *Old Testament Form Criticism*. San Antonio: Trinity Univ. Press, 1974.

Johnson, M. D. *The Purpose of the Biblical Genealogies*. 1969.

Maertens, T. *A Feast in Honor of Yahweh*. Notre Dame: Fides, 1965.

McEvenue, S. E. *The Narrative Style of the Priestly Writer*. Rome: Pont. Biblical Institute Press, 1971.

Noth, M. *The Laws in the Pentateuch and Other Studies*. Philadelphia: Fortress Press, 1967.

————. *Leviticus*. Philadelphia: Westminster, 1965.

————. *Numbers*. Philadelphia: Westminster, 1969.

Otto, R. *The Idea of the Holy*. Oxford: Oxford Univ. Press, 1970.

Plastaras, J. *The God of Exodus*. Milwaukee: Bruce, 1966.

Snaith, N. H. *The Distinctive Ideas of the Old Testament*. New York: Schocken, 1964.

von Rad, G. *Old Testament Theology*. Vol. I, 223-279. New York: Harper & Row, 1962.

Westermann, C. *The Genesis Account of Creation*. "Facet Books"; Philadelphia: Fortress, 1964.

The Yahwist Theologian

Blenkinsopp, J. "Theme and Motif in the Succession History (2 Sam. XI 2ff) and the Yahwist Corpus" *Supplements to Vetus Testamentum*, 15 (1966), 44-57.

Brueggemann, W. "David and His Theologian" *Catholic Biblical Quarterly*, 30 (1968), 156-181.

————. *In Man We Trust*. Richmond: John Knox, 1972.

Calderone, P. *Dynastic Oracle and Suzerainty Treaty*. Logos; Manila: Loyola House of Studies, 1966.

Clements, R. *Abraham and David. Studies in Biblical Theology*. Naperville: Allenson, 1967.

Coats, G. W. "The Joseph Story and Ancient Wisdom: "A Reappraisal" *Catholic Biblical Quarterly*, 35 (1973), 285-297.

Cross, F. M. *Canaanite Myth and Hebrew Epic*. Cambridge: Harvard Univ. Press, 1973.

Daube, D. *The Exodus Pattern in the Bible*. "All Souls Studies"; London: Faber & Faber, 1963.

Ellis, P. F. *The Yahwist: The Bible's First Theologian*. Notre Dame: Fides, 1969.

Flanagan, J. W. "Court History or Succession Document? A Study of 2 Samuel 9-20 and 1 Kings 1-2" *Journal of Biblical Literature*, 91 (1972), 172-218.

Kirk, G. S. *Homer and the Epic*. Cambridge: Cambridge Univ. Press, 1965.

Leach, E. *Genesis as Myth and Other Essays*. London: Jonathan Cape, 1969.

Lohfink, N. "The Song of Victory at the Red Sea" *The Christian Meaning of the Old Testament*. Milwaukee: Bruce, 1968.

Lord, A. B. *The Singer of Tales*. Cambridge: Harvard University Press, 1960.

Maly, E. *The World of David and Solomon*. Englewood Cliffs, New Jersey: Prentice-Hall, 1966.

Miller, P. D. *The Divine Warrior in Early Israel*. Harvard Semitic Monographs; Cambridge: Harvard Univ. Press, 1973.

Moscati, S. *The Face of the Ancient Orient*. Garden City, New York: Doubleday, 1962.

Nielsen, E. *Oral Tradition. Studies in Biblical Theology*. Naperville: Allenson, 1954.

Noth, M. *A History of Pentateuchal Traditions*. Englewood Cliffs: Prentice-Hall, 1972.

Speiser, E. *Genesis. Anchor Bible*. Garden City, New York: Doubleday, 1964.

————. "The Wife-Sister Motif in the Patriarchal Narratives," *Biblical and Other Studies*, ed. A. Altmann. Cambridge: Harvard Univ. Press, 1963.

von Rad, G. "The Joseph Story and Ancient Wisdom" *The Problem of the Hexateuch and Other Essays.* New York: McGraw-Hill, 1966.

———. *Genesis.* Philadelphia: Westminster, 1961.

Whybray, R. N. "The Joseph Story and Pentateuchal Criticism" *Vetus Testamentum,* 18 (1968), 522-528.

———. *The Succession Narrative: A Study of II Sam. 9-20 and I Kings 1 and 2. Studies in Biblical Theology.* Naperville: Allenson, 1968.

The Elohist Theologian

Derousseaux, L. *La Crainte de Dieu dans l'Ancien Testament.* Paris: Cerf, 1970.

Dion, H. M. "The Patriarchal Traditions and the Literary Form Old Testament 'Oracle of Salvation'" *Catholic Biblical Quarterly,* 29 (1967), 198-206.

Fretheim, T. E. "The Jacob Traditions" *Interpretation,* 26 (1972), 419-436.

Jenks, A. W. *The Elohist and North Israelite Traditions.* Dissertation; Harvard University, Cambridge, Mass., 1965, available in microfilm.

Maly, E. "Genesis 12: 10-20; 20: 1-18; 26: 7-11 and the Pentateuchal Question" *Catholic Biblical Quarterly,* 18 (1956), 255-262.

LaVerdiere, E. A. "The Elohist 'E'" *The Bible Today,* 55 (October, 1971), 427-433.

Noth, M. *A History of the Pentateuchal Traditions.* Englewood Cliffs: Prentice-Hall, 1972. 35-36; 38-41; 223-235.

Wolff, H. W. "The Elohistic Fragments in the Pentateuch" *Interpretation,* 26 (1972), 158-173.

The "D" Theologian of Original Deuteronomy

Baltzer, K. *The Covenant Formulary.* Philadelphia: Fortress Press, 1971.

Beyerlin, W. *Origins and History of the Oldest Sinaitic Traditions.* Oxford: Blackwell, 1965.

Freedman, D.N. "Divine Commitment and Human Obligation" *Interpretation,* 8 (1964), 419–431.

Gerstenberger, E. "Covenant and Commandment" *Journal of Biblical Literature,* 84 (1965), 38–51.

Harvey, J. *Le Plaidoyer Prophetique contre Israel Apres la rupture de l'alliance.* Studie 22; Bruges – Paris – Montreal, 1967.

Hayes, J.H. (ed.). *Old Testament Form Criticism.* San Antonio: Trinity Univ. Press, 1974, 99–134.

Hillers, D. R. *Covenant: The History of a Biblical Idea.* Baltimore: Johns Hopkins, 1969.

Huffmon, H. "The Exodus, Sinai and the Credo" *Catholic Biblical Quarterly,* 27 (1965), 101–113.

McCarthy, D. *Old Testament Covenant: A Survey of Current Opinions.* London: Basil Blackwell Press, 1972.

———. *Treaty and Covenant.* Rome: PBI, 1963, rep. 1973.

Mendenhall, G. E. "Law and Covenant in Israel and the Ancient Near East" *Biblical Archaeologist,* 17 (1954), 2–23, 24–50.

Moran, W. L. "The Ancient Near Eastern Background of the Love of God in Deuteronomy" *Catholic Biblical Quarterly,* 25, (1963), 77–87.

————. "Deuteronomy," *New Catholic Commentary on Holy Scripture.* 256–276.

Nicholson, E. *Deuteronomy and Tradition.* Philadelphia: Fortress Press, 1967.

Nielson, E. *The Ten Commandments in New Perspective. Studies in Biblical Theology.* Naperville: Allenson, 1968.

Stamm, J. J. and Andrew, M. E. *The Ten Commandments in Recent Research. Studies in Biblical Theology.* Naperville: Allenson, 1967.

von Rad, G. *Studies in Deuteronomy.* London: SCM Press, Ltd., 1953.

Weinfeld, M. "Origins of Humanism in Deuteronomy" *Journal of Biblical Literature,* 80 (1961), 241–247.

————. *Deuteronomy and the Deuteronomic School.* London: Oxford Univ. Press, 1972.

Zimmerli, W. *The Law and the Prophets.* Oxford: Basil Blackwell, 1965.

The Psalms

Hayes, J. H. (ed.). *Old Testament Form Criticism.* San Antonio: Trinity Univ. Press, 1974.

Dahood, M. *The Psalms,* 3 vols. *Anchor Bible* Garden City, N.Y.: Doubleday.

Kissane, E. *The Books of Psalms.* 2 vols. Westminster: Newman, 1954.

Mowinckel, S. *The Psalms in Israel's Worship.* 2 vols. Nashville: Abingdon Press, 1962.

Oesterley, W. O. E. *The Psalms.* London: S.P.C.K., 1953.

Sabourin, L. *The Psalms: Their Origin and Meaning.* Staten Island: Alba House, 1969.

Westermann, C. *The Praise of God in the Psalms.* Richmond: John Knox Press, 1965.

The Deuteronomist Theologian

Albright, W. F. *Samuel and the Beginnings of the Prophetic Movement.* "Golden Lecture – 1961"; Cincinnati: Hebrew Union College Press, 1961.

Birch, B. C. "The Development of the Tradition on the Anointing of Saul in 1 Sam. 9:1–10:16" *Journal of Biblical Literature,* 90 (1971), 55–68.

Brueggemann, W. "The Kerygma of the Deuteronomic Historian" *Interpretation,* 22 (1968), 387–403.

Cross, F. M. "The Themes of the Book of Kings and the Structure of the Deuteronomistic History," *Canaanite Myth and Hebrew Epic.* Cambridge: Harvard Univ. Press, 1973.

Ellis, P. F. *1 and 2 Kings.* Old Testament Reading Guide. Collegeville: Liturgical Press, 1967.

Kearney, P. J. "Joshua," *Jerome Biblical Commentary,* 7:30-31.

McCarthy, D. J. "The Inauguration of Monarchy in Israel – A Form-Critical Study of 1 Samuel 8-12" *Interpretation,* 27 (1973), 401–412.

————. "2 Samuel 7 and the Structure of the Deuteronomic History" *Journal of Biblical Literature,* 84 (1965), 131–138.

McKenzie, J. L. "Royal Messianism" *Catholic Biblical Quarterly,* 19 (1957), 25–52.

————. *The World of the Judges.* Englewood Cliffs, New Jersey: Prentice-Hall, 1966.

Mendelsohn, I. "Samuel's Denunciation of Kingship in the Light of the Akkadian Documents from Ugarit" *Bulletin of the American Schools of Oriental Research*, 143 (1956), 17–22.

Mendenhall, G. E. "The Incident at Baal Peor," *The Tenth Generation*. Baltimore: Johns Hopkins, 1973.

Noth, M. *Uberlieferungsgeschichtliche Studien*. Tubingen: Max Niemeyer, 1948.

Simpson, C. A. *Composition of the Book of Judges*. Oxford: Blackwell, 1957.

von Rad, G. *Studies in Deuteronomy. Studies in Biblical Theology*. Chicago: Regnery, 1953.

Prophets

PROPHETISM

Craghan, J. F. "Mari and its Prophets" *Biblical Theology Bulletin*, 5 (1975).

Gerstenberger, E. "The Woe-Oracles of the Prophets" *Journal of Biblical Literature*, 81 (1962), 249–263.

Hayes, J. H. (ed.). *Old Testament Form Criticism*. San Antonio: Trinity Univ. Press, 1974.

Hillers, D. *Treaty Curses and the Old Testament Prophets*. Rome: Pontifical Biblical Institute, 1964.

_____. *Covenant: The History of a Biblical Idea*. Baltimore: Johns Hopkins Press, 1969.

Huffmon, H. B. "The Covenant Lawsuit in the Prophets" *Journal of Biblical Literature*, 78 (1959), 285–295.

Moran, W. L. "New Evidence from Mari on the History of Prophecy" *Biblica*, 50 (1969), 15–56.

Overholt, T. W. *The Threat of Falsehood. Studies in Biblical Theology*. Naperville: Allenson, 1971.

Rowley, H. H. (ed.). *Studies in Old Testament Prophecy*. Edinburgh: 1950.

_____. *Men of God*. London: Nelson, 1963.

Vawter, B. *The Conscience of Israel*. New York: Sheed and Ward, 1961.

Westermann, C. *The Basic Forms of Prophetic Speech*. Philadelphia: Westminster, 1967.

_____. "The Role of the Lament in the Theology of the Old Testament" *Interpretation*, 28 (1974), 20–38.

Zimmerli, W. *The Law and the Prophets*. Oxford: Basil Blackwell, 1965.

MAJOR PROPHETS

ISAIAH

Childs, B. *Isaiah and the Assyrian Crisis. Studies in Biblical Theology*. Naperville: Allenson, 1967.

Jeremias, J. and Zimmerli, W. *The Servant of God. Studies in Biblical Theology*. Naperville: Allenson, 1957.

Kaiser, O. *Isaiah 1-12. Old Testament Library*. Philadelphia: Westminster, 1972.

Kissane, E. *The Book of Isaiah*. 2 vols. Dublin: Brown and Nolan Limited, 1943; 2nd ed., 1960.

Knight, G. A. F. *Deutero-Isaiah*. Nashville: Abingdon, 1965.

McKenzie, J. L. *Second Isaiah. Anchor Bible.* Garden City, New York: Double-day, 1968.

North, C. R. *The Suffering Servant in Deutero-Isaiah.* London: Oxford Univ. Press, 1956.

Rowley, H. H. "The Suffering Servant and the Davidic Messiah," *The Servant of the Lord and Other Essays.* Oxford: Blackwell, 1965.

Smart, J. D. *History and Theology in Second Isaiah.* Philadelphia: Westminster, 1965.

Stuhlmueller, C. *Creative Redemption in Deutero-Isaiah. Analecta Biblica.* Rome: PBI, 1970.

Vriezen, T. "Essentials of the Theology of Isaiah," *Israel's Prophetic Heritage.* Fs. J. Muilenburg; eds. B. W. Anderson and W. J. Harrelson. New York: Harper, 1962.

Ward, J. M. *Amos and Isaiah.* Nashville: Abingdon, 1969.

Westermann, C. *Isaiah 40–66.* Philadelphia: Westminster, 1969.

JEREMIAH

Anderson, B. W. "The New Covenant and the Old," *The Old Testament and Christian Faith.* Ed. B. W. Anderson. New York: Harper & Row, 1963.

Bright, J. *Jeremiah. Anchor Bible.* Garden City, New York: Doubleday, 1965.

————. "An Exercise in Hermeneutics, Jeremiah 31:31-34" *Interpretation,* 20 (1966), 188–210.

Gerstenberger, E. "Jeremiah's Complaints" *Journal of Biblical Literature,* 82 (1963), 393–408.

Gottward, N. K. *Studies in the Book of Lamentations. Studies In Biblical Theology.* Naperville: Allenson, 1962.

Hillers, D. R. *Lamentations. Anchor Bible.* Garden City, New Jersey: Double-day, 1972.

Holladay, W. L. "The Background of Jeremiah's Self-Understanding" *Journal of Biblical Literature,* 83 (1964), 153–164.

Horowitz, W. J. "Audience Reaction to Jeremiah" *Catholic Biblical Quarterly,* 32 (1970), 555–564.

Rowley, H. H. "The Prophet Jeremiah and the Book of Deuteronomy" *Studies in Old Testament Prophecy.* Fs. T. H. Robinson; ed. H. H. Rowley. Edin-burgh: T. & T. Clark, 1946.

EZEKIEL

Brownlee, W. H. "The Aftermath of the Fall of Judah according to Ezekiel" *Journal of Biblical Literature,* 89 (1970), 393–404.

Craghan, J. F. "Ezekiel: A Pastoral Theologian" *American Ecclesiastical Review,* 166 (1972), 22–33.

Eichrodt, W. *Ezekiel. Old Testament Library.* Philadelphia: Westminster, 1970.

Zimmerli, W. "The Message of the Prophet Ezekiel" *Interpretation,* 23 (1969), 131–142.

MINOR PROPHETS

AMOS

Watts, J. D. W. *Vision and Prophecy in Amos.* Grand Rapids: Wm. B. Eerd-mans Publishing Co., 1958.

Wolff, H. W. *Amos the Prophet.* Philadelphia: Fortress, 1973.

HOSEA

Brueggemann, W. *Tradition for Crisis. A Study in Hosea.* Richmond: John Knox, 1968.
Craghan, J. F. "The Book of Hosea — A Survey of Recent Literature . . ." *Biblical Theology Bulletin*, 1 (1971) 81–100, 145–170.
Robinson, H. W. *The Cross of Hosea.* Philadelphia: Westminster, 1959.
Ward, J. M. *Hosea. A Theological Commentary.* New York: Harper & Row, 1966.
————. "The Message of the Prophet Hosea" *Interpretation*, 23 (1969), 387–407.

The Chronicler Theologian

Ackroyd, P. R. *Exile and Restoration. Old Testament Library.* Philadelphia: Westminster, 1968.
Freedman, D. N. "The Chronicler's Purpose" *Catholic Biblical Quarterly*, 23 (1961), 436–442.
Myers, J. M. *The World of the Restoration.* Englewood Cliffs, New Jersey: Prentice-Hall, 1968.
————. "The Kerygma of the Chronicler" *Interpretation*, 20 (1966), 257–273.
North, R. "Theology of the Chronicler" *Journal of Biblical Literature*, 82 (1963), 369–381.
Smith, M. *Palestinian Parties and Politics that Shaped the Old Testament.* New York: Columbia Univ. Press, 1971.
Torrey, C. C. *The Chronicler's History of Israel.* New Haven: Yale Univ. Press, 1954.

The Wisdom Literature

WISDOM LITERATURE IN GENERAL

Brueggemann, W. "Scripture and an Ecumenical Life-Style" *Interpretation*, 24 (1970), 3–19.
Murphy, R. *Seven Books of Wisdom.* Milwaukee: Bruce, 1960.
————. "The Interpretation of Old Testament Wisdom Literature" *Interpretation*, 23 (1969), 289–301.
Noth, M. and Thomas, D. W. (eds.). *Wisdom in Israel and in the Ancient Near East. VTS.* Fest. H. H. Rowley, Leiden, Brill, 1960.
Scott, R. B. Y. *The Way of Wisdom in the Old Testament.* New York: Macmillan, 1971.

CANTICLE OF CANTICLES

Schonfield, H. J. *The Song of Songs.* New York: New American Library, 1959.
Murphy, R. "Form-Critical Studies in the Song of Songs" *Interpretation*, 27 (1973), 413–422.

PROVERBS

McKane, W. *Proverbs. Old Testament Library.* Philadelphia: Westminster, 1970.

Murphy, R. "The Kerygma of the Book of Proverbs" *Interpretation*, 20 (1966), 3–14.

Scott, R. B. Y. *Proverbs-Ecclesiastes. Anchor Bible.* Garden City, New York: Doubleday, 1965.

Whybray, R. N. *Wisdom in Proverbs. Studies in Biblical Theology.* Naperville: Allenson, 1965.

SIRACH

di Lella, A. A. "Conservative and Progressive Theology: Sirach and Wisdom" *Catholic Biblical Quarterly*, 28 (1966), 139–154.

JOB

Barr, J. "The Book of Job and its Modern Interpreters" *Bulletin of the John Rylands Library*, 54 (1971) 28–46.

Snaith, N. H. *The Book of Job.* Naperville: Allenson, 1968.

QOHELETH

Ginsberg, H. L. *Studies in Qoheleth.* New York: 1950.

Gordis, R. *The Wisdom of Ecclesiastes.* New York: 1945.

Zimmermann, F. *The Inner World of Qoheleth.* New York: Ktav, 1972.

THE BOOK OF WISDOM

Reese, J. M. "Plan and Structure in the Book of Wisdom" *Catholic Biblical Quarterly*, 27 (1965), 391–399.

Reider, J. *The Book of Wisdom: An English Translation with Introduction and Commentary.* New York: Harper, 1957.

Siebeneck, R. T. "The Midrash of Wisdom 10-19" *Catholic Biblical Quarterly*, 22 (1960), 176–182.

Wright, A. G. "The Structure of Wisdom 11-19" *Catholic Biblical Quarterly*, 27 (1965), 28–34.

The Midrashic Literature

Charles, R. H. (ed.). *The Apocrypha and Pseudepigrapha of the Old Testament.* 2 vols. Oxford: Clarendon Press, 1913.

Hals, R. M. *The Theology of the Book of Ruth.* "Facet Books"; Philadelphia: Fortress, 1969.

Landes, G. M. "The Kerygma of the Book of Jonah" *Interpretation*, 21 (1967), 3–31.

Le Deaut, R. "Apropos a Definition of Midrash" *Interpretation*, 25 (1971), 259–282.

Metzger, B. M. *An Introduction to the Apocrypha.* New York: Oxford Univ. Press, 1957.

Moore, C. A. *Esther. Anchor Bible.* Garden City, New York: Doubleday, 1971.

Strack, H. L. *Introduction to the Talmud and Midrash.* Philadelphia: Jewish Publication Society of America, 1931.

Torrey, C. C. *The Apocryphal Literature.* New Haven: Yale Univ. Press, 1945.

Vermes, G. *Scripture and Tradition in Judaism: Haggadic Studies.* Leiden: Brill, 1961.

Wright, A. *Midrash*. Staten Island: Alba House, 1965.

Zeitlin, S. (ed.). *Jewish Apocryphal Literature*. New York: Harper, 1950–.

Zimmerman, F. *The Book of Tobit. Jewish Apocryphal Literature*. New York: Harper, 1958.

The Maccabees

Dancy, J. C. *A Commentary on I Maccabees*. London: 1954.

Tedesche, S. *The First Book of Maccabees. Jewish Apocryphal Literature*. New York: Harper, 1950.

Daniel and the Apocalyptic Literature

Koch, K. *The Rediscovery of Apocalyptic. Studies in Biblical Theology*. Naperville: Allenson, 1972.

Porteous, N. *Daniel. Old Testament Library*. Philadelphia: Westminster, 1965.

Rowley, H. H. *The Relevance of Apocalyptic*. New York: Harper, 1946.

Russell, D. S. *The Method and Message of Jewish Apocalyptic. Old Testament Library*. Philadelphia: Westminster, 1964.

Sullivan, K. *The Book of Daniel, The Book of Jonah*. Old Testament Reading Guide. Collegeville: The Liturgical Press, 1975.

Students' Correlated Readings

The following correlated reading references aim to provide the student with
an awareness of the various types of literature relating to the Bible on a popular
level. Once familiar with the purpose, style and content of a particular volume or
series of volumes, a more complete and thorough reading will follow as occasion
calls for.

THE PENTATEUCH — *pages* 1-50

THE JEROME BIBLICAL COMMENTARY, pages 1–6; 671–702.
Jack Finegan: LIGHT FROM THE ANCIENT PAST, pages 3–138.
OLD TESTAMENT READING GUIDE, No. 9, pages 3–82.
Theodore McCown: THE LADDER OF PROGRESS IN PALESTINE, pages 18–53.
William F. Albright: THE ARCHAEOLOGY OF PALESTINE, pages 7–64.

LITERARY ANALYSIS OF THE PENTATEUCH — *pages* 51-127

OLD TESTAMENT READING GUIDE, No. 1, pages 3–64.
A NEW CATHOLIC COMMENTARY ON HOLY SCRIPTURE, pages 156–165.
Robert-Feuillet: INTRODUCTION TO THE OLD TESTAMENT, pages 71–117.
Michael Avi-Yonah: THE WORLD OF THE BIBLE, vol. 1, pages 127–176.
NEW CATHOLIC ENCYCLOPEDIA, vol. 2, *article* Bible, page 381ff.

PSALMS RELATED TO THE PENTATEUCHAL HISTORY — *pages* 128-169

Leopold Sabourin: THE PSALMS, vol. 1, pages 1–63; 179–243.
Edward Kissane: THE BOOK OF PSALMS, vol. 1, pages ix–xlii.
R. A. F. McKenzie: THE PSALMS (OTRG, No. 23) pages 3–128.
James B. Pritchard: ANCIENT NEAR EASTERN TEXTS RELATED TO OLD TESTA-
MENT, pages 365–401.
Martin Noth: THE HISTORY OF ISRAEL, pages 299–354.

THE DEUTERONOMIST'S HISTORY — *pages* 172-270

Eugene A. LaVerdiere: INTRODUCTION TO THE PENTATEUCH (OTRG, No. 1),
pages 3–64.
A NEW CATHOLIC COMMENTARY ON HOLY SCRIPTURE, pages 277–281.
Denis J. McCarthy: THEOLOGY AND COVENANT IN THE OLD TESTAMENT,
pages 160–164 in *The Bible Today Reader*.
Xavier Leon-Dufour: DICTIONARY OF BIBLICAL THEOLOGY, *articles*: Abraham; Adam; animals; ark; covenant; God; Israel; people; punishment;
prayer.
Jack Finegan: LIGHT FROM THE ANCIENT PAST, pages 139–220.

THE CHRONCLER'S HISTORY — *pages* **274-302**

Claus Schedl: HISTORY OF THE OLD TESTAMENT, Vol. III, pages 273–379.

James B. Pritchard: THE ANCIENT NEAR EAST IN PICTURES RELATING TO THE OLD TESTAMENT, pages 160–223 (with commentary on photos).

William F. Albright: FROM THE STONE AGE TO CHRISTIANITY, pages 200–333.

NEW CATHOLIC ENCYCLOPEDIA, vol. 11, pages 861–872.

Michael Avi-Yonah: THE WORLD OF THE BIBLE, vol. III, pages 93–203.

JUDEAN PROPHETS DURING THE EIGHTH CENTURY — *pages* **303-339**

Edward Kissane: THE BOOK OF ISAIAH, vol. 1, pages 71–149.

Madeleine-Lane Miller: ENCYCLOPEDIA OF BIBLE LIFE, pages 284–319.

Roland de Vaux: ANCIENT ISRAEL, pages 406–456.

Beek-Welsh-Rowley: ATLAS OF MESOPOTAMIA, pages 90–127.

A NEW CATHOLIC COMMENTARY ON HOLY SCRIPTURE, pages 563–567; 3–20; 53–60.

MESSIANISM, RETURN FROM EXILE AND POSTEXILIC PROPHETS — *pages* **340-419**

William Heidt: THE MAJOR OLD TESTAMENT THEME (OTRG, No. 31), pages 3–124.

John Bright: A HISTORY OF ISRAEL, pages 356–386.

Louis F. Hartman: ENCYCLOPEDIC DICTIONARY OF THE BIBLE, *articles*: Messiah; Messianism; Parousia; Sabbath; Eschatology; Esdra.

THE JEROME BIBLICAL COMMENTARY, pages 703–735.

Aharoni–Avi-Yonah: THE MACMILLAN BIBLE ATLAS, pages 11–23; 104–108.

THE RETURN FROM THE EXILE — *pages* **396-419**

Wilfrid J. Harrington: RECORD OF THE PROMISE – THE OLD TESTAMENT, pages 200–239.

Carroll Stuhlmueller: SECOND ISAIAH (OTRG, No. 20), pages 3–161.

Artur Weiser: THE PSALMS, pages 19–108.

D. F. Rauber: JONAH THE PROPHET, in *The Bible Today*, October, 1970, pages 29–38.

Frederick L. Moriarty: EZRA-NEHEMIA (OTRG, No. 11),pages 3–69.

LITERARY ANALYSIS OF THE CHRONICLER'S HISTORY — *pages* **420-471**

Edward Kissane: THE BOOK OF PSALMS, vol. 2, pages 1–8; 17–42; 60–65; 76–88; 121–123; 224–275.

Robert Feuillet: INTRODUCTION TO THE OLD TESTAMENT, pages 369–404.

David-Gehman: THE WESTMINSTER DICTIONARY OF THE BIBLE, *articles*: Zerubabbel; Seven; Old Testament; Jubilee; Jerusalem; Babylon.

Paul Heinisch: THEOLOGY OF THE OLD TESTAMENT, pages 92–101.

Roland de Vaux: ANCIENT ISRAEL, pages 457–517.

THE MIDRASHIC LITERATURE — *pages* **474-489**

H. Danby: THE MISHNAH, pages 1–75.

R. H. Charles: THE APOCRYPHA AND PSEUDEPIGRAPHA OF THE OLD TESTAMENT, vol. 2, pages 10–60.

Jack Finegan: LIGHT FROM THE ANCIENT PAST, pages 220–297.
Kathryn Sullivan: DANIEL AND JONAH (OTRG, No. 28), pages 3–119.
Leopold Sabourin: THE PSALMS, vol. 2, pages 257–331.

THE WISDOM LITERATURE — *pages 490-516*

Roland Murphy: SEVEN BOOKS OF WISDOM, pages 1–66.
Roger Schoenbechler: THE BOOK OF WISDOM.
James B. Pritchard: ANCIENT NEAR EASTERN TEXTS RELATING TO THE OLD
TESTAMENT, pages 405–466.
Wilfrid J. Harrington: RECORD OF THE PROMISE — THE OLD TESTAMENT,
pages 240–280.
William Heidt: INSPIRATION, CANONICITY, TEXTS, VERSIONS (ORTG, No. 30),
pages 3–68.

THE HISTORY OF THE MACCABEES — *pages 517-557*

Grollenberg: ATLAS OF THE BIBLE, pages 100–139.
Wright-Filson-Albright: THE WESTMINSTER HISTORICAL ATLAS TO THE
BIBLE, pages 73–80.
Negenman-Rowley: NEW ATLAS OF THE BIBLE, pages 115–138.
Baly-Tushingham: ATLAS OF THE BIBLICAL WORLD, pages 155–176.
Louis F. Hartman: ENCYCLOPEDIC DICTIONARY OF THE BIBLE, *articles*:
Machabee; Wisdom; Seleucids; Dead Sea Scrolls; Daniel.

THE BOOK OF WISDOM — *pages 558-574*

James M. Reese: WISDOM — ISRAEL'S WINDOW ON THE WORLD in *The Bible
Today Reader*, pages 249–252.
Ahroni—Avi-Yonah: THE MACMILLAN BIBLE ATLAS, pages 109–141.
Beek-Welsh-Rowley: ATLAS OF MESOPOTAMIA, pages 19–40.
Emil G. Kraeling: BIBLE ATLAS, pages 14–38.
A NEW CATHOLIC COMMENTARY ON HOLY SCRIPTURE, pages 131–138.

INDEX

Aaron, 32, 44, 193
Abel, 10, 93
Abednego, 544
Abdon, 192
Abel, 10, 93
Abiathar, 210
Abimelech, 192
Abiram, 44
Abishai, 206
Abner, 202
Abomination of Desolation, 530, 548f
Abraham, 11ff, 23f, 89ff, 101f, 172, 343f, 320f, 348f
Absalom, 205f
Abzu, 88
Achan, 184
Achior, 553
Achish, 201
Acre, 180, 182, 188
Acrostics, 131, 384
Adam, 9ff, 23, 93ff, 98f
Adaptation, 25, 30
Adonijah, 210
Age of the earth, 89
Agur, 501
Ahab, 214ff, 305
Ahasuerus, 488
Ahaz, 305f, 309ff, 360f
Ahaziah, 216
Ahijah, 214
Ahiqar, 491, 498
Ahitopel, 206
Ai, 185
Alcimus, 521
Alexander the Great, 519ff, 544, 556

Allegories of Ezekiel, 376, 378ff
Allegory, 226, 381, 410f
'Almah, 361f
Amasa, 206
Amaziah, 278
Amalekites, 183
Amen-em-ope, 491, 501
Ammon, 19, 181, 205
Ammonites, 192f
Amnon, 205
Amon, 322, 325
Ammorites, 45, 101, 115, 182
Amos, 217, 219ff, 537
Amphictyony, 104, 187
Anaphora, 131
Anathoth, 322
Angels, 285f
Anthropology, 81ff
Anthropomorphism, 98, 101, 119
Anticipation, 240, 251
Antiochus IV, 518ff, 533, 542ff, 551, 556f
Aod, 191
Apocalyptic, 383, 401ff, 533ff, 545ff, 551ff, 553ff
Apocrypha, 488
Apollonius, 521
Aquinas, 122
Ariel, 314
Ark, 31, 74, 186f, 193, 198f, 203, 211, 350
Ark history, 198, 203
Arnon, 179, 181
Arphaxad, 550, 552
Artaxerxes I, 398f

Artaxerxes II, 399
Asa, 219, 277, 280
Asahel, 202
Asaph, 166
Ashdod, 192
Asherah, 191, 357
Ashkelon, 192
Ashurbanipal, 263
Asshur, 100
Assyria, 100, 102, 218, 303ff, 327f
Astarte, 45
Athaliah, 217, 356, 359
Authenticity, 55ff, 389

Baal, 45, 214f, 329
Baal of Peor, 45
Baasha, 214
Babel, 11, 93
Babylon, 75, 89, 91, 100, 208, 320, 374, 506
Balaam, 45
Balak, 45
Ban, 184f
Banias, 181
Barak, 191
Baruch, 328ff, 488f, 492, 506
Bashan, 45, 181, 192
Bathsheba, 94, 205, 210, 356
Bel and the Dragon, 549
Belshazzar, 387, 543, 545
Ben-hadad, 215
Ben-hinnom, 329
Benjamin, 190, 193
Benjaminites, 193
Beer-sheba, 179f

Bethel, 12, 101, 193, 213, 220
Bethlehem, 182, 318
Beth-shan, 186, 188
Bildad, 509
Blessings of Jacob, 15f, 357f
Blood, 40, 42
Boaz, 194
Byblos, 180

CAIN, 10, 93, 353
Caleb, 44
Calf, 32
Cambyses, 400
Canaan, 12, 44, 92, 94, 96, 101, 186
Canaanite fertility cult, 351ff
Canaanites, 13, 99, 101, 115, 182, 185, 353f
Canticle of Canticles, 409ff
Canticle of Hezekiah, 427
Canticle of Moses, 19, 141
Carchemish, 328f, 373
Carmel, 180, 215
Centralization of cult, 105
Chaldea, 11
Cherubim, 34, 100, 377
Christ, 10f, 16, 21, 54, 120, 348
Chronicler, 80, 274ff, 397ff, 420f, 426ff
Chronicler's History, 274ff, 320ff
Chronicles, 116, 125
Chronicles, book of, 278ff
Chronology, 28, 178, 188, 209, 213, 277, 292, 294, 304, 321, 336, 372, 386, 397, 418, 519, 531, 543
Circumcision, 13
Cleanliness, 39
Climate, 181
Code of the Covenant, 20
Collective responsibility, 379f, 506ff
Collectivity, 379f
Commandments, 20, 108ff
Confessions of Jeremiah, 297, 323
Confucius, 75
Conquest of Canaan, 183

Cosmogony, 89
Court history, 93
Covenants, 12, 21ff, 33ff, 74, 91ff, 115, 172, 187, 479
Covenant theology, 292f
Creation, 9, 53, 85ff, 91, 98
Criticism, higher, 53
Criticism, textual, 53
Croesus, 387
Cult, 36ff
Cursing, 240f
Cyrus the Great, 373ff, 387f, 391ff, 403, 421f

D SOURCE, 57
Damascus, 305, 313
Dan, 179, 190, 193, 213, 220
Daniel, 365, 481, 492, 504, 508, 515, 517, 533ff, 541ff, 551, 553
Darius I, 398ff, 543, 548
Darius the Mede, 543
Dathan, 44
David, 16, 34, 93ff, 119, 186, 195ff, 200ff, 210, 262ff, 424, 440, 491
Davidic dynasty, 93, 175, 194ff, 203f, 214, 275, 279, 344ff, 351ff, 358ff, 421ff
Day of Atonement, 41
Day of the Lord, 225, 300, 322
Day of Nicanor, 532
Dead Sea, 13, 45, 179, 181
Dead Sea Scrolls, 476f
Deborah, 191
Decalogue, 20, 26
Dedication, 556
Demetrius I, 521
Demythologizing, 285
Deutero-Isaiah, 194, 307, 388ff, 534, 538, 543
Deuteronomic theologian, 103ff
Deuteronomic tradition, 102ff
Deuteronomist, 95, 103ff, 172ff, 186, 190, 233ff

Deuteronomist's history, 173ff, 232ff
Deuteronomy, 46ff, 55ff, 92, 102ff, 235f, 325f, 479
Deutero-Zechariah, 408f
Diaspora, 424f
Diatessaron, 54
Diodochi, 520
Divine pedagogy, 227
Divino Afflante Spiritu, 120ff
Documentary hypothesis, 56ff
Dynastic messianism, 344ff

E SOURCE, 57ff, 101
Early man, 9
Ebal, 180
Ebed-melech, 335
Ecclesiastes, see Qoheleth
Ecclesiasticus, see Sirach
Edom, 94, 181, 385
Edomites, 157, 183, 385
Eglon, 191
Egypt, 12, 95, 115, 313, 328
Ekron, 192
Elah, 213f
Elcana, 194
Eleazar, 207, 528
Eleazar Maccabeus, 524
Election, 109ff
Elihu, 505, 508ff
Elijah, 101, 215ff, 406, 519
Eliphaz, 508ff
Elisha, 101, 215ff
Elohim, 97
Elohist, 57, 74, 80, 92, 95, 100ff, 123
Elon, 192
El Shaddai, 97
Enlil, 89
Enemies, 240
Enuma Elish, 88f, 98, 285
Ephraim, 15, 101, 191
Ephraimites, 191
Epiphora, 131
Esau, 7, 95
Esdraelon, 180, 182, 555
Esther, 119f, 126, 481, 487ff, 542, 551f

504ff, 538, 542, 558, 567ff
Joel, 534, 539ff, 553f, 556
Johanan, 337
John the Baptist, 322, 406
Jonah, 119f, 126, 481, 482ff
Jonathan, 193f, 200f
Jonathan Maccabeus, 521, 525
Joppa, 180, 192
Jordan, 13, 42, 116, 180f
Joseph, 14ff, 93, 101
Josephus, 556
Joshua, 27, 44, 95f, 125, 174ff, 183ff, 236, 343
Joshua, book of, 183ff, 236
Josiah, 104, 178, 322ff, 507
Jotham, 306, 308ff
Jubilee year, 41
Judah, 14f, 57, 93ff, 191, 357
Judas Maccabeus, 519, 520f, 524, 530f, 544, 556
Judges, 93ff, 125, 174, 177, 188ff, 236, 357f
Judgment speech against individual, 287f
Judgment speech against nation, 288
Judith, 119, 125f, 550
Judith, book of, 550f

KADESH-BARNEA, 180
Karibu, 16, 100
Karkar, 305
Kings, book of, 125, 174f, 177f, 207ff, 237, 291, 520
Kingdom of God, 5f, 22ff, 30ff, 35, 468, 542, 544, 546
Kingship psalms, 468ff
Kingu, 98
Kiriath-jearim, 34
Knowledge of God, 228
Korah, 44

LABASHI-MERODACH, 387
Lachish letters, 334
Lamentations, 384f, 539
Lao-tse, 75
Law, 20, 92, 567

Legal holiness, 40
Legal purity, 39
Legends, 86f, 123
Lemuel, 492, 502
Letter of Jeremiah, 488
Levirate marriage, 49, 194
Levites, 43
Leviticus, 36ff, 55, 92, 102
Literary analysis, 52f
Literary forms, 86f, 115ff, 475ff
Lot, 12
Love, 40, 49, 102f, 149f, 230f, 301
Love commandment, 109ff
Lysias, 521

MACCABEES, books of, 125, 508, 517ff
Mahanaim, 202, 206
Maher-shalal-hash-baz, 306, 312
Malachi, 405f, 509
Mami, 98
Manahem, 217
Manasseh, 15, 101, 105, 192, 306, 315, 321f
Manna, 20
Marduk, 99, 373
Marriage, 411ff
Martyrs, 530
Mashal, 494
Mass, 39
Massah, 20
Mattathias Hasmoneus, 519ff
Medes, 327, 388
Megiddo, 182, 186, 188, 327, 556
Melchizedek, 12, 263, 265
Menahem, 217
Menelaus, 521, 528
Meribah, 20, 53
Meribbaal, 204f
Mernepthah, 19
Merodach-Baladan, 313
Messenger formula, 287ff
Messiah, 16, 184, 194, 204, 225, 261ff, 275, 298, 315, 318, 341ff, 382, 391f, 546
Messianic kingdom, 225, 301, 341ff, 543ff, 546ff

Messianic texts, 348ff, 359ff, 408f
Messianism, 340ff
Micah, 303, 316ff, 363f
Michal, 94, 201
Midian, 18
Midianites, 46, 191
Midrash, 119f, 276, 474ff, 544f, 550ff, 560f　,
Millo, 211
Miriam, 44, 101
Mishnah, 477
Moab, 19, 42, 45, 181, 183
Moabites, 45, 183, 194
Monarchy, 96, 115, 195ff
Mordecai, 487f
Moses, 4, 17ff, 30ff, 44, 47ff, 55ff, 101ff, 172, 183, 189
Mount Ebal, 180
Mount Gerizim, 180
Mount Gilboa, 180
Mount Lebanon, 179
Myths, 86
Myth-makers, 285

NAAMAN, 216
Nabonidus, 387, 543, 545
Nabopolassar, 305, 327
Naboth, 215f
Nadab, 214, 491
Nahash, 193, 199
Nahum, 305, 327
Naomi, 194
Nathan, 96, 203, 210, 344, 349
Nazarites, 43, 192, 198
Nebuchadnezzar, 305, 327f, 331ff, 373f, 388ff, 541f, 550, 553ff
Necho, 326ff
Negeb, 12, 44, 182, 191
Nehemiah, 125, 397ff, 406ff, 517
Neo-Babylonian Empire, 373
Neriglissar, 387
New Covenant, 228, 237, 324, 335, 347, 364, 376, 382f
Nicanor, 521, 528, 530
Nineveh, 305, 484, 552
Nin-gish-zi-da, 99

AUTHOR'S INDEX

Murphy, R., 409, 503, 504, 513

Nicholson, E. W., 105, 107
Nober, P., 265
North, C., 395
North, R., 185
Noth, M., 79, 232ff

O'Connell, M. J., 114
Orlinsky, H. M., 286

Pascal, B., 515
Pius XII, 90, 120ff, 126, 340

Plutarch, 518

Renan, E., 324
Robinson, H. W., 395
Rowe, S., 356
Rowley, H. H., 105, 110, 150

Schedl, C., 52, 373, 518
Skehan, P. W., 501, 504
Schoenberg, M., 518, 526
Shökel, A., 117
Strack-Billerbeck, 84
Stuhlmueller, C., 389, 403, 488

Sullivan, K., 541

Vawter, B., 85, 306, 331, 357, 361
Virgil, 40
von Rad, G., 78, 104, 106, 108, 111f

Wahl, T., 487, 550
Walters, S. D., 287
Weinfeld, M., 105
Westerman, C., 287f

Zimmerli, W., 395

MAP INDEX

PLATE I

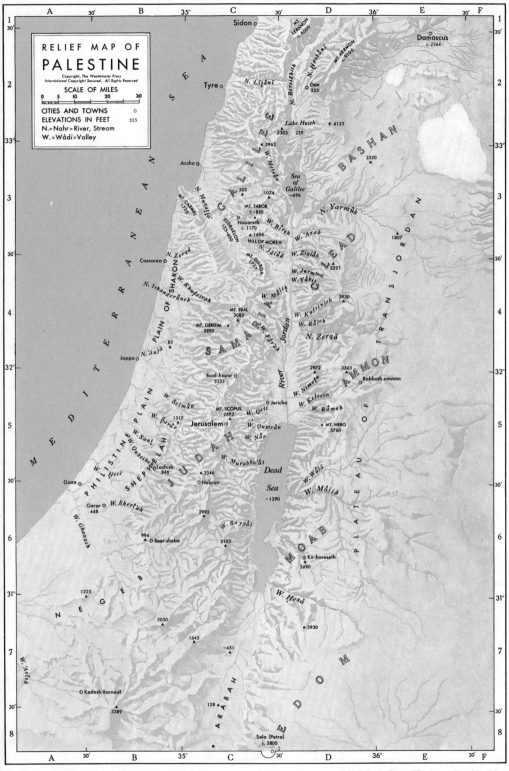

RELIEF MAP OF
PALESTINE
Copyright, The Westminster Press
International Copyright Secured.   All Rights Reserved

SCALE OF MILES
0   5   10   20   30

CITIES AND TOWNS   o
ELEVATIONS IN FEET   555
N.=Nahr=River, Stream
W.=Wâdī=Valley

Cartography By G. A. Barrois and Hal & Jean Arbo   Edited By G. Ernest Wright and Floyd V. Filson

PLATE II

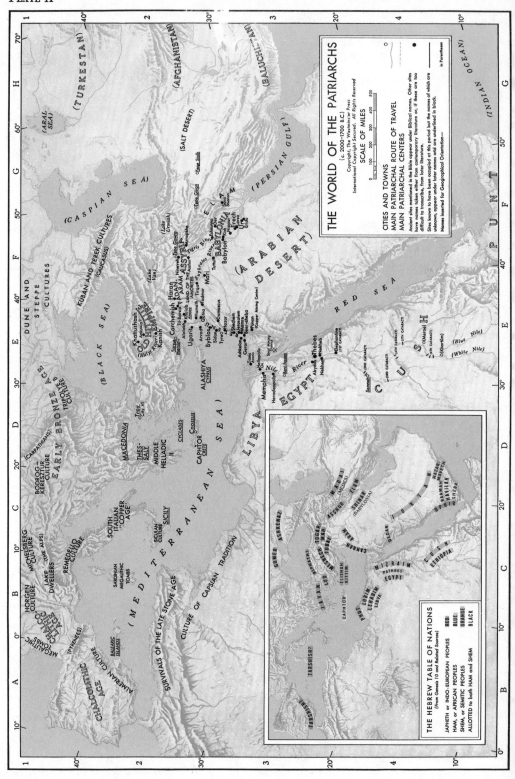

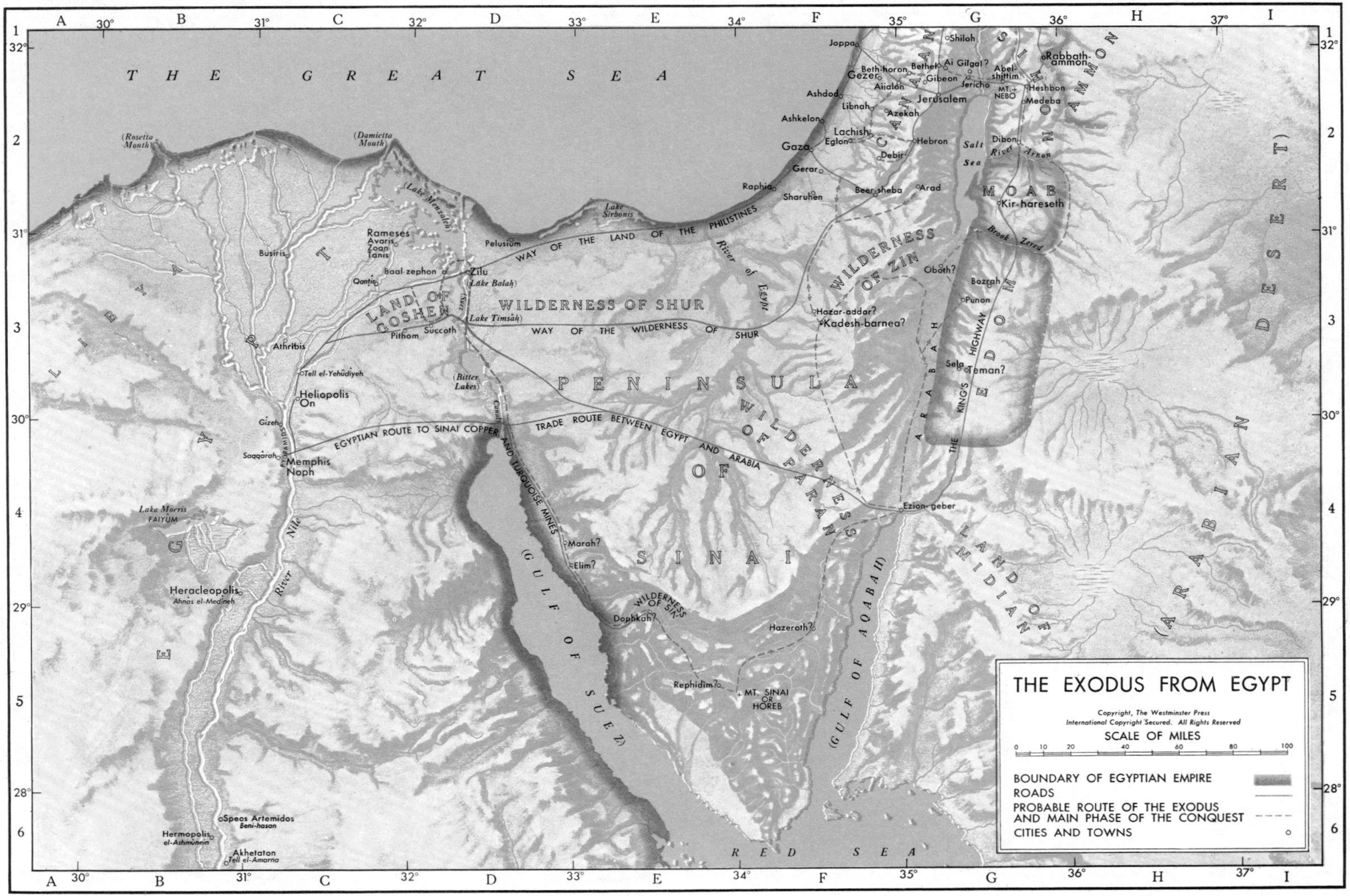

PLATE III

THE EXODUS FROM EGYPT

Copyright, The Westminster Press
International Copyright Secured. All Rights Reserved

SCALE OF MILES

0   10   20   40   60   80   100

BOUNDARY OF EGYPTIAN EMPIRE
ROADS
PROBABLE ROUTE OF THE EXODUS
AND MAIN PHASE OF THE CONQUEST
CITIES AND TOWNS   o

Edited By G. Ernest Wright and Floyd V. Filson

Cartography By Hal & Jean Arbo

PLATE IV

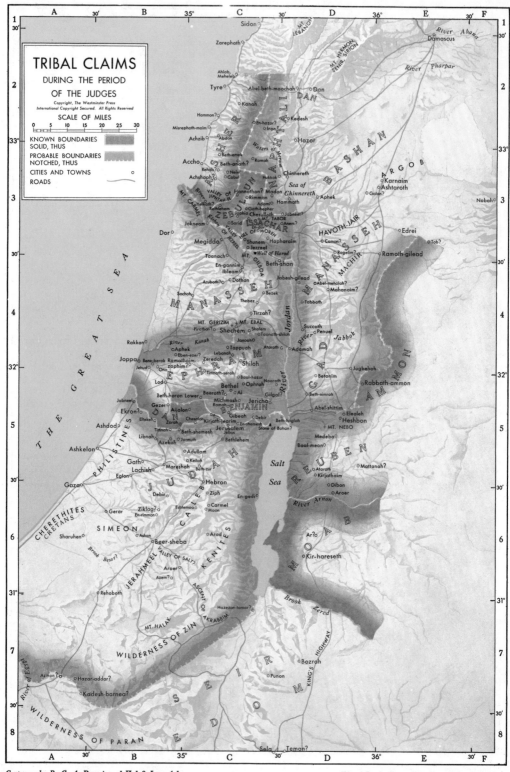

TRIBAL CLAIMS
DURING THE PERIOD
OF THE JUDGES

Copyright, The Westminster Press
International Copyright Secured. All Rights Reserved

SCALE OF MILES

0   5   10   15   20   25   30

KNOWN BOUNDARIES
SOLID, THUS

PROBABLE BOUNDARIES
NOTCHED, THUS

CITIES AND TOWNS   o

ROADS

Cartography By G. A. Barrois and Hal & Jean Arbo

Edited By G. Ernest Wright and Floyd V. Filson

PLATE V

THE EMPIRE OF DAVID
AND SOLOMON
(c. 1000-930 B.C.)
Copyright, The Westminster Press
International Copyright Secured. All Rights Reserved

SCALE OF MILES
0 10 20   40   60

BOUNDARY OF THE EMPIRE
INDEPENDENT PHILISTIA AND PHOENICIA
ADMINISTRATIVE DISTRICTS OF SOLOMON
TERRITORY CONQUERED BY DAVID
CITIES AND TOWNS   o

Cartography By Hal & Jean Arbo

Edited By G. Ernest Wright and Floyd V. Filson

PLATE VI

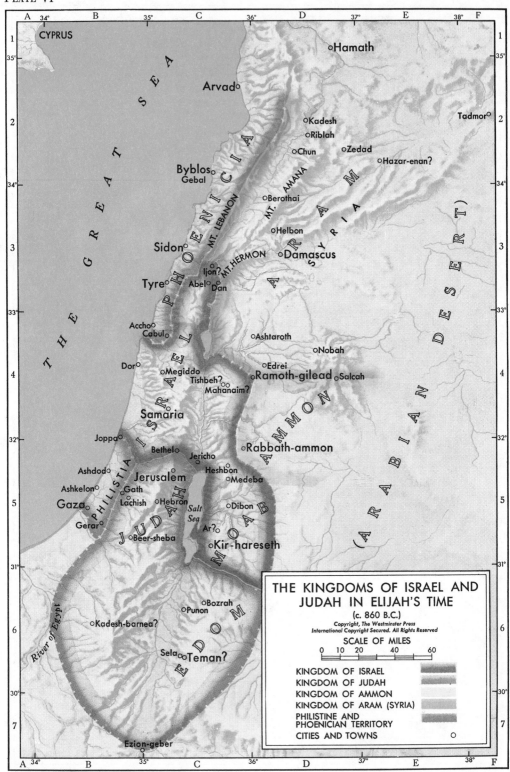

THE KINGDOMS OF ISRAEL AND
JUDAH IN ELIJAH'S TIME
(c. 860 B.C.)

SCALE OF MILES

0   10   20   40   60

KINGDOM OF ISRAEL
KINGDOM OF JUDAH
KINGDOM OF AMMON
KINGDOM OF ARAM (SYRIA)
PHILISTINE AND
PHOENICIAN TERRITORY
CITIES AND TOWNS   ○

Cartography By Hal & Jean Arbo   *Edited By G. Ernest Wright and Floyd V. Filson*

PLATE VII

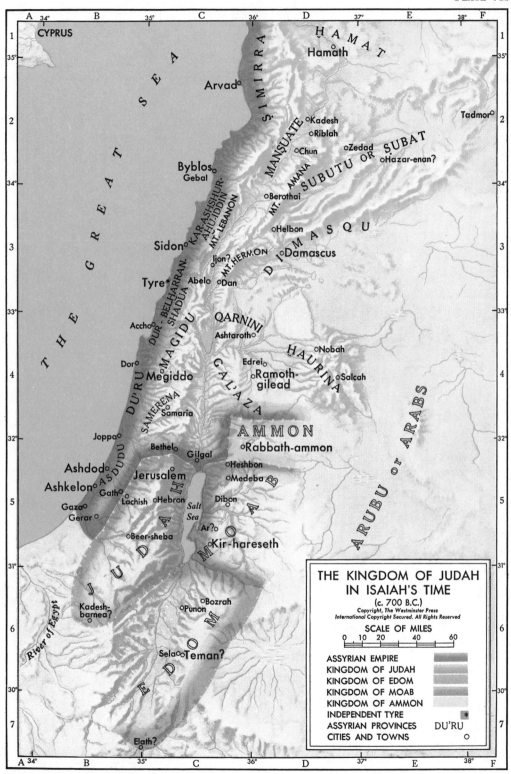

THE KINGDOM OF JUDAH
IN ISAIAH'S TIME
(c. 700 B.C.)
Copyright, The Westminster Press
International Copyright Secured. All Rights Reserved

SCALE OF MILES
0 10 20   40   60

ASSYRIAN EMPIRE
KINGDOM OF JUDAH
KINGDOM OF EDOM
KINGDOM OF MOAB
KINGDOM OF AMMON
INDEPENDENT TYRE   *
ASSYRIAN PROVINCES   DU'RU
CITIES AND TOWNS   o

Cartography By Hal & Jean Arbo

Edited By G. Ernest Wright and Floyd V. Filson

PLATE VIII

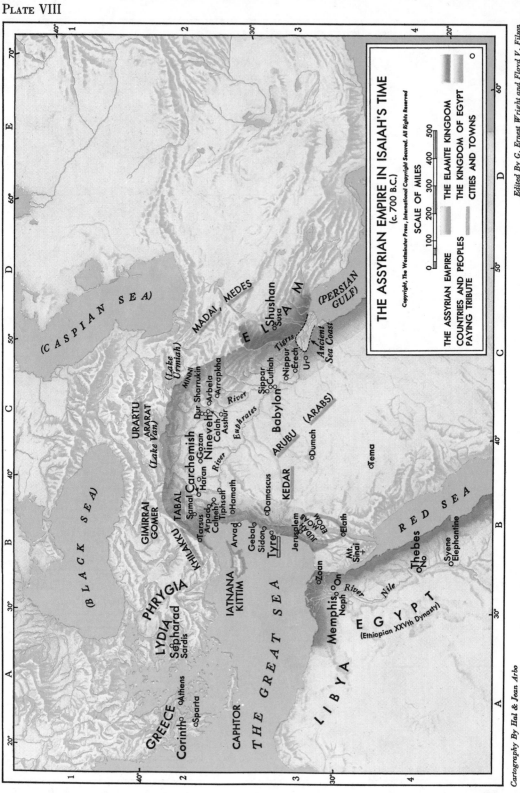

THE ASSYRIAN EMPIRE IN ISAIAH'S TIME
(c. 700 B.C.)

SCALE OF MILES

0   100   200   300   400   500

THE ASSYRIAN EMPIRE

COUNTRIES AND PEOPLES
PAYING TRIBUTE

THE ELAMITE KINGDOM

THE KINGDOM OF EGYPT

o CITIES AND TOWNS

Edited By G. Ernest Wright and Floyd V. Filson

Cartography By Hal & Jean Arbo

(CASPIAN SEA)

(BLACK SEA)

GREECE

Corinth o o Athens
Sparta o

CAPHTOR

THE GREAT SEA

LYDIA
Sepharad
Sardis

PHRYGIA

IATNANA
KITTIM

URARTU
ARARAT
(Lake Van)

(Lake Urmiah)

MADAI, MEDES

E L A M
Shushan
Susa o

(PERSIAN GULF)

Tigris
River

MINNI

GIMIRRAI
GOMER

KHILAKKU

TABAL

Carchemish
Gozan o o
Haran

Dur Sharrukin o
Nineveh o
Calah o
Asshur o

Arbela o
Arrapkha o

Sippar o
Cuthah o
Nippur o
Babylon o Erech
Ur o

River

Ancient
Sea Coast

Semal o
Tarsus o Arpad o
Calneh o
Tiphsah o

Euphrates River

(ARABS)

Hamath o

ARUBU
o Dumah

Arvad o
Gebal o
Sidon o
Tyre o

Damascus o

KEDAR

o Tema

Jerusalem o AMMON
MOAB
EDOM
o Elath

Zoan o

Memphis o On o
Noph o

Mt.
Sinai +

RED SEA

Thebes o
No

Svene o
Elephantine o

River Nile

EGYPT
(Ethiopian XXVth Dynasty)

LIBYA

PLATE IX

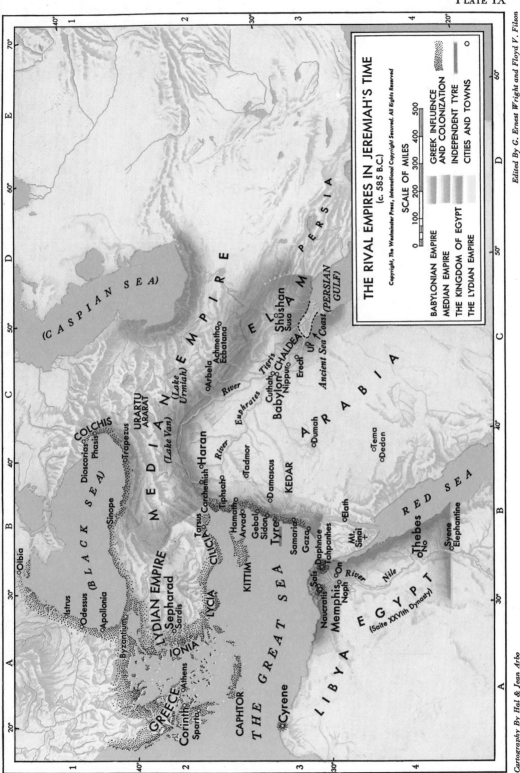

THE RIVAL EMPIRES IN JEREMIAH'S TIME
(c. 585 B.C.)

SCALE OF MILES

0 100 200 300 400 500

BABYLONIAN EMPIRE
MEDIAN EMPIRE
THE KINGDOM OF EGYPT
THE LYDIAN EMPIRE

GREEK INFLUENCE AND COLONIZATION
INDEPENDENT TYRE
CITIES AND TOWNS

Edited By G. Ernest Wright and Floyd V. Filson

Cartography By Hal & Jean Arbo

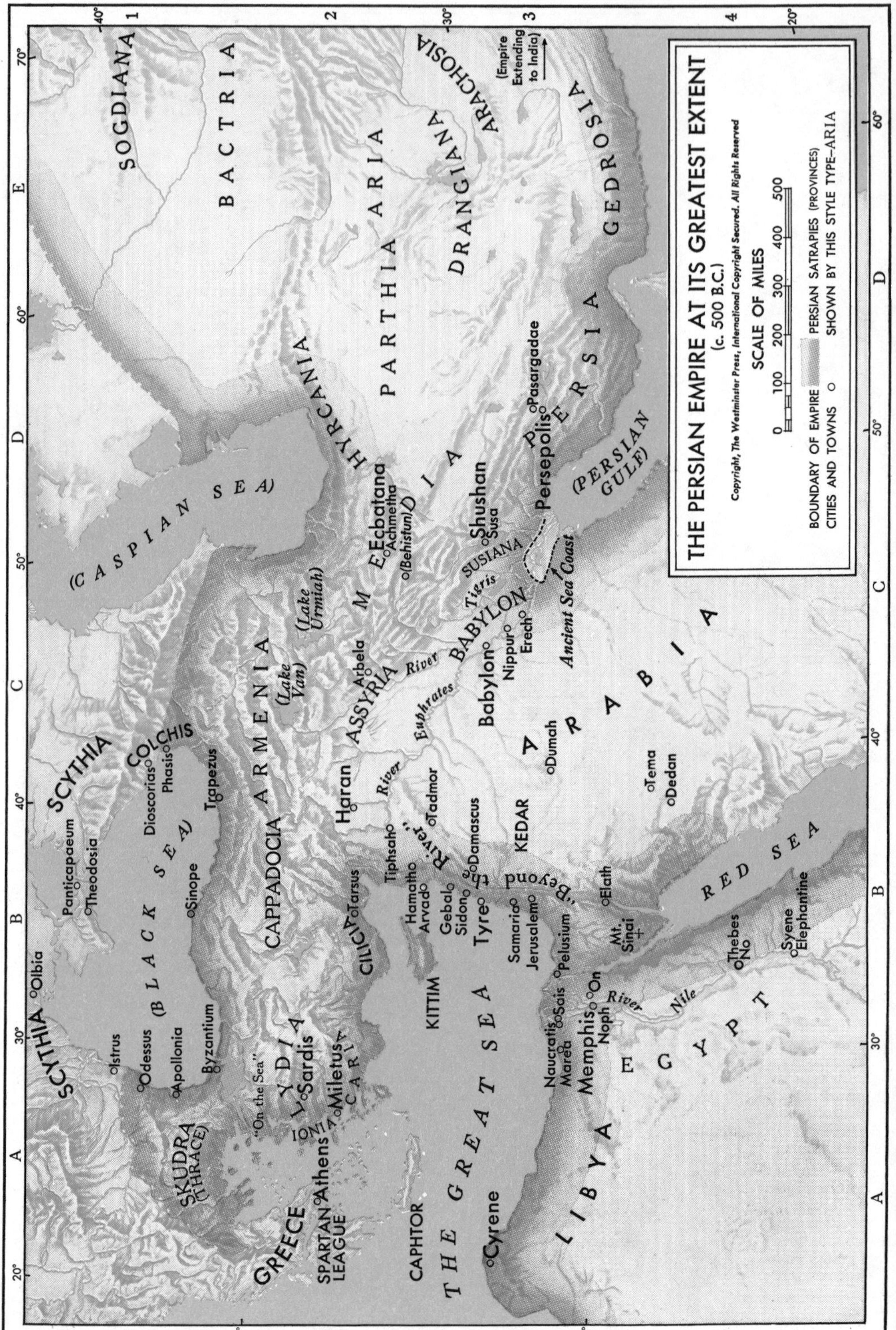

PLATE X

THE PERSIAN EMPIRE AT ITS GREATEST EXTENT
(c. 500 B.C.)

Copyright, The Westminster Press, International Copyright Secured, All Rights Reserved

SCALE OF MILES

0 100 200 300 400 500

BOUNDARY OF EMPIRE

PERSIAN SATRAPIES (PROVINCES)
SHOWN BY THIS STYLE TYPE—ARIA

CITIES AND TOWNS o

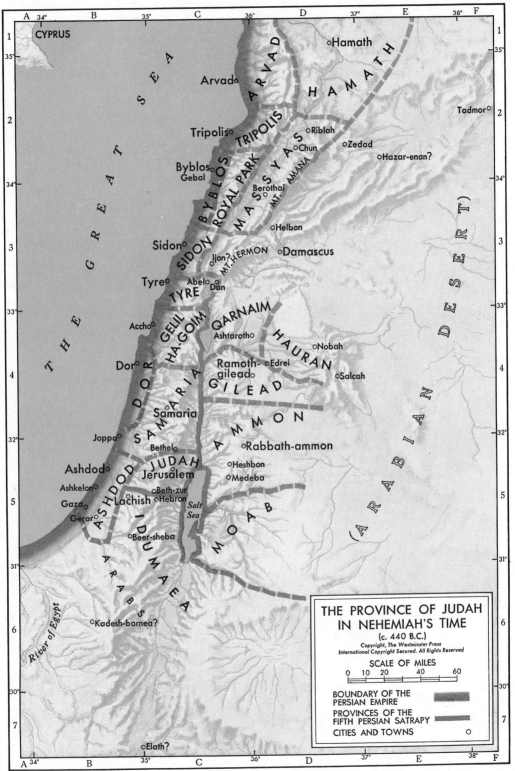

PLATE XI

CYPRUS

THE GREAT SEA

1 — 35°
34°
A B C D E F

Hamath

Tadmor

Arvad

ARVAD

HAMATH

Tripolis

TRIPOLIS

Riblah

Chun

Zedad

Hazar-enan?

Byblos
Gebal

BYBLOS

ROYAL PARK

MASSYAS

Berothai

MT. AMANA

Helbon

Sidon

SIDON

Ijon?

MT. HERMON

Damascus

Tyre

TYRE

Abelo
Dan

Accho

GELIL
HA-GOIM

QARNAIM

Ashtarotho

Nobah

HAURAN

Dor

DOR

Ramoth-
gilead

Edrei

Salcah

GILEAD

Samaria

SAMARIA

AMMON

Joppa

Bethel

Rabbath-ammon

Ashdod

ASHDOD

JUDAH

Jerusalem

Heshbon

Medeba

Ashkelon

Beth-zur
Hebron

Gaza

Lachish

Salt
Sea

Gerar

Beer-sheba

IDUMAEA

MOAB

ARABS

River of Egypt

Kadesh-barnea?

(ARABIAN DESERT)

THE PROVINCE OF JUDAH
IN NEHEMIAH'S TIME
(c. 440 B.C.)

Copyright, The Westminster Press
International Copyright Secured. All Rights Reserved

SCALE OF MILES

0 10 20   40   60

BOUNDARY OF THE
PERSIAN EMPIRE

PROVINCES OF THE
FIFTH PERSIAN SATRAPY

CITIES AND TOWNS   o

Elath?

Cartography By Hal & Jean Arbo

Edited By G. Ernest Wright and Floyd V. Filson

PLATE XII

PALESTINE
IN THE
MACCABEAN PERIOD
(168-63 B.C.)

Copyright, The Westminster Press
International Copyright Secured. All Rights Reserved

SCALE OF MILES

0   5   10   20   30

BOUNDARY LINE SHOWS MAXIMUM
EXTENT OF MACCABEAN KINGDOM
UNDER ALEXANDER JANNAEUS
(103-76 B.C.)

KINGDOM OF
ALEXANDER JANNAEUS

FREE CITY

CITIES AND TOWNS

Cartography By G. A. Barrois and Hal & Jean Arbo

Edited By G. Ernest Wright and Floyd V. Filson

PLATE XIII

PALESTINE
UNDER
HEROD THE GREAT
(40-4 B.C.)

Copyright, The Westminster Press
International Copyright Secured. All Rights Reserved

SCALE OF MILES

0 5 10   20   30

KINGDOM OF
HEROD THE GREAT

DECAPOLIS

FREE CITY

CITIES AND TOWNS

Cartography By G. A. Barrois and Hal & Jean Arbo   *Edited By G. Ernest Wright and Floyd V. Filson*

PLATE XIV

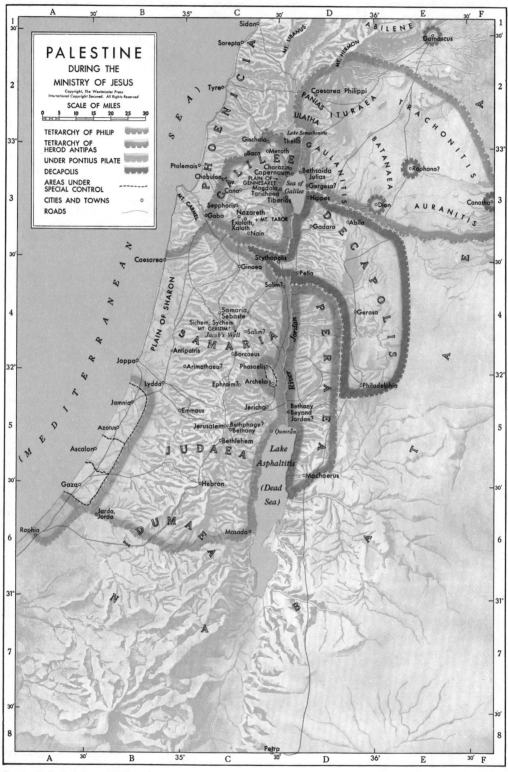

PALESTINE

DURING THE
MINISTRY OF JESUS

Copyright, The Westminster Press
International Copyright Secured. All Rights Reserved

SCALE OF MILES

0 5 10 15 20 25 30

TETRARCHY OF PHILIP

TETRARCHY OF
HEROD ANTIPAS

UNDER PONTIUS PILATE

DECAPOLIS

AREAS UNDER
SPECIAL CONTROL

CITIES AND TOWNS

ROADS

Sidon

Sarepta

Tyre

Ptolemais

Chabulon

Cana

Sepphoris

Gaba

Nazareth

Exaloth
Xaloth

Nain

Caesarea

Ginaea

Scythopolis

Salim?

Samaria
Sebaste

Sichem, Sychem
MT. GERIZIM
Jacob's Well

Salim?

Borcaeus

Antipatris

Arimathaea?

Phasaelis

Ephraim?

Archelais?

Joppa

Lydda

Jamnia

Emmaus

Jericho

Jerusalem

Bethphage?

Bethany

Bethlehem

Azotus

Ascalon

Gaza

Jarda,
Jorda

Raphia

Hebron

Masada

Petra

Gischala

Baca

Meroth

Chorazin

Capernaum
PLAIN OF
GENNESARET
Magdala
Tarichaea

Tiberias

Sea of
Galilee

Thella

Bethsaida
Julias

Gergesa?

Hippos

Gadara

Abila

Dion

Pella

Gerasa

Philadelphia

Bethany
Beyond
Jordan?

Qumrân

Lake
Asphaltitis

(Dead
Sea)

Machaerus

Caesarea Philippi

Raphana?

Canatha?

PHOENICIA

MT. LIBANUS

MT. HERMON

ABILENE

Damascus

PANIAS

ITURAEA

ULATHA

Lake Semechonitis

GAULANITIS

BATANAEA

TRACHONITIS

AURANITIS

GALILEE

MT. CARMEL

PLAIN OF SHARON

SAMARIA

DECAPOLIS

Jordan

River
Jordan

PERAEA

JUDAEA

IDUMAEA

N   A   B   A   T   A

(MEDITERRANEAN SEA)

+ MT. TABOR

Cartography By G. A. Barrois and Hal & Jean Arbo

Edited By G. Ernest Wright and Floyd V. Filson

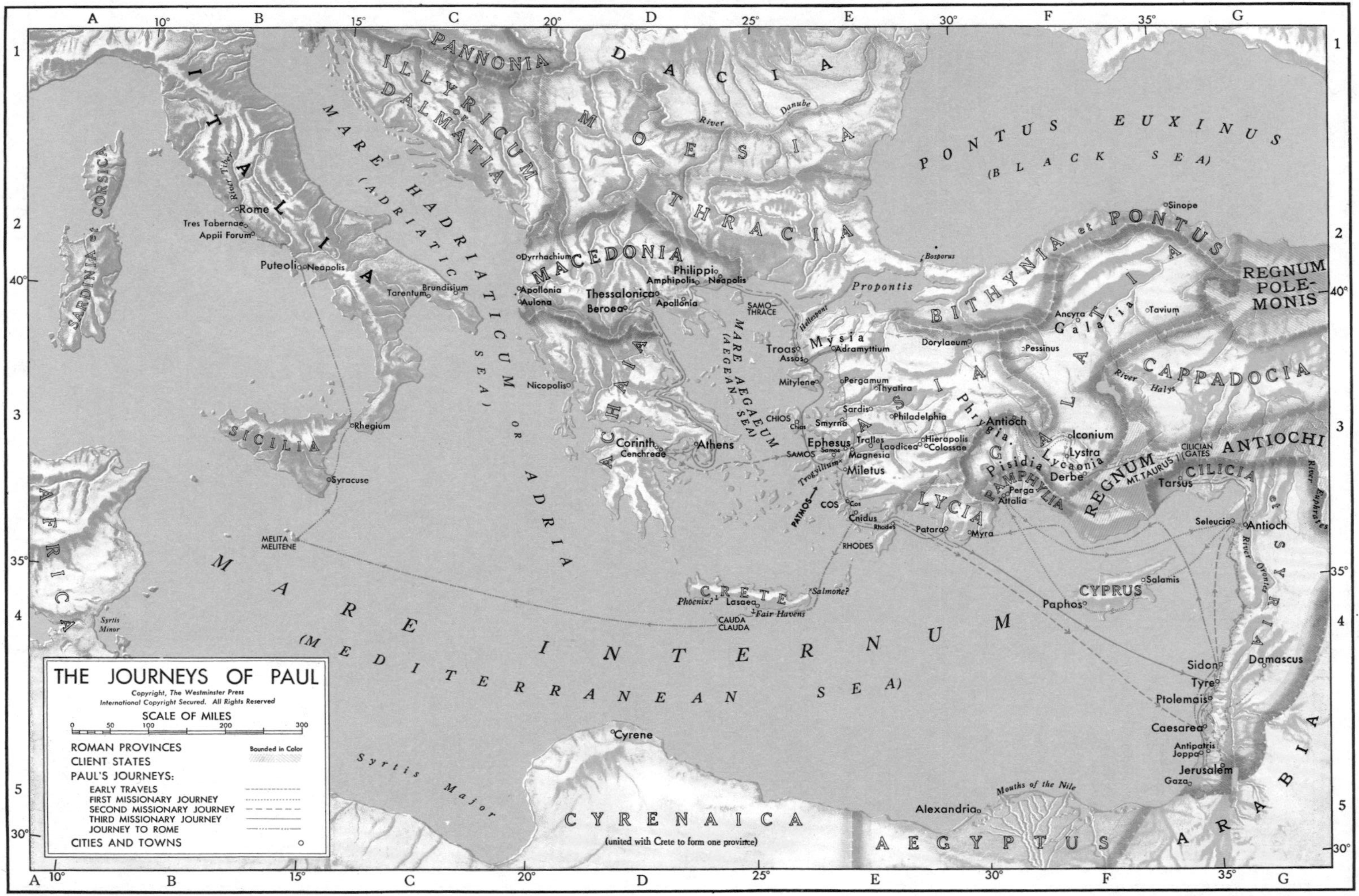

PLATE XV

THE JOURNEYS OF PAUL

Copyright, The Westminster Press
International Copyright Secured. All Rights Reserved

SCALE OF MILES

0   50   100   200   300

ROMAN PROVINCES
CLIENT STATES   Bounded in Color
PAUL'S JOURNEYS:
        EARLY TRAVELS
        FIRST MISSIONARY JOURNEY
        SECOND MISSIONARY JOURNEY
        THIRD MISSIONARY JOURNEY
        JOURNEY TO ROME
CITIES AND TOWNS   o

Edited By G. Ernest Wright and Floyd V. Filson

Cartography By Hal & Jean Arbo

PLATE XVI

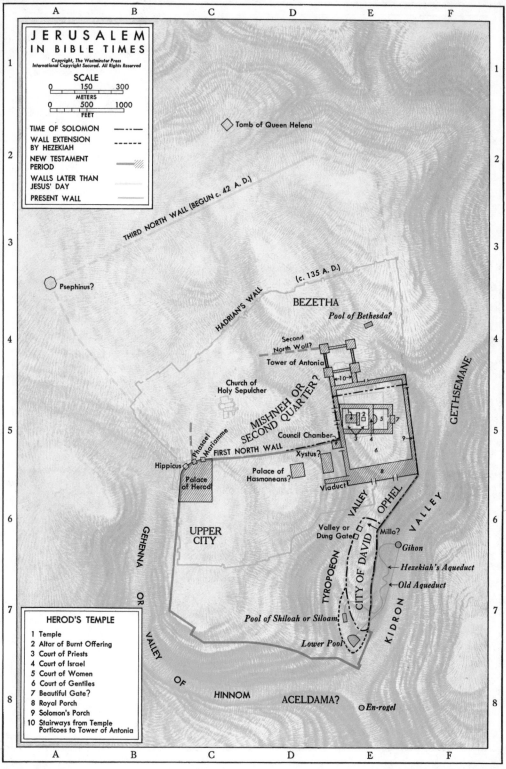

JERUSALEM
IN BIBLE TIMES

Copyright, The Westminster Press
International Copyright Secured. All Rights Reserved

SCALE

0   150   300
METERS

0   500   1000
FEET

TIME OF SOLOMON
WALL EXTENSION
BY HEZEKIAH
NEW TESTAMENT
PERIOD
WALLS LATER THAN
JESUS' DAY
PRESENT WALL

◇ Tomb of Queen Helena

THIRD NORTH WALL (BEGUN c. 42 A.D.)

⬡ Psephinus?

HADRIAN'S WALL

(c. 135 A.D.)

BEZETHA

Pool of Bethesda?

Second
North Wall?

Tower of Antonia

Church of
Holy Sepulcher

MISHNEH OR
SECOND QUARTER?

-10→

GETHSEMANE

Phasael
Mariamme

FIRST NORTH WALL

Hippicus

Palace
of Herod

Council Chamber

Xystus?

Palace of
Hasmoneans?

Viaduct

UPPER
CITY

GEHENNA

OR

VALLEY

Valley or
Dung Gate

TYROPOEON VALLEY

OPHEL

Millo?

CITY OF DAVID

◯ Gihon

← Hezekiah's Aqueduct

← Old Aqueduct

KIDRON VALLEY

Pool of Shiloah or Siloam

Lower Pool

HINNOM

ACELDAMA?

◯ En-rogel

OF

HEROD'S TEMPLE

1 Temple
2 Altar of Burnt Offering
3 Court of Priests
4 Court of Israel
5 Court of Women
6 Court of Gentiles
7 Beautiful Gate?
8 Royal Porch
9 Solomon's Porch
10 Stairways from Temple
   Porticoes to Tower of Antonia

Cartography By Hal & Jean Arbo

Edited By G. Ernest Wright and Floyd V. Filson